NEW LIFE OPTIONS

THE WORKING WOMAN'S RESOURCE BOOK

NEW LIFE OPTIONS

THE WORKING WOMAN'S RESOURCE BOOK

Rosalind K. Loring

University of Southern California
Los Angeles, California

Herbert A. Otto

National Center for the Exploration of Human Potential
La Jolla, California

McGRAW-HILL BOOK COMPANY

New York   St. Louis   San Francisco   Auckland   Bogotá
Düsseldorf   Johannesburg   London   Madrid   Mexico
Montreal   New Delhi   Panama   Paris   São Paulo
Singapore   Sydney   Tokyo   Toronto

This book was set in Times Roman by National ShareGraphics, Inc.
The editors were Robert G. Manley and Susan Gamer;
the cover was designed by Joan E. O'Connor;
the cover illustration was done by Thomas Lulebitch;
the production supervisor was Robert C. Pedersen.
The drawings were done by J & R Services, Inc.
R. R. Donnelley & Sons Company was printer and binder.

NEW LIFE OPTIONS: THE WORKING WOMAN'S
RESOURCE BOOK

234567890DODO783210987

Library of Congress Cataloging in Publication Data

Main entry under title:

New life options.

    Includes index.
    1. Women—Employment—United States—Addresses,
essays, lectures. 2. Women—Health and hygiene—
Addresses, essays, lectures. 3. Interpersonal
relations—Addresses, essays, lectures. 4. Women's
rights—United States—Addresses, essays, lectures.
I. Loring, Rosalind. II. Otto, Herbert Arthur.
HD6095.N39   301.41'2'0973   76-25092
ISBN 0-07-038742-7

Index

Contents

Preface

Until it reached this final form, this book went through many evolutions and changes. It began as an idea of one of the editors (Herbert A. Otto) and was first called "The Working Woman's Handbook." With the addition of the second editor and a closer look at the needs of women who work, the outline of topics was developed, discussed, and made final. Many women colleagues and students gave valuable ideas and insights which rounded out the list of issues. The decision by McGraw-Hill to publish the book as both a textbook and a book for the general public confirmed the present focus and title.

Each chapter is an original contribution by an expert, especially written for this book. Special thanks are due not only to the contributors but also to Barbara Datler, for early organization; to Jim Cameron and Aurline Emmett, for research assistance; and to Joan Benner Healy and Mike Loring, who stayed with us throughout, working nights and weekends, to edit and polish the manuscript.

We've enjoyed working on this book together and believe it is all the better for having two editors and for having the feelings and perspectives of both sexes represented.

Rosalind K. Loring
Herbert A. Otto

Where Women Have Options

Rosalind K. Loring
Herbert A. Otto

Rosalind Loring is Dean of the College of Continuing Education at the University of Southern California, which includes credit and noncredit programs, the summer session, overseas continuing education, and several major projects including the Davidson Continuing Education Conference Center, the American Language Institute, and the Experimental Admissions Program. In November 1976 she will serve as President of the Adult Education Association of the United States (AEA/USA), one of the largest adult- and continuing-education organizations in the country. For both the AEA/USA and the National University Extension Association, she has initiated sections on continuing education for women and caucuses on the status of women. She also created one of the nation's first programs for women, for University Extension, University of California, Los Angeles, in 1965, which included courses and counseling. Ms. Loring is a lecturer and writer and is coauthor with Theodora Wells of *Breakthrough: Women into Management* (Van Nostrand, Princeton, N.J., 1972). In addition, she was the producer of a series on National Educational Television, "Choice: Challenge for Modern Woman" (1964) and a film, "Women Up the Career Ladder" (1969).

Herbert A. Otto, Ph.D., is Chairperson of the National Center for the Exploration of Human Potential in San Diego, California. He was formerly an Associate Professor of the Graduate School of Social Work and Director of the Human Potentialities Research Project at the University of Utah (1960–1967). He is widely recognized for his pioneering work in human potentialities. His Developing Personal Potential courses, begun in 1961, are internationally known, and many of his techniques are now in the mainstream of the humanistic psychology movement. A psychologist, therapist, and marriage and family counselor, Dr. Otto has lectured extensively in the United States and abroad. He has published over sixty articles in scientific and professional journals and is the author or editor of fourteen books, including *Explorations in Human Potentialities* (Thomas, New York, 1966), *Guide to Developing Your Potential* (Scribner, New York, 1967), *Ways of Growth* (Grossman, 1968), *More Joy in Your Marriage* (Hawthorne, New York, 1969), and *Marriage and Family Enrichment* (Abingdon, Nashville, Tenn., 1976).

WORKING WOMEN: A RAPIDLY GROWING FORCE

Our concern for women who work began with a dazzling fact: over 33,650,000 women in the United States are currently employed.[1] In addition, we agreed with Anne Steinmann, who has said:

> Most women work at various stages of their lives, and all women are working women—those who work at home for the family and those who work away from home. For this book we will define "working women" as those who receive a salary and benefits not paid by the husband even though movement is now afoot to pay a stipend to the non-salaried woman who works at home. (Statisticians, census takers and others classify this group as "housewives".)[2]

Of course, we are also interested in the situation of women who are nonsalaried; most of the contents of this book will be equally helpful to women in either category. However, we intend to concentrate on the array of options available to employed women and to women who are about to become employed, and to suggest and even recommend approaches for dealing with these options. Each chapter contains insights into the current scene, information about what women and institutions are doing (and why), and resources for solving problems, acquiring skills, and improving behavior (your own or someone else's).

We know that some women work for money that is needed for essentials; others for an enriched family life; and others because they have invested so much in their education and want to recoup their expenditure of time and money. Still others work in order to express themselves, enhance their self-concept, or test and use their abilities. But in general women work for the same reasons men do—either because they must support a family, or because they want to contribute to

[1] *Monthly Labor Review,* U.S. Bureau of Labor Statistics, August 1975.
[2] Personal communication. Anne Steinmann is the coauthor of Chapter 17 (page 287).

someone's well-being, or because they enjoy the challenges presented. Age, income, education, skill, attitude, and the experiences of early childhood all have something to do with why women work—but not everything.

Many reports of research are included in this book. The interpretations are, obviously, those of the individual authors. The combination is a broad picture of the rapidly growing force which women exert in our nation, a force which influences decisions made in almost every area of national life.

The following statistics are presented to give an idea of the extent of career options exercised by (or available to) women:

One-half of all employed women (in 1974) were in the professions and related services (including educational and health services) or in retail trade.

Enrollment of women in colleges and universities increased by 29 percent; in 1974, women made up 44 percent of the total college population under thirty-five.

More women than men were in the professions and in service and financial occupations. Insurance and real estate also employed more women than men.[3]

Of all those employed in the United States, 39 percent are women. Occupationally, women account for:

7 percent of the total employed in mining
7 percent of the total employed in construction
28 percent of the total employed in manufacturing
22 percent of the total employed in transportation and public utilities
54 percent of the total employed in finance, insurance, and real estate
55 percent of the total employed in service industries
46 percent of the total employed in government[4]

In the past quarter-century women workers have increased from 33.9 percent to 46.2 percent of the total adult female population. Almost 90 percent of all women workers are employed in government, retailing, manufacturing, and services. Within services, women account for almost two-thirds of all workers in education and three-fourths of all workers in health and personal services (including domestic workers). But in spite of this, there are great discrepancies between the status and earnings of men and women: *Men still outnumber women by five to one in management jobs and by 600 to one in top management positions. In 1972 nearly two-thirds of all women who worked full time earned less than $7,000; less than one-fourth of all men workers earned below that level.* Thus there is a sharp difference between earnings of men and women—generally averaging about 40 percent.[5]

[3] *Current Population Reports—Population Characteristics Series,* U.S. Bureau of the Census, March 1975, p. 20, no. 279.

[4] Ibid.

[5] As reported in the Los Angeles Herald-Examiner, Thursday, October 30, 1975, quoting the economist William Burke, writing in *Business and Financial Letter* of the Federal Reserve Bank of San Francisco.

The economic impact of working women is seen in this fact: "From 1957 to 1973, the number of working wives rose 77 percent, to more than 20 million, and median family purchasing power increased 53 percent. This boosted the number of 'middle-income' families from 20 percent of the total population to more than 50 percent."[6]

These changes have produced other interesting figures: "One in every three mothers in the United States with pre-school children is employed outside the home. . . . Throughout the country there is space in day care centers for only 900,000 of the possible 6 million children."[7]

There have been various attempts to improve the economic status of women by quantifying their economic contribution as homemakers. The American Bar Association Family Law Section has proposed that upon divorce the court divide *in just proportions* "the contribution of each spouse to the acquisition of marital property, *including contribution of a spouse* as homemaker. . . ."[8]

The figures we have cited are not broken down by race, culture, religion, education, sexual preference, or inherited economic and social status. Actually, this book itself does not, on the whole, deal with the variations due to those factors. We decided early on that *while there are surely differences among subgroups of women, there are more often similarities.* For example, women, black and white, who are impoverished use the same governmental agencies for assistance and suffer equally when their families are in need. It is also true that wealthy women and top executives have similar, unique problems regardless of race, etc.

This does not mean that we do not recognize the additional burdens of, say, race, religion, or homosexuality. Often the situation is complex: for instance, black, Chicano, Indian, and Asian women are confronted by double discrimination (by sex and race); yet on the other hand they do not have to establish their autonomy and freedom to work outside the home. There has been a great deal of research on many such topics, but the data are still confused. In any case, these related problems are not really within the scope of this book. We will, however, make a few general comments. Many communities are hostile to people of foreign extraction different from that of the majority—Polish, Greek, Irish, Lithuanian, etc. Religious discrimination, especially against Jews and Catholics, is still uncomfortably common. If it is perhaps more subtle than racial discrimination, it is equally painful and equally disastrous to career development and personal identity.

We have noted from research reports and from our work in the field that such difficulties usually do not face middle-class and upper-middle-class "minor-

---

[6] "Squeeze in the Middle Class," The Reader's Digest, July 1975. (Condensed from *Business Week,* March 10, 1975.)

[7] Lynn Simross, "Day Care: The No Vacancy Sign Is Out," *Los Angeles Times,* January 18, 1976.

[8] *Recognition of Economic Contribution of Homemakers and Protection of Children in Divorce Law and Practice,* Citizens' Advisory Council on the Status of Women, Room 1336, Department of Labor Building, Washington, D.C. 20210.

ity" women. This, again, is an issue beyond the scope of this book. But it is important to note that research and commentary in this area are multiplying, and several significant theories are now proffered. Patricia Roberts Harris, an outstanding black lawyer and politician, has stated: "From these views of [the tiny fraction of educated black men and women] was developed a familial life style that accepts the equality of men and women, that is, the life style of the middleclass professional black family."[9]

Therefore, while the effect of economy and education is referred to in several chapters, we have not emphasized that aspect of women's lives. This book collects the experiences and convictions of contributors who represent a broad spectrum of age, race, political philosophy, feminist leanings, status, economic stability, marital and parental status, and geographical locations; therefore, we believe that it contains much which is appropriate for every woman. The resources listed and the approaches suggested to women as they manage their options will be helpful to both minority and majority groups.

Finally, we should point out that stereotypes are a burden for men as well as for women. Stereotypes create expectations, attitudes, and behavior in men much as they do in women; and men, like women, suffer from them. However, this book is for and about women, who are moving forward and whose roles and relationships are being realized in a way that men's are not. Where the problems of men and women are the same, we have tried to indicate this; but even in the absence of a specific comment, it should be borne in mind that many options and resources are not sex-linked.

For any change, the people involved must be ready. Many women today are ready to create new styles in all areas of their lives. Our contributors have joined with us in expanding and improving the quality of decisions regarding new life options.

HOW TO GET THE MOST FROM THIS BOOK

This book is divided into five parts, each of which is in turn subdivided into chapters.

The parts represent areas of life in which working women find themselves involved so frequently as to strain their energy and emotional well-being. Within the parts are chapters which select important elements and hold them up for closer examination. Naturally not all chapters apply to all women (some women may, for example, be too young to examine the implications of retirement; others no longer need be concerned about child care for themselves).

Which particular elements are selected and how they are assessed has been determined by the authors of the chapters, all of whom were invited to contribute because they had specific expertise. The editors' goal in this selection was diversi-

---

[9] Patricia Roberts Harris, "Achieving Equality for Women," *Women in Higher Education,* American Council on Education, Washington, D.C., 1974.

ty; thus the book really contains the richness of resources represented by contemporary American professional women (plus a few much-needed men). The range of contributors has, of course, resulted in a diversity of styles and approaches. Some authors are scholarly, presenting research findings; others have turned their experience into exercises and activities which the individual reader may utilize immediately. The combination, we believe, will be a good guide for making decisions.

The five parts are:

Part One: New Perspectives
Part Two: Getting the Best from Your Career
Part Three: Taking Good Care of Yourself
Part Four: The Potential of Your Relationships
Part Five: Managing Your Options

The content of each part and chapter is previewed in the following pages. This will enable you to select those specific chapters and sections which appeal directly to your own needs and interests; but we hope you will dip into all the chapters, for each has breadth as well as specificity.

PREVIEW OF CHAPTERS

As has already been noted, we have tried to group the chapters naturally, according to various activities of life. We must point out that because there is no consensus about what should be expected (or demanded) in any situation, alternatives are stressed throughout. Naturally, our contributors have their own opinions; consequently, each chapter contains only what its author feels is valid.

Readers who are considering employment outside the home—or who have already decided on it—will find Chapters 4, 5, 6, 7, and 22 of particular interest.

Part One: New Perspectives

This section deals with some broad social issues and trends facing working women today. New approaches are explored for establishing a good balance between home and career.

Chapter 1, Valuing the Quality of Your Life (by Rosalind Loring), surveys new trends in society and their impact on women's lives; it also examines how the new developments are related to values and to the choices confronting working women.

Chapter 2, When Women Work (by Judith Bardwick and Elizabeth Douvan), takes up external and internal forces affecting the working woman and presents some options and challenges.

Chapter 3, The Juggling Act: Home and Career (by Herbert Otto and Roberta Otto), has been written both for women who are considering employment and for those who are already employed. This chapter offers many creative ideas, suggestions, and experiences drawn from workshops and classes which the authors have conducted.

Part Two: Getting the Best from Your Career

In this section, we present many new career opportunities available to women, along with information on getting and keeping the job you want. There are also discussions of how to handle sexism and how to assess a working climate to see if it will be favorable to professional women. One chapter is provided for women interested in starting a business.

Chapter 4, Women Working: Opportunities Both New and Traditional (by Elinor Lenz), surveys many possible jobs, including the typical, familiar ones and new fields with potential for growth which are just opening up to women. The appendix to this chapter is a valuable list of resources.

Chapter 5, The Job of Job Hunting (by Priscilla Jackson), describes how to think about looking for a job. It should be helpful both to women who want to start work and to those who want to change jobs.

Chapter 6, The Range and Benefits of Volunteer Work (by Helen Feeney), contains up-to-date information on constructive uses of volunteer work and discusses how it can be of advantage in paid employment.

Chapter 7, Handling Sexism at Work: Nondefensive Communication (by Theodora Wells), faces an important aspect of modern society. The author suggests numerous constructive ways of dealing with sexism at work and in other situations, emphasizing clear and reasonable communication.

Chapter 8, Next Steps Up: Women as Peers and Managers (by Rosalind Loring), is a detailed account of the relationships working women must handle and of ways of improving them. A method is provided for evaluating the working climate at the personal level, the level of middle management, and the level of top management.

Chapter 9, Starting and Keeping Your Own Business (by Nancy Kuriloff and Arthur Kuriloff), is a concentrated but detailed introduction to this subject; it covers a wide range of topics from sources of capital to pricing and marketing.

Part Three: Taking Good Care of Yourself

The six chapters in this part are designed to help the working woman keep fit and in good health—mentally and physically. Information is included on family planning, birth, the care of infants, new ways of handling illness, and physical fitness.

Chapter 10, Maintaining the Best of Health: Nutrition and Diet (by Tomi Haas), emphasizes the role of nutrition in preventing health problems. The author, a public-health nutritionist, avoids food faddism and gives sound, down-to-earth advice, including a method for evaluating your present eating patterns.

Chapter 11, Family Planning: Medical and Legal Resources (by Helen Steiner and Alan Winters), presents the latest information on birth control, abortion, and legal issues. One of the authors is a social worker employed by a family-planning agency; the other is a physician.

Chapter 12, Birth and Baby Care (by Audrey Reid), gives recent medical information about how pregnant women should care for themselves and prepare for childbirth; sections on the resumption of activities after childbirth and on infant care are given. The author is a physician.

Chapter 13, Handling Illness: Health-care Problems (by Toni Michels), discusses valuable new ways of coping with illness and the personal and family problems that attend it. It also provides information on health-care services and common-sense health care.

Chapter 14, Your Mental Health and Therapeutic Resources (by Herbert Otto), discusses principles and practices for maintaining and improving mental health. There is a section on what types of therapy and counseling exist, and how to find a suitable therapist or counselor.

Chapter 15, Keeping Fit for Fun and Personal Development (by Olga Connolly), explores the benefits women can derive from developing more strength, energy, and endurance. It includes an excellent list of resources for starting your own exercise program.

Part Four: The Potential of Your Relationships

This section takes up a range of personal relationships; it includes discussions of living alone, the man in your life, child care, and working mothers. Many alternatives and options are presented. One chapter is devoted to the challenges and opportunities facing the single parent.

Chapter 16, Living Alone: Pleasures and Polarities (by Susan Osborn), is designed to help working women form a clearer picture of the complexities, problems, challenges, and pleasures of living alone, and to present creative ideas and suggestions.

Chapter 17, The Man in Your Life: Personal Commitment in a Changing World (by Anne Steinmann and Elinor Lenz), examines men's attitudes and male and female roles in modern society during the three stages of a woman's life. Current research, with its applications, is summarized.

Chapter 18, Coping with Child Care: Possibilities for the Working Mother (by Karen Hill Scott), should help the working mother make the best possible decisions concerning the care of her child or children while she is at work. A form for evaluating child-care agencies is given, along with information about alternatives.

Chapter 19, The Single Parent: Challenges and Opportunities (by Elizabeth Douvan), contains a great deal of information that will help the single parent cope with the various demands on her time and attention. The author is a well-known psychologist who has specialized in work with single parents.

Part Five: Managing Your Options

Included in this part are valuable professional resources for women. Among the topics covered are the development of the ability to handle finances (including property, inheritance, and credit); continuing education; the role of the law in the employment of women; assertiveness training; and responding positively to separation, divorce, and widowhood. Finally, there is a chapter on retirement.

Chapter 20, Assessing Self-Image and Training for Assertive Behavior (by Jane Berry), examines assertiveness training—a program, available throughout the nation, which improves the way people set goals and respond to others. The author has conducted many such programs.

Chapter 21, Continuing Your Education: Widening the Range (by Rosalind Loring), describes every type of institutional support for women's education. The innovations in educational programs now available are summarized; and examples are given which will enable individuals to ask for similar local programs.

Chapter 22, How the Law Helps Women's Employment (by Kathryn Heath), covers in some detail laws, directives, and judicial interpretations which affect the employment of women. The author, a well-known educator, emphasizes how a woman can use the law to help herself while employed.

Chapter 23, Legal Rights and Prospects: Property Inheritance and Credit (by Riane Eisler), gives general answers to questions of credit, community property, inheritance, and so on. The author is a lawyer. There is a section on administering an estate; and throughout there is stress on the importance of women's understanding their rights.

Chapter 24, Developing Financial Management Skills (by Helen Thal), contains valuable information on issues facing consumers. The author, who is a professor of home economics, suggests four steps in successful money management and also takes up budgeting, credit ratings, and debt management.

Chapter 25, Maximizing the Positive in Separation, Divorce, and Widowhood (by Herbert Otto and Roberta Otto), presents both theory and a series of experiences for extracting benefit from these three situations of change. Special attention is given to dealing with one's feelings and creating a supportive environment.

Chapter 26, The New World of Retirement (by Jaylee Duke), points out the many ways in which—or the many levels at which—a retired woman can begin a new life-style, with hopefulness and new sources of fulfillment. The chapter covers housing, economics, and employment as well as adjustment of one's life-style.

Epilogue

Finally, there is the Epilogue, Making a Political Impact as a Woman (by Patsy Mink). Congresswoman Mink gives a recapitulation of the political progress of women up to the present, and ends with suggestions on how women can help each other in the political arena. From her own experiences, she concludes that "women have a special contribution to make."

Today, more than ever before, new opportunities, new positions never before available, and new resources are beckoning to the working woman and the woman who is about to enter the work force. The women's movement has played an important role in this advance. However, to become fully and effectively able to contribute the broad range of her talents and capacities to society, the woman of today must continue to press for equal rights; a more humanistic approach to work, the working environment, and the worker; and equality under the law. These are some of the greatest challenges facing us.

Part One

New Perspectives

Chapter 1

Valuing the Quality
of Your Life

Rosalind K. Loring

For a short biography of Rosalind Loring, see the Introduction, page 1.

In the thirty-three days between November 16 and December 18, 1975, the dramatic changes taking place in women's lives were recorded in the newspapers. Taken together, the items quoted below describe the diversity of women's experiences today.

WORKING MOM OK, KIDS SAY
December 10, Chicago—The fact that working mothers are far more numerous than they used to be undoubtedly accounts for some new attitudes. . . . Children couldn't care less about statistics, of course. . . . It depends upon the quality of their relationship to their mother. . . .

WOMEN PRESS FOR EQUALITY IN CHURCH; CATHOLICS, PROTESTANTS SEEK STRONGER FEMALE IDENTITY
December 6, Detroit—Virginia Millenkott denounced what she called the misuse of the Bible by "Total Woman" and other groups that attempt to justify female submission through selected quotation of biblical texts. . . . Some 2000 (in separate locations) met to express discontent with traditional male leadership in churches, home and society. . . .

ALICE DOESN'T GET THE TOP POLITICAL JOBS
December 4, Los Angeles—"We're trying to look at the explanation of why male politicians enter the political system and move up," Dr. Judith Stiehm (political scientist and researcher at the University of Southern California) says, "and women come in and then move out. . . . Perhaps we'll find that women have to be trained to think big—to think about becoming senators and congresswomen. . . ."

WHY SO MANY BLACK WOMEN IN LAW
December 1, Atlanta—"We just seem like so many more, . . . since we're so visible. . . . We've always found the law a place to go when white liberals talk runs out," . . . reported a conference of women lawyers which met to discuss blocks to achieving goals.

THE LIBERATION OF CARDINALE
November 29, Rome—In recent months Claudia Cardinale has become a liberated woman—both personally and professionally. . . . "For more than 15 years I was considered and treated like an object or a project to be manufactured and merchandised. . . . It really is absurd to treat women this way—women, after all, are capable of more in life than making love." . . .

FRIEDAN LEADS RIFT IN N.O.W.
November 27, Chicago—Betty Friedan and twelve other past and present officers of the National Organization for Women have formed a group to . . . get that movement away from pseudo-radical rhetoric and back into the business of dealing with the real interests of women's lives, . . . the mainstream of economic priorities and personal relationships. . . .

FEMALE CRIME WAVE NOW ALL BUT IGNORED
November 27, New York—"Crime among women is on the rise, . . . but little is being done about it. . . ." Charles Work, Deputy Chief of the Law Enforcement Assistance Administration, said the criminal justice system, "is a system run by males, predominantly for males. . . . Few prisons offer any meaningful educational or vocational opportunities for women."

MOTHER FACES A "ROLE STRAIN"
November 16, Washington—A mother was talking about her 25-year-old daughter who had just . . . moved in—after a few years away at graduate school. . . . The mother had been . . . enjoying new styles of living and thinking. . . . But when her daughter settled in, so did confusion. . . . Mothers have few institutional or structural ways of establishing balance. . . .

PERCENTAGE OF FEMALE PROFS INCHES UPWARD
November 27, Stanford—A national survey shows . . . the proportion of women among American college and university professors has inched upward to 21% (from 19% in 1969). . . . [Women] spend more time teaching than men, they earn less than men, . . . receive less support for research and show a "striking pattern of segregation."

FIGHT FOR ABORTION LAW CONTINUES
December 10, Chicago—Sarah Waddington didn't realize it then, but her work to make abortion a legal option . . . was just beginning when she won a landmark

decision. . . . Since then the Texas lawyer and state legislator has . . . [worked] to stop the various states [which] have attempted to curb the scope of the abortion law. . . .

CORPORATE BOARDS ADDING MORE WOMEN

December 18, Chicago—Those women (lawyer Barbara Scott Preiskel, economist Norma T. Pace, and Sister Jane Scully, plus others)—all at the top of their professions—are a part of the . . . largest invasion of board rooms by women. . . . There are 296 female directors in the boards of the top 2,200 companies in the nation. . . . Most were elected during the last five years.[1]

Each of these stories describes in its own way the ferment in which modern women are caught up. Women are responding to national and worldwide events and trends by articulating their own particular concerns. Of course, not all women are involved in all the issues covered by such stories (nor do all women even care about all the events which might affect them). But it is equally certain that almost every woman shares some of these concerns and some sense of change. Few women today hold the same attitudes as they did five years ago. Although individualism is supposed to be characteristic of Americans, recent events have demonstrated that women, perhaps even more than men, are affected by social trends—that is, trends which have to do with roles and relationships. In the midst of so much activity, often what is experienced is "turmoil," yet for the majority of women the agitation has freed their minds to consider each decision freshly.

TODAY'S TRENDS

There are no longer "women's issues," but rather national issues. Whatever affects women affects everyone—in the family and the community, at work and play. Whatever impact women have upon the economy, political life, or the church, as these interact the repercussions are felt throughout society. In the past much has been made of the fact that women are more than 51 percent of the national population. But we can see from the news stories quoted above that women are subdivided by age, race, economic status, political concepts, religion, and philosophy. *Therefore, they should not all be expected to agree.*

What women face, however, is the recognition that while they may not agree, they do all respond to the same worldwide events. As we look forward to the 1980s and 1990s, there is a renewed awareness of the implications of so much change. Beginning with the relationships of people with each other and with the physical world, changes already in progress include the following:

---

[1] These news items are summaries or combinations of actual stories which appeared during the thirty-three days noted. During the past few years, the *Los Angeles Times,* the *Chicago Sun-Times,* and other major metropolitan newspapers have increased both the number of stories and the range of topics relating to women. Reports about women appear in feature articles and news stories: I, along with other women, am appreciative of the efforts of the print media to keep society informed about trends affecting women.

Change in the relationship of people to their governments, both in their expectation that they will participate in decision making and in their desire that government provide housing, food, entertainment, child care, education, etc.

Change in the relationship of people to "experts"—lawyers, doctors, educators, economists, and so on—accompanied by diminishing respect and increasing demands to share in decisions.

A growing interest in ecology, especially in better utilization of both the natural environment and human resources (which include women).

A greater search for personal meaning in one's life, often with self-renewal and self-expression as goals.

A questioning of the importance of *achievement:* what is its end? What is its price? What is to be done about the gatekeepers who control it? This is accompanied by a reevaluation of the typical use of the fruits of achievement—the rate at which the resources of the earth (comfort, luxury, food, drink, energy, etc.) are being consumed.

A redefinition of "work" and "leisure" and a renewed search for the meaning of both in humanistic and individualistic terms.

A growing dependence upon technology to save time, comfort, and energy (though surely not money, and probably not privacy); and a heavy utilization of technology to control one's own future (the pill and hormones, for example).

A widening gap between social, political, economic, and national groups and between nations.

An increasing need for integration and cooperation on some levels and issues by groups and governments.

Where decisions entail implementation by governments or other major institutions, the increasing importance of the question, How to decide? By consensus? By majority vote? By fiat?

The list is not, of course, complete; but it may be sufficient to demonstrate that women, seeking a better life and in the process establishing new goals, must do so within the framework of the society in which they live. Their concerns are bound to be influenced by the speed and the direction of changes. It should be noted that some women alone and a few women's organizations are attempting to change society drastically. But for most women, some limited societal changes (equal pay for equal work, or equal retirement benefits) are as much as they can tackle at this time. Fortunately, women's aspirations and abilities form a continuum, so that each woman can be free to work at her own pace while encouraging others to work at theirs.

An element which complicates the situation is the values which people hold and which come into play in times of stress and decision making. Thus, for the individual, ideals and rewards are forces which interact and combine to tell us internally "this is right" or "that is wrong." As a result of these forces we prefer one way of doing something to another, and we value some actions and not others. For women today, such values culminate in their right to make decisions unshackled by history, custom, or contemporary style. Basically, this means the right to determine one's sense of fulfillment, the freedom to choose one's role.

In the context of social change women must make decisions with understanding of their own values and of the consequences. In actuality, the complexity of the situation can be beneficial: in an ambiguous situation many new notions may be advocated and many innovations attempted. *It is only when we attempt to hold fast to the familiar that progress is not likely.*

The authors of *The Femininity Game*[2] state crisply (but with humor) our common folklore: that women are losers because in losing (to a man) a woman wins (a man). "Men don't love women who win." Of course, "everybody knows" that women want to be loved—all societal trends aside. According to the authors, the right to make decisions may not be perceived as so important, because women have been conditioned to avoid dealing with the marvelously intricate world of values, social trends, and their own behavior. But the news stories with which this chapter opened indicate that some changes are being made here. The "femininity game" is being played with new rules today. At least, there are some hopeful signs that women and men can accommodate to women's changing attitudes about challenge and competition and new relationships. More and more people are discovering, like Rip Van Winkle, that the world they live in today looks and is different from the one in which they spent their formative years. Women are viewing positively the value of winning—a game, a job, or a new way of life.

Psychologists, who have as much to say in the determination of values today as any group, have also joined in the demand for change by espousing new relationships between parents and children (similar to the changes sought in the relationship between government and citizen or expert and client). Anne Steinmann (coauthor of Chapter 17) and David Fox, discussing the development of adult lives (and values) independent of children, state: "In areas of social change involving reactions and responses as deeply rooted in the developmental process as are role responses and reactions, we do not expect reform and change to come in one step."[3] They do see reform and change in the relationships between parent and child (with less concentration on children's needs) and a comparable readjustment between husband and wife.

CHANGING NORMS AND ROLES

From the news items quoted earlier, it is apparent that mothers are reconsidering their role as Mother; not *whether* they shall be Mother, but *how* they shall be Mother. Steinmann and Fox have given cues—changes in norms and role changes by stages. To some the choice appears to be "either-or"; but actually that is not the way it works.

Rather, a few people lead the way to recognition of areas of nonfunctioning. Then others—pioneers—press ahead for real change—in laws, in attitudes, in actions and interactions. Still others ask questions about the necessity of maintaining what has been. ("Where is it written that women are better than men in

---

[2] Thomas Boslooper and Marcia Hayes, *The Femininity Game,* Stein and Day, New York, 1973.
[3] Anne Steinmann and David J. Fox, *The Male Dilemma,* Jason Aronson, New York, 1974, p. 283.

caring for children?" "Why does a woman have to be better qualified than a man for the same position?" "Since the nation is in such a mess, why shouldn't a woman be elected President or appointed Secretary of State?") Finally, there are those who quietly prepare themselves to actually do the job and are ready, waiting in the wings for the right time to appear. There are in fact so many in the last category that numerous listings of qualified women have been compiled and are available from all types of organizations. (See the list of resources at the end of Chapter 8.) Every professional group and guild is prepared to give names and addresses of women with specific qualifications. Private and public agencies stand ready to recommend women for all sorts of jobs.

As norms change, there are women actively engaged in changing their roles. The sociologist Armand Mauss has noted: "A 1972 national poll showed only 12% of the women and 15% of the men felt men should no longer be expected to open doors for women. . . . One wonders what the future will bring in such attitudes. . . . Actually, the present is a very ambiguous, transitional time for standards of behavior in male-female relationships. . . . Do women still like to have their beauty or sex appeal noticed by men, or will they respond with anger or indignation at being treated as sex objects?"[4]

Obviously, as usual it depends upon the woman. Not all women would qualify as sex objects; but—more important—not all want to do so. Many women share the conviction that the whistles and the gleam in the eye just aren't worth the cost. And, as a number of women executives have observed, a differential in salary of $5,000 to $10,000 per year is an expensive price for having the door opened for you.

On the other hand, this is clearly a time of transition, and the changing of norms is not as regularized a procedure as the changing of the guard at Buckingham Palace. Most women, therefore, have been attempting to be both old and new. They've prepared themselves to be specialists in transportation, public relations, or administration, but at the same time they are trying to keep up the standards of model American wives and mothers. Typically, career women of all races and economic conditions try to be more than adequate in each compartment of their lives—mother, wife, daughter, employee, employer.

Women in other parts of the world marvel at the stamina of American women and at their willingness to perform tasks which might as well (or better) be handled by someone else. Tender, loving care is the ideal; regardless of what else a woman does—whether improving the community or achieving personal status—she still feels compelled to perform the time-honored, ritualistic tasks of homemaking. Naturally, there are differences in degree depending upon circumstances. For example, when there is no father in the home more time is needed for the children; when one's income is low and one's work is hard physical labor, less energy is available for pleasant outings; when one's children have grown up and left home, there is more time for everything; and when one lives alone, there is more time to experiment with hobbies instead of household tasks.

[4] Armand L. Mauss, *Social Problems as Social Movements,* Lippincott, Philadelphia, 1974, p. 439.

It's interesting to observe that pressure to conform to the ideals (values) of the group is greatest in the middle and upper classes. Although Dr. Spock has finally released women from the pressure of always being present and accountable, there are still norms and enforcers of norms to provide guidance for appropriate behavior for women.

It is perhaps in the area of interaction between husband and wife that the greatest number of questions are arising. Mother goes to work to help buy a new car or a trip to the Orient or a college education for Jane, and so Father "helps" with *her* chores. The problem of finding time for conversation, sex, celebration of family occasions, and weekends out of town keeps cropping up. People who work with emerging women are full of stories about the accommodations made by women (and sometimes by men). The huge issues of ecology, war, integration, and the like are diminished by the daily decisions of work, home, and family. If most women are not politicized, it may well be because at that point their time and energy ran out.

BASIC NEEDS AND NEEDED CHANGES

In order to improve the quality of life, we must recognize two basic needs of working women:

- For all who work there must be fair and equal treatment—enforced by legislation if necessary.
- Regardless of whether a woman works because she *must* or because she *wants* to, there should not be any burden of guilt.

Guilt seems to be the heaviest burden a woman bears. In July 1975, the Purdue Opinion Panel[5] showed that a large proportion of male teenagers *disapprove* of women as governors (73 percent), as chairpersons of government regulatory agencies (75 percent), and as space scientists (67 percent). What is more, almost half agreed that men don't like to work for women. The mothers, of course, are to blame again. After all, they raised those boys, didn't they?

Here, then, is a central point—the unresolved question. Are the norms set by:

- The media, with their daily and nightly reinforcing of traditional roles for women and men?
- The textbooks, with their discriminatory illustrations and language?
- The attitudes husbands and wives brought with them as they formed new families?
- The almost all-male legislative bodies in state capitals throughout the nation as they repeat tired and inaccurate statements about the effects (real and feared) of the Equal Rights Amendment?

There is unlikely to be agreement on the answer. But the media, teachers,

[5] Arthur Snider, "Mother to Blame for Equality Lag?" *The Chicago Sun-Times,* January 27, 1975.

husbands, wives, textbooks, and legislators can work together to ease the replacement of old norms by new roles. Affirmative Action (see Chapter 22) is intended to accomplish this in work settings. But before that misunderstood and often mismanaged social invention can function, much work must be done. For example:

- The popular images of women must be changed by frequent visibility of women who are successful in nontraditional activities and who are comfortable in handling success.
- Women must be portrayed in the widest span of activities, performing as men do, functioning as experts *and* as people who are just getting by.
- The qualifications demanded of women as parents, workers, supervisors, religious leaders, and so on, must be the same as for men. The qualifications must be clarified so that those who judge and those who are judged agree on objective criteria.

Earlier, legal recourse was mentioned. Chapters 22 and 23 deal with this subject, but we should note here that women's economic, educational, political, and employment lives have improved markedly since the passing of civil rights legislation and its aftermath. While most women are reluctant to use the law to achieve their fair share of the nation's resources (suing someone is a most aggressive and unfamiliar activity), it is accurate to say that *enforcement of the laws* (in many instances as a result of legal action initiated by women) *has changed the quality of life for all women.*

FREEDOM TO CHOOSE

In 1916, Constance Markievicz said:

> Don't trust your 'feminine charm' and your capacity for getting on the soft side of men, but take up your own responsibilities and be prepared to go on your own way depending for safety on your own courage, your own truth and your own common sense, and not on the problematic chivalry of the men you may meet on the way.[6]

"Go on your own way" is an attitude many women think they're inventing today. (Constance Markievicz has not been much quoted since 1916.) In fact, to most women the current trend of exploring new options and selecting from among them is so new an endeavor that it feels radical and ground-breaking. For the individual woman it is radical to choose a new life-style:

> Says Saidie K., upon deciding to divorce her husband of twenty-three years, "Life comes by but once and I'd like to live a bit."

Or to choose a career:

[6] Quoted in an announcement from the TRW System's Opportunities for Women Committee, August 29, 1975.

"Why must a woman who aspires to a professional career be a non-conformist? . . . Why have so many been single?"[7]

Or to select her own values:

"I like the feeling of power when I decide who is getting which territory," reports Alice M., sales manager of a major food company. "And I refuse to worry any more about the morals of women 'out there' than I do the men."

Many women have joined in common objectives—to know themselves as they are and as they could be and then to be free to do as they decide. To be sure, freedom is an endless, and rather vague, quest. To be free enough to choose between possible options is perhaps a clearer statement of intent. To choose between an ever-widening assortment of real options is even closer to the mark.

Among the real options (and one still selected by many) is "occupation: housewife." Almost every woman is a housewife, although she may not be one full time. Thus for a large part of the female population the choice is still there: to work for pay full time or part time, or not to work for pay. It's significant that this choice is far more available to women than it is to men, even today. For women the decision to go out to work is conscious and deliberate; for men, the deliberate action would be not to do so. This again is an example of society's determination of appropriate behavior.

A number of other choices for women have been spoken of elsewhere in glowing terms. Social scientists, for example, have observed that technology has freed women from traditional household chores. Advocates of zero population growth are pleased that women can, as the result of chemical invention, control the population of the world. Advertising of the kind typified by "You've come a long way, baby" has created the impression that life has improved magnificently for women. However, as of this writing, some of these developments are mixed blessings. For example, contraceptive pills, long touted as a primary emancipator of women, have recently been revealed as potentially hazardous to health: current research strongly indicates that oral contraceptives may contribute to heart attacks in older women and to cancer. Higher education, the aspiration of all emerging subgroups, is now open to women, who are admitted in some numbers to professional schools and nontraditional curricula. But the programs of compensatory preparation which are necessary in order for women to be successful are woefully absent, and advances in status have been slow (again, see the news stories at the beginning of this chapter).

Seeking financial restitution for past discrimination is a possibility for some women who have been long employed; and it has paid off magnificently for some. One major discovery in this regard is that women can avoid risking their careers when they bring lawsuits as groups rather than as individuals. Here, many women's organizations are ready to help.

Between the small daily freedoms and the huge occasional ones which

[7] Cynthia Fuchs Epstein, *Woman's Place: Options and Limits in Professional Careers,* University of California Press, Berkeley, 1970, pp. 98–99.

change life-styles altogether are an array which enrich life and provide bonuses as one grows older. Systems of social support—friends—activities which keep the mind and body nimble, and working toward independence from societal pressures are all helpful in the present and will enrich life during widowhood or retirement.

VALUES IN CONFLICT

The many large-scale and small-scale "conflicts"—strikes and walkouts; hostility between parents and children; divorces—are at base due to different concepts of what is important, what has priority. The problem of how to achieve a more stable society is replicated within each woman. Every step toward the often-mentioned goal of liberation is a step away from being protected. Movements for freedom are frequently accompanied by the agony of decision. And change, which is so characteristic of the 1970s, requires so much flexibility that fatigue is often the result.

Pragmatic values are constantly being tested:

"I believe people should be qualified in order to be selected for a position. . . . *But* I recognize that most women have not had the opportunity to become as qualified as men."

"I believe in honesty and am tired of playing the expected stereotyped feminine games. . . . *But* I like men (love some) and really want to be appealing to them."

"I know that the situation for most uneducated women is worse in a time of inflation. . . . *But* I haven't the energy to develop my own potential and theirs too."

"I can see my husband (or the men I work with) feeling less confident as I become more independent. . . . *But* I feel so strong with my new-found confidence."

And so the inner dialogue goes. The trade-offs seem continual and certainly are numerous.

One value still seems to be firm—in the last half of the twentieth century there has been almost complete consensus about the value of work. Now, however, the discussion moves to another level:

"Are all kinds of work outside the home equally valuable?"

"Why is it more acceptable to have to work for economic reasons than to have to work for psychological completeness?"

"Am I fulfilling my potential by working as a girl Friday?"

A number of married couples have reported to interviewers that when both partners have careers and equity of treatment is thus required, stress is placed on each partner. When both maintain exciting and demanding careers, "their lives are subject to career pressures and domestic upsets that drain their energy and absorb their time. . . . (But the way of life is one they chose freely. . . .)"[8]

[8] Mary Bralove, "Working Partners," *Wall Street Journal,* May 13, 1975.

"You'd Be So Nice To Come Home To" is the title of a song of the 1940s. The physical and emotional softness of women were a relief highly valued by men oppressed by the war and the concrete, glass, and hard edges of working life. Naturally, women enjoyed and appreciated being valued. Conflict arose in the women's world when being appreciated as a nonintellectual resource lost some of its charm. The education of women over the past hundred years has finally created another set of values—those of contemporary society.

CHOICES WOMEN HAVE

There are other choices working women face which are really not new. For example:

To have a typical life of home, husband, and family, *or* to remain single and face fewer demands from others for time and attention.

To have the warmth of friendships and the delight of helping others, *or* to make an impact by steadfast orientation to upward mobility, with no time for the sidetracks such as counseling and sponsoring others.

To conform to the moral code of Western religions, with their strenuous emphasis upon the importance of the family, *or* to work out relationships with men (husbands and others) in ways which are less traumatic but lead to a "solo" life.

Perhaps the most stressful of all conflicts in values for career women is the dichotomy between the idealized image of femininity and the traits of a successful working person. Competence, systematic organization, predictable behavior, emotional control, assertiveness, and a "cool" approach to problem solving are qualities desirable in professionals (and in mothers). The point is that women need not choose between these and "femininity" except in their priorities. The choice is one of emphasis or degree. In fact, that is true of all value conflicts— whether the basis for choice from among options is one's own internal set of convictions or a constant attempt to please many others.

WHAT WOMEN HAVE TO OFFER

It sometimes seems that women are seeking new options for the most selfish of reasons—their own satisfaction. That may well be true. But also to be noted are the views held by men and women about the contributions women can make in nontraditional fields. For example, several opinion polls have reported that as many as seven in ten Americans believe the nation would be governed as well or better by women. They believe that women in political office would be more conscientious and economy-minded and would have more integrity. Whether one accepts this or not, it is certainly reasonable to believe that government would be more representative with a better balance of men and women leaders.

While credit for hastening the end of the war in Vietnam must surely be shared by a number of subgroups in America, the organizations of women ("War is not good for children and other living things," etc.) were among the most vocal and continuously energetic in changing public opinion. Perhaps the best indication of the revised image of American women is the fact that at least a few have now been elected to public office in their own right, not as the widows of officeholders (formerly the only way women were elected).

The new breed of women politicians have introduced feminism as a part of their campaigns, and their activities once elected. They are, in fact, representing the needs and interests of women.

Women's commentaries on their own experiences have become more open and reveal still other concepts of women's worth. In a personal letter, a woman who had not been appointed commented on the recent appointment of a man as director in a large business firm:

> This is of interest because Danny D. worked in training at the same time I did in Kalamazoo. In fact, we were in the same Intern Program there. He is a nice guy and capable but not the heavyweight Jones said they were looking for. . . . The firm doesn't have a policy yet regarding collective bargaining even though the unions are visiting every department. Since I've taken the time to get that training, it just reaffirms my belief that we women have something to offer.

The "something to offer" is frequently a combination of training and experience which apply to a specific position, with an added ingredient—understanding or so-called "intuitive" awareness. It seems to me, contrary to commonly held conviction, that intuition is not a biologically inherited trait, but rather the result of lifelong listening. Early childhood training of girls includes a tacit but continuous effort to develop an "early warning system." Anxious to be pleasing, protective of children and parents and old people, women develop great skill at nurturing. This skill, more highly developed in most women than in most men, is of course transferable to the marketplace of work.

The excellence of a secretary, nurse, teacher, social worker, or librarian is often a result of the application of nurturing skills to an occupation. Some nurturing is exceedingly useful in managerial work. Unfortunately, beyond that "some," more nurturing is counterproductive in an increasing number of occupations. Thus, the uniqueness of this aspect of women's contribution, although highly valued in some jobs, works to their detriment in others. Much is written throughout this book about stereotypes and traditional and nontraditional roles and activities. Whether an occupation or a relationship is involved, at the core is a conflict between self-expression and the weariness produced by playing the same role all the time.

While the women's movement has received the most (if not the best) press coverage in this country, recognition of women's needs and contributions to society is now worldwide. Efforts are being made in almost all countries to improve the situation of women because they are valued as a potential national resource. Economists have struggled to quantify the value of women in the home and to society. (Money is always a way of understanding value.) Most pleas by the public and by politicians for widening opportunities for women are justified by the loss which results when women's capabilities are wasted or misused. "An underutilized resource" is the concept which makes governments and businesses change their patterns. The United States Agency for International Development has stated that "women are a vital resource in improving the quality of life in the developing world as mothers and producers of goods and services. . . . The United States Congress has encouraged programs aimed at improving the lives of women in the national economies of developing countries. . . ."[9]

In this country, too, there is a growing concern that women should be better prepared to make a contribution and, once prepared, that they should be fairly dealt with in all phases of work. (See Chapter 22, by Kathryn Heath.) Congresswoman Patsy Mink (see the Epilogue) has been a leader in congressional action regarding equity for women.

WOMEN'S ECONOMIC IMPACT

As has already been noted, numerous attempts have been made to determine the economic value of women in the home. If a husband had to pay for services normally performed by his wife, what would the cost be? Of course, the answer depends upon the minimum national pay scale at the time—if one lumps all household tasks at the bottom of the pay scale. Typically, however, women as homemakers perform tasks of varying complexity (and different women perform different tasks at various levels of proficiency); the calculation is therefore greatly complicated.

No doubt labor economists will eventually come closer to a fair figure simply because many divorce settlements will be based on an equitable division of sums earned by both partners during the marriage. Also, as more homemakers seek to establish a comparable wage when applying for work in the marketplace, a more accurate figure will be needed for all the forms and scales used by personnel managers.

Whether firm figures will ever be agreed upon is not yet clear. Meanwhile, since larger numbers of women control money (from inheritance, from husbands, or from their own earnings), investment companies have found it worthwhile to help women learn about wise financial planning. Women are now allowing themselves to be recognized publicly for their skills of money management and investment planning. Negotiating for higher salaries must surely be included in the so-called "nontraditional" area.

The economic impact of women is not limited to the possession (or lack) of money. It has also created concern by government, which in turn has produced federal laws and regulations. Social Security, welfare regulations, and tax policies as they relate to women have been reexamined, and further study has been requested. Legislation to ensure equal pay for equal work and equal employment

---

[9] As reported in *Guidepost*, published by the American Personnel and Guidance Association, December 5, 1975.

opportunity has changed the financial operations of innumerable firms and agencies, and women have been awarded large settlements for past discrimination against them.[10] Even more important, assurances that fair and full employment will continue are a major factor in personnel and financial policies. There is much concern for women at both ends of the economic scale—low-income and high-income. Their needs are vastly different, but great problems exist for both.

Through their organizations, women are learning how to use their economic power. The League of Women Voters changed its national convention site for 1978 from Chicago to Cincinnati because Illinois had not ratified the Equal Rights Amendment (which the League supports) whereas Ohio had. The financial contributions of thousands of women to the several organizations supporting the Equal Rights Amendment (ERA) have made it possible to continue the strenuous and lengthy battle for legal equality for women.

Concern for ways to resolve the problems of women has increased to such an extent that newspapers, magazines, researchers, and politicians all speak about this issue. The American Assembly of Columbia University focused their Forty-ninth Assembly (October 30 to November 2, 1975) on women and the American economy.[11]

All parts of life, the economic sphere included, naturally interact. Families differ from the average if they have more money (or if they suffer less from inflation), but in any event the cost of running a home tends to increase when the mother and father both work. The increase in the number of young married women in the labor force has resulted in fewer children and a change in relationships between men and women. Still, the discrepancy between men's and women's salaries continues to exist and is even growing. *On the average, women earn 56 percent of what men earn.* Enforcement of legislation should and must eventually eliminate that discrepancy. Similarly, the long-established tradition of seniority as the basis for retaining employees conflicts with Affirmative Action and must be eliminated. Another positive approach is to systematize the movement of more women from labor-intensive occupations (called "traditional") to fields which are newer, more sparsely occupied, and technologically more labor-saving. The increase in women's contribution to the gross national product is reflected in the mounting concern about facilitating this contribution.

UTILIZING TIME

We tend to speak of time as we do money and refer to time-saving gadgets, systems, and methods. Choices which are available for discretionary time or fixed activities are discussed throughout this book. Our values are seen in the ways we choose to manipulate the time we have. It is important to note that misuse of time

[10] *Business Week,* November 25, 1972, reported the following awards in equal-pay cases: Wheaton Glass, $901,062; G. C. Murphy, $648,000; Pacific Telephone and Telegraph, $593,457; Midwest Manufacturing, $238,695; Daisy Manufacturing, $209,905; Hayes Industries, $206,214; American Can, $149,927; RCA, $100,432.

[11] Juanita M. Kreps, *Women and the American Economy—A Look to the 1980s* (The American Assembly), Prentice-Hall, Englewood Cliffs, N.J., 1976.

is exploding the myth that unencumbered time is particularly desirable. Alcohol and marijuana are too often used to fill in dull minutes and hours; their cost in human waste can be added to the statistics about women's lives. Optimum use of time becomes a key concept in improving the quality of life.

As with other parts of existence, women regard their time as more or less valuable depending upon how it is regarded by others. A mother's time is likely to be spent in being available; consequently, it is always open to disruption, to change of plans or pace, and to unequal division depending upon the current crisis. (That is one reason why housewives can become such fine managers.) Unfortunately, many women who return to school soon discover that studying at home is impossible—there are too many interruptions.

Time spent as a volunteer has never been considered as important as time spent earning money. Again and again women find themselves persuaded that their time is thoroughly expendable and therefore that their efforts are not very valuable. It soon becomes apparent that *control of one's time is a clear signal of one's status.*

But that is usually true only until aging and retirement. At that point older women, like women whose children or husbands have left home, find they own a commodity which for them has little worth. Here again, specialists in human development emphasize the positive effects of the early establishment of interests that will continue in old age: hobbies, friendships, and community involvement.

POWER

Personal power is a desirable tool for everyone—man and woman. Indeed, some minimum of power is necessary if a person is to achieve control over his or her life—at work, at home, or in the community.

Women have always needed power, and they continue to need it; what is changing is the way women are filling their need for power. Questions about power—How much is good or evil? To what degree is it useful or necessary? In what is it to be exercised or stored? How is one to get it and keep it?—have been explored by philosophers for centuries. Most women have traditionally exercised power from "behind the throne." Or, in the American phrase, "Behind every good man is a good woman." The social commentator Gloria Steinem has pointed out that women traditionally get their power through men.

Most women have found this method of satisfying what appears to be a basic human trait reasonably comfortable. Here and there over the ages a few women have exercised power on their own—Lucia de Medici and Mary, Queen of Scots, for example. Only in this century have a representative number of women accepted the need for public recognition and the ability to use power. Perhaps of all the contributions of the women's movement, the most vital one has been the frank avowal of the value which personal power has in the life of a woman. The power to decide; the power to be free to do or not to do; the power to compete equally—all of these are now part of a woman's identity, and, while unsettling at first, do improve the quality of life.

Women are now beginning to achieve power through their own resources—

principally through careers and the attainment of important positions in govern-ment or in the community. An important difference, of course, is that women may now actively seek power; in the past, women could achieve it only surrepti-tiously—under the table, so to speak. Where women can now achieve power without dependence upon a man (or men), they receive a concomitant increase in independence.

Thus, women who are seeking to attain power are doing so as a part of gaining control over their lives and acquiring the ability to develop their own value system. In some cases this takes the form of making a place for yourself in an inner circle—a group of decision makers. In other cases, following through on personal convictions may entail leaving a warm but stifling atmosphere which does not allow for personal growth.

The planning group of "Pioneers for Century III . . . A Bicentennial Conference"[12] selected the theme "power among women and men" and ad-dressed three types of power: power in interpersonal relationships, power in orga-nizations and institutions, and power in societies and the world.

Michael Korda, in *Power! How to Get It, How to Use It,*[13] defines power as a very personal matter. After describing all various "power plays" (symbolic and actual—in sports, games, and exercises), he attacks the question of women and power. On the whole, his analysis is not very heartening. "Power is thought of as being essentially male." "Most of the successful women I know either try to charm or nag because they haven't found the authentic voice of power." The chapter on women is fascinating, even to women who have some power, and should be read if only to understand better the power ploys of men.

The uses and abuses of power hold a special fascination for women; there is excitement in consciously recognizing how much power one already owns and skillfully using such power. Both recognition and use of power are dealt with by various contributors to this book. Chapter 8 (Next Steps Up: Women as Peers and Managers) is predicated on the assumption that many women have far more potential power than they either recognize or will exert. Actually, all alternatives, options, or choices are ultimately based on power—the power to decide.

Conjoint with the urge to bolster the self-confidence of women and to im-prove their abilities so that they could decide has been the philosophy of quite a few women that the traditional decision-making process was inadequate for today's society. Strong women in positions of power have experimented with not repeating men's methods and have instead chosen to innovate, to create less hierarchical organizations and procedures. One interesting experiment is the ef-fort by Konnilyn Feig and Constance Carrol to accomplish the work of the College of Arts and Sciences at the University of Maine by means of "task forces and committees rather than leader fiat."[14]

---

[12] University of Cincinnati Conference "Pioneers for Century III: Power Among Women and Men," Cincinnati, Ohio, April 22–25, 1976. The conference was cosponsored by the University of Cincinnati Office of Women's Studies, the Ohio American Revolution Bicentennial Commission, and the Greater Cincinnati Consortium of Colleges and Universities.

[13] Michael Korda, *Power! How to Get It, How to Use It,* Random House, New York, 1975, chap. 8.

[14] Georgie Anne Geyer, "Shading the System," *Los Angeles Times,* October 30, 1975.

Other efforts to avoid the limiting, repressive, closed, politicized environment of many institutions managed by men have produced increasingly creative operational styles. Rather than waste their energy in continuous battle in an unfriendly locale, many women are starting their own firms (see Chapter 9 if that is what you want to do). The challenge of helping one another (known as "sisterhood" in feminist circles) is being met by urban communes for living or working and by ad hoc groups such as Women in Business, a Los Angeles organization of working professionals whose goal is to "get women together who can help each other." [15]

In academia, where change always comes slowly, the entry of women into responsible positions has been appallingly slow, although some academic women have found their lives changed. A report on women's political impact, together with recommendations for equalizing institutional power lines by fostering new organizational habits, is another hopeful sign.[16] There are numerous additional examples. In sum, they justify the conviction that, since change is so difficult in structures created and dominated by men, life would be better for everyone if the ground rules were revised.

POWERLESS WOMEN

The opposite of grasping for power or reorganizing it is represented by the woman who has been too long in a familiar and once favorable position. Such a woman is likely to be single and consequently dependent upon her salary as her only source of income; and she is unable to see potential power either in her current position or elsewhere. Actually, there may be more satisfaction, fulfillment, and growth in another position. But years of association with an organization, and the retirement systems of large and small organizations, seem to militate against change. Similarly, a married woman is often the sole source of income for her family, or finds that the years have sapped her feeling of power, with the same result—a wearisome, ineffectual, and dull work life which carries over into her personal and home life.

The ugliness and dismay of being powerless is too common to be ignored. Nor need it be endured. There are resources for women of all ages and stages, far more accessible than ever before. My own favorite example is the first class in "Developing Personal Potential" taught by Herbert Otto in 1966, of which one member was a woman of seventy-five.

AUTHORITY

Any discussion of power presupposes that a person or organization can, if necessary, use coercion in order to change behavior. Whether a manager, a mayor, or a military officer is concerned, the suggestion of force, subtle or overt, is present. Most women, perhaps because of past and present socializing forces, are repelled

[15] Lore Caulfield, President, Women in Business, Hollywood, California; personal communication.

[16] Florence Howe (ed.), *Women and the Power to Change,* A Volume of Essays Sponsored by The Carnegie Commission on Higher Education, McGraw-Hill, New York, 1975.

by the idea of applying this masculine model to their own behavior. Other women, including many of those who consider themselves "liberated," believe that since this traditional use of power has not worked well, they will be more successful if they develop other means of exerting influence. For them, a sounder, more rational approach seems to be use of authority as a vehicle for leadership. "Authority" in this sense is knowing—thoroughly, deeply, widely—all the elements of a given situation. Examples range from an executive secretary who can analyze the attitudes of others toward a planned change, to Rachel Carson, who influenced federal legislation because of her research into ecological decay. Completeness of knowledge is the center of such authority.

In the making and implementing of decisions, probably both modes of power are needed. There are some people who possess both qualities—charismatic and strong leaders who also are experts in their fields. Presidents of governments, organizations, and corporations who came up through the ranks hold both authority and power. But women need not wait to be "president" to exert influence, to affect major decisions. Few people in power can function for long without expertise. As our world continues to grow more complex and to use more technology, as bureaucracies continue to become larger and more complicated, and as values of different groups continue to compete, women will find new and challenging ways to demonstrate the authority they have earned and thus deserve.

VALUES IN ACTION

Dreams and fantasies, expectations and aspirations, the search for fulfillment—all stream from the cornucopia of the good society. It was possible for representatives of almost every nation in the world to meet in Mexico City during the International Women's Year (1975) and to find common threads of concern. The threads were not all closely woven, and their texture was uneven, but the need for institutional changes in the various nations was apparent. Changes in the delivery of health care, in the planning of education, in the establishment of economic stability, and in assuring the dignity and worth of individuals were inherent in the discussions.

Similar analysis in each community of this nation must follow, proceeding according to the World Plan for Action unanimously adopted by more than 100 governments at the United Nations World Conference in the International Women's Year.[17] While institutional life is being adjusted to the realities of the women's movement, each woman must make her own contribution to the improvement of the general quality of life, which inevitably effects the quality of her own life.

---

[17] The full text of the World Plan of Action can be obtained from the United Nations or the State Department. A condensed version is published and distributed by the Women's Equity Action League Educational and Legal Defense Fund, National Press Building, Washington, D.C. 20045.

BIBLIOGRAPHY

Boslooper, Thomas, and Marcia Hayes: *The Femininity Game,* Stein and Day, New York, 1973. A breezy, fast-paced book which educates and entertains, examining with humor the behavior and attitudes of women as they face or duck competition. Some resolutions of the age-old problem of dealing with competition are suggested.

Carter, Mae R. (ed.): *The Role of Women in Politics,* University of Delaware, Division of Continuing Education, Newark, Delaware, 1974. A compilation of papers presented at a conference held at the University of Delaware. Since the goal was to think about future roles of women in politics, the individual papers examine the problems facing women who aspire to political careers while encouraging such women because they are needed.

Epstein, Cynthia Fuchs: *Woman's Place: Options and Limits in Professional Careers,* University of California Press, Berkeley, 1970. A carefully researched but easily read book about how women view themselves and their career aspirations, with an excellent discussion of the importance of knowing about values.

Fox, Robert, Ronald Lippett, and Eva Schindler-Rainman: *Towards a Humane Society: Images of Potentiality,* NTL Learning Resources Corporation, Inc., Fairfax, Va., 1973. Three social scientists discuss the great possibilities of community organizations and action. The authors' experience in working with volunteers is reflected in their detailed recommendations of ways to bring more humanity into our cooperative ventures.

Maas, Henry S., and Joseph A. Kuypers: *From Thirty to Seventy,* Jossey-Bass, San Francisco, 1975. A report of data from a forty-year study of a group of middle-class residents of San Francisco which has produced extraordinary insight into the different ways people age. For our purposes here, the comments on women and the relevance of their early roles to their later life-styles are especially interesting.

McDonald, Donald: "The Liberation of Women," *The Center Magazine,* The Center for the Study of Democratic Institutions, Santa Barbara, California, May–June 1972. A clearly written summary of the rationale for the women's movement ("an effort to get at the truth"). The author uses the writings of women and men and makes his own comments. This supportive essay ends with an interesting list of recommended readings.

Chapter 2

When Women Work

Judith M. Bardwick
Elizabeth Douvan

Judith M. Bardwick, Ph.D., is a Professor of Psychology at the University of Michigan. She is also a consultant and writer and has served as a reviewer for nine journals. She has been a member of the National Science Foundation and the American Association for Science. She has published in such journals as *Psychosomatic Medicine, Psychology Today*, and the *Journal of Social Issues* and has contributed chapters to many books. Among her own books are *Feminine Personality and Conflict* (Brooks/Cole, Belmont, Calif., 1970) and *The Psychology of Women* (Harper and Row, New York, 1971).

Elizabeth Douvan, Ph.D., is Helen N. Kellogg Professor of Psychology at the University of Michigan. A consultant, lecturer, and writer, she has written for journals and professional publications such as *Psychiatry, Children, Contemporary Psychology,* and *Science;* she has also contributed numerous chapters to books. She is coauthor of a number of books, including *The Adolescent Experience* (Wiley, New York, 1966), *Adolescent Development* (Allyn and Bacon, Boston, 1969), and *Feminine Personality and Conflict* (Brooks/Cole, Belmont, Calif., 1970).

American women who work usually make a commitment to two major roles: wife-homemaker-mother and worker. This creates both logistical and psychological problems. Because of the traditional priority accorded to the sex-linked family roles and the heavy demands of these roles when children are young, most women leave work when their first child is born and do not return to work before their youngest child is in school. This general pattern is still true although a very significant number of mothers with preschool children are now in the labor force and although the number of years during which women leave the labor force has been declining. This pattern of employment has meant that most women's career development has suffered significant disruption. That is, *for the majority of women, work has been contingent on and constrained by traditional responsibilities.* While girls do very well in school, and while this enables them to know that they are in fact well able to learn and compete, they have tended not to take the competitive work commitment as seriously as that of the traditional role in the earlier years of their adulthood.

This means they have not planned for their career development or taken into consideration the effect of work upon the traditional role. The reverse is also true: women have given inadequate thought to the effect traditional responsibilities have on the possibility of a career. Basically, this happens because their motivation is mixed in early adulthood. The long-range consequences—the advantages and problems of both commitments—never become clear, and therefore solutions are deferred. Underlying this conflict of role commitments there is a conflict between thinking of the self in an egocentric way and thinking of the self in relation to others.

Today, the rise of feminism and widespread acceptance of feminist values, the emphasis on gratification of individual ambitions, the generally expanding economy which has absorbed more workers, an inflationary trend which creates pressure for wives to work, the increasing education of women, the new norm of a two-child family, decreased mortality for children and increased longevity for women—all these factors create an enormous motivation for women to enter and remain in the labor force.

What will it take to effect really significant changes in the number of women who do notable work, who initiate and decide, who are responsible and visible, who are autonomous and assertive, who are leaders, managers, and deciders? It seems that three factors are simultaneously necessary: (1) supportive legislation which can coerce; (2) real commitment to equal opportunity by high-level executives in organizations; (3) psychological changes in both women and men within organizations. For women, or at least for many of them, there has to be real change in motives and fears—and in their attitudes toward other women and toward themselves as women.

For the purposes of discussion we have divided the problems of the working woman into forces external to her and forces within the woman's own psychological system.

EXTERNAL FORCES

Logistical Challenges

For married women with children, the practical problems of managing two major
life commitments are the most salient and pressing issues. On one level these are
strictly logistical problems—who shops for food, who drives children to lessons,
who cooks or does the laundry—but at another level they involve symbolic issues
having to do with old habits and expectations, and with traditional divisions of
power and freedom. Many women, enlightened by the women's movement, are
pressing for the sharing of responsibilities at home as a normal procedure.

Traditionally, men have brought home money and have been exempt from
routine chores of home maintenance; but women who brought home money were
also responsible for all the routine functions involving house and children. Today, the clash over household logistics is the symptom of women's insistence on
the new view that when both partners bring home the bacon, who cooks it becomes an issue for discussion. Since these logistical problems are not seen as
matters of social policy but rather as something for individuals to solve, there are
gaps in the social structure: grossly inadequate child-care resources; insufficient
public transportation; no communal facilities for laundry, cooking, or cleaning;
and no public agreement that women's changing roles should make these a matter of social concern or legislation.

The most obvious solution to these household problems is for women to
initiate—because husbands and children are unlikely to volunteer—new patterns
of shared responsibilities. In our experience, clichés about new freedoms are
tossed around like salad greens, but the truth is that the old habits of divided
labor and privilege are difficult to dislodge. Characteristically, even when you
succeed in changing the pattern, the other family members act as though they are
doing you a favor—a situation that is enraging and may become exhausting. It
takes a lot of energy to continuously monitor these novel arrangements, and it is
difficult to resist the temptation to slip back into the apparently easier, uncon-
troversial older ways. It is draining to continually assert and insist on our rights:
it conflicts with our need to be loving and generous. We are still close in time to
a period when unusually liberal men "permitted" their wives to work.

There are other solutions, other arrangements of these everyday tasks which
require going outside of the nuclear family. Women's going to school or to work
is easier if certain tasks are pooled. The most radical solution is a communal
living arrangement, but relatively few Americans would be willing to give up the
degree of privacy and autonomy that this calls for. In our town there are a
number of shared work efforts that illustrate solutions of varying intimacy.

There are child-care cooperatives in which all the labor is provided by the
parents of the children under the general direction of a professional teacher.
There are also several play groups in which each mother agrees to take care of
four other women's children one day a week. In exchange, each mother receives
four days when her children are cared for by someone else. Neighborhood
groups, usually five or six families, have gotten together to plan menus and shop

for and cook dinners for all the families. Each woman is responsible for cooking one night a week; at 6 o'clock someone from each of the other five families arrives with pots to carry home their share.

As mothers of teenagers, we especially like a relatively recent development. Prodded by the shortage of jobs for teenagers, groups of two or three young people constitute themselves housecleaning companies and hire themselves out to women in their neighborhoods. This arrangement accomplishes several things: houses are cleaned, the isolation of housework is replaced by social cooperation, the work is paid, and housework becomes a recognized accomplishment.

Since most American women will have two children and also want to be involved in raising them, one realistic option is to lower the level of your ambition for about a decade. This does *not* mean abandoning one's professional commitment or perspective. *But if the commitment to children is free of conflict—as much as any large responsibility can be free of conflict—then a radical change in one's experience can produce positive outcomes because it involves growth and maturing.* Child rearing, if it is not regarded as a loss of opportunity, can be one of the truly significant experiences. Goals and conflicts for women can be clarified for those who want to be both wives and mothers and workers when their perspective is maintained and they understand the changing nature of commitments within the life span. From such an understanding women can create a sense that they are making decisions and controlling their lives. This, by itself, will reduce their ambivalence.

While one of the goals of serious feminists is the equal sharing of child rearing by fathers and mothers, that is an unlikely development for the general population. In the face of inadequate child care, parental anxiety, and maternal guilt, we think it constructive to emphasize that the period of heavy responsibilities in child rearing is relatively short, and that for the relatively unambivalent mother it can produce long-term personal gains.

We have spoken of the commitment to one's own children as a growth experience. For some women, involvement with children and with the community institutions related to child rearing may directly benefit their professional interests. As psychologists, we learned a lot from our children; it is not difficult to imagine linguists, physicians, educators, city planners, lawyers, architects, and others learning something real and relevant, gaining new insights, and establishing new professional priorities from interaction with, and support of, their children.

Some options now exist which allow a woman to continue her career development during the decade of most active mothering. These include part-time work; flexible working hours; work module arrangements; sharing of one job by two persons; and freelancing. Unfortunately, these options are not widely available. Therefore, an interesting alternative for this short period is professional work done on a volunteer basis or a serious involvement in nonprofessional volunteer work.

When unemployment is high, there is no pressure on employers to adapt to the unusual needs of working mothers. As a result, the choice tends to be full-time paid employment or nothing. Contributing your professional skills without pay may be damaging to one's ego, but it should be recognized that one is getting irreplaceable experience, maintaining skills, establishing professional contacts, and opening channels for reentry into the job market in a few years. If you cannot manage a professional job and no part-time job is available—and if you can afford it—unpaid use of your professional skills may be regarded as an investment in your career training.

The important point is to maintain your skills and develop others within the constraints of that period when children are too young for school. From that perspective, even volunteer work outside of your profession can have benefits which are usually overlooked.[1] For women who have not trained for professions, or for those with just a few years of work experience, volunteer work often offers more interesting, responsible, and independent opportunities than they would find in the job market. We know women who gradually assumed leadership of local organizations like Planned Parenthood, the League of Women Voters, political parties, parent-teacher associations, the Red Cross, and hospital volunteers. Characteristically, their involvement began slowly and gradually increased, and—sometimes to their surprise—several years later they found themselves leading the organization. In truth, they usually worked a full week; but psychologically they had the feeling that because the work was not paid, they could always get out. Some of these women became sufficiently visible in the community to be offered management jobs for which they had no formal qualifications. For other women, volunteer work has provided a sense of worth and competence, the accomplishment of goals traditionally important to women, and the sheer joy of a job well done. In our college community it is clear that many of the women who have returned to school, and later to work, gained the self-confidence to do so from their success in volunteer organizations. Because a broad, varied group of people are involved in community organizations, one is also likely to gain diverse and intricate connections within the community.

Connections with people, experience in managing and initiating, and the development of a sense of competence are obviously invaluable preparation for a serious career. The importance of volunteer work is that it offers significant opportunity and responsibility, under flexible conditions, without competition from professionals, with commitment a matter of choice. (See also Chapter 6.)

Facing the Organization

A central problem is that since there have been very few women leaders in nonvolunteer organizations, responses to women at work are likely to be governed more by myth and stereotype than by actual experience. Myths and stereotypes cannot be dismissed lightly even when they are wrong, because they affect

[1] On Standard Form 171, the Personal Qualifications Statement for applicants for Federal Civil Service positions, in item 20 there is the following paragraph: "Section 3311 of title 5, United States Code, provides that in examinations in which experience is a factor, credit will be granted for any pertinent religious, civic, welfare, service, and organizational activity which you have performed either with or without compensation. You *may,* if you wish, report such experience at the end of your employment history if you feel that it represents qualifying experience for the position(s) for which you are applying. Show actual time spent in such activity."

people's expectations so that behaviors which conform to the expectation are remembered more than behaviors which do not. Without real experience individuals in organizations, and thus the organization itself, are guided by the myths and are therefore likely to behave in ways which elicit the stereotyped behavior. As a result, a woman's behavior can be guided by a stereotype whether she yields to it or resists it.

Few of the myths about working women are flattering; women work for pin money, they get sick, they are bitchy, they are subject to raging fluctuations of hormones and wildly fluctuating moods, they are seductive and threaten the wives of the men they work with, they are thinking of their kids at home (which is where they ought to be), they lack ambition, they are not serious or reliable, and so on.

All of this leads to certain behaviors in institutions. Obviously, women's careers are not taken seriously; neither are individual women. More specifically, actions which in men are considered appropriate are interpreted in women as evidence of aggression, vindictiveness, emotionalism, and personalism. We might note that marginal employees of both sexes, feeling insecure in their position, are less likely than those who are taken seriously and feel secure to make work their major commitment, and they are more likely to personalize situations, anticipate threats, react emotionally, and either withhold aggression or explode with aggression instead of using measured, appropriate assertiveness.

Both men and women prefer not to work for or with a woman, in part because women are less respected than men. The expectation of inappropriate behaviors from women may contribute to this preference, but basically it exists because men—their accomplishments and their perceived personalities—are unthinkingly and automatically given more respect than women. We observe further evidence of basic sexism when we see men reluctant to act as mentors and patrons for women because they cannot bring themselves to acknowledge that their jobs, to which they have devoted a good portion of their lives, could be done as well by women: such a recognition is too threatening to their basic sense of masculine identity and self-esteem. Because of sexual overtones in a society where women are primarily sex objects, it is also true that the intimacy of a mentor-protégé relationship contains a possible threat to the man's relationship with his wife.

Partly because of sexism, few women have been promoted to important positions or hired as candidates for important careers. Thus few women can achieve responsible positions, and the few who do are always deviant. It is always difficult to become a leader; it is more difficult when there are no role models, when the organization—whether governmental, academic, or corporate—cannot perceive your potential, when you cannot enter the normal channels of promotion, when you are defined as ineligible, when successful women are considered exceptions.

As a result of all these forces, working women are always perceived as women who are employed and not as workers who are women. For women, gender is always significant.

What can women do to counteract and neutralize these limiting factors? We think that women in any organization must pool their efforts and insights to exert leverage within the organization. Women must learn the nature of the implicit structure and channels in the organization and learn to use these to achieve objectives which will ultimately help all women within that organization. We are suggesting that *sexism requires organized group effort*; the sum of efforts by individuals will not equal that of the group. Competitiveness between individual women will have to be muted. In the long run, individual goals will be realized most effectively and for more individuals through group effort. Without shared insights, individual women are all too likely to interpret their lack of success as evidence of personal inadequacy rather than the result of sexism.

We recommend that women in organizations form caucuses to clarify problems of particular interest and to suggest solutions. Such caucuses might, for example, take up child care, equal rights to overtime, the effects of protective legislation, possibilities for module scheduling, opportunities for job training, and ways to comply with federal regulations concerning equal opportunity.

Specifically, efforts must be directed toward increasing the number of women hired, especially in managerial positions, and getting more women promoted when their skills enable them to cope with increased responsibilities. We often find that women in large organizations do not have a clear understanding of the channels of promotion or of the training and experience required for promotion. Men are more likely to have picked up that information through their informal networks. Codification and clarification of the requirements can only help women because secrecy and obscurity always support and maintain the status quo. When requirements are not clear and open positions are not announced, promotions will go to people who are already visible in the establishment. Traditionally, these do not include women.

On a personal level, women must be ready to support the efforts of other women, to be especially attuned to their needs and to the merits of their work. Our society and the institutions within it are organized, in general, hierarchically; and the largest rewards go to those who compete successfully as individuals. Given the pressures for equal opportunity, especially in a recessionary economy when there are few job openings, able women are in reality being pitted against each other. It will take extraordinary dedication and creativity, and a long-range perspective, for women to resist the temptation of successful competition and understand the ultimate advantage of developing cooperative solutions. In our experience women in academia are sensitive to sexism in their institutions. But often women in beginning or middle management in business and industry seem unaware of sexism in their organizations, feel little commitment to other women, and are convinced that gender has had no impact on their careers. This lack of awareness has produced successful women in business, government, and academia who are convinced that sex is irrelevant. In their view only motivation, determination, talent, and ambition count. These women feel that if they could succeed, so can other women. By itself this attitude, while not helpful, is not injurious to other women. It becomes destructive when, like many successful men, a woman does not want the person succeeding her to be a woman; for the successful woman is likely to be in a position where she can effectively block promotion for other women. Many successful women enjoy the rewards of success and that special and delicious sensation of being extraordinary, even unique. Unfortunately, the fact that someone is a woman does not mean that she is necessarily a feminist.

INTERNAL FORCES

Taking Yourself Seriously

Perhaps the central problem for the working woman is a psychological one. You must learn to take yourself seriously as an individual. You must perceive yourself as an individual who is more than and different from someone's wife, daughter, mother, sister, or friend. When you are accustomed to thinking of yourself as you relate to others, it is an immense task to take on the responsibility for yourself outside of the matrix of your relationships. You must establish long-term goals, set priorities, make choices, and become comfortable with an ambition which implies making demands on others as well as on yourself. We are saying that you must develop a sense of yourself which is healthy but more egocentric than you are accustomed to.

You can expect a little guilt and a lot of anxiety. That is inevitable, given the fact that you will not be doing everything that you once did for others and, at the same time, you will be asking others to do things that they have not done before. You will be declaring your priorities and saying that they are as legitimate as anyone else's. This is true even for those women who are neither married nor mothers, since the traditional female role and the stereotyped personality qualities that define femininity hinge on qualities of selfless giving. Women who have glowed from the sense of giving, women who have never thought of themselves except in the context of roles that come from relationships, and women whose employers, husbands, parents, or children resist the development of their sense of independence—all such women will experience some fear. Women, however, have the advantage over men of being able to admit vulnerability and acknowledge dependency and to use this admission to guide them toward solutions.

To the extent that you become visible and successful in an organization or field where women are rare, you run the risk of experiencing psychological conflict between ambition realized and traditional femininity. Many feminists neglect this crucial conflict involving central values and basic definitions of the self. Few women can flourish in a situation where they are significantly deviant, ambivalent about their own values, and derided as men in skirts.

When a woman acts with appropriate decisiveness and assertiveness, her behavior is likely to be interpreted negatively because it contradicts definitions of what is acceptably feminine. When men act the same way, their behavior is consonant with our traditional ideas of masculinity and thus does not jar us or unsettle our emotions. For women, two factors are involved: which behaviors are appropriate and in which situations the behaviors are appropriate. Decisive, assertive, or independent behavior is antithetical to the traditional idea of femininity; in the work situation, where such behavior is critically important, it is never-theless forbidden to women insofar as women workers are still perceived as wom-en.

Women inexperienced in managing, leading, and deciding may act inappro-priately because management is a skill that takes a lot of practice and because those managed must be willing to be led. Particularly crucial is the ability to state one's position assertively, in a way which is definite but not aggressive, hostile, or passive-aggressive.

Assertive behavior is not hostile, because it is neither destructive nor person-al: you are not trying to humiliate or defeat someone else. Assertive behavior is not passive, because you are declaring your opinion overtly and are in effect saying, "This is my position and I am willing to be responsible for it." Women have been taught to use indirect, subtle, personal, and passive forms of aggression because these accord with expectations and because oblique forms of aggression allow one to avoid confrontation, with its risk of rejection. It takes some self-esteem, some sense of the legitimacy of one's own stance, and some experience that the sky does not fall down when one overtly takes a differing position, in order to make assertive behavior normal.

Women, like all other marginal people, will progress in leadership to the extent that they are able to give up hostility, for hostility provokes defensive behavior from those who are attacked. Similarly, women and other marginal people will be trusted to the extent that they give up passive aggression, which confuses and misleads those who are being led. Assertive behavior is objective, impersonal, and directed toward problem solving; issues of intimacy and person-ality (and thus of anxiety and defense) are intrusive and disruptive at work.

Any level of leadership demands that you accept responsibility for decisions which are public. It is necessary to acknowledge the fact that you will face com-petition and criticism. Most people will be uninterested in what kind of person you are; they will be interested in what you produce. While work can be a friendly place, it is intrinsically impersonal, and leadership tends to entail loneli-ness. When your commitment to work is serious, you must accept the fact that you have taken on a major obligation—to your organization, your field—and that this obligation often has priority over other obligations. Choosing to lead is also choosing to limit other freedoms.

Recent data on people's fear of success indicates that men and women are now roughly equal in this psychological dimension. In the recent past, women showed much more fear of success than men, and it was believed that this was because women were afraid that being very successful jeopardized their sense of acceptable femininity. That interpretation seemed especially compelling since the women who were most fearful of success were those who were placed in positions where they had to compete with men. Today it seems that there are many reasons to fear success, and anxiety about femininity is only one of them. When equal proportions of males and females demonstrate a fear of success, then it is plausi-ble to think that the origin of the fear lies in the realization of the costs to the individual of being intensely committed to success. Outstanding success is both gratifying and costly. Bardwick found that outstandingly successful men are disproportionately preoccupied with work and continuously generate conditions within work tasks which engross them, especially conditions which are risky but manageable.[2] Outstanding success probably requires this kind of preoccupation with work. When people covet outstanding success, they must acknowledge their motivation and they must expect gratifications which outweigh the costs in energy, loss of alternatives, personal relationships, and personal freedom.

There is some tendency for people who are inexperienced with success to dismiss past accomplishments as signifying success. They are also more willing to participate in efforts where success is not probable. Participation in group efforts allows them to deny their individual responsibility for the outcome. People who are outstandingly successful tend to take their commitment and time seriously. They do not participate unless they have made a conscious and deliberate choice, unless the effort is worth accomplishing, unless the effort has some reasonable chance of success. In this way, successful people assert their value and participate only in efforts which are likely to succeed. As a result, they are very likely to be successful again, and the new success will reaffirm their sense of their own value.

People who take on leadership cannot avoid criticism, competition, and conflict. These are outcomes of leadership itself, and they are antithetical to women's traditional roles. They are heavy burdens to anyone, but especially to people who do not have a secure sense of purpose, of self, and of self-esteem. Newer styles of management emphasize less competitive, more cooperative modes of interacting and problem solving. Still, competition from others for leadership positions and criticism and conflict about decisions are intrinsic to leadership. Leaders must accept the fact that, as Truman said, "The buck stops here" and "If you can't take the heat, get out of the kitchen."

Forming Supportive Relationships

Because stress is inevitable, we would again emphasize the value of sharing feelings of conflict, difficult problems, frustrations, and possible solutions with other women who face similar challenges. If the organization is not large enough to make a women's caucus feasible, it may be desirable to go to a group of women outside the organization. An occasional fortunate woman will be able to establish an honest, open, sharing relationship with an older, more experienced man or woman who will serve as a mentor. In our experience, this kind of honest intimacy is more easily found in a one-to-one relationship with a woman peer. While such a relationship may be used to explore business problems or family conflicts, it is, in fact, essentially a friendship and not a task-oriented partnership. In our own relationships of this nature, we find that we talk business only occasionally. When we do, we share irritations, complaints, and insights; we pool our observations and talk our way to a consensus about where our organization or own work ought to go. Mostly, there is a great deal of tacit sharing, because in our lives we

[2] Judith M. Bardwick, "The Dynamics of Successful People," in D. McGuigan (ed.), *New Research on Women,* University of Michigan Press, Ann Arbor, 1974, pp. 86–104.

have so many experiences in common. In fact, it is with the mentor-friend that we tend to do frivolous and spontaneous things.

In our society, friends of this sort may not be easily found; and in any organization, essential competitiveness may inhibit the growth of trust. But the value of such a relationship is so great that we recommend that women seek out places where real friends may be found. We are suggesting that such friendships are partly based on common problems, and that it therefore makes sense to seek out groups of women who are confronting the same issues and have gotten together to improve their work skills or to gain personal insight. Consciousness-raising sessions, classes in colleges, centers for continuing education for women, assertiveness-training courses, and management sessions for women are all sources of potential friendships.

With the growth of feminist awareness, many American women are either facing or anticipating the conflicts of multiple roles. It is therefore very likely that among your present friends, in your neighborhood, and even in your family you may begin to find a level of intimacy which can become supportive.

Just as conflict is inherent in leadership, so are envy and unmanageable idealization. It is difficult for the leader and the follower not to make the work relationship also a personal relationship. A personal relationship holds out the sweet prospect of being liked as well as respected, but it also holds out the possibility of feeling personally rejected when your work is criticized or your position is disputed. Women have been conditioned to be sensitive to personal nuances, to base their self-esteem on others' responses to them. It is therefore especially difficult for them to disentangle the personal from the impersonal. Women must learn not to seek signs that they are loved in the impersonal world of work.

It is predictable that women will seek approval from others, especially from men, partially because men's judgments are more respected and especially because affirmation from men has, for so long, been the gold at the end of the rainbow. This tendency to seek approval, common to people who are unsure of themselves, is one source of the idea that women are more emotional than men—an idea which is sometimes true. Women in organizations should remember that friendly relationships facilitate work but that intimate relationships can easily become disruptive. Intimate relationships with sexual overtones can be especially disruptive. Since organizations find the consequences of personal relationships intrusive, women's caucuses may benefit especially from training in this area and sensitivity to it.

When we run a management session, we find it useful to open the workshop by asking the women enrolled, "How do you feel about being in a class made up of women, led by a woman, focusing on problems particular to women? How do you feel about being labeled a minority person? Do you have any particular commitment to other women in your organization? Can you tell me how your sex has affected your career?" A significantly large number of women who have taken the initiative to enroll in the class nevertheless deny that being female has affected their work life in any significant way. That behavior is so paradoxical that it is easy to label it "denial."

In fact, many of the participants are aware that when education, skill, length of tenure, and experience are held constant, the only explanation for inequities in salary, promotion, and status is gender. In spite of the visibility of the feminist movement and statistics about inequitable treatment of women in academia, business, and government, many women find it threatening to acknowledge sexism and to identify themselves with minority groups.

It should be clear that significant change in the status of and opportunities for employed women will depend upon acknowledgment of sexism and cooperative group efforts directed toward change in the nation's laws and practices, toward specific goals within an organization, and toward the emotional buttressing of individual women who are experiencing the pain of changing norms, evolving self-concepts, and dealing with the uncertainties that always accompany extraordinary social change. The task is obvious for those few women who are pioneers. Women who are neither leaders nor pioneers, but who are still making some change in their role commitments, will also find it both exhilarating and painful to confront these issues and make choices. Consciousness-raising groups are evidence that people find comfort when they discover that their anxiety is both shared and normal. We repeat our belief that change will be best facilitated by deliberate cooperation among women.

THE PROMISE FOR WOMEN WHO WORK

In a psychological revulsion against the exaggerated idealization of women's traditional role during the 1950s, and because of real changes resulting from better maternal and infant care, increased education for women, an inflationary economy, a high divorce rate, and smaller families, the traditional female role has lost some of its power and significance and some of its certainty. It is no longer a haven of security or automatically a form of achievement. It is natural for American women, then, to turn to work. But now there is a new danger: that women will expect to find unmixed pleasure in the new commitment. It seems to us essential for women to be aware of the costs to them of the work commitment. If they are not, they will experience frustration, disappointment, and ultimately an alienation from work similar to the alienation from homemaking which is now being experienced by so many women.

It is easy to romanticize a role when one has no experience of it. As a result of perceptive, critical analysis of the traditional homemaker-mother role, we have witnessed a depreciation of women's traditional commitments and a concomitant idealization of the rewards of work. *But there are costs to every commitment, and work is no exception.* Today, the feminist movement remains middle-class, so that the work which is discussed is not simply jobs but careers which require education and imply a lifelong commitment. The costs of a job are easy to visualize, but the costs of a career—which are just as significant—may be overlooked. If you choose to succeed in a career you must get used to responsibility, to being assertive and competitive, to being respected rather than liked, to being independent and sometimes nonconformist, and to being criticized. If you want to succeed to an outstanding degree you will have to set goals and you will have to grapple with competitors, your own fluctuating motivation, and your attitudes toward other choices which are available to you. In many careers, outstanding success involves dominating others and using power. Becoming successful in a career involves getting used to being responsible for decisions which are highly visible, and taking on responsibility for other people. To the extent that the goal of success becomes consuming, you lose other options. When we discuss middle-class men this is easy to see; in the political climate of feminism, the cost to women is often denied.

On the other hand, there are obviously important gains to individual women when they engage seriously in the work life of their society. Americans, more than any other people, respect and esteem those who succeed in the competitive engagements of work. Women have tended to be cut off from opportunities to create a sense of self-esteem that derives, almost by definition, from the exercise of individual competence and achievement. Women who are committed to careers are especially prone to perceive work and family responsibilities as competitive and incompatible. We believe that much is lost when a choice is made between one and the other. Rather, we believe that women should participate in both roles, as men do. Women have been marginal in the work sector. Marginal people tend to cope differently, to perceive differently, from those who are within the establishment. When there are enough women in the establishment so that they feel free to act on their unique values, this very marginalism may contribute creative, new, valuable solutions.

It has been our personal experience—and it is our theory—that people grow when they are involved in more than one set of significant commitments. People become complex as they extend themselves, coping with and integrating the different demands of various spheres of life. People living complex lives become richer and more complex. As they shift from one set of obligations and investments to another, they are also able to clarify for themselves what aspects of their roles are beneficial and what aspects are costly. In the process they are better able to clarify their sense of self, their knowledge of who they are.

BIBLIOGRAPHY

Almquist, E. M., and S. S. Angrist: *Careers and Contingencies,* University of Massachusetts Press, Amherst, 1975. A report of a study of college women which makes clear the contingent character of young women's career plans.

Bardwick, Judith M.: "The Dynamics of Successful People," in D. McGuigan (ed.), *New Research on Women,* University of Michigan Press, Ann Arbor, 1974. This is a report of a study of successful men; it provides some information as to how they see themselves, set goals, form priorities, and affect the lives of their families.

————: "Some Notes About Power Relationships between Women," in A. Sargent (ed.), *Beyond Sex Roles,* West, St. Paul, Minn., 1976. The author speculates about why women are uncomfortable using power or dealing with powerful people, especially powerful women. Note is taken of the needs of women who feel themselves powerless, how this feeling influences their behavior, and how their needs and behaviors differ from those of people who consider themselves powerful.

————, and Elizabeth Douvan: "Ambivalence: The Socialization of Women," in V. Gornick and B. Moran (eds.), *Woman in Sexist Society,* Basic Books, New York, 1971. Here we discuss the normal development of women's need to participate in both traditional and working roles and how this leads to uncertainty, or widespread feelings of ambivalence.

Bernard, Jessie: *Women, Wives, Mothers: Values and Options,* Aldine, Chicago, 1975. Bernard, an eminent feminist and sociologist, discusses the current restructuring of the sex roles; the life patterns of women (especially as mothers); problems of age, class, ethnicity, and race; and the need and opportunities for women, within the new social forms which must develop.

Douvan, Elizabeth: "The Role of Modeling in Women's Professional Development," *Psychology of Women Quarterly,* vol. 1, no. 1, September 1976.

Huber, Joan (ed.): "Changing Women in a Changing Society," *American Journal of Sociology,* vol. 78, no. 4, January 1973. This is a special issue in which eminent sociologists, most of them women, discuss various aspects of change in the sex roles. Of special interest are Papanek's discussion of the two-person career; Komarovsky's discussion of sex roles and cultural contradictions; Epstein's analysis of the success of black professional women; Suter and Miller's discussion of sex differences in income; and Haven's discussion of women's marital patterns.

Knudsin, Ruth B.: "Successful Women in the Sciences: An Analysis of Determinants," *Annals of the New York Academy of Sciences,* vol. 208, March 15, 1973. This collection of papers resulted from a conference held in 1972. In addition to the formal papers there are some comments by participants in the conference. In Part I, women in different sciences discuss their lives. Parts II through VI contain twenty-one papers, most of which are extremely relevant to working women. We recommend especially the paper by Hennig on the development of achievement motivation and the paper by Bailyn on family constraints upon women's work.

Laws, Judith Long: "The Psychology of Tokenism: An Analysis," *Sex Roles,* vol. 1, no. 1, March 1975, pp. 51–67.

Liss, Lora: "Why Academic Women Do Not Revolt: Implications for Affirmative Action," *Sex Roles,* vol. 1, no. 3, September 1975, pp. 209–223. This article and the one by Laws discuss factors within women and organizations that enable individual women to deny their minority status and the effects of sexism.

Chapter 3

The Juggling Act: Home and Career

Herbert A. Otto
Roberta Otto

For a short biography of Herbert Otto, see the Introduction, page 1.

Roberta Otto is a writer, group facilitator, and trainer. At present, she is researching and coordinating a program in psychic energizing and healing for the whole person.

Everybody is a juggler. We are all juggling relationships, self-development, and growth. What do we hope to accomplish with this juggling? If we stop to analyze, we might discover that we want to create, to share our uniqueness with the world. We want to explore the many facets of life, and fulfill our needs and desires. We want to live the love, joy, creativity, and devotion that are in us—and our oneness with the universe—as fully as possible.

Life is in large part an adventure in relationships. If you can, visualize yourself as a center point, and see all relationships—with husband, partners, children, family, friends, business or professional acquaintances, and society—as extensions and variations of companionship, revolving around you. The people around you, too, are juggling their activities to accommodate their changing needs and desires. Reflecting back over the past year will no doubt show you how you juggled to allow for the changes that have taken place in your life. Change and the "balancing act" are part of life for everyone, and the changes in women's roles and possibilities for women are a part of what must be juggled in our lives today.

Thanks largely to the women's movement, a new, healthier view of the working woman has emerged: (1) The working woman is every bit as capable and deserving of respect, financial remuneration, and job opportunities as the man. (2) When a married working woman enters or reenters the labor force, she is no longer considered solely responsible for maintaining a smoothly functioning household. Shopping for food, housecleaning, laundry, preparation and serving of meals, family health, family social life, and so on, are now considered the joint responsibility of all the members of the household. With this new perspective, the contemporary woman has begun to understand that *it is not her function in life to meet everybody's needs all the time.* She understands, too, that she has the right to set her own priorities. In short, the new perspective is one of equal rights and shared responsibilities.

Although working mothers generally agree with this expanded concept of the role of women, many are not carrying it into their private life. They still rush home after a full day's work, expecting to prepare dinner for the family. Occasionally, some of the family may pitch in, but they are just *helping;* the responsibility for getting the meal ready is the woman's alone. It is not unusual to find the woman busy in the kitchen, while the husband has a beer and watches television and the children play. Many women worry about whether they will have any energy left to help their children with school problems, and even whether they will have energy left for their husbands and themselves. Such women are still playing the "mother game." They have lost touch with their own center of being from which their love flows.

The psychiatrist Eric Berne [1] has suggested that this game is played on two levels. Although it is natural for a mother to love, care for, and be supportive of her children, some mothers play a game of "ownership" with their children. They see them as their possessions and indulge in what we call "smother love." They have to do things for the children constantly to maintain this relationship. On the second level, the mother game is played with the husband, who is mothered excessively and consequently becomes more and more dependent and passive. This is typified by the remark, "He just sits around and lets me do things for him." Women who play the "mother game" are afraid to change, afraid to "let go." This is their way of feeling wanted and needed, regardless of the consequences.

Many women, and men too, do not seem to be aware of the far-reaching effects of equal rights and equal responsibilities. They do not understand that this new perspective has been, and can be, a way of freeing everyone in the family. Now, everyone has the opportunity to be recognized as an individual, an equal

[1] Eric Berne, *Games People Play,* Ballantine, New York, 1973.

partner in a family where all are dedicated to helping one another, where everyone is nurturing and nurtured, and where everyone feels needed, wanted, and loved.

This chapter is written for the woman who has been working for some time and for the woman who is about to go to work. It is meant for the working woman who wants to go beyond role playing to living her life fully, exploring all facets of her being. Much of the material used in this chapter has come from career women who have attended classes we conducted.

YOUR CHILDREN AND YOUR CAREER

Every working mother wants to feel the love and support of her family as she pursues her career. There is no doubt that in most instances she is aware of this support, or the lack of it. However, we have found that one of the paramount questions in the mind of every mother who is working or thinking about going to work is, "Will the personality development of my children be hurt in any way by my working?" Much anxiety and guilt is still generated by some aspects of Freudian theory that had currency in the early decades of this century. This theoretical approach stressed that the relationship of the mother and father to the child plays a dominant if not crucial part in personality development, especially in the early years of childhood, to the point where the temporary or prolonged absence of a parent was seen as harmful. Benjamin Spock, whose book on child rearing was a best-seller for decades, was strongly influenced by these Freudian ideas. Beginning in 1971, however, Spock has changed his approach; he has publicly expressed his regret over any guilt he aroused in working mothers. He now reassures his readers that if the mother works, this does not necessarily mean the children's personality development will suffer.

A great deal of contemporary research strongly suggests that *as long as children consistently have caring, loving adults to relate to, their personalities will develop in a healthy manner.* The experience of the kibbutz movement in Israel is an example. In the kibbutzim—collective farms—all adults work, and parents rarely see their children except during certain hours in the evening and on weekends. During the day, the small children are in child-care centers. These children evidently grow up to be healthy, well-functioning adults. They are in no way different from other Israelis who have spent most of their waking hours being looked after by their mothers.

In view of the Israelis' experience, it is not surprising that other current research indicates that there are some positive values in a mother's choosing to go to work. For example, in 1970 Ruth E. Hartley stated, "Data have indicated that a mother's working seems to have some very desirable effects on her children; daughters have more of the self-determination and spunk needed for modern living, take a less passive approach to the world outside the home and assume a more positive attitude toward the woman's role." [2] Researchers from the School of Public Health at Columbia University found that *the extent to which a mother*

[2] Quoted in Letty C. Pogrebin, *Getting Yours,* David McKay, New York, 1975, p. 35.

is satisfied with her role—as worker or homemaker—influences the mental health of both daughters and sons.[3] This strongly suggests that the attitude we have toward what we do is particularly important. The satisfied working mother can expect to be perceived more favorably by her children than the mother who stays home but is dissatisfied with her role in life. Finally, data gathered by the Women's Bureau of the U.S. Department of Labor indicate that a mother's working or not working does not cause juvenile delinquency: *it is the quality of a mother's care, rather than the time consumed in such care, which is of major significance.*[4]

Letty Pogrebin conducted an informal survey by asking youngsters for their views of their working mothers. Among her findings were the following:

- None of the children said they resent their mother's jobs and not one felt envious of friends whose mothers are at home.
- Each of the girls, from kindergartners to high school seniors, said she plans to combine family life with a career when she matures.
- All of the boys said they would not object if their own wives insisted on working, though most preferred that the woman stay home while the children are young.
- A great many children were critical of their fathers. They said they wished their dads would spend more time with the family, be more helpful in the house and more sensitive to their mother's needs.[5]

HELPING YOUR FAMILY ADJUST TO YOUR CAREER

There are some things you and your husband or partner can do to help the children adjust to the changes that are inevitable when you go to work.

Family Get-togethers

We suggest that you have your whole family (you, your husband, and the children) sit down together and begin talking about what is happening to them now that you are working (or about to go to work). Help each other express what you feel you need and what your feelings are about what is happening, as well as what is being done and not done in the family. Ask for suggestions and make decisions.

Listen carefully and try to understand the feelings your children have about the subjects that come up for discussion. Share your own thoughts and feelings with the family. Of course, all this is dependent on the age of the children, but many children as young as three and four have something to share.

You and your husband can talk about the advantages to the family of your working: the financial remuneration, job satisfaction, whatever applies to your situation. You may need several such family get-togethers to give all members an opportunity to express their feelings and bring about whatever changes may be needed. Here, as elsewhere, change in perception doesn't happen overnight.

Don't get caught in the "mother role." For family meetings to be most

---

[3] Ibid.

[4] See U.S. Government Publications Service for a compilation of these studies.

[5] Pogrebin, op. cit., pp. 20–21.

effective, share your feelings and concerns in advance with your spouse or partner. Discuss solutions to any problems you see. Your partner is an important and vital part of the family whose active participation is most important and a source of joy to everyone concerned.

The greater honesty you have in communicating your hopes, fears, and desires with your partner and children, the more open and close they will be in relating to one another. It has been proven time and time again that it is not the number of hours spent together that counts, but the quality and the nature of the time. A half hour sitting together watching the same television program is not as meaningful as a half hour spent lovingly sharing something that is important to each of you.

Family get-togethers on a regular basis have become a happy solution for many families, with or without working mothers. They seem to be especially effective when the woman is a working mother with a limited amount of time at her disposal.

Some families use the dinner hour as the time for sharing the activities of the day. Others have set aside one evening a week as a time of relating to one another. Any time when you can all get together and relax is a good time. This is a family decision you can make and, once these get-togethers have begun, the usual result is that everyone begins to look forward to this time of closeness.

The family that has had a few meetings to talk about needs and feelings usually finds it easy to continue family get-togethers. For ongoing meetings, here are some ideas which may be of value. You or your husband may want to lead off. We have found that it makes sharing easier if you start with a short phrase that you then complete. For instance, one family we know usually begins with, "The most important thing that happened to me was . . ." Other families we know have told us they begin with, "I feel good about . . ." or, "The happiest thing that happened to me was . . ."

Many families have agreed that it is a good idea to begin with a positive statement. It is a way of counting our blessings, of not being overshadowed by negatives. This does not mean that problem areas are not recognized and discussed; it just helps to balance our attitudes. Most of us have become so accustomed to looking for what is wrong about us and the world that we forget what wonderful, positive events and feelings are happening to us and are all around us. Finally, as a part of their togetherness, some families begin or end with a short prayer, with family members taking turns making up their own prayers.

"Family Joy Experience"

To eliminate a lot of guesswork, and to discover what you all enjoy doing, here is an experience (or game) that everyone can participate in. It tells everyone what you enjoy doing together. It also gives the family an opportunity to plan for future activities. We call it the "family joy experience," for it is based on everyone's recalling the most enjoyable times he or she has had with the family. It is fun to do, since it brings up happy memories.

Part 1 Begin by suggesting that everyone close his or her eyes; then ask the following question: "What have been the most enjoyable experiences we have had as a family in the past?"

You or someone else can volunteer to take notes and list the experiences that are identified. For example, the partial list of one family read as follows:

Picnic by creek—two years ago—Western trip
Fishing—time Daddy caught the big one
"Fantasyland"
Picnic by lake last year
Horseback riding—three years ago
Bicycle outing—Mom and kids
Deep-sea fishing trip
Visit with Clark family

The next step is to look over the list. Are there any patterns present? For example, the family whose list has been partially reproduced above, on looking over what they had written, found two very evident patterns—they enjoyed outings with fishing most, and picnics next. Even if there is no clear pattern, consensus can usually be reached about what type of event was most enjoyable.

Part 2 The next step is planning. You can begin by discussing the following questions:

How can we have more joy together?
What events shall we plan?

The whole family can plan at least one or more joyous events, setting dates and deciding on details. (Some families plan ahead for six months.) Everyone is encouraged to participate. If certain members are to have specific responsibilities, write these down if the event is some time away. They can be posted on a family bulletin board, along with additional suggestions.

Part 3 The final part of the experience is for everyone to experience joy *here and now*. Right after you have completed your planning, ask the following question: "What can all of us do *right now* that would make us feel good and be fun for everyone?"

Here is a list of activities which families have used to celebrate their love for each other:

Spontaneous dancing together
Playing a game together
Making candy
Surprise visit to another family, friends, or relatives
Getting some ice cream
Creating a family mural with magazine cutouts and crayon

By having a joyous occasion *here and now,* the experience ends on a positive note. Many families have found that this game can be used again and again. It seems to encourage good feelings as well as new suggestions. Use it as often as you wish, for experiencing joy together is a way of celebrating your love for each other.

"Now Communication Game"

Keeping lines of communication open between yourself and the rest of the family and among the other family members has a high priority. To help communication flow openly, we have designed the "Now Communication Game." [6] It consists of a rectangular plaque, 12 inches by 10 inches, made of heavy-duty plastic, that can be placed on a wall (like a dartboard) in the kitchen or dining room—any place where it is easily seen by everyone. On the plaque, under the subtitle "These are my communication needs right now," are ten different sections. Each section lists a different need, for example:

"I would enjoy being listened to."
"I would enjoy communicating in depth about something I will tell you about."
"I would enjoy praise and support."
"I am feeling good."
"I have some feelings I want to share with you."

The game is played like this: each member of the family places a token with his or her name written on it in the area that represents the appropriate need or feeling. (The tokens come with the game.)

As the children come home from school or play, or when you and your spouse or partner come home from work, you each place your token on the section that represents how you feel. For example, the section "I would enjoy being listened to" is very popular with children. Everyone's communication needs are out in the open, for the family to see. This is a direct method and eliminates a lot of searching. The children, especially, look forward to sharing their feelings. It has been found that after a short period of time they respond directly to each other, sensitively and quickly, without waiting for a parent to be there. The game has proven a boon to busy households, since everyone can clearly see where each of the family wants attention. It has helped many families to be more open to each other.

Before starting the game it is a good idea to discuss the different needs listed on the plaque. Children as young as four and five years old can participate in the game. We have received only positive reports from families using it.

Reorganizing the Household

You must understand that you will very likely overload yourself if you are working and at the same time carrying most of the homemaking responsibilities yourself. After a time, people who thus overload themselves usually become weary,

---

[6] The "Now Communication Game" is available from Holistic Press, 8909 Olympic Boulevard, Beverly Hills, California.

unhappy, and even bitter. This attitude begins to affect everyone and can be quite destructive to all concerned. It is in your own interest and in the interest of your family that you do not overload yourself but share the homemaking tasks with them. Cooperating in doing the cooking, cleaning, laundry, etc.—tasks that were formerly your responsibility—is a growth and learning experience for everyone.

Undoubtedly, your working has meant that many stereotyped sex roles and functions will have to fall, or have fallen, by the wayside. This means that habits established over a long period of time may have to be broken. Since it has been proven over and over again that habits establish attitudes, if you change the habits, new attitudes and new ways of doing things will emerge. Indeed, this is a time of change and challenge for all and contains the possibility of considerable personal growth for everyone. When such change comes to a household, there is an opportunity to create new arrangements that are better able to fulfill the needs of the members than the old ones. Your working can result in an increase in satisfaction for everyone.

In some of our classes, working women have reported feeling guilty as a result of initiating changes in their households so that they were no longer solely responsible for most of the homemaking chores. Discussing these feelings with a peer group seems to be especially helpful. (See also Chapter 25 for an exercise to help alleviate guilt.) Remember: *feeling guilty does not mean being guilty.* Also, feelings of guilt are often only a way of hiding inner resistance to a radical change in habits and life-style.

There is usually some opposition when habits and established routines have to be changed. Again, the best way to get everyone in the family involved is to start the family making a list of tasks and functions to be performed. You could make such a list privately, ahead of time, to help you think things through. Your husband can help with the distributing of homemaking functions, allocating the work to be done by the children (if any). The children can first be asked what they prefer doing and thus voice preferences. This gets planning started. Your husband or partner, of course, contributes his share, doing the tasks that he feels best equipped to do.

At the time of the planning session, or at a later session, write out a weekly schedule on a day-by-day basis. List what everyone will do on Monday, Tuesday, etc., and indicate the approximate time when things will be done. This avoids misunderstandings and disputes. It is also well to have a number of tasks that are rotated on a weekly basis. In most families, a rigid plan is not always advisable. Suggest that if a member of the family is busy and can't carry out his or her assignment for the day, tradeoffs should be made. However, the person assigned to a task has the responsibility for its completion. "Flexibility" is the key word, and family sessions are the times to express complaints and make necessary changes.

YOU AND YOUR PARTNER

Fortunately, men of today are more open than ever before to the needs of their female partners for self-expression and growth. The myth that having a family and children fulfills all a woman's needs for her whole lifetime is slowly disappearing. However, there are not many models of realized women and men. In relationships between men and women, especially, everyone is living with many expectations and fantasies. Everyone is forging a separate path.

Bringing an attitude of self-discovery and adventure to the man-woman relationship makes for viable partnerships. Some important elements are trust, open lines of communication, and talking about desires, values, and goals. Giving, sharing, feeling, and sensing keep a partnership alive. Because most of us have not been taught to be responsive and open, it is something we have to learn. For this reason, we believe a person's growth can be measured by the *ability to communicate needs effectively*. This ability requires self-respect, and appreciation of the unique values of you and your partner. It implies, too, a willingness to change.

All relationships are fluid. You and your partner have needs that you would like to have met. It is therefore important that you share your individual and common objectives and goals. For example, to make working feasible for both of you, your partner may have to participate more in household tasks and family responsibilities. Whether you have extra work to do, or need to have some privacy and rest, the sharing of responsibility helps. Even if there are no children in the family, your partner may be required to take a more active part in the functioning of the household. In some few cases this is not possible; but when it does happen, it can only strengthen the family and your relationship.

It will be important for you and your partner to work out a plan for what to do in certain emergencies. For example, who will pick up a sick child at school? By having contingency plans, much unnecessary tension and worry can be eliminated.

There are many other areas where understanding is needed. There may be times when you cannot be physically available to each other, where your partner will have to go without you to a football game, or where he will not be able to accompany you to an event you have planned. There may be additional expenses for courses, for clothing, etc. It is best to plan for this.

There may be times when sexual needs cannot be met. This happens in any relationship, whether the woman is working or not. However, it seems to take on larger dimensions if the possibility of its occurring has not been acknowledged.[7] Discussion beforehand helps to eliminate any guilt partners may have when they are not available. Occasional unavailability is part of any relationship.

Awareness of schedules and respect for different needs are part of the support you and your spouse can give each other. Built on a foundation of love, awareness and respect are an unbeatable combination.

Seeing yourselves as pioneers, as models that your children can follow, and as people who are living as truthfully as you can—this itself is worthwhile and

[7] Herbert A. Otto and Roberta Otto, *Total Sex,* New American Library (Signet Paperback 451–W5437), New York, 1973.

satisfying. It does not imply perfection. It just means going with the flow, and doing your best without getting overly tense or concerned. It means appreciating what you are and who you are, and loving the adventure it represents.

Once you have made up your mind to work, the issue of gaining your husband's support is before you. However, as some women in our groups have pointed out, it may be wise to first be fairly clear what type of career you are seeking.

> When I first decided I wanted to work I told my husband about it. I hadn't made up my mind what to do and he kept subtly discouraging me by playing on my uncertainties. It took me months to get over that. I talked it over with Helen and Jody, who helped me to see that I had the skills and qualifications and that I could get additional training if needed. I talked to my husband again after that and I was very positive about what I wanted to do. This made him positive and he agreed and gave me some good ideas.

To gain your husband's agreement, the following guidelines may be helpful:

1 Choose the time to talk things over—a time when both of you are rested, energetic, and feeling good about yourselves and the world.

2 Have a clear-cut "mental list" of both advantages and disadvantages as you see them. (You might write this list out beforehand to help you think things through in advance.)

3 Be open and listen to him—try to respond to his feelings as well as to what he says. (In all changes there is sometimes a fear of what might happen to the relationship.)

4 Have a clearly thought-out plan about how to cope with the disadvantages that might result from your working. Ask his help in finding other alternatives.

5 Have a separate session to think through and plan together the changes in household management and scheduling necessitated by your working. (Include the children as much as possible in the decision making.)

In the past, many men felt that it diminished them in their own eyes and in the eyes of their friends if their wives worked and contributed to the expenses of the household. Fortunately, this attitude is changing. However, if you believe that these are your husband's feelings, they should be brought into the open and discussed. Usually, where the additional income is not too important a factor, it is only one of the reasons for a woman's entering the job market. To many, a career is a way of fulfilling themselves, a way of expanding their knowledge and contributing to society. Regardless of why you want to seek work, you may wish to explore this topic with your family. In this connection, being completely honest and sharing the many feelings you have about yourself will help you and your husband—and your children—effect the changes you want to make.

This is a good time to expand your knowledge of family finances. Remember, you'll be adding to them. For example, how will working affect your financial picture? Will there be a great increase in expenses for clothes, transportation, taxes, eating out, etc.? Also, do you know where all the important documents are kept, such as stock certificates, bonds, deeds, installment contracts, leases, and insurance policies? How many of those have you read? This is not an area which you should simply leave to your husband. Are your accounts and documents held jointly? What are your rights in connection with them? Perhaps this is also the time to review certain fundamental questions, such as, Does your husband carry enough life insurance? Do *you* carry enough life insurance? Do you know your husband's lawyer, accountant, stockbroker? Have you and your husband made a will? What provision has been made for the children in the will?

It is well to explore these matters for another excellent reason: the fact that men die an average of 6.8 years earlier than women. Thus, by "thinking the unthinkable" and taking action (including talking this over with your husband), you can both gain more inner security and peace of mind.

YOU YOURSELF

Where are you in all this?

Are you rushing around in a whirlwind of activity, trying to be everything to everybody—the perfect mother, the perfect mate, the perfect lover, the creative homemaker, the inventive cook, the successful worker, the perfect hostess, the delightful guest, the good dresser, and so on?

Have you lost the real you?

It is easy to become fragmented as you rush from one activity to another. When was the last time you sat down and allowed yourself to be quiet and get in touch with yourself?

It is a common occurrence for all of us to lose sight of our goals, of our needs, of the very joy that is in us, as we frantically dash from one activity to another. There are a great many calls made on us daily that we feel obliged to answer.

We live in complex times, and it is easy to blur our guidelines. We lose the sense of the need to sit quietly to commune with one's own inner self. We begin to seek outside ourselves for the satisfaction of all our needs, forgetting that happiness reflects what is inside us.

We can only live from the center—the self—outward. It is only from our inner core that we can react to the stimuli we receive from our senses, from the outside world. We forget that, as Richard Wagner said, "Joy is not in things; it is in us."

The need to be quiet is being increasingly recognized as one of the vital needs of our time. We all need time to sit quietly and rest, to assimilate what has been happening, to recharge our batteries. A quiet time is a time for self-renewal. The reasons why we need such a time are obvious. Not only are there the demands of our daily activities; our physical environment is also demanding. We are being continuously bombarded by television, radio, traffic, advertisements, billboards, newspapers, magazines—all the accouterments of our civilization. They are fine in their place, but, again, there must be a balance to offset all this activity.

Walks in the country or on a beach, sitting quietly in a favorite spot, a short nap—these are very good and help us regain our equilibrium.

Questions to Ask Yourself

Am I a perfectionist?
Do I try to do everything myself?
Can I ask for assistance at home and at my job?
Can I accept mistakes in myself?
Can I accept mistakes in others?
Do I enjoy my day?

If you are a perfectionist and are happy that way, fine. However, if you are a perfectionist and insist that others do likewise, and if you feel harried and pressured by the amount of work you have to do, it is time you stopped and took a look at what you are doing.

If you are afraid of making mistakes, you are falling into a trap. Understand that making mistakes is being human. We learn by trial and error. Allowing for errors in ourselves and the people around us lets us be creative and adventurous and grow. If you have difficulty allowing yourself and others to make mistakes, you need to remember that *you can change if you want to.*

The awareness of damaging tendencies, and the desire to change, is the first step in the direction of change. As we mentioned earlier, all life is change. To be afraid of change, to be closed to life around us, to keep hanging on to a seemingly secure niche, is to grasp at an illusion. It can only lead to a sense of futility, to a feeling of defeat, to a joyless existence. Follow through on your ideas, and don't be afraid to make mistakes.

Other questions to ask yourself include these:

What is important to me?
What do I want to accomplish?
What is the meaning of life?

Answers to these questions are the guidelines we follow in our lives, consciously or otherwise. It does take time to sit down and think about these things, but once you do, it will give you a better understanding of yourself.

Some people see life as a spiritual journey, a means of realizing their oneness with the universe or with love as the source of life. Others feel that the highest expression of life is to be of service to their fellow human beings. To many, the journey of life means enjoying the moment without looking for meaning.

However, once begun, the search for meaning and the realization of your potential can be one of your most exciting ongoing adventures.

Your Own Space

Are you allowing yourself enough space?

It is not closet space for your clothes we are referring to, nor is it space for your papers, desk, or chair—although we hope you have made arrangements for these things in your household. We mean psychological and internal space.

Psychological space is a space where you can be alone to dream, to be inactive or active, as you choose. It is a place or time that is very specially your own, when you are not committed to anyone. It is a place in which you have the freedom to *be*.

Having your own space is as important as being quiet. It is something everyone needs—female or male, child or adult. Plan for your own space. Remember, it can have different forms, from taking a walk alone to being alone for an hour, a day, or a week. It is your own space and time. It can only result in a happier, more fulfilled you.

Evaluating and Reorganizing Yourself—For the Woman Who Is Starting a Career or Who Is About to Change Jobs

The time to begin evaluating yourself is the moment you decide to change your life-style and take up a career in addition to the homemaking that you are engaged in presently. Self-evaluation is also particularly valuable at a time when you are changing jobs.

Evaluating and reorganizing yourself is the best possible way to point yourself in the direction of becoming a career woman. This can be done in three steps:

1 Begin by recognizing and working with your feelings about going to work (or changing jobs).
2 Take an inventory of yourself.
3 Stage a "work rehearsal."

Recognize Your Feelings   Anyone who starts on a new course in life, or who is involved in changes, has many special feelings and concerns. It is best to get these out in the open, to recognize and face them. They can then be dealt with. When such feelings are put into writing, for example, they become more tangible and real. New perspectives, insights, and understandings often develop as a result of writing feelings out. As a participant in one of our classes put it, "Once I put my feelings down on paper I felt a sense of relief because I now had more of a handle on what I thought was bothering me. If it's vague, it seems more formidable."

Get a piece of paper and write your feelings under the following heading: "My feelings and concerns about going to work (or changing jobs)." As a part of getting in touch with your feelings, recognize how you are dependent on others. Again, recognition of dependency is the first step to overcoming it.

Once you have written down your feelings, put them aside for a day or two; then read them over. Make any changes and additions you wish, and then ask a friend or business associate to discuss them with you.

If you are a homemaker who is planning to begin working, ask a friend rather than your husband if possible. A friend often brings a fresh point of view and can be most effective in discussing your feelings with you at this beginning point. Your husband may be too close to you to be objective. After this ground-work with your friend, you can be more exact in talking with your husband. However, if you prefer to discuss your feelings with your husband first, by all means do so. You are the best judge of this.

Here are some examples of fears and concerns expressed by women who are planning to look for jobs.

Jane D., thirty-nine years old, married, with three children (ages twelve, eleven, and six), wrote the following:

> *My feelings and concerns about going to work:*
> I'm worried whether Leo, my six-year-old, will be unhappy.
> I hope I won't get too tired and not be able to enjoy my family.
> I don't know if I'll be able to find a job.
> I could use the extra money to buy things for the house and family.
> I would like to feel independent and be able to look after myself financially.
> I'm worried about how working will affect our marriage.
> I would like to continue my education—there is a conflict here.

The following is an edited taped conversation of a group discussion. A thir-ty-two-year-old woman, married for thirteen years, with two children (ages twelve and ten), talks about her feelings:

> I never realized how dependent I had become on my husband until I made up my mind that I wanted to work. I expected him to do the thinking for me and tell me what to do. He pointed this out to me—but even before that I had caught on to what I was doing but hadn't put into words.
>
> Then there is the children's dependence on me. A sticky subject. I imagine they depend on me less than I think they do. Excuses, excuses. I am also dependent on all my routines, my habits, all the familiar things at home. . . .

Lisa L., a twenty-nine-year-old college graduate, with no children, who is presently employed, wrote the following:

> *My feelings and concerns about changing jobs:*
> My basic concern is the people. Will I like them? Will they like me? I'm always very aware of other people's ego trips and I dislike intensely working with anyone who tries to make me feel inferior or who rushes and pressures me. I fear these situations on a new job.
>
> I wonder if my talents will really have a chance to be expressed. I like challenges and fear that a new job might lead to a dead end instead of an open road.
>
> Financial fears are similar—I fear that a change in job may not bring me the financial reward I hope for. I want to feel that I can grow financially as I assume greater responsibility.
>
> I fear that people in the new job will not recognize my worth, that they won't perceive how capable I am.

Take an Inventory of Yourself   An important part of evaluating and reorga-nizing yourself when beginning work or changing jobs is taking an inventory of yourself. This depends on recognizing two facts: (1) Self-knowledge is insepa-rable from the quest for self-realization. (2) An understanding of one's strengths and personal resources builds self-confidence and self-esteem, valuable qualities when applying for a job. The "self-knowledge inventory" given below provides a good starting point to help you obtain a clearer perspective of your assets and strengths. It is especially useful if you are undecided as to the area you would like to work in. (See also Chapter 5, page 111, for a listing of additional items.)

To make the inventory, get pencil and paper and find some "private time" where you will not be interrupted. (You may wish to schedule several sessions with the self-knowledge inventory.)

The self-knowledge inventory [8]

I   Work experience
    A   What types of jobs (part-time or full-time) have I held since I have been a teenager?
    B   What did I enjoy about these jobs? Why?
    C   What did I dislike about these jobs? Why?
    D   What kind of an employee or worker was I?
    E   What types of recognition or compliments did I receive from co-workers or bosses?
    F   What types of suggestions for improvement or criticism did I receive while working?
    G   What do I see as my ideal work or job?

II   Attitudes toward work
    A   What attitudes do I have that would be helpful in a job?
    B   What is my reaction to close supervision or to being continually directed?
    C   What is my attitude about monotony and repetition in a job (doing the same thing over and over, such as assembly or piecework)?
    D   What is my attitude toward the type of work where there is little chance of advancement, promotion, or recognition?
    E   Do I want to work every day, part-time, evenings?

III   Attitudes toward people
    A   Do I especially enjoy working with people and meeting people (as in reception, sales work, counseling, and social work)?
    B   What kinds of people do I get along with best?
    C   What kinds of people do I have some difficulty with?
    D   Do I go out of my way to meet different types of people?
    E   How many close friends do I have? Who are they and what do I like about each one?
    F   Do I have any preferences about working closely with men or women?
    G   How much contact do I need with other people?
    H   What are difficulties or arguments with other people mostly about?

IV   Attitudes toward myself
    A   What do I like about me?
    B   What are my strengths?
    C   What are my problem areas or weaknesses?
    D   What do I consider my outstanding achievements or accomplishments?
    E   Do I feel I have accomplished enough?
    F   What do I see as my biggest problem?
    G   What was the happiest period in my life? Why?

[8] Adapted from Andrew DuBrin, *Women in Transition*, Charles C Thomas, Springfield, Ill., 1972, pp. 63–67. We are indebted to Professor DuBrin for this adaptation of his "self-knowledge questionnaire."

     H What things do I dislike most in my life?
     I What bothers me the worst, and what do I worry about most?
     J What gives me the most satisfaction in life?
     K In what ways do I belittle or punish myself?
     L Am I curious?
     M Am I adventurous?
     N What motivates me?

V How others see me
     A What is the best positive remark or compliment my husband has addressed to me?
     B In what ways would my husband like to see me change or grow as a person?
     C What do people other than my family like best about me?
     D What do other people criticize me for?

VI Interests, hobbies, sports, etc.
     A What interests, activities, hobbies, and sports do I enjoy?
     B What interests, activities, hobbies, and sports do I actively participate in?
     C Which of the above do I get most excited about or like the most? Why?
     D Which of the above do I want to explore further?

VII Education and related areas
     A How far have I gone in school?
     B When did I last attend school?
     C Which were my best subjects?
     D Which were my poorest subjects?
     E What night or adult-education courses, workshops, classes, or other training have I had?
     F What travel or other educational experiences have I had?
     G Have I attended any consciousness-raising or assertiveness-training groups or classes?
     H What skills or abilities do I have now that could be applied to a job situation?
     I Do I feel I have the ability to take further education or training?
     J What are my plans for further education or training? Why?
     K How much time would I have available for further education or training?
     L How would my husband and children feel about my attending school?

VIII My future
     A What are my life goals or plans?
     B What are my goals for further personal growth?
     C What are my goals for further training or education?
     D What are my career goals?
     E What goals do I have related to interests, hobbies, and sports?
     F What are my plans and goals related to the people in my life?
     G What do I want for myself?

After you have completed the inventory, you may want to discuss it with someone close to you. Ask that person for his or her impressions on reading the inventory. If you have not yet decided on the type of work you want, the inventory may furnish some valuable clues. If you have made such a decision, filling out the inventory can result in increased self-understanding and a new view of yourself.

Stage a Work Rehearsal The final step in reorganizing yourself is to begin a "work rehearsal." For example, to facilitate your transition into the business world, set up a tight schedule for yourself and establish strict deadlines for specific tasks. As much as possible, simulate the work you will be doing by carrying out such tasks at home. Eat lunch at noon, and have a midmorning and midafternoon coffee break with no snacking in between.

If possible, arrange to visit the place where you will work before you start. Soak in the atmosphere and try to get more of an understanding of what you will be doing. Then, when you are back home, close your eyes and imagine you are at work. Visualize the place and rehearse your (possible) functions. All this will help make the transition easier.

YOU AND YOUR FRIENDS: OUTSIDE RESOURCES

Developing Support Groups

You can ask relatives, friends, and neighbors for help. Some churches, too, are now organizing support groups that church members can call on at a time of transition or change. Many working women have discovered that when they start back to work, people are especially eager and glad to help. (Neighbors, for instance, often offer to run errands, look after pets, etc.) This can serve to alleviate worry and anxiety and ease the period of transition. These support groups are also available to the working woman at a time of crisis or when pressures mount too high. We have also found that in our groups working women repeatedly discover, much to their astonishment, that children, husbands, and even pets are surprisingly able to take care of themselves and can manage quite well.

Keeping Up Friendships

Nurturing and maintaining friendships is always important. Because her time is often short, the working woman may encounter difficulties in this area. Yet many women appear to keep in touch with friends by lunching together, meeting for an hour or two after work, and talking by telephone.

When a woman starts working, there is the chance that for several weeks at least she may have less time or energy available for friends. A woman in one of our groups solved this problem by mailing each friend a greeting card with this message: "If I don't call you or see you in the next three weeks, it's not because I've dropped out—I've gone to work!" She said this helped her not to feel guilty when she was too tired to call her friends or see them. Once she had adjusted to the new work situation, she made sure to get together with each friend, and she reported many favorable comments about the cards she had sent. There is no question that the best way to maintain and nourish friendships is by keeping the lines of communication open and letting people know that you care.

Marriage and Family Enrichment

A rapidly growing new movement which represents a resource to the working woman is "marriage and family enrichment."[9] Its objective is to help a well-

[9] Herbert A. Otto (ed.), *Marriage and Family Enrichment—New Perspectives Programs,* Abingdon Press, Nashville, Tenn., 1975.

functioning marriage (or family) function even better and more lovingly, to strengthen family life, and to realize a family's potential. These enrichment programs are not meant for families or marriages that are in need of counseling.

The movement began in the early 1960s. Since then, more than half a million people have already attended one of its programs or classes. Marriage-enrichment and family-enrichment programs are usually weekend workshops. Children are expected to attend the family-enrichment programs. Most of the programs are sponsored by churches, and the larger denominations offer classes on weekends. The fees for enrichment programs vary but are usually quite reasonable.

Some Alternative Ways of Living

This may also be the time to explore some of the contemporary alternatives that are open to you as a working couple.

For instance, some couples are taking turns working. One year the husband will hold a job while the wife looks after the children and the household; the next year the roles are reversed.

Career sharing is another possibility. Here everything is shared on a fifty-fifty basis through the simple device of divided schedules. Her shift may begin at 8:00 A.M. and last until 12:30; he might find a job for the period from 1:00 to 5:00 P.M. In this way the partners share equally in work and household responsibilities in the course of a single day.

There are also a growing number of young and older couples who live apart during the week in separate communities and get together on weekends. Some couples are also trying communal living arrangements during weekends.

Another increasingly popular alternative is the family cluster.[10] The family cluster is a circle of three to five families with generally similar aims, goals, and values, meeting regularly and sharing specific family functions and services. Each family maintains its own house as a base. The major purposes of the family cluster are to strengthen the family and to foster personal growth and self-actualization. An important aspect of the environment provided by the family cluster is the help and support members give to each other. This includes help with children and household chores for members of the cluster who go to work. Another benefit is that no one is completely dependent upon the family for fun. It's easier this way to find someone to play cards, take a hike, or discuss politics. The family cluster can provide a framework that allows for the organic growth of love and caring: members, by loving themselves more, are better able to give to others. That perhaps is the greatest contribution this concept can make to the quality of our living.

Other alternatives include communal and cooperative living arrangements. Both of these usually involve a number of families or couples living in one dwelling. Most communes appear to be composed of members who have common values or a common ideology. This usually is not the case in cooperatives, where members have come together primarily for economic reasons or to make more

[10] Herbert A. Otto, *The Family Cluster,* Holistic Press, Beverly Hills, Calif., 1975, p. 2.

free time available by sharing tasks such as shopping, cooking, and child care. It seems certain that, over the years, more and more couples will seek out and sample some of these alternatives.

IN CONCLUSION

In any juggling act, the possibility exists that some of the items will be dropped, or that the juggler's timing will be off. No matter—the fun and the joy are in the juggling itself. It is in doing and seeking—often with trembling—that we experience the many dimensions of life.

BIBLIOGRAPHY

DuBrin, Andrew J.: *Women in Transition.* Charles C Thomas, Springfield, Ill., 1972. Written for homemakers who want to grow psychologically. The emphasis is on counseling.

Harbeson, Gladys Evans: *Choice and Challenge for the American Woman,* Schenkman, Cambridge, Mass., 1967. A scholarly study on changes in life and work patterns of the American woman. Many tables.

Higginson, Margaret V., and Thomas L. Quick: *The Ambitious Woman's Guide to a Successful Career,* American Management Association, New York, 1974. The chapter on "how to develop your boss as a resource to you" is especially good and provocative. Many new ideas.

Janeway, Elizabeth: *Between Myth and Marriage,* Morrow, New York, 1974. A collection of essays; of special interest are "Women's Place in a Changing World" and "Women in Business."

Pogrebin, Letty C.: *Getting Yours,* McKay, New York, 1975. Subtitled "How to Make the System Work for the Working Woman." The section on "Work, Home and the Family" is excellent. Outstanding resource sections.

Schwartz, Felice N., Margaret Schifter, and Susan S. Gillotti: *How to Go to Work When Your Husband Is Against It, Your Children Aren't Old Enough and There Is Nothing You Can Do Anyhow,* Simon and Schuster, New York, 1972. Includes an interesting "Career Baedeker" describing jobs, salaries, training needed, part-time possibilities, etc. A good resource book.

Part Two

Getting the Best from Your Career

Chapter 4

Women Working— Opportunities Both New and Traditional

Elinor Lenz

Elinor Lenz, M.A., is Director of the Western Humanities Center, University Extension, UCLA. Her professional activities include filmmaking, freelance writing, and lecturing; and consulting in media and program development. She has written extensively for radio, television, and films, and is the author of numerous articles appearing in national publications, among them the *New York Sunday Times, Spectator, Adult Leadership,* and *Change.* Her film credits include *Land and the Pursuit of Happiness, Powergame, Fire Myth,* and *Searching for Community,* produced for the Western Humanities Center. She is the editor of *The American Revolutionary Experience, 1776–1976,* a bicentennial collection published by the Western Humanities Center. She designs programs for UCLA Extension: *"Women in the West,"* a program dealing with women in Western history, is one of several she has designed in the field of women's studies.

TRIED AND TRUE JOB OPPORTUNITIES

But Can She Type?

A poster that began appearing in offices a few years ago consists of a photo of Golda Meir, the former Premier of Israel, with this caption underneath: "But can she type?" Here we have, in one picture and four words, the traditional view of women at work—tapping away at typewriters, performing the routine chores of our corporate society, serving as office support for the male executives. This is a view that reflects reality to a large extent: seven out of ten clerical workers are women, whereas only three out of ten are men.[1] As a result, the term "secretary," though in itself neuter, conjures up almost automatically a feminine image.

The ironic caption, however, fails to convey another reality—that many secretarial and clerical jobs require skill, training, and a mixture of such qualities as tact, good judgment, quick thinking, and the ability to keep things running smoothly under pressure. If these jobs have been held in low esteem in the past, it is at least partly because they have represented the narrow range of occupational choices available to women. As the range becomes wider and more diverse, secretarial and clerical jobs can be expected to acquire a more attractive image, one that conforms more closely to the facts of business life. In today's high-speed business world, good secretaries are highly valued and are often paid better than some of their co-workers who carry fancier titles. Many secretaries actually function as administrative assistants, although this is a title usually reserved for men, who may be performing essentially the same tasks as a secretary but prefer a job designation that is not identified as "feminine."

Even in today's changing social climate, with its growing emphasis on equal opportunity and the desexing of job descriptions, occupations continue to be tagged "male" or "female." When you think of the following, does the image of a man or a woman leap into your mind?—brigadier general, brain surgeon, forester, civil engineer, construction worker, truck driver; nurse, cosmetologist, model, elementary school teacher, librarian, receptionist. What would be your reaction if, on a transatlantic flight, as you were fastening your safety belt, a woman's voice announced: "This is your captain, Peggy Jones"?

The sex labels attached to occupations are so deeply rooted in our social consciousness that we tend unthinkingly to associate certain skills with men, others with women. Of course, most societies have had some form of division of labor between the sexes, although this may vary from one culture to another: in some cultures, for example, women do the hunting and men cook the food. In our Western industrial society, mechanical, management, and professional skills are attributed to men; clerical, nursing, and domestic skills, to women.

Traditional jobs for women, then, are extensions of what has been commonly accepted as "woman's role." These are the jobs in which one deals with people—the nurturing, helping, enhancing, supporting occupations that do so much to make life more livable and the world a more attractive, efficient, comfortable

[1] *Handbook on Women Workers,* Women's Bureau Bulletin #294, U.S. Department of Labor, Washington, D.C., 1969.

place. A list of these occupations would include nursing; teaching, especially at the primary level; social welfare; food preparation and service; selling; modeling; fashion design; cosmetology; decorating; and a wide range of clerical jobs from file clerk to executive secretary. Such jobs also include airline stewardesses, administrative assistants, bookkeepers, physical therapists, dental hygienists, court reporters—in fact, the majority of women working today, both married and single. Traditional jobs make up a vast and varied territory, calling for a diverse assortment of skills, aptitudes, and aspirations. Employment experts predict that many of these fields will continue to grow well into the 1980s. It is predicted that by 1980 there will be an increase in the percentage of people employed as systems analysts, programers, psychologists, medical laboratory workers, registered nurses, social workers, and clerical workers. Most of these are occupations that have been dominated by women.

Why Take a Traditional Job?

Why, in a world of expanding career options for women, do so many women continue to seek out these tried and true occupations? The immediate answer would appear to be, "Because they're there." These are, after all, the jobs that have always been most readily available for women—the jobs that, like a comfortable garment, a woman can slip into smoothly and wear with ease. But availability is only part of the answer. The traditional occupations we have been talking about are attractive to women for a variety of reasons—economic, psychological, sociological.

Let's take a look, for example, at what psychologists have identified as the "feminine fear of success." This concept was developed out of studies of college women which indicated that, in the case of many bright, successful women students, a funny thing happened on their way to the bachelor's degree—they changed their original career plans in favor of marriage or a more traditional type of job. A study of the top 1 percent of women students at Michigan State in the late 1950s and early 1960s indicated that, by graduation, most of the women who had originally gone into the sciences had switched to fields which they considered to be more compatible with the female role—social work, nursing, teaching, and home economics. More recent studies suggest that this is changing and that women students are showing an increasing tendency to stay with their original career plans.

However, the fact remains that many women (and a growing number of men) are not attracted to high-pressure, keenly competitive jobs. In 1972, the sociologist Amitai Etzioni asked, "Will they all end up dashing to work in a competitive world, seeking some elusive status and measuring their success against their take-home pay, to finally collapse at the end of the day in a neurotic exhaustion, using liquor and the television set as psychiatric first-aid for winding down?" [2] This description may seem exaggerated to women in high-level posi-

[2] Quoted in Armand L Mauss, *Social Problems as Social Movements,* Lippincott, Philadelphia, 1975, chap. 11, "Feminist Movements as Social Problems," p. 441.

tions who are enjoying their work and their families without any of the side effects suggested by Etzioni; but there are other women who view the upper level of business, industry, and the professions as Ulcerland and want none of it.

Aside from reducing the risk of ulcers, traditional jobs offer a number of other advantages. The training period is briefer and less expensive than in the professions and other more highly skilled and demanding occupations. Also, competition is less intense for these jobs than for those farther up the pyramid. Traditional jobs offer more possibilities for flexible time arrangements, a factor of great importance to working wives and mothers. And they provide deep personal gratification to women who enjoy caring for others and catering to the very human desire for comfort and beauty. While there is no scientific evidence that women are more responsive to such needs than men, this is generally assumed to be the case and may well be one of the reasons why more women than men are drawn to such occupations.

Furthermore, a traditional job can be a means to an end. It can serve as a port of entry to managerial positions or to some of the newer, more challenging fields of work. Although, as was noted above, a secretarial job can be satisfying in and of itself, it is commonly regarded as leading nowhere. Yet a leading film producer, the regional marketing manager of an airline, and the assistant director of a large import-export company all began their careers as secretaries. In the past, the chances of rising from secretarial to managerial positions have been in inverse proportion to the size of the firm: the smaller companies have offered better possibilities than the giants. Recently, however, General Motors, Pan American, and other large corporations report that they are finding talented managers in the secretarial pool and moving them along at a good pace.

Moving Upward

If you're planning to use your clerical-secretarial job as a rung on the career ladder, there are several ways to make the ascent smoother and speedier. As a start, you can choose a company that is dealing in products or services close to your own interests. Many of the "glamour" businesses—advertising, travel, publishing—are wide open to the upwardly mobile secretary. The same can be said of some of the large corporations which are moving into the so-called "women's fields" such as health care and education.

Once your foot is in the door, lose no time in learning all you can about the company—its history, the chemistry of staff and managerial relationships, and especially the problem areas. Enroll in any management training courses the company offers; if it doesn't offer any, look into extension or community college programs. If you're serious about making the move from an outer office to a private one with your name on the door, you'll have to keep upgrading your skills and your knowledge. Read the trade papers in the field, find out what the competition is doing, and stay on top of the latest financial data as well as the current office gossip. Of course, you'll have to let your employer know that you're ready, willing, and able to handle additional responsibility; after that, it should be just a matter of time, patience, and a little bit of luck.

Here are some other methods worth noting:

Aim for a job called "assistant to." Assisting an executive is not only the best way in the world to learn the job; it's the best place to be when that job or a similar one opens up. But be sure it's a true assistantship, offering you a chance to do important tasks—not merely a label hiding routine chores.

If merchandising appeals to you, starting as a trainee in a department store can lead to better things, though you may have to sweat it out for a while at a much lower salary than a secretary would earn.

If you are fluent in a foreign language, a job as correspondent with a multinational corporation would be a good springboard.

The way you choose to go depends on your particular talents and interests; but a traditional job can serve as a training ground to prepare you for a bigger and better-paying future.

Boobytraps and How to Avoid Them

Of course, the path to the upper reaches of today's corporate world is not strewn with roses; there are a few boobytraps along the way that are especially threatening to women. Let's look at two that seem to occur most frequently.

One might be called the "stopgap fallacy." It goes something like this: You have been working as a keypunch operator for two years but you consider yourself a writer and the job merely a stopgap; after all, you majored in English and had a story published in the college magazine, and your teacher in freshman composition said that your work "showed promise." True, you haven't written anything during the two years you've been punching the keys, but someday . . . At this point, stop, look, and listen to yourself. If you're serious about becoming a writer, you'd better hurry up and write something publishable. But maybe what you really are is a keypunch operator. Unless you're resigned to going on with what you're doing, you might consider entering a training program which will hoist you into another occupational level.

The other familiar trap, one into which executive secretaries are most likely to fall, may be referred to as a "case of confused identity." The heroine of this office drama is usually bright, capable, well-educated, no longer in her first youth, unmarried or married unhappily, or for one reason or another suffering emotional deprivation and therefore totally, unremittingly devoted to her job and to that person she works for, her boss. If the boss is male, the chances are that there is nothing sexual between them—he has, in fact, never been known to miss the 5:12 to the suburbs. But he accepts unquestioningly her loyal dedication to him and his interests. This may take the form of her assuming some of his job responsibilities, particularly when he has had one martini too many at lunch; but isn't that what executive secretaries are for? And hasn't she been rewarded adequately by small but regular increases, not to mention that makeup case he gave her last Christmas?

One problem here is that the scenario may, and often does, take an unexpected turn. For example, the boss may be forced into early retirement by ill health, and the person coming in to replace him may bring along his own faithful, devoted executive secretary. What happens now to our bright, capable, no longer young heroine? Of course, she can find another job, in time; but will it be commensurate with her actual duties and responsibilities on the old job? These were increasingly those of a top manager, but no prospective employer would ever suspect that from her title or salary.

If your job places you in a close working relationship with your superior, male or female, watch out for these danger signals: a tendency to confuse the boss's goals and achievements with your own; an uncritical acceptance of the boss's plans and instructions; a strong identification with the boss in all company matters, a "we two against all the others" feeling; a readiness to take on extra work for the boss without extra compensation, though you would never do this for anyone else; the conviction that working with or for anyone else would be boring and profitless.

If you recognize any of these symptoms in yourself, you may be falling into this boobytrap, and you should be thinking about moving on toward a job with better opportunities for self-realization. This may be a tough decision for you to make—something like deciding to get a divorce—but once you've struck out for independence, it won't be long before your abilities begin to assert themselves. From there on, the career you build will be your own.

The Big Three

Some experts predict that Americans will soon be living in a "postindustrial society" in which production of goods takes second place to the preservation and improvement of human and natural resources. What does this suggest about opportunities in those occupational areas that have traditionally been the "big three" for women: health, education, and social welfare?

Health Services In the field of health, the stress will be on rehabilitation. Nursing will continue as the number one profession for women, and there will be some upgrading of the nurse's scope and responsibility. An example of this trend is the nurse practitioner, who is actually a physician's assistant, qualified to conduct pelvic and other examinations and perform certain other diagnostic tasks. Her work may be concentrated in a family-practice center or in pediatrics, and she may also make "house calls," filling an important gap between the physician and the patient. The nurse practitioner, who must be an R.N., qualifies by taking a special six-month course and may in addition be required to have a preceptor, or guarantee of employment. Earnings in this position are about 25 percent higher than for the R.N.

The growing need for quality medical care, plus the mounting concern with rehabilitation of the physically and mentally handicapped, forecasts a favorable job climate for therapists. In recent years the proliferation of knowledge in this field has led to increased specialization. If you enter this line of work, you can choose from among a number of specialties, including physical therapist, occupational therapist, recreational therapist, speech and hearing therapist (also known as a speech pathologist or an audiologist). As a physical therapist, for example, you might spend your day something like this: training an elderly woman to walk with crutches; consulting with a neurosurgeon concerning a young paraplegic; preparing a twelve-year-old girl psychologically for surgery; visiting the hospital nursery to work on infants with birth disorders.

Therapists are required to have a B.A. with a major in their chosen field and to complete a one-year course, usually offered in connection with a hospital program. Therapists work mostly in hospitals and nursing homes, and the field is wide open. Currently, for example, there are approximately 17,000 speech pathologists and audiologists, but at least 40,000 are needed to help correct or reduce speech and hearing problems afflicting more than 8 million Americans.

There are several other promising careers in the vast and growing field of health care. These include medical and psychiatric social work, medical technology, pharmacy, dental hygiene, and public health.

The *medical or psychiatric social worker* helps patients and their families find practical ways to overcome social, emotional, and economic problems. A bachelor's degree is required, with a major preferably in psychology or biological sciences, as is a master's degree from a graduate school of social work accredited by the Council on Social Work Education.

The job of *medical technologist* requires precision and dependability and has always been attractive to women, who make up 90 percent of all registered technologists. Requirements: B.A., with an emphasis on science and mathematics; a blood-bank technologist must complete one extra year in an educational program approved by the American Association of Blood Banks.

A *dietician* supervises the nutritional care of individuals and groups. One of the primary responsibilities is training other professionals in a hospital in the importance of sound nutrition to patients trying to recover good health. This is a calling that goes back as far as Hippocrates (460–370 B.C.), who was a firm believer in treating disease through diet. Today, Hippocrates' ideas are gaining a growing number of adherents in the medical profession as new discoveries in dietetics vindicate them. A dietician should have a degree in home economics with a major in food and nutrition or institutional management. To qualify for professional standing, a one-year internship in a hospital, or two years of appropriate experience, is required. About half of the 33,000 dieticians in the United States work in hospitals; the other half are employed by universities, public schools, cafeterias of large businesses, food corporations, and the armed services.

Pharmacist: Advances in medical research and government support of health programs make this a promising field for both part-time and full-time jobs. Early aspirants should prepare for college with plenty of high school chemistry and biology. The college pharmacy program is a five-year course of study emphasizing chemistry, physics, mathematics, and physiology. Half of all pharmacists are in the retail business; the others are employed by hospitals or the government.

A mother of three in Denver who is a *dental hygienist* reports: "I work under the supervision of a dentist, but I work quite independently in my own office with many of my own patients and I regulate the hours I work each week, as long as I get in the twenty hours I agreed on with the dentist." Flexible working arrangements, plus the fact that a college degree is not required, make this an attractive field for women who are meshing a career with family responsibilities. It is expected that in the future there will be more jobs than hygienists to fill them. Some colleges and universities offer two-year training programs, and degree programs are available for those who want to go into research or teaching.

There is a range of *public-health occupations,* many of which do not require a college degree, including accountant, animal technician, engineering technician, laboratory assistant, radiation-protection specialist, research technician, statistical clerk, therapist aide, sanitarian, research analyst, health-program advisor. If your place is in the field of health services, you should select your specialty, train for it, and then apply to the appropriate agency or institution for a job.

Social Work   The need for qualified people in this field continues unabated as familiar values and institutions erode and alienation and loneliness spread throughout society, particularly in the large cities. Social workers help to provide some of the supports that an increasing number of people can no longer provide for themselves. They assist individuals and families with their problems and put them in touch with the public services available to them. Recommended training: a bachelor's degree with a major in the social sciences and a master's degree in social work. Though the master's degree is required for membership in the National Association of Social Workers, some states hire college graduates without an advanced degree and provide federally sponsored in-service training programs. Social workers are employed in community agencies, public schools, and hospitals, and psychiatric social workers in mental health centers and clinics. This is a traditional women's field which has been attracting men—as a result, the salaries are improving.

Education   Jobs in teaching have been declining for several years because of the leveling off of the "baby boom." The outlook for the immediate future continues poor. However, if you have set your heart on a career in education, there are several other possibilities. You might consider working as a writer-editor for a textbook publisher, as a researcher for an educational film maker, as an administrator in a corporation producing educational materials. If you enjoy working with very young children, you can work for, or open, a day-care center; this seems to be the wave of the future. If you are determined to teach, the specialties which seem to have the most promising future are continuing education for adults; bilingual education; and teaching the retarded, a career for which there are expected to be more jobs than qualified applicants as a result of increased federal funding.

Part-Time Work

For many women, a full-time job is, at least during their child-rearing years, impractical if not impossible. They may want to work for any number of reasons, including economic necessity, but at the same time find that they are unable to reconcile their domestic responsibilities with full-time work. Here, the part-time job offers itself as a solution, a way to counteract the boredom of domestic routine, keep skills from getting rusty, or earn much-needed extra money without unduly disrupting family life. At present, one out of every seven working women is engaged in some form of part-time work.

Part-time jobs come in all sizes, shapes, and levels of personal fulfillment but are more likely to be found among traditional occupations. The most familiar type is "temporary work," which you can find by registering with an agency specializing in part-time office help. You'll be expected to have the usual office skills and to be available for a specified number of hours per week. Your assignments will generally take you to smaller-sized firms, for whom "temporaries" are an essential economy measure, or occasionally to large corporations which take on part-time workers to handle peak workloads. The pay for these jobs, unless you have very special skills, is rarely much above the hourly minimum; and prospects for advancement in a career are virtually nil. But part-time work may be a welcome change from vacuuming the carpets, and it is of course a good way to pick up extra money.

Part-time jobs which pay well and require training include freelancing as a writer, editor, commercial artist, or translator; working freelance in certain professions, such as nursing, which require a combination of skill and training; the "split career," which you begin before motherhood, drop while your children are small, and resume when they are in school; and working at home, for example by designing jewelry, tailoring, or simply addressing envelopes for local merchants.

Recently, some efforts have been made to expand part-time options and convince employers that part-time workers can be a definite asset to an enterprise. The national nonprofit organization known as Catalyst,[3] which is dedicated to expanding employment opportunities for college-educated women who want to combine work and family, has devised an ingenious series of "flexible work schedules." Here are a few examples:

Job pairing. Two women divide one full-time job with equal responsibility for the total job.

Job sharing. Two women also divide one job between them, but each is responsible for only half of the work.

"Split-level" job. A position is divided into two levels of training or ability; the employer hires two part-time employees at different skill levels to provide full-time coverage, and pays them different salaries.

"Split-location" job. The job may be done partly at the office and partly at home.

Consultant or specialist. The job requires a particular type of expertise for a short period of time; the expert may be a permanent member of the work force on a regular but part-time basis.

A dissenting note on the subject of part-time jobs for women is offered by

[3] Catalyst, 14 East 60th Street, New York, New York 10022.

Alice S. Rossi, a distinguished sociologist who has devoted much of her research to careers for women:

> Part-time employment is this generation's false panacea for avoiding a more basic change in the relations between men and women, a means whereby, with practically no change in the man's role and minimal change in the woman's, she can continue as the same wife and mother she has been in the past, with a minor appendage to these roles as an intermittent part-time professional or clerical worker.[4]

But until the more basic change Rossi is calling for comes to pass, the part-time job in one form or another may be the answer for women who want to combine work with caring for home and family.

A Matter of Degree

Do I need a college degree in order to earn a decent salary at a job I enjoy? This is a question frequently asked by women, particularly those who married and began raising families or worked for a few years directly after high school and would now like to enter or reenter the work force. The vocational importance of a college degree has been a basic tenet of the American creed; aren't we all familiar with those statistics demonstrating that college graduates earn substantially more than high school graduates in the course of a working lifetime? It is only recently that a few voices have begun challenging this concept of college as a guarantor of bigger and better careers (see, for example, Caroline Bird's book *The Case against College,* Bantam, New York, 1975).

But although the college degree may no longer be as sacrosanct as it once was, there is still a strong connection between the B.A. and success in the job market. Studies of working women demonstrate a consistent relationship between level of education and employment. The more education a woman has, the more likely she is to be employed. In 1969, 49 percent of high school graduates were employed, compared with 30 percent of those who had completed grade school only. Of college graduates, 54 percent were employed. And 69 percent of those with five years or more of college were employed; of these, 83 percent were in the age group forty-five to fifty-four.

The relationship between higher earnings and education is less clear, mainly because women's earnings have been generally disproportionate to their training. But here, too, the evidence is in favor of education. Median income has shown an increase of between $300 and $500 per year for each additional level of educational attainment. There is a significant difference in median earnings of women with college degrees and women with one to three years of college—$1,800 more for the college graduates.[26]

But at the same time, it should be noted that there are a number of jobs in the traditional women's fields—such as interior decorating, merchandising, fash-

---

[4] Alice S. Rossi, "Barriers to the Career Choice of Engineering, Medicine, or Science among American Women," in Jacquelyn A. Mattfeld and Carol G. Van Aken (eds.), *Women and the Scientific Professions,* M.I.T. Symposium on American Women in Science and Engineering, M.I.T. Press, Cambridge, Mass., 1967, p. 53.

[5] Manpower Report of the President, U.S. Department of Labor, 1971.

ion design, and cosmetology—which do not require a degree and are more lucrative and more dynamic (if such a thing can be measured), and have at least as much potential for growth as many which do require the B.A. We have already seen that there are some good possibilities in secretarial and clerical work and health services for women without degrees. When we survey the newer, nontraditional fields in the next section of this chapter, we'll find that many of them, particularly in the trades, offer apprenticeship programs in lieu of college.

Of course, a college degree will always be essential for professional and technical occupations. And the kind of disciplined thinking that college training encourages is an advantage in any vocational or avocational pursuit. In a technological society which places a heavy emphasis on credentials, it makes sense to have as much education and special training as possible. But the question of a college degree has to be answered in terms of personal goals and aspirations; if a degree is needed, it can now be earned along the way—thanks to extension and other part-time programs—while holding a job or fulfilling household responsibilities, or both, depending on your motivation and stamina.

NEW CHOICES AND CHALLENGES

What's new about riveting, welding, tapering, writing briefs, riding in patrol cars, coding computer programs, repairing television sets, shingling roofs, editing films? Mainly, that women are now performing these jobs along with men. With equal-opportunity laws being enforced, jobs formerly labeled "for men only" are now more open to all qualified applicants without regard to sex. The work opportunities we'll be discussing in this section, then, are both traditional and new— traditional for men but new for women. If you are ready for some occupational ground breaking; for a job that will take you to the top of a building or deep into the forest, to a military base or an offshore oil rig; for hard work and irregular hours; and for a training period which in some cases may take several years— then there is a wide world of work opportunities for you to explore as you consider your choice of a job or profession.

During World War II, women entered the labor market in unprecedented numbers. Rosie the Riveter became a familiar symbol, and suddenly the arguments over whether a woman could combine a job with a domestic life were muted. Thus far, the situation was familiar. From the beginning of American history, in wartime women have been urged to come out of the kitchen and do their bit on farm and in factory to "support our fighting men." As the historian Dixon Wecter tells it:

> On the eve of the Revolution and during it, New England women particularly enjoyed more vocational freedom—as blacksmiths, tallow chandlers, soapmakers, tanners, coachbuilders—than afterward. The return of the soldier helped to oust them from such fields. Women struck their flag in prompt surrender, as happened again after Appomattox and the Armistice.[6]

After World War II, women again hoisted the flag of surrender. Between

[6] Dixon Wecter, *When Johnny Comes Marching Home*, Houghton Mifflin, Boston, 1974, p. 48.

June and September 1945, one out of every four women who had been employed in factories had either quit or been laid off. But something had happened. The war had proved to many women that they could successfully combine household responsibilities with a full-time job. Employers had discovered that many of their biases against women workers were unfounded. Even trade-union leaders, the majority of whom had always been opposed to admitting women into labor unions, began to think about including women in their long-range goals. As a result, except for a slight drop in women's employment at the end of the Korean hostilities, the trend has been steadily upward since 1947. Today, women represent over 38 percent of the work force, and 20 percent of trade-union members are women.

Industry

What are the opportunities for women today in the industrial labor force? From all indications, they range from good to excellent. Even in a postindustrial society, there will continue to be a heavy demand for houses and for automobiles, appliances, and other manufactured goods. And, as many women are discovering, the hourly rates for the trades often exceed wages in other jobs.

If you want to work as a tractor operator, carpenter, plumber, or electrician, what should you do? To begin with, enter an apprenticeship program in the trade of your choice. These programs have been opening up for women during the past few years and are offered through either the prospective employer, the trade union, or the state Department of Education. Apprenticeship programs vary in length but usually run for three to four years. They are conducted on the job site at predetermined rates of pay, starting at around $3 to $5 per hour (at the time of this writing). A written agreement between trainer and trainee spells out the terms of the training program. The usual requirements for apprenticeship are that the applicant be between the ages of seventeen and thirty-one, have a high school diploma or the equivalent, and have a commitment to learning the trade and staying with the course of training.

Once you've completed your apprenticeship, you are legally entitled to any job for which you have been trained, and changing attitudes on the part of employers and trade unions are also in your favor. However, one problem you may run into is the hostility of the men on the job. Women are still regarded as interlopers in many of these fields; and your male co-workers may give you a hard time—at least in the beginning, until you've proved yourself. As one of those rarities, a woman trade-union official, sees it, "This isn't a woman's problem; it's a man's problem. What we need is some good sound education for the men in the trades."

Educational and organizing programs for women are slowly gaining ground. The Coalition of Labor Union Women (CLUW) is an interunion organization which was founded in 1973 to provide a forum for identifying and discussing common concerns and taking action toward solving some of these problems. Groups like this one are particularly interested in the political education of women trade-unionists, since even in unions with many women members—such as the

Garment Workers Union and the Laundry Workers Union—the top elected officials continue to be men. Trade-unionists of both sexes agree that women will need to develop skill and experience in union politics if they want to expand their options and opportunities in this field of work.

Paraprofessional Work: The Indispensable Middle

The rising costs of professional services in recent years and, in some fields, a demand for these services that exceeds the supply have given rise to a new type of occupation—the paraprofessional (more familiarly, the "para"). Paraprofessionals, who act as a bridge between busy professionals and the public, have been finding their best opportunities so far in the legal profession. In a nation which prides itself on being a society based on law, the law is becoming too expensive for most people of average income. When you consider that hiring a lawyer to keep your neighbor's dog off your lawn can cost anywhere from $60 to $100 an hour, you can see why paralegals are becoming popular with lawyers and their clients. By taking over many tasks which would otherwise have to be performed by the lawyer, they make it possible for the fee to be substantially lower. As an example, where a lawyer's fee might be $60 an hour, the fee for a paralegal might be $30.

What precisely is a paralegal? First of all, she (so far, there are very few men in this line of work) is *not* a legal secretary. She occupies a middle ground somewhere between the legal secretary and the lawyer. In a large law firm, she may have her own office and will not be required to type. She can draft legal documents, comfort clients, sort and catalogue data, schedule meetings, and gather information; but she cannot appear in court or give legal advice.

Training programs for paralegals are growing and may be found in colleges, university extension divisions, and community colleges. University of California, Los Angeles, Extension offers a program, approved by the American Bar Association, which runs for four months and covers such subjects as corporations, probate administration, litigation, and real estate (four months are given to each specialty).

A paralegal might resemble any of these:

A thirty-seven-year-old woman with an M.A. in child development, who had been working as a general office typist in the ten years since receiving her M.A. She "hocked her diamonds" to put herself through the course, and ended up with a well-paying job with a respected firm in the Los Angeles area. She was hired almost immediately.

A fifty-four-year-old woman, married, with an ailing husband. She had course credits only from secretarial college. She completed the paralegal program while working part-time and then joined the same firm as a full-time employee. She had been a legal secretary previously. Now, she is actively engaged in the development of a national association of legal assistants. She travels extensively on behalf of the association.

A forty-nine-year-old woman, married, with a B.A. awarded eighteen years earlier. She had a little work experience, mostly with volunteer organizations; her paid work experience included only a few years of work as a medical secretary. She said, "If I were younger, I would attend law school. For me now the paralegal field is a practical and realistic alternative." During the course, one instructor noticed her exceptional work, and he hired her after graduation.

For some, a job as paralegal is a steppingstone to a career as a full-fledged lawyer. But for the majority in paralegal work, the job is an end in itself and one that offers its own satisfactions and rewards.

Potential employers of paralegals in addition to law firms are corporations, government agencies, unions, courts, and legal-aid groups. With the world becoming increasingly legalistic and the demand for legal services growing, the outlook for this field is excellent. A trend worth noting is the suggestion of the American Bar Association that paralegals be licensed. What this would mean is that paralegals would be hired by lawyers, trained by lawyers, and accredited according to standards proposed by lawyers.

Other professional fields are interested in this "indispensable middle." Paraprofessionals are making their way in social work, veterinary medicine, education, and especially in the health sciences as technicians of all kinds, such as dental aides and paramedics (who are much in demand by police and fire departments). It seems safe to predict that within a few years, wherever there is a profession, there will be paraprofessionals helping to extend its reach and improve its performance.

The Military

When a manpower shortage developed in 1942, the Army, Navy, and Air Force began looking to womanpower, primarily for administrative and clerical jobs. Since then, women have made substantial progress in the military. At present, out of more than 480 military occupational specialties (MOS), enlisted women are eligible for training and utilization in all except the 48 related to combat or direct combat support. Women aviators, surgeons, chaplains, and security officers are finding a welcome in today's armed services.

The three major service academies—Army, Navy, and Air Force—are accepting women applicants for the class of 1980. Women will take classes with men, and their training will be the same, with the exception of specific training for combat situations.

In weighing a career in the armed services, here are some points to consider:

Educational advantages. All branches of the armed services offer educational programs at bargain rates. The Army's "Project Ahead" pays 75 percent of tuition costs for college courses; under this program, if you're a qualified high school graduate you can get regular college credits for courses the Army provides and extra college credits for off-duty courses supervised by the college of your choice. After a three-year term of service, you can expect to have earned two full years of college credits along with your regular pay. The Navy's "Campus for Achievement" program is similar but requires a four-year enlistment. And the Air Force has the "Community College of the Air Force," which provides college programs for enlisted men and women through some 2,000 institutions of higher education.

Requirements. Age eighteen to thirty-four; good physical condition; high school diploma or the equivalent. Applicants under twenty-one years of age must have the consent of parents or guardians unless they live in a state which has granted legal emancipation at the age of eighteen. Enlistment is from two to six years.

Benefits. Women in the military receive the same pay, benefits, and promotion opportunities as men. All personnel on active duty receive medical and dental care and are included in Social Security benefits. Pregnancy is no longer a bar to continuing in the service. Enlisted personnel and officers are eligible for retirement after a minimum of twenty years of active military service.

In the all-volunteer armed services, opportunities for women will grow and diversify. An Air Force general recently announced a 150 percent increase in the number of WAFs to be recruited within the next two years. And the training and skills that are acquired in the services can be carried over to civilian life. In fact, the armed services, in providing women with opportunities to prove themselves in nontraditional jobs, have helped open up many new occupational areas for women in the civilian world.

For information on enlistment or appointment as an officer, write to your nearest recruiting office in the branch of the service that interests you.

Police Departments

In 1969, the Los Angeles Police Department graduated its last class of "policewomen." By 1973, a "unisex" program had been established which removed all previous limitations on the employment of women and replaced the job title "policewoman" with "police officer." This new policy, which is also being followed by some other police departments around the country, means that women must now meet the same requirements and pass the same examinations—including the rigorous physical tests—as the men applicants. The testing period runs from two to three months; to be eligible, a woman must conform to the department's standard requirements in regard to age, legal residency, citizenship, height, weight, and education. Once hired, she is given assignments without regard to sex. Women are now riding in patrol cars and performing the same kind of demanding, often dangerous tasks as men.

There's a lot more to police work than chasing criminals. Many women are working in such activities as recruitment, juvenile investigation, and community relations. Some of the jobs offered by police departments, particularly in community work, are held by civilians and can be applied for without going through the usual recruitment procedures.

Police work offers, in addition to a variety of challenging, active jobs, good pay (starting at around $12,000 in most major cities) and excellent health and retirement benefits. However, the selection process is a fine filter, and it's a case of many apply but few are chosen. In one major city in 1974, more than 10,000 persons were tested for the job of police officer; 2,500 passed all the examinations; and of these, about 500 were selected for appointment. But if you think you have the makings of a police officer, don't let this discourage you. Write or visit the recruiting division of your police department; you may find a rewarding career in which the dull moments are few and far between and the opportunities for community service are great.

Business

The invention of the typewriter brought women into business in large numbers, and the development of more sophisticated technology, such as the computer, is carrying them to new, higher levels in the business world. Aside from new managerial opportunities, which are dealt with in another chapter, there are a considerable number of staff or specialist jobs developing out of the growing complexity of today's business world. These include: accountant, computer programer, economist, geologist, market analyst, technical writer, researcher, translator. These are jobs requiring considerable expertise, so that a college education plus additional training is usually mandatory.

Fortunately, the Master of Business Administration (M.B.A.), which is the preferred degree for jobs of this type, is sufficiently flexible to accommodate a broad range of career goals. For example, an engineer with an M.B.A.—a combination of technical expertise and general managerial skills—finds little difficulty in getting an entry-level salary of $1,300 or more per month. Joint business and law degrees can be earned at many institutions and are also highly prized by large corporations. A new pharmacy-M.B.A. program instituted last year at the University of Utah will cut a full year off the time it ordinarily takes to earn both degrees. The M.B.A. would also combine well with the arts and education. Indeed, is there any field of human endeavor that wouldn't benefit from more imaginative, more efficient management?

A recent graduate of the Management Business Administration program at Columbia University exemplifies this new breed of businesswoman. Claire M., whose college major was English, was hired directly after graduation as a research analyst by a major New York publisher. Starting salary: $13,500. In this staff position, she helps the company to decide such things as which books to promote and what geographical areas are ripe for new bookstores. Within two years, she expects to move into a line job as a product manager; in five years, she expects to be in a top management position, earning around $30,000 a year. Expectations such as these are well within the realm of possibility; the chances of progressing rapidly in business today are very real, if you have the drive—and, equally important, the training.

Film Making

In the American dream factory, the motion picture industry, the final product has been largely the work of men. With few exceptions, women have been positioned in front of the cameras—as extras, or starlets, or stars. And though millions of American girls have dreamed of themselves as movie stars and many have followed the dream to Hollywood, only the minutest percentage of these fantasies has been translated into reality. Acting in the movies has always been reserved for those with an extraordinary amount of talent, luck, or both.

Meanwhile, behind the cameras, where the real action is taking place, the producers, directors, technicians, gaffers, cinematographers, editors—those who actually *make* the movies—have been almost entirely men. Women have been employed by the film studios mostly in clerical jobs. (The script girl who sits at the director's elbow marking the script as the shooting proceeds is actually a secretary with little or no responsibility for the progress of the film.) And a few women have built successful careers as scenarists and costume designers.

On the whole, this is a bleak picture. It is reflected in the stereotyping of women on the screen that has done so much to distort the image of the American woman around the world. But hopeful signs are appearing. In recent years, a few women have managed to break through the barriers and take their places behind the cameras. Of the more than 30,000 women presently employed full time in the industry, one-third are in the higher pay categories, which include managerial, professional, technical, and sales employees. This is a significant figure for an industry in which women were not so long ago relegated almost entirely to the lowest-paying jobs.

Surveying several women who are in top film-making jobs, we find that they have arrived by various routes. An associate producer at an independent film company started as a script supervisor. A writer-producer who won an Emmy for one of her productions held an assortment of nondescript jobs and got her start by selling a script to "Bewitched." A woman who had studied to be a crafts designer was asked to design products for television, developed a weekly half-hour program for children, and is now a leading producer of children's television shows.

As in most careers, there is more than one way to get there from here. And there is more to film making than Hollywood or television. Educational film making is a growing field; and industry and government are increasing their use of audiovisual media as an effective means of communicating with large numbers of people.

If you are attracted by the idea of working behind the cameras, you are strongly advised to enroll in a good film school to learn the trade. A list of film schools is available from the American Film Institute (see the list of resources on page 85). The American Film Institute (AFI), which is located in Beverly Hills, offers an internship program for promising new film makers and is also experimenting with a directing workshop for women and other projects to assist women in becoming directors of feature and television films. Life behind the cameras may not have the "glamour" associated with acting, but it offers a far better opportunity to translate a dream into an enduring career.

Professions

Women who are choosing medicine, engineering, architecture, law, and even the ministry as their life work are no longer regarded as social oddities, and the opportunities for women in the professions are getting better all the time. But keep in mind that the preparation is long, arduous, and expensive. Also—and this is of particular concern to women with families—these careers require an uninterrupted commitment: there are very few successful professionals who are practicing part time or who have been able to drop out for long periods in order to attend to domestic duties.

But if you feel you have a true calling and are willing to spend eight to ten years after secondary school preparing for it, you will find that the possibilities are virtually limitless. The sciences, which have experienced tremendous growth in research and development as well as in applied research, are looking toward women to fill their ever-expanding needs. Medicine is actively seeking women, particularly for such specialties as pediatrics and gynecology. Architects are beginning to recognize that the planning and building of houses have been entrusted far too much to men, considering that it is women who have been expected to convert houses into livable, functioning homes.

As for the law, there has been a vast change in attitude since the Supreme Court decided in 1873 that a woman could not be a lawyer, because "the paramount destiny and mission of women are to fulfill the noble and benign offices of wife and mother." [7] Today leading law firms are hiring women, and the number of women enrolled in law schools has increased from less than 2,000 to almost 17,000 during the past decade. Also, as with other standard entrance exams, women are scoring higher than men on the Legal Scholastic Aptitude Test (LSAT).

Whether you choose a traditional career or a newer one, there is certainly no lack of choice, challenge, or opportunity awaiting you. As an employment counselor specializing in careers for women remarked recently: "From a job standpoint, there has probably never been a better time to be a woman."

BIBLIOGRAPHY

Epstein, Cynthia Fuchs: *Woman's Place, Options and Limits in Professional Careers,* University of California Press, Berkeley, 1970. A thoughtful and comprehensive treatment of women's occupations from a sociologist's view, which focuses on the limits rather than the options.

Kievit, Mary Bach: *Women in the World of Work,* Center for Vocational and Technical Education, Ohio State University, Columbus, 1972. A useful synthesis of research on women as workers.

Kreps, Juanita: *Sex in the Marketplace: American Women at Work,* Policy Studies in Employment and Welfare number 11, John Hopkins Press, Baltimore, Md., 1971. A factual approach which examines when women work, at what jobs, and under what arrangements.

Lifton, Robert Jay (ed.): *The Woman in America,* Beacon Press, Boston, 1971. A fine collection of essays that cover a broad theoretical range. See especially Esther Peterson's essay, "Working Women."

[7] *Bradwell v. Illinois,* 83 U.S. 130 (1873).

Mattfeld, Jacquelyn A., and Carol G. Van Aken (eds.): *Women and the Scientific Professions,* M.I.T. Symposium on American Women in Science and Engineering, M.I.T. Press, Cambridge, Mass., 1967. Among the contributors are Bruno Bettelheim, Erik Erikson, Lillian Gilbreth, Mary I. Bunting, and Alice S. Rossi. Rossi's contribution offers a realistic picture of barriers and opportunities for women in the scientific professions.

Mitchell, Joyce Slayton: *I Can Be Anything: Careers and Colleges for Young Women,* College Entrance Examination Board, 1975. Though addressed primarily to young women planning their education and careers, the book is a handy compendium of new and traditional jobs. Describes briefly what the jobs are like, educational requirements, and future potential.

Superintendent of Documents: *Occupational Outlook Handbook,* U.S. Government Printing Office, Washington, D.C., 1975. The GPO publishes several other pamphlets relating to employment. *Occupational Outlook Handbook* is recommended as a summary and forecast of vocational trends.

Women's Bureau, U.S. Department of Labor, Washington, D.C., publishes various pamphlets on employment patterns, salary ranges, and requirements.

ADDITIONAL RESOURCES

General

For information about film schools:

American Film Institute
John F. Kennedy Center for the Performing Arts
Washington, D.C. 20566

For information about apprenticeship programs:

American Film Institute
501 Doheny Road
Beverly Hills, California

American Society of Medical Technologists
Suite 1600, Hermann Professional Building
Houston, Texas 77025

American Dietetic Association
620 N. Michigan Avenue
Chicago, Illinois 60611

For a list of courses and schools approved by the A.M.A. for physical and occupational therapy:

Department of Allied Medical Professions and Services
American Medical Association
535 North Dearborn
Chicago, Illinois 60610

Society of Public Health Educators, Inc.
419 Park Avenue South
New York, New York 10016

Office of Information
Department of the Army
The Pentagon
Washington, D.C. 20310

For information about apprenticeship programs in the trades:

Advocates for Women
564 Market Street
San Francisco, California 94104

National Association of Bank Women, Inc.
111 East Wacker Drive
Chicago, Illinois 60601

Data Processing Management Association
505 Busse Highway
Park Ridge, Illinois 60068

American Forest Institute
6255 Sunset Boulevard
Los Angeles, California 90028

National Association of Women Lawyers
1155 60 Street
Chicago, Illinois 60637

NOW Task Force on Labor Unions
National Organization for Women
5 South Wabash Avenue, Suite 1615
Chicago, Illinois 60603

American Society of Interior Designers
730 Fifth Avenue
New York, New York 10019

Local Resources

State Department of Employment
State Department of Human Resources
Career Counseling Centers
Women's Resource Centers

Chapter 5

The Job of Job Hunting

Priscilla Jackson

Priscilla Jackson, M.A., is President, Women-in-Conference; originator and Director of Place-finders Conferences; and chief consultant, Women-in-Management. In 1965 she founded the Continuum Center for Women, Oakland University, funded by the Kellogg Foundation. She was elected national chairperson for Continuing Education of Women, Adult Education Association, and is a consultant to several women's centers. She has worked with many vocations as Director of Conferences and as Assistant Dean, Oakland University; as Program Designer of management-education seminars for women, Graduate School of Business Administration, University of Michigan; and as a speaker at universities, professional associations, and women's organizations. Her publications include the *The Continuum Center: Education, Volunteering, Employment* (commissioned by the Kellogg Foundation), and articles written when she was a contributing editor for *Washington Newsletter on Women* (now *Women Today*).

You may have turned to this chapter because you want to enter what is sometimes called the world outside the home, the real world (as differentiated from schooling), or the labor market. Or you may have turned to this chapter because you want a different job in that world; or because you've been too long in a dead-end job and simply wonder how much effort it takes to change jobs.

Taking a new job is a significant change. You will remove yourself bodily from the place where you have been spending your life. You will venture into new territory, join a new set of people, and reorganize your work habits, schedule, clothing, and commuting patterns. You'll feel again the pangs of being a beginner. You will have to learn new customs. For example, in this laboratory they dress casually in jeans, but they expect exactitude in the experiments. In this office women wear heels and hose, but high-speed production is expected of them. You may clump into this construction site in clumsy boots, but you are counted on for agile judgments about massive machinery.

PRELIMINARIES

Define Your Reasons for Making a Change

If the idea of job hunting sounds exciting to you, you may be a person who relishes variety and exploration. If it sounds intimidating, you may be a rooted person. But either feeling is unimportant and will be temporary. More basic is facing the fact that, if you are looking for a new job, something is wrong where you are. Therefore, the first step is to define what is wrong: that is, why you want to make this change in your life.

What *is* wrong? Is it poverty? Boredom? Isolation? These conditions are familiar to women who are breadwinners, to women who are overqualified for their jobs, to women alone at home. Perhaps you just feel vaguely uneasy; an ill-defined weariness descends on workdays.

Why do you want to leave your present job? Are you crushed by a tyrannical boss or by an insufferable co-worker? Are you frightened? Exhausted? Enraged at discrimination? If so, wait. Some job is better than no job. Before you quit, calm yourself and tell the boss (or, if that fails, the boss's boss): "I'd like to keep this job, which has a lot going for it, but there is one thing I cannot tolerate. Can we change it?"

Perhaps what is wrong is nothing dramatic. Perhaps you've just been in one place too long. People tend to reach a plateau after an average of seven years in the same job, according to management studies. Your problem may be your success itself. You may have learned your job thoroughly, so that there is no curiosity; and worked out solutions for every eventuality, so that there is no excitement, no uncertainty. The work is flawless. In this case, you are a very valuable employee. But your success is now taken for granted, by you if not by the management. The process of accomplishment, which engaged your intelligence, is over. What you do now is easy for you—too easy. It no longer feeds your self-respect. Consider, though, whether you are bored enough to leave the satisfactions of approval, of a territory you know, of people you can cope with, of benefits, seniority, and so on. You may trade it all for too much uncertainty.

In assessing whether to go or to stay, consider the quality of your experiences during these best eight hours of your day. Watch your own physical responses. Do you grimace when the alarm clock rings? Do you dismiss with an offhand comment questions about what you do? Are you impatient when the boss is explaining something? Are you irritated by co-workers or disgusted when the same old problems reappear? Do you daydream about the weekends?

Perhaps your job is all right for the present, but you need a further goal. Can you progress to supervisor, officer, department head, principal, vice-president, chairperson, president? You wonder, Is your job on the route up? Are you moving along that route fast enough?

In order to decide whether your job is a dead end, study the culture of your organization like an anthropologist or sociologist. Analyze its elites, its specialties, its patterns of upward mobility. Like an economist, study its solvency, its management, its place in the industry. Like a social psychologist, observe its values, standards, expected behaviors, and successful mavericks.

Now place your own situation within this larger organization. If you decide that your job is not a dead end, you have now gathered data to prepare you for the climb up the hierarchical mountain. You can plan your ascent, find supporters, convince people that you can do it. Like a politician, you must present a positive image to the appropriate audience. Sit down and outline a campaign strategy. (And stop reading this chapter.) However, if you decide to leave, you not only know why, but you also know more about yourself, more about what to avoid in future jobs. Whatever your situation, define what is wrong. Name the problem in a single, concrete word or phrase. You are now on the way to the second step, defining what you want.

Define What You Want in a Job

If you need a job because you need money for food, you'll think these defining steps unnecessary. You are struggling for survival, the first level in the hierarchy of values developed by Abraham Maslow. But once you have a job, once you are fairly sure it will be secure for a while, then you will look for other good things from the job—interesting people, self-respect, variety, comfort, fun, excitement, news, influence, approval, and more money.

Consider whether this statement describes what you are seeking in a job: You are looking for a *place* (outside a home or bedroom), in which you can *help* a *certain* leader or boss achieve his or her purpose. In exchange you expect to receive money, a space, tools, supplies, security, an orientation, and a certain degree of civility.

These are expectations which both sides to the formal job contract understand. But there are also informal expectations known only to you. You may be expecting dates, a sense of usefulness, identification with a worthwhile purpose, a new territory, intellectual stimulation, or gratitude from clients or the boss. You probably mean all this when you say you are looking for an "interesting job." But how can the employer possibly know what is interesting to you? Athletes? American Indians? Polite people? Diamonds? What is news to you, and what is boring and obvious? Employers cannot know if you do not know yourself, or if you do not tell them. But employers know the penalty for *not* guessing what employees' informal expectations are: a high turnover rate. It costs the employer time and money to reinterview, reselect, reorient, retrain. The penalty for *your* not knowing your secret expectations is continual disappointment, and therefore continual job hunting.

JOB HUNTERS AND JOBHOLDERS

Much of what follows in this chapter may seem to be directed to the first-time job seeker—and it is. One assumes that experiencd job holders have held a series of jobs, and have therefore necessarily gone through a series of job hunts. But after a year of asking all kinds of people, "How did you get your job?" I am coming to the conclusion that for many people active, planned job seeking may be a once-in-a-decade or even a once-in-a-lifetime experience. Therefore, the "first time" job seeker is not only the worker new to the labor market and seeking an entry-level job. She can be anybody. Many experienced jobholders are inexperienced job hunters.

The new worker, and the person changing from one role or one industry to another, will have a bigger job than the experienced jobholder seeking a new job in her own field. The student leaving the world of schooling, the housewife leaving the world of the home, or the worker leaving an overcrowded or obsolescing field will feel like a stranger in a foreign land. She will have to discover the kind of people who inhabit this land and what they do. Are her past accomplishments useful to them, or irrelevant? Does she know their specialized vocabulary, their way of kidding? Finally, unlike the experienced worker who is job hunting in a familiar field, she will have no friends in this new country to act as her guides.

The experienced jobholder has a different problem. She is used to being considered a producing adult, to carrying her weight, to being depended upon, even to being taken for granted. Now she has to prove herself, convince others of her own value in spite of the fact that she has demonstrated it over and over again. That hurts.

If this experienced jobholder has been fired, or "eased out"—and most of us have been, or will be, at least once in a work career—she carries an extra burden of resentment. Her confidence is singed. She is not stretching toward growth, but scrambling back to the security she had. She is applying as an escape. Perhaps she is too angry to be an applicant at all.

Although the experienced jobholder will be familiar with many of the observations which follow, through others' job hunting if not her own, I think she will be surprised at how much plain work job hunting is. And she will be surprised at the feelings that flood her—just like those of the first-time worker.

The person who may bypass much of this chapter is the woman who has decided to move, but remains in a familiar field, bringing current skills that are in demand—the woman with experience, recommendations, acquaintances, and an overall view of the various organizations in her field. She knows the culture, standards, and requirements of the job which is the next step for her; or, if she does not know, she had better ask—not guess. She has the advantage of knowing whom to ask, of knowing that the woman at the next desk is not the horse's mouth. But her situation also has its disadvantage. She cannot, like the eager first-time worker, bustle around asking ingenuous questions. Since she is offering a work record which is to carry her beyond the entry-level job, she wants to carry herself with the dignity of proven accomplishment. If her boss considers job changers to be traitors, she will have to search discreetly. If she has resigned, she may shrink from eyes which wonder why she is jobless. In either case, she should force herself not only to attend every meeting of her professional association, but to use her free time intensively—offering to chair a committee, for example. She should also widen her knowledge by joining related professional associations and by taking courses in new but related fields.

FINDING A JOB

How to Be Offered a Job

There are two ways to get a job. You may embark on a job hunt, or you may be offered a job. Does being offered a job mean only "being lucky"?

Well, yes. But I am discovering that it happens more often than people realize. Here are six examples of housewives and mothers who returned to the world of work in just this way.

Bob Simone and Bill Stewart each start a business. Bob is an architect. Bill is buying a gas station. Both are working like mad producing the product or service and finding the clients or buyers. Neither has time for the interminable government forms—withholding statements, payroll records, documentation of income and inventory, income tax forms, licensing, business use, incorporation. But no money is left for another employee. So Janie Simone and Jill Stewart pitch in and learn to be bookkeepers and secretaries in a new family business.

Ann Fine took her child to nursery school and began to "help out." She was invited to work three mornings a week; and for her this was the perfect part-time job: close to home, and allowing her to be with her child during the preschool years. She learned that she enjoyed small children. She also noticed that the full-time staff had a professionalism that she did not have. So she took courses in early childhood education and did field work at the university experimental school, where she was asked to work part time (perfect while her children were in grade school). Now that her children have left home, she is the director of that nursery school. Should this be called luck?

Andy Wihelm is a manufacturer's agent. He is creative in the way he adapts plastics to his industrial customers' needs. He is also verbal, gregarious, mobile, dogged—a good salesman. But he hates paperwork. He asked his sister-in-law if she wanted to do some typing part time at home. Now she's his adminstrative assistant, his scheduler, and—he laughs—his manager (which she is).

Doris Scharf, a lively forty-five-year-old, came through our Continuum Center for Women at Oakland University. She'd had a couple of years of college and then married (a typical pattern). She was a natural student. Of our three routes to the world outside the home—education, volunteer work, and employment (EVE)—she was interested only in education. Because of her ability and enthusiastic, eager interest, her major professor invited her to help with his research. He urged her on to graduate school. Out of that came a graduate assistantship, a joint publication, a fellowship for her Ph.D., and his recommendation for her present job, as an assistant professor.

Minnie Tofske often took her mother to a home for the aged for companionship. But Minnie saw that the merely social events—meals, bingo—seemed to offer a plethora of play. She wondered if these older women would enjoy thoughtful discussions like those in the Continuum Center. She asked permission to start a discussion group. She was able to tell the director of the home that she had participated in such groups, had taken our group-leader training, and was "hearing a need." She recruited a group. It grew so important to the home that the director wrote a proposal requesting funding for this preventive mental health service, thus creating a job for Minnie.

How many construction crews are made up of a brother, a brother-in-law, two sons, perhaps a neighbor, with a woman relative managing the money, paying the crew? Remember the family farm, the "ma and pa" stores, cottage industries, owner-managed drugstores and restaurants? The people offered a job in such enterprises were simply *there*. The moral for the job seeker is to look for organizations which are small, local, nearby, just starting up. Hover around: *a job is sometimes at your fingertips.*

How to Embark on the Job Hunt

You must first accept job hunting as a job. Set aside the hours during which you intend to work. Set up shop at one place—a desk or table with telephone, stationery, files. Admit to yourself that this job hunt is likely to take from four months to a year. Recruit a friend or two who are also job hunting, or who are at least willing to explore with you.

Seek out a women's center. Call nearby colleges and community colleges and ask for their program or center for continuing education for women (CEW), as well as their women's resource center (which may or may not be chiefly for students). These centers may offer conferences, career counseling, and a library. Independent centers, such as Wider Opportunities for Women (WOW), are also springing up in several cities. Look also for the new services to women, supported directly by the fees of women who use them, such as employment agencies, our Place-finders Conferences, and so on.

The first rule in the job of job hunting is to help luck happen.

Rule 1: Tell Everybody   This is hard for women who have been conditioned to wait for dates to call, who would never invite themselves to a party or take the last cookie on the plate. But it is necessary in order to allow others to help you.

I found this out this way: When I was invited to work for a university as a part-time conference coordinator, it never occurred to me that I would ever be hiring anyone else. So I was surprised when a friend in the League of Women

Voters, Belle, mentioned that she'd worked for McGraw-Hill for a year before she was married (ten years before). I said if I heard of anything at the university, I'd let her know. I never did hear of jobs opening up in other departments. (Remember this when you think you're covered because you've "told somebody" at General Mills.) Two years later, however, I was suddenly inundated with conferences and deadlines for brochures. I remembered Belle and begged her to help part time. As often happens with part-time jobs, we were soon full-timers, and our careers have moved along interestingly since.

But I often wondered afterwards: why didn't I call any of my other friends? I know plenty of English majors, plenty of literary, responsible, energetic, pleasant women. Perhaps I thought that they might resent the implication that I thought they lived in secret poverty, or had empty, useless days to fill. Perhaps, not having worked before, they'd play at a job, and I'd be saddled with them. Perhaps they'd be resentful if the job were dull, saying I had lured them with the glamour of working for a university. Perhaps I resisted the effort of calling a long list of them on the off chance that one might be able and willing. I still don't know why, but I did call the person who had told me she wanted me to.

So tell all your friends. Ask women friends what their husbands do; ask them to ask about opportunities in their husbands' fields; say you'll call back Wednesday.

If you need money now, remind your friends (male and female) of your home-economics skills. Working people need help with housework; homemakers once had mothers, sisters, and daughters to help but now usually work in isolation. Offer to help with parties, or to bring casseroles to the door at dinnertime, or to alter clothing. If you need food and a bed, there is a tremendous need right now for live-in help in older suburbs.

Winston Churchill wrote letters and articles back to England from the Boer War. He rode up and down the marching column, meeting everyone, looking for ideas for articles, for contacts, for relationships. Luck, he said, comes in ratio to the number of exposures.

After rule 1—tell everybody—comes a caution: tell people clearly what you want and can deliver. If you say, ". . . anything with money today," will you, in fact, clean someone's house tomorrow? If you say, "I want two hours a day with no worrying responsibilities, but in a new place with people," will you go to the quilting bee? Will you be the evening cashier in a downtown restaurant? Will you file? Will you be a hospital volunteer? If you say you want a management job, are you prepared for overtime? What are you really willing to do?

Rule 2: Be Seen Twink Willett, who became the mayor of Birmingham, Michigan, happened into politics because of the muddy roads in her subdivision. She talked to neighbors, helped start the "what shall we do about it?" group, attended meetings of the city commission to find out where to complain. Selected to speak to the commission, she spoke. Once she had spoken, someone suggested that she run for the commission—and represent the group there. Fascinated now with government, she ran, learned, and grew.

Until I met a great cross section of women through our Continuum Center, I never dreamed how many American women are sitting home alone. During the twenty-five years that are left to us after our children are grown—now that science has given us such a long life—home is too private, too safe from irritation, discomfort, all the stimulations that keep us reacting and young. Young women—and men—who are unemployed can also hide in this haven.

Therefore, you must go out, in order to *be seen.* Once out, you must be more than a passive face in a crowd. You must be seen doing something—at least talking and gesticulating. Did you speak at the meeting, but no one suggested that you run for the city commission? Did they suggest that you run for club secretary? No? Then do something else. In order to find out what you are good at, *believe your feedback.*

Rule 3: Take Heed of Feedback   Don't dismiss it as flattery when someone says, "What a nice outfit." Wear it to all your interviews, especially if three people say it. When a woman friend says, "You're so well organized"; when her husband says, "That's a good company you worked for back there"; when an interviewer says, "You seem to have good experience in_____"—*hear* what they say. Capitalize on it at your next interview.

Rule 4: Look Locally   For new workers: Visit every shop in your town or neighborhood. Ask the people at the counter how they like working at that business. Many won't have time to waste. After all, they're working. But two or three sentences will start your grapevine. For experienced workers: Visit every organization where your skills are used, even though you don't want to work there. Inquire, learn, circulate, interview.

Understanding the New Environment

Housewives and students have spent their lives in homes and schools. The student has been only a customer in both—never a doer. The housewife was a customer in one and a doer in the other. Such people are as ignorant of the thousands of other worlds in our complicated society as the illiterate peasant is of schooling and the street urchin is of home life.

Unless you are a hunter and gatherer—or live on a subsistence farm making all your own food, clothing, shelter, education, entertainment, and transportation—you are part of a society in which we exchange tasks. That is, I farm and you build houses. We specialize.

The result—startling, and often disheartening to the uninitiated—is this: *the specialized world hires skills, not people.* This is particularly hard on homemakers. To their world of children, relatives, guests, club and church members, home-servicemen, local salesclerks, they extend warmth. But receptionists and interviewers are often cold by comparison. Why not? Scores of people pass in front of them, most of whom they'll never see again. Furthermore, why develop a warm relationship when it will only make rejection more embarrassing? They may answer the homemaker's smile with coldness, and if the interchange takes time, with impatience. The homemaker, thinking herself unlikeable, or impertinent for even applying where she is apparently so unsuitable, hurries home crushed. She may never apply anywhere again.

Importance of Skills   Civilization was built by one individual here and another there doing what was needed at the moment in the best way that person happened to think of. Necessity is still the mother of invention every day. Human beings remember successful solutions to problems: What grows? What keeps out rain? When there is too much for one head to remember, we specialize. Even in the Dark Ages there were architect-masons, a warrior class, an order of monks who built bridges. Therefore, in our highly specialized world, you need a named, identifiable, recognizable skill. You need to be called a barber, a technician, an aerialist, a navigator. Two stories will illustrate why this is so.

A well-educated, attractive minister's wife came to show me her résumé. Her husband had died suddenly, leaving her, at forty, with three children and a churchful of people anxious to help. Her résumé documented her education, her classes in painting and child care, her participation in organizations, her wide reading. And what was she offering employers?—A broad generalist; a conscientious, responsible citizen.

"Industry," she said, "is looking for generalists. Most professions are too narrowly specialized. Decision making in our society requires the wider view, particularly at the higher levels."

Perhaps executives—people already at the higher levels—say this when discussing "society today" with their ministers, or with professors at a university conference. Maybe it is even true. But I'll bet that the personnel files of the Ford Motor Company haven't a single job description asking for: "Generalist; only the conscientious need apply." After I'd broken this news, she mused, "The men in our church do keep asking me what I'd like to *do*."

Employment agencies place skills: that is, crafts, trades, vocations, professions.

I was querying a young personnel major in college who was also working in an employment agency. "You get a commission when you *place*," he said. "So you send over whoever has a trade to whatever openings have come in for that trade.—Do I fit the job and the person together carefully? Listen, the applicants want to interview wherever they can, and the employers want somebody *now*. If you don't send them a warm body in a couple of days, they'll call another agency."

"Well, what if the applicant is overqualified—or underqualified?"

He shrugged. "So they'll come back for another job, and the employer will want another employee fast. More commissions."

"Well, what if an intelligent, attractive, well-educated woman comes in. A— well—a generalist. You know she'll learn fast; could do anything; nice with people. Can't you call a few employers and sort of sell her?"

"Don't have time to bother with them," he said.

Making the Transition from School   I was interviewing people for the job of course coordinator (someone who arranges for rooms, registration, students, fees, coffee, etc.). A graduate student dropped by and engaged me in a lively discussion about his solutions for world problems. Suddenly I realized I had wasted an hour and a half. I felt vaguely bloated, as if I'd been eating air. I'd assumed that this student had come about the job and that he was showing me his intelligence and his ideas for new courses. But since he never mentioned the job, perhaps he hadn't. In any case, after discovering his preoccupation with global issues, I'd have been embarrassed to ask him to order coffee or check rosters. So I thanked him for stopping by. I never heard from him again. A brilliant student; a failure at job hunting.

The work environment is foreign to students in many ways. Students are taught to be critics—of writers, of politicians, and so on—and are used to working individually: many have done so since the age of four. If they excel, it is on their own efforts, seldom as part of a team. Getting help when it is really needed—at examination time—is called cheating. Authority figures praise students for the ability to select from among written or spoken statements, rather than from the welter of experience. Accountability has to do with "telling what you know," orally or in writing. The product is a paper or examination. The reward is a grade.

But authority figures on the job are not interested in what beginners know. Bosses are surprised to find that even beginners with vocational degrees offer information that is obvious or irrelevant, when what is wanted is good judgment about the action at hand. Furthermore, employers are paying for help in order to save their own time. They do not like to act as volunteer teachers. They do not remember that students are used to receiving approval for being eager, questing learners.

Students—like housewives and some managers—work on loose schedules: "do what you have to do in the time it takes." But for the most part organizations which hire by the hour, day, week, or month cannot work this way. They assume that you will get the job done, but they also assume that you will put in your time. Students who have graduated have proof that they can get a job done. But they may not know the ethics of the world of hours: "Give an honest day's work for an honest day's pay."

Specialization   Here are some sobering observations about the sophistication of the specialized society and why it is hard to enter it for the first time—or to change specialties within it.

1   Each generation adds an adjective to a named skill; e.g., "writer" becomes "technical writer," which in turn becomes "automotive technical writer."
2   Specialists are a decade ahead of the most alert lay person. I learned this through designing conferences with professional associations.
3   Specialists daily create their specialty. They stumble over obstacles, make mistakes, worry, try another way, evaluate, and share their successes with professional peers who know what they're talking about. This is how our advanced society developed.

Therefore, do not only think in terms of *jobs,* neat squares on organizational charts, with occupational titles, immutable, set. Organizations are, rather, a moving cluster of amoebas spreading and contracting, jostling each other and shrinking. Individuals within various job areas do the parts of the job they like and dab at others. They take over part of someone's else's job. They improve standards so much that they need an assistant, or they are found out filling time. Unfilled spaces appear between specialists who are developing in opposite directions. Job slots react to deadlines, departmental reorganization, new products, even new employees.

If you started reading this chapter by wondering whether you have been in your job too long, you may discover that you can change the job without leaving it. You can ask for more responsibility, suggest a new project, ask for an assistant so that you can take on another facet of the work. By looking at the overall purpose of the office, you may be able to show the boss that the purpose can be achieved better while at the same time making a valued employee (yourself) want to stay. That is creativity, and it is something no outsider can do. In the same way, if you seem to be in a dead-end job, you may be able to steer the job into the mainstream. Although this chapter has been written for the person who is seeking a new or different job, there is much to be said for remaining in the same organization and using your knowledge of the terrain to design the job that you really want.

Do not depend solely on your field of knowledge. Students file a collection of data in their mental computers. But as graduates, however, they often discover that these data do not, of themselves, lead anywhere. The information simply exists, in their heads. There turns out to be a great leap between it and the hiring office. For example, ecology is a field; it might be called on, say, in a health department. Unfortunately, teachers and professors are often ignorant of this leap, because they have always been in the specialty of schooling. As students themselves, they saw firsthand the route from consumer to producer; their product *is* knowledge; they were trained for their employers' requirements. However, the student entering another specialty is in a different position. Her product there is not knowledge collected in school, but judgment and action, and she was not trained for this employer's requirements—as any person in business will tell you. Furthermore, many specialties cannot use academic areas as such. For example, the field of botany is too general. It must be narrowed to flowers, or bulb flowers, or the iris, or the bearded iris. You might grow the bearded iris, or merchandise it, or photograph it, or describe it for a bulb catalogue or encyclopedia; you could paint it on china or crate it for export; you could teach its propagation or analyze its poison.

You should think in terms of institutions and companies rather than fields of knowledge. These "work arenas" are the large organizations, in any technologically developed country, in which heterogeneous specialties are employed to one purpose, and in one geographical place. Examples of arenas are the Miami *Herald,* Chrysler's Sterling Stamping Plant, Boston University, the Kellogg Foundation, Hutzel Hospital, Oakland County Courthouse, the Huron Pumping Station.

All arenas hire organizational maintainers: secretaries, finance people, administrators, janitors. Different arenas hire different specialties: hospitals hire doctors in sub-subspecialties, nurses in subspecialties, medical technicians of all kinds (respiratory therapists, x-ray attendants, x-ray technicians, radiologists, etc.). Arenas change constantly and at different rates. Not only do machines replace human beings, but the services performed by human beings change. Creative arenas are constantly making new combinations: some bartenders study counseling. Also, specialties split. Where there was once a professor of Oriental art, there may be now a professor of Japanese art and another of Chinese art.

Each arena has its own mood. You've heard of "cynical" newspapers and "bleeding-heart" social agencies. Those stereotypes may be false; they certainly are oversimplified. We've seen concerned journalists and uninterested social workers. But each arena does have a culture, ethics, a purpose, one kind of management. Do not judge it by its stereotype. You can judge it only by becoming part of it. That is why, during your student years, your job should be different each summer. For the same reason, taking a job you hate need not be a disaster; it can be a way of gathering information about yourself. Some arenas you will be comfortable in, some you will not. Also, arenas have their phases—of excited, rushed entrepreneurship; of neatening and consolidating; perhaps of stability, of rigidity, of death. You may be comfortable in one phase, but not another.

Entry Jobs Who is the buyer of paperback books for the second-largest wholesale distributor in the United States? A man who came there as an order-wrapper. Who manages the charming hotel in a college town? A woman who earned her B.A. as a waitress and her M.A. as a hostess, and discovered that she enjoyed giving hospitality more than her academic subjects. She stayed on after graduation as banquet manager. As convention sales manager, she enjoyed planning the right settings for group interchange. Now that she is the manager, she is "professionalizing" her vocation by continuing her education and serving as an officer in the Hotel Management Association.

I could give you fifty such illustrations, but you will find your own if you assign yourself the job of asking twenty established people how they found their area. "Well, it's funny—it just happened," they'll say. But scrutinize their *first* step. Were they "in" some arena? Did they (or someone) discover something they were good at? Did they enlarge their jobs with hard work, creativity, or both? Did they have an informal sponsor?

Why not just get in *somewhere*? Why not take an entry-level job that is indeed below the level that your education and upbringing have led you to expect? Submerge yourself in the new arena. When you come to the surface, it may be in a huge cavern that—from the outside—you never dreamed existed.

So beat the street, as the young people say. Apply in arenas which have *not* advertised openings. Take a lateral transfer to some other department in the same arena. Take a job that pays less than the skilled job you had risen to—because you'll enter some other industry.

And finally: Do a good job in that first job (as well as in the second or tenth), while you start looking around.

Describing Your Skills—Résumés

A résumé is a word picture of you, an unseen being.

First, everyone will look at what you can do. Large organizations will be checking specific requirements. Someone in the personnel office will have a job request just sent down from, say, Engineering: "Three years' experience in metal fabrication." She will try to match a résumé from her file with this requirement. She will also evaluate according to the standards of her organization: "Is this applicant's nurse's training from Littleville Hospital, or does she have a B.S. from Famous University?"

New organizations haven't yet compartmentalized themselves into neat boxes or may not be so choosy in their evaluations. Small organizations are run by people doing what needs to be done without realizing that they are "crossing functional boundaries." A small organization may use specialists to do general work, or may do without specialists, or may have amateurs doing specialists' work. For instance, the friendly, bustling women in charge of the small nursing home will order more paper towels, help the janitor with the broken glass, greet the new patient. But the director of a large nursing-care facility will have purchasing, housekeeping, and admitting departments.

Newer and smaller organizations, therefore, are looking for more general skills in your résumé. The smaller nursing home may be glad to know that you once worked as a payroll clerk, that you took a noncredit course in human development, that you know something about building repair because your father does construction work, that you play the piano as a hobby.

Second, everyone studying your résumé is wondering, What is she like? Will she be more trouble personally than her skills are worth? I once read that of every five people fired, four are fired for reasons having to do with personality rather than for lack of skill. I couldn't believe it—until I became a manager. The "human factor" is one reason we use machines whenever we can. (Would you prefer a washing machine or a washerwoman?) It is also the reason why (according to studies by industrial psychologists), the highest stress level in a plant is among foremen. (I have not seen data for the stress level of the "floor ladies" of textile plants around 1910, nor for more recent female supervisors.)

How do you put information about your personality on your résumé? Put yourself in the reader's shoes. For example, one person is responsible for a work project—whether that person is the owner, department head, supervisor, group leader, or whatever—someone who is already there. This person has to orient you. Can this person tell you once, and then get on with his or her own job? Or will you have to be told again and again, shown, corrected, coached? Anyone who has been through a few experiences like this wants to ask any applicant, "Are you dumb or bright?" This question cannot be asked; but your school record provides a clue. If your average was over 3.0, mention this.

Will the new employee sit slumped in her chair, waiting for someone to tell her every little thing? Well, here on her résumé it says, "Organized camping program for Cub Scouts."

Will she quit when the going gets tough? "Ran camping program for five years."

Will she get along with the others? (Remember the gossip who was always stirring up feuds?) Well, her résumé says, "Miss Popularity of the Badminton Boosters," or, more likely, "advisor to young people's program, 1968 to 1974."

Will she take responsibility, look around for what needs doing, let me forget her, and catch things I forgot to assign? Projects accomplished tend to indicate this, so mention that you served as chairperson of the charity drive or coordinator of the lecture series. Also, although neither male or female employers seem to realize it yet, the sole managership of a very small enterprise is the best possible experience in task-oriented responsibility. Unfortunately, it is hard to prove that twenty years' homemaking was *successful* management.

Finally, will she stay and grow with us? Of course, she is starting from the bottom; but we're teaching her. Will it pay off? Will she stay and run her unit excellently? Will she take on another unit? Such questions have to do with perseverance, responsibility, and leadership.

The housewife returning to work will find that writing a résumé is harder than she thinks. Here is a way to start. (You can find books of sample résumés by asking your local librarian and by consulting the references listed at the end of this chapter.)

First, list each year since you were in high school down the lefthand side of a piece of scratch paper. Jot down where you were and what you were doing, including childbearing, traveling, schooling. This will pin down dates and help you remember. You should list:

All your education: academic degrees or credits toward what degree and in what major; noncredit courses; music lessons; lecture series attended; conferences and conventions; on-the-job training; orientation to an elected or appointed office; independent reading (be sure this also reveals the *subjects* you know about).

All your experience and employment (whether paid or unpaid), giving exact titles and the names of the organizations. (Do not say, "volunteered at the hospital," but "Visitors' Receptionist, Deaconess Hospital, Dayton, Ohio, 1971–1973.") Include "invitations" to other jobs ("invited to return to former job as secretary to the Cement Workers Union") or to more responsibility ("was asked to serve as a nursery school aide"). Mention elected or appointed positions ("Bazaar Committee chairperson"); honors; awards; citations (such as a mention in the church bulletin or club newspaper). List anything that indicates mastery, like "teaching of_____," "speeches on_____," "writing on_____." Think: Did you orient (i.e., teach) the next Visitors' Receptionist? List professional memberships, offices, projects (by title), awards (with name, awarding agency, and date).

If necessary, coin a job title (in lowercase) to indicate what you did rather than saying you "helped" or were an assistant to some specialty. For example, surgical nurses and scrub nurses "help" surgeons but also have a skill of their own. If you helped a drug center raise money, you were a money raiser.

Now you may take your long draft to a professional résumé-writing agency. (With printing, this service costs nearly $100.) If you are going to do your résumé yourself, your next step is to simplify it. Group similar jobs, such as "Waitress; four summers" (unless you want those jobs to lead into restaurant management). List names of employing institutions (whether the work was paid or volunteer)— no address, just the city. Indicate what you did, if this is not clear from the title. Add extra responsibilities or projects completed after the job title. Add dates within ten years. Omit salary, supervisor's name, reason for leaving. Note that recommendations are available. Have them listed on a separate sheet to be given to any prospective employer who is interested (except on some standardized résumés, like teachers').

A one-page résumé is often recommended; and usually this is ample for a straightforward, one-skill career ladder. However, one highly active, creative, widely experienced professional woman came up with a five-page résumé, which, according to the head of salaried personnel at a major corporation, was one of the best he had seen.

What, then, is worth stating? What is "enough"? You won't know the answer to this yourself: those who haven't entered a foreign land don't know the customs of the natives. Therefore, ask. Show your résumé to several people who are as close to your field as possible.

Have your résumé professionally typed, on an electric typewriter, by someone other than yourself. Remember that the largest percentage of working women are in clerical-secretarial jobs. You can assume (1) that enormous amounts of recording and communicating are done in our interdependent, interstate, government-regulated society; (2) that employers in this society are used to professionally produced résumés; (3) that you are likely to have an acquaintance who is, or was, a working typist. If you do not know a typist, find a secretarial service. Such services are typing many résumés these days. Ask the typist there to help you change anything that sounds unprofessional, or looks unclear, or is set up inconsistently. There are other advantages to a professional typing job: one is that all your activities will look significant to you—and suddenly, your working self will emerge from the person whose skills are described. You will see yourself more objectively. You are not a nobody; you are a cluster of skills housed in an acceptable personality.

Send a short covering letter, an original, with each résumé. Send the résumé and letter to a person with a name—having called the secretary or personnel department to get it. Emphasize what skills are especially relevant to that company. Say that you will call about an appointment in a day or so. Do so. The person to whom you wrote will have been alerted to have a response ready. Even if you dread doing it, you must call, so that you don't wait and wonder. Sending out résumés without covering letters or follow-up telephone calls is like dropping leaflets from a dirigible; this is not serious job hunting: it is just a way of hiding from rejection.

Finding an Organization

Where in the world are the people or the organizations who want your skills enough to pay for them?

If you ask this question, you do not have a skill which is (1) certificated (like a textile designer, beauty operator, or pilot), (2) current, and (3) in demand. If you had a skill with these three characteristics, you would know what organizations to apply to (textile mills, beauty shops, airlines). If you must ask this question, you have reached the disheartening heart of the problem of job hunting—no matter what your age, sex, or ability. The problem is particularly difficult, perhaps, for those who want to make a change in mid-life, but it is hard for anyone who lacks a specific skill. Furthermore, you may be given less information than you need, because the people who are insiders in an arena might find it hard to understand how helpless outsiders are.

Lilli, an American girl who spent the summer in a tiny mountain village in Honduras, came back amazed at the ease of vocational choice there. All the women are mothers, she said. All the men are farmers, except for *the* priest, and *the* teacher, and outlaws. She came back to a good home in a safe suburb and to an excellent college. But, strangely, the vocational choices in the network of jobs, specialties, standards, and commitments which create that home, suburb, and college—these are not visible to her. All she sees is their facade—*as a customer.* And her mother may see little more: for example, active women often say that you don't discover your own church until you are put on a committee.

When we are outsiders, we really learn very little about what jobs are like from the inside. For instance, though television may show us the work clothes and workplaces of truckers and sailors and couturiers, it does not show us a pair of truckers evaluating a brake lining on a snowy highway, or a staff meeting to analyze a new hydraulic lift, or anger over slipshod loading, or admiration for efficient scheduling of shipments and routes. Most of us are physically walled out of the buildings where people work, and people who live in suburbs are often miles away from workplaces. And even if we could watch people at work, we could not understand their vocabularies. How can we possibly offer the skills that are wanted by worlds of which we are so ignorant? We see products and services, seldom creation. We see buyers and users like ourselves, seldom the makers. There is no village smithy, I am sorry to say, under our neighborhood chestnut tree. Thus we tell our graduates, "The world is yours; do whatever you want to do." But the graduates are, in effect, blindfolded. They have had schooling and maybe some sports. They have been taught some academic subjects and been made aware of some social issues. But they have not even visited in most of the worlds of our specialized society. They cannot see what there is to choose from, or what the world wants of them.

How, therefore, can you get to know this other world? By the oldest method in the world—exploring. Go to the personnel offices of large corporations—with a friend, if you like. You are not going to apply, just observe. Strike up conversations with people in the waiting room. Have a look at government agencies, manufacturing plants, brokerage houses, tree nurseries. Visit slow, stable utilities;

visit a hectic advertising agency. Everywhere you go, ask workers what they do and how they got their jobs. Meanwhile, examine your own reactions. Is the jail less callous than you imagined, or more? Is the neighborhood library a quiet backwater or a rapids of enlightenment?

Perhaps you have the skill most in demand—word processing. You may not want to be a secretary, but don't underestimate communication skills or their usefulness in holding an organization together. Being a secretary can get you into an organization and put you near the powerful people. It will also allow you to explore organizations while being paid. If you want to work part time, or hesitate to apply directly to employers, agencies like Kelly Girls, American Girl, Western Girl, and Manpower will job-hunt for you. One manager of Kelly Girls told me that she often sees women come up to their door and then go away. But agencies like this understand that the housewife will be rusty. If you could once type, let *them* decide if you need a refresher. And if you can't type, remember that they also place people with other skills. You may need people to motivate you. Don't sit home. If you need help exploring, let them help you.

Finding an Opening

Of course, if you are job hunting you will read the want ads of the largest newspaper in town. (The Sunday edition usually prints the most ads.) Circle possibilities, and circle ads you don't understand or ads for jobs you are not sure you could do. Remember, the perfect employee may not answer an ad; you may be the best qualified of those who do answer. Housewives and students tend to ignore ads for sales jobs ("national organization in town for two days at big hotel . . ."), but they circle all the jobs they could certainly do, like addressing envelopes at home. Call the possibilities right away, even on Sunday—often someone is there. When you find a really good lead, take your résumé and show up there on Monday morning. The early bird is also the bird in hand. What's more, go to that sales recruiting meeting—this is exploring, and their know-how may help you sell yourself, eventually.

You may consider an employment agency. Call up and ask what their charges are, where they place people, and whether they've placed anyone with your skills recently. Examine them coolly before you hire them, and don't hope for too much. *Only 5 percent of jobs that people find in the United States are filled through employment agencies.*

Another 5 percent of jobs are placed through state Employment Security Commissions (to find yours, look in the telephone book under your state government—e.g., Nebraska, State of). They handle job openings which require many people, and which many people can do with a minimum of orientation time, like assembly-line work, checkout monitoring, and machine operation. All that such jobs require, usually, is the human hand, the ordinary human brain, the ability to speak a little English, and simple arithmetic. But the fact that four abilities are widely dispersed throughout our population is no reason to be snobbish about the jobs in which they can be used. These entry-level jobs are the ones which brought—and are still bringing—thousands and thousands of country people and immigrants into the industrial cities. They lead into arenas where you can look around for the routes that lead up, where you can get into areas which are traditionally male, since many of these jobs developed from trades that once required muscle (like construction work, transportation, and heavy industry). These areas now seek women to fill the requirements of Affirmative Action, unlike many areas where the tools are words and the hands stay clean. From these jobs, you also may learn other skills, learn a business from the bottom up, and come to understand the experience of the people you may some day manage. Therefore, by all means visit your state employment agency. It also may have a professional section.

Fortune magazine once reported that 70 percent of jobs are heard about from people one knows rather than read about in ads. This is not the same thing as "pull." It means that Marilyn happens to mention at the bowling alley that Rose at the laundry is quitting. Everyone is part of some kind of network of communication. You must activate this network. Understandably, women who have once held good jobs may find themselves hiding from their professional friends as if joblessness were something to be ashamed of. But this is the time you need your friends most. Moreover, people like to help; let them bring you news. Meanwhile, as was suggested earlier, you arrange to be seen, tell everyone, look locally, and try to get in somewhere.

Avoiding Procedures That Are Not Very Helpful

Some things do not aid in job hunting as much as one would hope.

Sending Out Résumés "Cold" Who does anybody choose for anything? First choice: someone he or she knows to be good. Second choice: someone another employee says is good—and someone, therefore, whom the other employee will help orient, encourage, watch over. Third choice: someone a trustworthy outsider recommends. Fourth choice: someone who has been met informally and observed. Fifth choice: someone who has written to recommend herself.

Sending Out Résumés and Then Waiting for Employers to Call Do you have time to spend waiting and wondering on any paid job? No? Then isn't it the same for the job of job hunting? Therefore, on the day after you believe your résumé and cover letter will have arrived, call the person to whom they were sent, while you are still in his or her mind. Ask for an appointment. Calling is work for you—but also for employers. They resist it, just as you do. After all, you may be out; you may have already taken another job; you may sound unpleasant on the telephone. It is much easier for them to hire the person who is standing in front of their desk.

Putting Your Hopes on a National Directory Don't put much hope in a national directory, a computer printout of able women, a professional association's "available" listing. Instead, visit your college placement service. You will be more than a piece of paper to them.

Trying to Meet Important People   Don't waste much time trying to meet "important" people. It is true that the middle-class, middle-aged housewife often knows people, including her husband, who are at the stage in life where they may be hiring others. But the jobs that "important" people hear of are often at too high a level. Furthermore, in large organizations, top people are wary of reaching down into other departments' areas of responsibility. They are also wary of violating the principle of merit, "May the best one win." They believe in selection on the basis of excellence, not friendship. They are wary of arousing resentment or of leaving themselves open to charges of nepotism or patronage. They are wary of being used, of being stuck with someone's incompetent sister, of apple polishers. Owner-managers of small organizations may be freer in this respect, but they have few openings.

Relying Entirely on a Personnel Office   Don't count on a personnel office. For example, a student dropped out of a liberal arts college to explore various jobs, so that he could decide where to apply his energies as an adult and so decide what education was relevant for him (a very sound idea). To explore the arena of the hospital, he applied for a job as an orderly. No openings were listed by the personnel office. His sister, who worked in that hospital as a case aide, asked the unit manager of orderlies, who said, "I might be able to use another. Send him around." He was hired.

Send your résumé and covering letter directly to the department head whom you might work for, not to the personnel office.

Being Discouraged by Job Descriptions   Don't be defeated by a job description. Example: I wanted a public relations worker (and I didn't happen to know one who was available). The university personnel office would advertise and screen for me; it sent up a form on which to describe the skills I wanted them to look for. I thought carefully about what would help: at least two years' experience on a newspaper, so that she'd recognize news from the newspaper angle— preferably a local paper (southeast Michigan, in this case), so that she'd have contacts. She'd have to type her own releases; we couldn't afford to hire a typist too. Photography would make it unnecessary for us to hire a photographer; graphics would help on brochures and lettering. And of course she should be likable, an extrovert, a good salesperson, a hard worker, smart . . . Well, I couldn't expect all that; but at least two years' journalism. This is how job descriptions happen.

When a job description says "two years' journalism," the personnel office believes it. This is what the person in charge of the job thinks is necessary in order to save him or her the time of teaching a new employee.

But consider this. The three best women I have since come to know in public relations, who would have been available at that time, would have had the following experience on their résumés: Kay had done a few features for a Philadelphia newspaper; Barbara had had a year as a copy editor at McGraw-Hill, and had made hand-lettered Christmas cards and announcements for the Girl Scouts;

Audrey was interviewing people about community events on a tiny, new radio station. All three are alert, energetic, healthy, friendly, verbal, intelligent, hard-working, well organized; and I think I would have recognized these qualities if I had met them in person. But they wouldn't have been sent up to me by the personnel office—"two years' journalism." The moral is: Try to see the actual boss-to-be.

Interviews

There is nothing mysterious about job interviews. You've been selling yourself and your projects for years: asking club members to volunteer, co-workers to help, your husband to play bridge, your children to study. Women are nervous about interviews, believing—it seems to me—that if they "act perfectly" they will get the job, and that if they don't get the job they have somehow failed the interview. We are all nervous, because an interview is a cross between an oral examination and a proposal of marriage. The right approach is to act like a visitor in someone else's territory—which you are. Then, it will be natural to notice where they seem to want you to sit, to respond with information they want—and not to go into a monologue about your successes and virtues. It will also be natural to look for signals (like shifting in the chair, stacking papers, and looking away from you) that mean "please go; I've learned what I need to know."

Some people who are being interviewed try to outwit the interviewer by finding out what is wanted and glibly giving it. To prevent interviewers from being manipulated in this way, some schools of business administration teach interviewing skills. One rule they teach is: Don't give clues. The result can be unsettling, as is shown in this example: A highly skilled professional secretary was reporting to our Place-finders Group last month about her job hunting. She had taken out eight years for mothering a son, but she was confident and had up-to-date skills. "But I can't believe the change in the interviewing," she said. "They just leave you sitting there like a clod. You don't know what they want. Pretty soon you feel you have to say something, but—they're blanks! It's humiliating, really humiliating." If this happens to you, don't just sit. Ask them about their company, and tell them how great you are.

If you're asked an illegal personal question—like "Are you pregnant?"—you do not need to answer. However, it is probably better to give some answer—not a retort, but something like, "I am making this serious effort to find a job, because I intend to work for several years." If you are asked, "Who will take care of your children?" you can say, "I see that you are concerned that my children have proper care. I am concerned about that also. Before I started looking for a job, I arranged for them to go to my neighbor's house after school until I come home from work."

Some entirely proper questions are nevertheless difficult. For example, you should prepare an answer to "Tell me about yourself." Mention some personal qualities—e.g., initiative—and point to the evidence on your résumé.

Don't hope for too much from each interview; and don't sit home waiting for a call. Instead, call them the next day. Say how much you enjoyed the interview, or how much you admire the organization. Say you are very interested in the job. May you call in three days to see if they have made a decision?

They may say, "Well, we've decided on someone else," or, "Better wait about a week to call," or, "Please don't call us; we'll call you." In the first two cases, you have succeeded in getting them to give you some information. No one wants to face the anger of an applicant who walks in only to be rejected in person; of course the third response is made to prevent exactly this. I'm not sure how to respond to it, but you might try this: "I really am interested in the job, but I will have to continue to look, so I may not be home to receive your call. Could I have your permission to call back in a week, just to see if I'm still in the running?" They might at least say—even if grudgingly—"Well, we can't stop you from calling, I guess."

Is this too pushy? Not at all. You *do* want the job. Therefore, when they call you, they can be assured of giving pleasure and receiving gratitude. Also, an interested employee is better than an uninterested one.

When you've been buoyed up by a pleasant interview, telephone for several more appointments. (You can always cancel them if you get the job.) After a discouraging interview, call a friend. Go over the interview. "What should I have said when she said that?" Besides warding off depression, this is good practice. It prepares you for similar questions in later interviews.

Interviews are emotionally draining, so don't overdo it. You cannot manage more than one interview in the morning and one in the afternoon. I consider three days a week quite enough, if you're not desperate. And you need the other days for such things as mailing and telephoning.

Do not accept a job, if one is offered, at a first interview. Say that you are pleased and flattered. Stand up, and ask when they'd like your answer. Then call or visit the next day and find out about benefits, vacations, and the like. Ask about opportunities for promotion. Next, discuss the job with two acquaintances. Simply describing it out loud can help you; you may hear yourself glossing over or apologizing for some aspects. Also, your friends won't be influenced by nonessentials—the enthusiasm of the interviewer or the looks of the building. Finally, always sleep on a major decision. If the decision seems awesome, tell yourself that it isn't so important; some people quit after one day. Think of it as exploring.

AFTER YOU'VE FOUND A JOB

Remember that you will almost certainly use the skills of job hunting again. According to a supplement in the *Christian Science Monitor* in March 1974, "Jobs in the Eighties," a person is likely to change jobs seven times during his or her work life. If you are leaving work to go to school or raise a family, remember that you will eventually leave school and your children will eventually leave home.

Therefore, keep your résumés. Keep your records, your contacts, your covering letters, your new friends, your mailing list, your association and union memberships, your city map. These are the tools of another skill you have acquired, the skill of job hunting. You never know when you'll use it again.

IN CONCLUSION

This chapter may have overstressed the embarrassment, the anxiety, the difficulty of job hunting. But even such aspects can perhaps be savored. In looking for work, you are experiencing the harsher end of the gamut of human emotions. This can make you more understanding of others. And after such a test, you will be stronger. You will also be closer to the friend or parent or husband or child you shared it with.

On the other hand, job hunting can have its pleasant moments. While you were working or staying home, you may never have had time to know your city. Now you are studying the city map, visiting new neighborhoods, entering unknown institutions. When you meet new people, you are quite as often surprised by their graciousness as by their gruffness. You find yourself talking with people different from those you are used to—like someone from a different ethnic group who is also waiting for an interview. You see new scenes—a city newsroom, for instance; it looks quite different from the movies. You hear people describe what they do, and learn about their feelings about it—from sober earnestness to offhand whimsy, from competence to disdain. You may be surprised, as I was, to discover so much expertise. You may be abashed, as I have been, to find how ignorant you are about other worlds.

Job hunting can be a humbling experience, but also an educational one; it can be a liberal education in the sociology of work. Occasionally, believe it or not, it can actually be fun. I earnestly hope that it may be so for you.

BIBLIOGRAPHY

Biegelesen, J. I.: *Job Résumés—How to Write Them, How To Present Them,* Grosset and Dunlap, New York, 1949. A quarto-size book with different styles of résumés for office, sales, management, technical, and professional jobs, and for trainee, summer, and part-time jobs.

Bolles, Richard: *What Color Is Your Parachute?: A Practical Manual for Job Hunters and Career Changers,* Ten-Speed Press, Berkeley, Calif., 1973. A revised edition is due in 1976.

Friedman, Sande, and Lois C. Schwartz: *No Experience Necessary: A Guide to the Female Liberal Arts Graduate,* Dell, New York, 1971.

Irish, Richard K.: *Go Hire Yourself an Employer,* Anchor, Garden City, N.Y., 1973.

King, Alice Gore: *Help Wanted, Female: The Young Woman's Guide to Job-hunting,* Scribner, New York, 1968. From one of the earliest women's centers, a book with a dated title, but following the life cycle of the majority of American women, from graduation onward.

Larson, Donald E.: *How to Find a Job,* Ace, New York, 1974. Clear, sensible, step by step, simplified; paperback.

Taylor, Phoebe: *How to Succeed in the Business of Finding a Job,* Nelson Hall, Chicago, Ill., 1974.

Women's Work. A bimonthly magazine published by Washington Opportunities for Women (W.O.W.). Editorial Board: Jane Flemming, Mary Janney, Christine Nelson. Subscriptions: 1111 20th Street, N.W., Washington, D.C. 20036.

Chapter 6

The Range and Benefits of Volunteer Service

Helen M. Feeney

Helen M. Feeney, Ph.D., is Associate Professor, Sociology, Queensborough Community College, City University of New York. She is a member of the Advisory Board of the Mayor's Council on Voluntary Action (NYC) and of the National Board of Trustees, Institute of Lifetime Learning (NRTA/AARP). A writer and consultant, she is the coauthor of *Volunteer Training and Development: A Manual* (Seabury, 1976) and *Learning by the Case Method* (Seabury, 1970), and a contributing author to *Priorities in Adult Education* (Macmillan, 1972) and *A Guide for Staff Training, Neighborhood Youth Corps* (U.S. Department of Labor, 1969). She has held office in the Adult Education Association of the U.S.A. and the Council of National Organizations for Adult Education, and is the recipient of a Fulbright Fellowship for the study of workers' and adult education in England.

Has volunteerism served to give women an illusion of participation in the world at large? Is volunteerism a threat to full employment? Are volunteers generally less qualified than paid workers? These are some of the insinuations heard about volunteering and volunteers. In many instances, it is the woman as volunteer that is the target of criticism. While it is true that in the past a large number of women were participants in volunteer activity, two unfortunate and often untrue stereotypes were formed: the middle-aged, middle-class, middle-of-the-road woman; and her earlier counterpart, the wealthy, well-meaning "lady bountiful."

The United States has more voluntary organizations for more diverse purposes than any other country in the world—or so we are described by historians and by visiting dignitaries. The picture of volunteer work in the United States today is changing, although it has changed so imperceptibly that many people have not been aware of the changes. Yet stereotypes persist in the mind of the public as well as in many women's perceptions of themselves when contemplating the job market. Just as she has so often said: "I'm only a housewife," a woman now adds, "I've *only* done volunteer work" or "I'm *just* a volunteer."

For years the traditional volunteer in hospitals and social agencies was a woman who gave unstintingly of her time and energy, first in being trained and then in being supervised by staff members as she worked without pay. Volunteering often provided such a woman a personal sense of satisfaction that was its own reward. Also, she did volunteer work on her own terms, which allowed her to schedule her time away from home and family in a flexible manner. There is no need to denigrate volunteer service as an extension of unpaid household work or as undignified because it is unpaid. *Volunteering is a tangible expression of a citizen's responsibility to the community and a commitment to improving the quality of life in a democratic society.*

VOLUNTEERING—A POSSIBLE BRIDGE TO PAID WORK

There may come a time in a woman's life, however, when she wants to trade her volunteer service and trained experience for paid employment, either returning to the labor force or entering it for the first time. She may be thinking about a second career and may need counseling, apprenticeship training, or refresher courses to prepare for the competitive job market.

Categories of Volunteer Work

In reviewing her potential skills and abilities, a woman should consider first the vast range of categories of volunteer service today and then evaluate what she has been involved in. For example, some of the overall categories are:

Civic affairs
Consumer education
Health services
Legal assistance
Aging
Education
Corrections (prisons and remand centers)
Drugs
Ecology

Within each of these categories are a number of subdivisions. For example:

Drugs:
Youth education
Community education
Counseling (youth and family)
"Hotline" or crisis counseling
Halfway houses
Emergency assistance

Appraising Your Assets and Areas of Competence

Any person who is trained and competent to carry out the activities covered by these categories, and many others, should be able to transfer his or her skills to paid work of some type. Volunteer jobs offer many learning experiences and opportunities; but women in particular often suffer from self-depreciation and lack of confidence when they try to describe their volunteer service. A number of chapters in this book deal with building your self-concept and self-image and in developing confidence in order to project your potential. The information and advice in those chapters can be applied here as you undertake to assess your skills and abilities. Career counseling can often be of assistance, if you have been away from the world of work for a long time; and self-help books and guides can help you make a practical appraisal of your abilities in writing a résumé of your volunteer work experience.

A good method of assessing skills, talents, and abilities is to trace back over the years and write down every volunteer job you ever had—from your teen years to the present. List every time you served on or chaired a committee, organized a block association or a street fair, ran a benefit dinner or planned the program for a class reunion. See if there is a pattern of interests linked with abilities—What did you *like* to do? What did you do *well?* Ask your family and friends to give you honest evaluations and write these down as well. Don't minimize the incidental tasks involved in such activities, such as meeting the public, keeping accounts, assigning tasks, and writing reports. Examine the overall picture in terms of a full- or part-time job, and list your achievements as though you were preparing a job specification. Ask yourself: Can I draw on my experience as a volunteer in a children's ward or as an organizer for the women's division of a local political party? Do I need training or a refresher course to be more efficient or to learn new methods?

You may be surprised at the number of marketable skills you already have, or the skills that might be sharpened by short-term training of some type. Consider, for example, the diverse tasks listed for volunteers working on a community intergroup program:

Conduct workshops and conferences to improve interracial relations; form coalitions among religious denominations; establish programs to reach inner-city people; and set up interracial home-visiting programs.

A volunteer engaged in such an effort over a period of time might well have experience and skills of communication useful in a community-relations job in a school, hospital, or social agency; or for developing and conducting staff training in intergroup relations for a commercial institution or housing project. There are innumerable opportunities for part-time consultant work in this field as well.

A group leader for a youth organization might find that she could list the following areas of competence, useful in a variety of jobs:

> Planning and coordinating activities for and with young people
> Organizing and conducting meetings for parents and the community
> Keeping records of individual and group progress
> Developing simple budgets and keeping financial records
> Obtaining resources for programs (people, materials, etc.)
> Teaching crafts, songs, dances, nature lore, games, and camping skills
> Operating filmstrip and 16-mm film projectors
> Preparing menus for a large group over a period of several days
> Teaching road and water safety
> Accepting responsibility for the welfare and safety of children and young people

In appraising your experiences and activities, it might be useful to compile a portfolio of samples, such as craftwork, photographs of trips or campsites, agendas of meetings, programs, budgets, reports, press clippings, and letters from parents and the community. A portfolio can be utilized to collect samples of your creative work as well (photographs, sketches, tape recordings). The very fact that you can compile such a portfolio should give you a better awareness of the scope of your abilities and make you more confident when approaching an employer. Take the portfolio along with you and practice talking about the various items as you expand upon what you *can* do and *how* you did it. You are actually playing the role of salesperson for your own wares; the more job interviews you undertake, the better you will be at selling yourself.

More and more employers are considering volunteer experience when hiring. "I write dozens of letters of recommendation to employers for volunteers who have worked here," says the director of volunteers of a large hospital.[1]

"For the lower-economic woman . . . volunteering offers opportunities for training and skills assessment, *an important step toward paid employment . . .* [italics added]," says the Executive Director of a metropolitan Voluntary Action Center; "Through volunteerism, new areas of paid employment have emerged, . . . non-professional tasks which later became paid para-professional positions. Hospital nurses' aides provide a good example."[2]

---

[1] Director of Volunteers, Los Angeles County-USC Pediatric Pavilion, quoted in Los Angeles *Times,* July 20, 1975.
[2] Executive Director, Mayor's Voluntary Action Center, New York City; in a letter to the *New York Times,* June 12, 1974.

Volunteer Credential Studies

A trend which may eventually help the volunteer or employer endeavoring to assess credentials is the studies now being undertaken by several organizations: The Council of National Organizations for Adult Education, the Federal AC-TION Agency, and the Educational Testing Service in Princeton, New Jersey. The Council has a task force examining volunteer accreditation. ACTION has a project designed to test a portfolio for the recording of volunteer experience. The Educational Testing Service and representatives from a number of national organizations with diversified programs have begun to analyze the abilities acquired by a volunteer researcher or advocate-lobbyist in the League of Women Voters, and a group leader, advisor-counselor, or educator-trainer in a voluntary youth organization, among others. It is proposed that credit be given for a specified number of years in a position with full responsibility—not an assistant or apprentice role.

In some parts of the country, colleges and universities give some form of academic credit for "life experience," community service, or experiential learning. For further information on this, see Chapter 21, *Continuing Your Education.*

MOVING FROM VOLUNTEER WORK TO PAID WORK

Some Case Histories

Some examples of women who have used their volunteer experience to move to paid employment may be helpful here. Of course, many more could be cited; but the women described here indicate how the scope and variety of volunteer work proved transferable to the job market.

National Board Member to Paid Administrator
Margaret, the wife of a professional man, had lived in various parts of the United States and in many countries abroad, volunteering her time to a national voluntary youth organization. College-educated and with considerable administrative ability, she became, in turn, committee member, chairperson of a statewide program, regional representative, and finally a member of the national board charged with responsibility for an international exchange program. In the course of her duties, she presided at meetings, planned and conducted training events, wrote reports, testified before state legislatures and congressional committees, and evaluated international programs concerned with children and youth.

When her children were grown, Margaret became interested in transfering her many-faceted skills to full-time, paid work. Various staff members and professional consultants in the organization had worked with her over the years; therefore, she had no difficulty in obtaining recommendations and references. Because the organization recognized volunteers as co-workers with its paid staff, she was offered a job with the organization when a suitable opening occurred. It might at first have been a little more difficult for Margaret to obtain a job in another type of organization or in business or industry, but she was able to do this several years later. Her combined record of volunteer and paid work experience helped to advance her rapidly in her chosen career despite a late start.

Author's Widow to Executive Secretary
The management of a household and wifely assistance to a prominent writer, while not actually in the category of volunteer work experience, serves as an example of the tasks and duties often overlooked when assessing one's personal capabilities. Alicia, an author's widow, tried looking for a paid job after her husband died. Analyzing the various tasks and duties that had filled her life, she was able to develop an impressive list for a résumé:

Typed manuscripts
Prepared travel schedules
Obtained airplane tickets and rental cars
Organized a wardrobe for a variety of events—press and publicity conferences, television appearances, speaking engagements, and dinners and other literary events
Prepared biographical notes
Assisted in taping interviews
Corrected galley proofs
Handled correspondence with publishers, editors, and lecture bureaus
Planned and acted as hostess for cocktail parties, dinners, literary teas, and receptions
Paid bills and checked royalty statements and expense reports for income-tax purposes

Presenting this list as an experience record, Alicia was able to convince her interviewer that she could handle the day-to-day duties of an executive secretary or administrative assistant.

Many women who have carried out similar tasks and responsibilities might appraise their experience in like manner.

Head Start Volunteer to Child-Care Staff Member
Maria is thirty-two and lives at home with her widowed father and two younger sisters. She has volunteered her free time at a Head Start program in her neighborhood for over four years. She likes children and relates well to preschool youngsters. Recently she received her Child Development Associate (CDA) credentials after having participated in a specially designed individualized training program. She went to school three nights a week for over a year and was evaluated for her work in the classroom and at the Head Start center. The CDA training improved her competence and gave her the confidence to try for a permanent job.

Several months after receiving the CDA certificate, she applied for paid work at a child-care center and was accepted as a staff member. She now plans to continue her education in the evenings as well.

Student Volunteer to First Job
"What do I want to do?" "What kind of work can I get?" "How do I earn an experience record when I can't get a job in the first place?" These and many other questions are raised by teenagers and college-age young people today. Some are goal-oriented or career-oriented and manage to enter their chosen fields. Others are bewildered and unfocused on a vocation or job. Volunteering can provide a young woman with the opportunity to experiment with a variety of job fields. Many colleges now have programs of work-study, internships, and community volunteer service.

Students work in hospitals, clinics, drug crisis centers, settlement houses, programs for the aged, neighborhood government offices, consumer education programs, and environmental programs. A responsible, meaningful volunteer job under proper supervision offers a young woman an opportunity to explore career options, with the added advantage of a written service record to present to an employer at some future time. The record, on an agency letterhead, should include type of work, job specification, hours worked per week, and evaluations of job performance by the supervisor at the workplace and the supervising faculty member at the academic institution. If the applicant has had different types of volunteer work or internships during school years, this overall record is useful to an employer. Volunteer experience will not guarantee a job to the newcomer in the job market, but it provides an important addition to an academic record.

Public Relations Committee to Assistant Casting Director
Norma had been a volunteer member of the Public Relations Committee of a national women's organization for five years. Her main responsibility was radio and television, and she had developed a reputation with the media for accuracy and dependability. She was aggressive in reaching program directors and producers of public-service shows, and she was not a time-waster. Her copy was concise, and she briefed the participants appearing on behalf of the organization on its program goals and on the requirements of the station.

The national organization employed a staff to produce films, filmstrips, and videotapes; but Norma assisted in the productions by supplying story material and often by securing locations for filming. Occasionally she arranged for members and clients of the organization to participate in the films. As a result, she gained considerable practical experience on casting, timing sequences, and editing scripts.

When she decided, because of the rising costs of her children's education, to try for paid employment somewhere in the mass media, she realized that her experience was mainly in the nonprofit area. Before applying to a radio or television station or an advertising agency, she enrolled in a university extension workshop that was cosponsored by an advertising women's organization. It was intensive training for several months, but she possessed a good knowledge of real-life situations which stood her in good stead.

Armed with her volunteer experience and her new training, she first made the rounds of radio and television stations and then tried several advertising agencies. It took a good six months or so before she finally found a job as assistant to the casting director in a small agency that specialized in products for the home. According to their personnel director, Norma's experience in the women's organization was the deciding factor in offering Norma the job.

Volunteer Chairperson to Staff Director of Volunteers
The position of "volunteer chairperson" in the community hospital had always been held by a woman who had been a volunteer for a number of years and who could give 2½ days a week to the responsibility. The position entailed recruiting, selecting, and placing volunteers (men and women); conducting training courses; and coordinating the work of the volunteer office with the needs of the hospital. This involved planning recreation programs; running the hospitality desk; selecting films for the recreation hall; supervising the candy-stripers; and meeting relatives, community members, and the clergy.

Dorothy had been elected to this office for several terms and felt that she was now ready to turn the responsibility over to someone else. Meanwhile, the hospital's patient load had increased by 50 percent and several city-based industries were planning to move to the suburban community. The hospital board decided to expand the volunteer program and realized that a full-time person would be needed. Dorothy was asked if she would be interested in the job. While she liked the flexibility of being a volunteer, Dorothy felt that this was a challenging opportunity not to be missed. She had never been employed before, but the position was merely an extension of what she had been doing. Her time would have to be organized to take care of home and other responsibilities, but she was an orderly person and felt that this could be done.

There were other volunteers in the program, reliable and worthy candidates, but Dorothy had actually carried the responsibility of heading the program for a number of years, and her record was excellent. She related well to people, and her knowledge of the needs of the hospital and its community was comprehensive. When the decision was made to create the position of Director of Volunteer Service, the board's first choice was Dorothy. This is not a unique situation; it is happening in many parts of the country as many agencies expand their services.

The Volunteer Professional

We should note here a new concept in volunteering, the "volunteer professional."[3] This seems to be a contradiction in terms; but the idea behind the expression is to identify volunteer workers who, while not paid, are "employed," trained, supervised, "promoted," dismissed, and given references as paid staff members are. The volunteer professional is given a written job specification, benefits and rights, rules regarding hiring and firing, training and supervision. An agreement or contract is then signed by both parties—employer and "employee" (the volunteer). Insurance benefits, tax deductions or tax credits, and even possible Social Security benefits for volunteers are some of the aspects being studied while an attempt is being made to "professionalize" volunteer service.

The formalizing of relationships, working conditions, and other benefits specified in these model "contracts" and agency guidelines should not be necessary in agencies which are "people-oriented" rather than job- or task-oriented. Women who volunteer for work in such agencies grow and develop in confidence, competence, and satisfaction, having chosen the activity *voluntarily,* not because of prescribed policies. The notion of development as "upward mobility" from unpaid volunteer to paid employee actually downgrades the volunteer who makes her contribution on a highly specialized, professional level.[4]

In this chapter I have tried to stress the concept of transfer of skills and areas of competence when and where the individual volunteer wants, rather than the concept of "promotion" to paid work. Many volunteers do not want to restrict their options and limit their time in paid employment. Others, of course, may find that at certain periods of their lives a change could be beneficial. Each should be free to make the choice. Often those who transfer to a more restrictive job continue to do volunteer work in areas where they find personal satisfaction.

WORKING AND VOLUNTEERING

Many employed women, married and single, can be found among the ranks of volunteers in all types of agencies, institutions, community services, and causes.

---

[3] See *The Volunteer Professional; What You Need to Know,* Straus Communications, Inc., New York, on behalf of WMCA: Call for Action, 1972.

[4] See Anne K. Stenzel and Helen M. Feeney, *Volunteer Training and Development—A Manual,* 2d ed., Seabury Press, New York, 1976, chap. 9.

They do volunteer work as museum guides, interpreters and visitors in hospitals, school board members, job developers, recruiters of the unemployed and untrained, and voter-registration aides.

Professional women and other career women can find challenges and rewards in these volunteer activities. They can contribute their special skill and talents to individuals or groups in need, and while the service is unpaid, it is highly valued by society.

A working woman whose job may be limiting or routine can seek stimulation and satisfaction in the many new volunteer opportunities now appearing. But of course she will need to explore these opportunities thoughtfully and with care in order to ascertain whether or not her work schedule and personal responsibilities allow sufficient time and energy to undertake this additional activity. Some volunteer jobs entail work on weekends and evenings; many can even be adjusted for women who have irregular working hours. Therefore, it is advisable to discuss with agency personnel or the recruiting officer the purpose of the agency and what the volunteer position involves. Signing up for a volunteer job in order to pass the time or to do something worthwhile can be disappointing. It is wise to inquire into how your special skills are to be used, how much involvement in policy and decision making you will have, and what opportunities for development may be available to you as an individual.

A skilled volunteer can make a contribution on a highly specialized, professional level; this fact should be recognized as such by the agency or organization. Financial payment should not create a barrier between volunteer or volunteer-professional and the paid staff member; nor should competence and ability be the attributes which distinguish professional workers from volunteers.

A volunteer should not be "used" or "required to do unpaid work" because of budget or personnel limitations, and interested persons are advised against volunteering in agencies where this happens. Career counseling services are careful not to refer people to this type of agency, however. Often the work is of a "dead-end" variety, no training or supervision is provided, and there is practically no job satisfaction.

Volunteering today offers women a vast number of opportunities to give service and to change society, for every volunteer has the potential to influence change and to create change. Working full time or part time at a paid job should not deter you from participating in the volunteer movement, which is basic to the foundations of a democratic society.

PERSPECTIVE ON THE FUTURE

The outlook for the transfer of volunteer experience to academic work and paid employment appears excellent. Many more people in all socioeconomic groups are volunteering today and may eventually wish to utilize some of their experience in a full- or part-time job. The women whose case histories were described in this chapter did not lose their interest in and commitment to volunteering after taking on paid work. Nor did their individual concern for service and their responsibility for community welfare stop when they became career women or qualified professionals. A number are carrying on some type of volunteer service in their spare time or intend to volunteer again upon retirement. The bridge between volunteer service and paid employment has been built. Differences in status and experience seem to be mythical. Understanding of both the volunteer role and the staff role improves as more and more people cross over from one area to the other. There is a need for both volunteers and paid staff in today's society.

BIBLIOGRAPHY

Catalyst Publications: *Self Guidance Series—G-1, Planning for Work; G-2, Your Job Campaign. Education Opportunities Series, Career Opportunities Series,* Catalyst, New York, 1973.

Fairbank, Jane D., and Helen L. Bryson (eds.): *Second Careers for Women,* vol. 2, Stanford, California, 1975. Chapters include Computer Science and Data Processing; Engineering; Health Sciences; Recreation and Leisure Services; Social Work and Related Fields; Writing and Editing; and Starting a Small Business. Available from P.O. Box 9660, Stanford, Calif. 94305.

Loeser, Herta: *Women, Work and Volunteering,* Beacon Press, Boston, 1974. A practical guide to volunteer opportunities; volunteering as a training ground for a career; advice on drawing up a résumé and finding a fulfilling volunteer or paid position. The subject is handled in an objective, intelligent manner.

Schindler-Rainman, Eva, and Ronald Lippitt: *The Volunteer Community,* 2d ed., NTL Learning Resources Corporation, Fairfax, Va., 1975. A thorough but concise report on volunteer work in the present and future. It stresses the creative use of human resources and discusses the relationship between democracy, volunteering, and personal growth and development. There is an excellent annotated bibliography.

Scobey, Joan, and Lee Parr McGrath: *Creative Careers for Women—A Handbook of Sources and Ideas for Part-time Jobs,* Simon and Schuster, New York, 1968. A useful paperback full of suggestions on finding a career, starting your own business, and finding opportunities in business and industry with emphasis on spare-time and part-time work. The appendix, however, may not be entirely up to date.

Scofield, Nanette E., and Betty Klarman: *So You Want to Go Back to Work! For the Woman Interested in a New and Satisfying Second Career,* Random House, New York, 1968. More ideas on types of jobs and how and where to get them. Useful and practical.

White, Martha S. (ed.): *The Next Step: A Guide to Part-time Opportunities in Greater Boston for the Educated Woman,* Radcliffe Institute for Independent Study, Cambridge, Mass., 1965. Useful information applicable to other geographic areas. It contains a step-by-step procedure for preparing a worksheet on skills and abilities, and a questionnaire for reviewing personal interests and aptitudes.

Women's Bureau, U.S. Department of Labor: *Continuing Your Education,* pamphlet No. 10, 1971; *Job Finding Techniques for Mature Women,* pamphlet No. 11, 1970; *Careers for Women in the Seventies,* 1972, U.S. Government Printing Office, Washington, D.C.

Women's Work. A bimonthly magazine published by Wider Opportunities for Women (W.O.W.). Copies and subscriptions available from W.O.W., 1111 20th Street, N.W., Washington, D.C. 20036.

Chapter 7

Handling Sexism at Work: Nondefensive Communication

Theodora Wells

Theodora Wells, M.B.A., heads her own firm, Wells Associates. She is also a communications consultant, focusing on individual, group, and organizational change, including change essential to implementing Affirmative Action programs. She is the originator of "Nondefensive Communication" programs, and coauthor of an award-winning book, *Breakthrough: Women into Management* (Van Nostrand, 1972). She produced a UCLA training film, *Women: Up the Career Ladder.* Since 1968 she has conducted a UCLA Extension course, "Management Development for Women." Nationally known as a speaker and conference leader, she has published in the *Training and Development Journal,* the *Journal of Contemporary Business,* and other journals and has contributed chapters to four books.

Sexism is a fact of life in most aspects of our society. At work, it is a primary factor in determining most decisions about virtually all aspects of employment. Traditionally, patterns of work for women have been different from those for men, with the pattern for men being vastly more favorable. This is sexism in action.

WHAT IS SEXISM?

Briefly, sexism is the preference of one sex over the other. Men are generally preferred over women for all jobs where higher-level skills and high pay are involved, and in all business processes at those high levels. We are a competitive society, stressing achievement and dominated by men. Access to precursors of achievement—education and employment—is more available to men than women. Men are expected to be high achievers; women are expected to support and value achievement in men, but not in themselves. Most work organizations are structured on these expectations, which act as a self-fulfilling prophecy. To recognize organizational sexism, look for these indicators:

Sex typing of jobs. Most jobs are predominantly held by one sex. Whenever this is so, sexism in hiring and placement is likely to be operating.

Different entry jobs for men and women. In most organizations, there is a barrier between nonexempt and exempt jobs. If more women than men are in nonexempt jobs, sexism is operating.

The invisible ceiling. This is the job level where one woman appears, with few women or none at higher levels. This ceiling sets the level beyond which women may not go.

Different meanings of "qualified." If women are expected to have more education and more experience, or to "prove themselves" longer than men or under different conditions, sexism in hiring, promotion, or both is operating.

Different rates of promotion. If men are generally promoted faster than women, sexism in promotion is operating. One indication of this is the woman who repeatedly trains her male bosses, who move on, while she doesn't get the chance to perform the job herself.

Different supports while "proving yourself." Often men have a year or so to prove their potential in a new job. But meanwhile they receive supports: a promotion is announced; status symbols are provided; and resources for information and staff assistance are made available. Women, on the other hand, often must prove more than their potential, and with few, if any, of these supports. Women are often promoted only after they *actually produce* for a year or so under much less supportive conditions. These women must produce by exercising influence instead of exercising formalized authority.

Different access to training and development. Educational supports are frequently more available to men than to women. Company-paid degree programs have only recently begun to be possible for a few women. Many programs are required to be "job-related"—a policy which discriminates against women by keeping them locked into their sex-typed jobs. Some companies are now using the concept of allowing "career-relatedness," which, depending on how it is administered, can reduce the sexist effect.

Tokenism. Managers point to the one woman at the invisible ceiling level: "See, we don't discriminate against women. There's one who could make it." This shifts all responsibility for promotion onto women and is an attempt to absolve others of exclusionary practices. It ignores the reality that cultural biases don't evaporate with a few acts. It is comparable to the remark: "I'm not prejudiced against women—I've been married to one for thirty years."

Differences in visibility. Most positions which women hold are behind the scenes, where one has few contacts with clients, customers, suppliers, or—internally—other managers and staff members. This makes it difficult for women's capabilities to be recognized, and they are therefore under close control by their supervisors. For example, if outside salespeople are men and inside people at the order desk are women, sexism is operating. Another example: If women are not sent on business trips where their expertise applies, but men are, the company may be acting *in loco parentis.* Whether or not this position is valid as applied to students, it is sexist as applied to adult women.

Behaviors which reflect sexist attitudes. These are common in most organizations, whether said or done by men or women.

Here are a few examples of sexist *attitudes:* (1) "She doesn't need the promotion; she's married" (when the same criterion is not applied to men). (2) "A family man is more dedicated to the job" (when a "family woman" is not assumed to be similarly motivated, even when she is head of a household). (3) "Well, if she's really qualified, I suppose she could be a manager if she wants to" (when "really qualified" is less exacting for a man; note also the implication that there's something strange about the woman who wants to be a manager).

Here are some examples of sexist *behavior:* (1) A supervisor shields a woman from criticism about her work because he's afraid of hurting her (often this means he's afraid she'll cry). This results in her not getting vital feedback on her job performance because of the *supervisor's* fears. It is also linked to sexual stereotyping: there is the suggestion that a male subordinate would be able to handle criticism. (2) It is assumed that women can supervise women but not men. The stereotype that people, especially men, don't want to work for women often prevents a woman from gaining vital experience and relieves men from responsibility for their sexist attitudes. (3) Heavy physical activity is part of a job, and it is assumed that all women are incapable of it. Even if it is true that comparatively few women have the required strength, the criterion should be passing a test for the kinds of strength needed, not a sex stereotype. (Not all men have the physical requirements for some jobs either.)

There is an infinite variety of such comments, actions, and situations. The above list will help identify sexism on the job and elsewhere.

PERVASIVENESS OF SEXISM

Whether or not you have directly experienced some or all of the situations just described, there is little question that sexism is indeed pervasive in our society, and therefore in the workplace. As we have seen, it is built into organizational policies and practices. Responsibility for its continuation rests with executives and managers who create the climate of work, men who perpetuate their advantages and women who go along with them. Clearly, it is not just a "women's problem"; it is widely shared. For the purposes of this book, however, let us look at those aspects of the problem for which women may take responsibility *without* taking responsibility for those aspects that belong to men, organizations, and society as a whole.

SEXISM AND DEFENSIVE COMMUNICATION

Sexism at work colors much communication between women and men, between supervisors and employees. While it is only one aspect of sexism, it is an important one. I believe that by analyzing how sexist communication operates, and by developing some ways to deal with it, a new competence among women can develop to reduce the negative effects of sexism.

It should be noted that since sexism has to do with power relationships, it can occur wherever there is a supervisor-subordinate relationship—that is, a dominance-dependence relationship. Clearly, power can be wielded by women as well as men. I shall focus primarily on the interpersonal "power plays," how subordinate behavior reinforces them, and how to become nonsubordinate without being insubordinate.

First, let's look at three patterns, predominantly in sexist communication: (1) sexist "put-downs," (2) double messages, and (3) the language and values of sexism.

1   Sexist Put-downs

A "put-down" is any maneuver in which one person tries to put himself or herself in a superior position to another—that is, to put the other person in a "one-down" position. (This is often called "one-upmanship.") A sexist put-down is a communication which implies that a person is "down" because of sex. Because women are valued less than men in our society, men can often use sexist content to put women down. Some women use this maneuver against other women or even against themselves. Often, sexist put-downs are unintentional and unconscious, but their effect is the same.

In many of my classes and workshops, I have asked women to complete this sentence: "I feel put down when . . ." When the hidden messages of their experiences are brought to the surface, they are consistent: a woman is less valuable, less important, less capable, less of a person. The key concept in the sexist put-down is *"less, because she is a woman."* Here is an example: A man asks me a question in my area of expertise, which I answer. He says nothing, but later asks a man who is not an expert and takes his opinion over mine, whether it's the same or not.

Some of the same ideas come through when men complete the same sentence ("I feel put down when . . ."), but men tend to experience a put-down as related to job-subordinacy, not sex-subordinacy. For example: "I feel put down when my boss ignores my opinions."

2   Double Messages

The "double message" is a communication in which there are two messages, one on the surface and one hidden. In the form of double message relevant to our discussion, the covert message is sexist. Actually, the sexist put-down is a common form of double message. But in a sexist put-down, there is little effort to keep the sexist message hidden. If the sender of such a message is confronted with the sexist content, it may be denied, but there is no great loss of power.

Other double messages, however, are more subtle. In these, there is a strong motive to keep the sexist message hidden. A double message may express an illegal stance, a rude implication, a crude attitude, or some other unacceptable viewpoint. For example: A woman is the best qualified person to be promoted to a vice-presidential position, but the top management group doesn't want a woman in its midst. The top managers ask their outside legal counsel how they can "legally" avoid promoting her.

If the hidden message here were brought to the surface, it could cost the sender a loss of power, prestige, or privilege, and possibly a loss of credibility. Therefore, it is in the sender's interest to deny that a second message exists. Let's take a close look at how this operates.

The Need to Maintain Covert Power [1]   The purpose of sending a hidden message is to maintain power over another person. To do this, the sender of the message must be seen as more credible than the receiver. Therefore, the overt— or surface—message must be one that is generally acceptable, so that the sender will be able to deny *credibly* that any covert message was actually sent.

In the above example, the sender, a male executive, would say that the top managers will select the most qualified person regardless of sex. He will then set about making the woman's qualifications *appear* less than those of the man they want to promote or hire; or the qualifications may be tailored to this man's experience. If the receiver, the woman candidate, questions the executive, a claim of innocence can be made.

The receiver must take an *overt,* usually defensive stance in the attempt to "prove" that more was actually involved. If this becomes a matter of the receiver's word against the sender's, the receiver usually loses for lack of equal or more credibility. In fact, more credibility is usually necessary, since the receiver is typically in the subordinate position. When the sender is male and the receiver is female, this increases the difficulty of overcoming the supervisor-subordinate relationship to bring the covert messages to the surface.

If the risk of exposure is great for the sender, then he or she will devise more than one double message to act as a smokescreen. Each additional message must then be probed to bring the hidden message to the surface.

If the sender is anxious to retain power in the larger context beyond the immediate communication, or if power is important to the self-concept of the sender, this will create additional motivation to keep the sexist message hidden. The sender would be emotionally involved in a "false accusation," since discovery could disrupt the network of power relationships already operating. When the sender is a man, this can be a powerful motivation, since men are often involved in one-upmanship, and in other competitive games considered appropriate to male roles.

If the sender can retain the "cooperation" of the receiver by so clouding the situation that the receiver is unable to sort out the messages (or if the receiver has

[1] Theodora Wells, "The Covert Power of Gender in Organizations," *Journal of Contemporary Business,* Summer 1973, pp. 55–56.

been conditioned not to ask questions about such messages), this gives the sender an additional advantage in maintaining his or her covert power.

3 Language and Values of Sexism

Here I have selected just a few of the more visible ways in which language is used to keep women on the defensive or out of competition. Language can reflect certain values of which it is vital to be aware. There are many subtle, as well as flagrant, ways in which language is manipulated; this section presents a sampling of these to provide a basis for later discussion of how to get *off* the defensive.

Structure versus Formlessness   Hierarchical structures, and the language appropriate to them, are often not central to the life experiences of women. Thinking in such terms frequently seems alien; yet women are often told that they must adjust to it if they want to get ahead. The options offered are "either-or": "adjust or adjourn." The feeling of alienation, though real, does not immediately suggest an alternative. Thus women are left with a sense of formlessness and perhaps a vague sense of fear; but these may be an essential part of the process of formulating new options.

Competitive Thinking   Many male role structures are based on "either-or" thinking, which uses the language of competition—either you die or I die. Language based on this kind of thinking is a sort of verbal fencing (which I call "duelistic thinking"). By limiting the options, it is possible to control thinking; George Orwell presupposed this when he envisioned Newspeak.[2]
Competitive or "duelistic" thinking is that of combat and conflict. The winner gains status, and the end justifies the means ("all's fair in love and war"—presumably the same). Words are used as weapons. Now, such thinking does have its place: the concept of adversaries is the basis for debates, and indeed for our legal system. But such thinking is often extended into areas where it is less appropriate; and wherever competition is considered essential to "manhood," there is often a thinly veiled contempt for women. The prevalence of competitive tests where there is no need for them may indicate a hunger on the part of men for combat and its resultant status.
Because competitive thinking is so prevalent, men often imply that they are helpless: "That's the way the world is. I can't do anything about it." Many men use sports and the language of athletic competition to deal with the system.[3]
This pragmatic approach often keeps men focused on "what is" rather than "what should be" or even "what's going to be." Women, on the other hand, often learn the idealistic "what should be" and have difficulty with the unfamiliar, uncomfortable "what is." Commitment to "what's going to be" is only recently forming on any wide scale among women, as new options unfold.

Male and Female Vocabularies   The use of harsh language by women is considered by many people to be unfeminine and in bad taste. It is supposed that

[2] George Orwell, *1984,* New American Library, New York, 1949, pp. 246–256.
[3] Martin Ralbovsky, *Lords of the Locker Room,* Peter H. Wyden, New York, 1974, pp. 21–36.

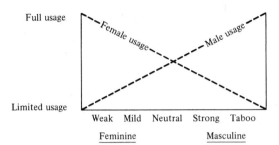

Illustration 1   Male and female vocabularies. *(From Mary Ritchie Key, Male/Female Language, Scarecrow Press, Metuchen, N.J., 1975, pp. 33–34.)*

certain aspects of language are appropriate to men; less valued aspects are relegated to women. This is another form of the power relationship. The issue of language has long kept women out of certain all-male jobs. One hears such excuses as, "Oh, we can't have any women working in here. We wouldn't be able to talk freely." Flimsy as these excuses are, they have worked.

Mary Ritchie Key has diagramed this concept as shown in Illustration 1. Examples of words at the left are "precious," "cute," "tummy," "sweet." Examples of words toward the right are: "blood," "guts," "belly," and scatological expletives and obscenities. Men who use the language at the left of the continuum are seen as effeminate; women who use words at the right are seen as coarse or worse.

It is interesting to note that words expressing power and action belong on the masculine side; words expressing passivity and niceness on the feminine side. This, of course, reflects sex roles, cultural expectations, and power structures. As a result, many women have learned language subsets. These include the language of *apology* ("I'm sorry, but . . ."); the language of *hyperbole* ("I could just *die* . . ."); the language of *permission* ("Is it OK with you if . . .?"); and the language of excessive *explanation.*[4] This is the language of subservience and deference; it fits well with the language of combat and status—no competition.

Dominant and Defensive Behavior   The list below provides examples of defensive and dominant behavior.

Defensive behaviors: subordinate	*Dominant behaviors: authority*
Explain, prove, and justify your actions, ideas, and feelings more than is required.	Prove you're right. *"I told you so . . ."* *"Now see, that proves my point."*
Ask why things are done the way they are when you really want to change them. *"Why don't they . . .?"*	Give patient explanations. *"It's always been done this way."* *"We tried that before but . . ."* *"There's no budget."*

[4] Mary Ritchie Key, *Male/Female Language,* Scarecrow Press, Metuchen, N.J., 1975, p. 37.

Defensive behaviors: subordinate	*Dominant behaviors: authority*
Ask permission when it's not needed. *"Is it OK with you if . . .?"*	Give or deny permission at any time. *"Oh, I couldn't let you do that."*
Give away decisions, ideas, and power when it would be appropriate to keep them. *"Don't you think that . . .?"*	Make decisions or take power as your natural behavior. *"The best way to do it is . . ."* *"Don't argue. Just do as I say."*
Apologize, feel inadequate, say *"I'm sorry . . ."* when you're not.	Prod people to get the job done. *"Don't just stand there. . . ."*

Power Plays   A "power play" is a double message (which, by definition, contains both a surface and a hidden message) that is used to gain or maintain power over a person or situation. Power plays are not always easy to identify because the surface message, by itself, could be a simple request for information or action. If the message is taken at face value, the hidden message is often not discovered until too late—when the power player is in a "one-up" position.

On the other hand, if the power play is accurately sensed but responded to disproportionately, the power player can credibly deny any hidden message, thus remaining in the "one-up" position. To stay out of a power play, you must sense it accurately *and* respond to it appropriately, "holding your own ground." The list below gives examples of power plays.

Overt words	*Covert messages*
"Can you prove that?"	*"I know you can't, but it'll be fun watching you try."*
"Now let's be fair. . . ."	*". . . By my rules."*
"Define your terms."	*". . . So that I can shift the discussion to show you that your understanding is totally inadequate."*
"It's either this or that. Which is it?"	*"Take a position at one end or the other. I'm cutting out the middle ground, controlling the choices."*
"Be specific. Give an example."	*". . . So that I can shoot it down and prove you wrong on the whole subject."*
"Now let's be reasonable. . . ."	*"I'll decide what's reasonable. I know best."*
"I'm not at liberty to tell you just yet."	*"And I can keep control by not telling you."* Or: *"The underlings can't know yet. They can't be trusted."*
"Now I think what you *really* mean is . . ."	*"I know better than you what you mean. No need to listen to you."*

Conscious Lies That people tell out-and-out lies is the conclusion of two public-relations experts—male—who conducted a survey of chief executive officers. According to these authors, the lies told by chief executive officers generally fall into these categories:

1 Outright lies
2 Evasions
3 Half-truths
4 True statements which lead to false conclusions
5 Silence
6 Literal truth when it's known that the inference will be wrong
7 The "non-answer" or non sequitur
8 The knowing smile accompanied by silence
9 An attack on the questioner to avoid answering
10 Answering questions with other questions
11 Ambiguity
12 Postponement
13 Obfuscation or gobbledygook (also called "chaff")
14 "Salted" paragraphs—a scattering of grains of truth in a quantity of falsehoods [5]

These are held to be consciously chosen masks, serving the needs of personal security or survival. Such lies are all forms of power plays and game techniques that are intended to divert or overwhelm the opponent—more forms of dueling.

Tone of Voice One's tone of voice may be used in various ways to control the behavior of others. As an experiment, try defining the meaning of the sentences below as the emphasis shifts—that is, as the tone of voice changes.

Subordinate	Dominant
"*I* didn't mean it that way."	"*What* did you do that for?"
"I *didn't* mean it that way."	"What *did* you do that for?"
"I didn't *mean* it that way."	"What did *you* do that for?"
"I didn't mean *it* that way."	"What did you *do* that for?"
"I didn't mean it *that* way."	"What did you do *that* for?"
"I didn't mean it that *way*."	"What did you do that *for*?"

Paying attention to how people use emphasis, how they raise and lower the voice to control the flow of dialogue, and how they adjust the speed and volume of speech can be the fastest way of learning how to recognize innuendoes given in this way.

Nonverbal Communication Much has been written about nonverbal communication. Three areas, however, remain relatively unresearched and unreported: the use of silence, the use of touching, and eye contact. Let us examine these briefly.

[5] From Otto Lerbinger and Nathaniel H. Sperber, *Key to the Executive Head,* Addison-Wesley, Reading, Mass., 1975, pp. 51–52.

Silence This has long been considered a prerogative of women. In fact, women have been commanded to remain silent by some of the more influential men in history, such as St. Paul. Historically, women were sentenced to silence because of their sex alone. Oddly enough, some were silenced by widowhood: in some cultures a widow was held to silence for a few days to a year. Women have learned to bear their pain in silence.[6] It is only within the last hundred years that it has come to be acceptable for women to speak publicly (and even today many men consider it acceptable only if the women say what men want to hear).

Silence comes in many forms. Many of us know the comfortable silence between two people experiencing love or close companionship. Others know the deadly silence following a blunder. There is also the tense silence between adversaries waiting for each other's next move. All of these are "active" silences.

The silence expected of women is, on the other hand, "passive." The expectation is that women should keep silent and smile. Women are not supposed to have feelings of anger or outrage, even when they receive outrageous insults. Part of being "nice" is to take other people's put-downs and keep smiling.

> Silence in woman is like speech in men; deny it who can.—*Ben Jonson*

> A wellbred woman may easily and effectually promote the most useful and elegant conversation without speaking a word—the modes of speech are scarcely more variable than the modes of silence.—*Blair*

The power to define to what extent, in what circumstances, and for how long certain groups of people must remain silent is always held by the dominant group (in our case, men). It is then perpetuated by the subordinate group (in our case, women) who need the acceptance of the dominant group for survival. Silence is often perceived as humility or long-suffering martyrdom. While it may seem manipulative, it often is one of the few ways by which women can adhere to their role and still exercise some control over themselves.

Touching This is a way of indicating status and refers to how much license is taken (whether or not permission is given) for one person to enter another's "personal space." In this country, the customary space within which we have learned to expect some bodily privacy extends just beyond arm's length. Status and power give some people the right to touch others without seeking their permission. Typically, therefore, there will be more touching of women by men than the reverse. It is considered presumptuous for a lower-status person to initiate touching of a higher-status person. But this becomes less rigid when status becomes less rigid, as is presently occurring between men and women.[7]

Eye contact This is an important form of nontactile touching. Here, too, there is a sex difference. Women tend to look at one another when they are in pairs more than men do when they are in pairs. This seems to be related to women's orientation toward inclusive interpersonal relationships. When women

---

[6] Key, op. cit., pp. 128–129.
[7] Nancy Henley and Jo Freeman, "The Sexual Politics of Interpersonal Behavior," in Jo Freeman (ed.), *Women: A Feminist Perspective,* Mayfield, Palo Alto, Calif., 1975, pp. 395–396.

and men interact, women use more eye contact to obtain clues regarding the acceptability of their behavior. Eye contact is also associated with listening. The prevailing pattern is that women listen more and men talk more.

While a mutual gaze can bring a sense of union, a prolonged gaze may become a stare that can be a signal for battle. A stare can also be a coercive look meant to control behavior. Because the direct stare is a common form of dominance, many women have learned to back down or look away when they receive it. Although women also use the stare, they often modify it by tilting their heads in a subtle, submissive ambiguity.[8]

Cooperating with Power Plays So far, we have been discussing how one is manipulated by other people. But it is also important to look inside ourselves to see how we cooperate with people who manipulate us, and how we make it possible for these games to continue working. The attitudes that cause us to cooperate and thus permit others to manipulate us might be called "hooks." These hooks exist because most of us carry certain rules around as part of our mental and emotional makeup. These are ideas about what we "have to" do. None of them are barriers in and of themselves: they all come from the work ethic and from expectations about male and female roles; many are valued and actively taught as part of the protocol of work. They become problems only when they are compulsive behaviors which tend to reduce one's options. The more we reduce our options, the more we can be controlled by others. What hooks do you have? Check yourself against the table on page 130. You may have others not listed; many people do. Add your own hook in the blank space.

One of the ways to avoid being manipulated is to be aware of these attitudes and put them aside when the games are being played. You may also want to see how you can bend and stretch such attitudes without violating your own integrity or setting up more risks than you feel comfortable with. For example, if one of your hooks is "I have to *be right*," you may want to consider other options, such as being wrong occasionally, giving yourself more latitude within your rules, and simply admitting to slight errors. Of course, there's always the possibility that you and the other person may both be "right."

The hook "I have to *be right*" is particularly important because the language of right and wrong is the language of "either-or," evaluative thinking. We need to use language less for evaluation and more for evolution if we want to get out of the deadlock which competitive thinking produces. The emphasis on cooperation is, perhaps, one of the really significant contributions of female socialization.

Limiting Sex Roles Many women learn to be subordinate by internalizing many self-limiting rules of the socialization process. Some of these rules are listed below. Not all women, of course, receive the same kind or amount of indoctrination. However, what *is* learned may be thought of as a gradual building up of

[8] Ibid., pp. 397–398.

"Hooks"

I have to *be right*.	I have to *win*.	
I have to *impress others*.	I have to *be a success*.	
I have to *be in control*.	I have to *do it by myself*.	
I have to *be responsible*.	I have to *finish it*.	
I have to *be liked*.	I have to *be informed*.	
I have to *produce and perform*.	I have to *be consistent*.	
I have to *prove myself*.	I have to *be on time*.	
I have to *earn the right* to play.	I have to *be logical and rational*.	
I have to *have the answers*.	I have to *be perfect*.	
I have to *be prepared*.	I have to *conform*.	
I have to *trust and obey authority*.	I have to *be able to take it*.	
I have to *go through channels*.		

layers. It takes considerable awareness and close attention to peel back these layers of learning, allowing one's individuality to emerge.

Never say no   Women are typically taught to accommodate the requests of others, especially bosses, parents, spouses, and children. Many never learn that the option "no" exists for them.

Smile no matter what you feel   The plastered-on smiles of many politicians' wives and beauty contestants are appropriate to the female role. But the constant smile can be a denial of one's own feelings.

Always try to improve   Soul-searching to find where we may have erred is taught early: We must keep *trying*, every day and in every way, to be better and better.

Never claim your strengths   Because attention is focused on searching for improvements to be made, little attention is given to noticing strengths, although these are needed to do the improving.

Protect the male ego   Early on, many women learn endless ways in which to set up and maintain relationships with men. Look up to men; let them look down on you. Be a fascinating woman, and you will live happily ever after.

Learn to react appropriately; do not act   If you notice the verbs used by traditional women, you may discover that many of them are "reactive" verb forms. They imply *being acted upon.* You can identify a woman who is emerging into individuality by her much more frequent use of active verbs, such as "I decided." She is learning that it really is all right to initiate action in her own interest as well as for others.

Don't trust your own experiences and perceptions   Because so much of role learning for women is reactive rather than active, women may learn to deny or discount their own experiences and feelings as less important than those of men, or not quite so valid. Rediscovering one's feelings and taking ownership of them is a central part of growth as a person.

Obey the "shoulds" and "oughts" of others   Obedience does not allow much practice in generating new options, or in learning to assess how much risk may be involved with a particular option. Consequently, women who are obedient may remain easily controllable and responsive to the dominant "either-or" thinking.

You can't trust a woman   Many women learn not to trust each other. This may happen because women learn to compete with each other for the attention of men. The woman who "takes your man away" can never be your friend. She can't be trusted because "she'll knife you in the back any chance she gets." These myths are so pervasive that it would be difficult not to absorb them by osmosis. Naturally, some *people*—women and men—behave in these ways; but this simply is not sex-linked behavior. Rather, it is part of the female role.[9]

GETTING OFF THE DEFENSIVE

In this section, there are three main topics. First, we will see how the role is not the person, and the person is not the role. Second, a "Choosing Process" will be offered which is a form of problem solving that incorporates and legitimizes feelings. Finally, the Choosing Process will be applied to a double message which is also a sexist put-down: "You're not one of those women's libbers, are you?" It will also be applied to a situation of being the one woman in an all-male work group for the first time.

The Role Is Not the Person; the Person Is Not the Role

The traditional roles for women and men consist of clusters of selected human traits that our society has deemed appropriate, depending on sex. But since all of us are first human beings, and only second one of two sexes, it seems eminently rational to permit human beings to choose for themselves the ways of being human which best suit their needs and purposes at any point in time. The options

---

[9] Theodora Wells, "The Psychology of Woman," in Arthur Warmoth and Barry McWaters (eds.), *The Art and Science of Psychology: Humanistic Perspectives,* Brooks/Cole, Monterey, Calif., 1977, pp. 16–21.

to re-choose can remain open, and the combination selected does not have to remain the same even from minute to minute.

Of course, feeling comfortable about using all the ways of being human implies that people must accept the fact that they are human. This is one of the psychosociological concepts of the present women's movement—that women (and men) can be whole persons. Because women don't yet have full equal rights under the law, and because women are often measured against male standards, it is easy to understand how some women and men may wonder if this is true.

Self-acceptance, instead of role acceptance, is the first step toward becoming a whole person. We are all born as potential whole persons. But on the basis of sex, certain expectations are taught from birth which tend to reduce this potential. For women, one such expectation is *not* to rely on valuing and accepting themselves, but rather to look to others—first parents, later men—for indications of their worth. When others determine our personal worth for us, we become dependent on their judgments and thus lose our sense of personal identity. Therefore, to become whole persons again, one necessary step is to move the source of acceptance from other people to ourselves: that is, to establish self-acceptance. As Thomas Szasz succinctly put it, "The proverb warns that 'you should not bite the hand that feeds you,' but maybe you should, if it prevents you from feeding yourself." [10]

The Choosing Process: Basic Concepts

The Choosing Process is based on a few concepts which we should first note.

1 It assumes that we have feelings and that we must deal with them as they occur, rather than automatically suppressing them in order to appear cool and mature. (Several options for dealing with feelings will be mentioned.)

2 It assumes that a desirable objective is to help create situations where all parties can gain something for themselves—a "win-win" situation. It assumes, furthermore, that most people want to contribute something valuable to their field and their organization, and that therefore when they gain something for themselves, they also gain something for the organization.

3 It assumes that put-downs are counterproductive, even when used in self-defense. It therefore tries to allow room for people to save face and maintain their dignity at all times.

4 It assumes that minimizing risks while maximizing gains may not always be the best procedure. It proposes instead the idea of taking the greatest risk that feels safe and comfortable. This is most likely to be optimal for the person taking the risk, for others, and for the organization.

The Six Steps in the Choosing Process

The steps in the Choosing Process consist of questions to be asked and answered. As you read this section, you may want to think of a situation which you would like to be able to resolve better than you have so far been able to do, and to try applying the questions to this situation.

[10] Thomas Szasz, *The Second Sin,* Doubleday, Garden City, N.Y., 1973, p. 45.

1 What Are Your Feelings? What feelings are you experiencing right now? (Or, what would be your typical reaction to the situation you are thinking of?) Try to name the feelings. Try to "own" your feelings—to consider it all right to have them, even if not to express them. Can you temporarily let go of the need to express the feelings (assuming that in your work environment you are expected to remain cool)? If you contain your feelings, can you release them later to reduce pressure before it builds up very much? Are your feelings mild enough so that you could report them, if you want to? Can you delay expressing them? Can you detach yourself from them—not so much that you become detached from what is going on, but enough to avoid a buildup of pressure?

If you can exercise one of these options, you are now in a position to choose what you feel, so that you can *act*—not just *react*. (This also helps you keep your sense of humor.)

If your feelings are getting in your way, you may need some space for yourself in which to release some of the built-up pressure that is not appropriate to the present situation. Or you may want to apply the Choosing Process separately to this situation, and generate many more options for handling this pressure.

2 What Is Your Purpose? Once you have determined that you are going to handle your feelings in a way which is comfortable for you, then a clear statement of purpose is needed. What do you *really* want to accomplish? What result do you want? If what you want is revenge, consider the risk involved in gaining that end, and consider whether you have any larger, longer-term objective. Be sure to *get something you want* out of the situation, while also leaving room for others to win or at least break even—but not lose.

3 What Are Your Options? List all the options you can think of without evaluating any of them. This is brainstorming with yourself. You may get many more options if you can include one or two close friends who are also interested in increasing their options. Be sure to get out *all* options, including those you think you would never use. Get out everything you'd really like to say or do. Sometimes farfetched options can be converted to practical ones. If not, it helps to keep a few options in reserve for dire emergencies: this has a strengthening effect.

4 What Are Your Risks? List your options in order, according to which seem most desirable for your purpose. Start with the least risky and list the options in order up to the most risky. Sometimes this simple rank-ordering helps to find the choice you want to make. If it doesn't, then you start with the option involving least risk, and make two lists: "What Are the Advantages?" "What Are the Disadvantages?" As you mentally weigh the pros and cons, you may decide that you could take more risk; if so, apply the same procedure to the next option. When you get to the option that feels too risky for you now, take the one just before this as your choice for now.

5 What Is Your Choice? When you have tentatively decided on the optimum-risk option for you, try to think, "What is the worst that could happen if I make this choice?" Then consider what would you do if the worst should happen. Would that still be all right with you? If so, you have found your optimum option. If not, you may need to go back to your list and try another, less risky, option.

It's usually helpful to keep one backup choice, just in case the predictions you made for your first choice do not come about.

6 Is Your Choice All Right with You? This is the final check on your comfort level. You must feel that the choices you make are appropriate for *you* in the situation, even if no one else might make exactly the same choices. No one else will live as closely with the consequences as you will. If things don't work out as you predicted, you can go back and discover where the predictions that influenced your choice were inaccurate. In this way, you can still have that option available again for another, different situation. You will not continually narrow your options by deciding, "Well, that's *one* thing I'll never do again!"

Applying the Choosing Process

Facing a Sexist Put-down First, let's see how this process can be applied to a typical, relatively simple put-down: *"You're not one of those women's libbers, are you?"* This is a double message in which the surface message is, "You really are normal, aren't you?" and the hidden message is a threat: "No man will want you if you are a women's libber." As I apply the Choosing Process, assumptions will be made about what the person is feeling, etc.; but naturally, actual feelings will be different for each person who is faced with this remark.

What am I feeling? "I feel put down. I'm not sure what is being implied, but I know I don't like it. There's a hook somewhere there. I feel stupid because I can't recognize it. I don't want that label. What's the matter with me?"

This person is now on the defensive, punishing herself for not being sharper. But she can simply say to herself, "I don't really know what to do right now about my feelings. I just want to feel more on top of this situation."

What is my purpose? One purpose—feeling more in control of the situation—has just been stated. Another might be, "I want to defuse the emotional load."

What are my options? Suppose this person now has a quick brainstorming session. The words she imagines herself using are in column 1. Column 2 shows her initial evaluation of each response. (Column 3 is dealt with below.)

(1) Possible responses	(2) Evaluation	(3) Risk rating
"What do you want to know for?"	Defensive?	-
"Isn't everybody?	OK	2
"What's a 'women's libber'?"	OK if really asking	1 (least)
"What's it to you?"	Defensive?	-
"Naturally. Aren't you?"	OK	3
"You'd better believe."	OK if true	4 (most)
"Screw you."	Out. No room to save face.	-

What are my risks? Let's assume that this person is a feminist and, though defensive, can get to the point of "owning" her views. Therefore, she has rated the risks as shown in column 3. Most of the possible choices would probably be reasonably comfortable for her in most situations, depending on her relationship to the person who made the remark, and on the nonverbal messages sent.

What is my choice? The least risky choice (rated "1" in column 3) is a request for information. This may be the best choice, provided that it is a genuine request. But if it is obstructive or defensive, it could be the most risky. Therefore, it is probably safest to choose the option rated "2" or "3."

Is this choice all right for me? Given the assumptions we have made, the answer seems to be "yes." The most unfavorable consequence is another put-down, such as, "What on earth do you want to be one for?" Her option there might be to say, "Don't knock it till you try it" as she exits (or looks down) to get back to work.

She has remained in control of the situation and herself without trying to put the other person down and without taking responsibility for the emotional content sent by the other person. Certainly she did not add any emotional load in her reply. All the applicable criteria for a nondefensive response have been met (assuming that her body language and tone of voice match the mood of the words).

Entering a Male Work Group as the One Woman Situation: you are a woman entering a work group of nine men for the first time. A meeting is about to start. You are greeted with a tentative, "Well . . ." as if they are waiting for the secretary to deliver her message and leave. Let's apply the choosing process to this problem.

What is your feeling? Let's say, for the sake of discussion, that you feel unwelcome, put down, and unimportant. You also feel somewhat defensive, angry in a muted way, and determined to make a success of what you see as a new opportunity for you and other women.

You decide that while you have many feelings about this situation, you are not going to express them or report them. You decide to delay expressing them until this evening, when you are with a close friend.

What is your purpose? Now, you can say that *being a success in this situation and in your job* is your purpose. But that might be too general. Perhaps a sharper definition would be that since a new group is now forming (by virtue of your arrival), there is a formation process to be gone through in which trust is a basic, desired element. Therefore, you may decide to make the *establishing of trust* your purpose.

However, this is still a bit fuzzy. What needs clarification is who is going to take the responsibility for establishing trust. So far, it appears that all the responsibility is likely to rest with you, the newcomer woman. Are you going to share that responsibility with the nine men who have been the regular members of this group? Since you all share responsibility for the group, your present purpose might be stated thus: *To behave in a trustworthy manner and determine whether or not the others are willing to extend trust initially to me as well.*

What are your options?   A brainstorming session might produce the options listed in column 1 of Illustration 2. In column 2, the options are ranked by risk, from least to most, as seen by you. No one else should be involved from this point on. (The risks are analyzed in the table on page 137.) Remember, this is just a hypothetical example; it is not meant to indicate what is "right."

What are your risks?   Applying a tradeoff analysis to this question might produce a table like the one below.

What is your choice?   Option 3 is the one chosen as most consistent with the purpose stated in step 2, given the risks as seen by you. It points in the direction of being yourself, being worthy of trust, and not taking responsibility for the behavior of the men. If they can't handle your presence, they will have to take the responsibility for that. You decide that you will hold to the line of being socially safe, hard working, discreet, and capable of confidentiality.

Is this choice all right for you?   If the worst happens, you will be excluded in such a way that you cannot do your job. If that happens, you decide that you will deal directly with the problem in the group, which also happens to include your boss. That seems all right for you; and if it doesn't work out, you can go up another level for help—to the personnel department for advice or a transfer. You prefer to stay and work through the problem, rather than appear to give up.

IN CONCLUSION

One dynamic way of handling sexism at work is the self-fulfilling prophecy. Most often it may work against us, since there are low expectations and stereotypes with which we must constantly deal. However, if we can go into these situations

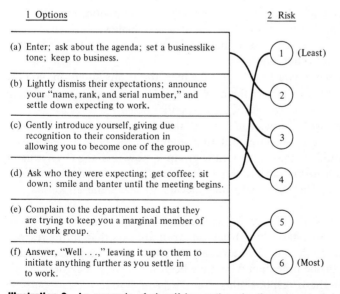

Illustration 2 An example of classifying options by the amount of risk involved.

Factors working *for* me	Factors working *against* me

Option *d*, risk rating 1 (least risk):

Factors working *for* me	Factors working *against* me
I can avoid getting them their coffee.	They may want me to get their coffee.
Smiles are seen as deferring. I feel good. I'm comfortable.	Smiles may confuse them, as I'm not always accommodating.
Banter is a good relaxer. I'm good at it.	I don't like small talk and banter.

Option *a*, risk rating 2:

Factors working *for* me	Factors working *against* me
No chance for small talk.	They like small talk, probably.
I set a "business only" tone for myself.	I may come across as more stiff or severe than I am.
	It's not "feminine."

Option *b*, risk rating 3:

Factors working *for* me	Factors working *against* me
An easy style for me, yet one that observes the amenities.	It may seem "too familiar."
Nothing phony.	Too businesslike, not easy going enough?

with the expectation of being accepted, of being able to handle reasonably well what comes up, we help make that expectation happen by our own attitudes. This is a positive use of the self-fulfilling prophecy.

Many men are not ready for this kind of change, even though they talk confidently. Most organizations have barely begun to revise the norms which give more supports to men than to women. In fact, in a survey of 5,000 readers of the *Harvard Business Review,* it was found that, "These managers do not see the organization as having any obligation to alter its attitude towards women [nor] to change [its] expectations of men."[11] Moreover, culturally ingrained attitudes which are reflected in our language add to the pervasiveness of preferential treatment of men. Coping with all instances of sexism would be an endless task.

However, we can make our own choices, to deal with what seems most important to us, to keep as many options open as possible, to take responsibility for ourselves, and to refuse responsibility for men or for organizational norms over which we have little control. If others fail to hold up their end of the shared responsibilities, we can take the necessary steps to ensure that this does not continue.

By working together, we can often create more "win-win" situations and make life more human for all of us who are trying to get through it with a

[11]Bensen Rosen and Thomas H. Jerdee, "Sex Stereotyping in the Executive Suite," *Harvard Business Review,* March-April 1974, p. 58.

minimum of unnecessary stress. We can, perhaps, even improve the quality of our lives through nondefensive, nonsubordinate behaviors whereby we can retain the optimum amount of power over ourselves.[12]

BIBLIOGRAPHY

Ferguson, Charles W.: *The Male Attitude,* Little, Brown, Boston, 1966. This book is out of print, but it gives an excellent historical perspective.

Henley, Nancy, and Jo Freeman: "The Sexual Politics of Interpersonal Behavior," in Jo Freeman (ed.), *Women: A Feminist Perspective,* Mayfield, Palo Alto, Calif., 1975. An excellent collection of sophisticated feminist writings on all major aspects of being a woman in America today.

Key, Mary Ritchie: *Male/Female Language,* Scarecrow Press, Metuchen, N.J., 1975. An excellent research report on the differences between male and female styles of language and their significance.

Lerbinger, Otto, and Nathaniel H. Sperber: *Key to the Executive Head,* Addison-Wesley, Reading, Mass., 1975. An exposé of executive behavior based on a survey done by two public-relations men, which reveals some behaviors not previously admitted to by executives. Highly readable.

Orwell, George: *1984,* New American Library, New York, 1949. A political satire which seems ever more relevant to our real lives.

Ralbovsky, Martin: *Lords of the Locker Room,* Peter H. Wyden, New York, 1974. A long overdue exposé of what Little League and high school coaches do to boys and young men in the name of sports.

Wells, Theodora: "The Covert Power of Gender in Organizations," *Journal of Contemporary Business,* Summer 1973. Further development of this theme is available here.

————: "The Psychology of Woman," in Arthur Warmouth and Barry McWaters (eds.), *The Art and Science of Psychology: Humanistic Perspectives,* Brooks/Cole, Monterey, Calif., 1977.

---

[12] The author is indebted to Caren Motzko and Laurel Campbell for their editorial assistance in preparing this chapter.

Chapter 8

Next Steps Up: Women as Peers and Managers

Rosalind K. Loring

"So I leave it with all of you. Which came out of the opened door—the lady or the tiger?"—Frank Richard Stockton, 1834–1902

To many—perhaps most—men who work with women as peers or managers, the question which seems uppermost in their minds is whether or not they will open the wrong door. They believe they can handle "ladies," but they know they are afraid of tigers. Tigers, of course, are defined by behavior—as are ladies. And an omnivorous, even man-eating, tigerish temperament has been freely attributed to assertive, competitive, no-nonsense women. Ladies, on the other hand, are considered to be gentle, docile, dainty, and quiet, with compliant behavior and traditional answers.

Women, too, face the question of which door to open. However, their interpretation of this old question has to do with constant selection: balancing the

Berry's World

© 1975 by NEA. Inc.

"Why yes, I am 'a little homemaker' — I'm in the construction business and I build small homes!"

Reprinted by permission of Newspaper Enterprise Association (NEA).

needs of a family with the demands of a career; choosing between time for pleasure and time for profit; knowing when to withdraw from the excitement of living fully in order to enter an inner zone of peace.

But the question itself may well be the wrong one. Women are sometimes ladies and sometimes tigers, just as men are capable of many styles of behavior. Women professionals and managers especially need to know that there are appropriate times for both styles. Often it's a matter of degree—for example, when aggressiveness would be experienced as a threat, or when compliance would be counterproductive. It's possible that either style can work against your predetermined long-range goals.

When men and women can better predict women's behavior, tension is reduced considerably. Much confusion is due to women's unplanned reactions to the politics, systems, and operations of the organizations in which they work. This chapter, therefore, concentrates on ways in which women can understand and analyze their work setting and their responses to it. Strengthened with such knowledge, women will be far freer to take their next steps as professionals and managers.

CHALLENGES FOR WOMEN

In addition to the other challenging areas for all women which are highlighted throughout the chapters of this book, for professional and managerial women the following progressions are frequently mentioned by women as being extremely important:

Moving from your own and others' stereotypes to nontraditional roles and relationships

Moving from a negative self-concept (a lack of self-confidence) to confidence in the transfer of skills to new settings

Moving from the achievement of personal success to managing the high price of working toward equity for other women

In an excellent article in the *Harvard Business Review,* Charles Orth and Frederick Jacobs, emphasizing the difficulties of establishing equal treatment, remind us that there are "traditional male attitudes toward women at the professional and managerial levels [which] continue to block change." But, they go on, "Many women are in fact ambivalent, confused or anxious about how they should relate to men in the competitive crucible of the typical business organization."[1]

This ambivalence can be seen in the interactions between women and men—or women and women—as institutional leaders. It occurs particularly in certain areas:

Implementing Affirmative Action programs[2]

Negotiating for jobs and salaries

Securing promotions, especially into management

Case studies, reports of surveys, and histories of programs have all indicated that these are still areas of considerable discussion (and often too little action) where any specific woman is concerned. This has meant that women who are high achievers maintain an extraordinary pace; and women executives give the impression that they have had to overcome ambivalence to a great degree. In negotiating to secure positions of leadership for themselves, women display different styles. Their current status demonstrates that acceptance of women at high levels is growing, but more slowly than women would like. In one report, a former employee of a major utility in the San Francisco area described in detail her attempts, from July 1969 to July 1973, to secure a position suitable for her education and experience.[3] Reluctant to use any legal recourse to solve her problem, she finally chose to leave the firm. But many women today *are* using the

[1] Charles D. Orth III and Frederick Jacobs, "Women in Management: Patterns for Change," *Harvard Business Review,* July-August 1971, pp. 139–147.

[2] "Affirmative Action" is the official term for a federal program for giving women and minorities equal opportunity. It is a complicated program in which governmental agencies attempt to (1) monitor the behavior of organizations which use federal funds and (2) enforce equal opportunity in recruiting, retention, training, promotion, and pay. For a full description, see Rosalind Loring and Theodore Wells, *Breakthrough: Women into Management,* Van Nostrand, New York, 1972, pp. 175–189.

[3] Personal communication.

law to secure not only more suitable positions, but also compensation for previous discrimination in pay and training opportunities (see Chapter 22).

CAREER COUNSELING

Career counseling is often the key to women's decisions about appropriate action for themselves. The field of choice has grown tremendously in the past few years and, combined with Affirmative Action, has at least opened many doors for women. For example, the Society of Women Engineers both at the University of California, Davis, and nationally is organized to inform its members of laws and employment opportunities and to provide a system of mutual support. The *Harvard Business Review* surveyed some of its corporate readers on managerial decision making and discovered that many employees receive both career and personal counseling from supervisors.[4] But another fact which emerged is that too frequently career counseling for men is vastly different from that for women.

It's apparent that young women entering college have been exposed to career counseling, either formally or informally. Alexander Astin, who reports yearly on trends in the career choices of college students, noted that since 1966 women freshmen have shown a steadily increasing interest in business, medicine, and engineering—certainly nontraditional and high-status fields for women.[5]

Counseling is available through colleges and universities, trade or technical schools, and professional organizations (e.g., the American Sociology Association and the National Association of Certified Professional Secretaries). In large cities there are growing numbers of private counseling firms, many of them especially directed to women's needs, interests, and abilities. Depending upon the sponsorship, the cost of counseling ranges from nothing, from a professional organization, to several hundred dollars or more, at a private agency. Throughout the country, continuing education divisions in colleges and universities have scheduled courses and made counseling services available day and night for career guidance (see Chapter 21).

PEERS AND MANAGERS

The concepts "professional," "peer," and "manager," as I am using them, can each refer to a different kind of status within an organization. A "professional" is someone with a particular field of technical expertise (such as computers, planning, or sales). Of course, a professional in this sense can work as a peer or manager. But in most if not all large organizations today, a manager's professional expertise is not the primary part of his or her job. Rather, managers spend most of their time and energy in administering policies and goals through the

[4] Benson Rosen and Thomas H. Jerdee, "Sex Stereotyping in the Executive Suite," *Harvard Business Review,* March-April 1974, pp. 45–58.
[5] Alexander Astin, Margo King, and Gerald Richardson, *The American Freshman National Norms for Fall 1975,* Laboratory for Research in Higher Education at UCLA and Cooperative Institutional Research Program, American Council on Education, Washington, D.C., 1975.

work of others. A "peer" is someone at or below the managerial level working with others of the same rank or status and therefore needing equal perquisites. These terms are sometimes interchangeable, in the sense that the same person can be described by all three.

Women working as peers have special concerns regarding equality in title, pay, opportunities, workload, power, and responsibilities. It should be noted that moving up from a peer position to a higher management position doesn't guarantee equity. According to a report by a task force of the National Council of Churches, salaries of women with managerial titles and responsibilities are still roughly *half* those for men in comparable positions.[6] Women working as managers face additional problems: attitudes of both other women and men to women supervisors. Lyle and Ross have noted that moving up in the same firm creates greater hostility than entering a new firm as a manager.[7]

Still, in spite of all this, there are a growing number of women in professional and managerial positions. Their ranks promise to be augmented by the many women currently preparing themselves to accomplish change in this area by either the "lady" method or the "tiger" method. In recent times, much has been learned about how to accelerate change, to speed up the evolution of women from workers concentrated in a few categories to workers in the full range of occupations. The very elements of challenge which have interested men in management have now become visible and attainable for women. The balance of this chapter presents guidelines and a system for self-help.

Of course, corporations, institutions of higher education, hospitals, and government agencies must be involved—in fact, they should provide the mechanisms for moving more women into responsible positions. *But women will need to provide consistent impetus and pressure in order to effect lasting change.* Meanwhile, women have still another option—to choose a work setting carefully and deliberately. Ladies and tigers, peers and managers, all need an environment which enables individual women to produce the best fruits of their labor.

GOOD WORK CLIMATES FOR WOMEN [8]

The quest for a work environment in which women can rise to leadership draws many women together in a common cause. I have studied management texts, examined the real-life experiences of working women, and speculated about the

[6] Task Force on Women and Corporations, *Women and Corporations: Issues and Actions,* National Council of Churches Interfaith Center for Corporate Responsibility, New York, 1975. Available from Mary Harvey, Interfaith Center for Corporate Responsibility, 475 Riverside Drive, Room 566, New York, N.Y. 10027.

[7] Jerolyn Lyle and Jane Ross, *Women in Industry: Employment Patterns of Women in Corporate America,* Heath (Lexington Books), Boston, 1973.

[8] I developed and presented much of the material in this section for two conferences for women in management: (1) The National University Extension Association, with the University of Iowa Extension, "Administrative Skills for Women," September 29, 1974, Iowa City, Iowa. (2) Jumbunna (an organization of businesswomen), "Breakthrough: Women into Management," Melbourne, Australia, October 22, 1975.

manner in which women, individually and in groups, can work to define and develop a helpful climate conducive to growth. I am convinced that we can, *in advance or on the job*, assess the potential of an organizational environment and determine whether or not the organization has possibilities for us. And we can determine whether or not certain changes in current working patterns seem possible. My own search has led me over the years up many paths and down a few byways—I've yet to encounter a highway. But I have assembled the results of these journeys into a way of thinking about possibilities for growth in the organization.

First, I recognize that efforts to improve the status of women vary in issues and emphases in different places around the world. For each nation and person, there is a continuum. Women, like many other groups, have rising aspirations; and, also like many other groups, seek to extend the range of functions and relationships available to them. Within each nation, state, and community, the spark has been lighted: women want to share in the development of better conditions—social and economic—within their own society.

Traditionally, women have been concerned about maintaining the most favorable environment possible for their families and their communities. They have espoused movements with names like "Save the Children," "Unpollute the Streams," and "Ethics in Government." For centuries, women have seemed bound to be "other-directed." What is new is that in the past ten years *many women have moved to public, open, action-oriented involvement in improving their own personal environment.* Nowhere is this more evident than in the goal of moving women into management—that most rarefied of organizational atmospheres.

As recently as five years ago, the management consultants Thomas Williamson and Edward Karrass reported that women clerical workers were more concerned about job amenities than with self-fulfillment in their work. On the other hand, men were less interested in amenities but rather looked for jobs which provided mobility and motivation.[9] Yet, times must be changing. In 1975 a coalition of people and organizations in Florida formed a statewide recruitment program for women entitled IMPACT (Identifying Management Potential and Career Talent). In 1974 the American Council on Education in Washington, D.C., established a Commission on Women in Higher Education. This commission recently conducted an "Invitational Seminar in the Identification, Recommendation and Placement of Women in Higher Education Administration." Other trends are communication workshops for women and men who work together on formal or informal teams; and an increase in traditional courses and seminars in management theory, interpersonal relations, and problem solving which are held on-site at the company's expense—these are now given just for women at the request of women employees seeking added skills to aid in their upward climb.

The fact is that a work setting conducive to growth for women and men is

[9] Thomas R. Williamson and Edward J. Karrass, "Job Satisfaction Variables among Female Clerical Workers," *Journal of Applied Psychology,* vol. 54, no. 4, August 1970, pp. 343–346.

the shared responsibility of both employees and management. Once this setting is well established, employees can move forward to participate through their own actions in forming their own future. *A concept of what should be must precede action;* therefore, women will not move (or be moved) into management until management and women work together. This is essential if we are to create the means and attitudes that will allow action toward equity to occur.

Necessary Elements

This climate we hope to create should contain all the elements we recognize as essential to the growth of any new venture, be it a flower, a child, a business, or a nation. There are five crucial elements:

A support system to provide sustenance
Nutrients for growth
Time for gestation and development
Absence of undue stress
Commitment by those involved

It is easy for us to agree that a business, for example, requires a support system in the form of a bank; that a flower needs fertilizer; and that a nation needs a century or more to become established. We know the penalties of undue stress such as accidents or illness in the life of a child; or the impact of wars upon the health of a nation. We recognize that every business requires the commitment of the owner. Now we need to remind ourselves and others that there is an analogy to each of these which relates to women in management.

To ensure the sound growth in the venture, the *support system* should be established initially by management and government. The second element, *nutrients,* must combine training, retraining, and more training with careful and unbiased evaluations and equal perquisites of rank (expense accounts, title, pay, office space, equipment, staff, etc.). The third element, *time for development,* has been almost totally disregarded; we know now that we must look for small steps, not giant leaps. Both management and women can expect that the experiences which lead to maturation will take some years. *Avoidance of undue stress,* the fourth element, is most frequently violated when the staff or their families—males and females—are unsupportive. Eleanor Schwartz, in *The Sex Barrier in Business,* reports on her survey of large and small organizations. She learned that the major difficulty women managers experienced was finding good employees who would work for them.[10] How difficult it is when well-qualified people refuse employment under a woman administrator! This compounds the problem, since every manager is only as competent as her or his supporting staff. To be a leader requires a group. We know from the behavior of prospective employees that this climate of which we speak is outside the organization—as well as inside—it's in the air we breathe (and evidently bring to work with us).

---

[10] Eleanor B. Schwartz, *The Sex Barrier in Business,* Bureau of Business and Economic Research, School of Business Administration, University of Georgia, 1971.

Element five, the capstone, is *commitment* by oneself as well as by management. It means commitment to the first four factors while avoiding too much competition too early. It also means searching for innovative, unique, and even risky methods to ensure the most fertile of soil and the best balance of human and technological resources.

Assessing Your Climate

In concentrating on women as managers, we must assume a certain level of age, experience, and education, together with some modicum of control over decisions. Consequently, I believe we can speak now of women's role in the selecting of their places of employment. "Select," "choose," "search out"—these may seem to be strange words in a sometimes dubious economy and in an employment market where there appear to be more women interested in management than there are serious recruiters from firms prepared for women managers. Nonetheless, anyone considering the possibility of management as a career has skills, experience, abilities, and attitudes which are as valuable as they are rare. The choice of where to invest your collection of talents finally rests with you.

The first step in creating a favorable climate is to assess carefully your current work setting and then other possible locations. Evaluation can start with the elements we have just been discussing: *support system, nutrients, time for development, predictable stress, and commitment of management.* Organize your ideas under these headings and check them against those of your colleagues or support groups.

Next, my system provides for explicit evaluation of the climate of any organization in terms of how compatible it is for women managers. Illustrations 1, 2, and 3 show how this system works. Let us examine each of them in turn.

Illustration 1: Organizational Climate   This concept encompasses operational patterns—how tasks and responsibilities typically are performed and what relationships exist. Organizational development is currently the most common method of examining a whole operation, rather than working with a single manager, in order to produce change and improve performance. It presupposes that any individual will affect the functioning of the entire organization only to a limited degree (although it's always possible that individual employees can make a considerable impact upon the organization). Hence, I start by viewing the complexity of the climate established by top management.

Without placing priority on any single item, we can say that the following are important elements which determine an organizational climate:

Top management's philosophy. This establishes the methodology of management and includes, but is not limited to, decision making, gathering and dissemination of information, problem solving, and rewarding and reprimanding of employees. It should be noted that in some management suites there exists a stated or implied philosophy of equality which is, however, not honored in fact.

The readiness of the organization to accept change. This depends upon

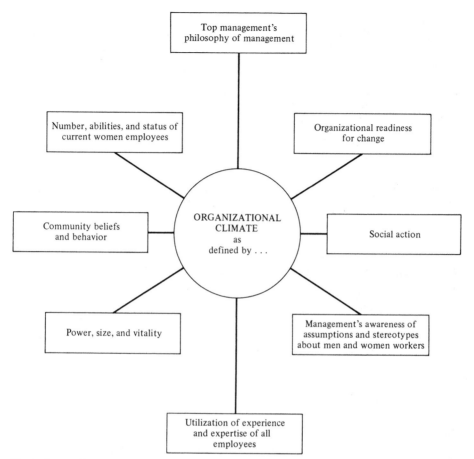

Illustration 1   Determinants of a favorable climate for women as managers and employees: the organizational climate.

management's previous experience and current expertise in recognizing when change is indicated, and its ability to respond appropriately in deciding on and implementing change.

Social-action activities. These activities benefit the undervalued and underprivileged—or attempt to correct the wrongs of earlier, less enlightened times. Usually they include some of the following: Providing better working conditions; providing especially designated training or educational programs and employment opportunities for women and members of minorities; extending the employment age at either end; and, of course, implementing Affirmative Action.

Management's awareness of assumptions and stereotypes about workers in general, and about differences and similarities between men and women. This is a response to myths and beliefs about why and how people work, and their physical, emotional, and social behavior; and it influences work assignments.

Utilization of the experience and expertise of employees. This has to do with the desire to use the potential of each person to perform a multitude of tasks and fill a variety of roles. How fully management explores and encourages the utilization of such abilities is a clear indication of its philosophy and commitment.

The power, size, and vitality of the organization. These affect the inner world of managers and their feelings about the risks they can "afford." Equally important is the outer world of other agencies and institutions, and the strength of the organization in dealing with them.

Community beliefs and behavior. The community interacts with the organization in the acceptance or rejection, understanding or denial, of the styles and actions of management and employees. Where the commitment from local government or ad hoc organizations is important, the stress involved in gaining cooperation is reflected in the work environment.

The number of women employed, their abilities, and their status. These factors inevitably indicate—on the basis of previous experience—the possibilities for growth for current women employees and for those who may join the organization in the future.

Illustration 2: Top Management's Philosophy of Management   This is just one element in Illustration 1. I've chosen to develop it in greater detail because of its importance in the evaluation of the organizational climate. Just as I judged the quality and capacity of top management in terms of my own goals, now I should look at a variety of *subfactors.* (Again, they are not necessarily listed in order of importance.) These subfactors also relate in some degree to other elements of organizational climate—in such areas, for example, as beliefs regarding workers' motivation and work patterns and the establishment and maintenance of clear standards. Of special note is consistency in maintaining the same rewards and punishments for men as for women. It is crucial that differences here not be allowed. The following are important indicators of management philosophy:

Management by objectives[11] and similar tools are valuable and often essential. In the system of management by objectives, managers' and supervisors' compensation and retention with the organization are tied to meeting objectives previously agreed upon. When one of the objectives is equal employment opportunities, consistent action on the part of all managers and supervisors is far more likely than otherwise.

Delegation to middle management. What decisions are delegated? How many decisions are delegated? How much autonomy is permitted?

The readiness of middle managers to deal with change is determined to some extent by their perception of how much is delegated to them. There are also other factors, of course, including personality and training.

The "view from the top" of women as managers and as peers. The willingness of top management to work directly with women is important. Typically, this can be determined by looking at the women near the top. If the women chosen make fine role models for other women, if they are strong and inventive and meet the criteria of growth—then the potential is stronger for other women. When there is only a token woman, then the possibilities are poor.

[11] George L. Morrisey, *Management by Objectives and Results,* Addison-Wesley, Reading, Mass., 1970.

Illustration 2 Determinants of a favorable climate for women as managers and employees: philosophy of management.

Beliefs about workers' motivations and patterns of work. Are any of these beliefs sexist?

Establishment of clear and equal standards. Standards for men and women should be the same.

Methods used to correct past discrimination. Is training offered? If so, is it provided by the firm on the site as well as in outside settings? Have job descriptions been rewritten? Are the criteria for selection of women the same as those for men as regards ability, drive, personality, etc.?

Convictions of management about the role of business and government in the solution of social problems. This and the following item denote a conceptual framework for the role of organizations in meeting the needs of society.

Convictions of management about the value of and necessity for change. This is a corollary to the preceding item.

In every aspect of our assessment, the concept of change is a vital factor—no doubt because the presence of more women in management is bound to have a great impact upon society. In value systems, attitudes, and activities, women do of course share many elements with men. Nevertheless, the introduction of any sizable number of women into management—a situation more rigorous in some ways than the one it replaces (there's no female counterpart of the "old boy" system, where friends receive recognition and benefits) and more vigorous in others (women have a longer life expectancy)—will change many patterns and thus the working environment as a whole.

Illustration 3: Middle Management's Readiness to Deal with Change   Let's now break down one of the subfactors into its components or sub-subfactors. I have chosen one element from Illustration 2—middle management's readiness to handle change—and have developed it further in Illustration 3.

Climate. Obviously middle managers respond to whatever climate is identifiable within the organization. If, for example, top management has made public statements regarding Affirmative Action, but does nothing within the work setting to implement or reinforce such statements, middle managers are quick to perceive the situation.

Compliance among managers. This is a sort of "domino theory." Managers amplify messages conveying either support or lack of it to subordinates. Behavior is seen as an expression of the real philosophy.

Awareness of personal values. This refers to an individual's self-knowledge about personal priorities and convictions.

Criteria for assessing ability. Middle managers (those who hold the gatekeeping positions) must be able to identify and correct sexist policies of recruiting, employing, promoting, and retaining. For these relatively new and often seemingly strange activities, each middle manager must be aware of his or her own values and attitudes and must consciously form patterns and criteria for assessing capability—based on function rather than sex.

Administrative autonomy. As with other newly learned behavior, any training providing tools and skills for middle managers must be accompanied by enough administrative autonomy to carry out the new-found ways of performing.

Experience with women as peers and supervisors. Finally, ease in relationships at work comes only with experience in working with women as peers and as supervisors. Obviously, this experience must be possible. When it is, it can be expected to be rough in spots but to smooth out as time passes. As the unknown becomes known, tension lessens.

Adapting the System to Your Own Needs   This system for assessment of an organizational climate is flexible and makes possible a close examination of any single factor. Just as Illustration 2 is an expansion of one facet of Illustration 1, and Illustration 3 expands on one facet of Illustration 2, so any other facet (e.g., social action or evidence of management's utilization of the experience and expertise of all employees) may be expanded in order to examine a specific working situation.

An important aspect of this evaluation is each person's own determination of the relative "weight" or importance of the separate elements. After all, few

Illustration 3 Determinants of a favorable climate for women as managers and employees: readiness for change.

firms have *no ability* to deal with change—but a firm may be less adept in this respect than in its other areas of operation. Each element in the illustrations may be expanded or contracted in relative size or importance. The result will provide you with a viewpoint which can be compared with the viewpoints of other employees, supervisors, or knowledgeable outside observers.

The next step in your evaluation is determining your personal "need factor"—the relative value to you of each facet of this multisided problem. Ask yourself such questions as these:

Is it important whether or not community beliefs are at variance with national beliefs?

Are the stereotypes held so important to their owners that they cannot be changed? For example, would I be unable to convince the plant manager of, say, my fiscal prowess (and would his stereotype be limited to my ability to balance the books)?

Would I prefer to gain experience in a relatively powerless organization in order to have the chance to be a manager? Or—even more to the point—will a relatively "powerless" organization take a chance on me?

It is reassuring to remember that events of the twentieth century have demonstrated the inevitability of change, and that therefore, *we must acknowledge that every managerial climate has the potential for change.* Armed with information about all the factors we have discussed, your choice (after your assessment) comes down to the amount of your time and energy you want to spend in creating or accelerating those changes.

EFFECT OF WOMEN ON CLIMATE

Thus far our concentration has been upon the "architectural" elements, the superstructure and the substructure. But the final assessment of the possibility for a successful meshing of an organization and an individual is still not complete. The missing piece is the impact of women, their share in the creation of climate. Much has been written and spoken about the problems of all women who work, but it seems that the difficulties are exacerbated by being a manager. Managers are both more vulnerable and more visible. Nonetheless, a woman can contribute much to the development process when she sees herself as capable; possesses both a strong self-image and a set of technical skills; and can provide for herself whatever is lacking within the system, whether it's continuing training, support, or motivation.

The teachers of workshops and courses for women at the University of California, Los Angeles, Extension, where "Management Development for Women" has been presented for ten years, find that building a good self-concept is the center of all training. Regardless of the title or the topic—whether communication, budget, or marketing—eventually the discussion returns to the theme of strengthening the self-concept. However, because the students are women managers, next in importance are ways of clarifying communication, both one's own and that of others—from nondefensive communication to active listening (see Chapter 7).

Illustrations 1, 2, and 3 are graphic depictions of an organization. Similarly, we can depict *you* creating a climate and moving yourself and other women into management. Illustration 4 does this. It demonstrates how you can clarify your own ability to contribute.

Illustration 4: The Woman Manager Defines Her Repertoire

The span of qualifications is expected to be as wide for a woman as for a man, so that she can contribute as fully as a man to the best functioning of the enterprise.

Most women include the following in their list of essential qualities (not necessarily in order of importance):

Ability to cope with awkward moments that are certain to arise
Acceptance of one's own identity

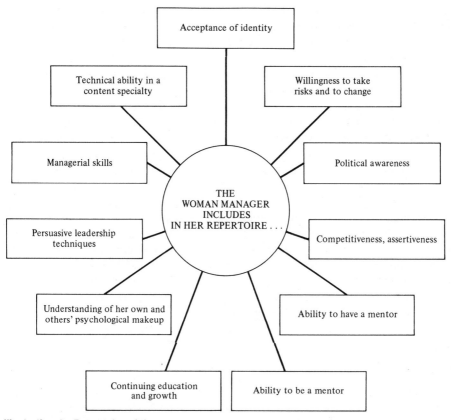

Illustration 4 Repertoire of the woman manager.

Willingness to take risks and to make changes
Political awareness (this includes politics within and between organizations)
Competitiveness and assertiveness
Interest in continuing to grow
Ability to listen and to communicate
Willingness to invest in further training
Understanding one's own as well as others' behavior
Technical ability in a specialty
Managerial skills (finance, marketing, sales, control)
Ability to predict and assess trends; willingness to be in the vanguard

There are other elements as well. For example, many managers set as a major objective having expertise in a specialty which is unique, or at least uniquely theirs in a particular setting. When everyone else catches up and they are no longer unique, they will have moved on into another specialty.

Furthermore, a woman should have a mentor, a sponsor who continues to guide and support her and alert her to organizational and political movements.

Later, she too must be a mentor, since this relationship is as valuable for those who provide assistance as for those who receive it.

Whether or not she has a mentor, every woman benefits from building her own support system related to her work. You must have able people whom you can call upon, whom you trust, and who will support you faithfully. This is not something the institution can build for you; rather, it is something you must do for yourself. As you move from one activity to another, there should be people you can call upon to help you make decisions; people who will tell you when you have misunderstood the process of a group. This is the reality of being part of a team. You must check with another person frequently and ask, "How am I doing?" Your support system should not be people who simply say, "Ah, you're wonderful," but people who will be straightforward.

The existing environment, then, makes a good beginning and provides a way of becoming a manager. But, there's more, much more—as we observe from those who are already successful managers. Jerolyn Lyle and Jane Ross, in *Women in Industry: Employment Patterns of Women in Corporate America,* conclude: "Not surprisingly, both women and men displayed most of the traits generally associated with success in management: *desire for achievement, drive for mobility; acceptance of authority figures; decisiveness; assertiveness; practicality—a tendency to look at facts;* and *a strong fear of failure.*"[12]

AND NOW FOR THE FUTURE

Promotions

The quest for satisfying work includes as a major factor the possibility of promotion. Indeed, people who are educated, trained, experienced, energetic, and creative are also typically ambitious. One obvious way to improve one's situation is to be promoted (that is, move to a higher, more complex, or more demanding position). It has always seemed to me that this urge is far more than fulfilling the American dream of "getting ahead." Rather, it appears to be part of the human condition, a psychological-biological response that has been demonstrated throughout the ages. People climb mountains "because they are there," or work long after they have enough money to support their needs. Promotions, then, indicate not only that one's worth is recognized but also that there are new mountains, fresh challenges which continue to draw on our unused abilities.

Unfortunately, for many women life has been filled with invisible ceilings—the steps up ended far short of the top. Even today, after the recent emphasis on equal opportunity, there are many statistics which prove that difficulties continue. But there have been some breakthroughs. There are today a few women who are presidents, vice-presidents, deans, hospital administrators, secretaries of government agencies, women who have achieved their status by their own efforts and not by inheritance. Their numbers can only increase in the near future, for *there are more women today than even a decade ago in middle management who will*

---

[12] Lyle and Ross, op. cit., p. 90.

soon be prepared by experience, education, and social attitude to take on the more complicated tasks of their professions.

How and when to risk seeking a promotion—like all the decisions we have discussed—is a very personal question. Ben Greco, in his comprehensive book, *How to Get the Job That's Right for You,*[13] outlines a number of reasons why people decide to make job changes. He says that *unavailable promotions* are one of the primary causes. He also suggests that before changing employers, it's useful to determine whether you can suggest to your present employer a new direction, product, or system which will benefit both you and the organization. I believe that economic and social pressures will encourage management to be far more receptive to such proposals from women, or at least more willing to listen.

Naturally, when a promotion is requested there are inner feelings and personal reactions on the part of both employee and employer. Assertiveness; nondefensive communication; and knowledge of the current job market, including the range of compensation, the qualifications really being sought, and the qualifications actually needed to do the work—all these are prerequisites to a decision to actively request a promotion. Certainly, two other crucial elements are your readiness to assume new responsibilities and the organization's capacity for promotion. When you're ready, it's time to move—up, or on to another organization.

Alternative Working Patterns

An atmosphere conducive to change can alter more than simply the structures and organizations within accustomed patterns. It can also allow new patterns to develop. One example, which is being tested for acceptance in government work, is the notion of "flexible time" or "flexitime." An early initiator of this idea, Lorraine D. Eyde, states:

> Management is constantly on the lookout for highly motivated, productive personnel who show low turnover. Such management bargains may be found among career part-time workers, but supporting evidence concerning worker effectiveness is largely anecdotal and comes from supervisors or part-time employees. Little in the way of hard data is available; however, research to date shows some promising results. . . .
>
> Recent experiments with the use of flexitime, a personnel approach allowing for flexible scheduling of full-time employment, have led government managers to identify some of the advantages of this employment practice. . . . Many of the benefits of flexitime also seem to hold for part-time employment. There appears to be a reduction in short-term absences. Employees seem to settle down to work faster and productivity increases.[14]

The criticism that part-time positions are unworkable at higher levels of responsibility has been quite adequately answered by several demonstration pro-

---

[13] Benedetto Greco, *How to Get the Job That's Right for You,* Dow Jones-Irwin, Homewood, Ill., 1975, pp. 87–96.

[14] Lorraine D. Eyde, *Flexibility through Part-Time Employment of Career Workers in the Public Service,* PS–75–3, U.S. Civil Service Commission, Personnel Research and Development Center, Washington, D.C., 1975, pp. 1, 2

jects. For example, one woman "has demonstrated that she can be an assistant vice president and economist at the Federal Reserve Bank while working a 20-hour workweek. She is able to carry supervisory responsibilities by sharing them with an economist in her section, thus creating a team management situation."[15]

Child-care arrangements and "long-distance marriages" are other trends making it possible for women to be successful without paying an exorbitant personal price. With all these factors, the number of professional women who are opening doors is increasing yearly. Although the growth rate has not accelerated as rapidly as many women would like, we can still point to the upper levels of professions and management, where the proportion of women in top positions has increased from 1% to 3% in ten years. Continued professional readiness, plus persistent vigilance, will undoubtedly create still greater numbers of qualified women in the next ten years.

BIBLIOGRAPHY

Gordon, Francine E., and Myra H. Strober: *Bringing Women into Management,* McGraw-Hill, New York, 1975. A compilation of presentations made during a conference at the Stanford Graduate School of Business for executives on the topic "Women in Management." It covers multiple issues, such as "The Issue of Sexuality," "The Law: Where It Is and Where It's Going," and "Institutional Barriers." Each of the chapters is brief, but the breadth of the male and female contributors' backgrounds is helpful.

Greco, Benedetto: *How to Get the Job That's Right for You,* Dow Jones–Irwin, Homewood, Ill., 1975. A manual on how to take the initiative in your own career development. The author covers knowing your own abilities and options better; the possibility of job changes; résumés and job interviews. Comprehensive list of resources: companies, directories, inventory, and other forms.

Higginson, Margaret V., and Thomas L. Quick: *The Ambitious Woman's Guide to a Successful Career.* American Management Association, New York, 1974. A compilation of strategies and techniques, all directed toward specific problem areas for women in the world of business. Some of the specifics are intended for lower-level positions ("dealing with someone who shouts"); while others have to do with upward mobility ("establishing your 'territory' when you gain promotion"). Practical, not philosophical.

Lippitt, Gordon L., L. This, and R. Bidwell (eds.): *Optimizing Human Resources,* Addison-Wesley, Reading, Mass., 1971. One of a large number of management texts published within the past several years. This one uses humanistic psychology as the basis for making management more productive. It should be helpful to women who want to understand how many "progressive" corporations apply certain psychological concepts in solving a manager's problems.

Loring, Rosalind, and Theodora Wells: *Breakthrough: Women into Management,* Van Nostrand, Princeton, N.J., 1972. This book concentrates on the factors involved in recruiting, training, and promoting more women for management. It enables career women to recognize the attitudes and behavior (often unconscious) which act as barriers to the full utilization of one's capabilities.

Nierenberg, Gerard I.: *The Art of Negotiating,* Cornerstone Library (paperback edition),

[15] Eyde, op. cit., pp. 7 and 8.

1971. Clearly, simply, but carefully written coverage of the process of reaching agreement in settling disputes or meeting diverse needs. It stresses communication, cooperation, and assumptions and then provides strategies for accomplishing the closest possible agreement. "In a successful negotiation everybody wins" (p. 23).

Tosi, Henry L.: *Theories of Organization,* St. Clair Press, Chicago, 1975. The purpose of this collection of summaries and extracts of works of many specialists in the field is to make available briefly and quickly a broad overview of organization theory. A good first look for anyone about to be initiated into management.

Publications

Barrer, Myra E. (pub.), and Barbara Jordan Moore (ed.): *Women Today,* Today Publications and News Service, Inc., National Press Building, Washington, D.C. 20045. Biweekly brief reporting on the latest events relating to women, including legislation, court decisions, activities of federal agencies, professional organizations, and programs and accomplishments of public and private institutions.

Business Week, U.S. News and World Report, Dun's Review, Forbes, Wall Street Journal. All these report with growing frequency on the changes in status of women. Example: "Up the Ladder, Finally: The Corporate Woman," *Business Week,* November 24, 1975, an article fully researched, packed with statistics and case studies.

The Conference Board: *Record: Reporting to Management in Business Affairs,* 845 Third Avenue, New York, N.Y. 10022. Frequent publications, monographs, reports, etc., discussing research in the fields of business economics and business management. Excellently written and researched by staff members. Example: Ruth G. Shaeffer, "New Approaches to Executive Staffing," 1972.

Davis, Susan (pub.), and Karen Wellisch (ed.): *The Spokeswoman,* 5464 South Shore Drive, Chicago, Ill. 60615. Monthly newsletter devoted to information about the work situations of women, including discrimination, political activities, and legal actions. It carries advertisements of professional and managerial positions.

Sandler, Bernice (project director): "Project on the Status and Education of Women," *Newsletter,* from Association of American Colleges, 1818 R Street N.W., Washington, D. C. 20009. Periodic newsletters carry comprehensive, well-researched, and well-documented reports on major issues affecting women. Specialties: Affirmative Action, women in professions, higher education management, political action, etc.

U.S. Government Printing Office, Superintendent of Documents, Washington, D.C. 20402. Publishes a variety of reports, pamphlets, statistical summaries, etc., including material from the Women's Bureau and the Bureau of Labor Statistics, U.S. Department of Labor.

Chapter 9

Starting and Keeping Your Own Business

Nancy Isaac Kuriloff
Arthur H. Kuriloff

Nancy Kuriloff, M.A., specializes in teaching adults at the college level. She has been a facilitator for a graduate women's project, an exploratory program helping women overcome psychological and institutional barriers to success in graduate school. This program was sponsored by the Women's Center and the Chancellor's Affirmative Action Office, University of California, Berkeley. Currently, she is an instructor at the University of California Extension; a conference leader for special programs at the Industrial Relations Center, California Institute of Technology; and a partner of Wordwrights, a management consulting firm in the San Francisco Bay region of California. Her poetry has appeared in *Atlantic, Ploughshares,* and other publications.

Arthur Kuriloff, M.B.A., teaches entrepreneurship, "venture initiation," and small-business management in the Graduate School of Management, University of California, Los Angeles, and practices as a management consultant. He brings to his practice an extensive background in starting and managing small businesses, in line management, and in consulting for industrial organizations. Mr. Kuriloff is the author of *Reality in Management* (McGraw-Hill, 1966) and *Organizational Development for Survival* (American Management Association, 1972) and of numerous articles dealing with management principles and practices.

"I was a novice in business when I started my bookstore. But I was lucky enough to hit on a way to build sales," said Barbara Markowitz, founder and former owner of Barbara's Bookstore in the Old Town section of Chicago.

"I'd always been interested in theater arts, the movies, the stage. But when I searched the bookstores in Chicago I found almost nothing on these subjects. So I built a stock of current books in this field and displayed them prominently in my store.

"I gradually compiled a list of customers interested in movies and the theatre. My store became widely known as the place to go for any book on the cinema or stage and on film makers, playwrights, and theater personalities. This specialty grew to a major and profitable part of my business."

Ms. Markowitz had neatly solved the problem that causes most small businesses to fail—lack of sales. And lack of sales almost always results from managerial incompetence. Fortunately, the skills you need to start your own business and run it successfully can be learned.

ASSESSING YOUR QUALIFICATIONS

If you have a burning desire to create your own business, you should start by checking your qualifications. Do you have the essential characteristics of the enterprising personality?

Entrepreneurs are a special kind of person. They see the world as a place where achievement is possible through the application of their own skills—and they have a strong need for achievement. However, they are not gamblers, despite what conventional wisdom says. They are realistic and optimistic. They want a moderate risk—large enough to be exciting, but with a reasonable hope of reward. They want prompt, accurate feedback on how they're doing. They work harder to reach their goal when they know what is right or wrong about the results they're getting.

Their thinking is more future-oriented than that of others. They tend to anticipate and plan, favoring logical predictions. Once committed to a task, persons with a high need for achievement become absorbed in it. They don't let go, because they can't forgive themselves for an unfinished project.

In summary, those who become successful entrepreneurs show a very high need for achievement. They are more realistic, persistent, energetic, and action-minded than people with other motivational patterns. To judge yourself you must ask the question: How well do I fit the profile of personality with a high need for achievement?

If you want to strengthen characteristics associated with the achievement-oriented, entrepreneurial personality, you can start by reading David C. Mc-

Clelland.[1] Some women have found assertiveness training helpful. Perhaps the best way is to follow Allen Wheelis's prescription: that we are what we do; if we want to change what we are, we must change what we do.[2] This means persistent practice in entrepreneurial behavior.

FINDING IDEAS FOR THE NEW VENTURE

The very worst new business is a "me too" business. Even by selling the same product cheaper, a new business cannot compete with established firms; they have too many resources and too much momentum to be bypassed by inexperienced competition.

You should start your business with a new product or service, or a better one. One way you can generate ideas for a business is to follow these procedures:

- Search for needs that should be filled; necessity often *is* the mother of invention.
- Explore the possibilities in your hobbies or personal interests.
- Anticipate trends in fashion, custom, or social behavior.
- Find deficiencies in the products or services of others.
- Answer the question, "Why isn't there a . . . ?"
- Start your business as a spinoff from your present occupation.
- Search through the patents owned by the federal government available for public use.

FINDING SOURCES OF MONEY

The woman starting a business of her own will need three kinds of money: capital money, short-term money, and personal money.

It's a discouraging fact that very few new businesses produce enough revenue in the first year to eighteen months to pay the owner a salary. You should therefore have enough money set aside to support yourself and your family if need be for at least eighteen months. Funds for personal support should be above and beyond those needed for the business.

Capital money represents funds required for permanent investment in the business. These funds are used for purposes such as buying fixtures and equipment, decorating, purchasing production equipment, and buying starting inventory.

Cash moves in and out of a business as customers pay their bills and the owner pays her suppliers of goods and services. The so-called "cash flow" of the business is the difference between the money coming in and money going out. It is usually figured by the month. If the business pays out more than it takes in, the entrepreneur can find herself without available cash.

The owner who has anticipated the need for operating money under these

---

[1] David C. McClelland, "Achievement Motivation Can Be Developed," *Harvard Business Review,* vol. 43, no. 6, November–December 1965.

[2] Allen Wheelis, "How People Change," *Commentary,* May 1969.

circumstances would arrange early for a short-term loan. Almost every business has the need for short-term money to cover temporary cash-flow deficiencies.

Indeed, this need is often a healthy sign. For example, when a business has built up a large backlog of orders for its product, it must buy quantities of raw materials. A new business that has not yet established a substantial credit rating must pay for these materials immediately. Yet payment for goods shipped to the customers may take an appreciable time to come in—perhaps sixty to ninety days, depending upon the custom in the particular industry. Under these circumstances the company could find itself badly short of cash. The solution is a short-term bank loan, usually thirty to ninety days, sometimes somewhat longer. To build the confidence of your bank in your business, pay off this kind of loan promptly.

Sources of Capital

The least troublesome way for you to raise start-up capital is from your personal resources: savings, or the sale of your stocks or bonds. You may also obtain funds by borrowing against securities and insurance policies, or by mortgaging property.

If your personal resources are inadequate, you might turn to relatives or friends who may be able to lend you the money you need, or who may want to invest in your venture.

In some cases a woman who has the capability and desire to own her own business can negotiate an Economic Opportunity Loan through the Small Business Administration (SBA), an agency of the federal government. To be eligible for this kind of loan, the total family income from all sources, other than welfare, must be insufficient to meet the needs of the family; or the woman must have been denied the opportunity to acquire adequate business financing through normal lending channels, on reasonable terms. The SBA can make a direct loan when funds are available and the circumstances are considered favorable; when funds are not available, the SBA can guarantee up to 90 percent of a bank loan if the prospects of the business warrant this.

Short-Term Funds: What Banks Can Do for You

It is essential for you to establish a solid relationship with a bank. Although banks do not lend money for capital investment in start-ups (". . . they all observe one rule which woe betides the banker who fails to heed it, which is you must never lend any money to anybody unless they don't need it"[3]), banks should be looked to ("because they perform a public service in eliminating the jackasses who go around saying that health and happiness are everything and money isn't essential . . ."[4]) for short-term loans that provide ongoing working cash. Short-term loans are available to help you out of cash-flow problems produced by seasonal bulges or the need to finance large orders.

---

[3] Ogden Nash, from "Bankers Are Just Like Anybody Else, Except Richer," in *The Face is Familiar,* Garden City Publishing Co., Inc., Garden City, N.Y., 1941. Copyright 1935 by Ogden Nash. This poem originally appeared in *The New Yorker.*
    [4] Ibid.

The first thing bankers want to know is how and when they will get their money back. Therefore, they want collateral as a secondary source of repayment if the primary source should fail. The secondary source may be collateral such as stocks or bonds, or a financially responsible person who will cosign the note.

In some kinds of business, banks will finance accounts receivable. Here they will advance you up to about 80 percent of the amount of the sale. Your customer is not notified and does not know that the bank has advanced you this money. As the borrower, you are still responsible for collecting the money due you from your customer. You must repay the bank whether or not your customer pays you. If your business is such that you can finance your accounts receivable, you must be sure that you deal only with reputable customers whose credit rating is high.

Although banks will not lend money for a start-up business, many will advance funds for this purpose on a loan guaranteed by the SBA. You can get approval from the SBA for a 90-percent-guaranteed loan *after* you have been turned down by the bank. Then, many banks will grant the loan because their risk is now limited to only 10 percent of the total amount advanced.

The most important aspect of your relationship with your banker is credibility. The better your banker understands your business and recognizes your integrity, the more likely it is that your bank will be responsive to your needs when you ask for a loan.

BASIC MANAGEMENT STRENGTHS YOU WILL NEED

Management is often said to be a combination of art and science. If you have the latent capabilities, the art emerges and develops with experience; the scientific aspects of management can be learned. Thus you can gain the knowledge you need to improve your chances for starting and keeping a successful business before you open your doors. The most critical functions you should learn—and the ones that many would-be enterprisers are woefully ignorant of—are these: management of the technical part of the business, that is, the functions that get out the product or service; marketing, as distinguished from selling; and controlling the finances of the business to keep it solvent.

The Product or Service

You should know the technical end of the business thoroughly—how to make the product or perform the service, in all details—before you start your own firm. To try to learn a business while starting it can be disastrous. There are too many other concerns that will absorb your time and energy. Know-how is hard to come by. If you do not have it, find a job in the business you want to enter. Work there for a year or two, keeping alert to every detail of what goes on. Learn all you can by observing the strengths and the weaknesses of the operation. Identify opportunities for improvement. Prepare yourself for your own business by studying and learning how to manage; pay special attention to marketing and financial control.

The benefits of this systematic approach can be enormous. You will learn the major pitfalls in starting and running a business; you will learn what to do to avoid them; and you will earn a salary while you learn.

Marketing

We have already said that most small businesses fail because of lack of sales. But you should be keenly aware that making the sale is the *last* step in a fundamental process of management called *marketing*.

The difference between marketing and selling marks a difference in point of view between what *you* want and what your *customer* may want. A strictly sales-oriented viewpoint can drive your company into bankruptcy, because it focuses on your needs. Marketing, on the other hand, focuses on the needs of your customer.

Becoming marketing-minded means that you will work to discover and satisfy the needs of your customer by providing a product or service the customer perceives as valuable. You must not fall in love with your product or service. Respect it; but, in the entrepreneurial manner, view it as objectively as you can. In one sense your product or service is a means and not an end in itself. The end is a profitable and viable business. The product or service is your means for achieving this end. Therefore, learn how to adapt your product or service to meet the needs of your prospective customers.

You need not necessarily engage the services of a marketing consultant to do a marketing study. You can take several steps yourself to learn a great deal about your product, its acceptability, and what to do to get it to the customer and sell it at a price that will make you a profit.

Why Would Your Customer Buy? The first question you should ask is: Why would a customer buy? To answer the question you must find out the tangible and intangible benefits a customer would get by buying your product or service.

A simple and effective way to start is to list the advantages and disadvantages of your product or service as objectively as you can. Do this with pencil and paper. Divide a page with a vertical line down the middle. Mark the left side "advantages." Under this title list all the benefits to the customer that you can think of. These might include such items as these: the economy of your product or service compared with those already on the market; its convenience as compared with other products or services; its special usefulness in performing a job that nothing now on the market can do; or its character as a status symbol for the buyer. Now mark the right side of the page "disadvantages." This list might include items like the following: the price is too high; use of my product or service would require a change in the customer's current habits; service and maintenance problems are hard to solve; the product or service is subject to rapid obsolescence.

Specify these advantages and disadvantages as cold-bloodedly as you can. This does some important things for you. It helps you avoid what is often called "marketing myopia," or shortsightedness, about your product or service. It forces you to seek ways to overcome the disadvantages and capitalize on the advantages of what you have to offer.

Having satisfied yourself on these points, the next step is to employ several *focus groups* to discover something about the reactions of prospective customers. A focus group is simply a small gathering of acquaintances you have asked to come together, perhaps for coffee or wine and cheese. It's probably best to invite acquaintances rather than close friends because you want to find out as objectively as you can what your group sees as advantages and disadvantages of the product or service you intend to market.

When the members of the focus group have settled down, you should tell them that you'd like to get their opinions about the product or service you're considering. Your task is to listen carefully to the comments without in any way trying to defend your product or any feature of your offering. You can ask questions to elicit honest answers, however. You might ask, for instance, "Can you see any way to make this widget easier to use?" Or, "Would you be willing to replace your present widget with one of these, even though the price might be a bit higher?" Eventually you might get some notion of what price to put on your product or service. You might ask, "Would you be willing to pay $75 for this widget in view of the advantages you see?" If the answer is no, you can arrive at a roughly acceptable price by further questioning.

By compiling the data from three or four focus groups you will have reasonably sound ideas about the advantages and disadvantages of your proposed product or service. You will have an idea of what an acceptable price might be. Admittedly, this group process is not a scientifically accurate procedure. But it will give you some guidelines to follow in improving the acceptability of your product or service and in setting your price.

Impact of External Forces in the Marketing Environment   Business is subject to a variety of continually changing environmental forces. These forces, unless recognized early and responded to, can damage a business severely. But they can also give the alert owner an opportunity for gain. Some of the more important forces that you must be alert to are economic, social, competitive, legislative, and technological.

Changes in the economy affect the way customers buy. During periods of recession, they become more discriminating; inflation produces the same effect. Customers want value for their money; they carefully assess what they buy. As the owner of a small firm, whether a manufacturer or a retailer, you can capitalize on this trend by offering intensely *personal* service. You can ensure that your customer not only *gets* real value, but also *appreciates* the value you're giving. What you want is "brand loyalty." You want your customer to be a steady, repeat buyer of what you have to offer. As the entrepreneur of a small business, you have a special opportunity to know and fulfill your customers' needs—and thereby to build a steady repeat business.[5]

[5] Benson P. Shapiro, "Manage the Customer, Not Just the Sales Force," *Harvard Business Review*, vol. 52, no. 5, September–October 1974.

Social forces include changing expectations, trends, manners, custom, and fashions. Any of these may offer you the opportunity to find a newer and more profitable thing to do. As an instance, current trends show an upswing in the popularity of do-it-yourself activities. People want the experience of participating in sports such as tennis, golf, hiking and backpacking, and scuba diving. Home gardening is not only a satisfying activity; it also gains popularity as vegetables increase in price.

Changing social forces can bring danger to your business as well as opportunity. A sudden shift in manners, custom, or fashion can leave you with an obsolete product or service. Therefore, you must keep on top of the positive and negative implications of social change.

It is an accepted fact that the entrepreneurial act of innovation, of bringing out an attractive product or service, is the basis for profitability in business. The firm that is innovative and successful automatically invites competition. Consequently, you must be continually creative and innovative if you want your company to remain prosperous and to endure. You must be ready to add attractive features to your product or service as your competitors bring out their copies. Or you must be prepared to launch new products or services as your existing offerings are copied or become obsolescent.

Legislative regulations demand that you keep specific records and observe legal requirements. You will be obliged to keep abreast of tax laws, labor laws, equal-employment laws, and many others. To do this you will want to rely on professional help, at least from your lawyer and your accountant, from the time you decide to set up a business. An old management maxim says that if you can't afford to hire a lawyer and an accountant to help you set up your business, you can't afford to start a business.

Constant awareness of technological forces is also imperative in starting and succeeding in business. This awareness is more important in some businesses than in others, but you will soon see that no business is free from the impact of changing technology. If you are making a product, you may find advantages in some form of mechanized inventory control. As your business grows, you may want to rent a computer terminal to use for storing and retrieving management information: in accounting, in cash-flow analysis, and in other financial areas. If you own a bookstore, you may want to use a tape-operated typewriter to turn out several hundred "personalized" letters describing new books to your customers. If you are in a technical field such as electronics, you will understand that keeping abreast of technology is crucial to survival. Profit and progress can come only from being aware of new ideas and taking advantage of them to satisfy your customers' needs.

Customers' Buying Habits   To aim your marketing effort effectively, you must know a great deal about your target customer. Your effort should be directed at defining the profile of your customer. To do this you must find the answers to the following questions:

● Who buys: age, income, race, location?

- What does the customer buy now—and how does my product or service fit or compare with others?
- How does the customer prefer to buy: impulsively, carefully; with cash, credit, deferred payments?
- Where does the customer buy: retail stores, wholesale outlet, mail order, door-to-door sales?
- When does the customer buy: seasonally, cyclically, frequently, or occasionally?

You can find the answers yourself for most of the practical purposes of your business, as the next section will indicate. When you have an adequate set of answers, you should check them against the information you have developed about your product or service and the impact of the external forces in the environment on your business. From this analysis you will be able to outline the buying profile of the typical customer for your product or service.

Demographics of the Intended Market Do not imagine that you can sell your product to every customer everywhere. It's not probable. The intent of the marketing method is to help you define the special niche in the marketplace where you can be successful with your special appeal—and your limited resources. You must understand in some detail the data that tell you where your potential customers are and whether there are enough of them there to support your business. For example, if you were setting up a retail shop, you would want to know how many families in the right age and income brackets live within a ten-minute driving range of it. Many sources of information are available to you. Among these are:

- The public library. Reference librarians are usually pleased to assist you.
- Graduate schools of business administration at universities have excellent reference libraries. Sometimes you can get the help of graduate students in a marketing study if you approach a professor of marketing who may be looking for real-life projects for students.
- Entrepreneurs successful in the field you're interested in. Most successful people enjoy talking about their experiences. If you tell a successful businessperson that you're setting up your business in another part of town, or in a different specialty, you can learn much about market conditions and marketing methods that have been successful—and those that haven't.

You can gather an impressive array of information from these sources and others that you will hit on along the way. Your task will be to study these data and to pull from them the specific information you need to identify your niche in the market and to assess its possibilities for profitability.

Criteria for Segmenting the Market Three criteria should be used for judging the worth of the segment of the market you have pinpointed. These are measurability, substantiality, and accessibility.

Measurability means that you should be able to put together a reasonable set of numbers about your segment of the market. These would include the number of potential customers, the average sale you expect to make in dollars, and an estimate of the sales you'll make per day, per week, and per month.

From these data you will be able to judge the *substantiality* of your intended market. You can then answer the key question: Is there enough potential for me to cultivate? In other words, are there enough possible sales dollars out there to give me reasonable assurance that I can launch a profitable business?

Finally, your study should tell you about the *accessibility* of your market—whether you can reach it through promotion and distribution. The specific business you enter will determine what you can do to promote it—through advertising in the local paper or over the local radio station; by direct-mail advertising; or by other means.

Every effort should be aimed at projecting the unique image you want—from the letterhead on your stationery and the design on the packing box in which you ship your product to the way your personnel answer the telephone.

Without the proper channels for reaching your intended customer, you have little chance for success. Different businesses have different channels of distribution. You must find out and use the best way of getting your product to market. You may need to use wholesalers, or other intermediates; to develop a door-to-door sales force; to sell by mail; or simply to open a retail store in a carefully selected location.

Once you have made decisions in these matters of promotion and distribution, you are ready to check and refine you marketing objectives. You should review your original ideas and concepts—your objectives—about whom you wanted as your customers and how you expected to reach them. You can check the results of your marketing study against the consumer evaluation profile you developed earlier. If your original objectives still look feasible and your estimated sales volume appears realistic, you have cleared a major hurdle on the way to setting up in business.

Pricing   One other consideration you must face in the marketing area is setting the price for your product or service. You will have gained some idea of the price range from your marketing study. You must now decide what price to set. You have two alternatives: you may set a high price, intending to recover your initial investment quickly; or you may enter the field at a low price, intending to penetrate the market with a high volume of sales. Much depends on the quality of your offering. If it is unique and attractive, you would be wise to set the price high. There are two reasons for this decision. You will "skim the cream" and get your investment back quickly at the high price. And customers judge quality—whether logically or not—by price. High price implies high quality.

It is always easier to lower a price than to raise it. As competition arises following your success, you will be able to counter it by dropping your price judiciously. By that time you should have recovered your initial investment and would be in a solid position to fend off the upstart competition.

Feedback from the Market Finally, study the signals that come to you from the moment you open your doors—or receive replies to your first letters. The reactions of your customers and the way your competitors respond to your entry are important feedback that will help you avoid difficulties you otherwise might not be aware of.

Do not overlook information from the people who work for you. They are often close to the customer. They develop ideas for improvements in the product or service. By asking them openly for this kind of data, you can often improve your operations.

Using feedback intelligently is a sure way to avoid marketing myopia.

Controlling Finances

The third managerial strength you will require in your business is the ability to control your finances. Financial control implies that you know where you are now, where you're going to be shortly, and where you want to be in the future. Several critical projections should be made before you actually start your business. Once the business is under way, you'll update these plans by inserting actual figures from operations, month by month, to replace the educated guesses you started with. In this way you'll gain intimate and accurate knowledge of the financial health of your organization—and by detecting the symptoms of dysfunction early, you'll be able to take corrective measures to prevent financial ailments from overcoming your firm.

The financial plans you should become familiar with include the following:

- Projected profit-and-loss statements and balance sheets for the first two years, by quarters and years.
- Cash-flow analysis for two years, by months.
- Breakeven statement for minimum sales goals for two years, by the year.
- Fixed-asset acquisition schedule, by the month; this will be needed only for building up the fixtures and equipment at the start.

The condensed scope of this presentation does not allow a detailed description of these important financial plans. You will find procedures for preparing them in the references given in the bibliography on page 169.

PROACTIVE MANAGEMENT FOR STARTING AND KEEPING YOUR BUSINESS

"Reactive" managers let things happen; "proactive" managers make things happen. Most managers are reactive managers; they spend their energies in coping with day-to-day problems, racing to put out one brush fire after another. If the idea of starting your own business has captured your imagination and you believe that you have the entrepreneurial spirit, you can start right now to be a proactive manager—that is, a forward-looking, forward-planning manager, one who makes things happen the way she wants them to. You will plan your business world to be the way you want it. You will support your business at the start, and it will support you in the long run. You will start and keep your business.

The following guide summarizes the key points that will help you to be a proactive enterpriser and business manager:

Identify a product or service that:

- Fills a potential customer's need
- Offers unique, attractive advantages and performs as specified
- You can produce with your resources
- You can sell at a price that yields a profit
- Pleases the customer so that you develop "brand acceptance"

Develop your managerial skills so that you are capable of:

- Analyzing your potential market
- Developing a marketing plan
- Testing your approach before making large investments
- Building customer appeal into your product or service
- Manufacturing in quantity with quality
- Managing financial affairs
- Making projections of sales volume, potential profits, cash flow, capital needed, and the facilities and organization required
- Building an organization capable of carrying out your plans
- Setting up controls so that you can measure your performance against what you've planned
- Avoiding the pitfalls that cause failure
- Capitalizing on your unique strengths

By performing the managerial act in a proactive way, with just a little bit of luck, you can make your dream of being your own boss come true.

BIBLIOGRAPHY

Levitt, Theodore: *Innovation in Marketing,* McGraw-Hill, New York, 1962. A classic presentation that tells how to avoid marketing myopia and offers valuable suggestions for developing new ideas for profit and growth.

McClelland, David C.: *The Achieving Society,* Free Press, New York, 1967. This paperback tells of McClelland's studies in entrepreneurship and the economic impact of enterprisers in various societies. Chapters 2, 6, and 7 are especially devoted to describing the achievement motive, entrepreneurial behavior, and characteristics of entrepreneurs.

Schollhammer, Hans, and Arthur H. Kuriloff: *Entrepreneurship and Small Business Management,* Wiley/Hamilton, New York, 1978. This textbook covers in considerable detail how to start a business and how to manage it successfully once it is started. An excellent source for learning in some depth the subjects in this chapter, including financial projections and marketing-feasibility analysis.

Steinhoff, Dan: *Small Business Management Fundamentals,* McGraw-Hill, New York, 1974. An excellent elementary text. The treatment of marketing analysis and financial planning is particularly suitable for beginners.

Part Three

Taking Good Care
of Yourself

Chapter 10

Maintaining the Best of Health: Nutrition and Diet

Tomi K. Haas

Tomi K. Haas, M.S., is District Director of Public Health Nutrition, Los Angeles County Department of Health Services. She is a lecturer, consultant, and writer, as well as a special program coordinator for television.

The emphasis today is on the quality of life rather than on just living longer. At present, the average life span for men and women in the technologically advanced nations is about seventy-three years. Immunization and better health care and diet add to longevity, and increased professional obstetrical care enables more infants and women to survive childbirth. As a result, reaching the age of seventy-three is no feat today—but reaching it with zest, strength, independence, and a healthy curiosity for the next encounter is another matter, and that is what, at any age, *living* is all about.

An old story illustrates this point. Three men—one seventy, one eighty, and one ninety years old—were rocking away on the veranda at a seaside resort. They were discussing how they would like to die. The seventy-year-old said, "I just want to slip away quietly, like this, while I am peacefully rocking." The eighty-year-old said, "That is not exciting enough for me. I want to go up in an airplane, have a grand crash, and that's it—go out with a bang, not a whimper." The ninety-year-old considered for a while. "You are both too tame," he said. "I want to be shot by a jealous husband."

The desire to have all one's faculties to the very end is a strong one for most human beings. It spurred Ponce de León to seek the Fountain of Youth, it makes us all respond to the idea of a Shangri-la. Just open a copy of *Vogue* or *Harper's Bazaar,* or any of the family magazines with their endless guides to beauty and physical fitness, and you will see that people are still looking for the secret of eternal youth.

That secret has never been found, of course; so far, the aging process cannot be reversed. However, it can be slowed down, and the prime of life can be lengthened, through good health care.

Taking care of oneself incorporates all the areas of knowledge implied by the term "good health habits." Rest, exercise, cleanliness, proper food (from before conception to the end of our lives), and regular immunizations all play their part in improving the quality of health. Most people in the United States today have little excuse for not making appropriate choices in these areas. For example, if one lives above the poverty level, one has access to an enormous variety of foods during all seasons. For the most part, readers of this book will have sufficient income to make the purchases that their health requires, and far more. In fact, in our affluent society, some people are eating too much of the more expensive cuts of meat, which contain a great deal of saturated fat.

Choosing foods which will contribute to, rather than undermine, health is a crucial part of taking care of oneself. The ability and the will to choose wisely are crucial to the improvement of health and thus to the improvement of the quality of our lives. Some people eat irregularly (coffee breaks, hasty lunches, snacks, and all the foods denied during the day crammed into dinner and the hours just before bedtime), and, as a result, elevate their blood cholesterol.[1] Others choose overly refined and processed foods (in the United States 102 pounds of refined sugar per person per year are consumed)[2] without a suitable amount of fruits, vegetables, and cereals; this decreases bulk and intestinal motility.

To help you know *what, where, when, why,* and *how* to eat, and to help you make better choices for maintaining health and the quality of life, is the purpose of this chapter.

HEALTH MAINTENANCE

To nutritionists, "health maintenance" means eating foods which provide the amount and variety of nutrients needed by the body to carry out its daily functions. The science of nutrition investigates all the body processes which incorporate nutrients; the foods which we eat are the source of these nutrients.

[1] Charlotte Young et al., "Metabolic Effects of Meal Frequency on Normal Young Men," *Journal of the American Dietetic Association,* vol. 61, no. 4, October 1972, p. 391.
[2] Richard L. Hall, "Food Additives," *Nutrition Today,* vol. 8, no. 4, July–August 1973, p. 20.

Some fifty to sixty nutrients are found in the body, of which many are known to be essential. Unless certain types of foods are eaten regularly, some of these essential nutrients—called "key nutrients"—may be missing. When this occurs, symptoms of deficiency appear.

In order to be sure that the key nutrients, and those whose precise need and function are yet to be discovered, are provided for in the diet, it is best for people to eat a *variety* of foods. Enough to eat, and a variety of food types, will ensure good nutrition. This is far better than any stringent and restrictive diet, which can be dangerous to one's health.

Some of the key nutrients are vitamins. Vitamins have been chemically isolated only in this century; before that, deficiency diseases such as scurvy, rickets, beriberi, pellagra, and certain eye diseases were not understood, although their presence was noted in ancient texts. Scurvy, for example, was rampant among sailors on long voyages, but when ships could put into ports where fresh foods were available, scurvy was minimal. Before long the correlation was made: with fresh foods, scurvy could be prevented.[3]

Immigrants to the United States who had come from the villages and farmlands of Europe worked to raise their social level. White bread was for them the symbol of upward mobility. They disdained the coarse, black bread of European peasants—with a consequent loss of nutrients. No program of nutrition education has succeeded in reversing this process. But by 1940, the major vitamins could be chemically produced, making it possible to fortify various foods. During World War II, to improve the nutrition of a population at war, and with food in short supply, a general program of fortification was begun. As long as white bread was preferred, the solution was to add to it the most important nutrients lost in the refining process. Thus thiamine (vitamin B_1), riboflavin (vitamin B_2), niacin (vitamin B_3), and iron were returned to white bread in the amounts naturally found in the whole-grain product. Margarine was fortified with vitamin A to make it equivalent to butter; milk was fortified with vitamin D because it is already a rich source of the calcium and phosphorus needed for bone and tooth formation in the presence of vitamin D.

To change people's food habits is a major undertaking. Age-old customs (such as the Oriental preference for white rice over brown), class-consciousness, and the pressures of mass marketing all influence food preferences. Only through education, social change (such as the insistence of many young people today on nutrition), and positive models in the mass media can food habits be altered.

KEY NUTRIENTS

If you want to be your own person where food choices are concerned, be sure you are clear about the thirteen established key nutrients. These, and foods in which they are found, are listed below and summarized in Illustration 1.

---

[3] Stanley Davidson and R. Passmore, *Normal Nutrition and Dietetics,* 4th ed., Williams and Wilkins, Baltimore, Md., 1970, p. 424.

FOOD FOR YOUNG FAMILIES

This chart summarizes the key nutrients, why each is needed, and foods that are good sources of each nutrient. It will help you understand why you should eat a wide variety of food to be well-nourished and healthy.

Nutrient	Why needed	Some important sources

PROTEIN

1. Builds and maintains all tissues.
2. Forms an important part of enzymes, hormones, and body fluids.
3. Supplies energy.

Proteins of top quality for tissue building and repair are found in lean meat, poultry, fish, seafoods, eggs, milk, and cheese. Next best for proteins are dry beans, peas, and nuts. Cereals, bread, vegetables, and fruits also provide some protein but of lower quality.

CALCIUM

1. Builds bones and teeth.
2. Helps blood to clot.
3. Helps nerves, muscles, and heart to function properly.

Milk—whole, skim, buttermilk—fresh, dried, canned; cheese; ice cream; leafy vegetables such as collards, dandelion, kale, mustard and turnip greens.

IRON

1. Combines with protein to make hemoglobin, the red substance of blood which carries oxygen from the lungs to muscles, brain, and other parts of the body.
2. Helps cells use oxygen.

Liver, kidney, heart, oysters, lean meat, egg yolk, dry beans, dark-green leafy vegetables, dried fruit, whole grain and enriched bread and cereals, and molasses.

VITAMIN A

1. Helps eyes adjust to dim light.
2. Helps keep skin smooth.
3. Helps keep lining of mouth, nose, throat, and digestive tract healthy and resistant to infection.
4. Promotes growth.

Liver; dark-green and deep-yellow vegetables such as broccoli, turnip and other leafy greens, carrots, pumpkin, sweet potatoes, winter squash; apricots, cantaloupe; butter, fortified margarine.

THIAMINE

1. Helps body cells obtain energy from food.
2. Helps keep nerves in healthy condition.
3. Promotes good appetite and digestion.

Lean pork, heart, kidney, liver, dry beans and peas, whole grain and enriched cereals and breads, and some nuts.

ASCORBIC ACID (Vitamin C)

1. Helps hold body cells together and strengthens walls of blood vessels.
2. Helps in healing wounds.
3. Helps resist infection.

Cantaloupe, grapefruit, oranges, strawberries, broccoli, brussels sprouts, raw cabbage, collards, green and sweet red peppers, mustard and turnip greens, potatoes cooked in jacket, and tomatoes.

Nutrient	Why needed	Some important sources

RIBOFLAVIN

1. Helps cells use oxygen to release energy from food.
2. Helps keep eyes healthy.
3. Helps keep skin around mouth and nose smooth.

Milk, liver, kidney, heart, lean meat, eggs, and dark leafy greens.

NIACIN

1. Helps the cells of the body use oxygen to produce energy.
2. Helps to maintain health of skin, tongue, digestive tract, and nervous system.

Liver, yeast, lean meat, poultry, fish, leafy greens, peanuts and peanut butter, beans and peas, and whole grain and enriched breads and cereals.

VITAMIN D

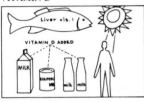

1. Helps body use calcium and phosphorus to build strong bones and teeth, important in growing children and during pregnancy and lactation.

Fish liver oils; foods fortified with vitamin D, such as milk. Direct sunlight produces vitamin D from cholesterol in the skin.

CARBOHYDRATES

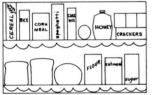

1. Supply food energy.
2. Help body use fat efficiently.
3. Spare protein for purposes of body building and repair.

Starches: Breads, cereals, corn, grits, potatoes, rice, spaghetti, macaroni, and noodles. Sugars: Honey, molasses, sirups, sugar, and other sweets.

FATS

1. Supply food energy in compact form (weight for weight supplies twice as much energy as carbohydrates).
2. Some supply essential fatty acids.
3. Help body use certain other nutrients.

Cooking fats and oils, butter, margarine, salad dressings, and oils.

WATER

1. Important part of all cells and fluids in body.
2. Carrier of nutrients to and waste from cells in the body.
3. Aids in digestion and absorption of food.
4. Helps to regulate body temperature.
5. Lubricates body joints.

Water, beverages, soup, fruits and vegetables. Most foods contain some water.

Illustration 1 Key nutrients. (*Developed by Extension Nutritionists of North Carolina, South Carolina, and Virginia Federal Extension Service, Cooperative Extension Work, U.S.D.A. and State Land-Grant Colleges and Universities.*)

Vitamins

The essentiality of each vitamin is proved by the fact that a deficiency disease occurs when it is withheld for a certain period of time.

Vitamins	*Foods*
A	Dark green, leafy vegetables; fruits and vegetables uniformly colored throughout: carrots, sweet potatoes, apricots, papayas
B_1	Cereals, breads, meats
B_2	Milk and its products, cereals, and breads
B_3	Cereals and breads
B_{12}	Foods of animal origin only
C	Broccoli, green peppers, citrus fruits, canteloupe, strawberries
Folacin	Green, leafy vegetables; cereals and bread
D	Fortified foods (e.g., milk), or sunshine

Minerals

Without calcium, the growth of bones and teeth (hard tissue) is not possible; the irritability of muscle tissue (including the brain and heart) is not possible; and the blood will not clot. Without iron, anemia becomes widespread, particularly among adolescent boys and girls and women of childbearing age.[4]

Minerals	*Foods*
Calcium	Milk and its products; some green, leafy vegetables
Iron	Meat (especially organ meats); cereals and breads; some green, leafy vegetables; dried fruits such as prunes and raisins

Calorie Producers

The calorie producers are protein, carbohydrate, and fat.

Calorie producers	*Foods*
Protein	Milk and its products; meat, poultry, fish, beans, nuts, eggs
Carbohydrate	Breads and cereals; sugar
Fat	Lard, oil, dairy products (butter and cream)

Protein   There are eight essential amino acids (ten with arginine and histidine) out of the twenty-two presently known. The body combines amino acids in infinite patterns to make the specific proteins which form the various body tissues—bones, skin, blood, hair, body organs, muscles, and so on. Eight of these amino acids cannot be manufactured by the body itself but must be acquired through the foods we eat.

[4] U.S. Department of Health, Education and Welfare, *Ten-State Nutrition Survey 1968–1970,* publication no. (HSM) 72–8130, Health Science Mental Administration Center for Disease Control, Atlanta, Ga.

When a food contains all the essential amino acids in the amounts required by human beings, it is biologically complete. Proteins from animal sources (meat, fish, poultry, milk, and eggs) are biologically complete. It is possible to meet protein requirements from sources other than animals by combining plant proteins (beans, seeds, and nuts) with cereal proteins (wheat, oats, and rice): in this way, two incomplete sources of protein combine and support each other to form a biologically whole source.

It is important that people meet protein requirements in periods of rapid growth. Thus for pregnant women, lactating women, infants, and adolescents, proteins are crucial. But it is also important for individuals not to overindulge in proteins, doubling and tripling protein intake beyond actual need. This is expensive and injurious. Protein which is used for energy undergoes a complicated metabolic process, and the excess is stored as fat. The degradation of amino acids in the process of converting protein to energy increases toxic substances in the body which need to be excreted. This adds an unnecessary burden to the kidneys. Another danger in a high-protein diet is an increase in saturated fat with an accompanying increase in cholesterol.[5]

Carbohydrates Carbohydrates, though much maligned, are essential producers of energy. Their caloric value is equivalent to that of protein (4 calories per gram). The richest sources of carbohydrates have been bread, wheat, rice, and maize for countless generations. A crop failure in any one of these foods can result in starvation for whole populations.

In carbohydrates are found essential vitamins and minerals, and supplemental protein. Carbohydrates are utilized by the body as glucose, the basic energy source for all internal body functions and gross motor activity.

A goodly intake of carbohydrates is essential to meet calorie requirements, but a very high intake of carbohydrates is unnecessary. The normal person may meet energy needs with about 300 grams of carbohydrate daily. Also, it is important to avoid carbohydrate-rich foods with little nutritional value—for example, sugar (the purest form in which carbohydrate is commercially available) in sweetened beverages or mixed with fat in such products as chocolate, cakes, cookies, and candy. Such products are high in calories but have little food value.

Fat The body processes require certain essential fatty acids. These are needed for the absorption and utilization of fat-soluble vitamins, for energy, and for keeping the skin supple. Most of us eat a great deal more fat than we realize as a component of cheese, meat, sauces, dressings, eggs, chocolate, bakery goods, and snack foods. Deep-fat frying can triple or quadruple the caloric value of a food. If Americans consumed less fat, many of our health problems would be reduced—obesity and heart disease, for example. Fat gives us the highest energy value of all foods: 9 calories per gram.

[5] American Medical Association, Council on Foods and Nutrition, "A Critique of Low Carbohydrate Ketogenic Weight Reduction Regimens," *Nutrition Reviews: A Special Supplement—Nutrition Misinformation and Food Faddism,* July 1974, pp. 15, 14.

The Four Food Groups

Many foods contain more than one nutrient and thus appear under more than one of the key nutrients in our lists. For convenience and simplicity in explaining a "balanced diet," nutritionists list foods in four main categories—the four food groups. All the needs of the individual for the key nutrients (as well as those nutrients not yet specified) will be met if sufficient foods are eaten daily from each of the four food groups.

Food groups	*Key nutrients*
Group I: Milk and its products	Protein, riboflavin, calcium, fat, vitamin B_{12}
Group II: Meat and its substitutes	Protein, iron, fat, vitamin B_{12}
Group III: Fruits and vegetables	Vitamin A, vitamin C, folacin (folic acid)
Group IV: Breads and cereals	Vitamin B complex, iron, carbohydrate, some protein

The amount of food necessary from each of the four food groups for people of various ages is shown in Illustration 2.

EVALUATING YOUR DIET

If you check your diet and find that it is balanced—that you are eating sufficient amounts from each of the four food groups—you will also discover that you have met two-thirds or more of daily dietary allowances recommended by the National Research Council.[6] However, if you omit any one of the four food groups and are low in another, you will find you meet less than half the requirements set by the National Research Council for most nutrients.

The standards of the National Research Council—the recommended dietary allowances—are no longer the tool of scientists alone; they have become a tool for many intelligent American consumers. The Labeling Act of 1974 requires that any food package which makes any nutritional claim such as "enriched" or "fortified" must display specific nutritional information about the product, expressed as percentages of the United States Recommended Dietary Allowances (USRDA) for a normal serving.[7] (See Illustration 3.)

The public demand for accurate nutritional information today has resulted in better labeling, more truth in advertising, and governmental regulation of the food industry. As the demands and the results become more widespread, a higher standard of nutrition can be achieved by all of us.

Now, what about you? Can you assess your own patterns of food intake? Do

[6] *Recommended Dietary Allowances,* 8th ed., Committee on Dietary Allowances, Food and Nutrition Board, National Research Council, National Academy of Sciences, Washington, D.C., 1974.
[7] Arletta Beloran, *Nutrition Labels: A Great Leap Forward,* FDA Consumer, DHEW publication no. (FDA) 74–2012, September 1973; O. C. Johnson, "The Food and Drug Administration and Labelings," *Journal of the American Dietetic Association,* vol. 64, no. 5, May 1974, p. 471.

Follow the Food Guide
Every Day

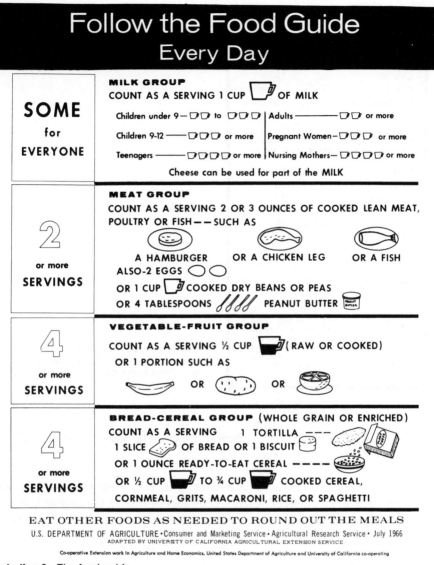

SOME for **EVERYONE**	**MILK GROUP** COUNT AS A SERVING 1 CUP OF MILK Children under 9— to | Adults ———— or more Children 9-12 ——— or more | Pregnant Women— or more Teenagers ——— or more | Nursing Mothers— or more Cheese can be used for part of the MILK
2 or more **SERVINGS**	**MEAT GROUP** COUNT AS A SERVING 2 OR 3 OUNCES OF COOKED LEAN MEAT, POULTRY OR FISH — — SUCH AS A HAMBURGER OR A CHICKEN LEG OR A FISH ALSO-2 EGGS OR 1 CUP COOKED DRY BEANS OR PEAS OR 4 TABLESPOONS PEANUT BUTTER
4 or more **SERVINGS**	**VEGETABLE-FRUIT GROUP** COUNT AS A SERVING ½ CUP (RAW OR COOKED) OR 1 PORTION SUCH AS OR OR
4 or more **SERVINGS**	**BREAD-CEREAL GROUP** (WHOLE GRAIN OR ENRICHED) COUNT AS A SERVING 1 TORTILLA 1 SLICE OF BREAD OR 1 BISCUIT OR 1 OUNCE READY-TO-EAT CEREAL OR ½ CUP TO ¾ CUP COOKED CEREAL, CORNMEAL, GRITS, MACARONI, RICE, OR SPAGHETTI

EAT OTHER FOODS AS NEEDED TO ROUND OUT THE MEALS

U.S. DEPARTMENT OF AGRICULTURE • Consumer and Marketing Service • Agricultural Research Service • July 1966
ADAPTED BY UNIVERSITY OF CALIFORNIA AGRICULTURAL EXTENSION SERVICE

Co-operative Extension work In Agriculture and Home Economics, United States Department of Agriculture and University of California co-operating

Illustration 2   The food guide.

you know where you stand in relation to the recommended dietary allowance standards? Here is a systematic way to find out.

Food Record

Keep a daily record of everything you eat from the time you get up in the morning until the time you go to bed at night. Keep your record under the following headings.

NUTRITION INFORMATION
Per 1 Cup Serving; Contains 4-1 Cup Servings

Calories	150
Protein	9 grams
Carbohydrate	14 grams
Fat	6 grams

PERCENT OF U.S. RECOMMENDED DAILY ALLOWANCE (U.S. RDA)

Protein	15
Vitamin A	20
Vitamin C	10
Thiamine (Vitamin B_1)	6
Riboflavin (Vitamin B_2)	8
Niacin	4
Calcium	*
Iron	2

*Contains less than 2% of U.S. RDA for this nutrient

INGREDIENTS: WHOLE WHEAT, BROWN SUGAR, CORN SYRUP, SOLIDS, COCONUT OIL, SOYA FLOUR, WHEY, SAFFLOWER OIL, SALT, ASCORBIC ACID, NIACINAMIDE, THIAMINE MONONITRATE, VITAMIN A PALMITATE, RIBOFLAVIN, ARTIFICIAL FLAVOR AND COLOR.

Illustration 3   A sample food label. *(John W. Gage*, The Guide to Better Nutrition, *Food Nutrition—Hoffman La Roche, Inc., Nutley, N.J.)*

Time   Record when you eat, how often you eat, and at what intervals you eat.

Food   Record the kinds of food eaten. This will reveal the quality of your diet in relation to recommended daily allowances for your age and situation. Be sure to list foods singly and not as a composite—for example, "bread, margarine, mustard, bologna, lettuce," not "sandwich."

Amount   Record in logical units of measurement, such as "cup," "teaspoon," "slice," "medium size (fruit)," and "cubic inch (cheese)."

Place   Record the place where the food was eaten: "at home," "in a restaurant," "in the kitchen," "at the snack cart," "at the refrigerator."

Position   Record your position while eating: "sitting at the dining room table," "standing," "sitting in a car," "lying down," etc.

Circumstances   Record the situation: "alone," "with company," "at mealtime," "because of boredom," and so on.

Illustration 4

Evaluating Your Food Record

Foods eaten, by food groups	Need	Amount eaten	To be added	Comments
Milk: ½ c milk 4 tbsp.milk Ice cream, ½ cup Milk equiv. = ½ of portion	2 (8-ounce cups)	1 cup	1 cup	Probably low in calcium; not made up for by other food choices.
Meat: Peanut butter, 2 tbsp. beef, 3 tbsp.	2 (2-ounce servings)	1½ servings	1 ounce	If calculated, total will probably come close to RDA by adding cereal protein.
Vegetables and fruits: *Vitamin A:* Carrot, 1 *Vitamin C:* *Other:* Potato, ½ on- ion Turnip, ¼	3 times a week 1 2 ½ cup, or 1 medium	1 0 2	OK None OK	No rich source of vitamin C. Probably low in Vitamin C, since potato and turnip would have been cooked for a long time.
Breads and cereals: Bread, 4 slices Cold cereal, ¾ cup	4 slices or ½ cup serving	5	OK	
Extras: Sugar, 5 tsp. Doughnut Jelly, 1 tbsp. Soft drink Candy bar Martini Cookies, 3	Slight			Total calories probably above need. Calorie value of alcohol, 7 per gram. If weight is a problem, control should be exercised here.

Source: Adapted from Tomi K. Haas, Eloise Jenks, Olympia Stapakis, and Sharon Wallace, *For Nutrition Counseling in Public Health,* Division of Public Health Nutrition, Community Health Services, County of Los Angeles, Department of Health Services, 1974.

Keeping a food record such as this for several days will not only help you analyze what you eat, but will also help you to understand your choices and habits. These patterns may turn out to be wise, or they may turn out to lead to irregularities, overweight, or loss of control over the food budget.

Food Evaluation Sheet

What is the *quality* of your food intake? To determine this, list the foods for any sample day on a food evaluation sheet such as that shown in Illustration 4. In this illustration, the following foods eaten have been listed by food groups:

8:00 A.M., at home, standing:
Coffee; sugar (1 teaspoon), milk (2 tablespoons)
Cold cereal (¾ cup), milk (½ cup), sugar (2 teaspoons)

10:00 A.M., at work, sitting:
Coffee; sugar (1 teaspoon), creamer (1 tablespoon)
Doughnut (1)

12 noon, at work, sitting:
Bread (2 slices), peanut butter (2 tablespoons), jelly (1 tablespoon)
Soft drink (12 ounces)

5:30 P.M., living room, sitting:
Martini (3 ounces)

6:30 P.M., kitchen, sitting at table:
Stew: beef (6 tablespoons); carrot (1), potato (1), onion (½), turnip (¼)
Bread (2 slices), butter (2 teaspoons)
Ice cream (double scoop)

10:00 P.M., bedroom, lying down, watching television:
Coffee; sugar (1 teaspoon), milk (2 tablespoons)
Chocolate chip cookies (3 large)

The food evaluation sheet shows how the food eaten can be analyzed in terms of the amounts necessary to meet the recommended daily allowances for a normal woman twenty-three to fifty years old. The analysis reveals several things. (1) Not enough *milk* was drunk to meet the need for calcium and riboflavin; and this was not made up for through other foods. (2) The *protein* intake from meat is sufficient, and the bread-cereal intake brings it up further. (3) The *vegetable-fruit* choices meet the vitamin A requirement, but may lack sufficient vitamin C—although potatoes and turnips would provide vitamin C if they weren't cooked too long. (4) Sufficient *breads and cereals* were included. (5) The addition of unnecessary high-calorie food with low nutritional value (5 teaspoons of sugar, a doughnut, jelly, a soft drink, a candy bar, a martini, cookies) has raised the total calorie intake beyond normal need. A judicious amount of these may be necessary to meet total calorie requirements.

This same intake might just meet the calorie needs of an active eighteen-year-old woman, but it would still not ensure good nutrition because the recommended amount of food from the four food groups was not eaten. If these foods were consumed by an inactive sixty-year-old, the calorie intake would be excessive (this would lead to obesity), and the basic RDA standards would not be met. A diet this high in sugar and fat could easily lead to obesity, which might predispose an older woman to diabetes and heart disease. Poor food choices only compound the stress, competition, and added responsibilities which characterize women's lives today.[8]

[8] William B. Kannel, "The Disease of Living," *Nutrition Today,* vol. 6, no. 3, May–June 1971, p. 2.

Better food choices should ensure good nutrition, and thus better health; using a food record and a food evaluation sheet may be a necessary step toward getting a realistic picture of one's own food habits.

NUTRITION AND DRUGS

Increased information is now available on the inhibiting influence of drugs on the availability of nutrients. The side effects of drugs on the flora and fauna of intestinal mucosa are known. (We will not consider malnutrition or undernutrition, or the result of interaction between drugs and nutrients which may make a drug ineffectual.)

A drug commonly used by women is the oral contraceptive pill. This depresses the tissue and serum levels of folic acid (folic acid is an essential vitamin; its deficiency results in a form of anemia), pyridoxine (vitamin B_6), vitamin B_{12}, and vitamin C. When a woman is taking an oral contraceptive, her physician should periodically test her blood levels of these vitamins and prescribe supplementation if necessary.[9] Aspirin taken just after a meal is slowly absorbed and can irritate the intestinal mucosa, causing ulcerations. A good rule is to take a drug 1½ hours before or after a meal. Antibiotic drugs sterilize the gut of positive bacteria which aid in the digestion, production, and absorption of many of the vitamins.[10]

When specific drugs are taken for disease, their effect on the nutritional status of the patient must be considered, as must the effectiveness of the drug when taken with certain foods.

SOCIAL FUNCTION OF FOODS

Food functions socially in various ways: as nourishment for a population, as a means of meeting needs for essential nutrients, as a way to maintain the strength of a population, and as a way to resist disease. It also has certain cultural connotations.

We are increasing our knowledge of the interaction and interdependence of nutrients during the metabolic process which turns food into the chemical substances that enable us to function. Isolating these substances, and reconstructing them in the laboratory, has enabled medical technologists to treat certain diseases. It has also enabled food technologists to introduce these chemical substances into foods to make them more nutritious. We have already mentioned how white bread, margarine, and milk are fortified. The enrichment of white flour with the B vitamins has eliminated beriberi and pellagra in the South. Vitamin D in milk has made rickets a disease of the past. Another example is iodized salt, which has practically eliminated goiter, a condition once endemic in

---

[9] *Oral Contraceptives and Nutrition,* Committee on Nutrition of the Mother and Preschool Child, Food and Nutrition Board, Division of Biological Sciences, National Research Council, National Academy of Sciences, Washington, D.C., 1975.

[10] Helen Cates, "Food and Drug Interactions"; paper read at a seminar.

the Middle West. Sea salt, available at three times the cost of iodized salt, accomplishes little more.

Today, food technologists have gone beyond fortifying basic foods to develop manufactured foods, such as the sweet breakfast snack, which promise all the nutrients of a balanced meal. But depending on a special food like this has the same flaw as depending upon a multivitamin pill—it lulls the consumer into believing that she is meeting all her nutritional needs and can therefore take license on what is eaten for the rest of the day. There are numerous trace elements in a balanced diet impossible to account for in any manufactured food item or pill. Nutrients act in concert and need the proper environment to be utilized in the body to the best advantage.

Food is more than what we eat. It can be ritualistic; it can be something around which certain cultural attitudes form. It can also be used as a social medium—either for exclusion or inclusion. In our own time, particularly since World War II, food habits have responded to affluence and technological advances. To many consumers, convenience is now more important than cost. Competition for consumers has caused manufacturers to proliferate products, to employ more expensive packaging, and to engage in expensive—even coercive—advertising. The culmination of marketing may be found in baby foods, which are flavored in accordance with the parents' tastes, not the infants'. There is, for example, no necessity for salt or for monosodium glutamate in baby foods, nor for sweetened desserts such as "blueberry buckle," a mixture of cornstarch and blueberry flavoring which can only lay the foundation for poor eating habits in which desserts play too prominent a part.

There are advantages, however, in today's prepared, bottled, frozen, canned, dehydrated, and take-out foods. A single person can get along very well by supplementing these with fresh fruits, vegetables, and milk. Prepared foods can provide speed, efficiency, and even economy. With only a refrigerator, an oven, and aluminum foil for preserving leftovers, one can manage quite well.

For the working mother, prepared foods can supplement her own meals. But the more completely prepared the product, the higher the cost; this makes extensive use of prepared foods impractical for a large family.

Prepared foods do not appeal to many people, because they seem to be evidence of the depersonalization and dehumanization of our society: "plastic food without individuality." For this reason among others, many people are again coming to regard cooking as an art. The pleasures of working with unprocessed ingredients and taking no short cuts have led to the revival of many old recipes and the discovery of many new and inventive ones.

There is also a growing realization that the food supply is finite. No longer are we able to assume that our choice of foods will always be unrestricted. We must face the fact that the world is one, and that food production can be outpaced by population. A scarcity of wheat in Russia means low wheat stores here; this forces food prices up all along the chain—cereal, grains, bread, cakes, cookies, and on into the animal products, owing to the cost of feed. The scarcity of one basic commodity in the grocery store affects how much money you spend. And the cost of convenience may be too great—it may be necessary to save money by making one's own salad dressing, breads, and desserts. We are now entering a period of conservation, or should be; we must learn how to get the most out of our time, money, and energy.

FOOD MANAGEMENT

Efficient management of food is particularly important for the wife and mother who is a worker, whether she has chosen this role or whether it is a matter of necessity. Whatever her reason for working, her contribution does raise the family's standard of living. An increase in the cost of running the household is inevitable: there is more use of convenience foods, commercial laundries, cleaners, and baby-sitters, and perhaps the addition of paid household help.

Cooperation among family members is essential if the family is to be fed adequately on a daily basis. Some of the steps which can bring order into the situation are as follows:

Menus should be planned a week in advance, taking advantage of the advertised "specials" of the two or three nearest supermarkets.

Each meal should be built around the main dish, which should be an advertised special.

Leftovers from one meal can form the basis of a second meal.

Box lunches for school and work should be planned for the week.

Take advantage of coupon discounts *only* for products you can use immediately, or soon.

Be sure that family members know which foods are "rationed." For example, half a cup of orange juice is enough to give the required vitamin C; therefore, one family member should not drink the whole family's daily supply.

Have inexpensive, nutritious foods available for nibbling (nuts, raw vegetables, cereals, fruits, etc.), and post a list of these on the refrigerator door.

Make out the shopping list with all these factors in mind, yet with enough flexibility to utilize unadvertised specials and accommodate sudden price changes.

Make it clear who is responsible for preparing each meal during the week. In assigning responsibility, take into account after-school and after-work activities and meetings of both children and parents. Consideration ahead of time avoids frustration and anger. For instance, when every member of the family is busy until suppertime, that is the day to use leftovers or bring home a take-out meal.

Preparation of complex meals can also be shared. If a dish (a roast, casserole, or stew, for example) needs long cooking, the person who will be home earliest can put it into the oven or on top of the stove. Make these arrangements ahead of time, assign each person specific responsibilities for the week, and post the assignments in the kitchen. The menus, with a written schedule of assignments attached, will not only save everyone's energy but will also spread responsibility equitably.

All housekeeping tasks should be similarly planned and scheduled around each person's school or work activities, capabilities, interests, and talents. Frus-

trations within the family will decrease when expectations are known and fulfilled. The role of coordinator is usually assumed by the mother, but it can be
delegated to whoever is most suited to it.

FOOD ADDITIVES

When we use convenience foods, we must expect to encounter food additives.
Preservatives, emulsifiers, and flavor enhancers make it possible to stabilize combinations of ingredients for mass production, and we should not be surprised to
find in reading labels ingredients such as "lecithin," "monosodium glutamate,"
"sodium ascorbate," "calcium propionate," and "BHT."

Are these safe for consumption? Various regulatory agencies (federal, state,
and local) have the responsibility for seeing that the food we eat is safe. The Food
and Drug Administration, the Federal Trade Commission, the consumer protection agency of your state health department, and the environmental health section of your local health center are all public agencies you may call upon for
information about any additive now in use. You may also let them know of any
situation in which a food or additive appears unsafe.

Many additives are natural food products, commercially produced for a
specific function. Lecithin, for example, originally isolated from eggs, was found
to be the substance in eggs which has a binding capacity (as in mayonnaise, in
which eggs are combined with oil into a stable mixture). Monosodium glutamate
is the salt of one of the amino acids derived from wheat protein; it has been used
in the Orient for generations as a flavor enhancer without discernible ill effect.
Sodium ascorbate is a form of ascorbic acid (vitamin C); its antioxidant properties are seen when lemon juice is sprinkled on apples or bananas to keep them
from browning. Other antioxidants are the tocopherols (vitamin E), BHT (butylated hydroxytoluene), and BHA (butylated hydroxyanisole): these retard spoil-
age. BHT and BHA are chemically produced and are used particularly in salad
oils and fried crisp products (dry cereals, potato chips, and crackers) to keep
them fresh and prevent them from becoming rancid. This is important because
rancid oils destroy vitamin E and in breaking down develop suboils which may
be carcinogenic. The levels of BHT and BHA in these foods are lower than the
allowable levels set by international standards.

Whatever your attitude toward food additives, you should be reassured by
Julius Coon's statement: "Most food additives are derived from natural sources
or are identical or closely related to chemical substances that occur in natural
foodstuffs. Much injury to human health has resulted from natural components
of foods, whereas no such injury can yet be attributed to food additives or pesticides when these agents or the materials to which they have been added have
been used as recommended." [11] We must remember that because of mass production and increased shelf life, food costs less in the United States than almost

[11] Julius Coon, "Natural Food Toxicants—A Perspective," *Nutrition Reviews,* vol. 32, no. 11,
November 1974, pp. 325–326.

anywhere else, and that our programs of food enrichment and food fortification have added to the nutritional value of foods.

However, Coon also notes: "An awareness of the toxic properties of essential nutrients and of the amounts present in foods being processed should also be maintained by the food industry so that it may avoid supplementation of its product with hazardous amounts of these agents." [12] Such controls are safeguards to the American public.

CHANGING FOOD HABITS

It is difficult to change ingrained habits, particularly those developed in childhood, as many food habits have been. Mothers give certain foods as rewards; other foods are associated with special occasions; special flavors take one back to the warm protection of childhood. There is also the influence of individual idiosyncracies, social customs, ethnic background, religious taboos—all shaping the individual's attitudes about food in relation to himself or herself.

Diets Based on Group Movements

Food today is used to nourish not only our bodies, but our souls. The consciousness-raising movement, for example, uses food as the social medium on which certain rituals and experiences are centered. Producing, procuring, preparing, and partaking of food may become the core of a group movement with its own taboos and rituals. There are many such groups whose diets, when analyzed, are excellent. One with a long history is the Seventh Day Adventists. Medical literature indicates that following their dietary precepts (no meats or stimulants) tends to increase longevity to better than average. Adventists do include milk and eggs and eat a varied diet otherwise similar to that of the general population. [13]

Another diet with a large following is Zen macrobiotics. This diet follows precepts set forth by George Ohzawa: "Man's diet is the integral component necessary to achieve clear thinking, eternal health, happiness, longer life and vital energy." [14] To achieve this, one must balance the physical, mental, and spiritual conditions of one's body. The symbol of balance is "ying and yang." Ying is the feminine, yielding element; yang is the masculine, strong element. Foods are placed in these categories, and some foods have both components. Even the way a food is sliced becomes an art, for one must include both components. [15] The Zen macrobiotic diet is essentially a vegetarian diet, but novitiates are allowed meat. Fish is often included. Soybeans are a staple. For those who have been adherents for some time, spiritual progress entails more stringent diet regulations. This is metaphysical eating: "It maintains that if one has followed the religious teachings, once food is ingested it is transmuted into elements needed by the

[12] Coon, op. cit., p. 331.

[13] Mervyn Hardinge et al., "Non-Flesh Dietaries," *Journal of the American Dietetic Association,* vol. 43, no. 6, December 1963, p. 545.

[14] Darla Erhard, "The New Vegetarians, Part II—The Zen Macrobiotic Movement and Other Cults Based on Vegetarianism," *Nutrition Today,* vol. 9, no. 1, January-February 1974, p. 20.

[15] Michael Abehsera, *Zen Macrobiotic Cooking,* University Books, New York, 1968.

body. This explains why one can thrive on an all rice diet." [16] Another macrobiotic precept is the sparing use of liquids.

When the ultimate level is reached, one exists on brown rice, with very little water. From studies on hunger, fasting, and starvation, we know that euphoric states and hallucinations result from such a regime. Extreme adherence to higher levels of the macrobiotic diet has proved to result in deficiency diseases and even starvation and death.[17] Pregnant and lactating women on a macrobiotic diet are urged to increase their protein intake (soybeans, soy milk, meat, fish, and eggs). Fortunately, the movement has become less compulsive about enforcing the upper levels of the diet. The lower-level diet appears harmless.

Another group which endangers its members through an eliminative diet is the Vegens. All foods of animal origin, including milk and eggs, are eliminated. This means a low consumption of calcium, iron, and riboflavin and no vitamin B_{12}. Deficiency of vitamin B_{12} affects every cell in the body; it affects tissue formation in the bone marrow, the gastrointestinal tract, and the nervous system. Symptoms are slow to appear, but it is essential that supplementary vitamin B_{12} be taken by those on a Vegens diet.[18]

One of the strangest phenomena in our culture has been that many people are prone to seek eccentric diets before they have any conception of what pattern constitutes a scientifically balanced diet.

Increasing Consciousness of Food

The new awareness of the importance of nutrition in health and well-being has exerted a positive influence. People are becoming more conscious of what they eat. Some people question their food habits and the pressures of advertising, and become more willing to change, to explore, and to learn about nutrition.

This new awareness surely accounts for the greater variety of foods available today. It accounts for greater interest in the foods of various ethnic groups—tofu, greens (collards, chard, kale, mustard, turnip, beet, bokchoy, chicory, cilantro, etc.), tortillas, filafa bread, string cheese, and so on. Often, exotic foods can be bought at a supermarket. Our choices are widening.

Remember that however wide you range in exploring new foods and food patterns, your basic awareness should be of the four food groups, which can be easily accommodated amidst all this plenty.

Megavitamins

Caution is the better part of valor. The excessive use of vitamins without medical diagnosis is absurd, expensive, and dangerous. The present emphasis on megavitamins has encouraged self-medication for all sorts of illnesses from arthritis to skin blemishes, but vitamins have not proved to be efficacious in this regard in studies reported by reputable institutions.

[16] Darla, op. cit., p. 22.
[17] "A Statement of the American Medical Association Council on Foods and Nutrition—Zen Macrobiotic Diet," *Nutrition Reviews: A Special Supplement,* July 1974.
[18] Davidson and Passmore, op. cit., p. 229.

A common abuse is high dosage of vitamin C, up to and over 4,000 milligrams per day. The recommended dietary allowance is only 45 milligrams. Today we know that a consistent high intake of vitamin C, abruptly halted, may lead to signs of vitamin C deficiency. When normal intake is resumed, these symptoms disappear within a month. Other destructive effects are the degradation of B_{12} in the system, the poor intestinal absorption of copper, and the increased formation of kidney stones.[19] "An orange or a potato a day" may be a better maxim than "an apple a day," for oranges and potatoes are excellent natural sources of vitamin C.

Vitamin E is also highly touted. But the curative powers which it is said to possess have not been demonstrated in humans. In the earliest studies, made on rats, its absence produced sterility. Its antioxidant properties prevent free radical damage to cells and seem to increase cell life. Consequently, it has become a glamour vitamin, said to prevent aging and increase sexuality. No studies on humans have demonstrated either of these capabilities; nor has it cured muscular dystrophy or heart disease, or been effective in healing wounds when applied externally. The normal diet contains, as far as we know, sufficient vitamin E; it is well distributed in such foods as whole grains, vegetable oils, and eggs.

SUMMARY

To maintain the best of health, you must meet at least two-thirds of the dietary allowance recommended by the National Research Council for your age, sex, activity, and condition. Your best plan is to do this by choosing your daily diet from the four food groups, which carry not only the key nutrients but also the trace elements whose importance is still unknown.

Specialized diets and nutritional supplements should be undertaken only after medical diagnosis and under medical care.

A nutritionally healthy woman is not only preventing illness but also improving the quality of her life. She is less likely to be susceptible to colds and virus infections, more likely to heal faster and to look younger than her counterpart of a generation ago. And that, as I have said, is what living is all about.

BIBLIOGRAPHY

Alfin-Slater, Rosalyn, and Lila Aftergood: *Nutrition for Today,* William C. Brown, Dubuque, Iowa, 1973. A concise and knowledgeable book on how, why, and what we eat. Includes sections on obesity, undernutrition, pesticides, and additives. Paperback.

Lappe, Frances Moore: *Diet for a Small Planet,* Friends of the Earth/Ballantine Books, New York, 1973. Explains the nature of protein clearly for lay readers. Written by a lay person (who has thoroughly done her homework), it covers all the sources of protein and their complementary relationship.

Naturally Occurring Toxicants in Foods, National Academy of Sciences, National Research

[19] Robert E. Hodges, "Megavitamin Therapy with Vitamin C," *Nutrition and the M.D.,* vol. 1, no. 7, May 1975; "Nutrition Misinformation and Food Faddism," *Nutrition Reviews: A Special Supplement,* July 1974, p. 39.

Council, Washington, D.C. Deals with the intrinsic chemical composition of food which may have detrimental effects on human beings. Quality, quantity, and nutrient-inhibiting factors are discussed.

Nutritive Value of Foods, U.S. Department of Agriculture Home and Garden Bulletin no. 72, Superintendent of Documents, Washington, D.C. A comprehensive analysis (calories, protein, vitamins and minerals) of foods popularly eaten, in normal serving sizes. Can be obtained for $.30.

The Use of Chemicals in Food Production Processing, Storage, and Distribution, Food Protection Committee, Food and Nutrition Board, National Academy of Science, National Research Council, pub. no. 887, Washington, D.C. The place of, need for, dangers of, and acceptance criteria for chemical additives in our foodstuffs.

Chapter 11

Family Planning: Medical and Legal Resources

Helen Steiner
Alan J. Winters

Helen Steiner, B.E., is the administrator of the Venice Family Planning Center and a former member of the Board of Directors of the Family Planning Centers of Greater Los Angeles. She is a lecturer and writer and has coauthored both articles and booklets about contraception and family planning.

Alan J. Winters, M.D., F.A.C.O.G., is a professor in the Department of Obstetrics and Gynecology, University of Texas, Houston. He is a diplomate of the American Board of Obstetrics and Gynecology and was formerly an Assistant Professor, Department of Obstetrics and Gynecology, the University of Texas Health Science Center. He is the author of seven articles which have appeared in scientific and professional journals such as the *Journal of Clinical Endocrinology and Metabolism*.

The birth of a child is almost always a significant event. Birth is a much awaited and desired occurrence for some, and a dreaded tragedy for others. It is the rare person for whom a child has little meaning. Ideally, every child should be a wanted child; therefore, the establishment of a pregnancy is as important as the avoidance or termination of a pregnancy.

Choice, not chance, should dictate childbearing. Before any woman considers having a child, she should realize that a large measure of her life will be given to rearing this child. Loving her baby means years of dedication and guidance to develop this child into a mature human being. As a cute and cuddly baby begins to walk, talk, and explore, constant observation and stimulation are required, in addition to the routine tasks of feeding, clothing, and health maintenance. Combining a career with motherhood is not always possible; and many women feel lifelong regret and resentment for having given up an opportunity because of the demands of a child.

It is a pity for a child to enter the world unwanted, unloved, and rejected, to be denied adequate care, education, and opportunity. Along with the advances of medical science there has come an increased confidence that a child will survive to become an adult. But we still need not simply *numbers* of human beings, but a *quality* of life commensurate with our ability to achieve the best for all, and about this we often cannot be so confident. A baby born into a crowded family is often neglected and occasionally mistreated. A parent who is overcommitted to other interests, whether they relate to family care or not, will not be able to give each child the proper attention, guidance, and education. Moreover, the basic needs of nutrition and health care may be overlooked. Even in an uncrowded situation, an unwanted child will detect the parent's resentment, and this will reduce the child's self-value.

In this overpopulated world, beset with the problem of shrinking natural resources, every pregnancy should be a desired event, not a mistake. Already there are many countries where an education and adequate diet are not possible for most people. On an individual basis, a woman must consider her own resources in terms of physical and emotional stamina and financial ability to support her offspring. The mother who delivers a child yearly may be unable to adequately care for her family, and of course the children suffer in such a case. Emotional immaturity is a similar problem. Pregnancy among young teenage girls is particularly disruptive. Additionally, "the teenage mother runs an especially high risk that her baby will be stillborn, premature, die in infancy or be born with a serious mental or physical handicap."[1]

BIOLOGY OF CONCEPTION

In order to control childbearing, an understanding of the process of conception is necessary. An egg, or ovum, is the woman's contribution to the onset of a preg-

[1] Jane Menken, "The Health and Social Consequences of Teenage Childbearing," *Family Planning Perspectives,* vol. 4, no. 3, July 1972, pp. 45–53.

nancy. The ovum contains the protein code which dictates the characteristics of the child. This, of course, is modified by the sperm cell, which is the contribution from the man. When a sperm penetrates an egg, fertilization occurs, and a pregnancy is begun. But before this, many other processes must take place. While the immature ova are in the ovary—the reservoir for eggs—development of a few eggs, ova, begins. One egg usually reaches maturity alone, and the others regress. At the proper time, a stimulus from the brain causes the mature egg to be released from the ovary. It is then picked up by the end of a tube called the "oviduct" and transported toward the uterus—the womb. Some sperm which are deposited in the vagina reach the cervix, the opening to the uterus, and are transported through this canal on a roadway of mucus provided by the glands in the cervix. The sperm travel through the uterus, and some reach the oviduct wherein the newly released egg resides. Many sperm must be deposited in order for one sperm to penetrate the egg. The fertilized egg, called a "gamete," then continues its trip through the oviduct and finally reaches the uterus. The gamete then attaches to the wall of the uterus, which has been prepared for this event. If the egg has not been fertilized, then two weeks after the egg is released, the uterus will shed its unused wall. This process is accompanied by some bleeding and is known as the menstrual period. In this way the uterus renews the inside wall for the next egg which may be fertilized. In a similar way, sperm are produced in the male testicle, but many billions of sperm will mature in the same time that only one egg matures. The sperm travel through a series of ducts until they reach the proper phase of development and location where they are ready for use. This sequence of events occupies some ninety days.

PREVENTION OF PREGNANCY

With this brief background in the biology of conception, we can explore the ways to prevent it. The methods of contraception are summarized below; in the following pages we will examine them individually.

A physical barrier can prevent the sperm and egg from meeting. A condom covering the penis or a diaphragm covering the cervix effects this barrier.

A chemical can kill the sperm before they penetrate the cervix and fertilize an egg. Foams, jellies, and creams which are placed in the vagina just before intercourse fall in this group.

A chemical can prevent the development and release of an egg. The birth-control pills and injectable hormones are in this group.

Changing the cervical mucus to create a hostile environment will prevent sperm from entering the cervix. Most birth-control pills and hormone injections also achieve this.

A mechanical device placed in the uterus may prevent the implantation of a fertilized ovum in the lining of the uterus. The intrauterine contraceptive device, IUD, is thought to work on this principle. This idea is not new, for the Bible refers to the placing of stones in the uterus of a camel to prevent conception.

Altering the length of time for transportation of the egg through the tube to the uterus may prevent fertilization or implantation. This is an alternative explanation of the effect of the IUD.

Sexual intercourse can be avoided during a woman's fertile days; this is the "rhythm method."

Breast-feeding frequently prevents conception by preventing the maturation and release of an egg. In many underdeveloped countries, women nurse their babies as long as possible, since this is the sole method of birth control available to them. It is one of the least reliable methods of birth control, however.

Other less reliable methods of birth control include washing the sperm away from the cervix by douching immediately after intercourse; and withdrawal of the penis from the vagina just before ejaculation (expulsion of the sperm).

Before using any contraceptive, a woman should have a medical examination, including examination of the breasts to detect tumors; examination of the genital organs, the uterus and ovaries, to detect tumors or other abnormalities; examination of the vagina; and a Pap smear, a test to detect cancer of the cervix. In addition, blood pressure must be checked to guard against any abnormality which may be aggravated by hormones used for birth control. Her medical history and that of her family should be reviewed. The counselor or physician should discuss the various contraceptive methods available, including their relative efficacy, the advantages and disadvantages of each, and contraindications for each. Subsequently, every woman should have her blood pressure checked at regular intervals and should have a complete physical examination, including a Pap smear, once each year. Any problems, symptoms, or complaints should be reported promptly to the physician who prescribed the contraceptive method.

Oral Contraceptives

Birth-control pills contain two hormones commonly found in high amounts in the pregnant female: estrogen, the female hormone; and progesterone, the pregnancy hormone. The pills prevent conception by fooling the body into thinking it is already pregnant, thereby suppressing maturation of the egg. Moreover, the cervical mucus is altered to create an environment hostile to sperm. There are several kinds of birth-control pills; most contain both estrogen and progesterone, but the amounts vary. Some pills, the sequentials, have estrogen only in the tablets taken during the first sixteen days of the cycle and combine estrogen and progesterone in the tablets taken for the last five days of the cycle.[2] The "mini-pill" contains progesterone only, and this is effective in blocking the entrance of sperm into the cervical mucus. Another variation in birth-control pills is the packaging. Some packets contain twenty-one pills; after finishing one packet, the woman must not take pills for seven days before beginning the next packet, to allow menses to occur. Another packet contains twenty-one contraceptive pills and seven tablets without hormones—the latter to be taken during the days of the

[2] As of 1976 the sequential pills have been removed from use by the Food and Drug Administration.

menstrual period; in this way, the woman does not stop and start taking pills each month. The hormonal effect of both types of packaging is the same.

Advantages of Oral Contraceptives Here we refer specifically to the pills which contain both estrogen and progesterone.

1 Protection is provided at all times.
2 There is no interference with intercourse.
3 The pills are virtually 100 percent effective if taken as directed.
4 Directions are easy to follow.
5 Most women whose menstrual periods were irregular find themselves having regular episodes of bleeding.
6 Women who have been suffering from menstrual cramping—dysmenorrhea—often have less discomfort.

Disadvantages of Oral Contraceptives Here again, we refer to the pills that contain estrogen and progesterone.

1 Some women experience symptoms similar to those of early pregnancy, such as nausea, vomiting, tenderness or fullness of the breasts, and bloating. Some women gain weight, sometimes a large amount. Although the pills have no calories, they can stimulate the appetite and also cause water retention, edema. Usually the body adjusts to these discomforts, which generally present no significant hazard to health.
2 Spotting or bleeding—commonly referred to as "breakthrough bleeding"—may occur during the cycle. Unless bleeding is persistent and very heavy, the physician usually advises the woman to continue with the pills, because this side effect, although annoying, will frequently disappear.
3 Oral contraceptives must be taken regularly. The omission of pills can cause spotting or bleeding, and may also allow the development and release of eggs, thus exposing the woman to the possibility of pregnancy.
4 A small number of women develop a spotty mask-like darkening of the skin across the cheeks and above the upper lip. This is called chloasma and is intensified by exposure to sunlight. The condition is observed on some women during pregnancy.
5 A few women experience less common side effects such as dizziness, changes in appetite, fatigue, nervousness, and an increase or decrease of scalp or body hair.
6 A number of women do not have periods for several months after discontinuing use of the pills. However, if menses were regular before using the pills, they will become regular again afterwards, and fertility is not affected.
7 Nursing mothers may find a decrease in their milk supply while using oral contraceptives. It has not been definitely established whether the baby will be harmed in the long run if the mother takes pills while nursing. A nursing mother must consult her physician before taking oral contraceptives.
8 Menstrual bleeding often is considerably decreased and sometimes even stops while a woman is taking oral contraceptives. This may cause fear and, in some women, real emotional problems. Lack of menses, amenorrhea, is not dan-

gerous to health; but since women have been conditioned to expect a regular and fairly heavy menstrual flow, many become very upset if an expected period should fail to occur. If two months elapse without a period, even without having omitted any pills, the woman should have a test to rule out pregnancy, if only to put her mind at ease.

9 In a very young girl whose full development has not been completed, taking hormones may inhibit growth.

10 The only serious danger that has been reported is the possibility of developing a blood clot that could travel to the heart, eye, lung, or brain and cause disability or even death. Statistics have shown that this is a small risk. Edward Tyler, a pioneer in developing and testing the pill since 1956, has reported that "the chance of death associated with pregnancy is 17 times greater than with pill-taking."[3] Obviously, any person who has had a blood clot, from any reason, should not take oral contraceptives.

11 Recently, the Food and Drug Administration reported that women in their forties should not use this method of conception control, because they may run an increased risk of stroke and heart attack.

12 Women who are diabetic or who suffer from kidney disease, asthma, or depression should use caution when taking the pills, since these conditions may be aggravated by the hormones.

The "mini-pill" contains a very small amount of one of the synthetic hormones, progesterone, and eliminates the estrogen. While the contraindications are the same as for pills with estrogen, the side effects are minimal. The main problem seems to be a tendency to spot-bleed, to skip periods, or to have frequent periods. This can occur sporadically. The woman must be prepared to tolerate this harmless effect if she takes this form of oral contraceptive; in exchange, she is unlikely to experience the usual side effects associated with the two-hormone pill. Of course, since the mini-pill contains a very low dose of hormone, there is a slight chance of pregnancy, and it is of the utmost importance that these pills be taken on a strictly regular basis. Yet there is a smaller risk of conception with any pill than with any other method of birth control.

Contraindications   As noted above, the contraindications are the same for two-hormone pills and the mini-pills.

1 A recent history of active liver disease such as hepatitis or jaundice, unless special liver-function tests indicate that the liver is normal.

2 Any previous blood clots, especially in legs, lungs, or brain (this does not refer to the blood clots during menses).

3 Migraine headaches, fainting spells, or blurred vision.

4 Previous cancer of the breast or uterus.

5 History of high blood pressure, unless the woman is under the care of a doctor who is controlling it with medication.

6 Untreated thyroid disease.

[3] Edward T. Tyler, "The Pill Is Safe," *Look,* June 30, 1970.

A woman taking oral contraceptives should report any of the following developments to her physician:

1 Any lumps or growths on the breasts.
2 Persistent and frequent headaches or vomiting.
3 Sudden pains in the chest, shortness of breath, or coughing up of blood.
4 Visual disturbances, dizziness, or fainting spells.
5 Unexplained continuing pain in the legs or numbness in legs or arms.
6 Unusual swelling of the ankles.

Despite some sensational publicity in the press, on radio, and on television maligning the pill, millions of women continue to use this method of contraception successfully. The only birth-control measures that are more effective are sterilization and total sexual abstinence. As a reassurance to those women who have heard that cancer can be caused by this method, there is no scientific proof that this is so.

Hormone Injections

In addition to administration by tablets, hormonal contraception may be administered by injection. A long-acting synthetic progesterone, Depo-Provera, has been used successfully by many women. This method is not widely used, because return to ovulation and menstruation may take years, and indeed childbearing may be permanently affected. This method, which has been used in clinics in Los Angeles, California, for ten years with much success, is thought to inhibit ovulation. No breast cancer has been noted in any of the patients; some have taken the shots for as long as nine years. None of these women has become pregnant while taking the injections. A private practitioner in Los Angeles, Dr. Edgar A. Guess, Jr., calls this method "the Cadillac of contraception,"[4] and has said that he has no reservations about it.

Although Depo-Provera has not yet been marketed as a contraceptive in the United States, it is used extensively in more than eighty countries and is often given to a woman right after she gives birth. The United States Food and Drug Administration has had reservations about using Depo-Provera, since an experiment on beagles produced an increased incidence of breast cancer in these animals. However, the beagles were given dosages 25 times greater than the human equivalent, and beagles are known to be particularly susceptible to breast cancer; consequently, some investigators do not consider this a valid test. Nevertheless, any patient who wants to use this type of birth control must be made aware of the possible danger and must sign a consent form stating that she has been told about it.

[4] "Evaluating the 'Cadillac of Contraception,'" *Los Angeles Times,* part IV, p. 10, March 8, 1974.

Advantages   Depo-Provera injections have the following advantages.

1   There have been virtually no pregnancies among women taking these shots.
2   There is nothing to take or do for three months at a time.
3   For some patients, there may be an absence of periods for many months; many women find this a relief.

Disadvantages   However, there are also some disadvantages to the Depo-Provera injections.

1   Menstrual irregularities, such as continuous spotting or no periods for months, may occur.
2   Some women have difficulty becoming pregnant after discontinuing these shots.
3   An occasional patient gains a very large amount of weight which is very hard to lose, even after discontinuing Depo-Provera.

For the worldwide problem of overpopulation, the injection might prove to be one answer. In northern Thailand, for example, the injections are now being given to roughly 50,000 women. As Tyler has said, "A long-acting injection is probably the closest thing yet to a practical mass contraceptive agent; it is easily administered, long-acting, requires no continuous motivation, and is acceptable to women in many parts of the world."[5]

Intrauterine Devices

Many different kinds of intrauterine contraceptive devices (IUDs) are available today in various shapes and sizes. Some are made for the woman who has never delivered a child and some are for the mother of many children. There is no definite knowledge about how the IUD works, but there are various theories: for example, that it creates an inflammation in the lining of the uterus, preventing the fertilized ovum from being implanted; and that it speeds up the passage of the egg through the fallopian tube, so that the egg passes through before it can be fertilized. The devices are made of soft, flexible plastic. One has copper thread around the stem; its manufacturer claims that the metal is released in minute amounts and thus prevents conception. A new device, recently approved by the Food and Drug Administration, contains progesterone in its stem. It is shaped like a T and is small and comfortable. The hormone, which is continuously released, changes the cervical mucus, thus preventing the sperm from penetrating. The device itself holds the progesterone in place in the uterus. As the hormone will be used up in about a year, the device should be removed and replaced after that time—a disadvantage of this particular IUD.

[5] Edward T. Tyler, *Mankind's Great Need—Population Research,* Population Crisis Committee, 1730 K Street, N.W., Washington, D.C., p. 38.

An earlier IUD had a stem that was designed to protrude slightly out of the cervical opening so that a woman could insert her finger into her vagina, feel the end of the stem, and be assured that the device was in place. However, some of the male partners complained of being scratched or poked during intercourse. The modern IUDs have soft nylon threads which hang out of the cervix into the vaginal passage. These can be felt by the woman to reassure her that the device is in place. If the strings are so long that they hang out of the vagina, or if they cannot be felt at all, the woman should see her physician as soon as possible. The device may have been expelled. Also, if the partner complains of feeling the hard end, the device is lying too far down. An x-ray can be used to locate the IUD if no string can be seen or felt.

The IUD is usually inserted during a woman's menstrual period, thus avoiding insertion in a pregnant woman. Also, it is less uncomfortable for the IUD to be inserted at this time.

Contraindications   An IUD should not be inserted in certain situations. These are as follows:

1   Pregnancy.
2   Unexplained abnormal bleeding.
3   Suspected cancer of the cervix or uterus.
4   Overt disease of the reproductive organs.

Advantages   If the IUD is not contraindicated, it can provide several advantages.

1   Relative simplicity; there is nothing to remember before sexual intercourse.
2   Effectiveness—almost as high as that of contraceptive pills.
3   Permanence—it can be left in place for years.
4   Absence of the side effects associated with pills.
5   Reversibility; after removal, pregnancy occurs readily in fertile women.

Disadvantages   The disadvantages associated with IUDs are:

1   Cramping, sometimes so severe as to necessitate removal. However, aspirin can often relieve the discomfort.
2   Persistent bleeding, often clotting.
3   Expulsion.
4   Rarely, perforation of the uterus. If this occurs, surgery is needed to remove the IUD.
5   Risk of pregnancy. Pregnancy does occur in a very small percentage of women wearing an IUD. If the device is removed during pregnancy, there is a possibility of an incomplete abortion; the patient may then require hospitaliza-

tion. Many obstetricians advise leaving it in place; they say that the baby develops normally and that the IUD comes out at the time of delivery with no harm to the child. However, the Food and Drug Administration recommends removing the IUD if pregnancy should occur.

Diaphragm

The diaphragm is still being requested by many women despite the newer and easier methods available today. Some patients cannot tolerate an IUD and have had bad side effects from contraceptive pills or should not take them because of medical contraindications. Some simply say, "I don't want to put any drugs into my body, and I do not want a foreign object in my uterus." And some women, or their male partners, are allergic to spermicides.

The diaphragm is a physical barrier preventing sperm from entering the uterus. It has been used for over forty-five years and was the first medically accepted contraceptive. It is a rubber cap, strong and lightweight, with a thin round metal spring covered by rubber. It is compressed and placed easily in the vagina. Then the spring is released, and the cap expands to cover the cervix like a lid. A spermicide, which kills sperm on contact, should be put inside the diaphragm and around its rim for maximum efficacy. The diaphragm is inserted before intercourse and should be left in place for at least six hours after intercourse. It is removed by placing a finger between the diaphragm rim and the vaginal wall; it is then pulled down and out. After use, the diaphragm must be carefully washed with a mild soap and water, rinsed, dried, and powdered with a baby-type powder for storage.

Diaphragms come in many sizes and must be fitted properly, because women vary in the distance from the back wall of the vagina to the pubic bone. The doctor measures this distance during a pelvic examination, and it is a painless procedure.

Advantages   The advantages of the diaphragm are as follows:

1   It does not affect fertility.
2   It has no side effects.
3   It is painless.

Disadvantages   The diaphragm also has certain disadvantages, however.

1   It is not as effective as the pill or the IUD.
2   It must be inserted before sexual intercourse; some patients complain that this "spoils the spontaneity of intercourse."
3   It must be left in place at least six hours after intercourse.
4   It must be handled gently and cared for conscientiously.

Condom

This is the only contraceptive available today, other than sterilization, for which the man takes the responsibility. With all the methods available for women, condoms still are used by millions of couples in this country and are the first choice in many foreign countries. If used properly, a condom is a very satisfactory and reliable method of birth control, considered by many to have as high an efficacy rate as the diaphragm.

The condom is a thin stretchable sheath that fits over the penis. Some condoms are made of rubber; some, called "skins," are made from animal membranes. Those made from membranes allow a very high degree of sensitivity, as they permit a greater transfer of heat. But because they are packed in oil, they tend to be rather messy; and they are more expensive than rubber (latex) condoms.

Advantages   The advantages listed below apply to both rubber and membrane condoms.

1   They are harmless to the health of both male and female.
2   They have no side effects.
3   They can be bought without a prescription and are widely available.
4   They are easily carried in pocket or handbag.
5   They are comparatively inexpensive.
6   They can help increase the control of men who experience premature ejaculation.
7   They are ideal for impromptu sexual encounters.
8   If used properly, they are very reliable.
9   They may prevent the spread of venereal disease.

Disadvantages   Again, the disadvantages are the same for rubber and membrane condoms.

1   The condom can break if improperly handled or pulled on too tightly.
2   Seepage can occur from the top if the open end is not held as the penis is withdrawn after ejaculation.
3   Many men find that their sensitivity is dulled.
4   Occasionally, the vaginal tissues of the woman are irritated.
5   The condom must be put on just before actual intercourse, interrupting foreplay. This spoils the feeling of spontaneity for many couples.

The degree of protection provided by the various grades of condoms does not depend on price. Rather, price depends on the sensitivity allowed by the sheath. Some condoms have a pouch at the end to receive the sperm after ejaculation; this helps prevent breaking and spilling. Some condoms are prelubricated by an oil-based or water-based solution or by a dry lubricant made of a smooth silicone powder. These are helpful if the woman does not have enough natural lubricant during sexual excitement.

When a woman cannot take birth-control pills, cannot tolerate an IUD, or cannot be fitted with a diaphragm, the use of a male contraceptive such as the condom is indicated. The condom also provides protection when a woman has any kind of vaginal infection, such as monilia (yeast) or trichomoniasis, or the more serious problem of venereal disease.

Spermicides

A foam, jelly, or cream containing chemicals that kill sperm on contact can be used to cover the cervix with an impenetrable film. Delicate vaginal tissues are not harmed by these preparations. Only one application is required before each act of intercourse; and an applicator is supplied with each spermicide, so that insertion is easy. One type of cream comes in prefilled disposable sanitary applicators, each one with a single measured dose. This is very convenient; there is nothing to fill or wash out, and since the dose is automatic, there is no mess. These prefilled applicators are somewhat more expensive than other forms, however.

Advantages   Spermicides have several advantages, as follows:

1   They are easily transported.
2   They can be purchased without a prescription at drugstores.
3   They can be inserted up to one hour before intercourse, so that there is no interruption of foreplay.
4   They present no danger to health and no side effects other than an occasional allergic reaction.

Disadvantages   The disadvantages of spermicides are as follows:

1   An occasional female, or her partner, is allergic to the chemicals. If an allergy exists, the spermicide should be discontinued and a doctor should be consulted.
2   Spermicides are inconvenient if the sex act occurs unexpectedly. Also, some women dislike the idea of using something just before intercourse.
3   The spermicides are somewhat messy and therefore offensive to some people.
4   The efficacy of this method is less than that of the contraceptive pills, the IUD, the diaphragm, or the condom.

Less Reliable Methods

Withdrawal   Withdrawal or *coitus interruptus* is sexual intercourse that is interrupted: the male withdraws his penis from the vagina just before ejaculation. It is one of the oldest means of preventing conception, but it has three serious disadvantages:

1   The lubricating fluids secreted from the penis during sexual excitement usually contain some sperm, even though ejaculation has not taken place.
2   A man must be considerably disciplined and experienced to withdraw in time, and completely, from the vaginal passage, and also to avoid any contact with the external genitalia.
3   Much frustration is a result of this method, and both partners can become extremely nervous as a result.

Douching Douches—feminine-hygiene products—are a poor substitute for a reliable method of birth control. Douching after intercourse is not reliable, because the sperm may penetrate the cervix immediately after intercourse. Douching washes the vagina, not the cervical canal or the inside of the uterus.

Rhythm Method This method requires abstinence from sexual intercourse during certain days of the month. It is acceptable to many people whose religious beliefs do not allow mechanical or chemical means of controlling conception. The days that must be avoided are the days shortly before, and during, ovulation. It is assumed that conception will be prevented because no sperm will be present in the vagina when an ovum matures. However, almost everyone using the rhythm method is relying on guesswork. It is very difficult to determine when ovulation occurs unless one is extremely motivated. Keeping a temperature chart for several months can help a highly motivated woman to determine, with her physician's help, which days of the month she may ovulate, if she menstruates regularly. The temperature must be taken every morning upon awakening, before eating, drinking, or going to the bathroom—in fact, before getting out of bed. It is charted to tenths of a degree on a special chart, starting with the first day of the period; and after several months a pattern may emerge, as the temperature dips, then rises and stays at a higher level until the next period. The time of change probably signifies ovulation. The pattern may change, though, as a result of illness, shock, worry, changes in surroundings, etc. The quality and quantity of cervical mucus may aid in ascertaining when ovulation may occur. The developing egg produces increasing estrogen, which causes an increase in the secretion of mucus from the cervix. A woman who is going to ovulate within a few days may feel wetter and stickier than at other times of the month. But even though a woman may have an idea of her "safe" days, sperm can survive in the woman's internal genitalia for a long time and thus be available when the egg matures.

Still, there are some advantages to the rhythm method:

1 Nothing is used, mechanical or chemical.
2 There are no hazards to health or side effects.
3 The method is acceptable to all religions.

The disadvantages of the rhythm method are as follows:

1 It depends upon chance to a large extent, because cyclic patterns can vary from month to month.
2 Most people find it difficult to abstain from intercourse at set times.
3 The pregnancy rate is high.

Abortion

Unfortunately, there are many women who rely on abortion as a means of birth control. Abortion should be used only when another method of birth control has failed, and in cases of unexpected, unprotected sexual intercourse, such as rape. For generations—before our laws regarding abortion became less rigid—women risked injury and even death to terminate an unwelcome pregnancy. In some cultures, this was accepted; in others, heatedly condemned. Controversy about abortion continues all over the world and involves political, cultural, and religious factors. Just a few years ago in the United States, many women seeking abortion went to Mexico for the operation or found illegal operators at home. The conditions under which illegal abortions were done were not always sanitary or reliable. A few fortunate women had the financial means to fly to Japan or Sweden, where laws were more liberal. Women who could not afford to pay anything, or did not know where to turn for help, often resorted to dangerous methods to terminate unwanted pregnancies themselves.

Recently, the legal status of abortion in the United States has been constantly changing. This is partly a result of increased sexual freedom and increased awareness of overpopulation. In addition, the surgery has become safer, with improved procedures and instruments and more use of antibiotics.

The technique which has been widely used to terminate a pregnancy of less than twelve weeks' duration is called "dilation and curettage," or "D and C." In this procedure the cervix is dilated and the uterus is emptied by scraping with a surgical knife called a "curette." A new technique has been developed in recent years which is quicker and safer than the D and C: the cervix is dilated and the contents of the uterus are removed by suction.

After twelve weeks of pregnancy, the procedure of abortion becomes more complicated and entails greater risk. A needle is inserted into the uterus and into the fluid-filled sac that contains the developing fetus, and a drug is injected which causes the woman to abort. Initially, a salt solution was used, but now more physicians are using a hormone of the prostaglandin group. After the injection, abortion usually occurs within 24 hours. However, almost 30 percent of women subjected to this procedure may experience great loss of blood, may develop an infection, or may have an incomplete abortion requiring suction of the remaining uterine contents. Rarely, the complications are so great as to require hysterectomy as a lifesaving measure. In marked contrast to the late abortion, the early abortion is safer than normal delivery of a full-term child.

Depending upon the circumstances, abortion may be performed in a hospital or in a physician's office; it may be done under general anesthesia or with only a local anesthetic with the woman fully awake. In any case, the earlier the unwanted pregnancy is terminated, the safer and easier is the procedure. However, repeated abortions are not advisable; future childbearing may be adversely affected, and the risk of any abortion procedure is always greater than that of using an effective method of contraception.

The "Morning-After" Pill

Another means of interrupting an early pregnancy is referred to as the "morning-after" pill. The time of administration is critical: this method must be used within a day or two after intercourse, before the woman or her physician can be certain that a pregnancy has begun. This drug is the much-maligned synthetic estrogen diethylstilbestrol (DES). After fertilization of an egg, some four days elapse before the fertilized egg will implant in the uterine wall. During this time, administration of high doses of estrogen will alter the uterine wall so that the gamete will not be able to implant and the pregnancy will be interrupted. The Food and Drug Administration has recently approved DES as an emergency method only, and has stressed that it is not acceptable for routine use. As with some other methods of contraception, there are unpleasant side effects, the most notable being a high incidence of violent nausea and vomiting. Moreover, if this method fails to terminate the unplanned pregnancy and the baby is female, that child is at risk of developing a virulent form of vaginal cancer most commonly detected at the end of the second decade of life.

Sterilization

When a person or couple has decided that childbearing is no longer wanted, sterilization may be considered. The decision to end the possibility of future childbearing must be well considered, for all methods of sterilization are considered permanent. Although some sterilization operations may be reversed, the return to fertility is not common. Whether a woman has many children or none at all, her decision to be sterilized must be respected. The desire to give birth to a child is a very personal decision, as is the desire to avoid all possibility of pregnancy, permanently.

Several methods of sterilizing a woman exist, and each has its proper place and use. The surest way to effect sterilization is to remove the uterus. This operation, called a hysterectomy, may be performed through the abdomen or through the vagina. If the uterus itself is of normal size, but other considerations dictate its removal, the vaginal operation may be preferred.

Another form of sterilization is to interrupt the passage of the egg to the uterus by tubal ligation. Three general methods exist to accomplish this. First, the abdomen may be opened and the tubes tied, cut, and separated. This may be done at the same time that a cesarean section for delivery of a child is performed. Second, in a woman who is not pregnant, an incision may be made in the back of the vagina and the tubes cut and tied through this opening. Third, there is tubal fulguration during laparoscopy. In this method, a laparoscope—a special tube with lenses and a light—is inserted just below the navel into the abdomen, and each tube is picked up and electrically burned so that a piece is removed. The patient is under a local or general anesthetic during the procedure. The recovery time after this operation is a matter of a few hours; frequently, the patient may be in and out of the hospital or clinic in the same day. Neither hysterectomy nor tubal ligation affects sexual response.

In most instances a woman may be sterilized without the consent of her husband or parents if she is at least eighteen years old. Anyone encountering problems regarding sterilization should write to the Association for Voluntary Sterilization, Inc., 708 Third Avenue, New York, N.Y. 10017. Information can be obtained from a physician or a local family-planning center.

Couples considering sterilization have an additional option. A man may be sterilized by interrupting the tubes leading from the testicle, where the sperm are developed, to the penis. This procedure, called a vasectomy, is done under local anesthesia in a short time. The man's scrotum is opened and the duct, called the vas deferens or vas, is elevated, tied, and cut. The procedure is then repeated on the other side. In contrast to sterilization of a woman, the vasectomy is not immediately effective. Several months may have to elapse before all the sperm are emptied from the ducts; therefore, some other form of contraception must be used during this time. As with hysterectomy or tubal ligation, there is no change in the sexual response. The ejaculatory fluid from the penis remains the same, except for the absence of sperm, which may be detected only with a microscope. After a vasectomy, many men develop an immunity to their own sperm; in the instances when a reversal of the vasectomy has been attempted, many men have remained infertile because the sperm heads stick together owing to this immunity. Before a vasectomy is performed, some men may want to store their sperm as a reserve measure. This can be done at a sperm bank, a facility for freezing and storage of sperm. Information concerning sperm banking is readily obtainable from the department of obstetrics and gynecology of any medical school.

INFERTILITY

It has been said that there are two kinds of women—those who want to become pregnant and those who don't. Among those who do want to become pregnant, a small but significant minority have little success establishing or maintaining a pregnancy. Many gynecologists can be of aid in overcoming the problems of infertility. In addition, there are some centers in the country that specialize in problems of infertility; one can be referred to such a center by a gynecologist. One important point should not be overlooked: almost half of all problems of infertility are due to a defect in the quality or amount of sperm. Therefore, any investigation of infertility must include both partners. The investigation is often time-consuming and expensive; but for those of limited income, family-planning centers offer information about programs that are subsidized so that the participants bear little or no expense.

LEGAL ASPECTS OF FAMILY PLANNING

The age at which a single or married woman can be given contraceptives, have an abortion, or be sterilized varies from state to state. New laws are being enacted and old ones liberalized in the United States, and in most other countries of the world. Despite this, however, and despite the recent advances in contraception, many women are still prevented from fully exercising their right to plan births. Often, they cannot obtain the necessary information, materials, or services. Poor women and rural women are at an especial disadvantage.

In the past, many women have been forced to resort to dangerous and frequently ineffective methods of terminating unwanted pregnancies. In 1973, the

Supreme Court ruled that a woman has a constitutional right to choose to abort a pregnancy within the first twenty-four weeks. Since that time, legal abortions have replaced illegal abortions. During the first three months of pregnancy, a woman may decide to have an abortion without any interference from the state. The decision is hers. Any woman who decides against abortion after counseling is free to continue the pregnancy. Since abortion on demand has been legalized, there has been a decline in the maternal death rate, infected abortions, and abandoned and illegitimate babies. These statistics do not tell the whole story, for there is also an improvement in the quality of family life and a decline in human misery.

The controversy over abortion continues, however. Both houses of Congress are continually besieged with antiabortion measures. By fighting the use of public funds for abortion, the antiabortion groups seek to deny the poor a right which more affluent women enjoy—the right to continue or terminate a pregnancy.

Sterilization is available to any legally competent adult. Before any such operation, each person must be informed about the anticipated procedure, its potential side effects, and its irreversibility. The consent of parents or a guardian is usually required for the sterilization of a minor.

In many states, anyone, including minors, may obtain birth-control information and services without parental consent. Furthermore, condoms and spermicidal jellies and foams may be purchased at a pharmacy without a prescription.

The current women's liberation movement has done much to dispel the image of a woman as only a homemaker, sexual object, and producer of babies. The woman is emerging as a full participant in the economic and social life of her community. Her health, that of her children, and her right to pursue an education and exercise her social, economic, and political options are affected by her ability to plan her family, space her children, limit their number, or decide to have none at all.

BIBLIOGRAPHY

Boston Women's Health Book Collective: *Our Bodies, Ourselves—A Book by and for Women,* Simon and Schuster, New York, 1973. This is a collection of articles for women, informing them about social and psychological aspects of being female. It explains anatomy, the physiology of reproduction, sexuality, venereal disease, birth control, and abortion.

Dixon, Ruth B.: "Women's Rights and Fertility," *Reports on Population/Family Planning,* no. 17, January 1975. A publication of the Population Council. A woman's control of fertility is discussed as it affects her status in education, employment, public life, and the family structure.

Endres, Michael E.: *On Defusing the Population Bomb,* Wiley, New York, 1975. An examination of the effects of economic development and birth control on overpopulation. This is suggested reading for undergraduates studying population and social science.

Lieberman, E. James, and Ellen Peck: *Sex and Birth Control,* Thomas Y. Crowell, New York, 1973. (Paperback, Schocken, New York, 1973.) Sexual freedom for young ple; what they most want to know; and what their responsibilities are where birth control is concerned. There is a list in the appendix of places and addresses in many communities where help can be found.

National Center for Family Planning Services: *Family Planning, Contraception, and Voluntary Sterilization: An Analysis of Laws and Policies in the United States, Each State and Jurisdiction,* Department of Health, Education, and Welfare, Washington, D.C., 1974. Conditions are discussed under which minors can receive services in various states; the laws, regulations, and policies regarding contraception are cited.

Osofsky, Howard J., and Joy D. Osofsky: *The Abortion Experience: Psychological and Medical Impact,* Harper & Row, Hagerstown, Md., 1973. Twenty-one articles reviewing the medical, psychological, and legal effects of abortion in the United States. Ideas for further research in all areas are offered.

Whelan, Elizabeth Murphy: *Sex and Sensibility: A New Look at Being a Woman,* McGraw-Hill, New York, 1974. This book, written in the language of the teenage woman, discusses contraception and both the familiar and the new in the area of female and male reproductive systems.

Chapter 12

When You're Having a Baby

Audrey Y. Reid

Dr. Reid, married and the mother of two children, is a practicing pediatrician in Pasadena, California. She is currently enrolled in the UCLA School of Public Health, working toward a graduate degree in International Health. She and her husband intend to spend part of their lives helping to provide health care in developing countries.

During the reproductive years, the possibility of pregnancy is foremost in the minds of most women who have missed a menstrual period following sexual intercourse.

MECHANISMS OF REPRODUCTION

In the chronology of reproduction, in the middle of the menstrual cycle an egg is extruded from one of the ovaries into one of the fallopian tubes. In the average woman, this occurs on about the fourteenth day after the start of the preceding menstrual period. If the egg is met and penetrated in the tube by an enterprising sperm, the egg is fertilized. The egg slowly travels downward to the uterus, or womb. If it has been fertilized, it becomes implanted in the womb within eight to ten days. Identical, or monozygotic, twins result when a single egg has been fertilized and later divides. Such twins are always of the same sex. Fraternal, or dizygotic, twins result when separate eggs are fertilized by separate sperm. For the most part, the multiple births produced by "fertility pills" occur because an overactive ovary extrudes multiple eggs.

SYMPTOMS OF PREGNANCY

Because many body systems are affected by pregnancy, it is accompanied by a variety of symptoms. Some of the symptoms, however, are not fully explained on physiological grounds. The most prominent symptom is amenorrhea, or the absence of menstruation. This is due to chorionic gonadotropin, a hormone which is produced by the placenta and which, by accumulating in the blood and urine of the pregnant woman, becomes the basis of most reliable pregnancy tests.

Morning sickness—nausea, vomiting, and a distaste for some foods—is experienced by about 50 percent of women during the first three months of pregnancy. This symptom is not, in spite of its name, limited to the morning hours; and it may last longer than the usual three months. Emotional upheaval is thought to be a factor, but hormonal changes are also a cause. Hormonal changes also account for the tenderness of the breasts that occurs after the early weeks. So far unexplained is the lethargy most women experience soon after conception. In the later months, constipation and hemorrhoids may result because the enlarging uterus displaces and compresses the intestines. Similarly, because there is pressure against the bladder, frequent urination occurs.

At approximately eighteen to twenty weeks of gestation, the expectant mother feels the first movements of the fetus in the womb; this is called "quickening."

Another symptom of pregnancy is weight gain, most of which is accrued during the second trimester. (For obstetrical purposes, the period of pregnancy is divided into three-month segments called the first, second, and third trimesters.) Other symptoms include deepening of the pigmentation of the nipples, enlargement of the breasts, and vaginal discharge.

All these symptoms, including quickening, may occur in the absence of pregnancy; gas passing through the intestines may simulate fetal movements. In the condition called pseudocyesis or "imaginary pregnancy" (which occurs mainly in women who are overwhelmingly anxious to have children or are extremely apprehensive of becoming pregnant), all the symptoms do appear, but of course there is no enlargement of the womb and tests for pregnancy are negative. Disturbances in the menstrual cycle occur under a variety of circumstances, including emotional stress. For example, gynecologists are often asked to perform pregnancy tests by college women whose menstrual periods have been delayed by the pressures of final examinations.

DIAGNOSIS OF PREGNANCY

With modern laboratory techniques, a diagnosis of pregnancy may be made several weeks before the enlarged uterus can be felt by an examining physician.

The basis of the tests is the accumulation of hormone, beginning soon after the fertilized egg is implanted in the womb; this may be detected in the urine or blood. In most cases, the test will be positive within a few days after the first missed period. The hormone reaches its peak level at fifty to ninety days after conception. Some women who have had negative results from pregnancy tests will produce positive results as more hormone accumulates.

Pregnancy tests may be done quickly in a physician's office; a report can be had within minutes. But this means of testing is less accurate—that is, it gives more false negative reports—than the test done by regular laboratories, whose results are usually available within twenty-four hours. The test costs about $8 to $10 (at the time of this writing). When it is done as part of an office visit to a physician, the cost of the visit must be added. If this physical examination represents the initial visit to the particular physician, other tests, such as a complete blood count (blood type and Rh factor are also determined), an analysis of the urine, the VDRL test for syphilis, a culture for gonorrhea, a Pap smear for cancer of the cervix, and a rubella titer for German measles, are likely to be added. The simplest way of finding out ahead of time what the cost will be is to ask the receptionist at the time the appointment is made.

A pregnancy test may also be obtained in a commercial laboratory, which can be found by consulting the "medical laboratories" section of the yellow pages of the telephone directory. The examination by the physician and the other laboratory studies, however, should be done, particularly if the pregnancy test is positive or if an irregular menstrual cycle is a problem. Such examinations, as described, at least once a year, are recommended for all women.

A less frequently used method of diagnosis is the administration, either by injection or orally, of the hormone progesterone, which in nonpregnant women will cause withdrawal bleeding within a few days.

OPTIONS FOR THE PREGNANT WOMAN

When the test is positive, the working woman has several options. Early in pregnancy, the choices include abortion, which is discussed in Chapter 11. One might choose not to abort, even though the pregnancy is unwanted, for various reasons such as religious convictions or late discovery of the pregnancy (after twenty weeks, abortion is medically unsafe and illegal in most states). Emotional factors are often important: some women abhor the thought of abortion, and emotional disturbance could result if it were forced upon them. Under these circumstances, psychological counseling is desirable, and usually it is wiser to proceed with the pregnancy. If the problem is money, free clinics have been established in most cities to help women to whom the expense of abortion would otherwise be prohibitive.

A third choice, in addition to abortion and keeping the baby, is to give the baby up for adoption. This choice is not limited to single women. Some women who are married but do not wish to add a child to their present families, will choose this option. The decision to give an infant up for adoption should be examined from all angles, and arrived at rationally, preferably before the delivery. Most women who decide to give up a child for adoption will choose not to see or hold the infant after delivery and during their hospitalization, fearing that contact with the child might make them waver in their decision. Of course, the nurses taking care of the baby must be aware of this situation. Pediatricians have often seen a worker from an adoption agency leave the hospital empty handed after a prospective client has been allowed once to hold her newborn. Before deciding on adoption, a woman should examine her emotional outlook thoroughly and seek professional help if necessary.

A single teenager, who decided against adoption, told me that her emotional makeup was such that to give her child over for adoption would destroy her life—whenever she heard a baby cry, she would have wondered about her own child, and not knowing would haunt her all through her life. That young woman saw the pregnancy through but kept her professional goal in mind, and, with the emotional support of her family, worked toward it. But another young woman in the same position chose to give her baby up for adoption to a family who sincerely wanted a child. She reasoned that whereas the infant would be a hindrance to the attainment of her own professional aims, it would be a joy to the adoptive family, who could well afford the added cost of a child. Both women have since achieved success in their careers and have also made successful marriages to men who respect them for, among other things, the decisions they had made under difficult circumstances.

A woman who elects to place a child for adoption should avoid making her own arrangements. Instead, she should use a reputable agency which will transfer the baby directly from the hospital. A telephone call to the adoption society in one's own city will serve to set the system in motion. In state-run agencies, the infant is placed in one or more foster homes before finally being settled with the permanent parents. This system eliminates contact between the real parents and the adoptive parents and thus avoids some of the problems that might ensue from such an encounter. It must be emphasized that a trustworthy agency—public or private—must be sought and used. To find a trustworthy agency in your locality, consult with an official of your local United Fund Organization, with officials of your local planned parenthood agency, with the Department of Social Services, or with any clearinghouse organization for social agencies in your community.

PERSONAL CARE DURING PREGNANCY

Morning Sickness

If a woman, single or married, elects to continue with a pregnancy, there will be some changes in her routine. Morning sickness can be a source of physical discomfort, but to keep this at a minimum, work schedules can sometimes be rearranged. For instance, if symptoms are present in the early morning hours, a pregnant woman in some occupations might be allowed to work during the evening hours and rest at home in the mornings. Of course, in many types of jobs this plan would be inconvenient; women in such jobs must rely on antinausea drugs. Since certain drugs are teratogenic—that is, they may cause physical abnormalities in an unborn child—it is essential that the physician's choice of drugs be relied upon during these months.

Weight Gain

Weight gain, almost universally present by the later months of gestation, is another source of concern. The ideal weight gain has been accepted as 20 pounds. When a woman gains more than 25 pounds, she increases by 25 percent the risk of toxemia—a condition which consists of elevated blood pressure, swelling, and protein in the urine and which is accompanied by a high degree of serious complications for both mother and infant.

Maternity Clothing

It is impossible to predict when maternity clothes will be needed, because women vary in their body contours and in the amount of weight they gain. Usually, sometime during the second trimester it becomes desirable to wear looser clothing—from the standpoint of both comfort for the wearer and aesthetics for the viewer. Certain styles of clothing, such as loose shifts and smocks, can continue to be used when the pregnancy is over; these are more economical. If the baby is to be breast-fed, buying brassieres that can later serve as nursing bras is also economical. Low-heeled shoes which give good support are practical and safe.

Nutrition

Unless there is excessive weight gain, the caloric intake during pregnancy should be about the same as usual. According to the Food and Nutrition Board of the National Research Council, the normal intake should be approximately 2,500 calories a day, and this is the same as for lactating woman and women who are not pregnant. Larger amounts of certain nutrients are required, including protein; calcium; iron; vitamins A, B_1, B_2, C, and D; and niacin. Metabolic activity increases in the latter part of pregnancy, but this requires no extra caloric intake since there is a lessening of activity at this time. The National Research Council recommends 85 grams of protein a day for the pregnant woman and 100 grams a day for the lactating woman (for women who are neither pregnant nor lactating, 60 grams a day is recommended.) At least two-thirds of the protein intake should be of animal origin—meat, milk, eggs, poultry, and fish, for example—to supply essential amino acids. Vegetable protein may make up the remaining one-third.

Exercise

Exercise is desirable both physically and psychologically. Childbirth classes are given around the country; these are set up with planned exercise as a part of the routine. The concentration is on exercises which will help control of the muscles of the lower part of the body and thus help make the delivery smoother. Many women who have participated in such classes have told how much satisfaction and help the class afforded them during labor. The expectant mother should avoid sports which involve any risk of physical injury but should engage in some form of planned activity. Naturally, she should not exhaust herself.

Effect of Smoking

Many investigations into the influence of maternal smoking on unborn infants have demonstrated that mothers who smoke during pregnancy deliver infants of low birth weight. A newborn weighing less than 2,500 grams (5 pounds, 8 ounces) is considered premature if the length of pregnancy was less than thirty-seven weeks but "low birth weight" if the pregnancy has been of normal length. On the average, a woman who smokes runs nearly twice the risk of the nonsmoker of delivering a low-birth-weight infant. Smoking which is discontinued before the fourth month of pregnancy does not appear to influence birth weight.

Infants of smokers have a faster growth rate in the first six months of life than the infants of nonsmokers. This is thought to represent the removal of the infant from a toxic influence which before delivery had retarded the infant's growth. Apart from toxic influence, it is also suggested that, among other mechanisms, smoking might decrease the appetite of a pregnant woman, causing her to gain less weight, with adverse effects on the fetus. Low-birth-weight infants are predisposed to a variety of problems, beginning with stillbirth. Surviving infants are predisposed to hypoglycemia (low blood sugar), which, if not treated early, will cause convulsions and coma; to hemorrhage in both the lungs and the brain; and to infection.

Narcotics

Among the problems associated with the use of heroin is the cessation of menses (when the drug is stopped, menstruation eventually resumes). A pregnant woman who uses heroin is at great risk of having a miscarriage or of delivering a stillborn or low-birth-weight infant. Surviving infants are, for all intents and purposes, addicts, having had a constant supply of narcotics in the womb. Even before they are born, such infants, when they need a "fix," make their mothers aware of it by increasing their activity; they quiet down after the heroin has been supplied. At delivery, the drug supply is cut off; and sometime between delivery and the fifth day of life, most such babies will go through a "cold turkey" withdrawal, which, if left untreated, endangers their lives. The infant undergoing withdrawal will exhibit irritability, restlessness, and tremors which might progress to convulsions, coma, and death. Difficulty in breathing, vomiting, and diarrhea also are prominent and dangerous symptoms. Similar complications may arise from the use of codeine, cocaine, barbiturates, and methadone by pregnant women. Amphetamines are also reported to cause problems in newborns, and infants born of alcoholic mothers may experience withdrawal symptoms. Some research has indicated that marijuana causes chromosome damage, which results in birth defects and hereditary diseases. There is some conflicting evidence; but in order to be safe, it is wise to avoid using marijuana during pregnancy.

Sex during Pregnancy

The average woman may indulge in normal sexual intercourse until the last month of pregnancy. There have been a few cases in which sexual intercourse caused early labor during the last month; therefore, although intercourse is probably harmless for most women, the usual recommendation is to avoid copulation during those last weeks.

Work

As with exercise, the expectant mother should avoid work which results in fatigue. A woman may continue to work throughout her pregnancy if the pregnancy is normal and uncomplicated, if the employer allows it, and if the occupation involves little danger or discomfort. I have known several professional women who have left work only when the labor pains began, with no adverse effects on mother or infant. Of course, this is not possible in occupations that require a great deal of physical exertion; and some employers will not allow a woman to work beyond the second trimester, often because their insurance or workers' compensation arrangements do not allow for the added risk. For secretaries and receptionists, the awkwardness of sitting behind a standard-size desk presents a problem. Avoiding excessive weight gain might be a key to holding onto such jobs for a longer period of time.

EMOTIONAL SUPPORT DURING PREGNANCY

The months before the delivery of the first child have been said to be one of the happiest times in the life of a woman. This holds true, for the most part, if the pregnancy is wanted, if financial support is not a serious problem, and if the expectant mother receives much-needed emotional support. Such support may be obtained from a variety of people. Usually the father of the child provides it; but in his absence, or if he is unable to provide it, parents, other relatives, and close friends may substitute. Single women in the same condition may elect to live together, thereby reducing their expenses and providing emotional support for each other. The obstetrician can also provide support; areas of concern should be brought to his or her attention.

Fear, usually about her own health, about possible malformations of the infant, and about labor pains and hospitalization, are normal for almost every woman during pregnancy; but the desire for the baby, when the pregnancy is wanted, usually outweighs these fears.

A married woman whose husband does not want a child might find it more difficult than even her single counterpart to get help in maintaining a positive mental state. Jealousies related to the child may emerge, and in some cases there is even resentment of a wife's contacts outside the home. Also, household duties tend to occupy more of the nonworking hours of a married woman than of a single woman. A married woman who has these problems may come to depend mainly on her physician; in such a case, the wisdom of continuing the pregnancy might have to be reconsidered. But psychological counseling can help; and group gatherings, such as childbirth classes, can prove especially helpful.

FINANCES

For the working woman, pregnancy and childbirth represent added expenses with which the family budget must cope. Such expenses begin with a physical examination and laboratory tests as soon as pregnancy is suspected, and do not end with the birth of the infant. Money is probably the greatest concern in the decision to have a child. Learning to sew will help cut down the expense of maternity clothing and the layette. Cribs, playpens, and other such equipment for the baby are no problem for parents who are handy with tools. Also, much of this equipment can be bought secondhand, painted, and reconditioned. During the early weeks of the baby's life, a large box or a drawer from a dresser, placed on a firm surface and padded with a blanket or comforter, can substitute for a bassinet.

Monthly visits to the physician for the first six months of pregnancy, semi-monthly visits for the next two months, and weekly visits for the ninth month are an added expense; most physicians, however, will include these visits in the total fee for labor and delivery (this cost, at the time of this writing, was in the neighborhood of $450 but varies from doctor to doctor and from community to community).

If finances are a problem, this should be discussed with the obstetrician at the start, and he or she will be able to offer suggestions for possible solutions. In most states, the medically indigent, though working and able to support themselves otherwise, may apply for assistance from Medicaid, a program in effect since January 1971 and supported by federal and state funds. The obstetrician is able to contact a social worker who will set this system in motion. This plan will also help medically indigent families with hospital bills.

Currently, the average time of hospitalization for an uncomplicated delivery is three days. Separate charges are made for the mother's room and the nursery. One can check with the prospective hospital ahead of time to get an estimate of costs (in the Western United States, at the time of this writing, the total was $650 to $1,000; in the East, it was perhaps slightly lower). There is an extra charge for the delivery room (at the time of this writing it averaged $120 to $230).

A cesarean section entails more expenses, as it requires two more days of hospitalization and higher operating-room costs. The charges of the anesthesiologist (the doctor who administers the spinal or general anesthesia) and the pediatrician (who takes care of the infant during the hospital stay) are not included in the bill for hospitalization or the obstetrician's bill. When the delivery is complicated, all the charges are increased, and the pediatrician might be required to stand by in the delivery room to resuscitate the infant at the moment of birth if necessary.

If the infant (as happens in some complicated cases and in prematurity) requires long hospitalization or admission to an intensive-care unit for newborns, the bill might be enormous. Many insurance policies do not cover obstetrical care and other expenses related to pregnancy. Some other policies, including employees' benefits, do cover pregnancy but do not cover the newborn until thirty days after delivery (since this period is the time of highest risk for newborns). The fine print in insurance policies must be carefully read for information regarding coverage. In a catastrophic situation where the infant needs intensive care, often the Crippled Children's Services will cover the costs.

Paid maternity leaves are rare in business organizations. Thus it may be wise to save sick days and put them together with regular vacation time; this will give as much paid leave as possible.

PREPARATION FOR DELIVERY

Most hospitals which have a delivery-room service, and many local health departments, have set up childbirth classes to teach expectant mothers about the events surrounding the labor and delivery. Parents' organizations have set up Lamaze birth classes in various communities. Classes employing the method of Bradley and others are also available. Basically, these sessions prepare the expectant parents psychologically and physically for natural childbirth by means of a series of controlled breathing and exercise techniques. It is understood that should the mother require some assistance with drugs, that will be available. In some classes, husbands are very actively involved, learning to time the labor contractions and give the commands for starting and ending the breathing and exercise maneuvers. In cases of home delivery, these techniques become doubly important. Such classes are recommended in the third trimester. For more specific information, see the bibliography at the end of this chapter.

Some women choose hypnosis as anesthesia during delivery. A physician competent in hypnosis should be sought; and in the absence of a definite referral, one might be found by telephoning the local chapter of the American Psychiatric Association. Preparation for delivery by this method must be worked out between physician and patient, since not all women are suitable subjects for this form of anesthesia, and for suitable subjects a system of signals and responses must be worked out.

Home Delivery

In many countries, including the Netherlands—which is reputed to have the lowest infant mortality[1] in the world—home deliveries, mainly supervised by midwives, are a way of life. Hospitalization is reserved for high-risk births. The United States ranks fifteenth among the nations in infant mortality, but most deliveries in the United States take place in hospitals. Midwives, although legal in some states, are not utilized in the management of pregnancy, labor, and even delivery nearly as much as in many other countries.

But more and more young families are turning to home delivery for the psychological well-being it affords, the family involvement it allows, the ability it creates to have the delivery performed in familiar surroundings, and the economy it provides. Home delivery requires good natural health, adequate psychological preparation, and the absence of high-risk conditions. When these requirements are met, complications occur very infrequently.

Still, most obstetricians regard the procedure as an unnecessary risk and will not participate. The complications most feared are hemorrhage in the mother (since in this situation blood and other lifesaving intravenous fluids are not immediately available) and conditions in the infant which necessitate resuscitation (since hospital-based equipment and trained personnel are not immediately available). Companies which insure physicians against malpractice suits might be unwilling to cover clients who habitually subject themselves to this risk, and hospital staffs might also be hesitant to accept them as members.

Having evaluated the pros and cons of home delivery, a family wishing to deliver at home will still be hard put to it to find a physician who will help them

---

[1] The infant mortality rate is expressed as the number of deaths per 1,000 live births occurring during the first year of life. However, the great majority of infant deaths occur during the first twenty-eight days.

do this. The physician chosen should be competent in obstetrical techniques and infant resuscitation and, if not a staff member of a hospital with facilities adequate to handle any complications, should work in conjunction with an obstetrician who is. If there is such a physician in the community, referral is usually by word of mouth: from friend to friend, sometimes by the teacher of the childbirth class, and (as one family pointed out to me) sometimes by inquiring at a local health-food store.

High-Risk Pregnancies

From the standpoint of the survival of the unborn child and the well-being of the mother, certain conditions constitute states of high risk. In such cases, it is crucial to have proper health care and to follow the advice of the attending physician closely. Furthermore, the delivery must take place in a center equipped to cope with any emergency that might arise.

A high-risk pregnancy exists when the expectant mother is malnourished or addicted to narcotics, when labor is premature, when the membranes (or the so-called "bag of water") rupture early, when toxemia of pregnancy is present, when the woman has diabetes (whether or not it was acquired during gestation), when there was bleeding during pregnancy, when there is a multiple birth (because of the possibility that the infants will be of low birth weight), and when the possibility of a birth defect exists. A high-risk pregnancy also occurs when an Rh-negative mother becomes sensitized by an Rh-positive fetus, so that she produces antibodies which destroy the red cells of the infant. This rarely occurs during the first pregnancy. At the present time, an Rh-negative mother, after delivery of her first child, is given Rhogam, a drug used to prevent sensitization in the future. If, however, Rh incompatibility between mother and child is likely to pose a health hazard, the physician will do several tests on the mother to determine the level of sensitization and, if necessary, induce an early labor, thereby lessening the danger from this source. In these circumstances, a cesarean section might be done before the expected date of delivery on an elective basis rather than an emergency basis (with arrangements made weeks in advance). A similar method of delivery might be elected in other conditions which pose a threat if the pregnancy is carried to a full term, such as diabetes and cephalopelvic disproportion (where the mother's pelvic outlet is inadequate for the delivery of the head of the baby), or when the mother has had a previous cesarean section.

DELIVERY

The contractions of the uterus during labor are divided into three stages. During the first stage, the cervix, or neck of the womb, becomes effaced and dilated so that the baby may pass through. During the second stage, the baby actually proceeds down the birth canal and out into its new world. The third stage is the delivery of the placenta, or afterbirth. The length of time of each stage as well as the entire labor differs with each woman and is therefore not predictable, except as judged by the frequent vaginal or rectal examinations done during labor.

By and large, the woman in labor will arrive at the hospital during the latter part of the first stage. There she is examined and then prepared for delivery. Such preparation, in most institutions, consists of an enema to empty the rectum, a catheterization to empty the bladder, and shaving of the pubic hair for purposes of asepsis. There is no definite proof that shaving off the pubic hair is necessary in order to have a sterile field for the delivery; and some institutions will modify the procedure if the woman objects to it, shaving only the areas likely to require suturing.

With more fathers wanting to participate in the experience of labor, more hospitals are allowing fathers to stay with the laboring mothers. This can afford great psychological support for the woman. Also, the father can give the signals for the breathing and exercise techniques learned in preparation for delivery. Here again, the pregnant woman must exercise her options.

Childbirth without medication is greatly to be desired, since the infant delivered without medication is at the least risk of being physiologically depressed after leaving the womb. It is here that the relaxation techniques have the greatest value. In the hospital setting, analgesics and anesthetics are available; but the drugs do cross over to the baby, and while the majority of infants show no effects, there are those who have respiratory distress immediately after birth, or have learning disabilities years later. In premature labor, no analgesics or anesthetics are used because of their depressing effect on an infant who already is handicapped by being immature.

General anesthesia is least desirable for delivery of the baby. Regional anesthetics include the spinal, which involves injection of the anesthetic agent into the spinal cord; and the epidural and caudal, in which the drug is injected in the nerve roots outside the birth canal. These forms of anesthesia appear to be an improvement over general anesthesia; but research indicates that even in the most dedicated hands regional anesthesia can compromise the well-being of the mother and her infant. For example, the drugs may cause lowering of the mother's blood pressure, and this affects the infant's circulation. They may also lessen the mother's ability to push the baby's head out of the birth canal, thus increasing the chances that forceps will have to be used to extract the infant. During the delivery, local anesthesia may be used to prepare an area for an episiotomy, a laceration that is made to widen the vaginal outlet. This form of anesthesia is harmless; but unnecessary episiotomies are often performed.

Fathers are permitted in the delivery room in some institutions and by some obstetricians, but are frowned upon by others, because the practice can pose a hazard to all concerned. The danger of infection, previously thought to be a major factor, no longer represents the threat it once did. However, fathers have been known to faint at the sight of blood. One hospital administrator told me of such an occurrence in one of the delivery rooms at his hospital. The personnel, busy with the mother and baby, were encumbered with the additional task of taking care of the father, and the danger of infection was increased when medical assistants entered the delivery room to wheel him away. More disconcerting for the administrator was the fact that when he fainted, this father had struck his head; this raised the possibility that he would sue the hospital.

In spite of these drawbacks, if expectant parents believe that there are emotional gains to be derived from being together during the delivery, they should certainly discuss this with the physician. He or she might be able to arrange it. Physicians appreciate patients who truly take an interest in their own welfare; and if the patients' requests, even though unorthodox, are reasonable, the physicians will try to comply. This is a two-way street, however: the patients must also be willing to listen to the physicians' reasoning. Working together, they are generally able to arrive at solutions which would have been unworkable had demands been made on either side. Of course, there are a few doctors who assume that their word is law and entertain no discussion. If this is unsatisfactory to a woman, her only alternative is to find another physician.

AFTER DELIVERY

Once the baby has arrived, more options are presented. The first is whether to have the baby stay in the hospital nursery with only brief feeding visits to the mother, or to have the baby "room in" with the mother. An increasing number of mothers want "rooming in." Proponents of this arrangement feel that the infant needs to be aware of its mother's closeness in the first twenty-four hours of life; while those against it feel that the mother needs to rest after labor and delivery. Most hospitals allow mothers to have newborns room in with them, but the women may return their babies to the nursery whenever they wish. Since the nursery is the home base of the baby, no expense is saved by this plan. If the mother or baby is ill, rooming in is contraindicated; and if the mother has had a cesarean section or other difficult delivery, it is probably unwise.

In the matter of the infant's nutrition, the mother must again make a choice. For many years, formula feeding has been popular; but mothers are now returning to breast feeding, and more evidence to support its superiority is being uncovered. Besides the well-known closeness provided between mother and child, it has been found that mother's milk contains antibodies which protect the baby against certain diseases. Also, infants who are breast-fed have fewer allergies. A mother who intends to return early to her job might breast-feed until then; or, when she returns to work, she might supplement the breast with a prepared formula.

Around the third day of life, many newborns develop jaundice, or yellowing, of the skin and eyes. This, in the absence of blood-group incompatibility or other diseases associated with jaundice, is termed "physiologic jaundice." It results from the inability of the immature liver to handle all the breakdown products of red blood cells presented to it as a normal function of life. A minor setback is thus experienced by some infants. The jaundice may necessitate extra days in the hospital, where continuous phototherapy with light in the blue-green spectrum is used for treatment.

The mother, soon after delivery, may feel a letdown, a condition known as "postpartum blues." Here, again, she needs support from her family, her physician, and the hospital personnel. If she has had a spinal anesthetic, a spinal headache might occur; if an episiotomy has been performed, the sutured area might be painful. For the latter problem, a heat lamp is useful.

RESUMPTION OF NORMAL ACTIVITIES

On an average, mother and baby are discharged from the hospital on the third day after delivery. In cases where finances are low or other problems exist, the physician might be persuaded to discharge them on the second day, provided that adequate arrangements for follow-up care are made.

Housework should be kept at a minimum for the first few days. For several weeks, heavy work and lifting should be avoided, since undue bleeding could result from such activities. Many mothers find it comforting to have friends or relatives around to help during this time, especially if there are other children in the family.

Though it is advisable to wait until after the first checkup (this takes place four to six weeks after delivery) to resume a normal work load, many women return to work earlier with no untoward effects. When I graduated from medical school, there was one young woman who had given birth on the previous day, right after her last examination; she then began her internship the next week. Another classmate arranged her pregnancy so as to give birth during the Christmas vacation; at the end of that two-week period, she was back in class with the rest of us.

Sexual intercourse is best postponed until after the first checkup. Social activities, especially where large crowds are involved, should be avoided because of the danger of transmitting infections to the baby. Relatives and friends will want to see the baby, but anyone with a cold should not be allowed near the newborn.

INFANT CARE

When the mother plans to return to work, the question of a substitute for her arises. In the United States at the present time, no uniform system for child care has been set up; and parents may have a difficult time making suitable arrangements. A relative who is retired may be willing to take on the responsibility; this can work well if his or her child-rearing practices match those of the parents. The parents should not assume that a relative who cares for their child does so "out of the goodness of his or her heart." If the relative expects to be paid, that should be done.

If the work schedules of the parents differ, they may be able to take turns caring for the baby. A single woman may make some such arrangement with other single parents. In a family situation, this kind of arrangement can, however, have a deleterious effect on family life.

A live-in housekeeper is the most convenient arrangement if there is ample room in the home. It is also the most expensive. An older person, such as a widow, who wants to share family life can sometimes be found. Naturally, anyone given this responsibility must be thoroughly investigated beforehand. After a prospective baby-sitter's references have been checked, he or she should spend a few days with the infant while the mother is still at home, so that the proper observations can be made.

Another arrangement is to have a baby-sitter who takes care of the baby in the infant's own home during the parent's working hours. This is a bit more expensive than transporting the infant to and from the house of a baby-sitter (another possible arrangement).

Another possibility, in selected cases, is for the baby to go to work with the mother. An acquaintance of mine had her son accompany her to work every working day for the first six months of his life. He slept in a crib in her office, was fed at regular intervals, and was changed when he was wet. Others I know have done likewise, not on a regular basis, but when no baby-sitter was available. My own child has pleasant memories of the numerous nights she has spent in the physicians' lounge of hospitals where I was on duty.

The department of social services in most counties has listings of the licensed day-care centers in the area; it also serves as a source for referrals.

There are those who feel that a mother's place, twenty-four hours a day, is in the home—until the last child goes off to school. While this is suitable for some families, it is by no means universally desirable. I have known many full-time mothers who failed to engage in activities with their children, forever reasoning that "there is tomorrow." Conversely, many working mothers realize the limits of the time they have with their children, and therefore plan ahead on a regular basis for family activities and companionship. If the mother is doing work she enjoys, her emotional well-being carries over to her home and truly makes her a happier, better mother. This is not to say that every woman, to be happy, needs to work outside the home; but every woman should engage in whatever activity best suits her. With proper planning, women are able to combine meaningful employment with pregnancy, childbirth, and the responsibilities which follow.

BIBLIOGRAPHY

Arms, Suzanne: *Immaculate Deception,* Houghton Mifflin, Boston, 1975. Deals with the problems surrounding childbirth in the United States; has a good discussion of home deliveries.

Cherry, Sheldon H.: *Understanding Pregnancy and Childbirth,* Bobbs-Merrill, New York, 1973. A comprehensive guide to pregnancy and childbirth with a condensed home course in the Lamaze method.

Department of Health, Education, and Welfare, Public Health Service: *The Health Consequences of Smoking,* Washington, D.C., 1973. The seventh report in a series dealing with the scientific evidence linking smoking to disease and premature death.

Dick-Reed, Grantly: *Childbirth without Fear,* Harper & Row, New York, 1972. A revised version of *The Original Approach to Natural Childbirth.*

Haire, Doris: "The Cultural Warping of Childbirth," *International Childbirth Education Association News,* Spring 1972. A report on various obstetrical techniques used in the United States, with a critical review of each.

Liley, H. M. I., with Beth Day: *Modern Motherhood,* Random House, New York, 1966. The author, a physician and mother, discusses pregnancy, childbirth, and infancy from the viewpoint of both mother and child.

Chapter 13

Handling Illness:
Health-Care Problems

Toni Michels

Toni Michels, M.S.W., is a licensed clinical social worker in private practice and Director of Mental Health Services at California Medical Group,
Los Angeles, California. A consultant, teacher, and lecturer, she is the
author and coauthor of numerous articles, some of which have appeared
in such journals as the *American Journal of Psychotherapy* and the *Journal of the American Academy of Psychoanalysis*.

"If I'm sick, who will take care of everybody?"

"Isn't it nice someone's going to take care of me for a change?"

"What a dirty trick on my husband (me, my child, my family)!"

"I'm worried about my health. And who's going to pay the bills?"

"When I get sick, my children don't come running, because they think I'm so
strong. And that hurts."

"When I'm sick, I feel so rotten about myself—as if I'm a failure!"

These statements were made by productive women who became sick. There
is nothing unusual in becoming sick: illness is a common hazard of life. However,
in some of the remarks there is a realistic acceptance of an unpleasant, possibly

frightening, state of affairs; in others, there exists the potential for an emotionally laden, volatile situation which could become a crisis.

RESPONSES TO SICKNESS

The experience of sickness evokes a multitude of responses and reactions which are both intrapsychic (within the self) and interpersonal (involving a relationship between two or more people). Some of these reactions may be supportive. Others may be counterproductive or even destructive.

Intrapsychic Reactions

How does it feel to be a working woman who gets sick? She loses, at least temporarily, her most valuable resource, her health and strength. If she is single and living alone, there is no one to take care of her. A simple need, like getting tea or chicken soup, can seem overwhelming when one is sick. Feeling weak, yet being totally dependent on one's own efforts in order to stave off hunger or dehydration makes one exquisitely sensitive to the true meaning of being mortal and alone. It is invaluable to have friends close enough to call during an emergency—if only to negate the feeling of isolation that being sick engenders. It is also important to feel entitled to extra pampering at times of need. Sometimes it is difficult to ask for help and even harder to accept it. But illness removes the capacity for normal functioning and entails a period of inactivity, a dependency which resembles childhood. To some, this may seem like a regression to an inferior status; to others a freedom from responsibility. Either attitude may be complex.

Illness can represent an attractive solution to social pressures or stresses; a legitimate way to escape a culture which reinforces activity and independence either externally or through one's own internalization of societal values. All of us, men as well as women, have a latent need for dependency which clashes with our concept of the ideal adult. Women who are strong enough to compete successfully in the economic "man's world" may perhaps have the most complicated defenses against giving in to the covert need to be taken care of. Illness is a challenge to those defenses. That is why taking a day off because of a cold, or contracting a more serious illness, can produce feelings of guilt. A woman may react to her own illness with excessive intolerance, continuing to measure herself in terms of productivity at a time when she is least able to work. She may become depressed because of her loss of autonomy. Lowered self-esteem may follow feelings of impotence. If, in addition, she needs hospitalization, even more adjustment is required. The strange impersonal milieu of a hospital often reactivates childhood fears of separation from parents that can add panic to current fears of chronic illness or death.

Illness, even when mild, can be perceived as a threat to one's identity and integrity, and severe anxiety can result. It can also mean a loss in terms of income and vitality—and loss is the most common cause of depression. If, to make matters worse, one has had previous experiences of pain associated with sickness, this latest burden may be met with pessimistic attitudes which preclude success-ful, energetic problem-solving approaches to the situation. Obviously, such reac-tions are not limited to the single, working woman; and they are enormously more complicated when a woman is concerned not only about her own emotional and physical health but also about her husband or children.

Husbands, too, must be prepared for many unexpected reactions within themselves. Sudden feelings of helplessness may be extremely difficult to tolerate. Being burdened with unfamiliar domestic decisions as well as fear about the health of a loved one; economic problems; feelings of insecurity which may be reactivated from unresolved problems of the past—all this emotional confusion may combine into anger at the wife—anger which is reinforced by the husband's own dependency needs.

The illness of a wife and mother can be a very disturbing event because she is often the emotionally supportive member of the family. This means that the husband and children lose her strength when it is needed most. The invalid, the husband, or the children may become depressed: among the symptoms are diffi-culty in eating and sleeping, irritability, anxiety, and withdrawal. For those who have never dealt with depression, it is hard to believe how intolerable it can be. Depressed people can be overwhelming. Their needs seem insatiable; their atti-tudes appear completely narcissistic; they can be manipulative; their moods swing irrationally from clinging dependence to alienating rejection, a process which is sometimes accompanied by rage. Depression can also be experienced by a family as a frightening, passive withdrawal from life, regardless of external stimuli. It is important for the family to realize that the depressed person also can be frightened at the self-defeating or self-destructive behavior and the lack of control. In severe cases, a husband may be unable to continue working; this, of course, adds immeasurably to the economic and psychological stress.

If, in addition to these problems, the woman's illness may be fatal, the family may experience general shock. Each person involved may try to deny the potential danger in order to avoid the necessity of dealing with the painful pros-pect of death.

These intrapsychic reactions, disturbing in themselves, can also disrupt inter-personal relationships, so that important sources of support may become weak-ened or invalidated.

Interpersonal Reactions

Two out of three women who work almost completely support themselves or others. Dependents have a profound effect on the woman's attitude toward her-self, as well as on her ability to cope with problems, when she is ill. But her dependents also have personal problems in such a situation. They have to try to help her while attempting to deal with their own emotional reactions to her illness. How deeply their lives are affected is contingent on how much dependen-cy is involved in the relationships.

Everyone in a family has both a structural and a functional role. The struc-tural roles of mother, father, brother, etc., are obvious and unchanging. The functional roles are flexible and are either assigned or assumed in response to various needs of the family. If these roles operate complementarily, the family is said to be maintaining its equilibrium. If not, antagonism can result. Roles can be interchanged, and one might say that a healthy family has the least resistance to predictable or inevitable change. Parents should be able to nurture each other as well as their children, and their ability to do so strengthens the tolerance and flexibility of each member of the family.

When the mother falls ill, even though she has been partially absent because of her work, the family system is out of balance. This means that everyone has to make a serious adjustment. Although the contingency of sickness may have been prepared for, a period of some confusion and resentment may ensue. Previously accepted methods of coping with stress or tension may have to be altered because they are now useless. This fact alone may cause panic or self-defeating behavior because the patient or her family has not had time to develop new methods of coping with this new problem. The situation then becomes emotionally hazardous. It is the handling of this critical period that can make the difference between eventual success or failure.

Effects on Children

When the mother is seriously ill, children are frequently sent away, so that in actuality they may experience loss of the father also—at least temporarily. Young children are particularly vulnerable to separation anxiety, as Bowlby and others have demonstrated,[1] and we have learned that this method of coping with a family crisis often results in more stress rather than less.

If separation in the form of illness is forced on a family, it can be tolerated better, with less trauma, if it is planned for in advance when those involved are not under emotional stress.

It seems obvious that continuity of child care is crucial to the child's optimum development. That, however, does not mean that the mother who must work should feel that she has in any way failed to consider the child's best interests. That feeling, in itself, can lead to such concern that the mother may be unable to continue work. For the mother who is working but who becomes ill and must arrange emergency care for her child, the resultant guilt can exacerbate an already anxiety-laden situation. This reaction is both unnecessary and unproductive. A disruption of the mother-child relationship can be handled so that there is a minimum of trauma. Even Bowlby—who certainly is a strong advocate of the child's need for one stable, intimate relationship—has said that children can be gradually taught to tolerate separation from their mothers and to trust other adults; they thereby become better prepared to deal with a lengthier separation should it be inevitable. However, the training should not be forced and, if possible, should be appropriate to the psychological and social developmental phases through which children mature.

---

[1] John Bowlby, *Maternal Care and Mental Health,* World Health Organization, 1951; John Bowlby and M. Ainsworth, "The Effects of Mother-Child Separation: A Follow-up Study," *British Journal of Medical Psychology,* vol. 29, 1956, pp. 251–254.

FACING A CRISIS

Stages of growth are an important concept with respect to resolving crises. As one develops, one encounters problems and gains mastery over them by learning ways of coping with them. Families also encounter problems and develop methods of dealing with them. These problem-solving techniques, however, may be inapplicable or inefficient for the new situation of illness which must now be faced. One can see, then, that a crisis can elicit two types of responses: healthy and maladaptive. The healthy response is for the individual or family to learn new coping mechanisms which will then be added to previously learned techniques, resulting in an ability to face life even more successfully than before the crisis occurred. When the response is maladaptive, the stress may continue or become more severe because of failure to solve the problem. Both types of response have long-term effects and may become models for future problem solving. This means that successful resolution of any problem creates optimism, motivation, and energy for solving the next problem. But if the crisis was experienced as failure, the attitude toward future problem solving becomes more pessimistic, and feelings of hopelessness and helplessness may interfere with, or even preclude, strong efforts to correct the situation.

Added to the emergency is the possibility, mentioned above, that a crisis may reactivate emotional problems out of one's past which were thought to have been totally or partially resolved, so that one may find oneself suddenly, inexplicably, reacting in the present with regressive tactics, faulty past perceptions, inappropriate coping mechanisms, or childish ways of interrelating with other members of the family. I am referring not only to the invalid but also to every other member of the family. Each person faces a crisis as an individual. But the whole family system as a functioning unit is also facing a hazardous situation. It is precisely through the experience of crises that families can disintegrate or can develop resources and strengths for dealing with the serious, unexpected hazards that are a part of life. Thus, children or adults who are overprotected lose the opportunity to reinforce and add to their strengths.

Research by Erich Lindemann and Gerald Caplan of the Harvard Medical School, augmented by that of others in the field, has developed our knowledge of crisis management. The main reason why these studies are so vitally important is that we have learned not only *how* to manage crises but also *when* to help. Observation has shown that "during the period of upset of a crisis, a person is more susceptible to being influenced by others than at times of relative psychological equilibrium."[2] Referring to this increased susceptibility, Caplan suggests that "from a preventive psychiatric point of view, this is a matter of supreme importance because by deploying helping services to deal with individuals in crisis, a small amount of effort leads to a maximum amount of lasting response."[3] To be even more specific about the timing, we know now that early identification of

[2] Gerald Caplan, *Prevention of Mental Disorders in Children,* Basic Books, New York, 1961, p. 13.
[3] Gerald Caplan, *Manual for Psychiatrists Participating in the Peace Corps Program,* Medical Program Division, Peace Corps, Washington, D.C., 1962, p. 82.

problems is vital because "both individual and family reactions to such threats as prolonged illness are fashioned from one to four weeks after the diagnosis is confirmed."[4]

RESOLVING A CRISIS

The importance of these findings cannot be overemphasized. They indicate that individual and familial responses or reactions to crises need not be seen as rigid. They can be modified with education and early application of the proper techniques. They are not predetermined by "character" or emotional makeup or strength alone but also by the timing and type of help received. And that help need not necessarily be professional; it can come from "significant others" such as friends, other family members, and community agencies. Reaching out to one's social network or to medical resources should be perceived as widening the choice of alternative solutions, and not as weakness, emotional instability, or mental illness by either the individual, the family, or the community. If for any reason there is hesitation or inability to seek help, then the most strategic time, when a little help can go a long way because of the susceptibility of the people in the crisis, will be lost.

Basically, there are five principles of crisis resolution which apply to family systems as well as to individuals. According to Caplan, these are as follows:

1 Help to identify the problem. This is a truth-seeking, data-gathering activity that is a healthy response to trouble. If the crisis seems multifaceted or overwhelming, this will help to break it into smaller units which are more tolerable and can be resolved gradually.

2 Give no false reassurances. This is difficult because everyone involved— those in need and those trying to help—may want to deny the seriousness of the situation. But the only safe kind of reassurance is faith that the crisis will be managed eventually.

3 Don't encourage anyone to blame others, because this is another way to avoid learning from one's own actions. Responsibility must be accepted before coping mechanisms will be developed and put into operation.

4 Help each person to accept help. Difficult though it may be, it is better to acknowledge that one has a problem than to pretend that no problem exists. Helping someone deny a potential danger will not encourage that person to get needed support.

5 Help with everyday tasks. Do not belittle this. A crisis disorganizes and disorients one's energies, and simple concrete help is very valuable.

Acceptance of Feelings

Throughout all these steps, communication and ventilation of feelings are vital. People involved in crises need to talk about their fears, hopes, and frustrations, about the terrible situations in which they find themselves. They need to be

---

[4] Gerald Caplan, *Principles of Preventive Psychiatry,* Basic Books, New York, 1964, pp. 39–54.

helped to express feelings, even those they may not approve of and those that they are not aware of having. For example, the invalid may be thinking, "Why me?" This indicates anger at her fate. Others in the family may be feeling guilt because they are thinking, "Thank God I'm not the one who's sick!" Freedom to express emotions is felt only when there is a strong sense of being accepted as one is—without pressure to be different or to change. It is experienced when someone cares and can listen without judgment, without cutting off the communication by trying to make one "feel better." No one wants to be labeled, lectured at, or interpreted.

It is difficult to share fears about financial insecurity, illness, loss of a job, problems with children, and other personal matters. One tends to withhold feelings in frightening areas, even from one's mate. It may be equally frightening to listen to someone express these worries, especially if one feels responsible or cares deeply for the person in distress. But these fears and the inhibitions resulting from them can preclude intimacy. It is almost impossible to screen out certain "taboo" feelings selectively and consistently, so that they are not discussed, and to remain honest and open in other areas. The result is usually an emotional incongruence or social distance which creates loneliness and which makes the unmentionable fears even harder to bear. Emotional support, then, is absent when it is needed most. Resentments are fostered and grow; and the more that supportive intimacy is needed, the more its absence is felt. A vicious circle is created because the cause of the emotional distance may be lost or forgotten, and then resolution becomes more difficult in the hostile climate that ensues.

Children's Feelings and Problems

Children, as well as adults, need a chance to ventilate their feelings, and their confidences must be respected. Otherwise, there is a danger that, in this crisis, their ability to develop basic trust will be threatened. Problems of shaken trust can affect a person throughout adulthood. Children should not have imposed upon them the additional problem of "being brave" or not crying. Tears are a normal, healthy response to fear or sadness at every age. Everyone is entitled to the so-called "negative" feelings at a time of stress. Children may feel, and need to express, their fears more at night when everything looks darker and more frightening. This should be expected and prepared for through a special time alone with the father or mother, if her illness permits, or a good friend who can be a temporary, surrogate parent.

Talking should not be forced. But it should be realized that the feelings and emotions aroused by a threatening illness, or disruption in family life, are devastating only when they pile up without a way of sharing the burden. One way of supporting is to offer physical expressions of caring or closeness. A hug is worth many words and is rarely misinterpreted.

Children must know they count as people. Immeasurable damage results when a child is treated like a "nonperson," cast aside in a crisis by well-meant but insensitive adult reasoning such as, "He's too young to know what's going on," or "Mary is playing and doesn't realize the seriousness of this crisis." I think that children do know what is going on and should be included, to some degree, in the group problem solving. This will lessen their feelings of impotence and isolation. They can benefit from family crises by learning that their feelings are important and, with help, can learn how to cope with problems through the experience of watching adults cooperatively search for solutions.

On the other hand, if there is an air of mystery, children may panic because they imagine a situation much worse than the reality. Or, through the process of "magical thinking," they might feel responsible for a mother's illness and suffer guilt. They may feel unsupported and become angry. Children can also feel rage at a mother who has "abandoned" them even though, on a different level, they are quite capable of understanding the reality of the fact that she was forced to leave them to go to the hospital. They may feel loss, leading to depression. They may feel unfairly punished. Some of the anger and frustration experienced by the adults may be displaced onto the children, adding to their fear and panic.

These are powerful emotions, and may be very difficult for a child to bear alone. But children cannot share these frightening emotions unless they are confident that they will be accepted as normal. The concept of ambivalence should be understood, so that a temporary feeling of hatred is recognized as occurring not necessarily alone but along with contradictory feelings such as love and caring. Anger can be described as a normal response to fear, and even a very young child can understand and be relieved by a discussion of aroused feelings. Fears are usually aggravated when children are not allowed to visit their sick mother. If it is possible, even a brief contact by telephone can be very reassuring to the anxious child.

The child who has difficulty expressing any feelings at all in a period of deep stress can be helped by an adult who suggests gently, "It's scary when mothers are sick," or "It's hard to talk about it." This "permission to feel" may open the door to the relief or ventilation that the child needs. It is a way of communicating the fact that one's feelings are acceptable without pressuring for more verbalization than is comfortable at the time.

A child who was unable to discuss his or her fears during the crisis should be given additional opportunities when the problem is over—even if it was resolved happily. Denial during a crisis is common at any age and does not mean that when everything is all right again, ventilation is no longer necessary. Sometimes it is only after the situation returns to normal that one can express the deep panic one was hiding even from oneself. Of course, the trusted adult must continue to keep all such sharing completely confidential and to remain trustworthy.

Occasionally a parent is reluctant to share feelings of loneliness or sadness with the child for fear of seeming weak, or for fear of arousing some anxiety in the child which does not seem to be present already. I think such sharing is not harmful to the child in appropriate amounts. It is one of the ways in which we model humanness and caring. It is one of the paths to a capacity for true intimacy. It enables people to share experiences rather than to feel abandoned or isolated. Relationships should meet the needs of those involved and should be gratifying and flexible. When feelings are shared, children learn to identify their own

emotions more clearly, feel less helpless, feel more involved, and are better prepared to meet future stresses and make necessary adjustments. Throughout all,
there should be an attitude of realistic hope and pervasive optimism. Being able
to share one's emotions is a protection against despair or rebellion. When one's
own feelings are respected, one learns respect for the feelings of others, and
awareness and sensitivity in interpersonal relationships are increased.

Although I have focused this section on the child, the principles I have
discussed apply equally to adults in the family under stress. Not only are children
people, but adults under stress can be childlike in their needs.

Parents may experience many of the same feelings the child has in addition
to concern for the anguish of the child. Responsibility for the child exacerbates
the mother's anxiety and guilt, and she may strongly resent the burden of these
feelings when she herself needs support. She may need to consider herself first
just when it is most difficult, because she knows that her family is suffering. Yet
all may benefit if she accepts that right. It would be ideal if both parents could
have a philosophical attitude that the crisis is a normal event in the process of
development, something to be handled and adjusted to, like any other matura-
tional task of the individual or the family, such as going to school, managing on
a tight budget, or moving to a new job or location. Then, perhaps, parents could
learn to accept whatever is inevitable, and be as matter-of-fact as possible under
the circumstances. In such an atmosphere, the child would also relax and the
family team could proceed to identify the problem, search for fresh solutions, and
learn new ways of coping with difficulties.

Family Communication

Lack of honest communication, or obstacles to communication, will weaken family relationships just when they most need to be strengthened. The result is distrust, and the failure of subsequent efforts to cope with problems. Family relationships should be reciprocal: members of a family facing a crisis are expected
to help the other members, and individuals who are having problems expect
others in the family to help them. The needs of people undergoing stress may be
emotional, physical, or simply practical. If they are ignored, especially when
there is a condition of "legitimate dependency," the result is resentment or hostility, which then reinforces the lack of mutual support. This situation may be the
result of previous improper communication, the expectation of failure, or the
family's perception of the professional woman's strength. However, the "strong"
mother may be experiencing depression as a result of her feelings of inadequacy
because she is ill. She may have regressed to the point of expecting fulfilling and
instant gratification, much like an inadequate, helpless, "legitimately dependent"
infant. She may be incapable of asking for help in an adult manner—and she
may silently or loudly resent what she perceives as a lack of response from those
she loves.

Ongoing disequilibrium or interpersonal conflicts in a family may not reflect
a crisis. They may represent a more chronic problem. In fact, the discord may be
of such long duration that its source may have been forgotten. This kind of

hostility can immobilize a family if a crisis occurs. It is the type of problem which should be dealt with through therapy so that one member does not become the scapegoat as the family tries to set things right.

Some people require more time to express their anxieties about illness. Just spending time with the person under stress will help. If suicidal feelings develop, they should be dealt with as a natural phase in the process of grieving; but anyone who is that depressed should be watched carefully to determine how deep or strong these feelings are. Perhaps suicide-prevention centers should contain units which deal with families in stress. Then dependency needs could be met during periods of depression and regression, even while people were encouraged to use their potential for autonomy and strength.

People should not live anonymously. Families, no matter what their size, should not allow themselves to be isolated in a community. Activities which help newcomers become integrated are important, so that support systems are accessible when a problem develops. We need more family service agencies and professional services within reach of the large working middle class. Education should also be available, because the ability to cope with problems can be taught—not only to those in trouble but also to those who might be asked for help.

AVAILABILITY OF HEALTH-CARE SERVICES

I suppose one cannot think about the effect of illness on the working woman without examining our institutions as well. Women have certainly proved themselves to be stable factors in the nation's economy. There seems to be no evidence for the widely held belief that women workers have higher rates of absenteeism. Yet the fear of economic, physical, and interpersonal instability seems to be greater for women workers. This is partly because such women are juggling professional and personal responsibilities and partly because of social attitudes and attitudes of the women themselves. Also, women earn less than men, which means that they have less money to spend on health care.

If a woman is married, it is assumed that her primary loyalty and concern is for her husband and family. Women also accept this priority, even over and above their personal needs for financial security. Thus, many women leave their work after eight hours to begin a second job as housekeeper or mother. It seems natural to assume that there is an axiomatic correlation between good health and plenty of rest and relaxation. Yet in our drive toward achieving equal pay for equal work, we have neglected our need for equality in rest, leisure, medical care, and household duties. For example, if there are children in a family where both parents work, and if we are moving in the direction of greater egalitarianism in child care, why is there not more flexible scheduling for the father, so that he can be a really equal parent? And where are the high-quality day-care facilities which would enable women to work more freely?

Health care is one of the largest industries in our nation. Yet our health-care system is frequently called a nonsystem, because there is no organization of preventive medical services. The constitution of the World Health Organization states, "Health is not only the absence of disease and infirmity, but also a state of complete physical, mental, and social well-being." This implies an ability to be active, to cope successfully with life. If this idea were actualized, it would mean the end of paternalistic medical authority exercised over a dependent, passive, childlike patient. It would mean education of the public to use health-care facilities in an active way, emphasizing the prevention of disease and the maintenance of health.

Health care should be a basic right, available to all. Obviously, our priorities need rearranging. Yet there seem to be few moves in that direction. The ways in which our health needs are now served depend more on what insurance companies will cover than on efficiency. For example, a well-equipped outpatient clinic could provide much preventive medicine and health maintenance; but available health-insurance plans may pay only for hospitalization. The medical supply industry is also geared to inpatient treatment. As a result, we have large hospital plants, not easily available to all, that operate mainly in response to immediate needs.

Women consume the largest proportion of health services. They make an average of 25 percent more visits each year to the doctor than men. If visits of mothers with children are included, the proportion increases to 100 percent more than men. Women also take 50 percent more prescription drugs, and they are admitted to hospitals much more frequently than men.[5] Yet women are discriminated against in a very subtle way by our health-care system. A report of the United States Department of Health, Education, and Welfare indicates that women are treated differently from men with respect to the value placed on their health, the respect given to their complaints or requests, and the general way in which treatment is prescribed and administered. Many of women's complaints are labeled "neurotic" and ignored, "sometimes until physical diseases are beyond treatment."[6]

COMMONSENSE HEALTH CARE

Women must learn how to manipulate the health-care system in order to feel safe and to get better care. Common sense dictates the following measures:

1 Gather information to protect yourself from iatrogenic diseases (those which are produced by or are inherent in the medical treatment).
2 Know and state your allergies.
3 Know your rights with respect to consultation.
4 Investigate alternative medical procedures with your doctor.
5 Ask for honest communication from your doctor.
6 Know your right to refuse treatment until your questions are answered.

[5] *Health Policy Advisory Center Bulletin,* March 1970, p. 1.
[6] *The Report of the Women's Action Program,* GPO–922–425, U.S. Department of Health, Education, and Welfare, Washington, D.C., January 1972.

7 Learn techniques of health maintenance, including education in parenthood; do not depend solely on treatment of symptoms.

8 Take responsibility for your own health; don't leave it to your doctor.

9 Beware the "omnipotent" doctor who encourages complete dependence, sometimes by offering barbiturates and tranquilizers without a clear exploration of the problem.

Another commonsense measure is following simple, well-known paths toward health: giving up smoking, for example. According to the American Lung Association, of the various forms of cancer, lung cancer is now the third major killer of women. Heart disease and sudden death due to heart failure are increasing among women at such a rate that they soon may be as common as they are among men. If people stopped smoking, the incidence of lung cancer would be reduced by 70 to 80 percent and the rise of other smoking-related illnesses would be reversed. Statistics show that women seem to have more problems with smoking than men. If you can't quit forever, at least try to lengthen the periods during which you cut down.

Food is also directly related to your health. (For a detailed discussion of nutrition, see Chapter 10.) One of the reasons why women have weight problems is that they feel they must have perfect figures. Rigid dieting in order to attain this ideal results in resentment that frequently leads to rebellious overeating. Another source of problems in this area can be boredom on the job or a feeling of being stuck at a point of minimum satisfaction. Workers trapped in dull, repetitive jobs suffer great occupational stress. They feel anxiety and depression, and these emotions can set off appetite disturbances. Feeling forced to conform by dieting increases one's perception of being manipulated and deprived. Then, eating seems like a much-needed reward. Food thus becomes the symbol of many feelings and is misused as a result. The next time stress develops, think in terms of alleviating it in other ways. Maybe a movie, a hot bath, a good cry, or a long talk with a friend would serve the same purpose.

Learn to hesitate to assume that any hurt you feel in a relationship was deliberate or directed at you. Innocent remarks can be taken personally and used to verify insecurity or an already painfully low self-concept. Learn to share and clarify your feelings as soon as possible before anger and hurt become destructive. It's very important to find out what you need to maintain good health and to seek it in a determined way without worrying about what others will think of it—whether it be yoga, abstaining from liquor, or standing on your head. The most important aspect of this process is caring for yourself, the feeling that you and your health are very important—important enough to deserve a regular expenditure of time and energy.

Cultural Influences

To a large extent, the culture of an individual determines his or her attitude toward health care. Family roles, religious attitudes, medical roles, and personal values all stem from the culture which one internalizes as one grows up. Even one's language about illness, health, and family varies with one's culture, and meanings may differ widely.[7] Cultural beliefs are deeply rooted and continually reinforced by the social milieu. The suspicion and distrust frequently encountered by doctors is also reinforced by the high cost of medical treatment, by the pain and strangeness that are sometimes involved, and by the frequent demand that the patient give up autonomy. Attitudes toward health care can determine the success or failure of medical treatment. One important factor is that communication may become difficult because of assumptions made by the patient or the doctor. The patient may have cultural beliefs directly in conflict with the doctor's choice of treatment. The doctor, unaware of this, experiences only the patient's resistance, and may react with hostility. But with time, patience, and caring, these problems can be expressed, heard, and dealt with intelligently.

Some Practical Points

Obviously, everyone handles illness differently. What is of minor importance to one person may be a calamity to another. Missing work, for example, can evoke various extremes of reactions. For that reason, some invalids are "a pleasure to take care of" and others are "impossible." Personalities are not easily changed, but planning ahead can ease temporary discomforts.

Choosing a Physician   It is especially important to be prepared in the area of medical services. Choosing a doctor or a hospital should not be left to chance or until an emergency occurs, unless this is unavoidable. The ideal, of course, is to have an ongoing relationship with a trusted primary-care physician. He or she, then, becomes your guide through the complicated maze of special problems or hospitalization. If you have not established a relationship with a physician or if for some reason you do not want to consult your previous doctor, you can get a list of staff physicians from a good local hospital or call the county medical society. Most county medical societies have a twenty-four-hour telephone service. If you would prefer a prepaid comprehensive health plan such as is described on page 239, get in touch with the Group Health Association of America, 1321 Fourteenth Street, N.W., Washington, D.C. 20005.

Choosing a Hospital   Choosing a good hospital is much like choosing a doctor. In fact, the two choices are complementary. If you are in an outlying rural community, there are certain safeguards you can take. Ask the administrators of the nearest hospital about its accreditation, or write to the Joint Commission on Accreditation of Hospitals, 645 North Michigan Avenue, Chicago, Illinois 60611. If the hospital is affiliated with a medical school or has a teaching faculty, its quality is likely to be high. For further information, write to the Council on Medical Education and Hospitals, American Medical Association, 535 North Dearborn Street, Chicago, Illinois 60610.

---

[7] John M. Maclachlan, "Cultural Factors in Health and Disease," in E. Gartly Jaco (ed.), *Patients, Physicians and Illness,* Free Press, Glencoe, Ill., 1958, pp. 94–105.

Planning for Emergencies Before the need arises, you should make some arrangements for emergencies like future illness. Include details, such as who should do what and when and where it will be done. Don't forget prosaic things like marketing, cooking, transportation, and telephoning. Prepare a list of important telephone numbers to be posted in an obvious place. This list should include the numbers of the police and fire departments and the nearest hospital, as well as doctors, close friends, and family. Check hospital rates, availability of services, and how much payment is needed in advance. Hospitals vary considerably in these respects. If your friends or family are firmly supportive, ask your doctor about outpatient treatment. In some populated areas, special services are available which make hospitalization less essential. If you must go to the hospital, try to have someone close to you stay in immediate contact with your doctor and the treatment he or she is prescribing. Hospitals are frequently understaffed, and services can be dangerously inferior without supervision by someone who cares enough to be involved.

Talk about your desire to plan for possible future illness with those upon whom you may want to depend. You may alert them to their own needs, and you should know their limitations before an emergency occurs. Discussion beforehand will help everyone to remain calm when necessary, and this is vital. Panic can be contagious, and it precludes rational thinking just when it is most essential.

THE FUTURE

The United States is the only major industrial nation without a comprehensive national health insurance plan. Yet everyone seems to agree that we need a more efficient, more widespread system of health care. Many different kinds have been proposed. The question is whether a system operated by the federal government would be an improvement over the present "nonsystem." So far, large-scale social programs run by the government have not been noted for administrative sensitivity.

National health insurance is only one alternative to the traditional fee-for-service health care. Another is the concept of a health-maintenance organization. Organized medicine has been opposed to this for years, but the idea is now being backed by government funds as a possible solution to rapidly rising health costs. The Health Maintenance Organization Act of 1973 was enacted to increase the access of consumers to prepaid health plans. A health-maintenance organization (HMO) guarantees comprehensive health care by a team of doctors, including specialists, to enrolled patients for a prepaid, fixed fee that does not vary with the number of services actually utilized by the patient. The basic premise is that the patient is encouraged to seek early treatment of illness because it is already paid for. The doctors are on salary; this removes any incentive to provide unnecessary or possibly harmful services. Such plans emphasize and are oriented toward the prevention or early detection of disease, because illness increases the expenses of the organization.

The University of California School of Public Health researched the "preventive service index" and concluded that patients in two established HMOs in southern California received more preventive services than fee-for-service patients. Two studies involving a large HMO in New York found it significantly better than traditional medical service as regards mortality rates at birth and in the elderly.[8]

Women have come a long way in having their needs heard, understood, and filled. Proper medical care should be high on our list of priorities and approached with the same militancy as other concerns. There are lives to be saved and lives to be improved. The quality of life depends largely on health care, which should be perceived as a basic right to which all are entitled, not as a business in which profit is the only incentive. Health care should provide dignity, respect, compassion, privacy, education—everything that makes each person feel her own importance to herself and to the community. Passivity in this area is not feminine—it is self-destructive. Begin by critically observing your medical care. Explore other alternatives. Let your legislators know your needs. What we get will be the result of our own efforts, and it is time for us to take that responsibility.

BIBLIOGRAPHY

Arnstein, Helene S.: *What Every Woman Needs to Know about Abortion,* Scribner, New York, 1973. A complete guide, medical and psychological, through an abortion.
Boston Women's Health Collective, *Our Bodies, Our Selves: A Book by and for Women,* Simon and Schuster, New York, 1973. A description of a successful grass-roots women's health movement. It has a very extensive description of how women's bodies work and what to do when they're working wrong.
Clark, Margaret: *Health in the Mexican-American Culture,* University of California Press, Berkeley, 1959. An overview of how differences in belief systems relate to the preservation of health and the treatment of illness.
Forman, Carolyn (ed.): *Crisis Information Centers: A Resource Guide,* The Exchange, 311 Cedar Avenue South, Minneapolis, Minn. 55404.
Frank, Arthur, and Stuart Frank: *People's Handbook of Medical Care,* Vintage Books/Random House, New York, 1972. Very complete, explicit descriptions of illness and the medical system. Offers good advice and is useful and easy to understand.
Frankfort, Ellen: *Vaginal Politics,* Bantam Books, New York, 1973. This book explores the fascinating, sometimes frightening, relationships between women patients and their male physicians.
Gendel, Evelyn S.: "It's Your Body . . . Not Your Doctor's," *Redbook,* March 1974.
Grimstad, Kirsten, and Susan Rennie (eds.): *The New Woman's Survival Catalog,* Coward, McCann/Berkeley, New York, 1973. A reference book with descriptions of books, articles, women's health clinics, rape clinics, abortion, etc. By women, for women.
Hill, Reuben: *Families under Stress,* Harper, New York, 1949. A look at family crises and patterns of adjustment.
Horos, Carol V.: *Vaginal Health,* Tobey, New Canaan, Conn., 1975. Discusses medical

[8] *Consumer Reports,* October 1974, pp. 756–762.

problems and their prevention; includes a directory of women's centers, health-care clinics, and referral services for a range of problems from minor infections to venereal disease.

Kennedy, Edward: *In Critical Condition,* Simon and Schuster, New York, 1972. An exposé of the difficulty of, and problems relating to, trying to get good health care.

Krakauer, Alice: "A Good Therapist Is Hard to Find," *Ms Magazine,* October 1972, p. 33.

Loomis, Evarts G.: *Healing for Everybody—Medicine of the Whole Person,* Hawthorne, New York, 1975. Written by a physician; includes a specific section on nutrition and exercise.

Maddux, Hilary C.: *Menstruation,* Tobey, New Canaan, Conn., 1975. Deals with the physiological, psychological, and social aspects of this normal biological process. Offers candid, sound, and practical information.

National Institute of Mental Health, *Facts about the Mental Health of Children,* DHEW pub. no. (HSM) 7209147. Available for $.10 from U.S. Government Printing Office, Washington, D.C. 20402 (stock number 1724–0255). Brief, informative, and readable.

Rush, Anne Kent: *Getting Clear,* Random House, New York, 1973. All about women; with exercises for health, stimulation, and relaxation.

Samuels, Mike, and Hal Bennett: *The Well Body Book,* Random House/Bookworks, New York, 1973. Talks about your body as a three-million-year-old healer. The authors hold that we have the energy, tools, and material to keep ourselves fit.

Strax, Philip: *Early Detection—Breast Cancer Is Curable,* Harper & Row, 1974. A well-known specialist tells you how you can protect yourself against the disease all women fear.

"What Women Don't Know about Breast Cancer," *Consumer Reports,* March 1974, p. 264. This article lists twenty-seven breast-cancer screening centers throughout the United States.

Women in Transition, Inc.: *Women in Transition,* Scribner, New York, 1975. A feminist handbook on separation and divorce with a special section, "Taking Care of Ourselves," dealing with women as consumers of health care. Lists women's centers, clinics, rape crisis groups, etc.

XYZYX Information Corporation: *Home Emergency Ladies' Pal (H.E.L.P.).* Available for $1.00 plus postage from XYZYX Information Corporation, 21116 Vanowen St., Canoga Park, Calif. 91303. A useful and easy-to-read book on first aid.

CHAPTER 14

Your Mental Health, Vitality, and Therapeutic Resources

Herbert A. Otto

Today's changing society, with its many pressures, responsibilities, and tensions, has much to do with the emotional ups and downs and stresses to which working people in particular are subjected. Exposure to stress-producing forces is continual, and the effect is cumulative. Thus knowledge about available therapeutic resources, which may be needed at any time, is both pertinent and valuable.

In addition, any period of transition has its own combination of stresses, strains, and emotional demands. Starting work, changing jobs, and even the demands of work itself can create a condition of being which is often described as being "emotionally drained." At such times basic principles and methods of enhancing mental health and regaining vitality can be of particular value.

ENHANCING YOUR MENTAL HEALTH AND VITALITY

Basic Elements

Basic elements in enhancing mental health and vitality are *good nutrition, exercise,* and *love and sex.* These three elements are important at any time and particularly so at a time of change and transition or when one is under pressure or stress.

Good Nutrition There is a general tendency to neglect nutrition by taking it for granted. We tend to assume that what we eat is good for us and that we eat relatively little of what is not so good for us. Yet this is not always the case; and since what we eat does make a difference, almost any attention given to the improvement of nutrition by the working woman can be expected to yield positive results. For this reason, the reader is urged to read Chapter 10.

Exercise The health-enhancing effect of an ongoing exercise program cannot be sufficiently stressed. Studies have shown that, by and large, most people do not exercise their bodies sufficiently and fail to do the walking and "working out" which build and sustain good health. Exercise is especially important because much of today's work is sedentary and requires little movement for extended periods of time. Even as little as ten to fifteen minutes of simple exercises a day can make a dramatic difference. The following comments are typical of those made by women in our Developing Personal Potential groups:

> "I do ten minutes of exercises every morning in a gym suit with the window open in my bedroom. I do sit-ups, push-ups, knee bends, and running in place, and I can now touch my toes. My husband first laughed at me—but when he saw all the energy it gave me, he started too."

> "Every morning I start the day with fifteen minutes of yoga exercises. I got them out of a paperback book I bought at a newsstand. They set up the day for me. I feel great, and you can hear me singing when I dress. I wouldn't do without it!"

Chapter 15, Keeping Fit for Fun and Personal Development, contains an excellent exercise program which is easy to follow and lists books about yoga and other exercise programs which are both simple and effective and which can be used to special advantage by the working woman.

Love and Sex Giving love and affection and—equally important—being open and accepting when love is given can be deeply vitalizing and supportive. A home environment in which love and caring are abundantly given and received provides the type of emotional nourishment which is always important and which fosters mental health and well-being. The same can be said for a satisfying sex life. Every person has varying sexual and sensual needs, and these may diminish or increase—particularly during a period of change. But some people seem to have a tendency to use tiredness to mask their sexual and sensual needs. This is shown by the following excerpt from a tape recording of a group discussion:

> *Woman:* "I would come home too tired for sex. I had just started to work; I was bushed."
> *Man:* "That old gag—'Darling, I'm too tired tonight.'"
> *Same Woman:* "Wait a minute! Wait a minute! It was real. But I found myself getting more and more irritated. I was still too tired, I thought. Suddenly, it dawned on me: my sexual needs were there; I was using tiredness to hide them. This was not good for me. It showed in my nervousness and irritation. Once we had sex, that went away. I also felt less tired. It taught me a lesson. I now ask myself, "Is there something more behind the tiredness?"

Another Woman: "For me, it's a tension reducer. When I come home all up-tight and tense, a session in bed is the best cure. I feel so relaxed and loving."

These comments are by no means unusual. Many women (and men) find that sexual loving is vitalizing. It imparts new zest and energy as well as being deeply relaxing. At the same time, sexual communion strengthens the feelings of love and affection both partners have for each other.

Principles and Practices

Certain principles and practices of everyday living are conducive to good mental health. Some of the most relevant of these will be presented, and some of their uses and applications summarized.

Be Aware of Your Feelings and Needs As is evident from the group discussion quoted above, lack of awareness of feelings and needs can become the source of much frustration and emotional turmoil. One easy technique to help you become aware of feelings and needs which rarely takes more than a few minutes is called "centering." After you come home from work, go to your bedroom or any place in the house where you can be alone and undisturbed. Sit down, relax, and close your eyes. Now center your attention on your being and on the question, "What are my feelings now?" Let the answer come in. Next, ask yourself, "What are my needs now?" Always follow centering with a *course of action* designed to fulfill your needs or deal with your feelings if this is indicated.

Verbalize and Express Your Feelings For various reasons, repression and denial of feelings and needs has been characteristic of our culture. But the human potential movement and the women's movement have helped create a much freer, more open climate, more permissive of the expression of feelings and needs. Whenever possible, and depending on the circumstances (and your own good judgment), *give yourself the freedom to express your feelings, verbally and otherwise.* Tell people how you feel. If you wish, you can act out your feelings in the privacy of your room—stamp your feet, hit a pillow, scream or shout if you feel like it. As you are doing this, say to yourself, "I am getting rid of these feelings." (See also Chapter 25, pages 435 to 441, for specific experiences designed to help you express your feelings.)

Verbalize and Express Your Needs Make your needs known to people. Even if they cannot fulfill them, *it is better for the people around you to know what your needs are.* You will be surprised to find how often, once your needs are known by others, they will be fulfilled.

Ask for Help This principle is related to the previous principle. *It is important to risk asking for help and to develop the courage to do so.* Do this even if you have no clear expectation that anyone present can be of help in relation to a specific problem or circumstance. Jesus said, "Ask, and it shall be given you." In many, many instances, once you have indicated that you need help, it will be forthcoming—and often from unexpected sources. The secret is to get the word out to as many people as possible.

Use "Dynamic Listening"   When someone is talking to you, give that person your complete and undivided attention. Don't daydream or let your mind wander, or—worse—think of what you are going to say in reply. *"Dynamic listening" means giving complete attention and empathy to the other person and being aware of what that person is saying on a nonverbal level.* Be open to nonverbal clues—the compressed mouth, the clenched hand—and become aware of the person's feelings while he or she is talking. When someone close to you is angry with you, respond to his or her feelings, not just to what is being said.

Use the Technique of Self-Relaxation   If you come home tense, use self-relaxation to let go. Give yourself fifteen to twenty minutes of relaxation, and you will feel the difference. In the privacy of your bedroom, take off your shoes and any confining clothes (and eyeglasses), and stretch out full length on the bed or floor. Close your eyes and begin by flexing the muscles in your toes and feet, then relaxing them. (While you are doing this, silently say to yourself, "I am relaxing and letting go.") Next, flex the muscles of your ankles; then, in turn, flex the calf muscles, knees, buttocks, pelvic area, etc. Slowly work your way up your body until you are relaxing all parts of your face and the scalp muscles. Now keep your eyes closed and become conscious of your breathing. Flow with your breathing. You will become aware of a total sense of relaxation, with all tensions gone from your body.

Use the "Strength-Acknowledgement" Method   This simple method can transform the emotional climate of your home. In our culture, the overwhelming tendency is to point out to each other what we do wrong. We rarely acknowledge the many positive things that are done by the people around us. Yet, as everyone knows, it feels good when we hear someone saying he or she is pleased by what we have done. Using "strength acknowledgement" is easy and fun. *Whenever you see someone using a strength, acknowledge it by sharing your reaction.* For example, if a person has just finished arranging some flowers, you might say, "One of your strengths is your sense of beauty—I really like the way you did that." Consistently used, strength acknowledgement can build a very positive, loving, and caring home climate. Psychologists call the process involved in this method "positive reinforcement"; and in transactional analysis it is called "giving strokes," or "stroking."

You may be interested in collecting and using similar methods. If so, you may want to read Chapter 25, where other methods are discussed.

PREVENTION AND PREVENTIVE PROGRAMS

It is clear that good nutrition, exercise, love and sex, and the various principles we have been discussing are the essence of prevention. Translated into action, the principles we have been discussing become an effective preventive program. And an ounce of prevention is far better than a pound of cure.

An excellent resource is the weekend programs and classes offered by the more than 150 Growth Centers of the human potential movement. These are, for the most part, preventive in nature. The human potential movement is based on the hypothesis that the average healthy human being is functioning at less than 10 percent of his or her capacity. Most of the workshops or classes offered by such Growth Centers as Oasis in Chicago, Cambridge House in Milwaukee, and Cornucopia in Miami are directed by professionals and are designed to help people actualize more of their possibilities. The programs vary in price; many of the evening classes, groups, and "drop-in" events are inexpensive. (For the address of your nearest Growth Center, write to the Association for Humanistic Psychology, 325 Ninth Street, San Francisco, California 94103. Enclose $2 and ask for their updated Growth Center list.)

The consciousness-raising (CR) groups which are sponsored by the various organizations of the women's movement are also basically preventive in nature. *Consciousness-raising groups help clarify role conflicts and identify problems, raise self-esteem and self-confidence, and are often ego-supportive.* Many women learn, for the first time in their lives, how to trust other women and how to free themselves from trying to outrun female competitors to gain approval of men. Different topics—dependence and independence, mother-and-daughter relations, etc.—are taken up every week. The ground rules do not allow confrontation or criticism. Consciousness-raising groups are not set up to help women work through major emotional problems.

The psychologist Barbara Kirsch, who has made a study of these groups, places the consciousness-raising movement in a larger social context:

> Social-historical factors created latent role dissatisfaction in women and the women's movement was mobilized when contact occurred among women who perceived this dissatisfaction, and an ideology and organizational skill developed in the population experiencing sex role conflict. Consciousness-raising groups rose as resocialization agencies and alternative structures to psychotherapy for resolving role conflict. These groups are effective in developing an awareness in women of the culturally accepted feminine roles and behaviors. The rap groups encourage a critical evaluation of sex roles and of the attitudes and behaviors that perpetuate stereotyped roles. The groups offer alternative behaviors, attitudes and world view in a supportive atmosphere conducive to change. The conversion process motivates activity to change self, culture and social structure. Although consciousness-raising groups and psychotherapy are posed as alternatives and their major differences are stressed rather than similarities, in reality they often serve as problem-solving mechanisms for the same people, sometimes simultaneously.[1]

Many specialists in human behavior and psychology have now reached the conclusion that an important stress-producing element in women's lives is the

---

[1] Barbara Kirsch, "Consciousness Raising Groups as Therapy for Women," in Violet Frakus and Vasanti Burtle (eds.), *Women in Therapy,* Bruner-Mazell, New York, 1975, pp. 350–351.

roles and sex stereotypes which are still widespread in our culture. As Kirsch points out:

> As a culturally-defined minority group, women are delegated unprestigious roles and are taught devalued personality traits. There is nothing innately inferior with the wife-mother role complex or with such "feminine" traits as dependence, emotionality, nurturance and passivity; rather, *the problem is that such roles and traits are constricting when assigned to a group on the basis of ascription when the other half of society is freer to decide its roles on the basis of achievement.* (Emphasis added.)[2]

If these factors are taken into consideration, it becomes crystal-clear why attending a consciousness-raising group for a period of time is one of the best possible preventive programs for the enlightened woman. But, as has already been mentioned, these groups are not equipped to handle serious emotional problems or crises. For these, stronger supportive measures may be needed: this is the time to seek professional assistance.

DEALING WITH EMOTIONAL PROBLEMS

Selecting a Therapist or Counselor

The process of selecting a therapist or counselor usually involves a number of perplexing questions, such as these: "Is one type of therapy better for me than another?" "Should I have group or individual therapy?" "What are the professional qualifications of my (prospective) therapist?" These and other questions will be covered in this section in some detail.

Many schools and varieties of therapy and counseling are available today. There are Freudian, neo-Freudian, Jungian, Reichian, behavioral, gestalt, bioenergetic, nondirective, rational-emotive, and other treatment programs. Each school has a different focus or emphasis in working with the human personality. There are also eclectic therapists or counselors who use what they consider the best elements from a variety of schools.

If you are thinking about therapy, one of your first tasks is to acquaint yourself more fully with the various schools of therapy and counseling in order to select the one whose focus seems most relevant to you. For example, Freudian therapy has a strong emphasis on the past, on early sexual relationships, and on relationships between mother, father, and child. If your images and dreams are important and meaningful to you, you may wish to select Jungian therapy, which concentrates in that area. Gestalt therapy concentrates on repressed parts of the personality and involves considerable acting out or role playing. Bioenergetic and neo-Reichian therapies concentrate on body work. Behavioral therapy utilizes conditioning processes, reward systems, and contracts or agreements between therapist and client.

The choice of the school or type of therapy is less important if you are considering short-time counseling for a less serious problem. For example, you

[2] Ibid.

may feel that your mental health is fundamentally sound. However, because of a variety of pressures from your environment you need specific help for the specific situation in which you find yourself. On the other hand, you may wish to resolve problems which are traceable to your past, are of long standing, and have caused you repeated difficulties. In this instance, long-term therapeutic or counseling help is needed. Survey the various schools and select the one that suits you best. The bibliography includes a number of books which will be of assistance in this process. In any event, it is also most helpful to talk to as many friends and acquaintances as possible who have been in therapy and to get ideas from them.

There is a concept widely used by therapists: "We need to go most into the area where the resistance is greatest." This may have application to you when you are selecting a form of therapy. For example, if you have been "living largely in the head," if you are analytical and have strong intellectual interests, you may resist the idea of body or nonverbal therapy. Yet this may be the very area you need to work in, for a number of reasons—to create a more balanced personality, to experience new dimensions of yourself, and to make the best progress in therapy.

There is also the choice between private and group therapy or counseling. Both have advantages and disadvantages, and many contemporary therapists use both approaches as part of their treatment program. However, I believe that group treatment will be the preferred method in the future. This will be due to five major reasons, increasingly recognized by therapists: (1) Group treatment offers fewer opportunities for the unconscious manipulation of the therapist by the patient or client. (2) Group treatment offers more varied and effective ways of dealing with patients' defenses and resistances. (3) A variety of role models and health vectors can be utilized as a part of group treatment. (4) Group treatment is less expensive. (5) If used correctly, group treatment may reduce treatment time.

Regardless of whether the emphasis is on individual or group therapy, the personality of the therapist or counselor (and how his or her skills are used) are of the utmost importance in therapy. Naturally, however, the professional qualifications of the therapist must be carefully checked. Your local chapter of the American Medical Association, the American Psychiatric Association, or the American Psychological Association can be of help. Telephone them or write to them for information. Also, most states now have licensing programs which establish certain minimum professional and training standards for therapists and counselors. As a result, you are not as likely to encounter a quack. Do not be afraid to ask your prospective therapist about training or credentials. A qualified professional will welcome such inquiries. Again, you can get excellent leads by checking with your friends and asking ministers, social workers, and others in the professional community about who are the outstanding therapists in your area.

In selecting a therapist, your primary emphasis should be on whether you feel you can work with this person and whether you feel that he or she can help you with the problem you present. The professional qualifications and competence of a therapist or counselor are, of course, important, as I have just noted. However, far more important are the personality of the therapist and your relationship with him or her—that is, your feeling about the therapist and your confidence in the therapist as a person. Often a client will begin treatment with a therapist during a crisis, will be helped through the crisis, and will then discover that the therapist's personality and relationship with the client are not what was expected. The emotional intensity of a crisis may prevent a clear perception of this important factor. Clients often say something like the following in describing this variable: "When I first started therapy I was desperate. My first therapist helped some, but I became more and more convinced that he just wasn't right for me. He was a good therapist, but something in his personality prevented me from feeling close to him. We talked it over, and I changed therapists. What a difference! We clicked, and I really felt we would make progress." Do not be afraid to use your intuition and to change therapists—that is your option. The enlightened contemporary therapist has become increasingly aware that, in this connection especially, more often than not, *the client knows what is best for him or her* and can be trusted.

One of the things to be aware of in therapy is the tendency of some therapists to make their clients dependent on them. The psychologist Roberta Ellner says: "Demystify the relationship in terms of the power structure and be aware of the places where you buy into the authority-patient role. I heard a therapist in San Francisco describe his method for getting clients hooked on him. He sits and waits and just as a patient is about to make an interpretation, he makes it for them! The clients get dependent on him for problem-solving. Even, so the clients tend to get better. But it's very serious. In actuality the therapist is just a guide and the client has to do the real work for herself."[3]

Women face a particular problem in the selection of a therapist. Research has shown that many therapists (regardless of their sex) have sexist attitudes about what a woman is (or should be). If you believe that a woman's self-concept and her role in today's society are changing (and should change even more), then the therapist you select should not have conservative, traditional views, or a Victorian concept of womanhood.

To counter the influence of conservative, traditional views of womanhood held by many therapists of both sexes, and to offer the modern woman some alternative, feminist therapy collectives have sprung up all over the country. Staffed by qualified professionals, the collectives are groups of women who identify their mission as a feminist one:

> The members of some groups live together, but most do not share housing. In some places, collectives are *in effect, a group practice of therapists who possess all the traditional degrees but are applying their learning in untraditional ways.* Others combine paraprofessionals with women formally educated as therapists. . . . A feminist therapist does not believe that each sex must emit certain distinctive behaviors in order to be healthy, just because of gender. Clients who have been nudged back into conventional sex roles by the authority and values of many traditional therapists will get

---

[3] Quoted in Anne K. Rush, *Getting Clear,* Random House, New York, 1973, p. 133.

help from feminist therapists in doing some of the things they want to do. . . . Feminist therapists consider it beneficial to discover how you have been programmed to live down to sex-role stereotypes and then to overcome as much as possible your own conditioning.[4]

There is no question that a double standard of mental health and treatment exists. Not only do sex stereotypes obtrude into the treatment program, but women are seen both as the principal cause of sickness in others and as being sick themselves. Regardless of whether one subscribes to this point of view, there is evidence that women utilize mental health services of all kinds—including private and public facilities and institutional and outpatient facilities, considerably more than men do. (For example, in 1970 there were 69 men for every 100 women in the psychiatric wards of general hospitals and in private hospitals.) According to Phyllis Chesler, "From 1950 to 1970 women in America, England, Canada and Sweden have been seen and consider themselves more 'disturbed' than their male counterparts."[5] It is clear that the disadvantaged position of women in today's society contributes significantly to this fact.

The double standard in mental-health services also extends to the prescription of drugs. The psychologist Linda Fidell found that 67 percent of prescriptions for psychoactive drugs are received by women. "Since doctors tend to terminate interviews by giving prescriptions, it isn't surprising to find the sex with the greater number of visits receiving the greater number of prescriptions. The problem is that the numbers are disproportionate. *Women get more drugs than they make visits.* Therefore, a relationship that appears straightforward has, in fact, *a heavy overlay of sex-role stereotyping*" (emphasis added).[6]

The cost of therapy or counseling varies widely. By and large, psychiatrists charge the highest fees, followed by psychologists and other members of the helping professions. Fees range from $50 or more per session to $10 or less. The sliding fee is widely used. This means that the client and therapist together review the financial status of the client and arrive at a fee appropriate for the client's income and existing financial obligations. Lack of financial resources should not deter anyone from seeking therapeutic help. Not only is it possible to find a therapist in private practice (although it will take a little looking) with whom a financial arrangement can be made, but public resources are also available. These include local mental-health clinics. In many of the larger cities there are now "free" clinics (some are not actually free) as well as the feminist therapy collectives mentioned earlier. Most, if not all, of these agencies have sliding fees, and here the fee slides considerably lower and some free services are available. Finally, some of the larger churches now offer counseling services, and an increasing number of ministers are trained as counselors.

Marriage and Family Counseling or Therapy

When the two adults in a family are working, this can set up stresses and strains within a marital relationship which would not otherwise arise. (In this connec-

---

[4] Marilyn Elias, "Sisterhood Therapy," *Human Behavior,* vol. 4, no. 4. p. 58.

[5] Phyllis Chesler, *Women and Madness,* Doubleday, Garden City, N.Y., 1972. p. 56.

[6] Mary E. King and Sharland Trotter, "Why Do More Women than Men Think They're Sick in the Head?" *Vogue,* vol. 164, no. 4, p. 195.

tion, some of the exercises such as the "My Strengths Experience," the "Your Strengths Experience," pages 428 to 430, and the "Family Joy Experience," page 50, may be helpful.) If the partners are aware of marital difficulties, the best possible course is to seek marriage counseling early, before the problem becomes severe. Early treatment for marital problems not only saves cost and treatment time; it also prevents much unhappiness and pain which inevitably also affects the work of both spouses.

The American Association of Marriage and Family Counselors, which sets professional standards in the field, is an excellent source of help. By writing to their headquarters (225 Yale Avenue, Claremont, California 91711) you can obtain a list of qualified professionals in your community. The Family Service Association (national headquarters, the Family Service Association of America, 44 East 23 Street, New York, New York 10010) may have an agency in your community. They are specialists in family problems and offer professional services on a sliding-fee system. Mental-health clinics also offer family therapy.

If a child in the family has a breakdown or suffers an emotional illness and you live in or near a major metropolitan center, it may be well to obtain the services of a consultant. The consultant is usually a psychiatrist who specializes in diagnosing and assessing the severity of an emotional disturbance or illness as well as directing patients to the most appropriate treatment program or facility. Unfortunately, there are no directories of such consultants; however, the name of a consultant can be obtained from a reliable source such as the chairperson of the department of psychiatry in a medical school, the director of psychiatric services of a general hospital, or the director of a community mental-health clinic.

Symptoms of a serious emotional disturbance (a suicide attempt, depression, etc.) are the main indicators of the need for a consultant. In addition to finding the best possible treatment program, one of the major functions of the consultant may be to assess and coordinate the initial involvement of the family in the treatment process. In this connection, it is of interest that an increasing number of treatment facilities in the United States over the past years have come to the conclusion that *the best way of helping the emotionally ill person is to involve the total family in the treatment program.* There are some indications that this fosters earlier recovery and prevents a recurrence of the illness.

IN CONCLUSION

The best way to prevent emotional illness is by planning and beginning your own program to enhance your mental health and vitality. The first section of this chapter and Chapter 3, pages 56, 62, and 63, will furnish some basic guidelines useful in designing such a program. In the event of marital problems or emotional illness in your family, it is best to seek help at once. Qualified professionals are available in your community, and it will not be difficult to locate such resources as the first and crucial step toward regaining emotional health.

BIBLIOGRAPHY

Chesler, Phyllis: *Women and Madness,* Doubleday, Garden City, N.Y., 1972. A contemporary scholarly study of the reasons why women seek help through therapy or institutions. The author points out that sex-role stereotypes are at the heart of much of what we call "mental illness" and that a double standard exists in the area of mental health.

Corsini, Raymond: *Current Psychotherapies,* Peacock, Itasca, Ill., 1973. Twelve chapters, each written by an expert in the field. Technical, but understandable. There is also a paperback edition.

Deutch, Ronald M.: *The Family Guide to Better Food and Better Health,* Creative Home Library/Meredith, Des Moines, Iowa, 1971. A complete guide with special sections on weight control, growing up, aging, maturity, etc.

Geba, Bruno H: *Breathe Away Your Tensions,* Random House, New York, 1973. The author describes a five-week program of body relaxation and deep breathing for release from migraine headaches, nervous tension, insomnia, anxiety, depression, guilt, and other problems of living.

Harper, Robert A.: *Psychoanalysis and Psychotherapy,* Prentice-Hall (Spectrum), Englewood Cliffs, N.J., 1954. A concise yet comprehensive overview of thirty-six systems of psychotherapy by a well-known practitioner. Paperback.

Heck, Edward: *A Guide to Mental Health Services,* University of Pittsburgh, Pittsburgh, Pa., 1972. Offers guidance on the various types of mental-health service available, how to find a therapist, how to investigate his qualifications, and how to negotiate a contract for therapy.

Liss, Jerome: *Free to Feel,* Praeger, New York, 1974. Very readable; written by a young psychiatrist and subtitled "Finding Your Way Through the New Therapies." A special chapter, "The New Group Experience," has a valuable annotated bibliography.

Lomas, Peter: *True and False Experience,* Taplinger, New York, 1973. The book represents an attempt to understand factors that inhibit both patient and therapist from establishing a genuine relationship with each other. It also examines Freudian analytic theory in light of the post-Freudian and existentialist movements.

Loomis, Evarts G.: *Healing for Everyone—Medicine of the Whole Person,* Hawthorne, New York, 1975. Written by a physician who is also a minister. There is a special section on nutrition and exercise.

Miller, Don Ethan: *Bodymind,* Prentice-Hall, Englewood Cliffs, N.J., 1974. Subtitled "The Whole Person Healthbook." It has chapters on relaxation, exercises, food, etc., and emphasizes yoga, Zen, and other systems.

Rush, Anne K.: *Getting Clear,* Random House, New York, 1973. Subtitled "Body Work for Women." It covers a broad range of subjects through interviews with specialists. Chapters include "Relating to Your Doctor," "Pelvic Self-Examination," "Reclaiming Your Sexuality," "Childbirth, Children and You." There are sections on exercises, massage, etc.

Sobel, David S., and Faith L. Hornbacher: *An Everyday Guide to Your Health,* Grossman, New York, 1973. Covers all aspects of daily health care in considerable detail, including body rhythms and breathing exercises. Contemporary and profusely illustrated, it draws on many systems and has an excellent bibliography.

Turchetti, Richard J., and Joseph J. Morella: *New Age Nutrition,* Henry Regnery, Chicago, 1974. A full-scale treatment of diet and nutrition for the person who is confronted daily by the special stresses of modern life, a polluted environment, adulterated food, etc.

Chapter 15

Keeping Fit for Fun and Personal Development

Olga Connolly

Olga Fikotova Connolly, a former medical student at Charles University, Prague, is an Olympic champion in the women's discus throw and a record holder in the United States. She is the Director of Intramural Athletics and Recreation, Loyola-Marymount University, Los Angeles. Ms. Connolly has published numerous articles in magazines and journals and is the author of two books, *Vieraina Valloista* (Kirjäyhtimä, Helsinki, 1964) and *The Rings of Destiny* (McKay, New York, 1968).

"Do you know Mademoiselle Reisz?" Edna asked irrelevantly.

"The pianist? I've heard her play."

"She says queer things sometimes in a bantering way that you don't notice at the time and you find yourself thinking about afterward."

"For instance"?

"Well, for instance, when I left her today, she put her arms around me and felt my shoulder blades, to see if my wings were strong, she said."

"The bird that would soar above the level plain of tradition and prejudice must have strong wings. It is a sad spectacle to see the weaklings bruised, exhausted, fluttering back to earth." (From *The Awakening,* by Kate Chopin.)[1]

Our classification as human beings is based partly on erect posture. But, as somebody once said, women have yet to learn to stand up straight. Women's mastery of their own bodies, long overdue, can become the pathway to self-actualization.

Movement is basic to life and characteristic of one's personality. The question of how much expression through free movement a woman should afford herself is, therefore, far from irrelevant; and it goes well beyond the idea of exercise drills designed to protect people from dying young of heart attacks.

In 1888, the utopian novelist Edward Bellamy wrote, "Until woman comes to her kingdom physically, she will really never come at all. Created to be well and strong and beautiful, she long ago sacrificed her constitution. She has walked where she should have run, sat where she should have walked, reclined where she should have sat. She is a creature born to the freedom and beauty of Diana."

Had I known this quotation in 1957 when, fresh off the boat, I visited a high school in Massachusetts, I would have found it sadly fitting. During that visit I commented to the school principal that the girls' physical education program seemed to be so easy as to be ineffective.

"We don't believe in strenuous exercises for girls," the principal explained. "Our girls are different from the European women. You are much sturdier; to you, sports come naturally. American girls are brought up to play the violin."

As I stared at him in disbelief, I thought of the French concert pianist Micheline Ostermeyer, who was also the Olympic discus champion in 1948. I thought of Greta Garbo and Ingrid Bergman, who brought a new ideal of beauty to the United States—but how Americans ignored the basis of the Swedish complexion and figure, the rugged Scandinavian environment combined with a demanding program of calisthenics in every school. I also recalled a train journey I had made in January of that year, traveling with Czechoslovak and Soviet Olympic teams from Vladivostok to Moscow. All during the ten-day trip, women were shoveling tons of snow off the railroad tracks. The beauty of many of them could not be concealed even by the heavy layers of ugly clothing they wore to survive the cruel winter of Siberia.

My English was poor, so I said nothing. I only felt sorry for the girls at that high school, who were denied the opportunity to discover their own constitutions.

Now, twenty years later, such a conversation would not take place at a high school in Massachusetts. Women are coming into their own. They are loosening their girdles and tightening their muscles. They are fixing their own cars and paving their own driveways. They are finding that a woman, like a man, is born to build and to play.

Women who play volleyball are learning to deliver fast, well-placed spikes.

[1] Kate Chopin, *The Awakening,* 1899. Kate Chopin, an aristocratic Southern widow and the mother of five, was a promising writer of short stories. But *The Awakening,* which described the sexual and artistic awakening of a young housewife in New Orleans, was attacked by critics and banned by libraries; this abruptly ended her literary career.

Women gymnasts, through sweat and calluses, are defying gravity. In marathon races or the martial arts, women are proving that they are not quitters and are not physically or emotionally inferior to men.

WHAT IS FITNESS?

In 1953 Hans Kraus and Ruth Hirschland tested several thousand European and American children for strength and flexibility. They reported that whereas only 8.7 percent of the Europeans failed the test, 57.9 percent of the Americans failed.[2] Since then, physical fitness has become a topic of conversation as common as the weather. A never-ending string of reports on fitness and lack of fitness, with certain and uncertain conclusions, have followed: five out of seven Americans are rejected by the Selective Service, three for physical reasons and two for mental disability; one out of every two Americans is too fat; the pressure of a businessman's life, coupled with lack of physical activity, may cause a coronary failure at the age of fifty. National consciousness of fitness was created. An entire fitness business was born.

Nevertheless, "fitness" has remained a hazy term. A well-known scientist who loathes physical activity once told me that a person can be fit for only one life-style at a time. "I am fit enough to sit down in my armchair after work and read a good book," he said. "If I ever set my heart on climbing Mount Everest, I'll take up exercise."

"Fitness" is not synonymous with "trimness." A few months ago I had the opportunity to watch a breathtaking performance by a fire dancer from Hawaii who could most simply be described as a ball of fat. At incredible speed, she juggled flaming torches and thin-bladed knives in complicated rhythms and postures which required the utmost flexibility and body control from head to toe. At the end of her long performance she was barely out of breath. That young woman's body was not fashionable according to common American standards, but it was admirably functional.

Medical authorities usually define physical fitness in terms of the definition of health suggested by the World Health Organization: a sense of social, physical, and mental well-being. The President's Council on Physical Fitness states:

> Physical fitness is a broad quality involving medical and dental supervision and care, immunization and other protection against disease, proper nutrition, adequate rest, relaxation, good health practices, sanitation and other aspects of healthy living. Exercise is an essential element to achieve physical fitness.
>
> Strength, stamina, endurance, and other desirable physical qualities are best developed through vigorous activity. Physical fitness is achieved through a sensible balance of all these provisions adapted to age, maturity, and capacity of the individual.[3]

[2] H. Kraus and R. P. Hirschland, "Minimum Muscular Fitness in School Children," *Research Quarterly,* vol. 25, pp. 178–188, 1954.
[3] President's Council on Physical Fitness, *U.S. Physical Fitness Program,* John Dienhart, Chicago, 1963.

Gordon Rosenblum is a gynecologist in Southern California who is referred to by his younger colleagues as the "grand old man" of gynecology. He says,

> Ignorance of health and sex education can make girls and women less fit than flabby muscles. Is a person fit who can do fifty situps but who disseminates VD? . . . Unwanted pregnancies are still threatening many women's lives. . . . We cannot afford to have people ignorant about the physiological and sexual functions of their bodies and lacking the knowledge of how to behave responsibly. Sex education is a part of feminine fitness.[4]

Fitness, then, is the totality of many steps in many directions. Arthur Steinhaus, an eminent physiologist at the University of Chicago, once said: "We have to understand it on the level which separates us from animals." A fit human being must be fit on the level where physical, intellectual, emotional, and social factors cannot be separated. The search for such fitness must begin with the individuals' curiosity about themselves and about their inner and outer environments.

Intellectual fitness cannot be achieved without a study of some field or fields or without appreciation of the connections among disciplines of learning. It requires self-discipline; objectivity; and the ability to distinguish facts from hearsay, reality from superstition, and single-mindedness from lack of vision.

Emotional fitness can be achieved only by those trained to recognize their own strengths and weaknesses and to meet challenges by confronting and analyzing them.

Social fitness, based on mutual respect among people, might be characterized as the ability to freely interact with society without being swallowed up by it.

Intellectual, emotional, and social fitness all require the self-control and freedom which are acquired when individuals understand themselves and are comfortable with themselves. That is the point where physical culture plays an important role. For a normally developed person, bodily control is achievable and observable in a relatively short time. For a handicapped person, achievement of various degrees of bodily control often brings with it the discovery of more potential than was thought to exist.

WOMEN AND BODILY FITNESS

One good reason why any woman should cultivate bodily strength, endurance, flexibility, and coordination is that this will increase her confidence and security in the only environment where she can be completely in charge. A woman's own body is the one management position from which she can resign but cannot be fired. Age, bodily size or shape, marital status, and motherhood are irrelevant to fitness. All that matters is that you take a good look at yourself and pose certain questions, such as these:

How creative have I been with what is unmistakably mine?
Do I know the possibilities within myself?

---

[4] Olga Connolly, "Keeping Fit in a Sedentary Society," *Los Angeles Times,* July 12, 1970.

Do I understand the totality of my mind and body?
Do I know how to feel good without depending on outside sources?
Do I know how to relax?
Am I strong? What is "strength"?

Often I hear women say, "I wish I were taller"; "I wish I were . . ."; "I hate being so . . ."; "It would be great to be different." This sort of thing is a waste of time. It represents an estrangement from the time when the child discovered his or her body to be a creation of beauty, functionality, and comfort. Instead, ask yourself, "Is my body my best support, or is it a hindrance?" "Do I barely get through my usual daily activities, or do I have extra reserves on which I can draw either for fun or for emergencies?"

The Common Body Types

William Sheldon and his colleagues have isolated three major body types. They range from the thin, light-boned ectomorph, through the sturdier, broader, more muscular mesomorph, to the predominantly fat endomorph.[5] In individuals, these three basic body types are blended. Each person is therefore unique; and we all have a wide potential for making our bodies aesthetically pleasing or training them for a specialized function such as a sport. If one's body type makes one activity difficult, it will make for excellence in another one. For example, a pronounced ectomorph could hardly become a successful Olympic weight lifter but might well become an Olympic high-jumper.

For most people who strive for fitness at all levels, the possibilities are virtually limitless. To become fit, a woman needs to understand herself and balance her limitations and her strengths.

Posture

After consideration of one's body type, the next logical step is an appraisal of one's posture. Posture is defined as an arrangement of schematic body segments in a balanced column which ensures the maintenance of body balance with a minimum of energy expenditure and skeletal or muscular strain, as well as proper spacing of the internal organs so they may function to their full capacity. The segments are feet, ankles, and calves; knees and thighs; pelvis and hips; back and chest; shoulders, neck, and head. They all should be neatly stacked up one on another, shifted neither forward, backward, nor sideways.

If you stand with your back to a wall in properly aligned posture, the back of your head, your upper back, your buttocks, your calves, and your heels will all be lightly touching the wall. None will be actually pressing against. Try it. Stand tall, and enjoy the expansion of your breathing.

A fascinating analysis of posture and body types can be found in *Movement Fundamentals*, by Janet Wessel (see the bibliography at the end of this chapter).

[5] W. H. Sheldon, S. S. Stevens, and W. B. Tucker, *The Varieties of Human Physique*, Harper & Row, New York, 1940.

Weight Control   The chances are that before you begin to explore your body and its possibilities for creative expression through motion, you will consider whether you are overweight or underweight.

What are the facts involved in weight control? What is sensible, and what is faddish? Where should cosmetic considerations end; that is, to what extent should one try to match the norms of beauty in a given society? Where does a loss of functionality begin? When do you face the danger of the degenerative disease called obesity? Tables of standard weights, if used knowledgeably, can give you an idea. But they do not indicate the proportion of "active" tissue (bones, muscles, etc.) to tissue of limited usefulness—fat.

Fat is useful as a highly concentrated store of energy. It represents an emergency supply of body fuel and is an insulation against cold. The accumulation of fat depends on the kind of foods one eats and the kind and degree of physical activity one is involved in.

A pinch test indicates quite well whether you are storing too much fat. In a relaxed posture, perhaps lying down, gently lift your skin with your thumb and forefinger at certain places: the back of the upper arm; just below your shoulder blades; on the side of your lower ribs; at the top of the iliac crest; halfway between your navel and the top of your pubic bone. If the skin you can pinch at these locations is more than 1 inch thick, you are probably overweight. If what you can pinch is very thick, and if your body weight is more than 20 percent higher than the standard for your height and age, you are facing a struggle against obesity.

In a normal, healthy person, controlling fat is a relatively simple procedure which depends directly on a person's determination to give it some attention. No magician, miracle pill, or machine can do it for you. Taking diuretics or limiting your intake of water is foolish; this reduces not fat but the volume of your body's vital fluids. If you persist in dehydrating yourself, your body may get severely damaged; if you stop dehydrating yourself, the replenished body fluids will show up on the scales.

Fat cannot be rubbed away, pounded away, shaken away, melted, squeezed, dried, or hypnotized away. Fat can be lost only by being used as fuel for your energy output. In order to lose fat, you must take in less fuel than is needed for your output of energy. Since we supply new fuel every time we eat, we must eat less than we need to maintain our daily energy needs, and thus force the body to use its reserves. Or, you may consume the same amount of food, but increase your energy output, which will have the same effect. For example, if a woman adds a 2-mile walk to her normal daily activity without increasing her food intake, she will lose about 20 pounds a year. If at the same time she decreases her food intake by 200 calories a day, she will double that loss. Once she achieves a desirable proportion between lean tissues and fat, she must balance her food intake so that it covers all her energy needs, including the calories she is expending in the 2-mile walk. The walk will no longer serve as a means of reducing fat but rather will become a period of rejuvenation and relaxation.

People have claimed that combining exercise with their dieting makes matters worse because it increases their appetite, but the scientific evidence does not support this. Mayer et al. have shown that while a high degree of activity does increase appetite, moderate activity actually suppresses appetite.[6]

According to Herbert DeVries of the University of Southern California, and others, exercise is superior to dieting for control of fat. Weight loss through bodily training eliminates more fat and less lean tissue and water than dieting. There is another advantage to exercise. The main reason for energy expenditure during physical activity is the increase in metabolic rate. DeVries and others have confirmed that because of the increased metabolic rate, the fat-burning process continues for at least six hours following your workout.[7]

A most important consideration: Successful reduction of fat, which results in stabilization of one's weight for years to come, is best achieved not through a crash program but through a gradual, permanent change in one's living habits. The change from a sedentary to an active life should be accompanied by better understanding of your functioning.

For example, if you overeat, you ought to figure out why you overeat. One possibility is that you are a busy person who tends to develop a "sleep debt." Your body wants to go to bed and regenerate, but you try to substitute food for sleep. This is really a lack of communication with yourself, and it leaves you fatter rather than fresher. There are other reasons—mostly emotional—why people use food as a substitute for other things. Discovering such reasons and coping with them is critical not only for control of weight but also for personal growth and achievement.

Very obese persons whose organs and tissues have been weakened by the encroachment of fatty cells are strained by having to carry their own excessive weight. In order to determine if their heart, bones, muscles, joints, and ligaments can withstand the additional load of exercise, they should place themselves under medical supervision, choosing the physician carefully.

A word about being underweight is in order here. If you need to become heavier, you should reverse the thought processes connected with being overweight. In order to develop extra padding, you have to increase your energy intake beyond what is needed for your energy output. But exercise is also useful in gaining weight. Weight lifting is the best choice; combined with proper nutrition, it will result in increased muscle bulk (e.g., it will help you to fill in the spaces around your collar bones). Simply increasing your food intake can result in fatty deposits which may tire you out instead of making you sprightlier.

Some very thin people have a tendency to overexert themselves. Mastering the ability to slow down, relax, and sleep is of great value.

[6] J. Mayer et al., "Exercise, Food Intake and Body Weight in Normal Rats and Genetically Obese Adult Mice," *American Journal of Physiology*, vol. 177, p. 544, 1954.

[7] H. A. DeVries and D. E. Gray, "After Effects of Exercise upon Resting Metabolic Rate," *Research Quarterly*, vol. 34, pp. 314–321, 1963.

"**Instant-Body Shops**"   A few years ago I decided to explore some of the establishments that help perpetuate the notion that fat is synonymous with ugliness. Using my mother's maiden name, I made an appointment with a figure salon that promised completely effortless weight reduction and sensational improvement of the figure.

The manager assured me that I would receive individual attention. This establishment, before signing up a prospective client, photographs her, analyzes the pictures, and then designs a program that promises to help her body without hurting her pocketbook. And so my picture was taken, against the background of a white wall calibrated with large squares. On my photograph the manager marked what she said were excesses of fat, totaled up the "unsightly inches," and, in a subdued voice filled with sympathy, told me the verdict: I was quite bulky; I had been accumulating fat; I had been heading toward a loss of youthfulness and sex appeal. I could be saved, though, by undergoing their full battery of treatments for their highest fee.

Now, even though I am an athlete and even though I was there on a fact-finding mission, I felt quite shaken by this verdict. I accepted the free first session that was offered. The manager promised that it would be not only remedial but also thoroughly relaxing. Exuberantly, she introduced me to a couch-like machine made up of sinister-looking blocks. She made certain that I was resting on it *really* comfortably. And then she pushed the button.

I will never forget the moment when that mechanical beast sprang to life. It began to shake me, jolt me, and pull me in all directions, evidently with one intent: to end my career as a discus thrower prematurely by displacing my every bone.

About halfway between the beginning of the treatment and the time the machine succeeded in dislocating my back, the manager stopped by to explain that such violence was equivalent to five miles of horseback riding and that it would increase my circulation to a level where the blood would rip off the ugly fat cells and carry them away. I took my pulse, which was my usual 62 beats per minute, and I wondered (quite apart from the nonsense about the ripping off of the fat cells) how my circulation could be speeded up without my heart's pumping more vigorously.

The manager told me that I needed 150 hours on this machine, for a fee of $600. But, luckily, I qualified for a 20 percent discount. Had I not known that the California law (Civil Code Sections 1812.80–94) dealing with health studios fixed a maximum charge of $500 for their services, I might have believed this was a bargain.

More experiences followed. I visited a figure salon where women were wrapped up like mummies in acid-smelling, wet bandages, and stacked up on little cots to vegetate while their fat (and their money) shrank away. The contract for this service included a guarantee, but it had a condition: that the client must diet at home to a degree which, I considered, bordered on being injurious to health (this condition was not mentioned in the salon's advertised claims of effectiveness). The women who did lose weight did so because of their starvation, not because of the wraps; yet the salon robbed the women of the credit for success. Often, when these women finished their "cure," they returned to their old eating habits and remained inactive: $500 poorer, no wiser, and getting fatter by the hour.

In a chain of active-exercise studios the situation was not much better. The instructor took my measurements. Then he introduced me to certain exercises, which totaled about one-tenth of the intensity needed to increase my metabolic rate. An hour later the instructor gave me the benefit of a lecture on proper posture. Then he measured me again. I straightened up, having previously slouched over, and my waistline was 1 inch smaller and my bustline 1 inch bigger. This spectacular improvement, of course, had nothing to do with their exercises; anyone can produce such shifts in figure measurements by means of proper body alignment. (You can try it while experimenting with correct posture, using a wall as a guide. You'll like the immediacy of your figure improvement.)

For the sake of justice, however, I must emphasize that, besides the exploitative figure industry, there exist health clubs, usually smaller ones—and individuals within the big outfits—who have a background in athletics, body building, or physiotherapy, and who honestly educate their customers. They give their customers sound advice on the basic rules of conditioning and nutrition. They explain that the customers pay for being coached, for being encouraged to overcome their mental and physical weaknesses, and for having the opportunity to exercise in the company of others. These places allow their customers to grow through understanding what is happening to and within their bodies. An association with such a health club becomes a part of a person's schooling, and is therefore money well spent.

Women and Sports

American women have long had unfounded fears about participating in sports. I hope that the following discussion will help to dispel your insecurities in this regard.

Are you afraid of becoming muscular? You *are* muscular. Muscles are a part of your body and serve important purposes: they protect your bone structure from injury; they keep your posture erect and vibrant; they enable you to move.

Most orthopedic surgeons will confirm that a major proportion of lower back pain not explained by damage visible on x-rays is caused by a lack of muscular support in that heavily abused area.

Muscles are a natural girdle, though many women have been conditioned to replace them with foundation garments. Fine development of the stomach muscles (by sit-ups and leg-ups) and the lower back muscles (by back-ups) leads to good posture, a beautiful figure, easy childbirth, a painless back, and—believe it or not—a feeling of confidence that can last a lifetime.

Some women possess sharper, more masculine, bodily features. These are a matter of body type rather than a result of exercise. More typically, women's muscles are enveloped by a thin blanket of fat which softens women's muscular definition.

Your muscles are a part of you. It is inconceivable that while establishing yourself as a vital, vibrant, valid entity, you would allow any part of you to atrophy.

Menstruation, Pregnancy, and Physical Fitness

Both menstruation and pregnancy are a natural part of a women's physiology. They should be treated neither as sacrosanct nor as a hindrance or an illness. The evidence of research in Europe as well as in the United States is that exercise is not at all injurious to normal female functions. In fact, studies on strenuous training by women have shown that well over 80 percent of Olympic athletes who are mothers have gone through shorter labor than is normal for women who not are athletes, and that the incidence of cesarean section among these Olympic athletes was less than half of the average.[8] I competed in five Olympic Games over twenty years and four children, and can attest to the fact that the general and psychological conditioning derived from athletics has been a fine aid during pregnancy and recovery from childbirth every time.

Exercise and Age

There is little scientific evidence about the beneficial effects of exercise on aging organisms. But suitable calisthenics and rhythmic exercises, as well as stretches, have been used successfully in geriatric groups. According to DeVries, a person's limitations regarding exercise in the later years are largely self-imposed or imposed by a lack of continuity in exercise habits. Probably every activity which is mastered during one's youth can be continued well into old age, provided that it is practiced a minimum of three times a week.[9] The growing popularity of the masters' tournaments in track and field and in gymnastics corroborates this theory.

The onset of menopause is an undeniable sign of aging. But its message can be minimized by a woman's confidence in her physical strength and stamina. In our society, where an obsession with youth has made old age synonymous with uselessness, this is an invaluable psychological booster.

It is possible to start a program of physical conditioning late in life, or after years of inactivity. Several things are required.

A thorough medical examination.

Mental release from a socially imposed role (e.g., older people don't play soccer or jump).

A knowledgeably prepared plan for gradual, progressively more intensive conditioning.

Perseverance.

An understanding of fatigue.

[8] G. J. Erdelyi, "Gynaecological Survey of Female Athletes," *Journal of Sports Medicine*, vol. 2, pp. 174–179, 1962.

[9] H. A. DeVries, *Physiology of Exercise for Physical Education and Athletics,* Brown, Dubuque, Iowa, 1966, p. 296.

The last point—understanding fatigue—deserves a brief explanation. The sense of fatigue is as complex as the human personality. It may represent a diminished capacity for work because of actual tiredness—that is, a person's temporary inability to cope with a certain load. However, the feeling of being tired may also mean lack of motivation, lack of self-confidence, a feeling that youth is gone, or boredom with an uninspiring activity. Tiredness is a mental and emotional experience as well as a physical experience. Understanding why you feel tired and controlling that feeling are an important part of your fitness training.

THE BATTLE OF THE SEXES

Pitching women against men so that either side can prove its superiority is detrimental to mutual understanding and respect between the sexes. Women and men are built somewhat differently. These differences are significant, do not imply superiority or inferiority, and have to be understood in order to allow each individual to develop to his or her utmost potential.

Generally speaking, men's anatomical, physiological, and biochemical qualities provide them with greater potential strength, speed, and endurance. Women have greater potential flexibility, agility, and balance. But each sex also possesses the qualities of the other, though the degrees vary from individual to individual. Therefore, while all available qualities should be freely developed, in the competitions where the qualities dominant in one sex play a decisive role, men's and women's performances should not be compared. Here is an example: If a woman and a man of approximately the same size and weight undergo an identical training program, the man will soon surpass the woman in strength, endurance, and speed. Therefore, a woman who has just won an Olympic championship can defeat a less trained man in her event but cannot defeat a man who has just won an Olympic championship in the same event.

The ability to acquire skills coordination is equal between the sexes, as is neuromuscular coordination. Therefore, the man may win not because of superior artistry but because of greater overall physical stamina. Understanding this is part of an intelligent appreciation of sports.

A few sporting events—such as pistol shooting, aeronautics, and parachuting—in which power, speed, and endurance are not crucial invite mixed competition. They give everyone an equal chance, and can be called "unisex."

The lack of appreciation of women's athletic excellence is not women's fault. A society produces champions only in those areas in which it understands championship. It is up to women to educate both themselves and men in this regard.

No one would dream of asking a middleweight boxer to fight a heavyweight. Neither should anyone ask women to prove themselves by competing against men. A meaningful program in women's athletics can be achieved only if the many women who have had enough physical training to be able to appreciate perfection begin to appreciate one another.

A battle between the sexes is unproductive. Rather, fitness of both sexes is vital. Rudyard Kipling put it quite succinctly: "Nations have passed away and left no traces, and History has given the naked cause of it—one single, simple reason in all cases; they fell because their peoples were not fit."

A FEW IDEAS ON ACHIEVING FITNESS

There is no better beginning than taking a swift walk. You can walk in the morning, during your lunch hour, after work, while the kids are at school—where there is desire, there will be a twenty-minute opening even in a busy day. Take a walk with your family or a friend, or alone. A walk alone allows an undisturbed look at one's surroundings as well as at oneself. Besides, in order to participate fully in your conditioning—mentally and emotionally—you have to learn to enjoy being your own company.

Soon the desire to walk will become a desire to jog, then to try to run a bit and to stretch a bit and—finally—to explore one's whole range of movement. You can find competent advice, companionship, and guidance for further conditioning at a college department of intramural athletics, a community adult school, college continuing education classes, the city department of parks and recreation, the YMCA, the Sierra Club, etc. Several books which make enlightening reading and which are likely to be found in your local library are included in the bibliography.

Your final conditioning plan should match your individual needs and your personality. But it must follow a few basic rules:

1 The exercise must allow gradual progression from low levels to high levels of intensity and, therefore, of energy expenditure.

2 It must begin with a warm-up. This usually consists of slow stretches and jogging, possibly followed by stationary basket-shooting; light, rhythmical tennis practice against a backboard; some simple acrobatics; or the like. A warm-up takes you, bodily and psychologically, from the world of monotonous, limited, everyday movement, slow circulation, shallow breathing, and mental pressures into a world of revitalizing challenges, expanded bodily functions, and mental relaxation. A warm-up improves your concentration. It also improves circulation and oxygenation of tissues, thus protecting you from injury. A warm-up should take about fifteen minutes, or approximately the time you need to become lightly sweaty. Good music adds an extra, pleasurable dimension to the warm-up.

3 The actual training must be vigorous enough to result in increased body heat, as evidenced by perspiring. It must be based on the principle of overload, which means that you have to subject your body to a greater amount of work than it is normally accustomed to. This overload might be slight at first; but progressively it becomes greater. However, you should not risk injury to your bone structure, joints, and ligaments by overloading their capacity until it has been safely elevated.

4 Whatever your level of performance, the intensity of your workouts should be as high as possible at the time. In order to achieve reasonable progress, you have to find time to work out at least three times a week, no less than thirty minutes each time.

5 After you achieve a minimum level of physical fitness, start building a program for yourself around the activities you enjoy most. To make your conditioning an exploration, start with only controlled movements (calisthenics) and gradually add the more complex and more chancy moves of different sports, dance, or other physical arts.

6 End each workout with a warm-down period. It can be similar to your warm-up routine. This prevents or reduces muscle soreness on the following day and returns your mind to your other activities.

SOME QUALITIES TO BE CULTIVATED

Strength

A certain degree of overall strength is the foundation for the rest of physical training. Stronger muscles will enable you to move about with easier control, more efficiently, and more gracefully. Supple, toned-up muscles will help you withstand sudden stress without injury. They will enable you to perform more work with less fatigue. Your confidence in your strength will help stabilize your emotions.

People can improve their strength through regular work against a resistance supplied either by their body weight (e.g., push-ups, sit-ups, deep-knee bends, back-ups, etc.) or by various objects (dumbbells, barbells, medicine balls, bricks, books, rocks, etc.)

For a complete beginner the following isometric program might be useful: From toes to head, tense up every muscle group you are able to isolate. Keep the muscles of each group tensed up for about five seconds—remember, as tightly as you can. Then relax. Repeat five times.

Isometric tension will help tone up your muscles. But it will not give you muscular endurance, or improve your coordination. Therefore, as early as possible, start combining your isometric work with isotonic training—that is, moving an object of resistance along the entire range of motion of a given muscle group. (An example is lifting a barbell from shoulder level upward to the maximum extension of the arm.) This will help you improve your muscle endurance and dynamic strength. Excellent strength-conditioning programs are available from the California State Department of Education (see the bibliography).

For centuries women have been asked to stand out as restful islands in the sea of suffering and brutality. Even liberated women have to fulfill that role. But women have to understand that, in order to yield lifesaving fruits, an island must rest on rock. A weak island would be swept away by the sea.

Endurance

The most important quality of a well-conditioned organism is the ability to withstand prolonged activity or mental stress. In practice, strength training and endurance training often overlap. Running uphill, for example, strengthens the legs and at the same time improves endurance.

Nevertheless, general endurance—necessary to fortify heart muscle as well as to improve the efficiency of the cardiovascular, respiratory, and heat-regulatory systems—requires specialized training. In this, jogging, rope jumping, long-distance swimming, bicycling, and rowing are the more effective activities.

The principle of overload must be strictly adhered to. Calculating the sufficient overload is based on multiplying the basic pulse rate. To determine your basic pulse rate, take your pulse in the morning, immediately after awakening and before you get out of bed. It may be, for example, 65 beats per minute. In order to build endurance, you must undergo a workout strenuous enough to double that basic pulse rate. If the basic rate is 65 beats a minute, the rate at the end of a training period should be 65 x 2 = 130 beats a minute.

Overload can also be shown by perspiration. Forget your dread of sweating; forget the television commercials for antiperspirants. You should understand that perspiration acts as a regulator of body heat and as a cleanser of the skin. As perspiration flushes through the tiny pores in your skin, it removes most of the causes of unpleasant body odor—the impurities caught in the pores and embedded so tightly that they cannot be soaped away but can be forced out only by sweat.

The most popular method of endurance training alternates set periods of intensive activity (a given distance or time) and periods of easing off to permit recovery. For example: run 100 yards and then walk 100 yards. Or, swim the length of a pool, then climb out, walk to the other end, jump in, swim again, climb out, and walk back again. As your cardiovascular efficiency improves, you will need less and less time for recovery.

To determine when you have recovered, use your basic pulse rate again. You are sufficiently recovered when your pulse has slowed down from double the normal rate to slightly above the normal rate. If your basic pulse rate is 65, run until it reaches 130 beats per minute, then walk until it drops to about 80 beats per minute before you run again and bring it back to 130.

A strong cardiovascular system is difficult to keep up in today's sedentary kind of life, but it is essential in a world full of physical and psychological pressures. It is important to realize that your heart responds to emotional stimuli as sensitively as it does to physical labor. In the Symposium on the Meaning of Physical Fitness, conducted by the British Royal Society in 1969, Kenneth W. Donald of the University of Edinburgh presented the results of his study of people's cardiovascular responses to stimuli like common traffic situations. Even experienced drivers showed marked acceleration in their heart rate when they were about to pass another vehicle. Once they had made the decision and were engaged in the actual maneuver, the heart rate began to return to normal.[10]

Your heart is affected by many situations and must be abundantly conditioned.

Flexibility

The natural range of motion in different joints varies from one individual to another. There are no prescribed norms for flexibility. Experience has shown,

[10] "The Meaning of Physical Fitness," *Proceedings of the Royal Society of Medicine,* vol. 62, pp. 1180–1182, 1969.

nevertheless, that maintaining a full range of motion in all joints increases a person's agility and mobility throughout life, helps prevent strains and sprains, provides a youthful figure, and prevents a variety of aches and pains ranging from muscular aches to cramps caused by premenstrual congestion.

You can estimate the degree of your flexibility by simply exploring the ease of movement in your every joint. You may be annoyed to find tight spots, and decide to eliminate them through daily stretching.

Stretching does more than restore your flexibility. It also helps significantly in reducing tension. So-called "passive," or static, stretching, is more effective than the "active" loosening-up exercises which were once taught. Active exercises were based on bouncing or bobbing movements, such as the jumping jack, performed in rapid succession. But bouncing and bobbing movements elicit reflex contractions in the muscle fibers which tighten the muscle rather than loosening it up. Therefore, it is generally agreed that for loosening activities (warm-up and warm-down), for improving flexibility, and for reducing tension, static stretches are more effective.

Static stretching is a technique of reaching, gradually and smoothly, in one direction. At the point where discomfort sets in, the effort stops. The person remains motionless for a few seconds, then slowly withdraws and begins to stretch in the opposite direction. When the first movement is repeated, the original tightness has lessened and the point of discomfort moves farther away. Here is an example of a static stretch:

Rise on your toes and start reaching with your arms as high over your head as you can. Try to get beyond that point—another little bit—then slowly, smoothly, bring your arms down. Bend over while allowing your upper body to feel very flaccid, and reach with your arms and hands toward your toes. If you feel pain in the back of your legs before you touch your toes, don't try to use a bounce to get you lower. Just hang there for a few seconds; then start straightening up and rise on your toes again; reach upward, higher and higher—and when you reach the highest point, start downward again.

The chances are that before you feel the painful tightness, you will have reached farther toward your toes than you did at the first try. *Suppress the desire to bounce or move too quickly in either direction.*

Relaxation

A reasonable degree of flexibility is the key to muscular relaxation. (See the bibliography for readings that deal with this topic.) Basically, before you can learn to relax, you must learn to interpret certain messages signaled by your muscles—that is, develop some kinesthetic sense. For every physical activity, one should understand not only how it is done mechanically but—perhaps more important—what it feels like while it is being done.

Once I experimented with two beginning class tennis classes at my university. With one class, I explained in great detail the mechanics of the backhand: the footwork, the arm movement, and the follow-through. With the other, I spent a great deal of time creating images in the minds of my students about *what the backhand feels like.* This second class not only mastered the backhand faster but thought that it was "really easy." My first class did not really master the stroke until I switched to the "feel method" with them, too. This class thought that the backhand was "really hard."

Now, in order to learn to recognize relaxation, you must also learn to recognize tension. Two sample tension-relaxation drills follow:

> Isometrically curl your toes as tightly as you can. Then tighten them up more. Hold the tightness for a few seconds; then let go, and continue letting go. When you think there is no tension left, see if you can let go even more, until your toes feel very soft and warm.

> Close your eyes; wrinkle your forehead. Wrinkle it as tightly as you can; then tighter. Then start letting go—as evenly as possible. Relax; soften the fine musculature in your forehead, around your eyes, at your temples. Keep relaxing—letting go, letting go—until you feel overcome by a very receptive, open, peaceful sensation. Then open your eyes.

Like isometric exercises, tension-relaxation exercises can be used for every muscle group. Going through such a routine at night in bed often serves as a marvelous sleep inducer.

A headache is sometimes caused or worsened by muscular tension in the upper back, behind the neck and shoulders. It is a good idea to try your own resources before you open your medicine chest. Following are two samples of exercises to cure a headache:

> Lie on the floor on your stomach. While keeping your pelvis resting fully on the floor, as if disengaged from your waistline, push upward with your arms until you lock your elbow in full extension. Then allow gravity to suspend the weight of your upper body, neck, and head toward the floor.

> Lie flat on your back on the floor with your arms resting along your body. Raise your legs; bring them over your head and onto the floor behind your head. Close your eyes. Try to let go of the tightness that may appear in this position.

Relaxation is sometimes taught as a state you achieve by doing something. It may be more helpful to consider relaxation as ceasing to do anything. In letting go we are really trying to do nothing. The correct kind of breathing is being stressed. But if it is forced, it can work against your doing nothing. Breathe unhurriedly and naturally, and slow yourself down by taking your time while exhaling.

Experimentation with relaxation may be an experience that will yield new insights into your being.

IN CONCLUSION: FITNESS IN A HISTORICAL CONTEXT

A human being is a playful creature. No ancient, contemporary, primitive, or advanced society has been dedicated to toiling without a pause for games or dances. These are forms of human expression as natural as songs and music. And they need no justification for their existence.

Philosophers of every culture have advocated cultivation of the body and of the spirit, so that both would develop in perfect harmony and each could lean on the strength of the other in time of need. Plato and Aristotle themselves instructed young men in wrestling and body conditioning.

During the golden age of Greece, sports were participatory. Only the Olympic games attracted spectators. The Athenians never needed to plead the case of physical fitness with anyone. But at the height of the Olympic festivals, between 600 and 400 B.C., aesthetic and intellectual prowess was as much considered in determining a winner as athletic ability.

Where the Greek gymnasia were extremely simple, the Romans built lavish health and spa facilities. In fourth-century Rome every second day was a holiday. The races at the Hippodrome, part sport, part theater; the performances at the Circus Maximus; the lewd shows at the theater of Marcellus; and the butchery of people and animals at the Amphitheater accommodated half a million spectators every day. But as spectatorship increased, participation died.

Around A.D. 200, the leading physician of the day, Galen, found it necessary to begin to advocate exercise for health. But his efforts were engulfed by the general decay of Rome.

The delicate balance between training of the spirit and training of the body in conjunction with it was never fully recovered in the Western world. *Mens sana in corpore sano* ("a sound mind in a sound body") is a concept as shallow as it is popular. Fitness of the mind, which we have defined as intellectual, emotional, and social fitness, is not a product of a physically strong body. If it were, there might be no cheating or brutality in sports, and no athletes on drugs. The achievement of human fitness depends on the separate cultivation of each aspect.

Western physical educators have largely forgotten to stress the fact that physical conditioning by itself is not enough to prevent a human being from turning out lopsided. But this has been effectively explained by the teachers of yoga and the oriental martial arts. The great popularity of these forms of conditioning is not coincidental. It is born from the hunger of civilized human beings for a well-balanced development. Unfortunately, a detailed discussion of yoga and the martial arts is beyond the scope of this article. I can give only a brief outline of a few principles worthy of deeper exploration by the interested reader.

Unlike the kinds of conditioning described earlier in this chapter, *yoga* is concerned not with amount of movement but rather with type of movement. It entails lifelong training which includes some 840,000 different body postures. The intensive bodily discipline is accompanied by mental and philosophical training which is just as intensive. The amalgamation of the three ultimately leads the individual to understanding of the total human experience.

Yoga requires a great deal of self-motivation. It is a self-conquest in the sense of overcoming one's weaknesses and learning nonaggressiveness. It should produce increased self-awareness, self-confidence, and tolerance toward others, spiritual strengths which accompany impressively conditioned bodies.

A number of *martial arts*—judo, tae kwon do, hapkido, kung fu—have been introduced to the United States by serious teachers as well as by those who hope to exploit these activities commercially as means of self-defense. I believe that the martial art which contains the essence of all the others is aikido.

Aikido teaches that as an individual you are not drifting alone: you are securely interwoven in the spirit of the Universe. You must train yourself to receive this spirit and distribute it generously. Aikido teaches mastership of the spirit concomitantly with the mastership of the body. It must be understood not only as a gentle self-defense, but also as a superior training for strength, flexibility, and confident, graceful movement. The theory of aikido is that, just as at all times you need to know where your body is and be in control of its movement, you also need to know where your energy is and be in control of its movement. This makes sense, if you are willing to think about it.

I am convinced not only that the goal of total fitness through intensive training of separate components is applicable to Western physical conditioning, but also that without it Western physical training is doomed to failure. Hopefully, as people study the underlying theories of the martial arts and yoga, they will realize that sit-ups alone will not do, and that even basketball and football suffer from a lack of spiritual practice.

BIBLIOGRAPHY

Royal Canadian Air Force: *Official Exercise Plans for Physical Fitness* (rev. U.S. ed.), Pocket Books, New York, 1965. Two famous exercise plans for general physical conditioning: the XBX twelve-minute-a-day plan for women, and the 5BX eleven-minute-a-day plan for men.

Cheney, G., and J. Strader: *Modern Dance,* Allyn and Bacon, Boston, 1969. Presents modern dance as a multifaceted experience in movement, a discovery of new perceptions, and a vehicle for lifetime fitness.

Cooper, Mildred, and Kenneth Cooper: *Aerobics for Women,* Bantam Books, Des Plaines, Iowa, 1973. A do-it-yourself cardiovascular and respiratory conditioning program that works. Paperback.

Conrad, C. Carson: Series on Physical Conditioning, California State Department of Education, Bureau of Health Education, Physical Education, Athletics, and Recreation, Sacramento, Calif., 1969. Finely constructed conditioning programs.

DeVries, Herbert A.: *Physiology of Exercise for Physical Education and Athletics,* Brown, Dubuque, Iowa, 1966. A comprehensive and readable text on the effect of exercise on various body systems and on human metabolism. Application of sound physiological principles to physical conditioning.

Fox, Edward L., and Donald K. Mathews: *Interval Training: Conditioning for Sports and Physical Fitness,* Saunders, Philadelphia, 1974. A thorough explanation of principles and techniques of a highly effective method of endurance work.

Lindsey, R., B. J. Jones, and A. Van Whitley: *Body Mechanics: Posture, Figure, Fitness,* Brown, Dubuque, Iowa, 1974. Text-workbook exploring the human body at rest and in motion. Explains fitness, figure improvement, proper posture, care of the feet and back, nutrition, and relaxation.

Schwartz, Herman S.: *The Art of Relaxation,* Thomas Y. Crowell, New York, 1954. Presents techniques of relaxation and how to use them in everyday pressure situations.

Tohei, Koichi: *This Is Aikido,* Japan Publications, Tokyo, Japan, and San Francisco,

Calif., 1968. Thorough discussion of the philosophical principles of aikido, its history, and methods of training.

Wessel, Janet A.: *Movement Fundamentals: Figure, Form, Fun,* Prentice-Hall, Englewood Cliffs, N.J., 1970. A thorough guide to any woman's exploration of her capacities for movement.

Part Four

The Potential of Your Relationships

Chapter 16

Living Alone:
Puzzles and Polarities

Susan M. Osborn

Susan M. Osborn, M.S.W., is codirector of Assertive Training Associates, a consulting firm in Medina, Washington. She also works as a counselor-instructor at Bellevue Community College, where she teaches Assertive Training, Human Potential seminars, Career Exploration, and classes in the methodology of social work. As a social work practitioner, she has worked sixteen years in a variety of settings, including residential treatment centers, mental-health agencies, courts, and prisons. As an academician, she has taught at the University of Washington and has been a guest lecturer at Seattle University and at the Seattle Community Colleges. She is coauthor of *Assertive Training for Women* (Charles C Thomas, Springfield, Ill., 1975) and writes a monthly column, "Speak for Yourself," for *Pandora: The Washington Woman's News Journal*.

Living alone as a woman can be experienced as joyous and exciting; as a time of emancipation, freedom, and high energy; as a series of glamorous happenings. It can provide opportunities for meditation, reflection, and growth. It can furnish the ideal atmosphere for a woman to find her center, her soul, her *raison d'être*.

At the other extreme, living alone can be experienced as desolate and austere; as ostracism, rejection, and loneliness. It can provoke feelings of hostility, resentment, and isolation. It can provide fertile ground for seeds of mistrust, suspicion, doubt, and paranoia. It can accentuate the emotions of grief and pain to the point of rendering a woman immobile.

The most important determinant in whether living alone is seen as a time of independence and creativity, a time of stretching and flexing, or as a time of estrangement and desperation is the woman's attitude. Does she perceive herself as a strong, autonomous person embarking on an uncharted journey, or does she perceive herself as an undesirable alien who lacks skills, imagination, and creative potential? Does she regard others in her life as supportive and empathetic, or does she feel jealousy and envy for people who appear happier and more secure than she? Does she view her situation as providing an opportunity for personal growth, or does she see her own future as bleak? Does she look upon life as a challenge and learn from the results of her decisions, or does she feel overwhelmed by a multitude of unanswered questions and unknown territories?

Maintaining a positive personal attitude can be likened to keeping a sailboat on course. The individual woman's actions, feelings, and moods can be subtly influenced by a variety of social and political elements, much as the position or bearing of a boat can be easily shifted by wind conditions or rough waters.

A single woman's attitude about herself, her friends, her situation, and the world in general is colored and influenced by the interplay between her own inner world and the world that exists outside of her. For example, she may possess a high level of self-esteem and yet she can find herself being moved off course by the effects of stigmatization. Because she deviates from the norm or standard of the prevailing mode of group living, the nuclear family, she may be regarded as deviant and therefore given differential treatment.

Often, demeaning words are used in connection with women who live alone: "spinster," "old maid," "promiscuous," "perverted," "reject," "selfish," "queer," "weird," "rigid." By contrast, single men are referred to as "independent," "free," "adventuresome," "artistic," "unattached," "eccentric." For a single man, there is prestige attached to eligible bachelorhood, but no such prestige is attached to being a single woman.

A single woman walks a continual tightrope between doing what she thinks is right for her and responding to the opinions of others. Young single women often feel pressured by relatives and friends to get married and have children, whereas young single men are encouraged to develop careers. Single women who attend movies, plays, parties, dances, or nightclubs may be asked probing questions about why they couldn't find a companion to accompany them. Some restaurants will even refuse to seat a single woman, or will seat her after groups of people have been seated, because they object to her occupying a whole table. Single men are served much more readily, because people tend to assume that their time is valuable and that they are dining alone in between important business deals. Divorced women may be subjected to matchmaking even after they have repeatedly expressed a desire to remain single.

All people face certain emotional problems of living. Because the single woman is often a victim of stigmatization, the ordinary problems of living can become even more burdensome for her than they are for those who have other life-styles. The stigma which defines her as "deviant" gives others license to judge and criticize her behavior.

Awareness of the effects of stigmatization on her part can ease the personal impact of negative judgments and prevent her from engaging in destructive self-criticism. *It is also encouraging to recognize that today there is far less stigma attached to being single than ever before.*

By continually redefining her individuality in terms of her unique ideas, talents, and skills, a woman protects herself from internalizing the labels and judgments emanating from the stigma. To accept without question the judgments and opinions of others may mean giving credibility to negative views about herself based on stereotypes totally unrelated to her as a person. Fully experiencing her own fears and anxieties can also help her to understand why her life-style may be intimidating to others.

Often the pathway is so precarious that the only way she can survive is to focus on keeping her balance. Using the image of a sailboat that can capsize with a sudden gust of wind, it is possible to see how the attitude of a woman who is steering her life course alone can be easily influenced by the "weather" around her. To keep her ship on course—i.e., to maintain mental, physical, and spiritual well-being—she must learn how to achieve a sense of balance amidst the forces that pull her off center.

One of these forces has to do with decision making. For many women, major decisions begin to take on an "either-or" quality. Either she dates a lot of strange men whom she doesn't really enjoy or she sits alone at home, bored to tears. Either she puts her friends' needs ahead of her own or she has no friends. Either she works herself into a completely exhausted state on her job or she is unemployed. Either she visits her relatives regularly or she is labeled "selfish" and "uncaring."

All these problems can, of course, beset anyone; but they often take on a more vivid identity in the life of a single woman because she is unfamiliar with the decision-making process, lacks self-confidence, or fears being judged by those who see her through the foggy lens of stigma. How a woman will view single life has to do with the extent to which she is able to achieve a balance between various polarities. Learning to discover choices or options which fall between the extremes can mean the difference between achieving equipoise and feeling inner division and confusion. In all cases, the choice rests with the woman herself.

POLARITIES OF SINGLEHOOD

Living Alone or Living with Others

The initial choice that requires consideration is to live alone or to live with other people. Some women move through the stages of first growing up in a family, then moving in with friends, then getting married and initiating a new family constellation, without ever considering living alone. Others elect to live alone upon graduation from high school or college as a transition period before marriage. Many of these women never seriously consider living alone for an extended time until they are left alone by reason of death or divorce. Their time alone is bound to be radically different from that of the woman who has made an active choice to live alone. A woman who initiates living alone will tend to feel a greater sense of personal power and control over her life than a woman whose husband dies unexpectedly or a woman whose husband divorces her. But when a woman has not chosen to live alone, there are still areas of choice in her situation, and it is especially important for the woman who feels abandoned, rejected, or trapped to be able to recognize the choices available to her.

Because there are so many pressures directed against the single woman, it is a good idea to plan a strategy before leaving a group living arrangement, if possible. Some of the ways to plan strategies include the following: (1) Enlist the aid of friends, family, counselors, rap groups,[1] and single adults while deciding whether or not to leave. (2) Establish credit in one's own name. (3) Achieve a favorable standing at a local bank. (4) Obtain a car in one's own name. (5) Make certain that community property is equally divided on all legal documents. (6) Have money in a savings account to use for emergencies. (7) Establish several close friendships with reliable, supportive people. (8) Line up one or two places to stay in case of need. (9) Have sufficient income to meet basic expenses.

Often the major concern is finances. Establishing credit is a process that requires time and financial resources. For example, a woman may accumulate enough money in a bank account to support herself for one year, and then separate from her husband. She knows she can pay her bills, and yet she will have difficulty securing credit because she is unemployed. By the same token, women who have paid cash for everything all their lives are shocked to learn that they cannot get credit. A necessary institution that is spreading throughout the country is the feminist credit union. Women who are members of such unions will be able to secure low-interest loans.

For those women who worry about starting on their own with very little cash, it is advantageous to accumulate some funds before making a major shift. Straitjacketing oneself to the point where one cannot do anything pleasurable or buy anything but food with food stamps hardly forms a base for freedom and independence. A good way to get an estimate of financial needs and resources is to reduce expenditures to the bare minimum to learn what is actually required for self-support. Many women are happy to discover how little money they can actually get by with.

Security needs can also be met in other ways. One can build a sense of social affinity through friendships. Taking courses encourages the examination of one's skills, talents, and potential. Attending classes or groups in which other single people are present is a way to broaden one's perspectives and to develop a range

---

[1] A rap group is a discussion group which emphasizes the importance of sharing personal experiences.

of possibilities. Additionally, peers can serve as role models. Finally, one can draw on spiritual or religious resources.

Before making a permanent move it might be useful to try a short-term experiment in solo living by taking a vacation alone; staying at the Y.W.C.A. or in a women's center that has rooms; or renting a room for a month. For many women, a brief period by themselves is sufficient for clarifying their thoughts.

Living alone need not turn one into a cloistered recluse. However, it will require energy on the part of a single woman to initiate and maintain social contacts, as there seems to be a greater tendency for people to be attracted to other groups of people. Single adults usually have to work harder because they can't rely on the natural exchanges that occur among members of group living arrangements.

Being able to count on old friends is exceedingly significant. The fear that friends will disappear when one is divorced or separated has some basis in reality. If marital partners are regarded as a "package deal" by their friends, they may suddenly be seen as nonentities should the partnership dissolve. In other instances, separated or divorced people are treated as pariahs because they become a threat to those persons who are afraid to look at the fragile nature of their own marital commitments.

One of the most exciting developments in terms of opening up new pathways for friendships among women of all ages is the women's movement. Rap groups, consciousness-raising groups, problem-solving groups, women's centers and services, work and living collectives, communes, and political organizations are all bringing women together. The growing sense of solidarity among women is making it much easier for single women to find the kind of support and intimacy that historically has been found primarily in nuclear families.

Taking Responsibility for Oneself or Depending on Others

When a woman lives alone, it becomes apparent that to a large extent she is responsible for what happens to her. It can be a relief to be able to see the results of one's actions clearly, and it can be refreshing to be able to explore one's own power. This experience can be intoxicating.

Little by little, however, this sense of power and control over one's own life may begin to erode. The "honeymoon" period following the departure from a very dependent situation to an independent one often causes the single woman to appreciate the degree to which mutual dependency, reciprocity, and an interchange of resources is necessary for survival. While being dependent gives rise to feelings of weakness and entrapment, attempting to be utterly self-reliant is unrealistic.

Just as she accepts the fact that she is the originator of every choice she makes, the single woman must accept the reality of moments of fatigue, doubt, inadequacy, pain, and need. Developing the ability to ask for help assertively in times of stress and not to disparage herself for needing others furnishes an avenue for healthy dependency.

The idea of taking responsibility for oneself is not synonymous with being totally self-sufficient, nor does it imply that one has absolute power and control over all aspects of one's life. It is important to recognize the limits to one's personal power and the various ways that social and economic conditions affect one's life. The impact of external political elements can be tremendously debilitating unless a woman is able to set apart those conditions over which she has no personal control and which require widespread social change. For example, guilt and self-blame are inappropriate for a woman who has competed unsuccessfully for a job in a man's field, where discriminatory practices are well documented.

Solitude or Isolation

Living alone provides the opportunity to spend time alone or with others. When living with others, one may occasionally wish for solitude; but not much thought is given to whether or not having people around is desirable—they are simply there. When one bears the full responsibility for whether one spends time alone or with others, a great deal of thought is given to when, where, and with whom one will spend time.

The difference between solitude and isolation can be narrow and tenuous. If one allows too much time to be alone, one may end up feeling isolated and lonely. On the other hand, allowing insufficient time alone can result in feeling out of balance and off center.

Some women's lives are a frantic, dizzy whirl of activities aimed at meeting as many new people as possible, particularly men. Many businesses thrive on the loneliness of single adults, and anyone caught up in the "singles scene" risks feeling like a commodity. Participants in the game of singlehood soon become frustrated, desperate, and even more lonely. The game deadens the emotions and sexual interests of the participants and promotes an atmosphere of suspended adolescence.

The key to being socially active and yet not being enmeshed in meaningless engagements lies in exploring a variety of interests and activities, while scheduling time for oneself as well. It is important for any single person to discover things to do alone. The emphasis on two-parent families and heterosexual coupling results in a preponderance of activities geared for couples. Locating alternatives is sometimes difficult. Some possibilities are: (1) Enter activities which promote personal growth and provide social contacts, such as night school, extension courses, and weekend workshops. (2) Plan small get-togethers for genuine human interchange such as potluck dinners, literary discussions, informal teach-ins, folk or square dances, and film evenings (with rented films and equipment). (3) Join a singles group that sponsors varied activities. (4) Drop in at a singles resource center to meet other persons living alone. (5) Avail oneself of the resources provided by professional or religious organizations.

Should repeated attempts to establish intimate relationships fail, it is possible that the woman is looking in the wrong area for intimacy. The source of the difficulty may also lie in the fabric of society rather than within the woman's personality: that is, the problem may be alienation rather than isolation.

Isolation is feeling cut off from others: it has its roots in intrapsychic processes and interpersonal relationships. Alienation, a sociological concept, is a phenomenon which results when society fails to respond to the needs of the people: its roots lie in the sociopolitical structure of the culture. When a society itself is alienating, its members are alienated. Alienation thus has a structural base outside of individual personalities even though it has definite psychological consequences:

> When alienation exists, it encompasses most, if not all, social relations. . . . To be alienated is to experience a sense of not belonging and to feel that one's efforts are without meaning.[2]

It is important to recognize that there are limits to the steps which a woman can take to connect with other people. These limits are partially the result of a widespread feeling of alienation in our culture. With this awareness, women can work to transform those aspects of our society that cause it to be alienating by taking an active role in politics or by exerting pressure on organizations and institutions to be more responsive to people.

Accountability to Oneself or Accountability to Others

When a woman first begins to establish herself independently, she may tend to be self-indulgent. She often finds herself attending to her own needs and interests to the exclusion of other considerations. For a time, she may even be regarded by herself and others as selfish.

Being selfish and pampering oneself may be a good thing for a while, particularly since one can always change. Another salient point for any single woman to bear in mind is that there is a difference between being selfish and practicing the art of self-care. To be selfish has the connotation of considering one's own comfort at the expense of that of others, or failing to consider others. To engage in self-care is to have regard for one's own mental and physical well-being.

Given the extent to which our culture indoctrinates women to be loving, considerate, and nurturing toward others, it is understandable that indicators of egoism would be interpreted as frightening. It is also fitting that for a period of time a woman experiment with her freedom to locate a workable balance between satisfying some of her own personal needs and acting on her genuine concern for others. It can be reassuring to know that self-interest is not, in and of itself, a sign that a woman will forever follow a narrow path of living for herself alone.

Finding a Man or Making a Life of One's Own

The conflict between the enjoyment of one's freedom and increasing self-development and the nagging quest for someone to share it with commonly reduces itself to a manhunt without due consideration of the wide range of other options. This internal problem is magnified by external assumptions. It is hard for many people to believe that any woman in her right mind would choose to live alone.

---

[2] Amitai Etzioni, *The Active Society,* Free Press, New York, 1968, p. 620.

Out of sympathy, well-meaning friends subtly press the single woman to attend social functions where single men will be present. Or, they "fix her up" with a male acquaintance of theirs, unaware that their good efforts might be interpreted by her as an indication that they don't think she's capable of finding a man on her own.

The most agonizing aspect of this problem is the fact that many single women have a suspicion that they must find a man in order to feel whole. An interesting theory that describes this phenomenon suggests that every woman fantasizes about finding a "soul-mate," her "other half," or her hero. In fantasy, this male image takes on the attributes of a "ghostly lover," which represents a collective or universalized picture of man as he has appeared through the centuries of human experience *in relation to woman.* The ghostly lover or "animus man" is a projection of the woman's soul onto a man as though half of herself were in him. She longs to find him and consciously assimilate him in order to avoid suffering the pain and distress of lacking the male balance to her feminine existence.[3]

The fantasy is useful in that it can lead to increased awareness on the part of a woman of the "masculine" attributes she wants to expand in her own personality. It becomes destructive when a woman desperately attempts to locate one man in real life who measures up to her fantasy. Because finding one man to fulfill this fantasy is impossible, the fantasy may continue to operate at an unconscious level, resulting in frustration, anger, and despair for the woman. *The goal of finding a man must therefore be examined carefully by each individual woman over a period of time in order to evaluate how much of her desire stems from genuine feeling, how much is a result of social pressure, and how much is based in fantasy.*

Designing a social life for oneself takes energy, motivation and courage, initially, but it offers a viable alternative to the pointless pursuit of "Mr. Right," and an alternative to getting enmeshed in meaningless engagements engineered by others. Specific courses in assertiveness training for women on their own can help one learn how to plan and initiate contact with others, how to handle rejection when invitations or overtures are refused, and how to present information about oneself in a positive way so as to stimulate and encourage social interchange.

Workshops on sensuality and sexuality offer instruction and feedback regarding ways to feel more comfortable in intimate relationships. Communications workshops provide aids for enhancing verbal and nonverbal exchanges in a genuine, honest manner that can short-circuit the destructive games that go on between people.

Such skills are important if one is to find a balance between utter isolation and hectic dating. As more women seek recognition and economic independence and become open to living arrangements other than marriage, a new subgroup will continue to gain members: that of mature, free, sexually active single women who are more attuned to self-awareness and self-discovery than to falling in love or finding mates.

[3] M. Esther Harding, *The Way of All Women,* Harper & Row, New York, 1933, 1970.

Spontaneity or Self-Control

When a woman changes from a placating, submissive attitude to one of emancipation and assertion, she may go overboard in her spontaneous expression of feelings and opinions. Therefore, it is a good idea to achieve a balance between being honest and open about every single thought and emotion and holding everything inside oneself in the belief that one ought to work out one's own difficulties without assistance.

Being assertive includes being tactful and considerate. In learning to be honest with others, one must take into account the possible outcome of one's actions. Will an honest expression of anger or hostility toward another person be creative, or will it destroy a relationship that cannot be rebuilt? If one is more concerned with expressing negative emotions than with the eventual outcome, it may be more productive to find alternative avenues of emotional release.

Some women who have advanced in the business world confuse independence and assertion with the license to be tactless and unkind. They use their increased power and expertise as permission to "speak their mind," no matter what the consequences. They misuse their power partly because they have felt powerless for so long and partly because they are assimilating the prevailing model of male power, which entails domination and gaining the upper hand. At the opposite extreme are professional women who have assumed a mantle of masculinity: they may refrain from expressing any real feelings out of a fear of being seen as weak.

A degree of caution must be exercised in expressing positive emotions spontaneously in social situations. Friendliness and openness can be misinterpreted as seductiveness. For her own self-protection, a woman needs to consider the possibility that welcoming a new male acquaintance with open arms will be perceived by him as sexual interest and availability.

Out of nervousness, a desire to appear open and honest, or an interest in making conversation, some women disclose more about themselves than is in their best interest. It is practical to establish a strong level of trust with a man before revealing extensive personal information. To blindly take for granted that a man will accurately read verbal and nonverbal behavior on the part of a woman is highly unrealistic.

A practical problem that most single women worry about is the chance of being attacked or robbed. Getting acquainted with the police officers in one's area and informing them of one's single status can decrease fear and increase the sense of physical security. Meeting neighbors and knowing that they can be called on in an emergency also provides security. Rape relief centers are developing in the major cities to provide instruction on preventive measures and services for victims. Assertiveness training and karate teach specific ways that women can develop the physical skills to better protect themselves.

Living in the Present or Living in the Past or Future

There is a strong emphasis, emanating from humanistic psychology, on living in the here and now, on "getting into one's feelings," on "letting things flow." This approach can be very useful in helping a woman to extricate herself from the past and to stop worrying about the future.

Some women hold onto the past so tenaciously that they are blind to what is going on around them. Many women constantly look back over their lives and think about how they might have done things differently. They berate themselves for being so long-suffering, so stupid, or so forgiving. Widows are particularly susceptible to living in the past. After the death of one's husband, one occupies a somewhat dignified position and is permitted to grieve over the loss. But after that relatively short period of time, the widow is forgotten and shunned. She shares none of the glamour and attractiveness associated with being divorced. The present is lonely and the future looks hopeless. In situations of this sort, "grief workshops" can be tremendously helpful in working through past emotions so as to enjoy the present. Another group of women who may find themselves dwelling more in the past than in the present are women in intact marriages whose husbands are gone most of the time. Such women are neither fish nor fowl. They are seldom invited to couples' gatherings or to activities for singles. Many women in such a situation have negotiated contracts with their husbands with the understanding that they intend to participate in social functions whether the husband is home or not.

On the other hand, some women tend to live in the future. Women who are constantly making plans for the future hesitate to engage themselves with people unless there is a good possibility of a long-term commitment. No matter what they are doing, they are focusing on the future results of their actions. It is easy for young women to become addicted to making plans for the future. In elementary school, they imagine what it will be like to attend high school. In high school, they fantasize about college or marriage. In their early twenties, they are planning their families, their jobs, or their homes. If they have children, they are planning futures for them.

A play called "Waiting" has been presented at Womanhouse in California. It consists of vignettes representing the things women wait for throughout their lives: waiting for boys to call, waiting for boys to ask them to dance, waiting to be beautiful, waiting to fall in love, waiting for sex, waiting to get married, waiting for the first baby to come, waiting for children to come home from school, waiting for children to grow up and leave home, waiting to lose weight, waiting for the menopause, and waiting for life to begin.[4]

Living in the present is a beautiful way to begin appreciating feelings and experiences moment by moment. It can eliminate needless worries and enable a woman to gain insight into her own thoughts and emotions, as well as insight into the emotions of people around her.

Again, it is important to maintain balance. Living in the present to the extent of forgetting to consider the past or plan for the future can be just as much of an entrapment as being completely oblivious of the present. A woman who is living alone in an effort to find a totally new identity will encounter frustration should she attempt to disregard and devalue her personal history; and a woman who

---

[4] Judy Chicago, *Through the Flower,* Doubleday, Garden City, N.Y., 1975.

regularly spends her entire income on luxury items would do well to deposit some of it regularly in a savings account.

PRODUCTIVE USE OF TIME ALONE

Living alone can provide time for, and an atmosphere conducive to, self-exploration and self-discovery. We all need some protected time to "hear ourselves think," to ponder, to assimilate, and to create. Physical separation allows us to clarify which resources we can develop for ourselves and which ones we must depend on others to supply. It is thought that one reason why car pools are often unsuccessful is that people need a time alone driving to and from work.

Most people need practice in learning to use the time they spend alone. Although our value system strongly advocates individualism, we are constantly bombarded with literature on how to achieve closeness, intimacy, and companionship. We are encouraged to join social groups and organizations. Our lives are crowded with people and events.

And yet, groups actually do not provide insurance against feeling alone and isolated. Even in the company of others, we often have anxieties about not belonging. In fact, being surrounded by others from whom one is estranged can bring intense feelings of loneliness.

If living alone were a planned phase of every woman's life, it could serve as a foundation of internal security from which could grow relationships based on true mutuality and interdependence. In the struggle to liberate oneself, it is of crucial importance to learn who one is in terms of personal power and specific skills. There is no doubt that a woman living alone will gain awareness of her strengths and weaknesses and of her individual identity. Finally, if it became a common practice for people to incorporate sabbaticals, retreats, and secluded intervals into their schedules, the stigma currently associated with being a single woman would be reduced.

In working alone to achieve a state of equipoise among polarities it helps immensely to see each decision as an experiment. Rather than being a final, everlasting, rigid formulation, making choices is only part of the whole decision-making process which consists of thinking, deciding, acting, and evaluating. When one choice has been made but another choice becomes more attractive, it may be wise to make a change and to accept being fallible. Two of the most liberating beliefs that a woman can hold are that it is all right to be wrong and that it is all right to change one's mind.

Finally, time spent alone can be used to examine the extent to which one is caught up in one's own drama and to appraise the work one needs to do to grow, to change, and to improve. It can be a time for spiritual renewal that increases one's self-respect and self-confidence and expands one's awareness of and appreciation for others.

BIBLIOGRAPHY

Bengis, Ingrid: *Combat in the Erogenous Zone,* Knopf, New York, 1972. A book about love, hate, and sex among men and women.

Chesler, Phyllis: *Women and Madness,* Doubleday, Garden City, N.Y., 1972. The author details the damage that psychiatry has done to women and offers valuable documentation and new insights.

Chicago, Judy: *Through the Flower,* Doubleday, Garden City, N.Y., 1975. This is the candid, powerful autobiography of an artist determined to bring her total identity as a human being and a woman into the practice of her art.

Crystal, John C., and Richard N. Bolles: *Where Do I Go from Here with My Life?* Seabury Press, New York, 1974. A systematic, practical, and effective planning manual for career seekers and career changers.

Gerson, Noel B.: *George Sand,* New England Library, London, 1975. A biography of the first modern liberated woman.

Keyes, Ken: *Handbook to Higher Consciousness,* Living Love Center, Berkeley, Calif., 1973. A guide to greater perceptiveness, wisdom, and oneness for effective and happy living.

Osborn, Susan M., and Gloria G. Harris: *Assertive Training for Women,* Charles C Thomas, Springfield, Ill., 1975. This book includes an examination of the rationale for providing assertive training groups for women, a discussion of areas of application, an overview of related research, and a presentation of innovative techniques.

Rush, Anne Kent: *Getting Clear,* Random House, New York, 1973. An integrated collection of awareness and body exercises.

Taves, Isabella: *Women Alone,* Funk & Wagnalls, New York, 1968. A practical handbook for widows and divorcees.

Thurman, Judith: "Living Alone," *Ms.,* July 1975. A first-person account of the thoughts and conflicts of a woman living alone.

Chapter 17

The Man in Your Life: Personal Commitment in a Changing World

Anne Steinmann
Elinor Lenz

Anne Steinmann, Ph.D., a pioneer in research on female and male concepts of their roles, began her psychological studies in 1952. She is founder-coordinator of the Maferr Foundation, Inc. (Male-Female Role Research), an institute for conducting research on male and female roles and associated psychological and social problems. Maferr is affiliated with the Research Department of the Postgraduate Center for Mental Health in New York City. A clinical psychologist in private practice, she is also a member of the Sexual Dysfunction area, Psychiatry Department at New York Medical College; she was formerly an assistant professor at Hofstra University and a lecturer at the New School. She has written over forty professional and other publications. Her book *The Male Dilemma* (Jason Aronson, New York, 1974), which she wrote with David J. Fox, Ph.D., received the Family Life Book Award from the Child Study Association of America.

For a short biography of Elinor Lenz, see Chapter 4.

In today's fast-changing world, roles and relationships that once provided anchorage for men and women, for their sense of self and place in the world, have shifted, casting both sexes adrift in a sea of ambiguity. As a result, the male-female relationship, that basic and universal human connection, is in a state of flux. A bewildering range of choices and challenges are opening up which affect men as well as women, and nonworking women as well as working women. And for both sexes, there is little guidance to be had from past generations: men and women today are leading very different lives from those of their grandparents, responding to pressures and experiencing life-styles that would not even have been dreamt of by people living a hundred or even fifty years ago.

Today, marriage is only one of many life-styles available to men and women. Living-together arrangements may take any number of forms, according to the needs and desires of the people involved. In a panel discussion at Princeton University, the following was suggested as a model of the various life-styles and relationships that people can develop in the course of their lives: first, living alone for a time after leaving the parental home; then living with someone of the opposite sex; this to be followed by marriage, not necessarily to the person one had been living with; later, following the dissolution of this marriage, moving on to sharing a home with a friend of the same sex; afterwards, a second marriage in which the partners spend only part of their time together; and finally, in the later years when one is again alone, living as part of a group in some type of communal arrangement.[1] In some parts of the world, notably Sweden and Denmark, informal ad hoc living arrangements are on the rise as traditional marriages decrease, a trend which some social critics regard as healthy since it may mean that the legal unions will have a better chance of success.[2]

The growing social acceptance of such variations and combinations is a reflection not only of our more relaxed, more open society but—more profoundly—of the breakdown of such institutions as the extended family. As ties of kinship have dissolved and life has become increasingly impersonal and bureaucratized, many people have become so disconnected from their sources of personal identity and stability that their world appears to have, in the words of a character in Saroyan's play *The Time of Your Life*, "no foundation all the way down the line."

The offices of therapists in the fields of psychiatry, psychology, social work, and other counseling services are crowded with people asking: "Why? Where did it all go wrong? Why do I feel so alone, although there are people all around me? Why is my life so empty, although I have all the things I always wanted? Where am I going? What can I believe in?"

In this chapter, we shall explore these and related questions in the course of analyzing the role of personal commitment in the working woman's life. Today, whether or not the working woman wants a man in her life is a matter of choice.

---

[1] Leslie Aldridge Westoff, "Two-Time Winners," *New York Times Magazine*, August 10, 1975.
[2] Jan Trost, "Married and Unmarried Cohabitation: The Case of Sweden with Some Comparisons," *Journal of Marriage and the Family*, vol. 37, no. 3, August 1975, pp. 677–682.

We will be discussing the working woman who has chosen to have a man in her life. In dealing with her concerns, we will be applying the insights and perspectives gained from research in sex roles, marriage, and family life, as well as from research in psychology, sociology, and anthropology; we will also draw upon actual life situations of men and women whose personal commitments are in disarray.

CONFLICT AND ACCOMMODATION

> "Let me not to the marriage of true minds
> Admit impediments."—William Shakespeare, Sonnet 116

Throughout the normal course of our lives, we make a series of commitments that are like invisible filaments woven into a network of relationships within which we develop our sense of identity. Of all these commitments—to family, to friends, to co-workers—the one to which we bring our highest expectations and upon which we make our greatest demands is the union of a man and a woman, which, whether it takes place within or outside the legal bonds of matrimony, continues to serve as the basis for our social structure.

During the past decades, we have seen this structure shaken to its foundations as divorce rates have gone up; transient pairings have replaced enduring relationships; juvenile delinquency has spread through all layers of society; and a variety of social ills, particularly alcoholism and drug abuse, have indicated increasing alienation, loneliness, and personal disruption. One of the theories that is repeatedly put forward to account for these problems suggests that they are a direct result of so many women's moving out of the home into the work force. This neat rationale, supported by recurring waves of nostalgia, evokes a cozy scene from the yellowing pages of an album, of a tightly knit family group in which each member was firmly aware of his or her immutable role. The woman in the picture received only enough education to prepare her for marriage and motherhood; she married early and thereafter devoted herself to the needs and interests of her husband and children. In her later years, when her children were grown and had families of their own and her husband was perhaps no longer living, she kept herself busy with her grandchildren and good works.

Although this portrait bears little resemblance to the reality of working women throughout most of human history, it continues to exercise a strong influence on the male-female relationship. Within this framework, in which sex-linked roles and duties are assigned at an early age, men and women have been expected to work out their tensions and differences. Today, however, in view of women's rising aspirations and expectations, these outworn images and patterns of yesterday are being rapidly discarded. Since custom and tradition are no longer as powerful as in the past in governing male-female behavior, the commitment between the man and the woman must stand on its own; the burden of proof is now on the individuals who have made the decision to join their lives. In place of the traditional rules, they must develop their own "social contract" which will set out the terms of the agreement, and they must recognize that, from the moment this contract is entered into, neither party can have everything his or her own way. As in all contracts, certain considerations are required on both sides.

It is a curious feature of our society that, although we are a highly legalistic people and enter readily into contracts covering a variety of activities, we are reluctant to spell out the terms of agreements involving sexual relationships, regarding this as "unromantic." But regardless of how blinding the love and sexual attraction, both parties should recognize a contractual nature in their intention to live together and should talk openly and freely about their hopes, plans, personal habits, and—most important—their expectations for themselves and each other. Since every deep relationship must rest upon deep understandings, it would be wise for couples planning to make a life together to consider the following aspects of their proposed partnership. (These suggestions for the contract are just that—suggestions. The details of a contract must vary according to the particular needs and desires of each couple.)

Decision making—general:
Which decisions should be shared?
Which decisions are hers alone?
Which decisions are his alone?

Decisions relating to everyday life:
Where will they live? Country? City? Suburb? House? Apartment? Loft?
How will the home be furnished?
How will finances be handled?
What will they do with their leisure time?
How will household responsibilities be shared?

Decisions relating to work:
What happens if one partner's job requires a transfer to another part of the country?
What adjustments will be made for irregular working hours of either partner or both partners?
How much of their working lives will be shared? Which areas will remain private?

Decisions relating to parenthood:
Do they both want children? If yes, how many? If they do not agree, how will they resolve this difference?
How do they want their children raised?
What do they consider the most important contribution each can make to their children's upbringing?

Decisions relating to self-realization:
What does each require in order to achieve personal fulfillment?
What are their sexual patterns?
What is needed for each to retain personal identity within a shared commitment?
What are their plans and aspirations, as individuals and as a couple?

Which tastes and interests (e.g., music, literature, movies, sports) can they share? How will they deal with those which they do not have in common?

Decisions relating to human relations:
Must all friendships be shared, or can there be exclusive friendships?
Can partners have friendships with those of the other sex, exclusive or other?
What are the needs and plans concerning relations with parents and relatives?
How can the individual need for privacy be realized without the partner's feeling rejected?

Decisions relating to values:
What are their views in regard to politics? Religion? Sexual fidelity?
How will they resolve a basic value conflict?

These are the kinds of decisions that should be considered as early in the relationship as possible. But even when there appears to be complete agreement and mutual understanding at the beginning, this does not preclude the possibility of conflict. Human beings are not static; they change and develop in different directions, and the "contract" will be a continuous reflection of their changing lives. Along the way they must expect to incorporate into their experience both conflict and accommodation; these are the two essential elements in any living, breathing human relationship, and the way they are worked through and resolved will determine the nature and durability of that relationship.

Although conflict is commonly associated with hostility, it can be a constructive force. Creative conflict occurs when there is a legitimate difference between two people who care for and respect each other, and when each is willing to listen to the other. As long as a dialogue can be developed and maintained, there exists the possibility of accommodation. For accommodation is not passive acquiescence; it is an active effort to negotiate which can bring benefits to both parties by providing an emotional learning experience and a deeper understanding of their mutual commitment. Even when no resolution has been achieved, the channels of communication have been kept open, and both have gained an expanded awareness of themselves as individuals and as a couple.

The potential for both conflict and accommodation can be placed in clearer perspective when we consider that the interaction of man and woman represents more than the sum of two individual reactions. Each partner brings to the union a cultural-biological inheritance accumulated over many generations; within this heritage are characteristics passed on through the genes, and thus inherent in the organism's "nature," and others handed down through social conditioning, or "nurture." As regards nature, the reality is that men and women are physiologically different. This is a difference that is easy enough to identify: the man's reproductive organs are external, and his sexuality primarily rests with them; the woman's reproductive organs are internal, and her secondary physical sexual characteristics provide her with more outlets for her sexuality. But what does this tell us about the comparative psychology of the sexes? There are no physiological or psychological measurements for "masculinity" or "femininity"; nor is there any evidence that women differ from men in their capacity to think and do productive work. Although biology, and particularly the reproductive process, places different demands upon males and females at various stages of their development, these differences are complementary and do not force us into molds.

As regards nurture, we have two people attempting to merge their separate sets of personal habits, attitudes, values, and expectations without blurring their individual identities. Even when the man and the woman come from similar backgrounds, the resulting mix may be highly unstable, especially when, as in our time, there are no fixed codes of behavior to provide cohesion and continuity. It is in this area of cultural conditioning that so much of the divisiveness between male and female arises.

In every society there is tension between the real and the ideal: as the real moves farther away from the ideal, the tension increases. In our society, the ideal has been developed in accordance with white, middle-class, male-oriented standards. Charles Ferguson, the author of a historical study of male attitudes, suggests that our educational system at all levels has been designed to reflect male criteria for intelligence. This system emphasizes measurement and competitive achievement, constantly tested by examinations. "The creature who finishes the curriculum in our schools and colleges is thoroughly indoctrinated in male traditions and methods and values and is bound to speak from the male point of view, whether he or she knows it or acknowledges it."[3] Although these standards are being challenged on many fronts, they are so much a part of our collective consciousness that they will continue to permeate our thinking and behavior for some time to come.

But although biology emphasizes differences, and cultural conditioning produces tensions and strains, the means for maintaining a balance are always present in the human capacity to reason and communicate. It is communication that opens the door to better male-female relationships. In today's social climate, however, with its shifting roles and fluctuating value systems, communication is often impeded by the guilt, confusion, and ambivalence both sexes are experiencing. A study by the Center for Policy Research in New York revealed that "communication adequacy," to use the technical term, is a key to marital satisfaction; yet a recent study of married couples in the United States found that on the average, marital partners talk to each other only twenty-seven minutes a week.[4]

This communication gap shows up in the disparity between what men and women want for themselves and what they believe the other sex wants them to be. Clinical research in male and female role and identity problems has demonstrated that women want men to be sensitive to women's needs, to be family-oriented, and at the same time to be strong and self-assertive.[5] Yet men want to be more aggressive and self-assertive but feel that women want them to be less so. The women participating in this study indicated that they wanted to expand from

[3] Charles Wright Ferguson, *The Male Attitude,* Little Brown, Boston, 1966.
[4] Donald Szantho Harrington, "The Real Revolution in Family Life," pamphlet series, no. 4, New York, 1974–1975.
[5] Anne Steinmann and David J. Fox, *The Male Dilemma,* Jason Aronson, New York, 1974.

their roles as wives and mothers, to become more self-sufficient, to take a larger part in work and in community affairs; but they felt that men didn't want them to. But the men insisted that they would like to see women moving in this direction. This disparity increases where women have more education and higher-status jobs.

How can such misperceptions exist between two people who share a home and a common language? Failure to communicate is at the heart of the male-female problem. We perceive the world through images which shape what we expect of others and what we believe they expect of us. Since we have not yet developed new images and symbols to replace the outmoded ones, a vacuum exists, and communication between the sexes is conducted without the aid of dependable signals and cues. This failure in communication will continue until men and women learn to listen to each other as sexual human beings rather than sexist stereotypes.

THE DOUBLE LIFE

"Wandering between two worlds, one dead,
The other powerless to be born."
—Matthew Arnold, "Stanzas from the Grand Chartreuse"

How can working women deal with the conflicting demands that arise out of the exigencies of their double life? Since we believe that the majority of working women are "not individuals who wish to pursue a competitive vocation [and] accept singleness as the price of the prized career,"[6] we are operating from the premise that the working woman, in order to be free and comfortable with herself and her work, must be able to deal freely and comfortably with the man in her life. The working woman's "most important source of support or hostility for [her] participation in professional work is her husband," according to a study of marital satisfaction in relation to employment in working mothers. This study reported that marriages tended to be happier when the husband found satisfaction in both career and family than when the husband was either career-oriented *or* family-oriented.[7]

The premise of this study is supported in an article written by a working wife and mother who poses the question asked by so many women today: "Can a woman be liberated and married?" This writer answers the question in the affirmative and goes on to say that she thinks it is easier for her husband and herself than for some other couples she knows because "we started out with a set of expectations that weren't so far apart. He knew that I wanted to be a reporter as much as he wanted to be. We both knew we wanted children. I'm convinced that a liberated marriage, like ours, isn't just luck or a gift of Providence. It has a lot

[6] Judith Stiehm, "Differences," *New York Times,* July 3, 1975.
[7] Lotte Bailyn, "Career and Family Orientations of Husbands and Wives in Relation to Marital Happiness," *Human Relations,* vol. 23, no. 22, 1969, pp. 97–113.

to do with what the bride and bridegroom think they are at the outset and what they think they want to be."[8]

Other studies of male attitudes indicate that a woman's job does not necessarily threaten the masculine status of the man in her life. As one researcher states, "Husbands of working wives differ from husbands of non-working wives in their perceptions of and attitudes toward working wives. The husband whose wife works seems to have a more liberal view of the wife's employment, her economic equality, and her privilege of individual sexual expression."[9] Most of the men surveyed, however, had reservations about the effect of the wife's employment on her role as wife and mother.

The woman's motivation for working is another factor that enters into the man's perception of his wife's double role. A study on the marital happiness of working wives found that:

> Both partners are less happy if the wife works because of economic necessity than if she participates by choice. This finding holds across educational levels, stages in the life cycle, and part-time and full-time employment. Among the less educated, the strain comes from an increase in tensions for husbands and a decline in sociability for wives; while among the better educated, husbands and wives both experience an increase in tensions and a decrease in sociability. A woman's decision to work strains the marriage only when there are pre-school children in the family. At other stages in the life cycle, her decision to work makes little difference in an individual's assessment of her own marriage happiness.[10]

The studies of working women do not show a consistent pattern of better or worse marital adjustment whether the woman works or not, or whether she works from motives of economic necessity or self-realization. One consistent pattern does emerge: that it is important for the working woman to share her two worlds with the man in her life. We have heard women say that they hesitate to bring their work home with them for fear of appearing overly committed to their jobs. But our research shows that when women and men share their expectations and feelings, women will find that men will share in the joys and satisfactions as well as the problems and difficulties of their wives' working lives. As a matter of fact, the working wife might find that men need and want to share their wives' work problems.

While the working woman's double life expands the possibility of potential conflicts in her relationship with the man in her life, it can also open up opportunities for accommodation through understanding and sharing an active communication. However, the path to accommodation is often blocked by the petty irritations and frustrations that are built into the working woman's double bind.

---

[8] Caryl Rivers, "Can a Woman Be Liberated and Married?" *New York Times Magazine,* November 2, 1975.

[9] Leland Axelson, "The Marital Adjustment and Role Definitions of Husbands of Working and Non-Working Wives," *Journal of Marriage and Family Living,* vol. 25, no. 2, 1963, pp. 189–195.

[10] Susan Orden and Norman Bradburn, "Working Wives and Marriage Happiness," *American Journal of Sociology,* vol. 74, no. 4, 1969, pp. 392–407.

The exaggerated importance of apparently trifling things—the baby-sitter who doesn't show up on time, the repeatedly late dinner hour, the disarrayed house—arises out of the ambivalence concerning sex roles which we have noted. If a woman is concerned about her femininity or her husband about his masculinity, they will seek for clearer definition wherever they can find it. The question, then, of who does the dishes becomes freighted with symbolic significance.

The result is that communication turns into a game of hiding behind trivia, and small annoyances mask deeper disturbances. A remark such as, "Why can't he (she) put the top back on the toothpaste tube?" translates into, "Why can't he (she) be more considerate; I work hard enough all day; etc." The problem is compounded by the fact that, in this turbulent transitional time, men and women are communicating in two different languages—to paraphrase Matthew Arnold, one dying and one waiting to be born. The dying language is a residue of the past, when men and women worked together in mutually sustaining, intimate settings and in which women found fulfillment in work performed at home. The language waiting to be born is one that reflects a technological world of competing individuals in which women are striving to find their place.

And in this new world, it is the male who is at a disadvantage, for it is women who are advancing and men who are retreating. The domain which men had accepted as their own—the world of the marketplace with its masculine rules and codes—is being invaded by women. At the same time, men are now expected—in fact, required—to take more responsibility for the domestic sphere, for child care and household routines which have not, for the most part, been considered their proper concerns. The male identity has been shaped by the principle of dominance in the arenas of family, work, and sex. As women claim an equal place in these arenas, the male is left wondering who he is and how he can perform as a sexual being.

Is it any wonder that men sometimes echo Freud's famous question: What does a woman want? But the question should be rephrased: What do men *and* women want? And if the answer is that they want what so many people seeking marital counseling say they want—companionship, a loving attitude, and common interests and goals—then the next step is to begin developing patterns of accommodation. These patterns, which grow out of open communication between the sexes, should be sufficiently flexible so that they can be adapted to changing needs and expectations during the three stages of male-female interaction.

THREE STAGES IN A WORKING WOMAN's LIFE

"Everything has its appointed hour. There is a time for all things under heaven."
—Ecclesiastes 3:1

In this section, we are concerned with personal commitments in three stages of a working woman's life; as we shall see, each stage has its distinctive characteristics and each presents different facets of the split existence familiar to women with jobs. In general, these chronological stages will vary according to each woman's physical, psychological, and social milieu. Consequently, we have not strictly defined the ages for each stage.

Stage One

This is the period before marriage and after marriage, until the birth of the first child. It is a good time to have fun with the decision-making contract and its translation into a loving relationship. At this time, the young woman is preparing for a future which she may as yet only dimly perceive. Until recent years—when such developments as higher education for women and the women's movement brought about a sharper awareness of the options and objectives available to women—most girls considered marriage and motherhood a primary goal; a career was only secondary. As a result, they did not make career decisions as early in life as boys did. Today, although the majority of young girls intend to combine marriage and a career, it is still probable that a girl in her teens or early twenties will be shopping around, trying one job after another, postponing any definite occupational decisions or commitments.

According to available data on the subject, if she is attending college, she will begin during her junior and senior years to think more seriously about how she is going to earn her living. She will start narrowing down her choices; by the time she graduates, she will very likely have decided on the job or profession she intends to pursue. In making this decision, she may have been influenced by any or all of the following: family, friends, college counselors, the media, financial pressures, the current man in her life. If she is thinking about marriage and children, her choice will also be affected by this consideration—that is, she may decide on a career that offers flexible hours and possibilities for part-time work.

At this time, her emotional life will also be in a state of flux. There is a good chance that at some point, she will enter into an "arrangement"[11] with a young man, who may also be a student. Neither she nor her roommate will be thinking very far beyond the present. Their "arrangement" will represent a convenience, a way of satisfying their sexual needs and, beyond that, perhaps an experiment in living with another person. They consider that living together in this way is very different from marriage, since it imposes no long-lasting obligations or responsibilities.

However, couples responding to Decision-Making and Behavioral Surveys[12] and describing themselves as not legally married did not reveal responses different from those of the legally married respondents. The problems of making a life together are not basically affected by the legality of the union. It is the nature of the commitment that is significantly different: most marrying couples at least

[11] An "arrangement" is any plan by which male and female live, sleep, and, if they are students, study together. As the Swedish study mentioned earlier suggests, these "arrangements" are not only on the rise, but may in time become a social institution with the aim or function of serving as a test or trial marriage.

[12] When the Decision-Making and Behavioral Surveys are cited, this is a reference to research conducted by the Maferr Foundation, Inc. (Male-Female Role Research), affiliated with the Research Department of the Postgraduate Center for Mental Health, 124 East 28th Street, New York, N.Y.

intend to make their partnership a lasting one and, therefore, tend to regard the "contract" as more binding.

Certainly, the young woman's relationship with her "live-in" partner does not at this stage represent more than a transitory experience, nor does it seriously affect her plans for a career. Should she decide to marry while still in college, the picture will probably change. Though the proportion of college dropouts is the same for both sexes—approximately four out of every ten who enter—the reasons are different: boys leave because of academic difficulties or problems of personal adjustment; the most frequent reason given by girls is marriage.

Since the average age for marriage today is twenty-one for women and twenty-three for men, a man will probably have completed at least his undergraduate studies by the time he marries, but a woman is likely to be still working toward her degree. She may now begin thinking about a home, a place which someday could accommodate a child or two; this vaguely formed thought, together with the priority our culture places on a man's career over a woman's, may propel her toward a job that pays well enough to support the two of them while he completes his training. The job may have no relevance to her own career plans; but later, she tells herself—when they are settled, when he has made his start—later, she will pick up where she left off.

Unfortunately, as we have seen from many couples seeking counseling later on in their marriage, this fairly typical behavior pattern in young marriages can set the stage for misunderstandings and resentments in the years ahead, particularly if the couple do not make their objectives clear at the time they enter into their "contract." Many a woman in her mid-thirties or early forties pours out her bitterness at a husband who has asked for a divorce: "I gave up my own education and career possibilities. I thought it was right because in time I would have my turn. Now this is my turn—out in the cold."

For such a woman, the sense of martyrdom and betrayal is unbearably painful; she feels she has been cheated and denied the chance for a life of her own. And her husband? "I was not prepared," he may tell the counselor. "I knew nothing about what women wanted, what they felt. I hadn't the remotest idea what was expected of me. I thought I was supposed to be the breadwinner, that I was doing the right thing. We never talked about her plans or ambitions." Our society should be devising ways to prepare the young for living together as we now prepare them for earning a living. Sex and marital counseling should be made as readily available to them as curriculum and employment counseling.

But suppose a young woman does not marry when she is barely out of her teens, a possibility which is increasing, according to recent figures among women from twenty to twenty-four, the proportion remaining single rose from 28 percent in 1960 to 40 percent in 1975. As a single woman, she manages her own finances, arranges her own social life, and serves her sexual needs as she sees fit. If, however, she decides to marry later on, her adjustment may involve certain difficulties. She has become accustomed to being her own woman, to making all her own decisions. She may have developed views, tastes, and habits which she has no intention of changing. Of course she intends to go on working; her work is as important to her as a man's work is to him, and she thrives on the sense of power and achievement it affords her. Will she be able to share her life successfully with a man?

Much depends on the ability of the partners to work their way through the ambivalence and distorted perceptions which showed up in the Behavioral and Decision-Making Surveys. We have seen women who are strong and successful in a career who feel, when they are attracted to a man, that they should conceal their so-called "masculine" traits. But as research on male and female roles suggests,[13] women who behave in this way may be ascribing to men a set of standards for women which men do not actually hold. This poses a question: Does the belief arise from an ambivalence within the woman? Does she, wishing to achieve success on her own and at the same time retain some of her "femininity," project onto the man the image of a dependent female which she has in her own life rejected?

Such ambivalence is understandable in a transitional time like the present, and it presents particular difficulties for the woman with a job. But we should also note that the independent working woman has some important advantages in achieving a good relationship with the man in her life. Recent studies by psychologists and sociologists have indicated that when both partners work, the husband is more likely to help around the house and the wife to take a more equal part in decision making for the family.[14] Also, the assumption of the role of provider by the wife reduces tension because her economic contribution takes some of the financial pressures off the husband.[15]

Essentially, this early stage of the relationship is a time of growing accustomed to each other's physical and emotional needs; of learning when to move in and when to withdraw into what the poet William Carlos Williams calls "the secret gardens of the self"; of taking nothing for granted and asking the questions that need to be asked. It is a time for exploring, testing, discovering—a time when social and sexual patterns are being established, when the "contract" is being revised and adjusted to conform to the growing realities of everyday living together. It is a time when both parties can negotiate in terms of their individual and common needs and interests. With the birth of the first child, this situation begins to change.

Stage Two

This is the time when the children are being born and growing up. For many couples, these are the years of fruition, of creating and building together and sharing in the rewards; but they are also a time when the relationship is strained by heavy new pressures. The transition from working wife to working mother,

---

[13] Steinmann and Fox, op. cit.

[14] Jacob Jack Finkelman, "Maternal Employment, Family Relationships, and Parental Role Perception," unpublished doctoral dissertation, Yeshiva University, New York, 1966.

[15] F. Ivan Nye and Lois Wladis Hoffman, *The Employed Mother in America,* Rand-McNally, Chicago, 1963.

which is dealt with in detail in Chapter 18, introduces into a woman's life a number of difficult problems, emotional and financial.

If a woman decides to follow the pattern which has become customary in middle-class families and give up her work for a number of years while her children are in school, she may be exchanging one set of frustrations for another. As a student or a woman with a job, she had become accustomed to having her achievements recognized. But as a full-time mother, she will have no tangible rewards analogous to grades or pay; instead, there may be a growing sense of isolation, of becoming stultified and cut off from the "real world."

Such a woman may also be aware of and troubled by her husband's sense of entrapment. In the Behavioral Survey conducted here and abroad, both men and women stated that men felt trapped by the responsibilities of wife, home, and children. A case in point is Anne Steinmann's experience with a family who have been in therapy with her for more than a year. The family consists of a father thirty-two years old; a pregnant mother, twenty-seven; and a young son, five. The father works in a law office and earns a respectable salary but so far has not been able to put away any savings. The job brings him little satisfaction; he describes himself as "dull, frustrated" and a "handmaiden" to his superior. He feels there is no way for him to make any progress, since his superior never gives him any opportunity to assume responsibility. He says, "If I didn't have my wife and child and another coming, I would venture out—try something else." During sessions with the wife and husband, when the husband's unhappiness with his job came up, the wife said in a hollow voice, "Of course, Marty should do what he really wants; but what do we do in the meantime?"

There has been some experimentation in Canada with a program to provide loans for families in this predicament, to "untrap" men who wish to strike out in a new direction.[16] Similar programs might be undertaken to "untrap" working mothers; assistance could take the form of day-care facilities to be made available through educational institutions and places of employment. Many marriages in the child-rearing stage could be strengthened and preserved if the man and woman were able to fulfill themselves as human beings rather than filling sex-typed roles within the family.

The sense of entrapment carries with it another malaise of the middle years, which can be summed up as "bed and boredom." This is the time when the excitement of the early years has been muted and passion and impetuousness have been absorbed in daily routine. The principal preoccupations of this marital stage are nesting and breeding; and in our child-centered society parenthood has a way of pushing aside most other interests and activities, including the kind of carefree and spontaneous sex life that the couple enjoyed in their early years.

A psychologist has noted: "The number one topic of conversation in America today is not politics, sex or football. It is children. Americans are obsessed

---

[16] Program conducted in Canada under the direction of the Department of Manpower and Immigration, Ottawa.

with children as no society has ever been. The frustrations of child-raising have caused it to be listed as the second leading reason for divorce."[17] He goes on to cite the proliferation of books, articles, and courses on parenthood and a parent-training program that has 8,000 instructors.

Somehow, the raising of children—once accepted as a matter of course—has become a highly complex, sophisticated, professionalized activity. Married couples with growing children find that their interaction with each other revolves around their offspring. The working woman finds that the children's needs, demands, and well-being are all-controlling. For the sake of the children, the parents may move from city to suburb, though the city may be where their work, friends, and interests are. Once in the suburbs, the children must be chauffeured to school, to music lessons, to the riding ring, to the tennis courts, to their friends' houses. And there is the never-ending anxiety about how the children are doing in school, whether they are keeping up their grades and making a good showing on the athletic field.

In the shuffle of parenthood, a man and woman who once interacted as individuals may lose their sense of themselves. They may become extensions of their children, who meanwhile are growing away from them into a segregated culture of youth. It is one of the ironies of our time that children who were once thought to be the tie that binds marriages together should now be partly responsible for untying the knot. But it is understandable in view of the erosion that takes place in the lives of men and women when much of their thinking and planning are concentrated on the rearing of their young, to the exclusion of their own growth and development. The woman who works has at least one advantage here, since her job provides her with access to stimuli beyond the kitchen and nursery. During these stressful years while she performs a professional "juggling act," she will need to take advantage of every opportunity to continue her personal growth and encourage the man in her life to do the same.

These middle years are a time when, as the statistics indicate, one out of every three marriages will ultimately be dissolved. But the rising divorce rate is accompanied by a rising rate of remarriage. Of the 1 million people who are divorced in the United States every year, four out of five remarry. The result is what sociologists call the "blended" or "reconstituted" family—that is, a family group including children who are "hers," "his," and, in time, "theirs." Although many people who remarry claim that the second time is a great improvement over the first, the fact is that second marriages are no more enduring than first marriages. The average duration of second marriages that fail is six years, compared with seven years for first marriages that fail.

What happens to the working woman who finds herself living alone after several years of marriage or an "arrangement" with a man? If she has children to care for—and this is true of the majority of divorced women—her life will be more complicated than before. As a single parent, her roles and responsibilities

[17] Richard Farson, "Here Comes a New Liberation Movement," *Los Angeles Times,* October 19, 1975.

have doubled: she is now father as well as mother. And she must do it all on a reduced income; if formerly her earnings were the icing on the family's financial cake, now they are very likely the bread and butter. There is also loneliness to deal with, as well as the problems of everyday living. A recent study of depression found that divorced and separated women were more depressed than divorced and separated men. Among both sexes, those with children were more depressed than those with no children. The younger the children, the greater the depression.[18] (It is Steinmann's experience that such depression is measured by degree rather than incidence.)

And yet, despite the stress and difficulties of this stage, the working woman and the man in her life have many things going for them. They can both take satisfaction in their work as well as their home life, thus providing a good basis for companionship. They can add meaning and depth to each other's lives by sharing their separate working worlds. And if they are sensitive to each other's feelings, they can bring a vitality and variety to their relationship which will enrich and expand both their lives.

Stage Three

Stage three is the later years. This is the time when a woman is released from the demands of biology. With the end of menopause comes a new kind of freedom—freedom to enjoy sexual intercourse without fear of pregnancy, freedom from the time-consuming and energy-consuming responsibilities of motherhood. "Menopause is one of the great eras in a woman's life," a prominent gynecologist has said.[19] And a study conducted under the auspices of the Committee on Human Development of the University of Chicago found that women who have been through the menopause have a more positive view of it than women who have not.

But menopause is also a time of anxiety, particularly for women who work. A woman who has built a fine career suddenly finds herself competing with younger women. She begins to doubt her abilities and wonders if she can go any further in her profession. Or she looks in the mirror and sees pouches and wrinkles—and panics at the thought of losing her job. Who will hire her at her age?

In addition, there are new disruptions in her relationship with the man in her life. She is now at the peak of her sexual powers, whereas his may be declining. (However, it is increasingly recognized that the decline in male potency and vigor during these years is due to cultural conditioning and the acceptance of social myths about age and sexual activity.) Their careers are also out of phase. Most working women, their energies released when their children are grown, begin to go full speed ahead in their jobs or professions at just about the time when their husbands are ready to let down and relax. This imbalance is aggravated by the

[18] Jessie Bernard, "Note on Changing Life Styles, 1970–1974," *Journal of Marriage and the Family*, vol. 37, no. 3, August 1975, pp. 582–593.
[19] Luigi Mastroianni, Jr., chief of obstetrics and gynecology at University of Pennsylvania Hospital, quoted in Sally Olds, "Menopause—Something to Look Forward To?" *Today's Health*, May 1970.

fact that women tend to marry men several years their senior, so that when the men have reached retirement age, their wives still have a good many working years ahead of them.

One way of preparing for this imbalance is for the partners, in their contractual communications over the years, to discuss and encourage the man's interests and resources other than his work. In other words, he should have another occupation, or avocation, that he can phase into at the right time.

It is not until late middle and old age that men and women have a chance once again to find each other. Now both may be retired,[20] and if their health is good—which is very possible in these days of improved health care—they can enjoy their time by developing new interests together. Since the working wife has enjoyed a balanced relationship with the man in her life and is accustomed to communicating with him as a peer, they have a sound basis for making the most of their leisure time.

In this youth-oriented culture, the sexuality of older people tends to be ignored. Actually, if the partners have communicated openly with each other and have been able to express their full sexuality throughout their lives, their active sex life can be prolonged far into so-called "old age." This is the stage of life, in fact, when many couples, if they have set the pattern of discussing their contractual obligations openly and lovingly, can understand for the first time in their lives the deeper meaning of companionship.

THE SEXUAL HUMAN BEING

> The pleasures of sex are the pleasures of company—the head is where every sexual safari musters, where the trip is conceived, where the exploration begins. The mind is the most important of all the erogenous zones, both temperate and torrid—it provides context and meaning, appetite and appreciation. Unless it is exercised, every other sense becomes flabby and out of condition.—Philip Oakes, "The Pleasures of Life"

The woman who works is first and above all a woman, a sexual human being whose sexuality, like a man's, originates in her mind, and at the same time is diffused through her genitalia and her entire body. The working woman and the man in her life are capable of complete satisfaction in the enjoyment of their sexuality if they recognize that both male and female are capable of sensitivity, assertiveness, warmth, and just plain fun. And as the English writer Philip Oakes states: "Sexual pleasure is not taught but communicated, and always, person to person."[21]

Joy in each other and in each other's sexuality comes from a total feeling of understanding, trust, and respect which some call "love." But does this always occur? How can it be obtained?

---

[20] We are using the word "retired" because it is commonly accepted. But we feel the word should be retired. There should be freedom from a set pattern of work and from financial worries, and a sense of security—but no retirement from life.

[21] Philip Oakes, "The Pleasures of Life," series in the *Sunday Times Weekly Review*, London, August 10, 1975.

Freud tells us that sexual repression is the price we pay for civilization, a theory that has been challenged by several psychoanalysts. But whether we subscribe to the Freudian theory or not, we know that many of the discontents of civilization are related to sex. In America today, we are moving rapidly away from a period of a tighter, more private concept of sex to an era of sexual openness and freedom. However, this new liberation does not seem to have lessened our discontent or to have brought about a sexual Utopia in which male-female interaction is happier, healthier, and more enduring. On the contrary, sex-related problems are increasing, and the number of men and women seeking marital and sexual counseling is also steadily increasing.

How can we account for this paradox? Why hasn't the sexual revolution lived up to the general expectations? Should we abandon the new morality and, if so, what can we put in its place? The old morality with its rigid, sex-typed codes is obviously not the answer, and as Kinsey demonstrated, it bore little resemblance to human sexual behavior. But what, then?

These questions are troubling many women today whose expanding sexual options make them feel as though they are wandering through uncharted territory without the aid of a compass. The woman who works and who wants fulfillment in bed as well as in her job is beset by confusions; she has greater access to a variety of sexual opportunities than the woman who stays at home. And in today's permissive atmosphere, why shouldn't she take advantage of whatever opportunities come her way?

There are no easy answers to questions like these. But in the interests of clarity, we can begin by making a distinction between "sex" and "sexuality." "Sex," by our definition, refers specifically to a sex act—the physical act of bodily pleasure. Sexual intercourse is an example. "Sexuality" is the total interaction of a man and woman in every aspect of their living together, with a daily appreciation of their individual sexual, emotional, and intellectual drives. The sex act is part of sexuality, but it should never be isolated from the "pleasure of company." For sexuality represents a completion—a wholeness and continuity of affection and communication between two people. It is a life force, or, in the words of the philosopher Henri Bergson, an *"elan vital."*

Unfortunately, we have tended in recent years to isolate sex and remove it from the context of sexuality. The media bombard us with messages urging us to become sexier by driving a certain car, smoking a certain cigarette, or using a certain deodorant. Books and articles on sex, like those dealing with child care, are multiplying rapidly, and most of them are in the "how to" category. All sorts of helpful tips are offered by these works: detailed instructions on positions, techniques, strategies, approaches guaranteed to turn you overnight into a sexual virtuoso. One can't help wondering how the human race managed to get any pleasure out of sex during all those millennia before print was invented.

The danger in this emphasis on technique is that sex begins to resemble an athletic performance, to become a matter of training, agility, and prowess. It's not how you feel but how you do it that counts—and what you get out of it for yourself. Giving is not as blessed as receiving. If you don't have the orgasm many of these books and articles emphasize you're entitled to, maybe, according to their authors, there's something wrong with your style. You may begin to think that you're reading the wrong books; and, we say, you are. Qualified people who counsel or write about sex deal with it as part of a whole person and a total relationship.

The attempt to measure up to a set of arbitrary sexual standards produces feelings of guilt and inadequacy, and this is particularly hard on the working woman who lives in a split-level world of work and home. If she is to realize the full potential of her personal commitments, she will need to do all she can to integrate sex into sexuality.

IT TAKES TWO TO MAKE ONE

> Marco's leg slid forward against mine and my leg slid back and I seemed to be riveted to him limb for limb and after awhile I thought, "It doesn't take two to dance, it only takes one."—Sylvia Plath, *The Bell Jar*

A successful relationship requires two equally involved partners: it takes two to make one. That one is not indivisible. It is divided or—in today's high-pressure world—fragmented into various roles and responsibilities, and these are increasingly being determined by human rather than sexist needs and objectives. In the mathematics of mating, one and one adds up to an indeterminate number, for each of us consists of many changing, growing selves which include masculine as well as feminine attributes; and these many selves need a chance for expression if we are to develop as fully realized human beings.

It has been suggested that one of the new life-styles we might be moving toward is the "symmetrical family," in which both partners would have absolute equality. This would mean that one would work in the morning and the other in the afternoon, with each being free to spend the other half of the day caring for the children and running the household.[22]

In the article on liberated marriage mentioned earlier, the author describes how she and her husband have worked out their version of a "symmetrical life-style." Before the birth of their first child, both wife and husband had worked on newspapers as reporters. There was complete "equality" in their lives. With the birth of the first child, the husband now had to be the main support of the family while the wife did freelance writing at home. With the birth of the second child, time for the mother to write had to be carefully "hoarded." She felt frustrated. Meanwhile, the demands of the husband's high-pressure job gave him the sense of being cheated out of the pleasures and rewards of family life. Then, these partners decided to switch roles. Now he writes at home and goes through all the complications and disorders of trying to do creative work while taking care of two small children. She has a full-time job teaching at a university, and it is her income which supports the family of four. This is an example of the reversal of male-female roles with no corresponding loss of identity. The wife sums it up, "If

[22] Shirley Summerskill, from an address delivered in Oslo, September 18, 1975.

I am a free woman, and I believe I am, it is due in no small measure to the fact that I have lived with—and loved and been nurtured by—free men."[23]

A truly free man, in our view, is one who can express has the so-called "feminine" attributes of nurturance, just as a free woman has the "masculine" attributes of drive and achievement. The working woman, in liberating herself from sexual stereotypes, is also liberating the man in her life. Her double commitment, to work and home, means that she can bring to both worlds the vitality and richness she gains from living a dual life. And the contribution she makes to her family and her community *can*—and, we think it safe to predict, *will*—have far-reaching effects on society and its values.

BIBLIOGRAPHY

Astin, Helen S., Nancy Suniewick, and Susan Dweck: *Women—A Bibliography on Their Education and Careers,* Human Service Press, Washington, D.C., 1971. Comprehensive, annotated bibliography of the literature on women's training and occupations and how they mesh with the role of wife and mother. The large number of studies attests to a growing interest in working women and their expanding role in society.
———et al.: *Sex Roles,* Center for Human Services, Washington, D.C., 1975. An expanded and updated version of the preceding reference.
Braudy, Susan: *Between Marriage and Divorce—A Woman's Diary,* William Morrow, New York, 1975. A searching and sometimes painful self-analysis; the author gives an account of the breakup of her marriage and her struggle to make a life as a woman and as a writer.
Deutsch, Helene: *The Psychology of Women,* 2 vols., Grune and Stratton, New York, 1944, 1945. A classic work on the growth and conflicts of women. Deutsch presents clearly what she has learned from patients, and this helps give a deeper understanding of women. This book engenders controversy but is nevertheless a pioneering work.
Ferguson, Charles Wright: *The Male Attitude,* Little, Brown, Boston, 1966. A fascinating study of the male drive for dominance—its history, and how it has distorted the male-female relationship.
Freud, Sigmund: "Some Psychical Consequences of the Anatomical Distinction between the Sexes," in *Standard Edition,* vol. 19, Hogarth Press, London, 1925; "Female Sexuality: The Oedipus Situation in a Girl" and "Femininity," from *New Introductory Lectures,* in *Standard Edition,* vol. 22, Hogarth Press, London, 1932. Freud's papers on women have been both attacked and defended; one must read him and judge for oneself. In the paper on femininity, Freud himself admits that his remarks are partly conjectural and expresses the hope that science will give us more information: "If you want to know more about femininity, inquire from your own experiences of life, or turn to the poets, or wait until science can give you deeper and more coherent information."
Fromm, Erich: *The Art of Loving,* Perennial Library, Harper & Row, New York, 1974. Fromm defines love as "the capacity of the mature, productive character." Since he regards loving as an art, he suggests that it—like other arts—requires discipline, concentration, and patience.

---

[23] Rivers, op. cit. The author uses the plural "men" here to include her father, who also took a nonsexist view of women and their roles.

Howard, Jane: *A Different Woman,* Dutton, New York, 1973. Through interviews with women of various backgrounds, the author shows how all of them have in some way been affected by the rising tide of feminism.

Klein, Viola: *The Feminine Character—History of an Ideal,* International Universities Press, New York, 1949 (first published in England, 1946). A scientific but immensely readable outline of various approaches to the understanding of women: historical, biological, philosophical, psychoanalytical, anthropological, and sociological.

Lederer, William J., and Don D. Jackson: *The Mirages of Marriage,* Norton, New York, 1968. A presentation of Jackson's central ideas about the nature of the marital relationship, for a popular audience. The foreword, by Karl Menninger, describes it as "bibliotherapy: therapeutic help derived from the reading of books."

Maferr Foundation, Inc. (Male-Female Role Research), affiliated with the Research Department of the Postgraduate Center for Mental Health, 124 East 28th Street, New York, New York. For over twenty years the Maferr Foundation has been conducting studies on the lack of communication between men and women, which seems to be prevalent in many countries and cultures.

Mead, Margaret: *Male and Female: A Study of the Sexes in a Changing World,* William Morrow, New York, 1949. From an account of sex roles among Pacific peoples, Mead proceeds to a provocative analysis of sexual patterns in the United States.

Oakes, Philip: "The Pleasures of Life," series in the *Sunday Times Weekly Review,* London, August 10, 1975.

Slater, Philip: *The Pursuit of Loneliness,* Boston Press, Boston, 1970. An examination of the underlying assumptions and themes of our culture. "If I had to select a single book by which to tell a stranger what life in this country has become and why, it would be this one. It is even more useful in telling us about ourselves."—*New York Review of Books,* June 4, 1970.

Steinmann, Anne, and David J. Fox: *The Male Dilemma,* Jason Aronson, New York, 1974. The Child Study Association of America, in giving this book the Family Life Book Award, noted its "balanced analysis of the issue of sex roles and its perceptive examination of the profound implications for males, females, families, and child-rearing in the years ahead."

Unger, Rhoda K., and Florence L. Denmark: *Women: Dependent or Independent Variable,* Psychological Dimensions, New York, 1975. Until recently, most psychology has been defined in terms of males and oriented toward males. This book intends to help define a new field of study—the psychology of women.

Chapter 18

Coping with Child Care: The Working Mother

Karen Hill Scott

Karen Hill Scott, Ed.D., is currently Assistant Professor, University of California, Los Angeles, School of Architecture and Urban Planning. She wrote her doctoral dissertation on the process of day-care planning in a Los Angeles community. She has developed an ethnically oriented curriculum and training program, has published a monograph on the children's television program "Sesame Street," and has contributed to *Essence* magazine. Ms. Scott is also Executive Vice-President of The Planning Group, a nonprofit planning and consulting organization and was recently appointed Project Director for the Joint Center for Community Studies, affiliated with UCLA.

In the best of circumstances (where husbands share fully in the rearing of children) and in the most difficult circumstances (where a woman raises her children alone, without help from any source) the problem of finding child care usually ends up as the mother's responsibility. Unfortunately, finding good-quality child care is not a simple matter. It is a complicated problem that requires a great deal of thought, organization, and planning on the part of the mother to locate the most suitable arrangement for her particular child-care needs. This is because there is no centrally organized system of child care which offers various types of services to all segments of the population. What exists is an ad hoc system of services, none of which come under the same set of regulatory or licensing procedures, and some of which should be, but are not, licensed at all. The working mother must sift through alternatives until the appropriate child-care solution can be found.

Many mothers are in this predicament. In 1970, it was estimated that there were 21,332,000 children under the age of six in the United States. Of these, 6 million had working mothers, most of whom were working out of financial necessity.[1] If one considers that there is yet an additional need for child care for children over the age of six, the figure increases accordingly. Who is taking care of these children? It is estimated that from 60 to 75 percent of them are taken care of through informal baby-sitting arrangements. Another 20 to 25 percent are cared for in an out-of-home arrangement such as a day-care center or a family day-care home. And approximately 3 percent—about 18,000 children—are "latchkey kids," on their own without adult supervision.[2]

The public response to the needs of the working mother has generally been poor. Day care has experienced widespread support only during times of national crises (such as World War II) when the male work force was decreased. Otherwise, meeting the need for day care outside the family has historically been regarded as a function of social welfare agencies established to protect children from troubled or disintegrating families.[3] However, during the last ten years a dramatic increase in the number of working mothers has created a new need for widely available child care. In 1960, only 19 percent of all mothers worked; in 1970, 30 percent of this group was in the work force. Concurrently, many parents began to realize the value of a preschool education for their children. Thus, in 1970, 38 percent of all three-, four-, and five-year-olds were in preschool. These children came from all socioeconomic groups, although 48 percent of them came from homes with annual incomes over $10,000 which were also headed by a college graduate.[4]

It is apparent from these figures that as parents' education increases, the demand for preschool education will become greater. Also, many of the children of working mothers, particularly those who make less than $10,000 a year, are not in the preschools but are in other day-care arrangements. As a consequence, the actual increased need for extrafamily care and social awareness of the value of a preschool experience have attracted attention to what is now regarded as a national problem.

To deal with the problem of day care, various bills have been proposed in

[1] Pamela Roby, "Child Care—What and Why?" in P. Roby (ed.), *Child Care—Who Cares,* Basic Books, New York, 1973, p. 3.

[2] Mary D. Keyserling, *Windows on Day Care: A Report Based on Findings of the National Council of Jewish Women,* National Council of Jewish Women, New York, 1972, p. 13.

[3] I. Lazar and M. Rosenberg, "Day Care in America," in Edith Grotberg (ed.), *Day Care: Resources for Decisions,* Office of Economic Opportunity, Washington, D.C., 1971, p. 73.

[4] Roby, op. cit., p. 4.

Congress since 1969. All these bills build upon existing federal programs, such as Head Start, where because of legislative guidelines the priority is necessarily given to low-income families. The major piece of legislation for child care to self-sufficient families was the Comprehensive Child Development Bill of 1971, proposed by Senator Mondale and Congressman Nelson as S2007, the 1971 Amendment to the Economic Opportunity Act. They proposed a Title V to the Economic Opportunity Act which would authorize the Department of Health, Education and Welfare (DHEW) to make grants to prime sponsors of child-development programs. In addition to existing Head Start funds, $100 million would have been authorized for planning in 1972, and $2 billion would have been authorized for actual programs in 1973.[5] Both the House and the Senate passed the bill, but it was vetoed by Richard Nixon, who was then President. Nixon stated: "Neither the immediate need nor the desirability of a national child development program of this character has been demonstrated." He felt that the proposed outlays were excessive and considered the bill to be "the most radical piece of legislation to emerge from the Ninety-second Congress" and to have "family weakening implications."[6] Although similar bills have come before Congress since then, none has become law.

The working mother is caught "between a rock and a hard place." There have been increases in child-care services since 1960, because new proprietary day-care centers were started and the federal government has provided services to families whose need is extremely great. But by no means have these increases been large enough, nor has the quality of care been good enough to consider our national need as being met. In this chapter, I hope to make it clear that the working mother, as a consumer of child care, should not only be appraised of the various options that may be available to her; she must also fully understand that her individual need is tied to a national child-care problem, where quality and quantity of care are salient issues. The chapter will provide the working mother with a means of assessing child-care services. Finally, because the emotional aspects of coping with child-care arrangements are rarely discussed, some thoughts on this topic will also be offered.

QUALITY OF CARE

One of the first questions raised by the working mother when assessing child-care services is, "What am I supposed to be looking for?" Working definitions of the three qualities of care currently found in day-care settings may be helpful. These will be followed by a discussion of four widely used child-care arrangements.

Custodial Care

Custodial care ensures at a minimum the general supervision and physical safety of the child. There are usually no planned activities for children in this type of

[5] Erika Streur, "Current Legislative Proposals and Public Policy Questions for Child Care," in P. Roby, op. cit., p. 58.
[6] Economic Opportunity Amendments of 1971—Veto Message (H. Doc. No. 92-48), December 8, 1971.

day-care situation and no opportunities to build a sense of self-worth or to promote intellectual development.[7] At its best, custodial care provides to some extent for the emotional safety and happiness of the child. That is, although the child-care setting may not have an organized program of developmental activity which will assist the child's intellectual growth, there is nothing in the setting that will harm the child or retard the child's growth in any way. By and large, many child-care services which purport to offer preschool programs are actually centers with good custodial care.

Developmental Care

The second type of child care that can be provided, which is also endorsed by the DHEW Office of Child Development, is developmental care. With this kind of day care, a child is provided many opportunities for physical, social, and intellectual growth. There are planned educational and recreational activities, and the child is supervised by trained workers. There are three types of trained workers in a developmental day-care setting: the day-care director, the teacher, and the teaching assistant or aide. These workers have varying levels of formal education and working experience with children, are paid accordingly, and are certified appropriately by a regulating agency. A developmental child-care program will offer meals—at least lunch and two snacks—and is sometimes able to provide the child with a yearly medical and dental exam. Parents are encouraged to participate in a developmental child-care program.[8]

Comprehensive Care

The third quality of care is called comprehensive care. In comprehensive programs, the widest possible range of educational, health, and counseling services is made available to the children and their parents. Almost every need, from family counseling to complete medical and dental care, is met.[9] There are very few comprehensive child-care programs in the country, and it would not be possible to offer these services on a large scale because the costs are prohibitive.

DHEW Standards

It is important to note that in addition to defining quality of care, DHEW has also issued a set of recommended standards for group day-care centers. However, these standards are only proposed and are not legally binding. There are also various federal, state, and local requirements which attempt to regulate day-care practices. But these requirements are not always consistent with each other; they vary from place to place, and they do not apply to all child-care facilities. Furthermore, with the exception of the Federal Interagency Requirements on Day Care, most state licenses specify only fire and safety requirements. They do not include judgments about the quality of programs. Thus it is highly probable that a licensed child-care service meets only the minimum standards for custodial care.[10]

[7] Edward F. Zigler, "The Need for Day Care," *Children,* Winter 1972, p. 2.
[8] Ibid.
[9] Ibid.
[10] Mary P. Rowe and Ralph T. Husby, "Economics of Child Care: Costs, Needs and Issues," in P. Roby, op. cit., p. 99–119.

Issues of Cost and Quality

In 1972, government estimates of the average cost per year for each type of child care were as follows: $1,800 per child for custodial care; $2,300 per child for developmental care; $3,500 per child for full-day, full-year care. Adjusting for inflation at 7 percent a year, the figures for 1976 will be, respectively, $2,359; $3,015; and $4,588.[11] Since the majority of parents pay from $1,300 to $2,080 per year for child care, it is apparent that working mothers are probably very poorly served.[12] As the Westinghouse-Westat study (1970) indicated, most day-care centers, for example, cut the costs of personnel, service, and overhead by increasing the number of children, lowering the requirements for teaching jobs, and operating out of poorly equipped facilities. Thus, rather than having one adult for every five two-year-olds, there may be one adult for every seven; the supervising adult may not be a certified preschool teacher; and the children may have no space for indoor play. Often only one person on the entire staff may be certified, even by the admittedly minimal regulatory standards currently in existence. In family day-care homes, some costs may be automatically reduced because fees do not pay for auxiliary services or administration. However, less than 7 percent of such day-care homes are licensed.[13] Therefore, the quality of care and services offered is almost totally unregulated and is highly variable.

The combined issues of cost and quality are too complex to be discussed fully here. There are some regional differences and some differences between rural and urban settings, as well as extremes of cost which are not reflected in a discussion of averages. However, this brief discussion should serve to illustrate that in most cases the cost of care is directly and positively correlated with the quality of care. This is because about 50 percent of the child-care dollar is spent on the direct costs of teaching and care. The remaining 50 percent is spent on food (11 percent); health, social services, and transportation (10 percent); administration (16 percent); and building overhead (13 percent).[14]

CHILD-CARE ARRANGEMENTS

If a mother realizes how important her judgment of quality care is, then she is in a better position to make a choice regarding child care. If she is informed about the key issues in quality of care, she will not be easily deceived. For example, she will not think that a licensed but poor center is necessarily better than an unlicensed family day-care home. A mother should also understand the differences among child-care arrangements. In this section I have drawn upon the three

[11] These adjusted figures fall within the current federal cost specifications for full-year developmental day care under Title IV-A of the Social Security Act.

[12] Based on a communication from the Los Angeles Commission on Day Care, National Survey of Costs, 1975 (unpublished report).

[13] Westinghouse Learning Corporation and Westat Research, Inc. (Westinghouse-Westat), *Day Care Survey—1970. Summary Report and Basic Analysis,* Westat Research, Inc., Rockville, Md., April 1971, pp. 203–207.

[14] Abt Associates, Inc., *A Study in Child Care 1970–1971, vols. 2 and 3,* Abt Associates, Inc., Cambridge, Mass., 1971.

major studies of child care in America: Westinghouse-Westat, *Survey of Child Care* (1970); the National Council of Jewish Women, *Windows on Child Care* (1972); and Abt Associates, *A Study in Child Care* (1972). These studies describe four types of child-care arrangements. Together, they give an overall picture of the available resources in day care.

In-Home Baby-Sitter

The first, and perhaps oldest, child-care arrangement is the in-home caretaker. Fifty years ago, when the extended family was more common, and stronger, a relative would often take care of a working mother's child. This arrangement still exists when family networks remain strong. But today, many mothers hire sitters (related or not) to come into the home, and most mothers express a preference for this arrangement, expecially for the child under three. For example, in a survey of the Mount Pleasant community in Washington, D.C., Zamoff and Lyle found that home-like settings were preferred for infants and toddlers, whereas day-care centers were preferred for three- to six-year-olds.[15]

The advantages of the in-home sitter can be great, provided the right person has the job. First, the child is at home and in familiar surroundings. If the child is sick, care can still be provided, and exposure to the illnesses of other children can be minimized. Also, for some families, the in-home sitter may provide other services, such as cooking and housekeeping. Under the best of circumstances, in-home care provides a full-time person to handle a fair amount of household and child-care responsibilities. However, such an arrangement is both rare and expensive. Usually the in-home sitter simply provides custodial care, but in the child's own home. If the home lacks space, ventilation, play areas, and equipment, the in-home sitter may be a disservice to the child. A more formal arrangement in a developmental day-care center might be more suitable. Also, there are no requirements which qualify a person to be a good baby-sitter. If the parents cannot find a reliable, responsible person, the turnover rate of baby-sitters is likely to be high, and the mother is plagued with having to frequently find a new sitter or general housekeeper. This turnover rate puts the child in an unstable situation and puts the mother under undue pressure and worry about finding satisfactory child care.

The costs of in-home care vary. I have heard about a range of rates from nothing to upwards of $100 a week. If the baby-sitter is a relative or close friend, the parents often feel they should pay much less than they would for a sitter hired outright. In the Mount Pleasant survey, for example, 13.7 percent of the respondents felt that they should pay nothing for care offered by a relative or friend. Yet 16.1 percent were willing to pay a hired sitter $28 a week or more. The average cost range for in-home baby-sitting (with light or no housekeeping) is from $25 to $50 a week.

---

[15] Richard Zamoff and Jerolyn Lyle, "Planning and Evaluation of Day Care at the Community Level," in Dennis R. Young and Richard R. Nelson (eds.), *Public Policy for Day Care of Young Children,* Heath (Lexington Books), Boston, 1973, pp. 71–90.

Family and Group Day-Care Homes

In a family day-care home up to six children are kept in the home of one adult caretaker who is not related to any of them. The group day-care home usually cares for up to fifteen children and should have another paid adult to assist the adult who provides the service. A group day-care home should occupy a larger physical facility than a family day-care home.[16]

Day-care homes are the largest providers of formal day care today, and it is estimated that from 850,000[17] to 1.8 million[18] children were cared for in over 450,000 homes in 1970. About 90 percent of these day-care homes were unlicensed, a fact which makes it difficult to locate them for one's own use and even more difficult to accurately estimate the number of children served.

According to the survey by the National Council of Jewish Women (NCJW), some of the poorest and some of the best care was in day-care homes. In the majority of cases, though, both the NCJW and Westinghouse surveys report that day-care homes offer a custodial, or strictly baby-sitting, service. The advantages of the day-care home are similar to those of the in-home baby-sitter. The child is in a homelike setting which is usually very close to or in the child's own neighborhood. Care during illness may be provided; but the possible exposure to infectious diseases is of course increased. About 60 percent of the children in day-care homes are under the age of three, both because some parents prefer the small, cozy arrangement for very young children and because there are few centers which offer care for children of this age.[19]

The major disadvantage of day-care homes is inconsistency and unpredictability of service. Although 35 percent of the homes in the NCJW survey offered adequate custodial care, another 65 percent offered only fair to poor care. Without good regulatory measures, and a standardization of personnel requirements, parents may have to endure a few bad experiences until the right day-care home can be found. And since most day-care homes are unlicensed, parents will have to rely on word of mouth or other informal means of communication to locate a decent service.

Day-care homes are supported by fees and by public subsidy if they serve welfare families. The average range of fees is from $25 to $40 a week. It is interesting to note that these fees are high for the custodial care that the children receive; these same high fees would pay for better care in a child-care center.

Potentially, the day-care home could be a high-quality source of child care. That is, with more stringent licensing procedures and regulatory practices, and the special training of personnel, the day-care home could help meet the current shortage of child-care service in this country. It has been proposed that if large day-care systems were to be established, the day-care homes could serve as feeders to day-care centers. The homes would serve infants and toddlers, while the centers would serve the toilet-trained preschool children.

---

[16] Keyserling, op. cit., pp. 130–166.
[17] Westinghouse-Westat, op. cit., p. 203.
[18] Keyserling, op. cit., p. 130.
[19] Richard Nelson and Michael Krashinsky, "The Demand and Supply of Extra-Family Day Care," in Young and Nelson, op. cit., pp. 9–20.

Day-Care Centers

Day-care centers serve 25 or more children; are housed in various types of physical facilities (homes, schools, churches, self-contained units); and employ three or more adults who are responsible for administrating and maintaining the center, supervising the children, and preparing food. Day-care centers may be proprietary (profit or nonprofit) or non-proprietary (publicly subsidized or sponsored by a voluntary organization).[20] The source of funding is often a critical factor in the quality of services provided. This is because the publicly subsidized center must meet federal requirements for developmental care and therefore is supported entirely by the government or receives supplements to fees.

Because of the availability of public funds for preschool education, there has been a rapid expansion of licensed day-care centers. The Westinghouse survey estimates that there was an increase from about 4,400 centers in 1960 to about 17,500 centers (serving 575,000 children) in 1970. The children cared for in most of these centers were between the ages of thirty months and six years. About 14 percent of all centers offer extended day care for children up to twelve years, but very few centers offer care for children under the age of two.[21]

In a day-care center, the child meets and plays with a larger group of children of various ages. Care is provided for an average of ten hours a day, although some centers are open for twelve hours a day. Usually lunch and two snacks are served; some nonproprietary centers also offer breakfast. According to the NCJW survey, even those centers which are custodial try to offer some education. Because most centers are not financially able to retain a professional staff, their educational programs are not very successful. This is especially true of the proprietary centers, where the median ten-month salary of a day-care teacher was $3,580 in 1972. Professional workers cannot be hired at these salaries, and consequently these programs tend to be weak. It is estimated that about 25 percent of all centers offer a good developmental program and the rest are fair to poor.[22] On the other hand, the Abt Associates study, which tended to select more exemplary programs for study, describes, in detail, some good developmental programs.[23]

The major disadvantage of the day-care center is cost. According to a national survey recently completed by the Los Angeles Commission on Day Care, fees in proprietary centers now range from $25 to $40 a week for each child.[24] Usually a nonproprietary center will have somewhat lower fees because some services, some staff work, or the physical facility are provided "in kind," donated by a philanthropic organization, or supported by revenues other than fees. In publicly subsidized day-care centers, parents pay fees on a sliding scale which is adjusted to income. In California, for example, most public day care which is funded through the state has an actual cost of $1.14 per hour for two- to five-year-olds and $1.35 per hour for infants. The full fee for the average fifty-hour

[20] Rowe and Husby, op. cit., p. 124.
[21] Emma Jackson, "The Present System of Publicly Supported Day Care," in Young and Nelson, op. cit., pp. 21–46.
[22] Keyserling, op. cit., p. 119.
[23] Abt Associates, op. cit.
[24] Personal communication from Vivien Weinstein, Chairperson of the Commission.

week ranges from $57 to $67.50 per child.[25] However, under the 1976 Title XX regulations the maximum fee actually paid by families who have the maximum income proportionate to family size is 49 percent of the full cost to the state, or $28 to $38. It is apparent, from this example, that without large-scale well-organized public subsidy of all day care-programs, for most working mothers developmental care will be difficult to find and to afford.

"Latchkey Kids"

This arrangement is really a nonarrangement. In this situation, the child takes care of himself or herself and sometimes siblings while mother works. It is estimated that 18,000 children are in this category.[26] I do not advocate this plan (nor does anyone else in the field of child development), because it offers the child no developmental advantages and can lead to serious family problems.

Some parents use the latchkey system because they honestly cannot find child care. Others use it because they believe that a child who has reached school age can be self-reliant. There are also those who cannot afford to pay for any kind of child-care service. And there is a small group of parents who have willingly abdicated their child-rearing responsibility except for providing the minimum necessary for survival. Regardless of the rationale for using the latchkey system, the child suffers. It could be argued that for children of nine and older, one or two hours alone a day is not irreparably damaging and can even teach responsibility. But the preadolescent does not have a mature sense of judgment about strangers, about accident prevention, or about what to do in emergencies. Thus, the latchkey plan is very risky, even though the risk may be lessened as the child becomes an adolescent.

ASSESSING CHILD-CARE PROGRAMS

The main theme in the discussion of each child-care arrangement is that developmental child care is the exception rather than the rule. The working mother must "shop" for the child-care plan that offers the best service in relation to its cost and convenience. There are six areas in which a parent can rate a child-care service: the physical facility, including space and equipment; program organization (including the educational component); staff; auxiliary services; parental participation; and cost. After discussing each of these areas, I will offer a checklist for rating child-care services and for making informed decisions about quality care.

Physical Facility, Space, and Equipment

A parent should determine if there is adequate space for the number of children served; if the facility is safe, well-ventilated, and well-heated; if it has enough toilets, a clean kitchen, and child-sized furniture. Also, check for safe outdoor

---

[25] Funded by Title IV-A of the Social Security Act (regulated under Title XX) through the California State Office of Education under the California Comprehensive Annual Services Program Plan—Public Law 13647.

[26] Keyserling, op. cit., p. 13.

play equipment, a sandbox, and a grassy area. Find out if there are balls and blocks, tricycles or bicycles, and musical instruments and toys in working condition. These items, in sufficient quantity, are the absolute minimum necessary for the physical facility. Nicely painted and decorated interiors with lots of storage, a good open floor plan (partially carpeted), a garden, and a small animal center would enhance a developmental program. The facility may be old and cluttered, but it should not be dirty—taking into account that with more than one child around, it is difficult to maintain a spotless place.

Programs (Including Educational Component)

Once a mother is thinking of child care in terms other than simple baby-sitting, the program offered is the heart of the child-care service. You will find a range of offerings from general enrichment activities (such as games and field trips) to well-planned lessons aimed at intellectual and emotional development. At a minimum, children should be talked to; taken places (even places as simple as the grocery store); and taught some very basic skills such as their names and addresses, parts of the body, how to tie shoes, and how to count and say the alphabet. For infants, the "program" is not directly educational but rather cultural. Toilet training, feeding, weaning, and becoming self-sufficient are major tasks which should be jointly worked on and carried out in a similar way by the mother and the caretaker. This point cannot be overemphasized, as inconsistency in caretaking patterns is likely to confuse the child and produce anxious behavior. Even a strict disciplinarian should give warmth and affection to all children, and discipline should be worked out jointly by parent and caretaker. For the school-age child, a "homework helpers" program is useful. Of course, if a child-care service purports to offer any kind of education program, parents should check to see if the appropriate materials—such as ability-graded books, puzzles, and toys—are at the center. When a mother wants her child to receive developmental care, she should also consider her personal feelings about what is important educationally (self-concept, racial pride, cooperative behavior, and preacademics, for example). Developmental curricula are different from each other—and all are equally valid approaches. The important thing is what the parents feel the child needs.

Staff

The third area a working mother should be concerned about is staff. Here the parent would want to know about how many staff members serve the children and what their qualifications are. In the case of nonprofessional personnel, a mother should seek firm but compassionate persons who enjoy children. According to the Federal Interagency Requirements, certain ratios of children to adults should be adhered to:

For children of two years and younger: No more than ten children with a professional and sufficient adult assistants for a 2:1 ratio.

Three- and four-year olds: No more than fifteen with a professional and sufficient adult assistants for a 5:1 ratio.

Four- to six-year-olds: No more than twenty with a professional and sufficient adult assistants for a 7:1 ratio.

Since the staff impart the program to the children, a parent should not be afraid to ask questions about the training and previous work experience of the staff.

Auxiliary Services

Auxiliary services include all health, social, and transportation services provided by a center. Nutritional services are usually considered a mandatory part of the regular program and should include at least one hot meal and two snacks a day.

Participation by Parents

Child care is not child rearing. Therefore, parents must be involved to some extent with the practices of the child-care service. Perhaps the closest involvement should come with the care of infants, as their very survival depends upon the caretaking program. Even the parent who wants her responsibility clearly separated from that of the caretaker should be involved enough to know what is happening to the child each day. Higher-quality services are obtained when there is a partnership between the parent and the caretaker. In fact, a good child-care center welcomes the involvement of parents.

Cost

Finally, there is the subject of costs. Because very few people can afford the developmental care all children need, the cost of a child-care service must be weighed against the benefits a parent and child receive from it. I estimate that good custodial care under any arrangement now costs about $25 to $30 per child per week (at the time of this writing). Since these fees are high for most working parents, a mother should find out if she is eligible for subsidized child care or if she can deduct the costs of child care for income-tax purposes. A working mother should also examine several child-care services at about the same price to see what they offer in comparison to each other. The goal is to get the best care relative to the price, not just to find cheap child care.

Rating Sheet

This assessment tool was developed to help parents select a child-care arrangement. It consists of a representative group of items for each area of concern. Some other questions or items could be added to make the checklist exhaustive. The rating sheet uses forced-choice categories: each aspect of child care is rated "acceptable" or "unacceptable." This approach is offered because individual choices concerning day care are usually based on acceptability rather than on a complex system of scoring. The checklist should be used in the following way:

1   Either ask questions or take notes for each item on the checklist.
2   Mark your findings "acceptable" or "unacceptable" or "not applicable (NA)."

3 Each "acceptable" gets 1 point.

4 A category labeled "intangible" gives the parent the opportunity to record an intuitive feeling about a child-care setting.

5 You may give a child-care service up to 5 points for a really good intuitive feeling, and you may subtract as many as 5 points for a poor feeling.

6 A child-care service must have at least 35 points total across all categories to be acceptable in terms of the criteria discussed earlier in this chapter. A service whose total is 35 points, or not much more, is minimally acceptable.

Acceptable   Unacceptable   NA

Basics
Is this program licensed?
How many children are served?
How long are the hours?
Is there a waiting list?

**Physical facilities, space, and
    equipment**[27]
Space
Toilets
Safety (no exposed nails, broken
    windows, etc.)
Clean kitchen
Ventilation and heat
Child-sized furniture
Safe outdoor equipment
    Bars
    Slide
    Swing
    Jungle gym
    Tires
    Tricycles
    Wagons
    Large blocks

Indoor equipment
    Books
    Working toys
    Dress-up clothes
    Play kitchen
    Record player and records
    Musical instruments
    Blackboard
    Puzzles
    Dolls

[27] Although one's own judgment can be used, requirements of each state and the Federal Interagency requirements specify "minimum square feet per child."

Other supplies
  Colored paper
  Children's scissors
  Glue
  Nontoxic paints and crayons
  Clay or play-dough
  Educational materials (such as
    large numerals and letters)
  Maps
  Pictures and posters
Floor plan (easy flow of traffic)
Storage
Child's own space
Interior decor (carpet and
  child-sized furniture)

Program organization
Is there a schedule of activities?
Is anything of value to you (as a
  parent) taught to your child?
    Name and address or telephone
      numbers
    Parts of the body
    Counting
    Alphabet
    Writing
    Phonetics
    Other academics (science)
    Values and social skills
Are there any field trips?
Do the children have special projects?
Is there a garden?
Are there pets?
How are the children taught?
  Planned lessons
  General exposure
For infants only:
  How do you toilet-train?
  Will you follow my feeding
    schedule?
  Will you keep me informed of all
    developments and problems?
Discipline:
Not harsh
Compatible with, though not
  necessarily the same as, parents'

Staff
How many staff members to how
  many children?

Training of staff members (number
  at each level of training)
  High school diploma and
    experience
  Some college and experience
  B.A. degree
  Advanced degree

Auxiliary services
Nutrition
  Breakfast
  Lunch
  Snacks
  Supper
Health service
Transportation
Social services
Family counseling
Sick care

Participation by parents
How much involvement of parents is
  there?
What kind of involvement do
  parents have?

Costs
What is the fee?
Is there a reduction for more than
  one child?
Is the fee set by the week?
Is a portion refundable if the child is
  sick?

Intangibles

Total points

COPING TOGETHER AS A FAMILY

When there is no full-time person available to be totally responsible for the home, every family must make organizational and emotional adjustments. Although many families experience unique difficulties, there are some similar problems faced by all families when the mother works.

Redistribution of Responsibility

In order to understand how adjustments can best be made and how families can cope with their situation together, it might be useful to identify the responsibilities that are usually involved in home management. There are child rearing; household management, including paying for and buying groceries, planning meals, etc.; home maintenance, which includes the care and cleaning of the interior and exterior of the home; actual financial support of the family; family entertainment; and family education. If the family can be viewed as an organization or small system, which consists of parents and children, one can see that the responsibilities can be distributed throughout the organization in a variety of ways. When a change occurs in the system—when one person does not carry out the expected role, for example—responsibilities in that system must be redistributed. Gradual changes, such as children getting old enough to dress themselves, are absorbed in the system rather easily. More abrupt or emotionally charged changes, such as a mother going to work outside the home, are often more difficult to accommodate. Thus, when mothers do work outside the home, this change in the normative (not necessarily "normal") role can present problems for the entire family unit. Ideally, the responsibilities once held by the mother should be redistributed to members of the family unit who are physically and mentally capable of handling them. Perhaps two examples will illustrate what is meant.

1. A single parent with a very young child would have no choice but to assume all of the responsibility for child rearing, household management, etc. This would be the most difficult situation, and the parent in this case must get some outside help for one of the functions in the system. Extrafamily child care is a necessity which, when found, will make a small redistribution of responsibility.

2. A married woman who works may be able to offer a portion of her previous responsibilities to her husband and to her children. Or, one of the responsibilities of the home, such as child care, may be given entirely to a new person or resource. This has the effect of enlarging the family system.

If we take this organizational view of the family, we can see that various types of adjustments are often made not deliberately but by default or by accident. We can also see that many working mothers are actually carrying twice the responsibilities of nonworking mothers. Rosalind Loring points out that this double duty has negative effects on the entire family, not just the mother. Of particular importance, she feels, is the denial of an opportunity for the father to enjoy and actively share the responsibility of child rearing.[28]

Even when family responsibilities are redistributed in the organization once the mother takes a job outside the home, working mothers still carry a greater psychological responsibility for the family welfare. These feelings are reflected in a mother's guilt about leaving her children, about not being physically available; in her feeling that the children will be less stable emotionally because of her absence from home. These feelings are real but are based on popular misconceptions about the emotional consequences of working and using extrafamily care.

Mother-Child Relationship

One problem of a working mother is that she thinks she does not have enough time with her child to create an effective relationship. However, research over the

[28] Personal communication.

last five years has shown that the quality of a parent-child relationship is far more important than the quantity of time spent with the child.[29] Research has also shown that the relationship between working mothers and their children is as good as, and sometimes better than, the typical relationship between nonworking mothers and their children.[30] Thus, it is important to distinguish between caretaking and child rearing. The parent-child attachment is made when a relationship is intense and loving and is not merely a matter of routine maintenance of the child.

Another important aspect of the parent-child relationship is consistency and continuity. It is therefore important that the child perceive some general similarity in caretaking styles between the home and the child-care service. One danger that is thought to exist with day-care arrangements, and with extended-family relationships, is that the child will perceive several mothers: no firm attachment can be established to any one of the mother figures. This, however, is very unlikely to occur in children in day-care centers; research by Ainsworth and others indicates that the children of working mothers are no different in measures of attachment and emotional warmth than children of nonworking mothers.[31]

Meeting Internal Standards of Motherhood

Some of the difficulties in coping with day-care arrangements are really problems within the mother herself. Often women, because of cultural socialization, find it very difficult to work outside the home without feeling that they have denied their children something valuable. Some of the internal conflicts that might occur to women include feeling social pressure to be at home, particularly when there are young children; experiencing contradictions between internal standards or beliefs about motherhood and one's own actions; being unable to deal effectively with a husband's uncooperative attitude; trying to explain to the children why their mother may not be around as much as other children's mothers; in the case of a woman who has been at home for a long time, explaining why she has suddenly left the home to work; and coping with nonworking mothers who deride either the working mother or her job.

The solution to each of these problems must fit the individual needs of the mother. However, there are two important general responses that can be made. First, there is nothing in the research to indicate that working mothers are inadequate mothers. What is inadequate is the support systems—such as child care—which enable people, in general, to work outside a home. Second, whether a woman works from choice or necessity, the decision to work has been made. The family adjustments which follow will *have to be made.* If the mother and her family can work together, these changes can flow smoothly, and emotional struggles or guilt about working outside the home can be discussed. In fact, these struggles should be irrelevant once the internal conflict about deciding to work can be resolved.

[29] Greta G. Fein and Alison Clarke-Stewart, *Day Care in Context,* Wiley-Interscience, New York, 1973, pp. 143–190.

[30] Lois Hoffman, *Working Mothers: An Evaluation of the Consequences of Work on Husbands and Children,* Jossey-Bass, San Francisco, Calif., 1974, p. 29.

[31] Fein and Clarke-Stewart, op. cit., pp. 62–64.

Establishing Trust

Perhaps the most difficult problem encountered by the working mother is finding a caretaker she can trust with her child. As a parent, the mother feels ultimately responsible for anything that happens to her children. She must feel confident that the caretaker will not abuse her children, will supervise them closely, and will contact the mother immediately if there is an emergency. When the caretaker is untrained and is not a relative, the incidence of problems in all these areas increases. The horror stories about many day-care homes reported in the NCJW survey reflect both the gravity of the problem and the need for standardization and regulatory procedures for child care.

It is no wonder that mothers indicate the highest degree of satisfaction with day-care centers, half of which must meet either the Federal Interagency Requirements or a similar state guideline.[32] It is also highly unlikely that child abuse would go unnoticed in a federally subsidized center for fifty children with six staff members; and at least one person on the staff of such a center would know how to handle an emergency. With a day-care center, the mother is not personally burdened with hiring and firing caretakers, and she may also feel that there are formal channels of recourse if there are problems in the service. While the mother is responsible for her child, the center is directly responsible to the parent for providing adequate care. Perhaps satisfaction with day-care homes would increase if similar federal regulations were established for them.

Increasing numbers of women are working mothers. Their need for quality child care has become great enough to warrant national attention. Without public interest in a national day-care program, only the wealthy will be able to afford developmental care; and the working poor and middle-class mothers will continue to pay the highest price, proportionate to income, for average to poor child-care services. As a consequence, children will continue to lose the opportunity for a stimulating start in life.

A call is being made for a national mechanism to meet the need for extrafamily care. Admittedly, nationalizing day care will entail a complex legislative process and bureaucratic reorganization. But without it, a gross lack of standardization in service, costs, and policy will continue to plague us. Again, it is the children who suffer—some of them are cared for in potentially dangerous circumstances, or are not cared for at all.

Finally, there is the issue of setting some priority on providing all human beings a basic quality of life. In theory, this is our highest priority—but in reality, it is one of our lowest priorities. There are those who fear that by looking outside the family for the protection and development of children we will seriously threaten the future of American society and family life. However, in coordinating child care we may be better able to ensure a diversity of high-quality child-care arrangements with family involvement. Certainly, this path will help produce effective citizens. We know that the existing approach to child care, particularly for the low-income, high-need family, has produced the opposite result.

[32] Westinghouse-Westat, op. cit., p. vii.

BIBLIOGRAPHY

Day Care and Child Development Council of America, Inc., 1012 Fourteenth Street N.W., Washington, D.C. 20005. This organization not only serves as an advocacy office for day care and children's rights but is also a major distributor of and clearinghouse for day-care information. A list of publications is available, and monthly newsletters are sent to members.

Fein, Greta, and Alison Clarke-Stewart: *Day Care in Context,* Wiley-Interscience, New York, 1973. This book is probably the most detailed and comprehensive review of child-development literature as it relates to emerging day-care programs. Very scholarly in tone, it is aimed at the professional in child care.

Keyserling, Mary D.: *Windows on Day Care: A Report Based on Findings of the National Council of Jewish Women,* National Council of Jewish Women, New York, 1972. A descriptive survey of the national day-care situation. Offers facts, figures, and anecdotal material on four types of day-care arrangements. It is particularly useful as a reference (though dated), as it condenses voluminous records down to a manageable and readable report.

Roby, Pamela (ed.): *Child Care—Who Cares,* rev. ed., Basic Books, New York, 1976. This book is an indispensable reference. It covers every topic pertinent to day care in a direct and thorough manner, is well documented, and aptly summarizes major surveys of national day care. In addition to a thorough look at day care in America, one section of this book reports on day care abroad. Paperback.

Young, Dennis R., and Richard R. Nelson (eds.): *Public Policy for Day Care of Young Children,* Heath (Lexington Books), Boston, 1973. This book takes the emotion out of day care and addresses serious questions of financing, planning, and organizing a national system. It offers an excellent analysis of legislative trends (up to 1973) and makes policy recommendations within a brief 119 pages. Excellent.

Chapter 19

The Single Parent—
Challenges and Opportunities

Elizabeth Douvan

For a short biography of Elizabeth Douvan, see Chapter 2.

Single-parent families occur for three reasons: death, divorce, and childbirth among unmarried women. Divorce is by far the most common cause, and apparently we can expect both divorce and single-parent households to be even more common in the future.

A characteristic which almost all single-parent families share is lower-than-average income; indeed, many of these families are at the poverty level. Households headed by women are overrepresented in the lowest income categories. And in Morgan's study of poverty, it is clear that the single most important force in determining movement into and out of the poverty category is family composition. Divorce pushes many people below the poverty line, but the recomposition of families or the formation of new households by grown children tends to lift them over the poverty line.

We can expect, then, that single-parent households will tend to bear more than ordinary burdens—economic, social, educational, or psychological. One lawyer I know advises any couple who come to him for a divorce to consider first the financial implications of divorce. His general initial warning is that "only Rockefellers can afford divorce." And he outlines for his clients the reduction in living style which will inevitably follow after they split their resources to take care of two households.

But despite all the practical reasons for maintaining a particular marriage, human affairs are not conducted altogether rationally, and marriages do end. Divorce has increased to the point where many social theorists are predicting the end of the family as we have traditionally conceived it. They envision various alternatives: serial monogamy; two-stage marriages, in which the partners agree to a more permanent arrangement and children only after having lived together long enough to test their compatibility and desire to make the larger commitment; and communal arrangements in which children become the concern and responsibility of some social group larger than a couple, and the adults conduct their personal and sexual relationships separately from child raising.

We may indeed witness new and experimental arrangements within the next few decades. In the meantime, however, women raising children alone are a major area of social concern and a situation occurring with increasing frequency. In this chapter we will look at some of the problems women confront under these conditions and offer some suggestions for handling them. Since single parenthood occurs most often through divorce, and since divorce creates a more complex set of problems in some areas, the central thrust of this article is on the problems confronted by the divorced woman with children. Special problems of the widowed mother and the unmarried mother will be mentioned briefly only where they are different from those faced by the divorcee.

FINANCES

For both the divorced woman and the widow, the ruptured family situation is likely to highlight the nature of her previous role in the family and to make shockingly clear either her competence in dealing with finances or the degree to which she depended on her husband in this area. The woman who has not had a clear understanding of family resources—who has left support and finances entirely in the hands of her husband—will be at a disadvantage when she is faced with financial responsibility for herself and her children. Her incapacity can be a great handicap, as she is likely to discover quickly. Widows bilked by unethical advisers or lawyers, and divorced wives who settle for an insufficient financial arrangement because they have no clear knowledge of the family financial resources, are too common to be ignored. Such cases should remind all wives that they have an obligation to themselves and their children; as competent adults, they must have a clear and exact understanding of family finances, so that they can participate equally with their husbands in financial planning and decision making. Few human beings are exempt from the possibility of family disruption, and while financial survival may not be the only, or even the most important, challenge implied by such a disruption, it is one aspect of the situation for which preparation is both possible and sensible.

In very rich families women usually have sufficient motivation to maintain access to financial knowledge. Centuries ago, under feudalism, no lady could escape detailed training and understanding of her husband's holdings, since she might be called on to manage them whenever he was off to war or crusade. But today thousands of middle-class wives accept without question a position of dependency and ignorance regarding family finances which—when disruption comes—leaves them bewildered, vulnerable, and usually in financial straits. Along with training in assertiveness (which I will discuss later), women's need for financial skills is probably the most important general issue the feminist movement has raised and clarified for the large majority of middle-class women. The educational efforts of the movement in these two areas have enormous potential for increasing the welfare of women.

With knowledge of family resources, the woman enters divorce negotiations with some trump cards to play. She will also do well to retain the services of an excellent and honest lawyer. There is a movement for "self-help" divorce—that is, divorce without the services of a lawyer, a response to the unconscionable fees of some divorce lawyers—but in most communities a woman can find an ethical lawyer whose fee is not exorbitant. Low-cost and public-service lawyers are increasingly available in urban areas. The self-help movement has also gained support from women who have had particularly unpleasant experiences with sexist lawyers. Fortunately, feminist lawyers are also increasingly available.

The self-help divorce cannot serve one of the critical functions of a lawyer: the reduction of raw power, hostility, and vengeance as guiding forces in the divorce and financial settlement. In most divorces, the partners are going through the last stages of a failing relationship. They are bruised and angry, and are not in a position to deal well with the real issues at stake. A sensitive lawyer may be both compassionate and strongly identified with a client's position, and yet be objective enough to negotiate effectively for the long-term welfare of the client— more effectively than the client could, since the client is likely to be experiencing depression, anger, or guilt. Women are often so eager to get out of a marriage, because of fear or hurt or anger, that they settle for considerably less than they should or could have. A good lawyer can take some of the pressure of negotiating off a woman's shoulders, and reduce her involvement with her husband during the negotiations which may be necessary to win a decent and just settlement.

The woman with dependent children will have two areas to negotiate: child support and support or a settlement for herself representing her share of the family's assets. For most couples in our society the husband's earning capacity is significantly greater than the wife's, and would not have been so great without the supportive services of the wife; therefore, courts have often awarded some alimony or support for the wife above and beyond a sharing of accumulated holdings at the time of the divorce. In some states it is still common for alimony to continue until the woman remarries. But this practice has come under more critical analysis in the light of the feminist movement. In a society which systematically excluded women from access to good jobs and the training required for these jobs, and in which sex discrimination in pay was commonplace, some contribution from the former husband which allowed the woman to maintain a standard of living not greatly lower than she had had in the marriage may have been justified. But with changes in legislation and increasing opportunities for women, arrangements other than alimony are developing to supply the same needs without some of the degrading aspects of the alimony arrangement.

Ideologically advanced divorce lawyers urge their women clients to think through certain plans for their future lives before settlement negotiations are opened. The woman is asked to think through the following questions for herself: *"What work would I eventually like to do—work which would hold intrinsic interest and gratification for me and would provide me with an earning capacity adequate for the life-style I want? What training do I need to prepare for such work?"* Once the woman has settled on a career and knows the training she will need, her lawyer has a basis from which to negotiate realistically with the husband for support payments, over a limited period, which will effectively equip the woman to be self-supporting. This system seems more humane than unlimited alimony and also has the advantage of building and reinforcing the woman's independence and self-esteem. It is no favor to any person to imply that she is incapable or that she deserves limitless support simply for having married at some time in her life.

Whether she decides that she needs a doctorate or an apprenticeship, a two-year course to become a court reporter or an EEG technician, psychotherapy or driver training or capital to open a business, the woman's clarification of her future life before she enters divorce proceedings will help her attorney by providing him with a realistic perspective from which to begin settlement negotiations. It will also obviously have great potential benefits for the woman herself in helping her to clarify the options she has and to plan a future life that holds both hope and independence.

Women faced with divorce often find the need to make choices on their own a new experience, and a difficult one at first. A woman's lawyer—by encouraging and supporting her efforts to clarify each step—can be of great assistance to her psychologically as well as practically. If the choices are still too overwhelming, some professional counseling may be necessary to help outline and clarify the problem and support the woman in her efforts to come to terms with the decisions facing her.

Aside from this support for herself and provision for training—which obviously will include baby-sitting and other services that will allow her to become independent—the woman who has dependent children will need to negotiate the issue of child support. In many states this aspect of the settlement will bring into the negotiations the Friend of the Court, a lawyer or social worker attached to the court who counsels and negotiates with parents in divorce cases to guarantee the children's welfare. Depending on the specific economic situation of the couple and the attitude of the court worker, this involvement can be a help or a liability. Knowledge of options (that is, of when the court must be included and when the support payments can be handled without involving the court) is crucial for the woman. At least in some areas, organized social pressure to effect changes in sexist practices of the Friend of the Court offices may be called for.

When there is doubt about the father's good will and intention to meet his child-support obligations, requiring payment through the Friend of the Court may add some authority and power to collection. Unfortunately, where income is low (the very cases where default is most likely) the fee for collection is a significant part of the payment and may seriously undercut the support.

The amount of support necessary to maintain a child will, of course, vary with the age of the child. In initial agreements it is crucial to state specific stages in the child's development when the amount of support will be renegotiated. *Aside from normal expenses, the support statement should cover special expenses for emergencies, health insurance, uninsured medical and dental bills, special or private schooling, and some commitments concerning postsecondary education.* Clearly the beginning of college is a stage at which support arrangements must be renegotiated, since the cost of particular schools and the relative ability of the two parents and the child to contribute to the cost will not be known before the time of college entrance approaches.

PRACTICAL PROBLEMS

The practical problems of the single parent do not end with finances. Even when the financial arrangements are adequate, the mother raising children alone and trying to work or train herself for eventual work faces the possibility of overload. Time and energy are limited, and the demands of a work life combined with total responsibility for home and family maintenance add up to a task load that will test the most organized and energetic person. Two general admonitions seem obvious: (1) You must ask for help and use help whenever and wherever it is available. (2) You must reserve some time—however limited—for yourself, to allow you a moment of quiet or an evening out or some other activity that will refresh your spirit and allow you to regain a sense of control over the complications of your daily life.

The mother alone will face varying practical problems depending on the age of her children. Although the mother of older children will face financial problems and the special psychological strains of adolescents, practical problems usually are most serious when the children are of preschool and elementary school age. If the mother has the resources to allow it, this period will obviously be more manageable if she can limit her involvements outside the home. Part-time work or school, or any commitment that is relatively flexible in the face of emergencies, is preferable to a full-time, inflexible job. The period in a child's life when full-time care and supervision are required is brief and early. Through the first years of elementary school, the problems of after-school supervision and care during childhood illnesses and school holidays continue. Beyond the fourth or fifth grade, the child is less vulnerable, more mobile, and more capable of independence. Day care for little children is the major practical problem reported by single parents.

Child care and home maintenance are problems for all working mothers, and they have been dealt with in some detail in Chapter 2, along with various suggestions for handling them. But the single parent who works has fewer options than the woman who shares responsibility with a spouse. Though it may be difficult for the working wife to break established patterns and introduce greater sharing of responsibilities with her husband, the woman alone cannot improve her situation at all in this way. There is no spouse to share with.

For a single parent, more radical and innovative solutions which depend on cooperative arrangements with people other than family members are much more to the point. One possibility is actually combining households with one or more other women in the same situation, so that child care and finances are handled by pooling the resources of several adults. Another possibility involves living in the same neighborhood or apartment building with several other single-parent families and managing some of the major tasks cooperatively. These seem the most promising arrangements for parents alone with dependent children. Meal cooperatives, in which a number of families plan, shop for, and cook their major meal cooperatively and with rotating responsibility, offer real help to single working parents. These have become popular in student housing developments, particularly among single-parent families. In this plan, any one parent has responsibility for meal preparation only one night during the week (other nights, she simply arrives at one of the other houses at mealtime and carries home her family's share of the community meal). Thus she has extra time on off nights to take care of errands, enjoy some family activities, or put in an extra hour on work or studies. Children's play groups, nursery cooperatives, and baby-sitting cooperatives often have much the same organization and are especially important for the single parent. Clothing and furniture exchanges are other innovations which ease the financial pressure on the single-parent household.

Assuming that the woman and her former husband maintain a relationship having to do with their children and that the father has some share in their custody, he will have the children with him during some period during the year. Depending on the distance between households, this can vary from one relatively long visit during the school holiday each summer to casual visits back and forth each week. The mother whose children spend every weekend or every other weekend with their father has an experience which married mothers rarely have—that is, a certain amount of time when she is absolutely alone, without responsibility for the children.

At least at first, such time is likely to be a mixed blessing, since it leaves the woman both free and lonely. With a little familiarity and practice, however, she can probably make especially good use of this time for work or for her own relaxation and refreshment. The children's father or other members of his family may also be willing to help with child care in emergencies—when the child is sick or during school holidays which do not correspond with the mother's work holidays. To the extent that she can accept such offers of help, the woman increases her own options and reinforces family ties for her children. Especially where the nuclear family has been disrupted, children probably benefit from clear, stable, and strong relationships with members of their extended families.

Because of the long history of sex discrimination in certain classes of jobs, it is men who may at times hold jobs which create especially serious difficulties for parenthood. For a man raising children alone, work on the assembly line or a foreman's job—jobs which have traditionally excluded women—often make it impossible for the parent to be available even by telephone during work hours, and thus cut him off from the kind of access necessary when older elementary school children are alone at home. Any parent whose work is inflexible in this respect, making contact in minor emergencies impossible, faces a need for some adult neighbor or friend to supply this kind of minimal care even when children are normally able to care for themselves.

One last point about the practical situation of the single mother. The jobs of maintaining a home and an automobile—the heavy mechanical and repair jobs which men traditionally handle—are very expensive when hired out to professionals. Partly because they are male skills, they command a higher fee than the cooking and laundering which a man alone may have to pay for. The woman may know someone in a communal neighborhood, in her extended family, or among her friends who can help her with these jobs. And the feminist emphasis on improving the skills of women in home and automobile maintenance has led to the establishment of many short courses and self-help clinics. While a mother raising children alone can probably not imagine having the time to do her own automobile repairs, knowing enough at least to diagnose a problem and check on the work of someone she hires is a great advantage to any woman.

Underlying all the suggestions for handling the practical complications of single parenthood—for managing the heavy workload of a double commitment— is the assumption that *the woman has a support network*—family or friends who will lend a hand or will enter into cooperative arrangements. But how does the woman who has no established support system find other women with whom to form housing, cooking, or child-care cooperatives—women who share her situation and problems?

Over and over again, in discussing this problem with women in a middle-sized university community, I have been struck by an experience which many of them have had. New to a neighborhood or housing development, the woman alone initially has the feeling that she is probably unique and deviant. Whether she lives in graduate-student housing or in the community, her sense is that the world is made for traditional families (by and large a realistic assumption) and that she is deviant. After a period of time, she may meet one other single parent who introduces her to others in the neighborhood who are in a similar situation. Or at a community event she discovers a number of people who share her life situation. The point is this: when you are isolated, it is easy to begin to think of your situation—whether you are a single parent or a bachelor or a married professional woman—as more deviant than it in fact is. Though the statistics may indicate your pattern to be rare, it is not unique. The chances of finding one or more other people who share it—and even one other person can help enormously in reducing feelings of isolation and deviance—are reasonably good.

Nonetheless, in urban settings, community events and communication among neighbors may simply not occur. In that case, the individual woman will need to find friends and collaborators through more formal organizations. Fortunately in the last decade a number of formal organizations have been created specifically out of the felt needs of single-parent families. Parents Without Partners and MOMMAS are organizations which offer practical and social help to parents alone and provide a setting for meeting potential friends and allies. Churches often have special groups for single parents. And social agencies in the community can often put a woman in touch with these groups as well as other resources. The Friend of the Court office should be able to supply a list of family agencies.

PSYCHOLOGICAL PROBLEMS

Psychological problems—like practical problems— will vary with the age of the children and the particular circumstances surrounding the family disruption. If the divorce has followed a stormy relationship and has created anger and bitterness, children, particularly small children, will in all likelihood show the effects of the conflict in minor or more serious problems. If they have lost a parent through death, children will experience mourning and must be helped through their grieving at a time when you as the remaining parent have your hands full managing your own grief. The situation of a child born to an unmarried woman has problems of its own—which will come when the child begins to grasp the fact that his or her family is different and to ask questions and answer questions raised by other children. There is no shortage of problems; there are plenty to go around. In this section I will emphasize some of the psychological challenges faced by all single parents, and some that arise particularly where parents have been divorced.

While divorce does not always occur in conditions of intense anger, bitterness, and recrimination, it often does; and at best it is likely to cause some damage to one or both of the spouses. Our society perceives almost all areas of human existence as systems of achievement, and marriage is no exception. Involvement in divorce is likely to be experienced as a personal failure, reflecting on one's value as a person. In many cases one member of the pair—traditionally, more so than now, the woman—feels rejected and damaged. Divorce is rarely without serious costs in lowered self-esteem, depression, and guilt.

What to do about these costs? Obviously the first thing a woman needs in such circumstances is support and sympathy from friends. Even one friend who will listen sympathetically and act as confidante will help with the initial problems of objectifying the situation and ventilating some of the hurt and confused emotions.

In addition to sympathetic friends, one needs to engage in activities and relationships that affirm one's identity and self-esteem. In the most simplified terms, *nothing helps an individual to forget the hurt of a bad relationship as much as the discovery of a new and better one.*

I am *not* recommending rushing headlong into a new marriage to soothe the hurt of a bad one. The new relationship can be with anyone—friend, colleague, relative—of either sex. What I am suggesting is that the experience of being responded to as a good, valuable, and attractive human being will help restore self-esteem damaged by a divorce.

Responding to yourself in this same way—as a good, attractive, and valuable person—is what we mean by self-esteem. Any experience—friendship, achievement at work or school, involvement in art or music, athletics or other physical activities—*which affirms one's pleasure in life and oneself* is the salve that is needed when events have threatened one's sense of self.

The most serious damage occurs when the divorce has been a unilateral choice and when the rejected partner's self-concept was too exclusively defined by the traditional family roles. If all you are and all you enjoy is captured in the role of wife and mother, then loss of the role threatens loss of self. If you have established a self based on many roles—friend, sister, worker, citizen, and believer, as well as wife and mother—clearly the loss of one role will not as radically disrupt your sense of self. Phyllis Chesler has described the fate of older women who have overinvested in motherhood when their function diminishes: they too often succumb to depression.[1]

If a woman is to weather a divorce with relatively little self-damage, then, the bases of her self-concept and self-esteem must be varied and stable. The woman who has a strong and complex self-concept will manage the blow of divorce with normal self-help and the support of her network. The woman who is devastated by divorce may need professional help. But in all likelihood she could have used such help during the marriage as well—to enlarge her self-concept and capacity for a full experience of life, and to secure her self-esteem through self-exploration and development.

What must the woman alone give her children during and after family disruption? She must, first of all, give them some basis for understanding *that they are not to blame for what has happened; that their father did not leave because they were bad or because he did not love them.* Too often children—and particularly young children—take on responsibility and guilt for events which they did not cause and over which they have no control. Even when a parent dies, young children sometimes feel that they are responsible.

How you explain the family breakup to a child will depend on the nature of the situation and the child's age and capacity to understand. The goal should be to communicate to the child the fact that the problem exists between the parents and that the child is not responsible for it, that the parents still love the child and will continue to be her or his mother and father.

In some divorces, a parent may actually feel that an adolescent child has caused the problems leading to the breakdown in the marriage. Events as critical as divorce rarely stem from one cause, however, and hundreds of thousands of marriages have survived the raising of difficult adolescents. Consequently, the breakdown of a marriage cannot be attributed to one problem or person. If a parent actually accuses a child of causing the problem, the child may require more than ordinary reassurance, perhaps professional counseling. Surely such a parent needs some help, but the chances of his or her actually seeking it are slight since the very fact of blaming the child indicates the use of psychological defen-

---

[1] Phyllis Chesler, *Women and Madness,* Doubleday, Garden City, N.Y., 1972.

ses. People who externalize responsibility for their problems in this way are not likely to recognize their own limitations or need for help.

Some of the difficulty which many single parents report in relation to their children stems from the parent's own guilt about the divorce and its effects on the child's life. Mothers particularly often try—at least in the early stages—to be superparents, feeling that they must be both mother and father, taking on more obligations than they can realistically manage. Here again the help of a friend— sharing the problem with someone else who has faced it—can be useful in developing realistic expectations and overcoming feelings of inadequacy and frustration. In this and other ways, the parent alone must clarify her own self-knowledge, her understanding of her needs and capacities. This self-knowledge plus the ability to ask for help from others—to assert one's own needs and goals—can be forces for growth for the woman raising children alone.

Many women see, in retrospect, that divorce led to individual growth and family growth. Women who had highly traditional marriages often feel that divorce represented the first time in their lives that they had both control over, and full responsibility for, their own choices and actions.

Children can also benefit from the mother's recognizing that she cannot do everything, that she has limits and needs like everyone else. Children benefit from a relationship with a human being rather than a saint or perfectionist. And children benefit from being asked to help—to share the work and responsibility of family life. They develop a sense of competence and individuality from participating in real work and knowing that their help is valued. Even very young children can help with cleaning, laundry, and cooking. When children know the reasons for demands made on them, they respond with more spirit, work more effectively, and develop more independence than we sometimes think possible. Children who are really needed in a family organization often have a greater chance to learn independence and competence than children who live in families where the adults can manage all the responsibility and give children busywork that is not really crucial to the life of the family.

The mother's responsibility, again, is to recognize what needs to be done, to organize tasks, and to state her expectation—the work obligations of each child— clearly. This requires clarification of her own goals and standards and a certain degree of assertiveness. Clarifying for the children what expectations they must meet—and checking that they have done so—organizes their world in ways they can understand and cope with. Too often we hold unformulated, vague expectations, communicate them ambiguously or not at all, and then react with anger or passive aggression or guilt when children do not meet them. Clarity and openness reduce confusion and facilitate family interaction.

CHILDREN'S RELATIONSHIP WITH THE OTHER PARENT

Assuming that custody and visitation arrangements have been worked out satisfactorily, you will now face the necessity of working out a new relationship with your former spouse—a relationship which will make it possible for you to meet occasionally (as when one of you picks up the children) to develop some consistency in child-raising goals and practices, to discuss problems which arise in the children's lives. You continue to share a central area of your lives although you no longer share a marriage.

At the outset it must be said that in many cases the presence of children helps people to behave more decently than they would if they had no children. Even when a divorced couple feel bitter toward each other, they often avoid acting out their anger and resentment because they are sensitive to the welfare and well-being of their children. Over the years, many divorcees who thus constrain their behavior discover that the former spouse is quite an acceptable person with whom to share friendship if not marriage. Behaving civilly for the sake of the children has opened these people to more objective exchanges and so often allows the growth of good will where only anger and hatred had existed.

Nonetheless, a number of problems can arise for the couple and for their children from the fact that the children are now part of two distinct families. Two of the most important kinds of problems can be classified as those in which the parents use the child as a pawn in their relationship, and those in which a child uses the parents in a game of manipulation and power.

Parents Using the Child

When the divorced partners feel a residue of hurt and anger toward each other, they may compete with each other for the child's affection, or each may try to alienate the child from the other. In either case, the child is being treated not as a person but as a pawn to be manipulated in a battle with the former spouse. The outcome of such treatment is almost certain to be bad, and the parent who recognizes such tendencies in himself or herself should use the help of a friend or counselor to try to eliminate them. If your own life is satisfying, taking revenge on your former spouse should become unnecessary. If you continue to need revenge, the most constructive response is to ask what is wrong in your own life that makes you persist in such strong feelings about a person who should no longer be central to your life. It is your life—and your children's life—which should be important; and making it as satisfactory as possible should be your goal. *To damage or misuse your children in order to hurt your former partner is both inhumane and self-destructive.*

Growing up in the complicated modern world is hard enough even when two adults love you and give you that special central attention that defines nurturing, responsible parenthood. It is also good for a child to have at least two adults to emulate and admire. Irrespective of the two parents' feelings toward each other, it seems crucial not to interfere with the child's chances for a loving relationship with both. *To damage the child's image of or relationship with the absent parent is to reduce the child's resources for developing normally and happily.* So long as the other parent wants the relationship and is good to the child, one's own feelings about the divorced partner must be secondary to the interests of the child.

Children Manipulating the Parents

If the relationship between the divorced parents is bad or cool, children will sometimes use the distance between them to promote interests of their own. Even in intact families, of course, children are quick to observe differences between their parents and to play on them skillfully. We are all likely to be familiar with a situation like this: The child asks one parent, "May I go to Billy's to play?" The parent says, "Ask your mother." The child then says to the mother, "Can I go to Billy's house? It's all right with Dad."

Actually, some of this sort of thing supports growth. Children note differences in parents' attitudes and styles, in what works with them. But they also discover areas in which there is complete unanimity—between mother and father, Grandma, Aunt Lil, and even Mrs. Quimby next door. In this way children apprehend that some things are matters of taste and style while others involve norms that are shared by people of widely different tastes.

But too much of this manipulation can lead to habitual misuse of people. When children know that their two parents dislike each other and communicate poorly if at all, they may play the parents against each other in a competitive game to win privileges which should not be granted and would not be granted under other circumstances. "Mother lets me stay out till eleven" may be only a moderate elaboration on the truth (the truth being that mother once let me stay out until eleven the night my school class and teacher were returning from a visit to a city 80 miles away). But if it becomes a signal for a competitive bid for the child's affection, or if the responsibility for setting effective limits gets lost somewhere in the communication gap between the parents, then a serious problem is created. Clearly the solution is the maintenance of open communication and solidarity between the divorced parents on issues involving their parental responsibility.

Other Problems of Children

Other problems which arise have no obvious solutions. Here is an example: A divorced woman with an eight-year-old daughter and a seven-year-old son has begun to face a reluctant son each Saturday when the children are to leave for their father's home in a city some 35 miles away. Her former husband, with whom she has maintained a friendly and thoughtful relationship, remarried several years ago and has a new family into which he welcomes his first two children on most weekends and some holidays. The seven-year-old's change of feeling about these visits has to do with his father's recent conversion to a fundamentalist religious sect. From the time the father joined the sect, the children began to spend a good part of each weekend at church; and while his sister doesn't mind, the little boy finds it uninteresting and alien to his experience. He has been raised by his mother, whose religious views are skeptical and liberal.

The mother now faces a dilemma. She wants her son to have a continuing relationship with his father, and she knows that her former husband both wants and enjoys his little boy; yet forcing the boy to go to his father (and the church) regularly is not consistent with her own feelings and attitudes. In addition, it does not seem to promise a continuing good relationship between the boy and his father. She has tried to discuss the issue with her former husband but finds his new religious fervor incapable of compromise. When real differences in values exist, they cannot be easily resolved—there is no formula for solutions.

The important goal in such a case must be *to allow the child some freedom of movement without creating a situation that alienates him from either parent.* Eventually the child will choose his own values and will have to work out a means of living with differences between his own values and those held by people who are important to him. But seven is too early for such critical choices. The boy is reacting to the constraints of his father's religion, not to his religious values as such. His mother has so far handled the problem with ingenuity. She has tried to arrange some visits on school holidays other than Sunday and has let her son skip some Sunday visits. She recognizes that this compromise is merely a staying action and that eventually some more stable solution will have to be found. They may need to obtain the help of a professional to work out a solution that accommodates them to each other without violating their individual belief systems.

There is also the problem—again resistant to any facile solution—of the parent who has indeed been thoroughly irresponsible, who has deserted the family, mistreated or abused the children, or in other ways failed to meet ordinary standards of loyalty and responsibility. How does the other parent help the children to come to terms with such a reality without undermining their trust or their chances of developing and living meaningful and satisfying lives?

The important thing to communicate to children in such circumstances is that such behavior is not the daily coin of human exchange. In addition it seems necessary to preserve the child's respect for the *idea* of the other parent—though not for the despicable behavior—whenever possible. An abusive or deserting parent is a sick parent; and if the child is old enough to understand that alcoholism or mental illness can make people behave in ways that they would not normally, such explanations may help the child to survive painful experiences and preserve love and respect for at least that aspect of the lost parent which lives on in the child's own memory.

MALE MODELS FOR CHILDREN

Women raising children alone—when the father is functionally no longer part of the children's lives—often worry about the lack of a male model for their sons. The fact is that men other than the father—uncles, grandfathers, a neighbor, a minister—can provide such a model; and as the boy grows, he will come into contact with admirable men at school and in the community. The crucial thing for the mother in this situation is to remember that since she is the major adult in the boy's life, her attitude toward men—and toward the boy's maleness—will also count heavily in his idea of himself and what he will grow up to be. The temptation to damage the father in the child's eyes—or simply to express one's own resentment toward an ex-husband who may indeed deserve it, will be more easily avoided if the child's welfare is always one's prime consideration and goal.

SOCIAL LIFE AND SEX

The whole area of social life and relationships with men—leading perhaps to remarriage—represents a concern for many single mothers. Concerned with their children's development, they wonder how freely they can seek social relationships, how social they can be, whether they can and should go out with men, and what effects their social and sexual lives may have on their children.

Again, there are no pat or specific answers to these questions. The answer will vary for particular women and for women whose children are in different stages of development. But certain general outlines and considerations can be made explicit which may help a woman find her own answers.

The first consideration is that being a single parent does not mean that you are selfless or a saint or that you don't have normal needs for companionship and love. If you want and enjoy friendships with men, your happiness counts. If your life is gratifying, you will also be able to make a more gratifying life for your children.

You are, however, not an adolescent, and you can't take on adolescent norms. Your object is no longer to be the most popular girl on the block or the most attractive to men. You have responsibilities which you did not have as an unattached woman. Your relationship with a male friend or male friends will serve as a model for your children—teaching them something about how to relate to other people and what relationships are about. You will, then, communicate your values about people and relationships through your own actions. If you want your children to relate to other people as whole persons; to respect other people and themselves; to regard love, intimacy, and commitment as the optimum conditions for meaningful sexual expression; to view their sexuality as a normal and good part of life but not as the whole of life—then clearly your actions must reflect these same values.

Expressing and governing your sexual needs no longer concerns only you and your own fulfillment. It also involves your children's sexual development. Obviously, then, you will want to consider your children, their developmental status, and their need to gain sexual knowledge and knowledge of your sexual nature at a pace consonant with their developmental stage, their capacity to face and understand sex without being either overstimulated or overwhelmed.

At certain points in their development, children are more vulnerable to overstimulation than at others. In the oedipal stage, around the age of four or five, and again in early adolescence, the child's own heightened sexual impulses and fantasies make any extraordinary demands (like sharing the mother with a strange man about whom she seems peculiarly excited) difficult to cope with. The child may act out the problem directly by sulking, making scenes, or having tantrums whenever the man arrives. Some children begin to have problems—with sleep, school, or other areas—which may reflect preoccupation with sexual fantasy or fear.

In such situations the mother can usually handle the problem by special thoughtfulness toward the child—for example, making sure that the child gets to know her male friend and spend time with him, and sharing with her child some special time and special activities that do not include the friend. If the problem does not dissolve under normal care and consideration, the parent may want to seek advice or counsel from a professional or from an experienced and wise friend who has faced similar problems.

Here is one last example of the special circumstances you face in forming sexual or romantic liaisons when you are a single parent: a very attractive divorced woman with four children, aged four through ten, met and fell in love with a man in the process of being divorced. The relationship progressed with great intensity, and seemed to offer the promise of long-term and deeply committed love. The man was a great charmer, and the children took to him as much as their mother did. The hook in the situation was that the man had a history of manic depression complicated by quite heavy drinking. The woman knew of his problem, and for some months felt that perhaps their relationship was having a therapeutic effect. When eventually he began to behave erratically, it became clear that the problem was not so easily solved. After numerous very serious efforts to solve the problem—including his entering therapy—the woman decided that she could not marry him. If she had been alone, she felt, she could devote herself to a joint long-range search for health with this man whom she deeply loved. But his very serious disturbance—and its manifestation frequently in violent aggressive behavior—precluded marriage because she did not feel that she could place the fate of her young children in the hands of someone so unstable.

The point, then, is simply that when you have children you are not choosing for yourself alone and unencumbered. You are responsible for the lives of others, and their fate and welfare must necessarily enter the equation that determines your choice in anything as crucial as a serious love relationship or marriage.

This same woman had a number of experiences with men during the period before she remarried. Among them were a number of unattractive, even frightening, encounters. She was a target for the advances of immature and predatory men. She also attracted a man who was not predatory but truly loved her and yet was unable to offer her anything beyond a love affair because of his own marital status. The crucial issue in this instance was that she had to either accept or reject the relationship as it was offered. And this meant that she had to assess her own situation, her own needs and desires, and to choose.

IN CONCLUSION

The woman alone is faced continually with this need to make choices and to extend and clarify her own self-knowledge—her own internal criteria—in order to make them.

It is this necessity, and the growth which sometimes occurs as a result of facing it, which sometimes leads social-service workers who deal with single parents to conclude that divorce is sometimes a first step toward family growth. Of course, these are the successful cases, the ones in which the woman does meet the challenge and grow rather than retreating into some new dependency. Nonetheless it is encouraging to know that such cases are numerous enough to fix this impression in the minds of experienced people in the field.

And it makes sense: Just as the challenge of dual roles stimulates the woman who has both a career and a family to develop, mature, and enlarge her psychological being, so the challenge of being on one's own, responsible for one's own life and the lives of dependent children, can stimulate new solutions, a new and more complex integration, a more competent self.

To meet this challenge, one must have support and services available. One must be able to assert one's own legitimate demands, and one must also be willing to enter into interdependence with others who can give and take assistance cooperatively.

We might once more reiterate what supportive services are needed by the single parent and where and how one is most likely to find them.

Depending on the ages of your children, you will need help with child care— to free you during specified times to attend school or work or simply to refresh your spirits and your perspective. Use all the resources you have available: the children's father and members of his family, your family, hired help, and your friends and community. Cooperative child care brings you into contact with other parents and thus has benefits beyond free time.

You can use help with the routine jobs of family maintenance. Cooperative food preparation provides extra time and additional ties to neighbors. Informal exchanges of home and automobile repairs may be available in the neighborhood or in your circle of friends. Even if you pay for such services, they are likely to be less expensive than services provided through normal commercial channels.

And, most important, you will need friends—for refreshing your view after a day alone with little children, for companionship when the children are older and busy with their own activities and friends, for help and advice and comfort when you face problems with your children or your own life.

Where do you find all these friends and community resources? If you can't find them in your established circles, you will want to join groups in the community which are likely to include people in similar life situations who are facing the same problems and challenges that you face. Church groups for single parents and organizations like Parents Without Partners and MOMMAS will offer activities, resources, and support. You may find that somewhere along the way you will also want some professional counseling for yourself or other members of your family. Organizations for single parents, and friends you meet through them, are good resources for references to appropriate professionals—professionals who have been helpful to others in your situation and whose fees are within your reach.

Finally, you will need a good deal of strength and bounce. But that is true in any situation in life which is challenging and stretches—and expands—your personal capacities.

BIBLIOGRAPHY

Epstein, Joseph: *Divorced in America: Marriage in an Age of Possibility,* Dutton, New York, 1974. A consideration of the meaning of marriage and divorce in modern America.

Gettleman, Susan, and Janet Markowitz: *The Courage to Divorce,* Simon and Schuster, New York, 1974. A general treatment of the problems and positive outcomes that make a divorce in many cases a constructive social act.

Wheeler, Michael: *No Fault Divorce,* Beacon Press, Boston, 1974. An analysis of the social movement for no-fault divorce, of situations in which it is relevant, and of the transaction of a no-fault divorce.

————: *Women in Transition: A Feminist Handbook on Separation and Divorce,* Scribner, New York, 1975. A very detailed and helpful description of the problems and considerations that arise in divorce, and suggestions for resources and solutions.

Part Five

Managing Your Options

Chapter 20

Assessing Self-Image and Training for Assertive Behavior

Jane Berry

Jane B. Berry, Ed.D., is a writer, lecturer, and consultant who lives in Mansfield Center, Connecticut. She was formerly Assistant Dean of Continuing Education at the University of Missouri; and she has published extensively in such journals as *Adult Leadership, Personnel and Guidance Journal,* and *National Vocational Guidance Quarterly* and has contributed chapters to four books.

YOU AND YOUR SELF-IMAGE

How do you feel about yourself most of the time—today, every day?

Simply stated, your self-image is your view of yourself and your behavior in all the situations of life in which you participate. Your self-image or self-concept has to do with your personal psychological organization. This organization has developed over time and is the direct result of your experiences and the patterns of reaction—your reactions to others, and theirs to you—which have evolved from and been reinforced by those experiences.

Most of us describe or talk about our self-image upon occasion by calling forth a few clichés and generalizations such as: "I'm an easy mark" or "I can't say no to anyone." In other words, many of us tend to go along from day to day with only a general impression of ourselves. We may think, for example, that we are timid, meek, lonely, submissive, or maybe too unselfish for our own good—or perhaps all of these.

Girls and women in our society have been conditioned to behave by simply *responding* to what is happening to them or around them, rather than trying to influence what is happening. In other words, many women have accepted passive roles in both family and work settings. Until very recently, girls and women have been encouraged to take secondary roles in most sectors of any society. Self-images of sacrifice, surrogate lives, and selflessness have been reinforced over and over for the majority of females.

Working women today are just beginning to be aware of different life options, new possibilities, and techniques of behavior modification which can make the self-image more positive and more satisfying. These skills and techniques are known as "assertive behavior." The following are characteristics of the assertive woman; you might try considering yourself and women you know in light of these qualities:

The assertive woman feels comfortable about expressing her feelings.
The assertive woman reacts in a positive manner.
The assertive woman is able to express her feelings without violating the rights of others.
The assertive woman possesses self-respect and strives for the respect of others.

SELF-ASSESSMENT

How do you feel about your ability to respond to other people? Do you regard yourself as an assertive person? That is, how do you honestly see yourself, in terms of the characteristics of the assertive woman?

Assessment of oneself in specific situations can be very helpful. For example, you might begin with your job. Are you able to recognize when your rights are being violated, by your boss or by your co-workers? For example, how do you deal with the situation when your boss asks you to do "one more thing" or when he or she seems to be asking you to do extra work that is not required of others?

Recall your response pattern in such situations. Do you agree to do the work, even though you may be seething inside? Do you do the work and then spend the rest of the week wishing you had refused?

How do you deal with co-workers who impose on what they regard as your "good nature"—which is in reality your inability to say no, to speak up for yourself and your rights. You may try to assert yourself in such situations but find that somehow you can't. The words seem to catch in your throat, and you find it easier to make an unassertive response. You seem unable to act on what you feel. This is so for many women.

You will also want to examine your situation at home, with your family. Are you able to respond as you feel? Do you tend to "take just so much" and then burst out angrily, so that you feel self-contempt? Do you brood over your inability to speak out effectively for yourself and your needs?

Cultural traditions inhibit many women's responses, particularly at home and in social settings. You may feel inadequate or unimportant. You may wish at times that you could escape all your commitments and do something you want to, the way you want to.

Perhaps you have identified this problem in your own life; you may often think, Why didn't I say what I *really* thought? Why didn't I stand up for myself? Somehow, you want to assert yourself but do not know where to begin.

Perhaps you are feeling what has been called "gender anxiety." This results from the idea that women should be submissive, passive, and selfless. If you grew up with that idea, it may have such a hold on you that it automatically determines your responses. If so, you are not alone.

Many women in the 1970s are caught between the old pattern of passivity and newer possibilities and alternatives. We hear more and more about women's rights—about human rights, if you please. Women today hear on every side that they have new freedoms. But nevertheless, many still feel that as individuals they are unable to speak up, to act in their own behalf.

Awareness of new opportunities is only part of the answer. In fact, such awareness can produce more frustration than satisfaction for some women. They want to react differently at work, at home, and in the community, but they do not know how. Also, women believe that assertive behavior is risky. Some are afraid of being called "aggressive." Indeed, there is often confusion about the difference between assertiveness and aggressiveness.

ASSERTION AND AGGRESSION: DEFINITIONS AND DIFFERENCES

It is important to understand the meaning of the word "aggression." Aggression is commonly defined as an attack or an act of hostility. The aggressive person is one who dominates in a militant style which is frequently indifferent to the rights of others. There is a common tendency to regard aggressive behavior as bad or undesirable. This can confuse the woman who is attempting to become more assertive and self-directing. The truth is that aggressive behavior, considered as positive and initiative, is very important in the promotion of you and your ideas.

There is a subtle relationship between "assertion" and "aggression." Assertion is a positive declaration of a position which affirms one's own rights and convictions and which, at the same time, takes into account the rights of others. The assertive woman, while standing up for herself and expressing her feelings without violating the rights of others, may also be initiating actions and activities which are in the best interest of herself and others. Assertive and aggressive responses may be closely linked in situations which invite or require self-reliance and movement in new directions.

Aggressive behavior may be entirely appropriate and in fact necessary for the assertive woman when it is creative and when it generates and sustains goal-directed activity. But aggressive behavior is not useful when it is negative: when it creates combat, disrupts interpersonal communication, or is generally self-defeating.

The challenge is to develop and cultivate assertive *and* aggressive behavior which makes you feel good about yourself and produces positive responses from your associates.

ASSERTIVENESS TRAINING: THE CHOICE

Times are changing. Women's roles, options, and opportunities are changing. Many women are working in a man's world.

You may be mulling these matters over in your own mind. Perhaps you have been passed up for a promotion or have failed to get a position for which you feel you were well qualified. Quite naturally, you are prompted to consider your own horizons and possible opportunities. What are your avenues for advancement or promotion? Periodic self-assessment can be helpful to most women, and it naturally leads to a consideration of your behavior, your self-concept, and how you believe others respond to you and your efforts.

You may begin to feel disgruntled or disatisfied with yourself. You begin to think more about your *own* feelings and reactions to your own behavior. Once again, you examine your self-image; and you may not feel very good about yourself. You experience gnawing, vague feelings of depression whenever you allow yourself to think about these matters.

You may therefore decide that you want to change your self-image—or at least do something to improve the way you seem to be operating, your style of interaction with others. It may occur to you that you should be doing something active about your self-development. Perhaps you can change your behavior—make it more attractive and productive so that you can feel better about yourself, your boss, your co-workers, your spouse, or others. It is here that assertiveness training can help.

Assertiveness training has been developed and refined; and during the past few years—coincidently with the development of the women's movement and extended opportunities for women in business and industry—it has offered an avenue for self-development. Assertiveness training grew because psychologists, social psychologists, psychiatrists, guidance counselors, and others in similar fields felt a need for it. It is designed to help women bridge the gap between traditional, limited roles and new opportunities, personal and professional.

Assertiveness training—now frequently referred to simply as "AT"—is based on psychological and therapeutic practices which have demonstrated that behavior can be learned and consciously changed. It is a systematic attempt to help persons change behaviors which cause difficulties and interfere with self-satisfaction. Such training has become widespread and popular throughout the nation. There are intensive courses, extended courses, sequences of courses, one-day seminars, weekend workshops, and rap groups. Many companies are sponsoring workshops for their women employees; but many women are organizing and paying for their own training. Assertiveness training is discussed in books and magazines. It is seen by many as a very positive experience; and for many people it is even something of a fad.

Assertiveness, and particularly assertiveness for women, is seen as generating new attitudes and changing life-styles. People are talking about their new assertive skills and abilities. Some of these are far from earthshaking; in fact, many seem to involve quite ordinary matters—for example, not always agreeing to make coffee for everyone in the office, or simply finding the courage to speak up to a superior about an idea or suggestion.

This may sound interesting to you, especially if you have been the "girl" making the coffee, collecting the money for the boss's Christmas present, and so on. But you should consider two points: Is assertiveness training right for you? Is it right for you at this time? The purpose of this chapter is not to urge assertiveness training on you, but simply to explain assertive behavior, the possibilities of assertiveness training, and the connection between self-image and assertion. The decision to investigate and enroll in a training program is, finally, yours. Certainly such a decision would be in line with the many new choices and possibilities for self-improvement that are developing in response to the needs and goals of women. But you may ask yourself, Can habits really be changed? You may also be uneasy about learning theory and conditioning procedures. Is this what you really want to get into? There is also the matter of other people's reactions: Would you be troubled if people did not understand or were hostile? Some fears about assertiveness training are rationalizations; but for any particular woman, some may be substantive. What is right for you must be your own decision.

As has been noted, there are an increasing number of formal training programs. You can find out about such programs from the local YWCA; from the continuing-education program at a nearby community college or university; from women's centers sponsored by educational, religious, and community agencies; and from the personnel office where you work. Bookstores and public libraries are another source of information, for there are many books now available on this subject. If for any reason you are unable to locate a training program or a rap group in your area, you can write to either of the following national offices; they can put you in contact with someone in your area who is familiar with local assertiveness training programs: Impact, San Luis Obispo, California; American Personnel and Guidance Association, 1607 New Hampshire Avenue, N.W., Washington, D.C.

ASSERTIVENESS TRAINING: THE PROGRAM

This section will briefly describe some aspects of assertiveness training (AT) programs, to give you an idea of what to expect if you decide that you want to investigate AT for yourself.

Emphasis is placed on speaking up in a manner which is forthright and neutral without being aggressive or provocative. Certain assertiveness training courses have a particular focus and help with a combination of skills. For example, a course offered at one university is called "Assertiveness and Confrontation Skills for Women." Other courses are called "Self-Assertion Skills," "Assertiveness Training and Your Job," and "Creative Management of Stress." One popular approach is the combination of management training and assertiveness training; such curricula have been found to be very effective.

Some specific parts of assertiveness training programs are detailed below.

Self-Development and Self-Control

This involves conscious identification of situations where you seem to lose control, where you fail altogether to be assertive, or where you fail to be as assertive as you would like. Special attention is given to development of the ability to speak out and express feelings effectively.

Body Language

Here the emphasis is on understanding physical reactions (such as sweating or a "nervous stomach") which occur when one feels less than effective in a situation. Assistance is provided in developing the ability to relax physically and to attain calmness which will permit clear thinking and more productive interaction with others.

In addition to these involuntary physical reactions, there is also the analysis of voluntary body language. This is important. You are already aware that body language, or nonverbal behavior, can convey at least as much as verbal behavior. AT programs examine and interpret nonverbal behavior as it relates to assertiveness. For example, unassertive body language is commonly said to include giggling inappropriately, casting the eyes down, slumping the shoulders, wringing the hands in despair, shrugging the shoulders helplessly. Assertive body language includes erect but comfortable posture, an attentive look, a confident expression, and obvious alertness.

Effective Behavior in the Job World

Here, training is directed toward controlling general anxiety on the job as well as specific anxieties associated with specific tasks. Assertive techniques for job seeking may also be explored. It is probably true that one cannot be as assertive when one is looking for a job as when one is an employee. This matter needs further research and investigation, but it seems clear that a job seeker does not have rights to assert in the same sense that an employee does.

Techniques

Paper-and-Pencil Exercises   Simple exercises involving assessment of one's self-image and assertive reactions are frequently employed to initiate assertive training sessions. These give participants insights into their own responses.

An example of such an exercise is a rating-sheet device which describes simulated life situations. Following the description of each situation are five possible reactions. Trainees are directed to select one of the five statements which most accurately represents their response to each situation. Responses vary from those which are uncertain and ambivalent to those which take a positive and confident stand in terms of the simulated situation. Self-image inventories utilizing a checklist format are also helpful in providing a profile of a trainee's self-assessment of selected personality traits. Such exercises can be used at various points during a training sequence and are a measure of how a woman is coming to change her feelings about herself as a result of increased understanding of assertive techniques.

Reinforcement Activities   These activities follow the introduction and practice of assertive skills and are very important. Reinforcement exercises can be practiced in group settings or by the individual alone. For example, one reinforcement technique is saying something good to yourself after you have made an assertive response which was effective and embodied your new understanding of assertive style.

I have given, of course, only a very brief look at AT formal programs. In addition to such programs, there are many other avenues to assertiveness training—and it should be pointed out once more that the choice is yours. There are numerous books and articles describing assertive skills, and these make do-it-yourself training possible. You may want to use such materials on your own, to see what you can learn and practice by yourself. Later, you might consider a formal training program.

ASSERTIVE STYLES

Style is a subtle thing. Your style is your general manner: your physical appearance and actions, your way of speaking, your characteristic reactions, and the way you relate to others. Your style is you; quite simply, it reflects and projects your image of yourself.

It might be said that assertive style may combine body language and modes of expression. For example, standing tall—*not* rigid, but giving an impression of confidence and openness—is desirable. This style means that you have a good idea who you are and why you are behaving and speaking as you are. On the other hand, a self-conscious person is beset with a tight, "on stage" feeling which often has physical manifestations: a "dry mouth," turning red, or even shaking or swaying from side to side.

It is always desirable to work toward a personal style that seems right for you—a style which is generally consistent and which seems to feel comfortable most of the time. There are a number of checkpoints for viewing and reviewing one's style as it is perceived by oneself and others. These include:

Lack of self-consciousness
Feeling accepted by individuals and groups with whom you are interacting
Ability to listen and respond with concern
Appreciation of self-disclosure (sharing your hopes, fears, and dreams with others)

Techniques involving the use of videotape can assist in the assessment and improvement of assertive style. It can be very helpful to observe yourself and others in both work and leisure settings. Videotape makes this possible and is used by several AT programs.

As your understanding of self-assertion develops, you will discover that you are observing assertiveness in others. Quite simply, your "assertive consciousness" will be raised. You will find that you are assessing yourself and others in terms of assertive competence. You will also observe that assertive behavior is not an isolated characteristic but rather an important component of your total personal style.

Cultivate flexibility in your effort to become more assertive. Avoid the temptation to try out your new-found assertive skills in such contrived and obvious ways that you appear to be wearing a sign which says: "Beware—I am the new assertive woman." Some women are so enthusiastic about their new-found assertiveness that they overdo it; often, they then exhibit inappropriate behavior.

A FEW WORDS OF CAUTION

Some words of caution are in order. First: You cannot be the "timid soul" one day and assertive the next. Your goal should be a gradual understanding of yourself and of appropriate and responsible reactions. Remember, assertive behavior is controlling yourself. Moreover, assertive capabilities are like other capabilities—they fall along a continuum and cannot be separated out.

Second: Avoid "testing" behavior. Assertiveness does not mean standing up for yourself at all times in all circumstances. You stand up for yourself and your rights when you are right *and* when it is right for you to stand up for yourself.

Third: Anticipate reactions to your new behavior. Don't go overboard. "Instant assertiveness" can be both troublesome and traumatic. People with whom you interact at home and at work have long been accustomed to expecting a certain type of behavior from you. When you change, your associates may not know what has happened and may not be prepared for your assertive behavior. It may not only surprise them but also irritate and bewilder them. It is important to anticipate such reactions. It is also important to avoid the temptation to use your newly found assertiveness for "shock effect." Assertive behavior should reflect your self-concept and should seem appropriate to others as well as to yourself.

IN CONCLUSION

The assertive woman is a perceptive realist. She recognizes that there are different situations and different social realities—different kinds of relationships with different people. Her assertiveness is modified and adjusted as she moves from one situation to another. I have already noted, for example, that reacting within a job is different from seeking a job as far as assertiveness is concerned.

The key is to integrate assertive skills with other interpersonal reactions, such as empathy and autonomy, and not to expect miracles: you will not always be totally pleased with yourself as an assertive person, any more than you were with yourself as a timid person.

Assertiveness is something to be understood and developed over time, with a sense of moderation and a sense of what is comfortable for you. Make a creative compromise between sitting down and taking it and standing up and saying it.

And finally, examine your motives. Why do you want to be more assertive? Where does assertiveness fit in your plan for self-development? For example, does it interest you simply because you want success? Begin with such questions. Examination of motives should also include an assessment of how assertive you are now. Try to recognize the areas of your life where you are already assertive, if any. Identify and practice assertive responses that you are already making, and see whether they result in more satisfying and productive behavior.

Today's women want to feel good about themselves. Individual women are discovering that new opportunities require new behaviors, as well as the ability to cope with the consequences of one's behavior. Assertive behavior can enhance self-development and create confidence. There is an important link between a healthy self-concept and creative assertion.

BIBLIOGRAPHY

Assert, The Newsletter of Assertive Behavior, Box 1094, San Luis Obispo, Calif. 93406. Six issues per year, $2.50. Up-to-date information about new assertive programs, techniques, and activities.

Angras, W. Stewart: *Behavior Modification,* Little, Brown, Boston, 1972. Provides understanding of behavior-modification techniques and their potential for growth, development, and changing personal styles and habits.

Bailyn, Lotte: "Career and Family Orientations of Husbands and Wives in Relation to Marital Happiness," *Human Relations,* vol. 23, 1970, pp. 97–113. Enhances understanding of marital interaction and encourages understanding of conflict caused by perceptions of individual and family goals.

————: "Family Constraints on Women's Work," in Ruth Kundsin (ed.), *Women and Success: Anatomy of Achievement,* William Morrow, New York, 1974. Review of problems faced by women oriented toward success and achievement.

Bloom, Lynn Z., Karen Colburn, and Joan Pearlman: *The New Assertive Women,* Delacorte Press, New York, 1975. Describes recent approaches to assertiveness training and provides examples of productive programs and techniques for enhancing assertiveness.

Eisler, Richard M., Peter M. Miller, and Michel Herson: "Components of Assertive Behavior," *Journal of Clinical Psychology,* vol. 23, no. 3, 1973, pp. 295–299. A basic analysis of assertive behavior and related psychological considerations.

Fensterheim, Herbert, and Jean Baer: *Don't Say Yes When You Want to Say No,* David McKay, New York, 1975. A comprehensive and significant review of assertiveness in personal life as well as job-related situations.

Horner, Matina: "Femininity and Successful Achievement: A Basic Inconsistency," in M.H. Garskoff (ed.), *Roles Women Play,* Brooks/Cole, Belmont, Calif., 1971. Review and interpretation of important research linking early female socialization and the lack of development toward satisfying achievement.

Jakubowski-Spector, Patricia: "Facilitating the Growth of Women through Assertive Training," *The Counseling Psychologist,* vol. 4, no. 1, 1973, pp. 75–86. Thoughtful explanation of and philosophical perspective on assertive training and its ramifications.

————: "Non-Assertion and the Clinical Problems of Women," in Diane Carter and Edna Rawlinds (eds.), *Psychotherapy for Women: Treatment towards Equality,* Charles C Thomas, Springfield, Ill., in press.

Knox, Barbara: *Trends in the Counseling of Women in Higher Education, 1957–1973,* National Association for Women Deans, Administrators, and Counselors, Washington, D.C., 1975. Review of programs and materials designed to assist women in anticipating obstacles and opportunities in planning for education and employment.

Lazarus, Arnold, and Allen Fay: *I Can if I Want To,* William Morrow, New York, 1975. Positive, down-to-earth, how-to suggestions for becoming aware of positive and negative effects of one's personal behavior in everyday situations.

National Organization for Women: *Assert Your Self,* Seattle, Washington, 1974. A sound basic explanation of assertive behavior combined with a review of techniques, programs, and resources for enhancing one's assertiveness.

Phelps, Stanlee, and Nancy Austin: *The Assertive Women,* Impact, San Luis Obispo, Calif., 1975. A useful handbook describing assertiveness training, self-image, and the practice of assertiveness in real-life situations.

Smith, Manuel J.: *When I Say No, I Feel Guilty,* Dial Press, New York, 1975. Enhances understanding of behavior orientation which can be self-defeating. Gives suggestions, exercises, and examples for consciously increasing personal satisfaction and effectiveness in relationships with others.

FILMS

Assertive Training for Women, Part II. Available from American Personnel and Guidance Association, 1607 New Hampshire Avenue N.W., Washington, D.C. 20009.

Assertive Training: The Teaching of Appropriate Behaviors. Available from Atascadero State Hospital, Atascadero, Calif. 93422.

Symposium: A Multimedia Demonstration of the Various Uses of Assertive Training. Available from Oxnard Community Mental Health Center, Oxnard, Calif.

The Use of Assertive Training in Creating New Roles for Women. Available from Ventura Center, Oxnard, Calif.

Chapter 21

Continuing Your Education: Widening Your Range of Options

Rosalind K. Loring

Evidently Cinderella's beauty and youth were not enough, for her fairy godmother, having decided to give her an "equal opportunity," dressed her in finery and gave her an elegant coach and horses, but nonetheless warned her to return at midnight. Even then, in the origins of myth and fairy tale, something more substantial was needed. The secret (which the fairy godmother neglected to tell Cinderella) was that she could do much more to help herself. She didn't need to wait endlessly to be rescued from a miserable life. Nor did she have to suffer so much from a lack of self-confidence. The same is true of women today.

Today almost every woman in America has a wealth of resources available to her which were lacking in earlier times. These include a range of continuing education programs which hold almost as much promise as the glass slippers did. From all accounts, continuing one's education makes it possible to change conditions brought about by being underprepared, underexperienced, and undereducated. It also helps people to change careers, deal with their everyday personal and family problems, and work to improve the community and the environment. And, equally important, continuing education can be a source of delight. Philoso-

The Now Society

Yes, Bruce, you are the man I married. But since then I've improved my memory, lost thirty pounds and quintupled my reading speed. *

©Chronicle Publishing Co. 1975

phy, the arts, literature, languages—these can help us to live more fully, more deeply, with greater appreciation and enjoyment. The variations and benefits of continuing education are as numerous as the needs and interests of adults (and, for our purposes, especially of women) and can affect every area of one's life.

Although Abigail Adams reminded her husband in 1776 to "remember the ladies and be more generous and favorable to them than your ancestors . . . ,"[1] it has taken almost two centuries for educational opportunities for women to approximate those available for men. But since World War II there has been a dramatic increase in the amount and variety of education appropriate for women or especially created for them.

BENEFITS OF LEARNING OPPORTUNITIES

Juanita Kreps has stated that "guidance offered through continuing education programs for the past two decades was the only assistance from the education world to women returning to work."[2] The importance of continuing education for women is, by now, widely recognized.

On April 15, 1975, the United States Supreme Court ruled that the State of Utah may not discriminate against women by establishing a different age of

[1] Kathryn G. Heath, "The Female Equation," in U.S. Dept. of Health, Education and Welfare, *American Education,* Washington, D.C., November 1974, pp. 20–32.

[2] Juanita Kreps, *Sex in the Marketplace: American Women at Work,* John Hopkins Press, Baltimore, Md., 1971, p. 88.

majority for males and females: "If the female is not to be supported so long as the male she can hardly be expected to attend school as long as he does, and bringing her education to an end earlier coincides with the role-typing society has long imposed."[3]

Change magazine reported in November 1975 that of the "500,000 women ranging in age from 21–80 plus [who] are turning or returning to college . . . the point of entry [for many] is the adult education program, while still others turn to continuing education for women's programs."[4]

A counselor for a university extension advisory service reported of one woman client: "She is fifty-two years old, a widow and black. She had a handful of credits in 1950–1951 with poor grades. After her husband died, she was motivated to go back to school and did very well. From fall of 1968 to fall of 1974, going to school during the day, she completed an A.A. [Associate of Arts] degree. Now she works nights for the Postal Service at the airport. We are helping her in this office by indicating the extension classes for her to take that will make her eligible to enter the university as a junior."[5]

Many accounts could be given of power gained, relationships restored, skills sharpened, and new knowledge acquired. The simple fact is that women have learned that immediate as well as long-term needs can be better met if educational experiences are used to understand, analyze, and evaluate, so that there is greater control over one's destiny. Alternative ways of learning increase every year. The data show that women in ever-increasing numbers are discovering the potential and the dimensions of *lifelong learning*.

Actually the 500,000 women mentioned by *Change* are but a fraction of the number of women who are partaking of the rich resources now available to them. It is estimated that the sum of all adults in some learning setting now exceeds 50 million. Of these, well over half are women.

For women of every age and background—economic, social, or educational—and for women with all sorts of objectives, interests, and issues in mind, there is a continuing education experience somewhere available. And women especially stand to gain from such programs. Long-established institutions of higher education, private firms, informal coalitions of women, individual entrepreneurs, and professional and community organizations of all types have "discovered" women and have made plans to welcome them. Naturally, no single institution makes available the entire range of courses, but the totality in large communities—and the growing diversity in smaller ones—combined with opportunities for independent study, can now meet almost any need.

A major factor in bringing this about has been the women's movement, which has changed the attitudes of women and men regarding the the importance of education in the lives of women. As Patricia K. Cross remarked, "Whether the

[3] Susan Davis (pub.) and Karen Wellisch (ed.), *The Spokeswomen,* vol. 5., no. 11, May 15, 1975. (This is an independent monthly newsletter published in Chicago, Ill.)

[4] Elizabeth Stone, "Women's Programs Grow Up," *Change* magazine, November 1975, pp. 16–20.

[5] Personal communication.

primary purpose of education is career training or liberation of the mind and the enrichment of life, it is hard to argue that the education of women is less important than that of men."[6]

Costs, and sources of financing, will be discussed later; but the point should be made that women who work stand to benefit enormously from continuing their education, whether formally or informally. Yet as a result of home and family responsibilities, working women in the past have participated less than women of school age, elderly women, and women whose primary work is homemaking.

For the working woman who wants to improve her educational status, either for her career or for her own enrichment, even the most cursory investigation will uncover a rich selection of choices. Educational institutions, by and large, are actively recruiting women students. In business and industry, more and more forward-looking employers recognize the positive results in their businesses when employees are encouraged to improve themselves. Many employers offer substantial financial incentives for employees who continue their education as a recurrent, developmental process.

OPPORTUNITIES FOR DEGREES

The options for continuing one's education exist in traditional and nontraditional forms and settings. Traditional programs in traditional settings are the programs at colleges and universities leading to the bachelor's degree; and the programs at universities leading to the master's and doctor's degrees. Even in the most traditional schools, the exigencies of meeting the needs of many diverse students have brought about some innovative programs. These include the "extended" and "external" degree programs, in which courses are arranged at special times and locations; such programs are convenient for the fully employed woman. Some institutions award credit toward degrees for "life experience."

For the working woman who is close to a degree and has flexible working hours, the traditional programs offer many choices. Community colleges have expanded their offerings to include much more than the usual business-oriented Associate of Arts (A.A.) degrees that were originally expected of them. For example, they now give the A.A. for nursing and hospital procedures, landscape gardening, financial services, merchandising, photography, technical illustration, and urban studies.[7]

Many colleges and universities are offering interdisciplinary bachelor's and master's degrees as an alternative for those who want as broadly based an educational experience as possible. One example is a degree in liberal arts; another is a master's degree in management of the arts, combining business, management, and fine arts.

Traditional programs in new settings include such choices as degree credit

---

[6] Patricia K. Cross, "The Woman Student," in *Women in Higher Education,* American Council on Education, Washington, D.C., 1974.
[7] P. Burkel, *College Blue Book,* Yonkers-on-the-Hudson, N.Y., 1975.

for correspondence courses, television courses, on-the-job training programs (this includes apprenticeships), gaining credit units by examinations, and validated work and life experience. In traditional school settings, on campus, nontraditional programs are proliferating rapidly. In fact, college catalogues have difficulty keeping up with the changes; as a result, college counseling services are daily inundated with flyers and brochures announcing experimental programs of admission, experiential learning programs, compensatory courses for women (often in mathematics and the "hard" sciences), and scheduled classes held at extended times—day or night, weekdays or weekends. New programs for women, however, tend to emphasize back-to-work skills and are highly work-related. Pressure is being put on the educational institutions to increase part-time study, accelerated programs, and independent study and to make arrangements for child care.

Degrees for Part-Time Students

The most noticeable change in educational programing seems to be greater flexibility in scheduling of classes. Every effort is being made to provide classes at times convenient for working people. Santa Monica College in Santa Monica, California, for example, has a program called Saturday One Day College. Students may be fully matriculated (twelve units) or on a limited matriculated status (seven or fewer units). Examples of the courses available are Beginning Design, Human Ecology, Introduction to Business, Introduction to Data Processing, Power and Speed Reading, Consumer Education, Real Estate Principles, and Conversational Spanish. Mundelein College in Chicago has designed a weekend college where students arrive for classes on Friday night and leave for home or work on Sunday afternoon. This is a realistic approach to providing education at a time when young mothers and older women can take advantage of it.

Memphis State University at Memphis, Tennessee, has a "weekend university" for part-time degree students, with classes in accounting, economics, marketing, and journalism. It also has a "mini-college" for women over twenty-five, to ease them back into the school experience; no entrance examination is required.

Pepperdine University in Los Angeles offers a bachelor of science degree in administration designed particularly for working women; classes meet every third weekend for eighteen weekends a year. It takes about two years to complete the upper division, or third and fourth years' work.

The College of Continuing Education of the University of Southern California in Los Angeles has offered a master's degree in liberal arts since 1970, recognizing that adults appreciate the interrelationships of all academic fields. This interdisciplinary course of study has been designed mainly for those already established in professions who want to round out their education. People who are employed can earn the degree in two to three years by taking one or two courses a semester (usually in seminars limited to fifteen students). USC also offers part-time degrees for people interested in specializing in a profession. In a number of locations (which include the campus in Los Angeles as well as Sacramento, Washington, D.C., and overseas), credit toward a master's degree and sometimes a doctor's degree may be earned in such fields as journalism, public administration, education, computer science, cinema, business, international relations, and an array of engineering specialties (civil, mechanical, chemical, electrical, geological, systems, environmental, and aerospace). Because needs vary from place to place, not every program is available in every location.

So great and so wide-spaced is the interest in developing better methods for providing nontraditional students with opportunities to learn what the students feel they most need, the United States Office of Education, Fund for the Improvement of Post-Secondary Education, is providing funds for experimentation and evaluation. For example, the University of Utah has undertaken a program of "educational trade-off" so that full-time workers may seek a college degree and full-time students may secure practical on-the-job experience to augment their formal classroom training. One major objective of the program is to devise a curriculum based on competence, which will allow the workers an opportunity to demonstrate already achieved skills and knowledge.[8]

Another trend is the collaboration of groups of colleges, universities, or both within a given region to present a wider selection of classes, courses, and degree programs. For instance, the California State College and University system has formed a consortium with an office in Los Angeles. A degree will be granted from one of the nineteen campuses, but some courses may be taken at other campuses. Since the institutions involved range from northern to southern California, this arrangement constitutes a thousand-mile campus.

Most such developments in colleges and universities have been called "extended" or "external" degree programs. They have sprung up all over the country because of the demand by the adult working population for a practical route to academic skills. A program of this sort will generally begin with the bachelor's degree, and the first requirement for eligibility is the equivalent of the first two years of college. Degrees in business administration and liberal studies seem to be the most common. For the woman working in business and industry, a degree in business administration is eminently practical, as it offers broad knowledge including management and supervisory techniques and organizational behavior, as well as business basics. The liberal-studies degrees tend to be cross-disciplinary and are therefore useful in many areas, such as prelaw.

Off-Campus Study

Upper Iowa University in Fayette, Iowa, has an extended degree program that allows a student to complete most of the work off campus through the use of cassette tapes and tutoring; however, students are required to live on campus for four to eight weeks before graduation (a typical requirement of most "off-campus" programs). The bachelor's degree is offered in public administration and business administration at the time of this writing, but there are plans to expand the program. A service called "Portal Program" is offered by California State

[8] More information is available from Dr. Robert Guilliam, Project Director, or Ms. Gertrude Peterson, Academic Coordinator, Human Resources Institute, University of Utah.

University at Dominguez Hills; it has not only a master's degree in business administration for the fully employed but also a special program for those who have not completed a bachelor's degree. The student who successfully completes specified classes in a sequence of undergraduate courses is certified and has the opportunity to move directly into the master's program, but will not receive a bachelor's degree.

Another approach which has found favor is the "University without Walls." This is a consortium of about thirty institutions throughout the country that offer degrees on the basis of a "graduation contract." The student, with the approval of the school, plans a curriculum with a faculty advisor and proceeds at his or her own pace. Some schools like Goddard have a residency requirement, which means spending some time at the campus. Others, like Antioch, do not require residency at the parent school.

The University of the State of New York has an extremely flexible program, called the New York State Regents External Degree Program, for earning an A.A. or a B.S. degree in business administration. Credits toward these degrees can be earned by (1) successful completion of regular college courses as verified by official transcripts; (2) recognized proficiency examinations; (3) special assessment of knowledge gained from experience, independent study, or other non-traditional approaches; (4) any combination of regular college course work, proficiency tests, and special examination or assessment. Similar programs are offered by Thomas A. Edison College in Trenton, New Jersey, and by the Board for State Academic Awards in Hartford, Connecticut; and degrees from the New York Regents External Degree Program were made available to students nationally in the fall of 1976.

The receptivity of many institutions to giving credit toward a degree for life experience offers many women a short cut that may make the difference between getting a degree or giving up in despair. This decreases not only the length of time required for a degree but also the cost. Volunteer work, creative writing, work in political campaigns, and work as a teacher's aide or translator or interpreter can add up to about the equivalent of a year of college credit, if such experiences are documented. The Life Equivalency program at Queen's College, New York City, is a fine example. Usually this kind of program is found at a small private college, but it is worth investigating every school in your area to find any such program that exists or to encourage the development of one.

Courses by Television

More and more courses for credit are beginning to appear on television. Under the sponsorship of national television networks and public broadcasting, viewers have been presented with such series as "Classic Theater," "Search: The Quest for Personal Meaning," "Introduction to Physical Geography," and Jacob Bronowski's "Ascent of Man." These are being presented in the Los Angeles area by the Southern California Community College TV Consortium, a cooperative enterprise of thirty-four Southern California community colleges, as college credit courses on open broadcast television; there is no tuition charge for students who are legal residents of California. Students view the programs, complete study assignments, and may attend one or more review meetings. Midterm and final examinations are taken at one of the cooperating colleges. Courses in psychology, humanities, art, consumer education, and child growth and development can also be taken for credit. Similar plans—though usually for a fee from colleges and universities which are not so well funded by local or state tax dollars—are available throughout the country. It may well be worthwhile to pay the standard fee for such a course from a college or university in your area if the credit thus earned has more value when applied to a degree.

Credit by Examination

The College Level Examination Program, known as CLEP, is a nationwide network of over 800 test centers that give tests in about forty college subjects. Some 1,500 colleges and universities award credit on the basis of these CLEP examinations. The amount of credit allowable and minimum acceptable scores vary from school to school. These tests are helpful for determining placement of adults in special or innovative new programs and for licensing or certification requirements, and they present an alternative way to satisfy requirements for job advancement. The University of Iowa, the University of Missouri on its several campuses, and a growing number of other American colleges and universities in the nation[9] have authorized CLEP general examinations as a way for students to meet graduation requirements. Many women can find this a quick and expedient way to validate their informal educational experience. At the time of this writing, one test costs $20; two cost $30; and any three to five cost $40.

Independent Study

Independent study programs are plentiful, and most offer college credit although relatively few grant degrees. There is a Universal College Program sponsored by Azusa Pacific, a small private college in Southern California, which grants an A.A. degree: video cassettes of course material are sent to those who cannot attend scheduled classes. The degree program can be completed in two calendar years. It costs $800 for the first semester of four courses and $600 for each four-course semester thereafter. Costs include texts, workbooks, videotapes, and a playback machine. Correspondence courses are available from most large universities. Degree programs, however, are hard to find. One of the few is offered by Syracuse University, which has a correspondence program that will lead to a B.A. in liberal studies or a B.S. in business administration; it costs about $1,500 a year. Independent study requires discipline and perseverance, as well as a clear-cut idea of your goals, and should be undertaken if you have a degree in mind only after consultation with a counselor at the institution from which you intend to secure your degree.

There are too many experimental programs to list in detail here. Two others

---

[9] For a listing of colleges and universities which participate in CLEP, write to College Entrance Examination Board, 8881 Seventh Avenue, New York, N.Y. 10019. (Since examinations are given periodically in specified locations, ask for the schedule as well.)

may be noted, however: the Cooperative Assessment of Experiential Learning (a joint effort of the Education Testing Service and 160 institutions) and the American Council on Education together with the New York State Board of Regents' Project in Noncollegiate Sponsored Instruction. As the *Carnegie Quarterly* has stated:

> Education, to be sure, reflects the needs and desires of society. By any measure we are demanding that more people have opportunities to lead the good life—to have access to better jobs, higher social status, a secure future for their children. And since higher education is a pathway to these benefits, colleges and universities have been under pressure to open their doors to ever greater numbers.[10]

NONDEGREE OPPORTUNITIES

Growing as rapidly as degree programs are the multitude of noncredit, nontraditional courses, conferences, workshops, and seminars known as "adult education" or "continuing education." The length of time and the commitment involved vary widely, from one-day workshops to a year of classes. Typically these are educational experiences which focus upon one specialized issue or topic. Most are short-term and part-time, but there are a number of programs which are highly concentrated and even full-time for as much as four to six months. As with almost every other option women have in education, the duration and the content depend upon the methodology and the institutional affiliation of the planners.

Certificate Programs

Certificate programs offer a documented record of learning acquired for job improvement. Here again the choice seems almost limitless. For example, the University of New Mexico offers three programs of about six courses each. One is in real estate, one in small business operation, and one in social service technology. Other short-term certificate programs can be found throughout the country in such fields as air conditioning, bookbinding, cabinetmaking, computers, cytotechnology (cells), drafting, fashion, interior design, financial management, and metallurgy.[11] In the health sciences some courses are given at hospitals and are convenient for nurses, medical aides, and others with flexible working hours.

Certificate programs which offer intensive rather than broad educational experience are frequently the mechanism for high-level paraprofessional training. In 1975 the American Bar Association approved training programs for paraprofessionals in corporate law, litigation, real estate, and probate law given by a number of public and private institutions.[12]

Equally, certificates are a way of designating that those who are already professionally educated or trained have kept current in their field or thot they are branching into some new variation of a previously established career. Certificates

---

[10] *Carnegie Quarterly,* Carnegie Corporation of New York, Fall 1975.
[11] Burkel, op. cit.
[12] For specific information about fees, time, prerequisites, and so forth, write directly to the American Bar Association.

in interior design, purchasing, industrial relations, psychiatric nursing, childhood education, and other highly skilled fields are growing in importance because the concept of lifelong learning is valued and because knowledge increases at such a rapid rate.

Not to be overlooked is the liberal education available in one-day and weekend seminars that facilitate upward mobility for the enterprising woman. The variety of such courses is almost endless: titles of programs include Women in Management, Leadership, Decision Making, How to Profit from a Job Change, Selling, Graphics, Memory Training, Problem Solving, Group Counseling; in fact, there are courses in everything from how to assert yourself at work to how to write more effective memos.

Women whose pay is high are concerned about money matters and are taking courses in accounting, financial management, and investment. Women who are searching for a career and a way back into the work force are helped by such courses as Creative Writing for Publishing (Drake University, Iowa), Practice of Equal Employment (George Washington University, in cooperation with Federal Publications, Inc., Washington, D.C.), and Family Health Worker: An Intensive Training Program (New School for Social Research, New York City). The list of topics and titles has multiplied rapidly to match the growing individuality of American women and their interests and needs. Jean Wells, Special Assistant to the Director of the Women's Bureau, U.S. Department of Labor, commented in 1974, "It is now estimated that there are over 500 sources of programs for adult women."[13]

Adult Education in High Schools

Community and adult programs in the public schools usually operate on a similar schedule. Typically, each school conducts evening classes from 5:00 P.M. to 10:00 P.M. and frequently schedules a much smaller offering during the daytime. Persons enrolling in the courses may pay a small registration fee per semester for one or more subjects, plus some incidental fees. Each school maintains its own guidance and counseling service. Besides completing requirements for a high school diploma, an adult student may also earn certificates in a variety of occupational training programs or prepare for the examination to become a United States citizen.

A sampling of the subjects available includes English composition, public speaking, effective communication, speed reading, foreign languages, government, citizenship, history, bookkeeping, accounting, shorthand, typing, computer programing, dressmaking, cabinet and furniture construction, plumbing, arts and crafts (such as ceramics, jewelry, drawing, and painting), art history, sign language, self-defense for women, and investments. There is even a course in powder-puff mechanics.

Most public school systems throughout the country offer adult education courses, and those listed above are typical. The range is limited only by community interest and funding. Classes tend to meet once or twice a week and are

[13] Jean Wells, *Continuing Education for Women: Current Developments,* Women's Bureau, Employment Standards Administration, U.S. Department of Labor, Washington, D.C., 1974.

short-term or given by the semester. Each local high school will have a listing of its offerings.

Vocational and Technical Schools

While all school systems have at most levels educational programs which are vocational in nature (law, management, secretarial skills, paramedicine, etc., can be so defined), there are institutions which specialize in preparing people for occupations which frequently require physical skill or manual dexterity. Plumbing, electricity, hairdressing, carpentry, television repair, automobile mechanics, and a host of other trades and crafts may be learned. (See Chapter 4 for greater detail about possibilities and potential hazards.) Often such preparation is necessary in order to take a state examination for licensing, to be accepted for apprenticeship by a union, or to acquire enough competence to perform certain tasks.

For women with mechanical aptitude, these fields offer opportunities for better pay than is typical for some white-collar jobs and for personal satisfaction (e.g., working outdoors, using one's dexterity, and seeing immediate results). Furthermore, the cost of instruction frequently is relatively low since the time required may be a year or less.

Note that these types of education are provided by public and private schools, most of which specialize in training for specific occupations (secretarial schools, trade and technological junior colleges, etc.). It is wise to check both the contract you sign to pay for costs of instruction and the accreditation of the program and the institution. There are many fine proprietary schools, but unfortunately there are also far too many which charge substantial fees without providing high-quality education or the potential for employment after training.

Continuing Education at Community Colleges

Local community colleges have not only degree programs (A.A.) which may be applied toward a college or university degree, but also "community service" programs which are noncredit. The noncredit programs attempt to meet the interests of the local community and provide service to adults in their residential and work settings. Here again the span of methodology, course content, and location is extraordinarily wide, and there is great concern that students be well counseled. Many community colleges are open day and night, accept all students who are over sixteen (or eighteen in some states), and emphasize reaching and aiding adults of the inner city. There are compensatory programs and programs providing college credit for advancement into four-year institutions. There are also specialized courses such as women's careers, literature of black authors, Chinese cooking, and parent-child relationships. Most community college districts (and quite a few public school districts) operate specialized vocational and technical facilities.

Continuing Education at Colleges and Universities

As was mentioned earlier in this chapter, the separate units of continuing education in institutions of higher education were responsible for much of the pioneering work in helping mature women to move forward by providing education which was appropriate, useful, and designed for various levels of experience and sophistication. Even today these academic program units specialize in designing activities for "targeted" adult students, emphasizing the special character of each subgroup.

The range of programs offered naturally varies from one institution and state to another. The following course description is typical:

> *The Professional Development Seminar for Secretaries:* A special program designed for those employed in secretarial or clerical positions at *other* than administrative-assistant or executive-secretary levels. The seminar is a refresher course; it will improve the efficiency of your office as well as offer new and creative ideas and skills. Topics will cover written communications, professional development, the value of empathy, a personnel-problems clinic, and techniques for effective teamwork.

Sue Gordon, Coordinator, Women's Programs, Continuing Education, Oregon State System of Higher Education and administrator of the program just described, says, "If she's good enough to be your secretary, she's worth investing in." Here are two other typical descriptions:

> *Continuing Education and Community Service Programs in Gerontology:* The Pennsylvania State University has a long history of continuing education programs and cooperative extension services in gerontology. Within recent years, programmatic efforts in gerontology have emerged directed toward these goals: To provide problem-oriented, in-service training for the rapidly growing corps of relatively untrained providers of human services to the elderly. To lend ongoing technical consultation to service agencies in the planning, development and evaluation of gerontological programs. To develop training mechanisms for community-based, extended-degree programs in gerontology for existing service providers.[14]

> *The Female Client:* An elective course in the University of California Irvine Extension Human Services Certificate Program. The ten lectures in the series cover such issues as: "The Traditional Woman in the Labor Market"; "Female Sexuality"; "The Stages of Motherhood"; "Women from Other Cultures (Black, Chicano, Asian)"; and "Women Alone."

In Virginia, a consortium of colleges and universities throughout the state offers evening courses, most of them for teachers, in subjects related to students and administration.

Proprietary Institutions and Other Sources

In addition to the institutions we have been discussing, almost all community and voluntary organizations, governmental agencies, and business and industrial organizations make continuing education available in the form of on-the-job training, television programs, or annual meetings. One private organization whose business is continuing education specializes in producing audio cassettes which are sold as sets or "presentations."[15] An assistant professor from Michigan State

---

[14] For more information write to Gerontology Manpower Development Project, Amy Gardner House, College of Human Development, The Pennsylvania State University, University Park, Pa. 16802.

[15] Affective House, P.O. Box 35321, Tulsa, Oklahoma 74315.

University is the author and commentator of one of their series, described as follows:

> *On Women* is a self-contained program that describes and explains aspects of existing sex discrimination. Also explained are reasons why sex discrimination exists and is perpetuated. You are given information that will help you to effect change. Women can help themselves and each other. Men (in education, in the church, in business and industry) can help to achieve equity. The program is not just documentation, but presents courses of action.
>
> 1 Sex Discrimination Exists and It Limits Women
> 2 Cultural Hangups with Sex Roles
> 3 Unwinding from "Traditional" Roles: What Can We Do?
> 4 Planning a Women's Group
> 5 A Women's Group
> 6 Group Exercises to Reduce Stereotyping
> 7 Group Exercises to Reduce Competitiveness
> 8 Assertiveness Training in Women
> 9 Group Exercises to Enhance Closeness
> 10 Sex Discrimination in Counselors
> 11 Sex Discrimination Workshop for Counselors
> 12 Counseling the Woman Student

Other nontraditional programs in nontraditional settings can be found at women's centers, at women's organizations, at conventions, and even on educational cruises planned by travel agents.[16] Other settings include places of employment, informal off-campus discussion groups, and government offices. The home has also achieved acceptance as a "learning center."

COUNSELING

All that has been written earlier in this chapter points out the wealth of resources available to women regardless of their occupation. But many women, surrounded by more options than ever before in history, need some assistance in choosing from among them. Questions relating to time, to cost, to matching perceived needs, even to diagnosing needs and developing the ability to succeed in completing one's education—all these become compelling in the selection of education programs.

Moreover, the planners of early programs in continuing education for women recognized that another set of questions were also part of determining a course of action by women planning to go to work or to take more responsible positions in the community. Family relationships, spouses' feelings, family income and

[16] Even vacationing can be educational today. With the burgeoning interest in ocean cruises, cruise lines are coming up with all sorts of ideas to improve your mind at sea. It could be a cruise of the Greek islands with a famous author to tell you about ancient Greek history; a Mexican holiday for archaeology buffs; or a weekend of psychology seminars. (If you would rather be on land, trips to historical or cultural centers abound, many for college credit.)

attitudes about it, health, and energy were all central to decisions and choices, and still are. In an effort to deal with these questions, several activities have become integral to women's programs and women's education.

Advisory and Counseling Centers

Career, educational, and personal counseling have been provided by a growing number of institutions through the creation of women's centers. In some universities these centers are specified as such, and a revised listing of these (now over 600 in number) has been prepared by the Project on the Status and Education of Women.[17] Such centers provide a wide range of services, from counseling on abortion to rap sessions on psychological concerns and questions of goals and identity. Some of them are staffed by professional counselors, some by volunteers; all attempt to provide practical assistance. The working woman should not overlook these centers, whether on local college campuses or sponsored by community organizations. One community group, the Home- and Community-Based Career Education Project, specializes in providing counseling services over the telephone. Very practical and detailed information is available on education, returning to work, and job trends.[18] Besides classes aimed directly at meeting her needs, any woman will find invaluable moral support in these centers from a group of women who share similar problems. This can sometimes encourage her to continue her education while working when difficulties have become oppressive. Moreover, many enriching classes such as arts and crafts are given which will add to the aesthetic, joyful quality of her life.

Some colleges and universities have general counseling centers with staff members who specialize in counseling women or returning, mature students. On many campuses each function is so compartmentalized that curriculum counseling is available only in the academic departments, health problems are the province of the student health department, etc. On some campuses an *ombudsman* is available for students who have difficulty with the system itself or with a specific aspect of college life (such as discrimination in the classroom).

In addition, many continuing education or extension divisions maintain advisory or counseling centers for a small fee or none at all. Some communities, through either government funding or sponsorship by a community agency, provide counseling services or referral and information centers. These centers, which vary widely nationally, include the New Haven Women's Liberation Center (Yale University); the Black Women's Institute (National Council of Negro Women); A Woman's Place (Athens, Georgia, and Champaign, Illinois); Span Place (Purdue University); the Women's Resource Center (Columbia, Maryland); and Everywoman's Center (East Lansing, Michigan).

Some women's caucuses of specialized professional organizations have concentrated upon improving counseling available to girls and women. For instance,

---

[17] Bernice Sandler, *Women's Centers: Where Are They?* Association of American Colleges, 1818 R Street N.W., Washington, D.C. 20009, September 1975.

[18] For further information, write to Vivian Guilfoy, Education Development Center, Inc., 55 Chapel Street, Newton, Mass. 02160.

the National Vocational Guidance Association's Commission on the Occupational Status of Women has now conducted three national workshops (held yearly); the one held in 1975 emphasized "Strategies for Action." Whether or not the organization's membership is made up of counselors, frequently the discussion revolves around the critical need for better counseling. One interesting feature is that usually these sessions are open to women other than members. There is a missionary-like zeal in those who work with these issues.

Counseling Courses

While centers most frequently provide their service to individuals, recently group sessions have been added in an effort to help greater numbers. One of the inventions of continuing and adult education was the development of courses which are introductory to further action and which, therefore, are rather short (usually ten to twelve weeks). Counseling courses—called Group Counseling for Women: Educational, Occupational, and Volunteer Opportunities—seem to have been developed simultaneously at three or four universities in the country. They are now ten years old, and are still the first contact many women have with educational institutions when they contemplate a dramatic change in life.

Speaking of the majority of institutions, Esther Westervelt, in *Barriers to Women's Participation in Postsecondary Education,* documented the fact that "research and commentary indicate that both girls and women are still victims of biased or inadequate counseling."[19] Every day brings new evidence that this is so, and yet it is also true that daily strides are being taken in terms of making counselors aware of sexist bias. Interest and ability tests long in use are now being challenged by women's organizations in an attempt to eliminate discrimination and poor guidance.

Whether the center is a program advisory service, a one-stop information center, or a total commitment for the duration of a woman's education, counseling is usually the key to greater ease in seeking educational experience.

COSTS

There are, of course, barriers to utilization of educational programs and pleasures. High on almost everyone's list is the cost of quality education or even of time spent away from home and family (transportation and child care, for example). In institutions not supported by taxes, tuition is charged. It is unfortunately true that many of the innovative special degree programs are located in institutions which must charge the student the entire cost of the program in order to present it at all. Women's financial vulnerability and their unique financial problems are well described in *Women's Stake in Low Tuition.*[20] It is often difficult for

---

[19] Esther Manning Westervelt, *Barriers to Women's Participation in Postsecondary Education,* National Center for Education Statistics, Education Division, U.S. Department of Health, Education and Welfare, Washington, D.C., 1975.

[20] Winnie Bengelsdorf, *Women's Stake in Low Tuition,* American Association of State Colleges and Universities, 1 Dupont Circle, Washington, D.C. 20036, October 1974.

women to get federal loans as part-time students; there are few work-study jobs, and in any case women have little time for such jobs; and, of course, women with lower incomes have less money to pay for education. Since money continues to be a problem, women must press for more scholarships, reduced fees, low-cost loans, and support from employers.

Most large businesses and industries include in their employee benefits some form of educational assistance. Even smaller companies with forward-looking presidents and directors will often encourage employees and staff to improve their education by offering financial aid. Some will pay entirely for job-related courses taken for credit. Some will pay half the cost of professional or career-advancement courses. And some will even support enrichment courses, on the well-documented assumption that anything that improves the employee improves the company. The clothing and interior-design industries encourage employees to go back to school to keep abreast of the latest trends. There are signs of growing cooperation between business and continuing education. The employee with ten or fifteen years' experience, but no formal education or degree, is particularly encouraged to go back to school. Some are offered prepaid education for an undergraduate degree or for a program that will give the foundation for a degree.

Affirmative Action (see Chapter 8) is pricking industry and business to help women by offering training. Such training can upgrade an existing staff—which is cheaper in the long run than hiring new people—or can serve as an inducement for new employees.

It is wise for any woman seeking ways to improve herself and move upward to investigate intervention by federal and local government, since many programs in industry are being subsidized. There is, for example, the Government Education Center (GEC) at Los Angeles, which is an organization completely supported by government agencies and educational institutions. GEC serves as a link between government agencies seeking to provide additional education for employees' professional, occupational, and personal growth and the educational institutions of the Los Angeles area capable of providing qualified learning programs at convenient times and places.

Many companies will set aside one day a year to invite schools in the area to present their programs to the company personnel. Often continuing education departments of universities will tailor-make courses for industry where there is sufficient demand for them. This is further evidence of the close cooperation between education and business in trying to meet the needs of all would-be students.

There are also many in-service and on-the-job training programs which could be beneficial to the woman seeking to improve herself. Telephone and electric power companies have planned and presented the largest number of training programs, according to a survey made by the Bureau of Labor Statistics in 1974. Some were apprenticeships, some on-the-job training, and some in the classroom. Like businesses, government agencies and utility companies cover the costs of their in-service training programs and frequently use their own employees as instructors.

APPRENTICESHIP: OPPORTUNITY FOR TRAINING

Apprenticeships for women should be explored, since many possibilities are opening up. According to a Manpower Research Monograph,[21] there are about 400 apprenticeship occupations in the skilled trades; examples of jobs in which women are succeeding are cooks, cosmetologists, barbers, lithographers, strippers and printers, bakers, television repairers, opticians, florists, watch repairers, draftsmen, sign painters, and musical instrument repairers. Apprenticeship requires a commitment to a specific period of combined on-the-job training and classroom work, usually for a minimum of two years. (It cannot be prepared for in full-time classroom situations.) A contract is signed which includes a salary with regular increases. After completion of the terms of the contract, the apprentice receives a certificate and is entitled to a full journeyman's salary.

As our society and the world of work become more technological, this type of training may be expanded to include even more specialized occupations such as dietetic cooks, medical-record techicians, and inhalation therapists.

During World War II the Department of Labor stated that few occupations were completely unsuitable for the employment of women (at that time, women were successfully operating cranes, tractors, and trucks, and working as riveters). Today the list of nontraditional jobs for women is growing again as pressures to allow them equal freedom of employment are increasing. Apprenticeships are certainly a logical consideration for the woman who is attracted to a nontraditional career and is willing to blaze some trails, especially if she is not interested in an academic degree.

EDUCATION PROGRAMS IN THE ARMED SERVICES

In time of peace, especially, the armed forces implement ways of providing education simultaneously with military service. The most recent plan is Project Ahead (Army Help for Education And Development), a College Entrance–Army Enlistment Program. The program offers an extension of "home" colleges and universities to men and women on active service who are stationed in the United States and throughout the world. Participating institutions admit a qualified person upon his or her enlistment in the Army. The school then provides counseling and records credits accumulated while the person is on active duty. (Admission policies and record-keeping practices may vary, since each school administers its own program.) The student participates in courses on or near Army posts, taught by fully qualified instructors from accredited postsecondary educational institutions. The educational institution is later a "home" for full-time studies as a veteran.

The Office on Educational Credit of the American Council on Education made a nine-month study of the feasibility of using the Army Enlisted Military Occupational Speciality (MOS) Classification System as a basis for both educational credit recommendations and advanced standing in apprentice training pro-

---

[21] *Women in Apprenticeship—Why Not?* Manpower Research Monograph no. 33.

grams. This implementation of recognition for on-the-job training, work experience, and independent learning may apply all the way up the ladder from vocational certificate to graduate degree.[22]

IMPACT OF EDUCATION

In the final analysis, your own motivation and determination will decide how far you want your education to take you. Nothing is better than your own ingenuity and enterprise in ferreting out special programs and educational opportunities in your own area. The local library, the women's division of the chamber of commerce, college and university information offices, and women's centers of information are good places to start finding out what is going on in your community. Judging by the length and breadth of the educational opportunities presented here, there is surely no reason for the working woman to feel unwanted in educational institutions or in the training centers of business and industry. Her goal may be to experiment in a nontraditional field, to upgrade her present skills, to add new ones, to finish a degree, or simply to continue her own personal growth and enrichment. Whatever her goal, as long as she is actively engaged in self-improvement and in broadening her perspective, she will find that she is becoming a more useful, more creative, and more interesting human being, to herself as well as to others.

The International Women's Year (1975) ended with the drawing up of an eleven-point program called the United States National Women's Agenda. Number two on its list of priorities is:

> Equal education and training (including enforcement of laws guaranteeing equal access to and treatment in all educational, vocational, and athletic programs and facilities, and the elimination of sex role, racial, and cultural stereotyping at every level of the educational system, including educational materials).

It appears that your future has the support of government as well as of individual women and women's groups. Finally, the one who benefits is you.

A woman may not have a fairy godmother; but the resources available to her are far better suited to the twentieth century. Given our conviction that we want control over our lives, the institutional innovations and the efforts of those who plan education combine to provide the vehicle for movement toward a fuller life.

SOURCES OF INFORMATION[23]

The examples of programs, typical and unusual, listed in this chapter are only a brief sampling. Every geographic area and community is different; it is necessary to seek infor-

---

[22] Jerry W. Miller, Director of Office on Educational Credit, American Council on Education, 1 Dupont Circle, Washington, D.C. 20036, will provide information about these expanded opportunities, which can save both time and money.

[23] The editorial assistance of Aurline Emmet in developing this chapter was invaluable.

mation locally regarding programs in which you are interested. You will find that the following are good local sources of information:

Colleges, universities, trade schools, school systems (both public and private)
State Department of Education
State Department of Employment
State Department of Labor
Employment training officer where you work
Professional or work-related organizations
Trade associations and trade publications (these will keep you abreast of a field in addition to giving you information about education programs)
Religious organizations such as the YWCA and B'nai B'rith
College alumna groups
Neighborhood counseling centers

In addition, information about national and local resources is available from the following:

Adult Education Association of the United States, 810 Eighteenth Street N.W., Washington, D.C. 20006
Adult Education Resource Center, Montclair State College, Upper Montclair, N.J. 07043.
American Association of University Women, 2401 Virginia Avenue N.W., Washington, D.C. 20037. Their List of Professional Women's Groups, August 1975, will give you names of people to contact, as well as addresses of most organizations which have a women's committee, caucus, commission, or task force. The list is large and impressive.
American Library Association, Adult Reference and Services Division, 50 East Huron Street, Chicago, Ill. 60611.
American Vocational Association, 1510 H Street N.W., Washington, D.C. 20005.
Association of American Colleges, Project on the Status and Education of Women, 1818 R Street N.W., Washington, D.C. 20009. Year-round research and publications relating to legal and governmental trends and actions and to issues important to all working women.
Association for Continuing Higher Education, Alban F. Varnado, President, University of New Orleans, New Orleans, La. 70122.
College Level Examination Program, P.O. Box 1824, Princeton, N.J. 08540.
Educational Resources Information Clearinghouse, Career Education, Northern Illinois University, De Kalb, Ill. 60115.
National Association of Black Adult Educators, Ernest A. Dow, Executive Director, 430 M Street S.W., Suite N206, Washington, D.C. 20024.
National Association for Public Continuing and Adult Education, 1201 Sixteenth Street N.W., Washington, D.C. 20036. In addition to a variety of other publications, the association publishes annually the *Public Continuing and Adult Education Almanac.*
National Home Study Council, 1601 Eighteenth Street N.W., Washington, D.C. 20009.
National University Extension Association, 1 Dupont Circle N.W., Washington, D.C. 20036.
U.S. Office of Education, 400 Maryland Avenue S.W., Washington, D.C. 20202. The

USOE supports a number of programs for adults. Queries may be addressed to the Commissioner of Education at the above address. *Note:* Each branch of the federal government also maintains some type of education or training for adults.

Women: A Select Bibliography, University of Michigan, University Library, Extension Service, 2360 Bonisteel Boulevard, Ann Arbor, Mich. 48105, 1975. Contains a diversified current listing of books, monographs, bibliographies, sources, newsletters, journals, media, and nonprint resources. Unannotated—names and addresses only.

Women's Bureau, Employment Standards Administration, U.S. Department of Labor, Washington, D.C., and regional offices. Many publications relating to women, their needs, and their educational opportunities. Example: *Get Credit for What You Know,* leaflet no. 56 (rev.), January 1974.

Chapter 22

How the Law Helps in Women's Employment

Kathryn G. Heath

Kathryn G. Heath, Ph.D., formerly Assistant for Special Studies, Office of Education, U.S. Department of Health, Education and Welfare, is now a consultant, lecturer, and writer. She has published in such journals as *American Education* and *Journal of the National Association for Women Deans, Administrators and Counselors* and has been responsible for Office of Education sections of many publications of the Department of Health, Education and Welfare and contributions by the Department or the Office to submissions by the United States government to international organizations. Her *Ministries of Education: Their Functions and Organization,* the result of a five-year study carried out with the cooperation of sixty-nine national governments, is unique.

The United States is a nation under law. Since 1964, the use of law to help women in employment has tended to mean using civil rights legislation to combat sex discrimination. This whole area, like racial discrimination, is emotionally charged and controversial. It is greatly influenced by cultural and social traditions; by the political and economic milieu; and by attitudes, beliefs, and value judgments. One complication is the difference between what conditions are, what some people think they are, and what others think they ought to be.

After the early settlers arrived in America, it was over 300 years before some legal prohibitions against sex discrimination were established. Even then, insensitivity to sex bias and foot-dragging by those in power made it difficult for women to get the legislation implemented. Bernice Sandler, speaking for the Women's Equity Action League (WEAL) on June 19, 1970, at a hearing in the House of Representatives on discrimination against women, succinctly stated why "massive" sex discrimination went "virtually unchecked, unnoticed, and unchallenged for so long." She said: "It is the last socially acceptable prejudice."

This chapter begins with an overview of the status of women before federal law began to include prohibitions against sex discrimination, and identifies a few of the laws which proved advantageous and others, intended to help women, which in fact worked against their interests as far as employment was concerned. Then developments of the last two decades are traced; the more significant legal mandates, and how they may be used in combating sex discrimination in the labor market, are discussed. The list of "Primary Resource Materials" on pages 389–390 will help readers locate the appropriate versions of laws (original or amended) for use in specific cases. The annotated bibliography on pages 390–392 cites sources which indicate the scope of the problems underlying actions to eradicate sex discrimination in employment.

BEFORE 1960

When the Constitution of the United States of America became operative in 1789, females had no rights and acquired none as "citizens" or as "persons." They were chattels without an established right to education or employment. If married, they normally could not own property, make contracts, sue in court, or even serve as legal guardians of their own children. If single, they were considered exceptions to the general rule, and laws for their special benefit were not contemplated.

Although civil and political rights tended to be the special prerogatives of a portion of the adult male population, from time to time women were incidental beneficiaries of some federal actions. Examples are the law of July 2, 1862, authorizing land grants; the law of March 2, 1867, establishing what came to be known as the Office of Education at the federal level; and the law of April 9, 1912, establishing the Children's Bureau. The first resulted in land-grant institutions of higher learning, which in time began to lower the barriers against women and thus broadened women's opportunities for education and for technical and professional employment. The second, by creating a federal entity for education in general, encouraged states to establish universal public education and opened the way for collection of data by the federal government on the educational preparation of females. The third, establishing the Children's Bureau, encouraged states to enact child-labor laws, which, in effect, freed more girls for schooling.

Later the Women's Bureau was established by a law of June 5, 1920. This created a means of exposing discriminatory practices which were keeping women on the bottom rungs of the employment ladder.

However, the federal government encouraged states to enact protective labor laws to improve the lot of working women. These well-intentioned but now disappearing state laws dealt with such matters as hours of work and weight lifting. In practice, they denied men the same protection and also served to exclude women as a class from most well-paying jobs and from overtime pay, promotions, and the like.

Sometimes individual women tried to break down barriers based on sex by challenging the constitutionality of laws when court actions were initiated for or against them. Either way they lost for many years. Tradition won before the all-male bar of justice, and women found themselves excluded from certain legal rights and benefits when courts interpreted state law to apply to men only or deemed federal constitutional provisions inapplicable or not violated in their cases. Other women used less formal means, and many were arrested. The following examples reflect what happened in formal and less formal struggles to improve the status of women.

Especially intimidating and damaging to women for more than a century was the failure of the Supreme Court of the United States to recognize any individual woman as a "person" entitled to "due process of law" and "equal protection of the laws" under the Fourteenth Amendment (added to the Constitution on July 20, 1868). The Court was unwilling to apply the Fourteenth Amendment when women's employment rights were at issue, although it did so for individual men, including aliens.

Specifically, on April 15, 1873, in *Bradwell v. The State,* the United States Supreme Court affirmed the judgment of the Illinois Supreme Court in denying Mrs. Bradwell's application to practice law although her character and professional qualifications were unchallenged. The Court held that there was no violation under the Fourteenth Amendment and, for that matter, none under section 2 of Article IV (on entitlement to "all Privileges and Immunities of Citizens in the several States").

The Illinois Supreme Court "regarded as an almost axiomatic truth" that "God designed the sexes to occupy different spheres of action, and that it belonged to men to make, apply, and execute the laws." The judgment of the Supreme Court of the United States includes a concurring opinion of three of the Justices which states: "The paramount destiny and mission of woman are to fulfill the noble and benign office of wife and mother. This is the law of the Creator." Only Chief Justice Salmon Portland Chase "dissented from the judgment of the court, and from all the opinions" which, for many years, so effectively barred most women from education, employment, and advancement in professional fields other than nursing and teaching.

In a franchise case—*United States v. Anthony*—Susan B. Anthony was arrested, tried, and convicted for voting in Rochester, New York, in the election of November 5, 1872. State law was interpreted as granting the franchise to men alone. Anthony's defense was based on the Fourteenth Amendment, but she lost in the U.S. Circuit Court on June 18, 1873. The decision of the Circuit Court effectively barred women in most states from use of the ballot box to encourage reform in employment or any other field for more than forty years.

Then Alice Paul conceived her strategy, which came to be known as militant nonviolent political action. For quietly picketing the White House to bring their cause to the attention of President Woodrow Wilson, women who were members of the National Woman's Party were attacked by men who tore down and trampled on their banners. The "Silent Sentinels," as they came to be known, refused to stop picketing, and were arrested, put in jail, and later force-fed after they went on a hunger strike to protest being treated as criminals rather than accorded the rights due political prisoners.

Like their more militant counterparts in England, these women refused to give up regardless of the indignities they suffered. As more of them were arrested, more came to picket in their places. Finally, the negative publicity could not be ignored by a nation at war to help save the world for democracy. The pickets were released from jail on November 27 and 28, 1917, and the President announced his support of woman's suffrage on January 9, 1918. The proposed Nineteenth Amendment cleared the Congress on June 4, 1919, for action in the states. Ratification by three-fourths of the states was completed on August 18, 1920, and the Amendment became a part of the fundamental law of the land when it was certified eight days later. Since August 26, 1920, sex alone no longer prevents women from voting in the nation.

In a labor law case—*Muller, Plaintiff in Error v. The State of Oregon*—relating to a law of 1903 prohibiting women from working more than ten hours a day, the Supreme Court held that sex is a valid basis for separate classification, and that rights under the Fourteenth Amendment were not involved. In other words, women as a class could be denied the protection of the Fourteenth Amendment when a protective labor law made no differentiation among them as a separate class.

In fact, it was only after the Civil Rights Act of 1964 became law that a substantial number of women, traditionally disadvantaged in the labor market, began to stand up for their employment rights despite ridicule, intimidation, reprisal, retribution, and—in most cases—considerable financial outlay. And it was November 22, 1971, before individual women were considered "persons" entitled to "equal protection of the laws." On that date, in *Reed v. Reed,* the Supreme Court found unconstitutional an Idaho statute which, because Mrs. Reed's husband was alive, automatically made him the one eligible to administer an estate. The Court made this judgment under the Fourteenth Amendment.

PRESIDENT'S COMMISSION ON THE STATUS OF WOMEN

Women had demonstrated their competence as workers during World War I and in World War II. But ability was not enough. Opportunity was also needed, and it ebbed away after hostilities ceased in 1945. Once again, men defined the role of women in sexist terms. Again, being female was an enormous handicap in the labor market.

President John F. Kennedy, who took office in 1961, all but ignored women when it came to his appointments. Smoldering anger caused some women to recruit Eleanor Roosevelt as their champion, and winds of change began to blow soon after she visited the White House. Executive Order 10980 (December 14, 1961) established the President's Commission on the Status of Women. This was a temporary body to review progress and make recommendations by October 1963. The work of the Commission encouraged the creation of other commissions—governors', county, and municipal—as well as what came to be known as the National Association of Commissions for women. Like the President's Commission, these bodies review progress and make recommendations. Some are statutory; all work for constructive action on a continuing basis. The Commission's report—*American Women*—was submitted to the President on October 11, 1963. It was supported by seven committee reports and summaries of four consultations; and it presented the first composite picture of the status of women in the United States as a whole. As was intended, the report was a basis for examination at the highest level, for policy development, and for programs. For example, it encouraged change in education to provide "practicable and accessible opportunities developed with regard to the needs of women."

Less than a month after the report was submitted, Executive Order 11126 (November 1, 1963) provided for an Interdepartmental Committee and a Citizen's Advisory Council on the Status of Women. Special reports, testimony on proposed legislation, and annual reports to the President attest to the Council's commitment to the elimination of sex bias and the improvement of the status of women.

During the deliberations of the President's Commission, *The Feminine Mystique,* by Betty Friedan, was published. In effect, it was this book which launched the modern women's liberation movement in the United States. At the same time, Commission members were pressing for enactment of a bill to provide equal pay for equal or similar work by men and women.

EQUAL PAY LEGISLATION (PUBLIC LAW 75–718; 29 U.S.C. 203, 206, 213)

After being introduced in every Congress since 1945, an equal pay standard was added on June 10, 1963, to others in the amended Fair Labor Standards Act of 1938. This amendment—the Equal Pay Act of 1963—aims to "prohibit discrimination on account of sex in the payment of wages by employers engaged in commerce." On June 23, 1972, the basic Act was further amended to extend coverage of the equal pay provisions to executive, administrative, and professional employees, including teachers. Related federal regulations to define and delimit these terms were published on May 7, 1973.

Legislative provisions call for the same pay for men and women doing work which is substantially the same and requires substantially equal skill, effort, and responsibility. Differentials in pay based on seniority are acceptable, as are differentials based on merit or systems measuring earnings by quantity or quality of production or factors other than sex.

How to File Complaints about Discrimination in Pay

Complaints about pay discrimination in employment covered by the law may be filed in person, by telephone, or by mail with the nearest Wage-Hour Office of the U.S. Department of Labor. To avoid reprisals against complainants, investigators reveal the source of a charge only when prior permission is given to do so. Most findings of violations are settled by negotiations between the Department of Labor and employers. However, the Department may take cases to court. In either event, the beneficiaries almost always are women.

TITLE VII OF THE CIVIL RIGHTS ACT OF 1964 (PUBLIC LAW 88–352; 42 U.S.C. 2000e ET SEQ.)

Provisions prohibiting sex discrimination were introduced in the House of Representatives in an attempt to defeat the bill which became the Civil Rights Act (July 2, 1964)—or in any case to defeat the portions of it which provided for equal employment. The attempt backfired in debate on February 8 and 10, 1964: Title VII on Equal Employment Opportunity prohibited discrimination in employment in the larger industries on grounds of sex as well as race, color, religion, and national origin.

In practice, however, the government concentrated on reducing racial bias. It demonstrated little interest in sex bias, although early charges by women in industry accounted for one-third of all the cases in which discrimination under title VII was alleged. Consequently, some women initiated court actions.

In *Weeks v. Southern Bell Telephone and Telegraph Company* (March 4, 1969) the U.S. Court of Appeals for the Fifth Circuit decided in favor of Lorena W. Weeks, who wanted to be a "switchman." This decision made possible an amendment (August 19, 1969) to the "Guidelines on Discrimination Because of Sex" (December 2, 1965). It narrows the interpretation which may be made of the phrase "sex as a bona fide occupational qualification."

The U.S. Court of Appeals for the Seventh Circuit included this interpretation in its judgment in *Bowe et al. v. Colgate-Palmolive Company* (September 26, 1969). Case law thus reinforces the narrow interpretation which, by inclusion in federal regulations, already had the force of law. Except in a few occupations, such as acting, women now can insist that they, like men, be considered on an individual basis rather than automatically denied employment because they are female.

Coverage under title VII was greatly expanded and the Equal Employment Opportunity Commission (EEOC) was given enforcement powers by the Equal Employment Opportunity Act of 1972 (March 24, 1972). Title VII is applicable to employers of fifteen or more employees; employment agencies; labor unions with fifteen or more members; labor-management apprenticeship programs; and private as well as public educational institutions.

The "Guidelines on Discrimination Because of Sex" were revised on April 5, 1972. They again narrowly interpret "sex as a bona fide occupational qualification," and they prohibit separate lines of progression (such as progression for women up to certain levels and a progression for men from those levels upward), separate seniority systems, discrimination against married women, advertising job openings under separate headings for males and females, discrimination in fringe benefits, and treating women as a class rather than as individuals in such matters as weight lifting, hours of work, and leave for childbirth.

How to File Charges under Title VII

Charges of discrimination under title VII may be filed in writing with EEOC by a complainant or on behalf of a complainant within 180 days after the alleged discrimination has occurred. Title VII covers discrimination in recruitment, employment, placement, conditions of work, insurance and other fringe benefits, training, promotion, seniority, enforced leave, layoffs, discharges, and the like. EEOC in Washington, or one of its thirty-two district offices, will notify the employer, employment agency, labor organization, or joint labor-management committee within ten days, citing the date, place, and circumstances of the alleged unlawful practice; but it does not make the charges public.

Where a state law or a city ordinance authorizes an authority to grant or seek relief or to institute legal proceedings, charges are referred for processing within sixty days (or 120 days if the agency has been operating less than one year). If action has not occurred in the specified time, jurisdiction returns to the Commission for processing of the complaint, and the sixty-first (or one hundred twenty-first) day becomes the official filing date of the charge. EEOC or any of its five commissioners may file charges. If efforts at conciliation are unsuccessful, EEOC may bring a civil action against the respondent unless a state or local government is involved. Then the case is referred to the U.S. Attorney General for civil action in the appropriate U.S. District Court. Preferably, a "Charge of Discrimination" form (available from any EEOC district office) should be used in filing a complaint, to ensure that sufficient pertinent information will be included for processing.

EXECUTIVE ORDERS 11246, 11375, AND 11478

In its report in 1963, the President's Commission on the Status of Women recommended advancing the principle of equal employment opportunity for women by an executive order relating to federal contracts. President Lyndon Johnson issued Executive Order 11246 under title VII on September 24, 1965, but it ignored sex discrimination in employment under federal contracts and federally assisted construction contracts as well as by the federal government itself.

The frustration of twenty-eight women leaders who attended the second Conference of Governors' Commissions on the Status of Women (June 1966) resulted in the formation of the National Organization for Women (NOW) on October 29, 1966. This was the first of many activist groups for women. (The address of the National NOW Action Center is Suite 1001, 425 Thirteenth Street N.W., Washington, D.C. 20004.) In 1971, it established a Legal Defense and Education Fund (9 West 57th Street, New York, N.Y. 10019) "for initiating and funding precedent-setting legal and education projects to free women and men from the shackles of discrimination."

NOW has grown rapidly. One of its initial successes, obtained by working through the existing power structure, is an amendatory executive order: Executive Order 11375 (October 13, 1967), which corrected the gross omission in Executive Order 11246 by inserting prohibitions against sex discrimination in federal contracts, federally assisted construction contracts, and the federal government itself. This was a major breakthrough for women. For women educators particularly, it constituted their first and only enforcement support for redress of sex bias in educational institutions having federal contracts.

The responsibility for enforcement is vested in the Secretary of Labor and rests with the Office of Federal Contract Compliance Programs in the U.S. Department of Labor. Responsibility has been redelegated to other departments and agencies to the extent of their areas of competence. All facilities of the contractor and subcontractor are covered if the employer has a federal contract of more than $10,000. Unlawful practices are the same as those under title VII of the Civil Rights Act of 1964. Related Revised Order No. 4 and later changes are published in title 41 of the Code of Federal Regulations as part 60-2. Contractors with fifty or more employees and a contract of $50,000 or more are required to have a written Affirmative Action plan in addition to taking affirmative action to set goals—not quotas—with timetables for the employment of women as well as members of minority groups.

The Federal Regulation on "Obligations of Contractors and Subcontractors" was amended on May 28, 1968, to prohibit sex discrimination. But the government moved with less than "all convenient speed" in issuing guidelines on sex discrimination under the amended Executive Order.

In November 1968, the Women's Equity Action League (WEAL) was formed. It spent a year gathering data on discrimination against women in institutions of higher learning and mapping its strategy for insisting on compliance with revised Executive Order 11246. (Its headquarters are in the National Press Building, Washington, D.C. 20004.)

On August 8, 1969, President Richard Nixon signed Executive Order 11478 on "Equal Employment Opportunity in the Federal Government." It supersedes those portions of revised Executive Order 11246 which were related to federal employees, calls for Affirmative Action plans and programs in the federal government, and vests responsibility for leadership and guidance in the U.S. Civil Service Commission.

By the fall of 1969, women had formed the first of many caucuses in professional societies to help accomplish one or more purposes. Particularly, they wanted an organized means of challenging the practices of professional bodies which expected them to pay full dues while usually ignoring them in nominating officers, in policy making, and in convention assignments. Through these caucuses women also sought to challenge discrimination against them in their professional employment.

On October 1, 1969, at the urging of Republican congresswomen, President

Nixon appointed his short-term Task Force on Women's Rights and Responsibilities. Its blunt and pertinent report—*A Matter of Simple Justice* (submitted to the President on December 15, 1969)—advised the President that the provisions in revised Executive Order 11246 regarding sex discrimination had not been implemented, although more than two years had elapsed since they had heen added by amendment. "It is imperative," the report stated, "that revised and updated guidelines be issued immediately and the Executive Order vigorously enforced."

The long-awaited "Sex Discrimination Guidelines" became a Federal Regulation on June 9, 1970, under amended Executive Order 11246—the same day the report of the President's Task Force was released to the press. Some government officials who had been apathetic over Senate hearings on the proposed Equal Rights Amendment (begun on May 5, 1970) found themselves scheduled to testify at the first Congressional hearings ever held on discrimination against women. The hearings opened on June 17, 1970, before the Special Subcommittee on Education of the House Committee on Education and Labor.

Two days earlier, the Department of Health, Education and Welfare had notified its regional Civil Rights Directors "that investigations of sex discrimination must be a part of all compliance reviews and that all affirmative action plans in the future must address themselves to overcoming patterns of sex discrimination."

How to Use Amended Executive Order 11246

WEAL did not wait for the revised guidelines to be issued. Its method became the model strategy for other organizations and for individuals in nonjudicial presentation of charges.

On January 31, 1970, WEAL used revised Executive Order 11246 as the basis for a letter to the Secretary of Labor filing charges of sex discrimination against the University of Maryland specifically and as a class action against all colleges and universities having federal contracts. Detailed supporting documentation was enclosed. In accordance with the revised order, WEAL requested that federal contract funds be withheld until the institutions took corrective action. Letters asking specific charges against several hundred institutions of higher learning were soon sent out by WEAL, on behalf of women educators, to the Secretaries of Labor and Health, Education and Welfare. On April 25, 1970, NOW filed charges against Harvard University. On October 5, 1970, WEAL sent a letter filing sex discrimination charges against all medical schools with federal contracts. The Professional Women's Caucus (P.O. Box 1057, Radio City Station, New York, New York 10019) was established on April 11, 1970, to provide expertise in any professional field to deal with women's problems. It filed charges on March 26, 1971, against all law schools having federal contracts.

How to Use Executive Order 11478

The U.S. Civil Service Commission issued instructions and suggestions to heads of departments and independent establishments on December 30, 1969 (Commission Bulletin No. 713–12), for development and submission of Affirmative

Action plans by January 30, 1970. Under these various plans, employees may consult on procedures with employment counselors and file written complaints of sex discrimination with their Equal Employment Opportunity Office or with another designated body for investigation, negotiation, and decision.

When the employees deem the result unsatisfactory, they are entitled to an impartial hearing and an internal, impartial review of the action considered unfavorable. If employees are still not satisfied with the result, they may appeal to the Commission for review and decision. They also may take their cases to court.

At the time of this writing, a new plan for federal employees was being developed by the Commission as a result of a court order. It provides for "consolidation of individual complaints of discrimination and/or reprisal." Such a class action may be assembled at the discretion of the employer (who combines several like complaints) or the complainant. Details of the procedure will be published in volume 41 of the Federal Register as subpart F of 5 Code of Federal Regulations 713.

INCREASES IN ACTIONS FAVORABLE FOR WOMEN

On January 25, 1971, the Supreme Court ruled in *Phillips v. Martin-Marietta Corporation.* In this case, the corporation held that it had refused to consider Ida Phillips for employment not because she was a woman but because she was the mother of children under school age. The Court ruled against this "sex plus" interpretation of equal-employment-opportunity law, holding that the law forbids different hiring policies for mothers and fathers of children below school age. Women no longer can be denied employment solely because they are mothers of young children, unless fathers of such children are also denied employment.

Public Law 92–65 (August 5, 1971) was the beginning of a growing list of laws including a prohibition of sex discrimination in specific programs receiving federal assistance—public works, economic development, water-pollution control, revenue sharing, military service, and the like. Among such laws, those concerned with education and training in a wide range of career fields are particularly far-reaching and significant. An example is Public Law 92–157 (November 18, 1971) amending the Public Health Service Act. It includes provisions prohibiting sex bias in admission to schools and training centers in medical and allied health fields that want to receive federal funds (and such institutions *do* want federal funds).

Thus the law put higher education on the defensive where women's rights are concerned. Some 1,400 colleges, universities, and hospitals found it necessary to give women an equal chance to prepare for careers in medical and allied health fields. As Alan Pifer, President of the Carnegie Corporation, put it in his address on "Women in Education" to the Southern Association of Colleges and Schools on November 29, 1971, a few days after the law was enacted: "Without the threat of coercion, it seems unlikely higher education would have budged an inch on this issue. Certainly it had every chance to do so and failed."

Again, there was a delay in promulgating federal regulations. Part of the trouble came in this instance because of a long controversy over the development of federal regulations relating to sex discrimination in the field of education as a whole. The specialized Regulations on "Sex Discrimination in Health Related Fields" were published on July 7, 1975, and became effective on August 6, 1975—nearly four years after the pertinent legislation was enacted.

Public Law 92–496 (October 14, 1972) expanded the jurisdiction of the fifteen-year-old Civil Rights Commission to include sex discrimination. The initial investigations of the Commission in this area offer little reason to praise the implementation of laws against sex bias; but its appraisal of laws and policies of the federal government is spotlighting instances where equal protection of the laws is denied because of sex.

Other legislative actions, in addition to the amendments to title VII of the Civil Rights Act of 1964, made 1972 an important year for women. They relate to equal rights in general and to equal rights in education in particular. In 1973 some major judicial actions began to put more money in the pockets of many working women.

EQUAL RIGHTS AMENDMENT

Beginning in the 68th Congress in 1923, the National Woman's Party (under the leadership of Alice Paul) led women's groups in getting members of each Congress to introduce joint resolutions proposing an Equal Rights Amendment (ERA) to the Constitution. After forty-nine years of effort, the proposal cleared the Congress on March 22, 1972, and went to the states for ratification. When thirty-eight states have ratified it, it will be added to the Constitution as an article specifying: "Equality of rights under the law shall not be denied or abridged by the United States or by any State on account of sex." Individual states and the national government will then have two years to rid their legislation of sex bias before the Amendment becomes operative. Some of the states, like the federal government, are getting a head start.

By contrast with the Fourteenth Amendment, which offers protection against abuse of existing rights, ERA will *add* a right: equality for the sexes. It applies to governmental action by establishing the legal underpinning for equal standing for men and women before administrative bodies and courts.

It *does not* hold that men and women are the same; hence it does not promote unisexism. It will *not* upset the principle of privacy in certain facilities, a principle which is implied by the Constitution and which has been upheld by the Supreme Court. Nor will it intrude on private relationships between husband and wife, or parent and child.

In fact, it will not render unconstitutional any law which differentiates on grounds other than sex. Only legislation discriminating against one sex will fall. Any law conferring a benefit (such as property rights) or fixing an obligation (such as jury duty or service to the nation) on only one sex will have to be extended to the other sex as well.

ERA will signal a national commitment to eliminate sex bias. It is the overall proposal, meant to obviate women's need to challenge discriminatory laws one by one, usually at considerable emotional and financial cost, to secure the same rights that men (the minority in the population) have considered their just due. ERA is a "matter of simple justice."

TITLE IX OF THE EDUCATION AMENDMENTS OF 1972 (PUBLIC LAW 92–318; 20 U.S.C. 1681 ET SEQ.)

Title IX of the June 23 Education Amendments of 1972, on "Prohibition of Discrimination," is a response to needs revealed in the hearings on discrimination against women in the House of Representatives and on the Equal Rights Amendment in the Senate in 1970.

With exceptions on admission to certain types of institutions, title IX states: "No person in the United States shall, on the basis of sex, be excluded from participation in, be denied the benefits of, or be subjected to discrimination under any education program or activity receiving Federal financial assistance."

Title IX also amended pertinent provisions in other laws. Prohibition of discrimination on the ground of sex was added to title IV on "Desegregation of Public Education" in the Civil Rights Act of 1964. And the coverage of the provisions regarding pay in the amended Fair Labor Standards Act of 1938 was extended to equalize pay of women and men in executive, administrative, and professional posts, including teaching.

Title IX was a controversial proposal in the House of Representatives and in the Senate. After enactment, it continued to be controversial as efforts were made over a two-year period to get sufficient support to take the first regulatory step by issuing the Proposed Rule for public comment; it was issued on July 20, 1974. Then an unprecedented number of written comments were received—nearly 10,000 sets—and considered, and countless consultations were held, before the new draft was approved by the President and published in the Federal Register on June 4, 1975, as the Federal Regulation (provided that the Congress interposed no objection within forty-five days).

The Regulation became operative on July 21, 1975 (part 86 of title 45 of the Code of Federal Regulations), despite concerted efforts by a few members of Congress to force it back for redrafting in keeping with their views or to gut part of title IX, on which it is based. Interim enforcement procedures are those established under title VI on "Nondiscrimination in Federally Assisted Programs" of the Civil Rights Act of 1964. Under title IX, women may file individual written complaints of sex bias with the Office of Civil Rights (OCR) in the Department of Health, Education and Welfare.

PROCEDURE FOR CIVIL RIGHTS ENFORCEMENT

A Proposed Rule was published in the Federal Register on June 4, 1975, as part 81 of title 45 of the Code of Federal Regulations, calling for a consolidated procedural approach to all the statutory civil rights responsibilities of the U.S. Department of Health, Education and Welfare. On September 29, 1975, controversy over this Proposed Rule resulted in a reopening of the period for public comment for forty-five days. The issue was whether to approach the solution to sex bias by identifying and eliminating systematic discrimination or by continuing with a complaint-oriented approach to secure individual relief for persons suffering from discrimination.

For the enforcing agency, the problem is one of having a manageable workload which will produce relief for the largest number in the shortest time. For the woman who suffers from sex discrimination, it is the resolution of her own problem which counts.

On March 16, 1976, the Secretary of Health, Education and Welfare announced that public comment on the Proposed Rule from "every organized civil rights group," other organizations "representing every point of view on the political spectrum," and individuals, "was overwhelmingly negative." Concern centered on individual citizens' having "no assurance of a response by the Department to complaints of unlawful discrimination." He withdrew the Proposed Rule in view of this "strong, clearly articulated public feeling" and enunciated the Department's policy "to seek a timely resolution of every complaint it receives."

The President's proposed budget for the fiscal year October 1, 1976–September 30, 1977, recommended funding for 150 additional positions to help fulfill the Department's responsibility. Even if the Congress approves, the Secretary pointed out, the augmented staff in OCR "will find it difficult to cope with the backlog and the rising volume of new complaints." Therefore, the Department published a "series of interrogatories" in the Federal Register (41 F.R. 18393, May 3, 1976) seeking public participation in the development of new approaches to civil rights enforcement and requested comments by July 2, 1976.

Before that date, a revised Order (Civil Action No. 3095-70) of the United States District Court for the District of Columbia was handed down on June 14, 1976, in a long-standing lawsuit *(Adams v. Mathews)* relating to discrimination on the basis of sex as well as race, color, and national origin in elementary and secondary schools in the seventeen Southern and border states. Precedent-setting new specific timetables for handling complaints and clearing up the backlog by October 1, 1977, were spelled out by the Order when plaintiffs (including WEAL) and the federal government failed to agree on a procedural format, as distinct from substantive issues that were already agreed upon.

The timetable for handling complaints specifies that OCR will (1) evaluate a complaint and reply within fifteen days of its receipt, (2) complete its investigation and determine within 105 days whether there has been a violation of civil rights, (3) complete its efforts to achieve compliance within 195 days if there is a violation, and (4) if negotiation fails, initiate formal enforcement procedures within 225 days or refer the case to the Department of Justice for legal proceedings. OCR issued a press release the next day announcing that the terms of the Order will be applied in all fifty states in the interests of uniform national policy. It also stated that the Order "does not pre-empt the action" dated May 3, 1976, which invited public comment on procedural rules for enforcement of those civil rights statutes which the Department administers.

CONSENT DECREES IN LIEU OF LITIGATION

The first of a growing number of Equal Employment Opportunity Agreements was signed on January 18, 1973, for recording as a Consent Decree in District Court in Philadelphia in lieu of litigation and judicial decision. This had important implications for industry.

Specifically, the largest private employer in the nation—American Telephone and Telegraph Company and its twenty-four Bell System Companies—agreed to make a multimillion-dollar one-time settlement giving back pay to women and members of minority groups who had been discriminated against in rates of pay; to adjust their present pay to bring it up to levels paid to others for equal work; to open more training and employment to them; and to revise promotion policies to bring these employees into the mainstream of the company.

This agreement was the model for others. For example, one was signed on April 15, 1974, with nine steel companies. Another was signed on June 8, 1974, with Bank of America, where 75 percent of the employees were women and almost none were officers. A unique feature of the latter is the bank's agreement to establish a $3.5 million trust fund for women employees for training, education, travel, sabbatical leaves, and other self-development programs commonly offered to men in banking.

These decrees are moving into many areas where low status for women has been perpetuated. For example, departmental seniority systems are falling in favor of industry systems; as a result, women may move from years of service in low-grade clerical positions to technical and professional posts in the same company without having to go to the bottom of the seniority list. Percentage limits on salary raises are also being removed, to prevent the widening of the pay gap between higher-paid men and lower-paid women doing the same or similar work.

EDUCATIONAL EQUITY (PUBLIC LAW 93-380, SEC. 408; 20 U.S.C. 1866)

Between July 25 and September 13, 1973, the House Subcommittee on Equal Opportunities held hearings on the proposed Women's Educational Equity Act; and on October 17 and November 9, 1973, the Senate held its hearings. This act became law on August 21, 1974, as part of the Education Amendments of 1974. It authorizes grants and contracts for a range of programs to promote educational equity, and thus can be expected to influence equity in employment. The related Federal Regulation (part 160 of title 45 of the Code of Federal Regulations) governing awards of the grants and contracts was published in the Federal Register on February 13, 1976 (41 F.R. 6420).

THE TASK AHEAD

Rare is the individual, institution, or association willingly ceding or sharing a traditional privilege taken at the expense of others. There are those who will lobby the Congress to water down legislation on sex discrimination, particularly when special interests are involved. There are those speaking and writing against ratification of the Equal Rights Amendment, on specious grounds which have been invalidated by law or upset by the courts. There also are difficult problems, still far from satisfactorily resolved, for employed women. Among them are a woman's status when she becomes pregnant and the need for satisfactory child care.

Vigilance and appropriate action to disseminate facts are needed to assure fair and equitable treatment for women. Women are on their way. They have organized, girded themselves for the task, and sought the cooperation of men in the interests of equity for women and men in the future. They have earned the right to support for their cause, and they intend to succeed.

PRIMARY RESOURCE MATERIALS

Published by the U.S. Government Printing Office, Washington, D.C. 20402, except as otherwise noted under "Judicial Acts."

Code of Federal Regulations: Federal Regulations arranged by title (3 The President, 29 Labor, etc.); codified to take account of changes, and listed by part number with subject.

Congressional Record: Proceedings and debates of the Congress of the United States with daily edition bearing volume, *issue,* and page numbers and day and date; and bound edition bearing volume, *part* (covering specified dates), and page numbers, which differ from those in the daily edition.

Federal Register: Federal Regulations (Executive Orders and Regulations applicable to department and agency programs) to implement law and having the force of law, Proposed Rules, and official Notices; published five days a week exclusive of holidays.

Judicial Acts: Federal case law with early Circuit and District cases in *Federal Cases;* later ones in *Federal Supplement;* and those in United States Courts of Appeals in *Federal Reporter, Second Series,* West Publishing Company, St. Paul, Minn. Early Supreme Court cases in *Cases Argued and Adjudged in the Supreme Court of the United States,* The Banks Law Publishing Company, New York; and later ones in *United States Reports.*

Legislative History Content: Messages from the President proposing or opposing legislation and signing bills into law or vetoing them; and bills and resolutions in the House of Representatives and Senate and related hearings, committee reports, floor proceedings, debates, and Conference reports on differences between House and Senate. A consolidated legislative history may be issued, as was done by the Equal Employment Opportunity Commission and the Department of Justice on title VII of the Civil Rights Act of 1964.

Opinions of the Attorney General: Official legal advice to the President and heads of departments and agencies in relation to their official duties; published individually and then by date in consecutive volumes.

United States Code: The Constitution; and public laws arranged by title (20 Education, 29 Labor, etc.) codified to incorporate changes; with an index of popular names of laws facilitating location when number and date are not known; published every six years with intervening annual supplements codifying changed portions.

United States Statutes at Large: Public laws published individually as enacted are compiled by number and session of Congress and organized in order of date under laws or under resolutions.

Weekly Compilation of Presidential Documents: Executive orders, proclamations, addresses and remarks, messages to the Congress, nominations, appointments, lists of legislative enactments and press releases, and other Presidential materials.

BIBLIOGRAPHY

All sources are published by the U.S. Government Printing Office, Washington, D.C. 20402, except as noted under Friedan.

Friedan, Betty: *The Feminine Mystique,* Norton, New York, 1963. This book sparked the modern women's liberation movement in the United States. It presents the discrepancy between the reality of women's lives and the image to which women were trying to conform.

Hearings

Congress of the United States, Joint Economic Committee: *Economic Problems of Women* (July 10–12, 24–26, and 30, 1973, in 93d Congress, 1st Session), 1973, Part 1; Part 2; Part 3. These hearings focus on economic discrimination in employment, earnings, credit, insurance, taxes, Social Security, and transfer programs.

House of Representatives Committee on Education and Labor, Ad Hoc Subcommittee on Discrimination against Women: *Oversight Hearings on Discrimination against Women* (April 26–27 and May 3 and 10, 1972, in 92d Congress, 2d Session), 1973. These hearings center on sex discrimination in the Office of Education and under its Grant and Contract Procedures.

———, Special Subcommittee on Education: *Discrimination against Women* (June 17, 19, 26, 29–30, and July 1 and 31, 1970, in 91st Congress, 2d Session), 1971, Part 1; Part 2. These, the first Congressional hearings ever held on sex discrimination, relate to section 805 (Prohibition of Discrimination) in H.R. 16098 (Omnibus Postsecondary Education Act of 1970). The Act did not pass, but the hearings are part of the legislative history leading to title IX (Prohibition of Sex Discrimination) in the June 23 Public Law 92–318 (Education Amendments of 1972).

———, Subcommittee on Equal Opportunities: *The Women's Educational Equity Act* (July 25–26 and September 12–13, 1973, in 93d Congress, 1st Session), 1973. These hearings relate to H.R. 208, to authorize the Secretary of Health, Education and Welfare to make grants to conduct special educational programs and activities designed to achieve educational equity. H.R. 208 and revisions—H.R. 10133 and H.R. 11149— were introduced by Patsy Mink as a follow-up of her H.R. 14451 in the 92d Congress. The result (August 21) is section 408 (Women's Educational Equity Act of 1974) in Public Law 93–380 (Education Amendments of 1974).

United States Senate Committee on Labor and Public Welfare, Subcommittee on Education: *Women's Educational Equity Act of 1973* (October 17 and November 9, 1973, in 93d Congress, 1st Session), 1973. The result of these hearings on S. 2518—a bill identical to H.R. 208—came on August 21 in section 408 (Women's Educational Equity Act of 1974) in Public Law 93–380 (Education Amendments of 1974).

United States Senate Committee on the Judiciary: *Equal Rights 1970* (September 9–11 and 15, 1970, in 91st Congress, 2d Session), 1970. These hearings, with Sam J. Ervin, Jr.—

an implacable foe of the Equal Rights Amendment—presiding, center on the constitutional system and the "various merited rights [such as protective labor legislation] and exemptions upon women" that he felt would not obtain if the Equal Rights Amendment (first passed by the House on August 10, 1970) were added to the Constitution.

————, Subcommittee on Constitutional Amendments: *The "Equal Rights" Amendment* (May 5–7, 1970, in 91st Congress, 2d Session), 1970. These hearings, with Birch Bayh—a sponsor of the Amendment—in the chair, were announced "to begin an all-out effort to secure a long overdue objective—equal rights under the law for men and women."

Reports

Citizens' Advisory Council on the Status of Women: *Women in 1975,* March 1976. Like earlier annual reports to the President, this sample details developments for the year and presents recommendations for action relating to women. Featured subjects are: International Women's Year, Equal Rights Amendment, employment, Social Security, education, credit and banking, media, female offenders, homemakers and the family, child care, rape, Public Law 94-167 (December 23, 1975) authorizing a National Women's Conference, Congressional Clearing House on Women's Rights (for the use of Senators and Representatives in their work and in helping their constituents), and indexes to Council recommendations in reports for the years 1970 through 1975 and to Council publications in the same six years.

National Commission on the Observance of International Women's Year: ". . . *To Form a More Perfect Union . . ."—Justice for American Women,* June 1976. This report under Executive Order 11832 (January 9, 1975) as amended by Executive Order 11889 (November 25, 1975) sketches the history of the women's movement; identifies "today's realities," including "strong laws and weak enforcement"; indicates where women are heading; makes 115 recommendations for legislative and other governmental and nongovernmental action in fifteen major areas including employment and such related areas as training and child care; and, in an appendix, offers a bibliography and a "revealing compilation" of pertinent legislative and statistical data. (The report was presented to the President in a ceremony attended by some 900 people on July 1, 1976. At that time, the President said that the correction of injustices caused by discrimination against women cannot wait for ratification of ERA. Accordingly, he ordered the Attorney General to coordinate a sweeping review of federal laws and regulations to determine the "need for revising sex-based provisions.")

President's Commission on the Status of Women: *American Women,* October 11, 1963. This report to the President, under Executive Order 10980 establishing the Commission, is an invitation to action relating to employment policies and practices, federal social insurance and tax laws, federal and state labor laws, differences in legal treatment of men and women, new and expanded services for women, and employment policies and practices of the federal government. Its recommendations are supported by committee reports in seven areas and by summaries of consultations on private employment, volunteer work, portrayal of women by the mass media, and problems of Negro women. The following publications of the Commission are the supporting reports: *Civil and Political Rights,* 1964; *Education,* 1964; *Federal Employment,* 1963; *Home and Community,* 1963; *Private Employment,* 1964; *Protective Labor Legislation,* 1963; *Social Insurance and Taxes,* 1963; *Report on Four Consultations,* 1963.

President's Task Force on Women's Rights and Responsibilities: *A Matter of Simple Justice*, 1970. This report to the President by his Task Force (appointed on October 1, 1969) was made on December 13, 1969, printed in April 1970, and released to the press on June 9, 1970, during the celebration of the fiftieth anniversary of the Women's Bureau. "Sex Discrimination Guidelines" under amended Executive Order 11246 became a Federal Regulation on June 9, 1970, in response to one of its recommendations. Among other recommendations are those calling for a White House Office and Conference relating to women; an Office of Education Unit relating to women; messages to the Congress in support of the Equal Rights Amendment, amendments to various laws (Civil Rights Acts of 1957 and 1964, amended Fair Labor Standards Act of 1938, and Social Security Act), child-care bills, and financing of State Commissions on the Status of Women; and as much concern by the federal government for sex discrimination as for racial discrimination. (Most of the recommendations have been or are being carried out. Instead of the recommended White House Conference, Public Law 94-167 of December 23, 1975, authorizes a National Women's Conference after state or regional meetings in 1976. After the Conference identifies barriers to women and sets timetables for action, it is to take steps to provide for a second National Women's Conference to assess progress.)

Chapter 23

Legal Rights and Prospects: Property, Inheritance, and Credit

Riane Tennenhaus Eisler

Riane Tennenhaus Eisler, J.D., is a lawyer and Founding Director of the Women's Center Legal Program of Los Angeles. A writer and lecturer, she has published articles in *Women's Rights Law Reporter, Social Action,* and *Everywoman.* She is the author of *Dissolution* (McGraw-Hill, New York, 1977).

In 1972 Ralph Nader wrote an article for *McCalls* called "How You Lose Money by Being a Woman." In it he explained how, owing partly to the unequal treatment of men and women under our laws, the approximately 7.5 million widows and unmarried women over sixty-five in the United States constitute the single poorest segment of our society.[1]

What can today's woman do to avoid taking the old routes that lead to this unhappy destination?

One important step is to become much more aware of our laws, in order to change the bad ones and also to take better advantage of the good ones.

---

[1] Ralph Nader, "How You Lose Money by Being a Woman," *McCalls,* January 1972.

Today, for the first time in Anglo-American jurisprudence, there is a strong trend toward treating adult women as independent, self-sufficient, and capable economic entities—in short, as our laws of property have traditionally treated men. This is in sharp contrast to the bulk of our earlier laws, which, rather than focusing on women's relationship to their property, basically approached the subject by defining women themselves as property.[2]

Although at first glance the comparison may seem extreme, throughout much of the nineteenth century, the position of women in our society was in many respects like that of slaves before the Civil War. In most American states, neither slaves nor women could hold office, serve on juries, or bring suit in their own names; and married women could not hold or convey property, make contracts, work outside their homes or retain any earnings from such work without their husbands' permission, or even serve as legal guardians of their own children.[3]

Since marriage was the main, and often only, career open to the vast majority of middle- and upper-class women—the women who would have any property to be concerned with in the first place—our laws effectively deprived most women of any real and active property rights.

Even today, when many of the more glaring legal discriminations against women have been or are in the process of being repealed, any discussion of women's property rights has to make a sharp distinction between the woman who is married and the one who is not.

In this chapter, I will examine separately the property rights of single, married, divorced, and widowed women, focusing on the legal characteristics of each group. I will also discuss some of the issues and problems that typically arise in the transition from singleness to marriage, and from marriage to divorce or widowhood, emphasizing how to plan these transitions from the standpoint of property rights. Wherever possible, specific practical matters will be dealt with. However, between the complexity of the subject, the limitations of space, and the enormous legal variations from state to state, the basic objective of this chapter can only be to give the reader a general introduction to and orientation in a legal area that affects and determines much of our daily lives but is all too often ignored.

SINGLE WOMEN

In legal theory, if not so much in practice, for the most part single adult women have the same property rights and obligations as adult men.

The customary property rights and duties of adults—such as the right to sell, buy, and mortgage real and personal property; the duty to repay borrowed money; and the right to control and manage wages, profits, or inheritances—general-

[2] See, e.g., William Blackstone, *Commentaries* (19th London ed.), vol. I, Lippincott, Philadelphia, 1908.
[3] See, e.g., D. Binder and R. Eisler, Brief for the Western Center on Law and Poverty and the Los Angeles Women's Center, as Amicus Curiae, *Perez v. Campbell,* 402 U.S. 637 (1970).

ly derive from two related and basic property rights: the right to legally hold and control property, and the right to freely enter into contracts.

There are for the most part no sexual distinctions as to the age when a person is legally considered to be old enough to hold property or to enter into a binding contract. Formerly, adulthood was defined as the age of twenty-one; but today the trend is toward making eighteen the legal age of maturity, and this is already the law in approximately two-thirds of the states.

At the point when a woman, or man, becomes legally recognized as an independent economic agent, some understanding of our laws of property is required, not only in order to invest money and manage property but also in order to carry out the many business dealings of everyday life. There are such matters as the legal requirements for a binding contract, the lawful interest rate for lending, and the use of a homestead as a protection against creditors, all of which will vary according to the laws of each particular state. There are many other legal issues, such as the availability of legal tax shelters and loopholes to minimize taxes; and there are also a myriad of legal procedures and business conventions and practices, such as how to stop a check, register a car, sell a parcel of land, or collect a debt, which anyone who owns any property should learn.

The single woman faces all the same legal situations and problems as a man, but in addition there are also a few that are peculiar to her status.

For instance, there are still some laws that treat single women and single men unequally. One glaring example is the fact that traditionally under our laws women are permitted to marry at an earlier age than men. Today approximately one-fifth of our states still permit girls to marry before boys without parental consent, and almost one-half of our states permit women to marry earlier than men with parental consent—usually at sixteen rather than eighteen years of age. There appears to be little rational basis for permitting women to enter into what is probably the most important contract they will ever make in their lives at a younger age than men. Some feminists hold that these laws seem to be remnants of a legal and social view of the sexes that would imply giving more protection to boys than to girls from marrying rashly, presumably on the rationale that girls do not have anything else to do with their lives anyway.

The view that women's main purpose is to marry, which is to some degree internalized by both women and men, is part of the traditional, "feminine" personal and economic dependence of women on men in our society. It is one of the unstated rationalizations for many of the discriminatory social conventions and business practices women still have to contend with, as well as for women's general lack of experience and exposure to the financial world, which has until recently been the exclusive province of men.

Once a woman recognizes that the responsibility for her financial affairs is really hers, she is well on the road toward overcoming many of these obstacles. By becoming more informed about laws and business practices, she can demand and obtain better—and less patronizing—legal and financial counsel. And perhaps most important, she will be able to plan ahead.

MARRIED WOMEN

Sound, informed planning is part of the process of making the multitude of legal and business decisions that must be made in order to properly invest one's money or just manage one's property on a day-to-day basis. It is also essential in making the very important transition from singleness to marriage, particularly since for many women that transition will eventually lead to still another one—either divorce or widowhood—where the consequences of the traditional unplanned romantic approach can be some very severe economic problems.

Under the early British common law, when a man and a woman married they legally became one person under the law, and that one person was the husband.[4] The vast majority of American states derived their marriage laws from Britain and are therefore governed by what is still known as the common law, even though much of it has by now been codified into statutory law rather than just case law. In eight of our states—Arizona, California, Idaho, Louisiana, Nevada, New Mexico, Texas, and Washington—marriage laws were modeled after those of Spain and France, and here the community property system, which at least in theory views marriage as an equal partnership, prevails.

Name and Domicile

In both community-property and common-law states, when a woman marries she loses her legal and economic identity in two important ways. Although only a handful of states have laws specifically requiring this, when a woman marries she legally assumes her husband's name. Furthermore, under the common law and the statutory law of most states, she must give up her legal domicile for that of her husband.

Besides their psychological and symbolic significance, the loss of a woman's name and domicile have some very direct economic consequences. As far as the former is concerned, there is the loss or failure to establish credit in one's own name. As for the latter, there are such practical issues as the loss of lower tuition rates for state residents at state educational institutions, eligibility for welfare, and other possibly disadvantageous results in such areas as taxation, probate, guardianship, and the legal residence required for purposes of divorce.

Marriage Contracts

Today, an increasing number of women are retaining their own names—and lines of credit—when they marry, and this practice is slowly being recognized by the business community. From a legal standpoint, a clause in a marriage contract to the effect that the woman will keep her name probably has a fairly good chance of standing up in court. This is so particularly in those states where either there is no precedent on the subject, or the loss of the woman's name is based solely on "established custom" rather than specific statutory law. The situation is somewhat more difficult when it comes to the matter of domicile, since the majority of our state laws specifically deny a woman the right to maintain her own domicile

[4] See, e.g., B. Crozier, "Marital Support," 15 B.U.L. Rev. 28 (1915).

when she marries. But even here the legal argument that a husband and wife should be entitled to make their own agreement can be made.

Marriage is, of course, always a contract. Whether a couple are aware of it or not, their relationship is always governed by the statutory and case law of their particular state. In most states, spouses are legally authorized to make some variations on the contract imposed by law by entering into an agreement of their own, either before or during the marriage.

Prenuptial marriage contracts dealing with property have been employed for centuries by royalty and families of great wealth. Even the type of egalitarian marriage contract that some couples are using today to deal with both economic and noneconomic matters has been employed before by such women as Lucy Stone, Mary Woolstonecraft, and Amelia Earhart. The economic provisions of these contemporary marriage contracts usually deal with the rights and obligations of spouses with respect to such matters as the ownership and control of property and the management of income and expenses during the marriage, and sometimes also in the event of a separation or divorce.

Whether a particular marriage contract will stand up in court is a complex and uncertain matter that will vary from case to case and from state to state. There have in the past been a number of decisions holding that if a contract is against traditional "public policy" (that is, contrary to traditionally accepted views of the marital relationship), or "in contemplation of divorce," it will not be enforced. There are, however, a number of more recent cases indicating a newer and less restrictive judicial view to the effect that every couple should as far as possible be entitled to make their own contract. In the light of our contemporary social realities of marriage and divorce, this approach should in the long run prevail.[5]

Common Law and Community Property

A strong case can be made that many of today's marriage laws are archaic. As late as 1966, the Supreme Court of the United States upheld a Texas statute denying a married woman the legal capacity to enter into a binding contract on her own.[6] That law has since been repealed, but unfortunately other economic discriminations remain, both in the forty-two states and the District of Columbia that have common-law systems governing property in marriage and in the eight states with community-property laws.

In both community-property and common-law states, as a general system of classification, there are two kinds of property owned by husbands and wives. One is separate property—property that belongs exclusively to a husband or wife—and the second is property which by law or agreement belongs to both spouses.

Under the community-property system, all property acquired before the marriage, as well as gifts and inheritances acquired after marriage, is separate property as long as it is kept separately—that is, unless it is put in the other

---

[5] For a comprehensive discussion of marriage contracts see L. Weitzman, "Legal Regulation of Marriage, Tradition and Change," 62 CAL. LAW REVIEW 1169.

[6] *U.S. v. Yazell,* 335 U.S. 464 (1966).

spouses's name or otherwise "comingled" with the community property. However, all earnings, investments, or accumulations from earnings after marriage are with a few minor exceptions the community property of both spouses, regardless of whose name they are in.

This is very different from the system of the common-law states, where everything a husband or wife earns and accumulates during the marriage is her or his separate property, unless it is specifically placed in the other spouse's name. One way of doing this is by making a gift to one's spouse. Another, more common, method is to hold the property jointly, either as tenants in common or as joint tenants—the main difference between the two being that under the latter arrangement the survivor automatically inherits the other's share.

Some legal observers believe that in practice the distinction between the common-law and community-property systems has been somewhat exaggerated.[7] One reason is that so many couples in common-law jurisdictions hold assets as joint tenants or tenants in common. Another is that until very recently, even in community-property states, the husband had exclusive management and control of the community property during the marriage. In anticipation of the proposed Equal Rights Amendment, which would invalidate laws discriminating on the basis of sex, Texas, Washington, and California have already amended their laws so that now "either" or "both" of the spouses have legal management and control. Since much depends on how these new laws are interpreted and enforced, it is very important that wives in these states acquaint themselves with the newly amended laws, to make sure they are respected by the business and financial establishments of their communities, and of course also by their spouses.

Support

In about half our states wives and husbands are required to support each other; but in the other half only the husband is required to support his wife. However, in practice it is debatable whether that discrimination against husbands means very much, since traditionally our courts have refused, as they put it, "to intervene in such matters while a marriage is still intact."[8]

One example is *McGuire v. McGuire,* one of the few reported cases where a wife actually sued her husband for support. The action was brought in 1953 by a housewife in Nebraska who alleged in her complaint that she had been married thirty-four years to a well-to-do farmer, "had worked in the fields, did outside chores, cooked and attended to her household duties, raised as high as 300 chickens, sold poultry and eggs, and used the money to buy clothing and groceries," but that she had to get water from a well, live in a house without a bathroom, and drive a 1929 Ford without a working heater, and that in the last four years her husband had hardly given her any money at all.

In dismissing the case, the Nebraska Supreme Court said that "to maintain an action such as the one at bar, the parties must be separated or living apart from each other" and that "the living standards of a family are a matter of

---

[7] Leo Kanowitz, *Women and the Law,* University of New Mexico Press, Albuquerque, 1969.
[8] See, e.g., *McGuire v. McGuire,* 157 Neb. 226, 59 N.W. 2d 336 (1953).

concern to the household and not for the courts to determine, even though the husband's attitude towards his wife, according to his wealth and circumstances, leaves little to be said on his behalf."[9]

Since in financial terms the traditional marriage contract is basically the exchange of a woman's sexual and economic services as a wife and mother for her husband's legal obligation to support her, the failure of our legal system to enforce the husband's obligation during the marriage constitutes a very real economic discrimination against married women. It is also one of the reasons that feminists have long advocated that homemaking and child rearing should be paid for as are all the other services that, unlike these activities, are included in calculating our gross national product.

DIVORCED WOMEN

With the advent of no-fault divorce—by which a marriage can be dissolved because it has broken down, not only (as in the past) because of some legally recognized wrongdoing such as adultery or cruelty by one of the spouses—has come the legal recognition that divorce is simply a fact of contemporary American family life. For the woman who has worked outside her home, built up a career, accumulated her own property, and maintained her own credit, there should be relatively few economic difficulties in the event of a divorce. But even in those states (about half) that have not as yet adopted some form of no-fault divorce legislation, for the housewife—the woman who has made her career that of wife and mother—divorce can be an economic as well as a personal trauma.

Spousal Support and Child Support

In the majority of American jurisdictions today, spousal support—or, as it used to be called, "alimony"—may be awarded to both husbands and wives. Despite the prevalent fear that women may lose their legal right to support if the Equal Rights Amendment is adopted, the consensus of legal authority is that the Amendment's ratification would simply result in the universal extension of the right to support to men.[10]

A widely held belief is that most divorced women are completely, or at least primarily, supported by their former husbands. But according to a report made in 1972 by the Citizens Advisory Council on the Status of Women, that assumption is completely out of line with reality, both present and past.[11]

Part of the problem may be that people tend to confuse rules of law with actual judicial proceedings and their actual results. Although there are of course great variations from state to state, in essence the laws governing spousal support usually provide that courts must consider such factors as the length of the marriage; the supported spouse's health, wealth, and work skills; the family's past living standard; and the supporting spouse's ability to provide. In jurisdictions

[9] *Ibid.*

[10] See, e.g., *U.S. Congressional Record,* S-472, vol. 117, no. 6, Washington, D.C., January 28, 1971.

[11] Citizens Advisory Council on the Status of Women, *The Equal Rights Amendment and Alimony and Child Support Laws,* Washington, D.C., January 1972.

without no-fault divorce, there is also the rule that a guilty spouse cannot be awarded spousal support, and conversely that in determining the size and duration of an award, the severity of the supporting spouse's guilt must also be taken into account. In awarding child support, in addition to considering the relative wealth and earnings of the parent who has custody and the one who does not, courts are supposed to consider the physical, emotional, and mental needs of the child or children.

In practice, however, awards of both spousal and child support have always been primarily governed by economic realities. For middle- and lower-class people, this usually means that you start with a determination of how much income the supporting spouse (usually the husband) may keep—so that, as courts often put it, "he will still be motivated to work"—and then you give what is left over to the wife and children.

For richer people, the wording of a particular law or statute is more often a factor, and it is from their often extended and costly legal battles that much of the case law on our books has been made. For example, when the new California Family Law Act (the first no-fault divorce act in the nation) was enacted in 1970, among the changes was language requiring that in awarding spousal support judges shall consider the supported spouse's ability to obtain gainful employment.[12] Although that factor had always been considered by courts, lawyers now argued that its specific inclusion in the new statute indicated a legislative intent that judges should give it more importance. What followed was that many ex-wives of wealthy men were awarded very little spousal support, and that only for a few years. Some of these cases were appealed and eventually reversed. In reversing such decisions, the higher courts often pointed out that after a marriage of long duration, and when a husband has a good business or profession, it was not fair to leave a wife whose only profession has been that of homemaker practically destitute. Nevertheless, despite these later cases, both in California and throughout the nation, today courts emphasize the woman's so-called "reentry into the labor force"; and most judges and lawyers agree that there is a definite trend toward lower and shorter spousal-support awards. In addition, since the lowering of the age of majority to eighteen, in many American jurisdictions today child support is awarded for three years less than it was in the past.

Once an award is made, the next problem is that of collection. According to the Citizens Advisory Council on the Status of Women, and a number of other studies, enforcement of spousal-support and child-support awards is extremely lax, and the delinquency rate is high. Although the problem does not seem to be a new one, it has certainly become much more visible and more frequent; and consequently there has also been an increase in the number of women and children who have had to seek welfare under the Families With Dependent Children (AFDC) program.[13]

[12] *California Civil Code*, Section 4801.
[13] See, e.g., M. Winston and T. Forsher, *Nonsupport of Legitimate Children by Affluent Fathers as a Cause of Poverty and Welfare Dependence*, The Rand Corporation, Santa Monica, California, December 1971.

One device to lessen this problem is laws like one recently adopted in California which authorizes courts to order employers to withhold delinquent child-support payments directly from a father's paycheck. For mothers who are already on welfare, another approach is to put pressure on authorities to prosecute defaulting husbands more vigorously, as they are already authorized to do under our present laws. But in many ways the problem is more social than legal, since basically it too stems from women's traditional economic and personal dependency on men and the cultural assumption that every woman has, or should have, a man to take care of her.

Division of Property

Like support, the division of property is determined either through an agreement between the parties (the so-called property settlement agreement, usually negotiated between opposing attorneys) or by litigation (where the decision is made by the judge).

The rules for the division of property vary enormously from state to state. As a general rule, the wording of most state laws usually provides a general formula: for example, that the division shall be equitable and just; or, in California, that it must be substantially half and half. However, in community-property states each spouse is entitled to a share in specifically defined property (the community property), whereas in common-law states the property subject to division varies greatly from jurisdiction to jurisdiction: some jurisdictions limit it to property held jointly, whereas others also include some property held solely in one spouse's name.

In 1970, the National Conference of Commissioners on Uniform State Laws first introduced the Uniform Marriage and Divorce Act as a model for reform of state family laws. They proposed that common-law jurisdictions adopt the concept of "marital property." Like community property, marital property would include all property acquired during a marriage—except by gift, bequest, or increases in value of property held before the marriage—but unlike community property it would come into play only when an action for "dissolution" (the new name for divorce) was filed. The proposal caused a great deal of debate in legal circles. To date, largely owing to the vigorous opposition of the powerful American Bar Association, it has not been adopted in any state.

Regardless of the legal ground rules, the property settlement in a divorce is (like support) always limited by the actual assets and liabilities in each individual case. Therefore, there is always the issue of determining just what you and your husband own. Here again, there is no substitute for having kept up with your family's financial affairs and having kept as informed about them as your husband. If you have not done this, once the action is filed your lawyer can try to use a number of "discovery" techniques, such as depositions, interrogatories, and subpoenas, to try to obtain the information. However, these legal tools (and the accounting services that are usually also required) are only second best to first-hand knowledge; moreover, they cost money. Consequently, particularly in lower-income families, there is frequently a choice between spending scarce family funds in search of possibly nonexistent assets, or taking the risk of ending up with less property than is actually there.

This dilemma, as well as the general question of economizing on attorney's fees, can be dealt with only on the basis of each individual case. There are certainly situations where lawyers have unreasonably escalated costs and fees. Nevertheless, if savings on legal fees are to be made, they should be made on both sides; and it usually makes little economic sense for a woman to let herself be intimidated into trading a "more generous" settlement for inadequate or no legal representation.

Credit

Since our basic social assumption has been that during marriage a woman will be economically dependent on her husband, the business community has traditionally been unwilling to deal with married women, even where the laws do not specifically limit their independent capacity to do so. This prejudice, coupled with the not totally unreasonable reluctance of business and financial institutions to trust an unknown entity, has resulted in a whole complex of problems for women who are divorced.

Particularly in an economy that is as heavily based on installment payments and charge accounts as ours, the denial of home mortgages, business loans, charge accounts, and other forms of credit places women at an extreme disadvantage. Fortunately this problem is beginning to receive some recognition in both the financial community and our legislatures. For example, California recently adopted a new law prohibiting discrimination against married women regarding credit; and under a recent amendment to our federal laws, credit may henceforth be based solely on ability to repay a loan, not on any criteria related to sex.

WIDOWHOOD

Inheritance

Perhaps nowhere is the necessity for proper planning more evident than in the transition from marriage to widowhood. The best insurance against the classic widow's syndrome of bewilderment, helplessness, and financial vulnerability is to become familiar with all your family's business and economic affairs—its assets, liabilities, and income—and to insist on participating in your husband's estate planning.

A myriad of legal and practical issues will arise, depending on the individual circumstances and the applicable state and federal laws. For instance, particularly in larger estates, one decision that must often be made is whether the bulk of the estate should be disposed of by will or by an inter-vivos trust, taking effect before either of the spouses dies. Other examples of crucial decisions relate to the appointment of an executor or trustee, the ages at which minor children shall have direct access to property bestowed by either inter-vivos or testamentary trusts, and whether the widow's state inheritance tax shall be borne by the entire estate or only her share of it.

Once an estate plan is adopted, it should be reviewed periodically. For example, wills usually contain a number of bequests to specific individuals, charities, or both, with the remainder going to the widow, the children, or both. With economic fluctuations such as inflations and recessions, it is obviously essential to review the will periodically to make sure that enough residual property remains to take care of the immediate family.

Proper estate planning requires expert help and advice. Here, as in the other subjects covered in this chapter, specific questions and problems must of course be discussed with a competent lawyer, accountant, or both. It is important for both spouses to attend these meetings. And, particularly in the case of women, it is important to ask questions and under no circumstances to accept pat reassurances or patronizing evasions. In the end, it is more often than not the widow who will have to deal with the consequences of a particular plan.

Estate Administration

One of the most important decisions in estate planning is who should be the executor or executrix. I believe that wherever possible the surviving spouse should fulfill that role; but, again, this makes it essential that a woman have a good deal of exposure to and experience in the economic world before her husband's death.

It is the job of the executor or executrix to manage the property of the estate until final distribution can be made. Besides making the usual financial decisions entailed in the management of any kind of property, the executor or executrix is responsible for notifying creditors of the death, for collecting all debts, and for paying all the federal and state estate, inheritance, and income taxes. This latter subject is extremely complex, and the taxes can be very high, so that good expert help and advice is a necessity, particularly for larger estates.

Here again, planning can make a huge difference. For example, it may be advisable to avoid the costs of probate by holding property as joint tenants. In such a case, the property usually passes directly to the survivor without having to go through any court proceedings. The same consequence usually follows if an inter-vivos trust (as distinguished from a testamentary trust) is properly set up during the lifetime of the deceased.

Another important factor that comes up during the administration of an estate is the widow's family allowance. Most states have provisions whereby a widow can receive either a lump sum or periodic payments for her support until the estate is finally distributed.

Unfortunately, under current law the distribution of an estate can take a year or even more. A number of model statutes, including the proposed Uniform Probate and Administration Act, contain provisions that would provide for a relatively quick settlement of small estates. In this connection, one important thing women can do to help themselves is to become fully familiar with our current laws and to work for better ones to reduce the present high expenses and delays of estate administration.

Protections and Discriminations

If a husband dies without a will, the laws of intestate succession, which award surviving relatives a certain share in the estate, come into play. In addition (again, the specifics will vary from state to state), as a general rule married women are protected by law from being completely disinherited by their husbands' wills.

In community-property states each spouse can will his or her half of the community property to anyone, but the other half still belongs to the surviving spouse. Any separate property can be disposed of as the testator wishes. If there is no will, then under the laws of intestate succession, the surviving wife and children will be given specific shares fixed by law in both the separate property and the decedent's share of the community property.

In common-law states, where each person's earnings and accumulations are her or his separate property unless title is held in both names, under the traditional rule of dower, a widow is entitled to a one-third share in her husband's estate, regardless of the provisions of his will. Today the percentage a widow must receive varies greatly from state to state, but under the rules of either dower or the more contemporary "nonbarrable forced share," husbands in common-law states may not completely disinherit their widows in their wills.

On the other hand, there are still a number of laws that directly discriminate against widows. For example, a recently repealed California law required that a widow's half of the community property had to be included in the probate estate, whereas no such reciprocal requirement was made if the husband survived his wife. For the most part, however, the majority of the hardships faced by widows today are more the result of the unequal social and economic treatment of women and men than of discriminatory laws. It would certainly help to have better laws and more vigorous judicial action, such as the stricter enforcement of the high fiduciary standard of care that our laws already require of executors and trustees. But in the last analysis, the "helpless widow" syndrome is a social and economic problem related to the dependent status and self-image of women.

It is hoped that the passage of the proposed Equal Rights Amendment will go a long way toward eliminating discrimination from our laws and changing many of the old, stereotyped, patriarchal notions about women and men. In addition, if any real progress is to be made in the immediate future, new, positive laws—laws with teeth in them—will also have to be enacted, so that business and industry will be motivated in the right direction. Furthermore, there is an urgent need for remedial laws and Affirmative Action programs to help those women who are trying to make the transition from their traditional roles to the new roles demanded of them by our society today. Another important, although largely ignored area is legislation for the public funding of massive educational programs to help both women and men overcome their sexist biases and self-images, as well as to help women acquire the skills that will allow them to function as both independent economic entities and self-sufficient human beings in the contemporary world.

LEGAL HELP: FORMS, INFORMATION, AND COUNSEL

Many large stationary and office-supply stores carry forms for some of the simpler legal transactions. Typically, they stock forms granting powers of attorney (by which one individual empowers another to legally act in his or her place), declarations of homestead (which when properly filled out and recorded prevent creditors from reaching your home, or at least that portion which is exempt under the law of your particular jurisdiction), and grant deeds (which are the written instruments required to transfer title to real property and which should be recorded in the county where the property is located).

Unfortunately, these forms are often out of date because legal requirements change frequently, both with the passage of new statutes and the decisions of courts. Although one can usually determine when a form was drafted from the printed legend at the bottom or on the back, even a recent date is in itself no guarantee of adequacy, for such forms are often prepared by business people with only an imperfect understanding of the law. Consequently, unless you know exactly what the legal requirements of your jurisdiction are, it is extremely unwise to use these forms.

A number of forms can also be obtained from legal newspapers. For example, in Los Angeles so-called "dba" ("doing business as") forms will be provided by the *Daily Journal* or the *Metropolitan News*. These newspapers help support themselves by publishing "dba" and other legal notices for the periods required by statute (thereby meeting the California requirement that to do business under any name other than your own, you must first give public notice). And of course it is at courthouses that you obtain complaints, summonses, and the myriad of other legal forms required to bring any kind of court action. Finally, bookstores, public libraries, and law libraries have publications containing everything from sample forms for drafting simple wills to the reams of questionnaires and applications usually required to form a corporation. Again, before a person should even attempt to use any of these on his or her own, it is imperative to be extremely well-informed.

Besides the federal and state statute books or codes and the official reports of court cases, the law libraries of most counties and law schools also contain many other types of publications. Most of these, like legal encyclopedias, treatises, and articles in law reviews, are meant primarily for the legal practitioner. Nevertheless, they can be useful to the lay person who wants to get some background in a particular field of law, since sometimes (as with the California Continuing Education of the Bar series) they at least try to treat technical subjects in a straightforward and comprehensible way.

There are also a number of books written specifically for the lay person. These range from general legal surveys such as Leo Kanowitz's *Women and the*

Law (University of New Mexico Press, Albuquerque, 1969) and Shana Alexander's *Women's Legal Rights* (Wollstonecraft, Los Angeles, 1975) to specific books dealing with a particular area of law, like Dacey's *How to Avoid Probate* (Crown, New York, 1965) and my book on divorce (*Dissolution,* McGraw-Hill, New York, 1977). Although some books for lay persons are well-written and carefully researched, unfortunately many are not. Furthermore, since laws change very fast and also vary enormously from state to state, even the good ones are useful mainly as sources for guidelines and information rather than for specific solutions to particular legal problems.

For example, a person who wants to make a will can profit from reading up on the subject, and may, in certain simple situations, be capable of drafting a simple instrument with the help of a number of books and forms. Handwritten ("holographic") wills are valid in most jurisdictions, as long as they are dated and signed, and do not contain any typed or printed matter whatsoever. In addition, unlike other wills, such an instrument generally does not have to be attested to by witnesses. However, the terms of such a will may be in conflict with a particular law, and in the end, if it is challenged, it may not stand up in court. Also, such a will may be so ambiguously worded that it will not be interpreted as the testator really intended.

Therefore, as a general rule, if you have a legal question or problem, it is best to seek legal counsel. If you have no money, free or low-cost legal aid is provided, at least in the bigger cities, by a number of federally or locally funded organizations, like centers for law and poverty and neighborhood legal-aid associations. Usually, however, there is a waiting period. If you can afford a private lawyer, but do not have one or are dissatisfied with the one you have, your best course is to ask around and try to find a friend or acquaintance who can refer you to one. Local bar associations will make referrals, but as a rule their lists are screened only for suspension or disbarment from practice. In some localities, women's organizations such as NOW and the YWCA have referral lists, but here too it is important to find out how carefully these are screened.

Basically, the task of finding a good lawyer is up to you. You may want to interview more than one; and it is always a good idea to make an appointment for a preliminary consultation, particularly when contemplating important and protracted matters such as a divorce or other litigation.

It is always important to ask about fees at the outset. Although it is often hard for a lawyer to predict time and costs completely and accurately, you can at least find out her or his hourly charges, as well as a general estimate of what your particular case may involve.

The choice of a lawyer, like that of any professional, is not a simple matter. Just as with doctors and plumbers, there are good, bad, and fair to middling lawyers. The initial interview will give you only a limited amount of data; and as in any other relationship, there is a lot you can learn only after you are actually in it. Nevertheless, before you entrust your case to a lawyer, you should have some idea of her or his intelligence, experience in a particular field, and—equally important—personal and social attitudes. You will want someone who can explain the legal issues involved to you, since ultimately the law will assume that you were adequately informed before you signed a particular document or agreed to a settlement of your case. You will also want someone who is genuinely concerned about your welfare, not just about a fee. And, particularly as a woman, you should have someone who will not patronize you or treat you condescendingly. In short, you should have someone who is at least somewhat aware of sexist prejudices and attitudes; who will not consciously or unconsciously act them out against you personally or in the conduct of your case; and who will help you, rather than hinder you, in becoming well informed, self-confident, and self-sufficient.

Chapter 24

Developing Your Financial Management Skills

Helen M. Thal

Helen M. Thal, Ed.D., is Professor of Home Economics Education, Pennsylvania State University. She is a former Director of Education Services of the Institute of Life Insurance, and has published extensively in such journals as *Vocational Guidance Quarterly, Forecast, Forum,* and *Journal of Home Economics.* She is the coauthor of *Youth and Money* (National Education Association, Washington, D.C., 1964) and author of *Your Family and Its Money* (Houghton Mifflin, Boston, 1968, 1973).

The truth about money is that there never is enough. And the truth about most people is that our wants exceed our income. All of this causes us to be anxious about money and how we use it, because in dealing with money we are forced to confront ourselves. In the final analysis, we are not managing money as much as we are managing ourselves.

MONEY MANAGEMENT: A PERSONAL AFFAIR

By following simple written directions, one can learn to change a tire, operate a calculator, or assemble a harpsichord from a kit. After a few lessons, one can learn to swim or play bridge or crochet. If so inclined, one can learn—through television—to cook like Julia Child or to bend and stretch like Bonnie Prudden. But learning to be a money manager is different: there are no simple directions for everybody or every situation; a few lessons from an expert can only give one some general guidelines; and the skills of money management do not lend themselves to exciting presentation on television. To be sure, we may hear money matters discussed on radio and television, and we have opportunities to enroll in personal finance courses—but such instruction and study are academic unless one recognizes where money management begins.

It might be of some help to know what money management is not, so that we can better understand why it frequently turns out to be frustrating and bewildering. First of all, managing one's financial affairs is not simply a matter of bookkeeping, although some simple record keeping is necessary. Nor is it merely a system for allocating expenditures according to a prescribed formula, although there is an element of allocation of funds inherent in any sound management program. Nor is it simply matching income with outgo month after month, *ad infinitum*, although matching money coming in with money going out is another of the pieces in the puzzle. And finally, money management is not simply a dollars-and-cents affair—although dollars and cents are the tangibles being managed, together with time, energy, and other resources.

Managing personal and family finances is unlike managing a business, but there is something to be learned from the business manager. In business, goals are firmly fixed, and the management system is directed toward those goals. The manager will be dispassionate in efforts to achieve the objective; mechanisms exist for operating and controlling the business so as to facilitate in every way the achievement of goals. For a business enterprise, that is how it must be. On the individual and family level, we find other factors that must be recognized and dealt with—such as emotions, attitudes, relationships, values, conflicting goals, and aspirations. Sorting these factors out and accepting them as part of reality is how personal money management must begin.

Knight, in his treatise on money, says it this way: "Most people are concerned, more or less continuously, consciously or unconsciously, with the solution of their private money problems; for money, some humans will do almost anything. Our concepts of money influence our conduct, aspirations, and emotional reactions to ourselves, our families and friends." [1] He goes on to say that the symbolic meaning of money is determined by one's upbringing; one's cultural background; one's religion; one's experiences; attitudes derived from parents, teachers, and—we might add—peers and significant others; and short- and long-range goals.

Money, in and of itself, is simply a medium of exchange, which we "translate into the beauty of living, a support in misfortune, an education, or future security." [2] By the same token, it can be a source of power, a status symbol, a measure of success; it can be a means to an end, or it might be an end in itself. We may use it to manipulate or control others or to improve the quality of life for our-

[1] James A. Knight, *For the Love of Money,* Lippincott, Philadelphia, 1968, pp. 11–12.
[2] Sylvia Porter, *Sylvia Porter's Money Book,* Doubleday, Garden City, N.Y., 1975, p.10.

selves and our families; it might be the instrument we use to assess our achievement or to weigh the worth of ourselves or of other persons. It is neither good nor evil—it has no inherent characteristics of its own that contribute in one way or another to individual or family well-being. It's what we do with money that counts—and what we do with it grows out of the emotional and psychological trappings which we attach to it, together with the image we have of what our life is and what we want it to be.

Consider then, what you want your life to be; and as you sort out your goals, reflect on your attitudes—not so much about money but about your life-style and the qualities you want to bring to it. In a way, you will be articulating a philosophy, and you will be determining those things that are important to you and to your family. Any financial plan you develop will then be directed toward achieving the goals that will contribute to your unique life-style. Because you are using your resources to create a style and way of life that are truly your own, money management can be looked on as a *creative activity*—indeed, a major creative activity.

Therefore, take time at the outset "to think out your own philosophy of living and your ambitions for the future." [13] Once that is accomplished, you will be ready to plan how you will get from where you are now to where you want to go. In effect, you will be designing a road map (or possibly a blueprint or a structural design) reflecting your values, tastes, and needs—all within the confines of your resources.

VALUES AS A FACTOR IN FINANCIAL PLANNING

Implicit in all that has been said so far is the presence of individual and family values in the process of management. Abstract as values are, the serious money manager can ill afford to ignore them. Let us examine briefly how your values influence your financial behavior. Our examination will be only a glimpse, although the subject deserves much more. (See also Chapter 1, which deals with the role of values in improving the quality of life.)

I have suggested that money management begins by sorting out priorities and setting goals. The outcome of that decision-making exercise will be dependent on your values; the road map or blueprint will emerge only as you have clarified your values and resolved value conflicts within yourself and within your family. The decisions that you will be making and with which you will be living for some time will turn out to be comfortable for you only if they reflect your values.

Values have been defined in various ways. In essence, we might say that values are the underlying beliefs which motivate us and from which we derive direction for behavioral decisions. The fact that you—like thousands of other women—made the decision to return to work reflects your value system. Why are you working?

---

[3] *Ibid.*

To increase the family income so as to improve your level of living?

To build a home, or renovate your present home?

To send your children to college?

To support your family or only yourself?

To support your parents or another relative?

To acquire some possessions that will enhance the beauty of your home?

To be with other professional or working men and women?

To get out and away from housework?

To help pay some family debts?

To add to the retirement income that you and your husband anticipate you will need?

To succeed or achieve in a male-dominated field?

To give expression to your own talents, abilities, and skills outside the home?

To practice your profession, or resume its practice?

To go into business for yourself?

How you respond to questions such as these will say something about what you value. It might be security, or education, or family, or success, or aesthetics; perhaps your answer will reflect economic need and social values, or the need for self-fulfillment and security. Values are personal, and we each devise our own ways of responding to them.

There are various classification systems designed by scholars and students which help us sort out individual values. For example, Allport and his colleagues at Harvard organized values in six categories:

Aesthetic:
Beauty
Harmony

Religious:
Reverence
Faith
Mysticism

Theoretical:
Intellect
Knowledge
Science
Reason

Social:
Justice
Concern for and service to others
Love

Economic:
Utility
Efficiency
Thrift
Conservation

Political:
Power
Prestige
Competition
Influence [14]

Less elaborate systems have been used to help clarify values. These tend to be more traditional and more family-oriented and home-oriented. Here is an example of a system with other categories:

Family-centered:
Health
Education
Affection
Security

Household-centered:
Convenience
Privacy
Orderliness
Utility
Comfort

Community-centered:
Altruism
Status
Prestige
Concern for others

Economic:
Thrift
Security
Productivity

As an exercise in identifying your own values, look at your canceled checks over the past two or three months—or even longer, if you want to give that much time to this project. What picture do you see? Is there a pattern that repeats itself every month? Are there certain large expenditures that seem to stand out? Is there a cluster of checks for personal pleasure or self-improvement (hairdresser, health spa, book club, subscriptions, lessons, athletic clubs)? Are there regular payments to charitable or religious institutions? You might analyze your checks and see what values are evident. Whether you recognize a pattern of values or not, this is a worthwhile experiment, for it gives an overview of oneself as a spender. In any case, it will tell you something about yourself. There is truth in

---

[4] Summarized from Allport, Vernon, and Lindzey, *Study of Values,* Houghton-Mifflin, Boston, 1960 (originally published, 1931). This work presents a scale for measuring the dominant interests in personality.

the challenge "Put your money where your mouth is"—for more often than not, we do.

Values have a pervasive quality that gives continuity to financial management and helps one maintain a reasonable degree of rationality in money matters. Conflicts over money will arise, however, as conflicting values meet. In every marriage there are *her* values and *his* values. Certain values will be shared; others will remain "his" and "hers." A case study, appearing in the *Washington Post* (May 13, 1973) and cited by Deacon and Firebaugh, illustrates how values can be consistent and at the same time conflicting within a marriage. The couple in the study have been married for eight years and have two children. Both are employed; he is a lawyer and she works for an architect. Their combined income amounts to $35,000. The wife says that it has only been recently that they have recognized and accepted their different values. She feels that her husband thinks her materialistic, and she accepts this.

> ". . . I am materialistic and I'm going to continue. . . . I mean it does matter to me to feel secure. It matters to me, not to have the things that other people . . . think are the important things, but things that are lovely. The things that I really like, I like to have. . . ." [5]

One final word on this subject: Once you have recognized and affirmed your values, you will better understand your financial decisions, and this will eliminate any guilt you may feel if your expenditures do not conform to the "average" or the "typical" expenditures which are cited frequently in magazines devoted to how America lives. Remember, the "average family" with its "average earnings" does not exist.

YOUR FINANCIAL PLANNING

As a working woman you will be juggling your resources in a way that may be new to you, especially if you are now returning to employment after several years as a homemaker. You have been providing all manner of services for your family: cleaning, marketing, meal preparation, entertaining, gardening, laundering, errands, baby-sitting, delivering goods or people—you can devise your own list. But now you are back to work. Seven or eight hours (or more) of every day belong to your employer. No longer do you have the time or the energy to continue serving your family and household as they may have become accustomed to being served. These services now must be given consideration in your financial plan, for you may very well have to buy the services, skills, and time of other persons in order to manage the household in a way that suits you and your family. You will buy more convenience foods; you will need different clothing; and your household routine will be altered. You may find that you can't count on other family members to share the housekeeping responsibilities. For your own

---

[5] Ruth E. Deacon and Francille M. Firebaugh, *Home Management: Context and Concepts,* Houghton-Mifflin, Boston, 1975, p. 147.

sake (and sanity), face up to these matters and allow for them in your management plan.

Basic Resolves

As a starter in creating your own money management plan, keep in mind three simple resolves:

1   It must be a partnership, if you are married. You both have a stake in the decisions you must make. Don't defer to your spouse—it is your money and your life as well as his.

2   It must provide personal allowances for you both. This money need not be accounted for to others in the family—it is yours to spend and it should be adequate to cover work-related expenses (lunches, for example) as well as spending money.

3   It must be a simple plan—easy to understand and easy to execute.

Your management plan is not "set in cement"—nor should it be. Keep it simple, allow it to be flexible, and don't be downhearted if at first it doesn't work. Try not to expect miracles—no financial plan is a panacea for all the troubles we have with money. None of us ever has enough money to accomplish everything we want to do, to have, and to be—especially in the first year we live on a budget. So if your first plan is not working, get rid of it and start again.

Keep in mind the nature of some of your goals and decisions: you are making financial commitments that extend well into the future, and you are committing money you haven't yet earned. Those commitments will be a part of your management plan for years—either they will be an albatross that you soon learn to hate, or they will be comfortably satisfying because they mean achievement of goals now or in the future.

To summarize: Your money plan starts long before you begin working with pencil, paper, and dollars. You have made some decisions about your goals, drawn some conclusions about how you want to live, faced the reality of your own values and how they influence your life-style, and identified the changes in your family living that result from your new role as a working woman. Now you are ready to look at your money. Let's begin with your paycheck and note certain deductions.

Your Money

Deductions from Your Paycheck   You already know that you never see a certain portion of your monthly earnings. But although you never see these dollars, they represent a financial asset worthy of consideration in your management plan. Therefore, a brief discussion of your deductions is included here, with the suggestion that you ask your personnel department for details as they apply to you.

Social Security   The benefits provided by Social Security are substantial, and the tax (the deduction) looks that way too. We will not look at the costs here, because the tax rate changes so frequently. But you ought to know what your money is buying, because Social Security benefits provide the foundation for your life insurance and retirement programs, and thus have real significance in your financial plans for the present and the future. Here are the benefits your Social Security taxes are buying:

1 Retirement income, starting at age sixty-five (or sixty-two if you wish), the amount of which is based on your average earnings over a period of years. The amount is not fixed once and for all—the monthly payments will increase as the cost of living goes up. Furthermore, income from Social Security is not subject to federal income tax.

2 Disability income, paid monthly after the first five months of becoming disabled. Again, the amount of income will depend on your average earnings, and the number of dependents for whom you may be responsible. Payments will continue until you are able to resume full-time work, if ever.

3 Survivors' benefits: that is, a monthly income to your dependent children if you should die prematurely. Benefits will be paid to your husband if he is over fifty, disabled, and at least partially dependent on you for support. A lump-sum payment of $255 will be paid to your beneficiary at the time of death.

4 Medicare, or hospital and medical insurance protection, beginning at age sixty-five.

To be eligible for Social Security benefits, you will have to be "fully insured," which means that you have worked long enough in "covered" employment to have earned the required number of "work credits." This means that you will have had to work at the most for ten years in a position where you were paying a Social Security tax.

For a detailed explanation of your Social Security benefits, contact the nearest Social Security office, where you can get informational booklets intended to help people understand the program.

Group insurance: life and health   It is the rule, rather than the exception, for employers today to make available to employees some plan for life and health insurance. Life insurance plans usually provide coverage in the amount of one or two years' salary; the cost may be shared by both employer and employee, or the firm may pay the whole cost. In the event that the employee shares in the cost, her contribution may not exceed sixty cents per $1,000 of insurance each month.

The group health insurance program may provide only hospital benefits, or you may be eligible for a plan that includes surgical and medical benefits, major medical payments, and loss-of-income payments. With the high cost of medical care, you can well appreciate why your group health insurance is a valuable asset. You should make it a point to learn exactly what benefits are provided and supplement the plan with additional health insurance if it appears inadequate.

About life insurance: If you are single and have no dependents, the group policy your employer provides may be all the life insurance you need at the present time—but don't count on it. Most group plans are effective as long as you are working for a particular firm; should you decide to stop working, or if you want to go into business for yourself, or when you retire, you will no longer be insured, and such times may be when you really need the protection. For the married woman, her group life insurance will help her family maintain the level of living they presently enjoy, and benefits from the policy will provide funds that she may be working to accumulate: college education for the children or some other important family goal. Your group life insurance should be considered in your family's life insurance program in exactly the same way as your husband's.

Retirement income or pension plan   The facts about your employer's pension program must be obtained from your personnel officer. In general, however, workers are eligible to retirement benefits either on a *contributory* or a *noncontributory* basis—either you share the cost or your employer pays the entire cost. If you are sharing, you are entitled to take your share with you, plus any interest, if you change jobs. If the company is paying the full cost, you may not be entitled to any benefits until you are "vested"—that is, until you have been an employee and a member of the plan for a specified number of years.

It will pay you to look into the plan you are part of and know its provisions. It may be worth thousands of dollars to you some day, and therefore should be considered as you plan your financial future.

FOUR STEPS TO SUCCESSFUL MONEY MANAGEMENT

You are about to create your blueprint for your present and future. Keep in mind that it may not work the first time—or even the second. You'll know that it is working satisfactorily when it (1) informs you where your income comes from, when it comes, and how much it is; (2) provides first for needs, then for improvements, and finally for luxuries if the money is there to pay for them; (3) provides a plan for savings and for paying off debts, plus the means for staying out of debt; (4) helps you acquire good habits for spending and saving. All this is not as difficult as it may seem.

Most financial counselors have agreed on four steps in the process of money management. The results will add up to a personal management plan that will actually work.

1   Know Exactly What Your Income Amounts To

Start with your take-home pay. Forget your gross salary—you may have been hired at $15,000 a year, but your paycheck may add up to only $11,500. It's that $11,500 that you have to work with. Treat your husband's income the same way. Add to your combined income any other money that will come in during the year—rent, dividends, interest, veterans' benefit payments, insurance benefits, money from the sale of property, unemployment payments, social security payments. Don't guess; don't exaggerate the facts. Be as honest as you can possibly be. Some money may be paid periodically (dividends and interest, for example); note what months those checks are received.

Now run a total for the year and divide by twelve. The answer will be the money you have to work with per month. If your salary is increased during the year, run a new total; or if there is a decrease, rework your figures. The important thing is to keep this income figure absolutely accurate—you are only fooling yourself if you do otherwise.

2   Know Exactly What Your Fixed Expenses Amount To

Everyone of us has certain expenses that must be made on a regular schedule— expenses that are unavoidable, and that are fixed in amount and fixed in time. Some of these will occur every month (rent or mortgage, commutation or bus fare, installment payments on a car or a television set, or other debt). Some of these fixed expenses occur only annually or semiannually (insurance premiums, taxes, membership dues, tuition). Remember your pledged contributions to a religious or charitable institution; don't overlook the little items: garbage collection, cable television, newspaper delivery service, magazine subscriptions.

Here is another item for your list of fixed expenses, and one you must treat with the same serious determination as your rent or mortgage: your savings. "Pay yourself first," say the smart money managers, and no matter how small your initial monthly savings deposit may be, deal with it just as you deal with other financial commitments. We delude ourselves when we believe we will save whatever is left over at the end of the month—too often we have no leftovers.

Your savings funds will be for two general purposes. First, you will need an emergency fund in order to meet the unexpected: a leak in the roof, an unexpected trip to tend to an ill parent, a special opportunity—your college alumni tour to Mexico, a special seminar offered for persons in your field of work or interest, the purchase of the carpet which you've wanted and which has now gone on sale, an unusual event that will be important to another member in the family. Your emergency fund should amount to about three to six months' income, and should probably best be kept in a savings account which is convenient and safe, and from which withdrawals may be readily made.

Your second purpose in saving is to provide funds for short- and long-range goals. You know you need extra money for vacations and at Christmas. You may know, too, that you are planning to send a child to college in a few years. And you know that you will sometime retire. As a matter of fact, these may be the very reasons you are now working, but unless you structure your financial plan so as to show how these goals are to be met, your income has a way of petering out.

The nature of this savings account will depend on the goal: if you know you are saving in order to have the cash for a child's college expenses, starting in seven years, you will consider a different savings medium than if your goal is to have retirement funds in twenty years.

You may accomplish these objectives through a payroll savings plan available through your employer. You may consider purchasing certificates of deposit at a bank or savings and loan institution; these usually pay interest in the neighborhood of 7 percent, compounded regularly. However you do it, get advice from knowledgeable financial advisors, select the course you believe will suit you best, and then start to do it. You will be surprised how a small amount of money saved regularly and consistently will add up over the years.

With your list before you, showing all fixed expenses including your savings deposit, run a total for the year. Divide by twelve, and you'll know exactly how much of your monthly income is needed for these unavoidable expenditures, which are more accurately thought of as financial commitments.

If you are just starting a system of money management, and you look ahead a couple of months or so and see that a life insurance premium of $375 is due three months from now, don't be discouraged. If need be, borrow the money for that payment, and stick with your plan. It will take a full year of operation before you will recognize how effective it can be in moving you toward a goal or series of goals.

3 Know Exactly What You Can Spend for Day-to-Day Living Expenses

You know what your monthly income is, and you know what your monthly fixed expenses are. Subtract the latter—the expenses—from the income. What you have left is the money you will need for day-in, day-out living. You know what these are: food (at home and in restaurants), clothing, transportation, liquor, entertaining, recreation, allowances, personal care, household supplies, gifts, electricity and telephone bills. You will probably have other items unique to your life-style. These needs are no less important than those you've met in figuring your fixed expenses; they differ in that these may be thought of as *flexible*. You can control them. You can use greater discretion in the supermarket, you can cut down on long-distance phone calls, you can use your car less and walk more, you can turn off the lights or turn down the heat or air conditioner. This monthly sum will be the more difficult to manage.

4 Know Exactly How You Will Budget the Day-to-Day Living Expenses

Here is where some records will be helpful. If you have records that can be used to reconstruct a picture of what you have been spending on some of these flexible items, get them out. If you have nothing to work from, start today to keep a record. After a couple of months' experience, you'll have a fairly good idea of how much you are spending and for what.

A word about your records. Be absolutely honest. Perhaps Saturday you spend $12.95 for a beef roast; $8.85 for a bottle of Scotch; $21, tips included, at the hairdresser; and $8 at the florist for a centerpiece. If these appear like extravagances, don't try to hide them. They may be very important in your scheme of things. The more accurate you are in these records now, the more accurate you will be in planning how you will budget your daily living expenses. Remember, you won't have to continue this particular kind of recording indefinitely—only long enough to get the picture.

From your records, you will be able to estimate how much money will be allocated for each of the items on your list of flexible expenses. Food will probably be the large item. Be as realistic as you can be, and be honest with yourself and your family. If you set limits that are too low, but look good on paper, your plan will not work—you'll quit because you feel you're in a straitjacket.

Probably your first budget will not work. If so, start over. Revise your limits. You will be working with estimates at first, and there are bound to be wrong guesses. Let other family members share in designing the plan—they all will then feel some responsibility for making it work.

Now a word about allowances. Each member of the family should have a certain amount of money that is strictly his or hers. How they use their allowances is up to each person; don't ask for an accounting. The size of the allowance will be determined by what the allowance is intended to cover: will the children take their Sunday school money out of it, as well as school lunches and after-school snacks? Decide in each case what the allowance is to provide. Pay the allowances weekly; and once they are paid, don't pry. If someone runs out of money, as a result of poor management, let it be one of life's hard lessons: money is not a limitless resource. If someone is short of funds for a reason that couldn't be controlled, you can help out. The allowance system, for children and adults, provides remarkably good practice in managing money and operating on a cash basis.

CONTROLLING THE BUDGET

This is where the battle of wants versus needs takes place. You have a sensible (or so it seems) budget neatly worked out on paper. But how to put it to work? Some system for controlling the cash flow is needed. What to do with income? How to manage outgo? Let's think, then, about banking your money. And let's think about two bank accounts as a minimum: a checking account and a savings account.

Savings Account

The savings account was mentioned earlier. Shop for the institution which pays you the best return and which offers the convenience you will need for maintaining your savings account—especially your emergency account. Here you need an account that is accessible and one where your money is paid on demand. You might be rewarded by examining the savings opportunities in your community. Consider a credit union or an account in a commercial bank, a savings bank (if savings banks exist in your state), or a savings and loan institution. Save where your money will earn the most money for you. Above all, do *not* try to *save* your money in your checking account: it won't be saved, nor will it earn any return.

Checking Account

Your checking account can be your bookkeeping system: through it you will channel all your funds—income and outgo—and if you are conscientious about it, your checkbook will tell you exactly where your money goes, and what funds you have available at any given time.

You will have your choice of two kinds of checking accounts, generally speaking: a *special* account or a *regular* account. Which kind you choose will depend on (1) the number of checks you write each month, and (2) the amount of money you will keep in the account. A special account requires no minimum balance, but there will be a charge for each check written. A regular account usually requires that you maintain a minimum balance—$100 or more each month. You will want to select the kind that will serve your needs most effectively.

Possibly you are married, and there are two paychecks per month. What to do? Again, you'll need to decide—together—what is the best method for handling your money. Here are some possibilities:

1 A joint checking account in which you both deposit your income, and from which you both draw funds and pay bills.

2 A joint checking account in which you both deposit *some* of your income—enough for fixed family expenses and household operations. The balance of each check will go into your personal checking accounts.

3 Two checking accounts, one for each of you. This arrangement means that you have a clear understanding of who pays for what each month. Who should pay for what? That's up to you. Tradition would have the man in the family paying for the mortgage (or rent), insurance premiums, automobile payments, and investments, and the woman paying for household operations, food, children's clothing, and other needs. You'll have to decide how you want it. The important thing is that you are each clear about your responsibilities. It is assumed, of course, that you each will be responsible for your own needs and expenses, and that you both will be contributing to a savings program.

If you live in a community where there are several banks, shop for the account and banking services that are best suited to your needs.

Shopping Skill—An Aid to Budget Control

The bank accounts can't do everything. Your behavior in the supermarket or shopping mall can make or break the budget, as you know well enough. A word of reminder, however—spending sprees can be disastrous if you indulge in them often. Develop some rules for shopping and stick with them if you can. Your rules well might include the following:

1 Make a shopping list, and stick to it. Curb your impulse buying and avoid being tricked into buying something you don't need, can't use, and don't want.

2 Compare before you buy. Shop around for major items if you have more time than money.

3 Shop for specials and items on sale, if what is offered is what you need.

4 Don't let charge accounts fool you into thinking that you are staying within the budget.

5 Buy the quality that suits the need.

6 Read the labels before you buy so that you know the quantity and the care or use the item will require.

7 Buy at shops where you have confidence in the management and merchandise.

These rules suggest how you and your family may control the outflow of money. You might add other rules that are especially pertinent to your family. Don't be so rigid, however, that you deny yourself the fun of a new lipstick or a flower for your desk—or a surprise for your husband now and then.

CREDIT

Five Guidelines

Credit, in the life of today's family, is simply taken for granted. When wants exceed means, there is the handy credit card. In our use of credit we differ dramatically from earlier generations, for whom debt of any kind was a disgrace—indeed, a sign of weak character and questionable morality. For the present generation, debt is a part of the American dream. In reality, debt is neither a curse nor a miracle. Manageable debt, secured for the right reason and responsibly handled, is an acceptable operating procedure.

Most of us use credit with caution, knowing full well that it costs money, and recognizing that the price we pay for it is not unlike the rent we pay for an apartment or for a space in the parking lot. In effect, when we use credit we are renting money. By so doing, we are able to have the use of something—a washing machine, an automobile, a lawnmower—while we are paying for it; and there's nothing wrong with that—as long as we need the washing machine, automobile, or lawnmower.

In today's market there are scarcely any goods or services not available on credit. Because it is so easy to obtain, credit has been a pitfall for some people who by overextending themselves are caught up in a cycle of overwhelming debts. Because it's easy to "charge it" or to contract for an installment-payment plan, we must learn to use credit with discretion. In that way we will enjoy it more and worry less.

Credit comes in a variety of packages and at a full range of prices, from the thirty-day charge account at a department store to the usurious services rendered by the loan shark. In between, you will find installment credit offered by the seller of durable goods, revolving accounts available from retailers or from banks, personal loans, and credit card accounts. And sources of credit are ever more numerous: banks, credit unions, small loan companies, savings and loan associations, and life insurance companies, as well as relatives and friends. (For a full discussion of credit, consult one of the references cited on pages 425–426.)

The purpose here will be to suggest some guidelines that are intended to serve you as you consider buying now and paying later. Remind yourself, as you may be staring temptation in the face, that any credit purchase commits a portion of your income that you have yet to earn. The payments will come due every month—be sure, therefore, that you will still want the merchandise as much in twelve months as you think you want it now. For the young family with one or two small children, the washing machine bought "on time" probably will be worth every cent of interest, and the monthly payments will not be a burden. On the other hand, that family may resent paying for last summer's vacation when

Christmas arrives. There is one hard fact about credit—once you have contracted to make monthly payments extending over twelve or eighteen months or more, you will have that much less money for other things you may want or need. Guideline 1, then, is: *Use credit to obtain the goods that will have some lasting value to you or to your family.*

Credit cards, whether from a bank, (e.g., Master Charge) oil company, retailer, or multipurpose agency (e.g., Diner's Club and American Express) are a convenience and let us avoid carrying large amounts of cash. It becomes an easy habit to pull out a card and walk away with a $40 blouse or $75 handbag. Ask yourself: Would I buy that blouse if I had to pay cash for it? Or would I shop for something less expensive? Guideline 2: *Use credit as you would cash, and avoid buying the more expensive items just because you can charge them.*

Because credit is readily available at so many sources, we may be inclined to run up bills faster than we realize, faster than we intended, and faster than we can pay for. For the inexperienced person, new to the world of credit, this is especially easy. For experienced users of credit, accustomed to buying on time and knowing how much credit they can safely carry, one debt is paid off before another one is started. Most of us can manage quite comfortably making installment payments on only one account at a time. It's when our accounts pile up and multiply that we are in trouble. Guideline 3: *Limit your installment payments to one or two accounts at a time; do not take on a new obligation until you've paid off the last one.*

Credit, as was already noted, is available from a variety of sources. For example, the automobile salesperson will offer you a payment plan. This may appear to be a good idea because the dealer's interest in your car will continue at least as long as you're paying for it. But in fact the dealer will probably turn your installment contract over to a finance company, and the payment plan may be more expensive than an automobile loan from a bank. Shop for credit in the same way you shop for the automobile. Guideline 4: *Search for the credit plan that is most in your favor.*

Credit has been defined as "man's confidence in man" (woman, if you will). The key word is "confidence." The lender—the creditor—has confidence in you and in your ability to live up to the terms of the loan. Confidence in you derives from your credit rating and from what has been learned of your character and reputation, and your money practices, and your job performance. In return for the lender's confidence in you, you have confidence in your lender. You know that if for some reason beyond your control you cannot manage your payments, the creditor should be the first to know. He or she will be the one person who can help you. Most likely, a way will be found of reducing the monthly payments, or another solution will be introduced. The important thing about this procedure is that you are protecting your credit rating—you have indicated your intentions to fulfill your agreement. Guideline 5: *Treat your credit rating with respect, because it is "money in the bank" in an emergency.*

Your Credit Rating: What Is It and How Do You Get It?

Everyone who has ever used credit has a credit rating. A person who has never borrowed money or maintained a charge account but has always paid cash may have difficulty in securing a loan, odd as this may seem. There is no record available on that person; consequently, the lender has little to go on in determining credit-worthiness. A credit rating is the record one has made as a user of credit, and it will count high among your intangible assets. How prompt you are in your payments, how stable your employment is, how often you change addresses, how you repay financial obligations—these are factors that enter into your record as a credit risk.

Lending institutions explain that their loan applicants are examined on three points:

Character: What they can learn about your sense of responsibility and trustworthiness.
Capacity: What they know about your ability to repay the loan. This will be based on your earnings, record of employment, and job prospects in the future.
Capital: What they learn about your assets—what you presently own: house, car, jewels, money in the bank, stocks and bonds, whatever will cover the loan you are applying for.

Because credit is so universally accepted as a way of doing business in our country, a favorable history (credit rating) is important to you as an individual. Even though you may not be a user of credit, some financial advisors suggest that you take out a small personal loan at your bank, repay it in a few months, and thereby get yourself on the books as worthy of credit. In that way, you will be able to get a loan in an emergency. All it takes to establish a credit rating is a small loan with a prompt record of repayment.

Until late in 1975, a married woman had to rely on her husband's credit rating, more often than not. Charge accounts and credit cards were issued in his name. It made little difference if the wife was employed and earning a substantial salary. But the Equal Credit Opportunity Act has changed that; it is now illegal for lending institutions to deny credit to anyone on the basis of sex or marital status. It would be to your benefit, therefore, if you haven't already done so, to establish a credit rating in your own name. Should the day come when you are separated, divorced, or widowed, you will already have a credit rating.

How Much Debt Can You Afford?

Unfortunately, there is no simple formula that tells you how much debt is enough; so much depends on you. But there are a few rules of thumb that suggest ways of setting limits on what you can safely owe.

1   Never owe more than 20 percent of your annual take-home pay—with the exception of a mortgage. Thus, if you take home $10,000 a year, a safe debt would be about $2,000.
2   Never owe more than 10 percent of the amount that you can pay per month for the next eighteen months. Thus, if your take-home pay is $1,000 per month, you can pay $100 per month. In eighteen months this would be $1,800— your debt limit for the year.
3   This one may be more difficult to reckon—never owe more than one-

third of your discretionary income for the year. Your discretionary income is the money you have left after paying all your basic living expenses. Thus, after determining your living expenses and subtracting them from your take-home pay, you have your discretionary income. One-third of it will approximate your debt limit.

What to Do When Overwhelmed by Debt

The answer is simple—get help, but not just any help. For example, "debt services" will be brought to your attention. These usually amount to little more than debt—taking on one large debt in order to consolidate your present debts.

If you need help, a good place to begin is your bank. The bank may provide a debt counseling service; if not, someone there may know where to send you. Or look in the yellow pages of the telephone directory for the Consumer Credit Counseling Service in your community. This is a nonprofit service, intended for overextended families, which is supported by banks, retailers, and other lenders. The service is aimed at working out plans that will get a family out of debt and on its feet financially. If you do not find a credit counseling service listed, write to the National Foundation for Consumer Credit, 1819 H Street, N.W., Washington, D.C. 20006, for the address of the nearest office. Other counseling services may be available to you through your union, or your church, or the personnel department where you work. The Family Service Association in your community may also have a service for the debt-ridden family.

Above all, don't hide or try to run away. Even your creditors will give you help if they know you need it.

IN CONCLUSION

This chapter has focused on financial planning and controlling the plan once it has been set in motion. The personal nature of money management has been discussed, and several paragraphs were given to the subject of credit, a factor that so often upsets the best-laid management plans.

But the subject—you and your money—is far from exhausted. You should also give some thought and consideration to a life insurance program; you may wonder what to do about investments; perhaps you are asking what to do about housing (to rent or to buy); if you have children, you may want some suggestions as to how to help them live in this world of money; or your chief concern may be retirement and how to be financially ready for it.

These matters are of utmost significance, and you are right in seeking some guidelines that will help you sort out your options. Because each of the questions we suggested is complex and because the answers cannot be dealt with in only a paragraph or two, you will best be served by consulting some of the references at the end of this chapter. But reading what professionals have to say may not be adequate; if so, continue your search by consulting experts in financial matters: your banker, your lawyer, your life insurance agent; you also may learn from experiences your friends can share with you. Possibly you will benefit by enrolling in a personal finance course at a nearby college or university or as part of a continuing education program available in your community. (See Chapter 21.) What is important is that you gather all the information you can as you plan, look ahead, and set your financial house in order. Don't try to make decisions in a vacuum.

On page 426 are listed a few sources of information or help for the consumer who may have a problem. In your investigation, do not overlook the extension service in your state; you will find that the specialists there will be able to give you free material on buying and on financial management. The state extension service operates out of a land-grant university.

Ultimately, however, the decisions will have to be made by you and your family. It all comes back to what was said at the outset—money management is a very personal affair. A prominent Southern bank said it on a highway billboard: "MONEY MATTERS—BUT NOT AS MUCH AS YOU."

BIBLIOGRAPHY

Blodgett, Richard D.: *The New York Times Book of Money,* Quadrangle, New York, 1971. Shows how to organize financial affairs in an efficient and rewarding way. Includes a chapter on the special financial needs and problems of women.

Deacon, Ruth E., and Francille M. Firebaugh: *Home Management: Context and Concepts,* Houghton Mifflin, Boston, 1975. A college text by two home economics professors (and deans) known primarily for their research on family management problems and practices. Chapters 4, 5, 6, 7, and 10—dealing with decision making, values, planning, implementing, and managing—will be helpful.

Fowler, Elizabeth M.: *How to Manage Your Money,* Little, Brown, Boston, 1973. Basic information and advice for the woman who wants to invest money, by a financial writer knowledgeable in the area of stocks, bonds, mutual funds, and other investments.

Knight, James A.: *For the Love of Money,* Lippincott, Philadelphia, 1968. The author, a psychiatrist and professor at Tulane University School of Medicine, has written a most readable treatise on the psychological meaning and emotional uses of money, and the symbols money carries into child rearing and family relations.

Porter, Sylvia: *Sylvia Porter's Money Book,* Doubleday, Garden City, 1975. The author, a well-known columnist and writer on economic and financial subjects, has produced what might be considered an encyclopedia on personal and family finance. This 1,105-page volume is highly readable, objective, informative, and authoritative—a good all-purpose reference on money matters.

Smith, Carlton, and Richard Putnam Pratt: *The Time-Life Book of Family Finance,* Time, Inc., New York, 1970. Readable and well-illustrated chapters dealing with money management and consumer problems. A clear, concise treatment of the two-income family, with thoughtful guidelines for assessing the financial benefits to be gained by the wife's returning to paid employment.

Wolf, Harold A.: *Personal Finance,* Allyn and Bacon, Boston, 1975. A college text by a university (Texas) professor of finance; thorough, comprehensive, and surprisingly nontechnical. The chapters on insurance, retirement planning, and home ownership are informative and objective.

SOURCES OF INFORMATION FOR THE CONSUMER

Bureau of Consumer Protection, Federal Trade Commission, Washington, D.C. 20580.

Consumers Union, 256 Washington Street, Mt. Vernon, N.Y. 10550. Publisher of *Consumer Reports* and an annual buying guide; does product testing.

Council of Better Business Bureaus, 1156 Seventeenth Street N.W., Washington, D.C. 20036.

Municipal bureau of consumer affairs. See the telephone directory for your city.

Office of Consumer Affairs, Washington, D.C. 20201. A government agency concerned with consumer problems of all kinds.

State consumer protective agency. This may be a division of the office of the attorney general, or it may be set up independently.

Chapter 25

Maximizing the Positive in Separation, Divorce, and Widowhood

Herbert A. Otto
Roberta Otto

At a time of crisis, the human organism, always in a state of flux, is more open to change than at other times. The crisis of separation, no matter what the cause, can therefore be used as a powerful agent in your life. You can use it to help you design a way to tap more of your human potential. Seen in this way, a crisis, or change in your life-style, offers you an opportunity for growth.

One of the best ways to begin the process of maximizing the positive factors—the opportunity for growth—in the situation is to be clearly aware of the "human potential hypothesis"—that in general people are functioning at between 4 and 10 percent of their capacity. From this awareness comes the recognition that *every person—and this includes you—has resources, powers, capacities, and strengths that are latent and not being used.* From the moment you realize this, the actualizing of your personal potential can become your most exciting lifelong adventure.[1]

---

[1] Herbert A. Otto, *Guide to Developing Your Potential* (2d ed.), Wilshire, North Hollywood, Calif., 1973. See also Herbert A. Otto, *Group Methods to Actualize Human Potential* (4th ed.), Holistic Press, Beverly Hills, Calif., 1975.

Maximizing the positives in divorce, separation, and widowhood is most effective if undertaken in the context of a person's strengths and resources. For this reason the first section of this chapter will deal with your strengths. Very few people have a clear idea of their own personal strengths and resources, largely as a result of having grown up and participated in an educational system that continuously stresses what we do wrong and what our problems are. We rarely hear enough about what we do right, and we receive insufficient recognition for our achievements. We are all members of a culture centered on pathology and problems, a culture that concentrates excessively on dysfunction and illness. On the other hand, knowing our strengths can give us a more balanced and realistic picture and a new perspective on many of the questions we are faced with during a time of crisis and change. *Knowing your strengths, and then working with any problems or difficulties in the context of this knowledge, is an important—indeed, a major—principle.*

A time of crisis is a time of strong emotions and feelings. These strong feelings can play a constructive or destructive role, depending upon the way they are utilized. Identifying these feelings and getting in touch with them is an important step toward transforming a crisis into an opportunity for personal growth. The second section of this chapter is devoted to this process.

The next step, discussed in the third section, involves working with these feelings and working them through to the point where they become a part of your dynamics of growth. Only by following this sequence can the positive elements present in the crisis be most effectively maximized. Specific experiences designed for this purpose are found in the final section of this chapter.

This chapter will be largely experiential—that is, it will be based on action—because the act of reading, by itself, is not sufficient to set in motion the process needed to maximize the positives in a crisis. It is through action that most change and growth take place. Thus each step will be discussed in terms of *experiences.* We originally conducted a series of classes called (like this chapter) "Maximizing the Positive in Separation, Divorce, and Widowhood," under the auspices of the National Center for the Exploration of Human Potential, San Diego, California. These were attended by residents of San Diego and La Jolla. The class sessions were tape-recorded, and the examples cited in this chapter are in general taken from the tapes. The examples given were chosen because they represent situations, problems, and responses typical of a separation crisis.

BEGIN WITH YOUR STRENGTHS

The first experience to help maximize the positive in separation, divorce, and widowhood is one designed to strengthen you.

The "My Strengths" Experience

We have been trained and brought up not to mention our positive qualities or personal strengths. It is part of our cultural conditioning to consider mentioning our strengths as "boasting." Yet it is important that we know this aspect of ourselves. *The process of listing our strengths is in itself strengthening.* This has been consistently reported by people who have used this experience. The experience takes approximately five to ten minutes to complete.

Part 1 Take a pencil and piece of paper and write the following heading: "The following are what I see as my strengths." Now list as many strengths as you can think of. Stop; do this now. *Do not read ahead.*

Part 2 Read over the following list of strengths (an example from a group brainstorming session) slowly and carefully. Then close the book and add those strengths that you realize you have left out of your list. Finally, post your list in a prominent spot (like your bedroom) where you can see it daily.

Personal Strengths

ability to give and receive
sense of humor
sensitivity
openness
courage
sensuousness
sexiness
intelligence
perseverance
trusting nature
attractiveness
loving nature
capacity for empathy
generosity
adventurousness
flexibility
imagination
health
love of life
energy, vitality
ability to write
ability to relate to people
ability to relate well to
  children
wide range of interests
respect of self and others
love of self
ability to listen
creativity
capacity for taking risks
intuition
sense of beauty
organizational strengths
spiritual strengths
"green thumb"
mechanical ability
mathematical ability
spontaneity
tenderness
responsiveness
faith
loyalty
business ability
sense of reality
leadership skills
sales ability
ability for public speaking
playfulness
ability for home
  management
inventiveness
curiosity
musical and rhythmic ability
sympathy
warmth

The "Your Strengths" Experience

For this experience you need a partner, preferably a friend or someone who knows you well. The "Your Strengths" experience will take about twenty to thirty minutes to complete. We like this experience. It is a way of having someone else tell you what he or she feels is good about you. It is a most supportive and enjoyable experience for you and your friend.

Part 1   To begin the experience, both partners read over the list of Personal Strengths. When you have finished, put away the list. Next, each take a pencil and paper and sit apart from each other so that you cannot see what your partner is writing. Now put your partner's name in the upper right-hand corner and write the following heading: "These are what I see as your strengths." List the strengths of your partner as you see them.

Part 2   When you have both finished, share your lists. As much as possible, point out to each other examples or evidence of strengths you have observed in each other. For instance, Jane R. told her partner, "I put down your sense of responsibility. You are a very dedicated person and you can be depended on to carry out or complete whatever you have said you would do."

The following is an edited tape transcript of a class meeting where people shared their reactions to the "Your Strengths Experience." Irene T., age forty-five (in the process of a divorce after eighteen years of marriage), said:

> "For the first time since the divorce began, I felt such a great glow of pleasure when Robert starting reading his list of my strengths. He has known both me and my husband for a number of years, and I feel he is trying to stay in the middle in this divorce, trying to be a friend to both of us, which must be pretty hard for him. Anyhow, he said he'd be glad to help me when I told him about what I was doing. When I heard him tell me I was kind and thoughtful and a warm and giving person, it was like a gift from heaven. I couldn't believe my ears. I thought he was faking it to be nice to me. But he insisted that he was telling the truth, and mentioned examples. Part of me knows and feels that I am this really warm person with an outgoing personality that Robert said I have. He also said I was bright and attractive; but I have been so lonely and miserable and complaining and unhappy for such a long time that I was sure nobody could see this in me."

After you have finished sharing your lists, give them back to each other. Put them aside for a few days; then look at them again and add strengths to your list which you know you have and which you consider important but which your partner may have left out.

By using the "My Strengths" and "Your Strengths" experiences, you become ready to get in touch with and work with your feelings. As was previously mentioned, this is part of the total process involved in maximizing positives—a process that takes place in the context of strengths.

IDENTIFY AND GET IN TOUCH WITH YOUR FEELINGS

A wide range of intense feelings are usually present during separation, divorce, or widowhood. The very intensity of the feelings triggered by such a change often surprises people: "I never expected to be *that* mad. I could spit nails." "I had some very bad, low moments and negative feelings." "The guilt feelings were the most terrible part. I've had nothing like it before."

This is just a small sampling of reactions. Experiencing such intense emotions while undergoing separation, divorce, or widowhood is normal, natural, and usual, and a valuable part of coping and adapting.

It is important at this time to get in touch with the whole range of feelings which are present—*especially the unrecognized or unacknowledged feelings.* Many people have a tendency to repress or bury feelings because they are unacceptable or because it would be disturbing to admit having them. These unacknowledged, unrecognized feelings can be the cause of severe problems. For instance, Joan T. (age forty-one, married twelve years) told us:

> "I had severe intestinal and stomach problems—indigestion and so on. It seemed like colitis to me, but the doctors couldn't find anything wrong with me. The third doctor referred me to a psychiatrist. I was desperate and lucky to find a good shrink. After three weeks in therapy I was much better. All my anger and hatred had been turned inside. Remember, I had told my friends we were having a friendly divorce, and I believed it! Nobody could have told me I was so angry with him that I could kill him. I was brought up to believe that nice people do not have feelings like that."

Lack of awareness of feelings and fears and misunderstanding of feelings are among the strongest detrimental forces and causes for poor functioning at a time of separation, divorce, or other major changes in life. It is therefore most important that you become aware of them. This is based on the principle that awareness of the feelings at work within a person is the first step toward working through these feelings, and thus leads to optimum functioning. The following are some of the most prevalent emotions encountered during this period.

Feelings of Confusion

A sense of dislocation, turmoil, disorganization, or bewilderment is usually prevalent at such times. People feel insecure, unsure, and confused about their future, their role in life, and themselves. Often there is a noticeable inability to concentrate or to perform routine tasks. However, this is usually a passing symptom.

Here, recognition of the basic psychotherapeutic principle that "confusion precedes growth" can be helpful. Confusion is often the mark of change and transition in the direction of growth. However, if the confusion is excessively prolonged and severe, it is best to seek counseling. (See Chapter 14, pages 247–251.)

Feelings of Fear, Panic, and Anxiety

At a time of crisis, occasional or more prolonged feelings of fear, panic, or anxiety are often present. In many instances these feelings are traced to the severing of ties of dependency, to doubts about one's economic security, to doubt that one can "manage alone," etc.

Lillian G. (age forty and married fifteen years) made these comments during a group meeting for singles:

"I feel as if I have been married my whole lifetime. When the children came, Fred and I agreed that my job was to stay home and look after them. I'm really scared now. I don't know what the future will bring, and I'm afraid I can't manage by myself. There's too little income. I'm panicking all the time. It's true that when I sit down and figure things out, I know I can manage somehow, and that we'll get along."

Feelings of Anger, Hostility, Frustration, and Resentment

The majority of people undergoing the separation of divorce report intense feelings of anger, hostility, and resentment. These feelings may also be present during widowhood; however, they are usually very quickly repressed. At times there may be strong feelings of anger directed at both the ex-partner and oneself or strong bursts of self-blame and hatred. It is important to recognize and be aware of such elements of hostility and resentment. If these emotions are repressed and not recognized and worked through satisfactorily, they may cause a state of depression or feelings of powerlessness.

Often too, repressing the recognition of anger or resentment results in a lack of energy or an outlook marked by indifference. Some people find it difficult to acknowledge their strong feelings of anger or resentment, while others are keenly aware of such feelings.

The accumulation of anger, hostility, and resentment is understandable, considering the circumstances surrounding the change in one's life. These feelings especially need to be worked with to keep them from becoming destructive. A number of specific exercises and experiences have been developed for this purpose and will be found in "Working With Your Feelings."

Feelings of Failure, Rejection, and Unworthiness

Feelings of failure, rejection, and unworthiness are often present. The sense of failure seems to be particularly strong among people who believe that a marriage or relationship should endure despite changes taking place over the years in the personality of both spouses and changes in circumstances.

The feelings are often especially acute in two circumstances: (1) when a partner has invested much time and effort to preserve an unworkable marriage or relationship and has not succeeded, and (2) when children are present and there is a belief that their personality development will be hurt or that they will undergo trauma because of the divorce.

Feelings of rejection and unworthiness are quite common. Many widows also experience these feelings quite keenly. The word "rejection" is often used to describe feelings of hurt due to the perception that one is unwanted, unneeded, or unworthy. Interestingly enough, sometimes a woman may have strong negative feelings about her spouse—in, effect, rejecting him. She may nevertheless feel rejected by her partner and, as a consequence, unworthy.

"Rejection, rejection, rejection! I kept saying that to myself, and it hurt. I was brainwashing myself by using the word. Then I realized that we had rejected each other—and for good reasons. What's wrong with that?"

"When he died, I felt very much rejected. After all, he had left me—I hadn't left him."

"I was a failure and unworthy because we were getting a divorce. I believed that for months and months, but I kept wrestling with it. Suddenly it came to me, out of the blue, that it took guts and a good sense of values on my part to get the divorce. That was the end of that 'I am unworthy' bit."

"I blamed myself for being a failure until during one of our discussions the kids said, 'We would be better off with a divorce.' "

Feelings of Numbness, Depression, and Grief

These feelings are especially strong at a time of widowhood. They are also present during a divorce or separation. The feeling of numbness often is associated with a person's repressing or "turning off" a variety of intense feelings. "Blue" or depressed feelings and feelings of self-pity seem to vary in duration and quality; they are reported to occur somewhat more frequently in the initial stages of losing someone.

"There was a general numbness. My whole body was numb and so was my mind. I could not think or feel much of anything."

"I never felt so blue in my whole life. I'd flip in and out of it like a yo-yo. Finally, it stopped."

Feelings of depression and numbness can often be helped by working with anger and hostility. The "Anger Release Experience" (page 436) can be particularly helpful. If a depression is severe and prolonged and seriously impedes or even immobolizes normal functioning, therapeutic and counseling help need to be obtained. (See Chapter 14, pages 248–250.)

Feelings of grief are often noted. These feelings may center on regrets about the dissolution of what had been, at one time, a close and satisfying relationship, or on grief over the possible impact of the divorce on the children, parents, etc. Grief may also be due to the lack of psychological support or to missing the closeness of a person. Again, some people are able to let themselves feel grief; others have to deny the emotion. As with other feelings, it is important to work with feelings of grief so that they will not have a harmful effect for a prolonged period of time.

Feelings of Guilt, Loneliness, and Isolation

Guilt and feelings of loneliness and isolation are universally reported. Guilt seems to be largely attached to a feeling of having failed in the relationship and being responsible for the "failure." Widows often have strong guilt feelings because they somehow blame themselves for the death of the spouse or blame themselves for having neglected to do something for the spouse that they believe they should have done. Again, there are often strong feelings of guilt about the effect of a divorce on the children. To a lesser extent, there may be feelings of guilt because of a stigma that society sometimes attaches to divorce.

Periodic feelings of loneliness and isolation are usual and realistic, during separation, divorce, or widowhood. Such feelings are often coupled with a feeling of loss, since a companion is now no longer available. While some people welcome solitude, many suffer from loneliness. Feelings of loneliness and isolation are often aggravated by the dissolution of friendships as friends of a couple "take sides" during a divorce.

Other Feelings

Sometimes feelings of bitterness and cynicism and an attitude of negativism develop. It is not uncommon to reach the conclusion that since a member of the other sex was in part or wholly responsible for a painful relationship or divorce (or even for separation by death), therefore *all* members of the opposite sex ought to be shunned because they may cause a repetition of the pain. Such statements as the following are by no means uncommon: "I avoided men for a long time. You know—once bitten, twice shy. Gradually I realized I was being unfair and missing a lot of fun."

All too frequently there is a tendency to hang on to feelings of anger, guilt, and bitterness for a considerable period of time. By holding on to such emotions and not working them through, these feelings can become part of a self-punitive and self-hurting cycle which can sometimes last for years.

During such times of change, physical symptoms of distress may be present; often these are traceable to emotional roots. Headaches, backaches, gastrointestinal disturbances, and other psychosomatic problems are often noticed. If they persist, professional help should be sought.

Positive Feelings

The feelings are not all negative. Positive feelings at times of crisis are by no means rare. Some people report a heightened sense of well-being and increased energy, creativity, and productivity. They also report moments of brightness, great joy, and gladness. The feelings of relief or release from an intolerable or abrasive situation and a sense of freedom and independence are often present. Sometimes, too, there are also feelings of concern, caring (and even love) for the partner in a divorce or separation.

It cannot be sufficiently stressed that *unrecognized, misunderstood emotions and feelings that are unresolved and not worked through are the major blocks that can keep a change from being the vital growth experience it could be.* Recognizing and working with the emotional processes encourages the emergence of new vitality and a fresh enjoyment of life. It marks the beginning of your personal growth and the development of your personal potential.

WORK WITH YOUR FEELINGS

Unless the range of emotions in a crisis are recognized and worked through, they become "unfinished business" that uses up energy and hinders present and future functioning. The psychiatrist Dorothy Baruch spelled out a principle in the late 1940s which is still pertinent today: "Let the negative feelings out so that the positive feelings can come in."[2] This is another reason for working with the feelings which may be present.

The working through of feelings consists of four phases: (1) Becoming aware of certain feelings. (2) Opening yourself to the full measure of these particular feelings, not holding them back or pushing them away. (3) Reexperiencing the incident, or incidents, that seems to have caused the feelings. (This means both understanding and fully entering into the emotions associated with each incident that may have been bottled up.) (4) Integrating the feelings—i.e., being aware that the full exploration and experiencing of these feelings has helped to diminish their force and reestablishes a balance in their relation to present reality.

The experiences described later are most effective if another person is present to help. Sometimes feelings are masked or hidden, and you may not be fully aware of them; however, the presence of another person helps many people get in touch with them. For example, a friend may know you well, be sensitive to your unconscious reactions, and point these out to you. (This could help you get in touch with the strong feelings you may not realize you were hiding or holding back.)

If you cannot find anyone to help you with the experiences in this section, *write out your feelings*. Another alternative is to *act out your feelings* by yourself and reexperience incidents that produced them. (You can stamp your feet, shout, cry, etc.) You can, of course, both write and act out your feelings.

If Feelings Persist

Sometimes in reexperiencing an incident that seems to have caused certain feelings, it may be necessary to "replay" or go into the emotions associated with the incident several times in order to let out and work through the feelings. This means that you may have to let time go by and then again return to the incident in order to fully work through the feelings involved.

If strong feelings persist every time your thoughts turn to an incident, even after you have worked with it and after you have followed the preceding directions, let some time pass. Then try the following experience.

Repeat the exercise from this chapter that you used previously: writing out your feelings, acting them out, or both. However, before beginning the experience, say to yourself aloud several times: "I am going to exhaust all these feelings *this* time and get rid of them."

Now repeat the exercise, going into the feelings, until you are physically exhausted. At this point say the following aloud a number of times: "I have now exhausted these feelings. They no longer bother me. I am through with them."

Get your whole body into the feeling of being finished with this particular reaction to the incident. Stand up and, using your hands, brush away imaginary pieces of anger, disappointment, frustration, etc., from all parts of your body. Repeat aloud: "I am through with this feeling"; "I am finished"; "It is gone"; etc. Do this to clear away the feelings from all parts of your body.

There may be times in the future when, owing to a series of circumstances,

---

[2] Dorothy Baruch, *New Ways of Discipline,* Whittlesey House, New York, 1949, p. 8.

certain situations or words may trigger the old responses. Since you have worked through and familiarized yourself with the situations and your reactions, you can make a decision whether or not to proceed in the old direction. At these times, you can say to yourself, "This is a trigger word (or situation) for me. I don't have to respond in this (the old) way," and *don't do it.* Relax, laugh, or begin humming a tune, and consciously change your response. *You can control what you do.* The causes are known. This is part of your increased awareness and growth.

Rewarding Yourself

Finally, whenever you have made any progress in working through hurtful feelings, *reward yourself. Congratulate yourself on what you have achieved, and give yourself something you will enjoy.* (Psychologists call this process "positive reinforcement.") Many people find it difficult to do something that gives them a lot of pleasure or to buy things for themselves. It is very important to respect and recognize your progress and your own worth. Giving something to yourself is a simple way of doing so.

A Little Help from Your Friends

If you are with a friend, your friend can help you in a number of ways while you are working with your feelings:

1 By encouraging you with such remarks as, "Go ahead and let *all* the feelings out—you are doing fine."
2 By helping you to be sensitive to other, related feelings that may be involved and by helping you to become aware of these feelings.
3 By comforting and assisting you.

It is well to know that exploring and expressing hurtful feelings is hard work and takes energy. You may need to be comforted. You may also want to rest and doze for a time or go for a walk between sessions of working on your feelings. (You may wish to read the preceding paragraphs to your friend before beginning any of the experiences in this chapter.)

Three "Anger Release" Experiences

Until quite recently (and this is still going on in many places) expressing certain feelings, particularly anger, was socially taboo. For example, the words "I'll scream," even used playfully during a discussion, seem to have a magic power behind them and will stop people in their tracks.

According to some authorities, women have more difficulty than men getting in touch with their anger:

> Most women are terribly frightened of their own anger. Largely this is because they don't know what will happen if it is released. It is as if their world might fall apart. The unfortunate truth is that when such women expressed anger as small children, they did pay an exorbitant price for it. Now they are defended against even *feeling* anger. . . .[3]

---

[3] Eleanor Hamilton, "Emotions and Sexuality in the Woman," in Herbert A. Otto (Ed.), *The New Sexuality,* Science and Behavior Books, Palo Alto, Calif., 1971, p. 65.

Fortunately, this type of emotional constriction is no longer as common, and the expression of feelings is now more widely accepted and practiced. Getting in touch with and expressing anger is the necessary first step in dealing with this emotion constructively.

It should be clear that many people have other ways of successfully handling hostility or anger. For example, some deeply religious people are able to neutralize or cancel out anger by drawing on their spiritual resources. Others use a different aproach to get rid of anger or to transform anger directed toward specific persons. Jill D. (thirty-two, an accountant with three children) made this comment, "When I find myself angry with anyone, I pray. This fills me with a deep peace, and anger disappears." Lillian R. (age twenty-eight, a successful dress designer) shared her way of coping with anger: "I discovered a good way to transform my anger. When I get angry with someone who has done me a bad turn, for example, I look at the weaknesses of that person and invariably find that the person is someone to be pitied rather than hated."

We need to recognize the positive uses of anger. Anger is not always negative. Anger can provide energy and trigger constructive or life-supportive activity. Anger can also operate to ease a separation. "The haggling I did with the lawyers made me so angry I began to see M's true colors. I'm definitely glad to be rid of M."—such feelings are expressed equally by both men and women. Anger may thus serve a very useful function during a divorce. However, when hostile or angry feelings become dominant or bothersome, it is well to deal with them.

Here are three experiences designed to help release feelings of anger. Read them over, and do one or all of them, according to your need. Have the experiences with a friend present, if possible, or by yourself.

"Anger Release" Experience 1: Part 1   Begin this experience by recalling incidents involving your ex-partner that made you angry. Talk about these situations. Get in touch with your anger. Let yourself feel the anger.

Part 2   Let out your anger. One way is to use a tennis racket, table tennis paddle, or rolled-up newspaper for an improvised club, and pound or beat on a bed, pillow, or stuffed chair. (You can also use clay to pound on.) Stamp your feet, and, as you experience angry feelings, scream, yell, or shout while you are hitting. Your friend can encourage you. When you are finished physically releasing the anger (or while you are doing it), say to yourself: "I am rid of this feeling. It isn't going to bother me any more."

"Anger Release" Experience 2: Part 1   "Replay" an argument or fight you have had with your ex-partner. This time, say all the things you didn't say before.

Part 2   While you are doing this, let *all* your angry feelings come out. Scream, stamp your feet, pound pillows, cry. Use whatever might help you to physically release your anger.

"I waited for a day when I was really angry with everything. Nothing was right. I remembered all the dishes and cups with cracks and chips in them that I had wanted to throw out. I took them to the basement and threw them against the wall one at a time as hard as I could. I kept yelling things like 'damn you' and 'nuts to you'—

whatever came to my mind. The crash was very satisfying and I had a very deep release." (Diane, age thirty-three, married eleven years.)

"I kicked that old chair hard and screamed at it and imagined I was kicking him in the butt." (Mary, age twenty-six, married four years.)

"My rolled-up newspaper was in tatters when I was through. I kept saying to myself, 'You're getting rid of this anger,' and it worked. I could feel it leave me. When it was over, I was peaceful and relaxed. This experience helped more than anything else." (Rosalie, age forty-nine, married twenty-six years.)

Part 3   To complete the experience, stand up. Brush away the angry feelings from all parts of your body, saying "It's over; I'm through with this," or whatever feels right to you.

Please note: You can get rid of your anger against yourself by using the same techniques described above.

"Anger Release" Experience 3   Writing out their most extreme fantasies of anger, hostility, or violence seems to help some people. In conducting the Developing Personal Potential groups,[4] we use a sign saying "Never feel guilty about your fantasizing." This is based on the principle that to communicate fantasies, to talk about them, to *get them out,* releases emotions. It is the repressed, pushed back, or "inadmissable" fantasy that causes trouble.

Part 1   Take a pencil and paper and write out the worst acts of violence you can imagine yourself doing in relation to the source of your anger. When you have finished writing out your fantasy in detail, read it over. Then tear it up and burn it. As you do this, say to yourself aloud, *"I am getting rid of these angry feelings."*

"The stuff I wrote was far out. Torture and sadistic stuff. I didn't know I was that full of hate. When I read it over, I had to laugh. Then I burned it after tearing it into a thousand little pieces. All that hatred went up the chimney. I felt better afterwards. It's silly to carry it around."

Part 2   After you have gotten to the bottom of your anger (if necessary, take several sessions to do this) talk over and explore the following question with your friend: "To what extent are these angry or hostile feelings a force in my life *now*?"

Finally, say to yourself out loud, several times: "I am finished with these feelings." "I'm through with these angry feelings." "I'm finished letting them bother me."

Part 3   Again, use your hands to brush away, in your imagination, all the angry feelings from all parts of your body.

---

[4] The Developing Personal Potential program was originally formed as part of The Human Potential Research Project, the University of Utah, 1960–1967. The program is being used by many colleges, universities, and schools in the United States and abroad, and over 1,000 group facilitators have trained in the use of these methods. (See also footnote 1.)

Remember—Reward yourself well as you make progress in working through your feelings.

The "Guilt Release" Experience   Many people have guilt feelings associated with separation, divorce, or widowhood. This experience can help you become aware of and work through such feelings.

Part 1   Begin the experience by writing out in detail *where you feel guilt in relation to the breakup of your relationship, to your family, to the divorce, to widowhood, etc.* (If you have no feelings of guilt about the foregoing, you have the option of writing out other types of guilt that may be present.) As you are doing this, be aware of your feelings.

When you have finished writing, put the material away for a day or two, saying the following to yourself aloud several times: "Writing out these guilt feelings helps me to get rid of them."

Part 2   While a friend is present, slowly reread what you have written and share the contents. (You may wish to read aloud what you have written.) As much as possible, let yourself enter into these feelings. (You may cry, shout, yell, etc.)

Janice (age thirty-one, married seven years):

"Those guilt hangups I had were something. I bought the trip my husband laid on me that I was the guilty one. I really felt it was my fault. Ted was always saying that I was not feminine, that I didn't understand him. He kept telling me that I was not keeping up my end of the marriage. I knocked myself out trying to please him. I would hurry home from work and rush to set the table and have dinner ready for him by the time he was home. He wasn't happy helping me with the dishes, and most of the time I would wind up doing them. He'd always be saying he had extra work to do, or was extra tired, or something. He'd sit at the television relaxing, and I'd be there cleaning up the house and getting ready for my teaching the next day. Maybe I didn't understand him, and I don't know what it is to be feminine. All I know is that I did the best I could. I got all the way into this stuff while talking to Nancy. It made me cry and be angry at the same time, but I did get rid of a lot of junk. The world is beginning to look beautiful again."

Part 3   Now talk over and explore the following question with your friend: *"To what extent are these feelings of guilt a force in my life now?"*

Many people like to complete this experience by saying, "I forgive myself and I forgive others." You can say this, or say to yourself aloud, several times; "I have worked through these guilt feelings; they are no longer dominant"; or "They no longer bother me."

As in the previous experiences, you can also use your hands to "brush away" the guilt and hurt from all parts of your body. While doing this, say, "I'm finished with these feelings"; "I am through with them."

The "Exploration of Loneliness" Experience   Loneliness is a universal feeling experienced by many during a time of life change. The intensity and nature of these feelings of loneliness varies widely. Most people find that the feelings will fade away as they become accustomed to a new life-style and find new friends and companions.

Part 1   Write out your feelings of loneliness. Do this in as much detail as possible. As you are writing, let these feelings enter you fully.

Part 2   You can now discuss these feelings with a friend who can help you get deeper into them. Next, you can discuss with your friend or determine by yourself *concrete actions you can take to deal with feelings of loneliness.*

Three people shared with us what using the "Exploration of Loneliness" experience meant to them:

> "I've always been most afraid of being alone, of having no one care for me. I realized I was worse off being married to someone who didn't care for me. I also realized how much I had been fooling myself. Talking this over with my friend has helped me in another way. I now know that somehow I will meet someone who will enjoy being with me. I am more optimistic."

> "Loneliness was one of my problems. When I wrote out what I felt about it, I reached the conclusion that it wasn't so bad after all. Everybody needs privacy, and you can't complain when the need is met. How much more positive can you get? I am also going to make more of an effort to go out and meet people."

> "Loneliness is a bugaboo, and I have to face it. Company is just a phone call away. We talked about it and came up with a whole bunch of ideas which I can use the next time I feel lonely."

The "Exploring Fears and Concerns" Experience   Fears and concerns appear to be an inevitable by-product of a change in one's life. Occasionally these fears are put into words, but usually they remain vague and unclear. It is the very indistinct nature of these concerns that lends additional force to such feelings.

Part 1   To begin the experience, take a pencil and paper and write out the following heading: "Fears and concerns I have at this time in my life."

Ask yourself these questions: "What am I worried about?" "What am I afraid might happen?"

Write out your answers in detail and, while doing this, open yourself to your emotions; sense how you feel.

Part 2   Next, take another sheet of paper and write this heading: "Some ways of handling my fears and concerns." *Write out as many ways of handling each fear and concern as you can think of.* Do not be critical of the ideas you are putting down. The objective is to get in writing as many alternatives as you can for dealing with your concerns. The emphasis is on the production of *quantity;* quality comes later. Do this "brainstorming" for every fear or concern you have listed. When you have finished, put your papers away for a day or two.

Part 3   Preferably with a friend present, review what you have written. Next, ask your friend for her or his ideas of ways to handle your fears or concerns. Add these suggestions and any additional ideas you may have to your list. Finally, go over the completed list together. *Underline what you see now as the best ways to handle your fears or concerns.*

The following comments are from people who used the "Exploring Fears and Concerns" experience:

> "I was very anxious and afraid when the divorce got started. It never occured to me to take a look at what I was afraid about. It was all very vague and nebulous. When I sat down and wrote out my fears, they started to evaporate. There was some solution for every fear."

> "Initially I did not want to do this exercise. Maybe I was a little afraid to face my fears." (Laughs.) "When I got the nerve to sit down and make my list, it wasn't so hard after all. I felt better just writing them on a piece of paper. I let two or three days go by and then looked at the list again and continued with the exercise. As I reread my fears, I noticed that a lot of things I had written were of the sort I call *'if this happened, then . . .' I am not saying it's not possible for those things to happen, but I was looking at all the negative things that could* happen in a situation once you put your imagination to work. This is the main thing I got from this excercise. My friend and I brainstormed the ways to handle some of the more real concerns on the list, and we came up with some good ideas." (Ruth M., age thirty-one, married seven years with two children.)

POSITIVE ELEMENTS

For the person who is single again, counting one's blessings and becoming aware of the positive elements in the situation is most valuable. Not only does it help you to gain a more balanced perspective of your situation, but becoming aware of these positive elements gives you a clearer picture of what to do and in what direction you need to move. Finally, many people have told us that the "Positive Elements" experience has made them feel better about themselves. Here, then, is the experience, which will help you realize the range of positive elements existing in your life today.

The "Positive Elements" Experience

Part 1 On a sheet of paper, write the following heading: "These are positive elements I see in my situation at this time."

Begin to list all the good things you are grateful for: your strengths, your resources, the supportive elements available and surrounding you—everything you can think of that makes you feel good. When you have completed your list, look ahead and read the sample lists of positive elements at the end of this experience. Add whatever additional positive elements may have come to your mind as a result of reading the sample lists. Now, when you have finished adding to your list, put it away for a few days.

Part 2 After you have let some days go by, take out the list and read what you had written. Add whatever new positive elements have occurred to you in the interval. Place the list in a prominent place, so that you can see it often every day. This also gives you the opportunity to add to the list often—every day or every second day—as new events occur or as other thoughts come to your mind, showing you how much more you have to be grateful for.

It is strongly recommended that you have a person close to you go over the list with you. He or she can suggest any additional positive elements you may have left out.

Jane's list of positive elements

"These are the positive elements I see in my situation at this time:"
I now have a chance to create a more harmonious life for my children.
There is the freedom to become a person in my own right.
For the first time I can make decisions I have never made by myself before.
I can shape my own life the way I want to.
Finally I have the chance to resume my education—starting in a small way (one class).
I have a good job.
I am loved by others.
I am a warm, loving person.
I am creative.

Rebecca's list of positive elements

"These are the positive elements I see in my situation at this time:"
My family supports me and my decision to get a divorce.
My children are settling down, and we are happier with each other.
I have a job that helps me.
I have good clothes and a car.
I am active in organizations.
Despite ups and downs I am basically optimistic.
Good health is one of my assets.
I am feeling attractive again.
I have a tendency to bounce back.
I do not have to move from my house.
I have a friend I can talk to.
I have a lot of interests that I can follow up.

Maximizing the Positive Elements

While working with the "Positive Elements" experience we became aware of a common thread running through the lists that people made. The sense of freedom to make your own decisions, of being responsible for your own activities and use of time and energy, seems to be universal. That is why this is an excellent time to begin to reevaluate and reshape many aspects of your life. This is the time you can begin to choose the direction in which you wish to go. The more consciously you make decisions, the more quickly a sense of direction and well-being emerges. This can happen effectively and without great stress when you begin to concentrate on and maximize the positive elements in your situation.

Here are a group of experiences that will help you create a more supportive and nourishing environment for yourself. Your total environment includes every aspect of your being—the people who surround you, your personal and spiritual resources, your home environment, and your value system.

Your Supportive Relationships   All of us have people around us we know— acquaintances, friends, family, co-workers, neighbors, and relatives. We are in fact cradled by human relationships. On closer examination we find that some of the people we know make us feel good to be around them. Others leave us feeling depressed, anxious, or gloomy, or questioning our ability to make decisions and carry on. Then there are people who seem to drain us and leave us without energy. On the other hand, *there are people who, when we are with them, foster our creativity—stimulate or challenge us.*

Recognizing that people do have an effect on us, now is the time to surround yourself with people whom you like and enjoy being with. An experience that can help you clarify and gain a clearer understanding of how your relationships with the people you know affect you is to ask yourself searching questions about these relationships. Analyze your friendships and relationships. How do you relate to the people in your life? How do you feel about being with these people? *It is especially important at this time to be with people who stimulate you, who care for you, and who are support you.* Spending more time with them and avoiding the people who make you feel uncertain and depressed will encourage you to attempt the things you want to do. These are the people who are "life-affirmative" for you.

Your Home Environment   In recent years psychologists have become increasingly aware of how the environment, and especially the home environment, affects people's attitudes, moods, and feelings. If you have continued to live in the house you shared with your spouse, certain areas of the house probably act as "emotional triggers" for you. In the case of divorce, these are often negative. Here are some experiences people shared with us:

"There in the corner was his chair and his reading lamp. Looking at them would make me either angry, or sad, or both."

"I want bright colors around me now; I'm trying to change the whole dark feeling of this place."

Often, changing the position of the furniture, obtaining inexpensive new wall decorations, or hanging the old ones in different places can bring a sense of freshness and renewal to your home. It is surprising how even the smallest change that you make in your environment can make it more pleasing and inviting to you, and thus make you feel better about yourself.

Use of significant symbols   Another important part of our environment is the symbols that we surround ourselves with. This includes the paintings, posters, souvenirs, photographs, knickknacks, etc., that have been accumulating over a long period of time. Now is the time to put away, give away, or sell those items which now have little or no meaning for you, or which do not recall happy memories. Once you have "cleared the decks," you can start discovering new things, obtaining and surrounding yourself with objects *that have positive meanings for you right now.*

Begin by introducing new, significant symbols into your environment. For example, treat yourself to a gift that will recall to you the first time you consciously used courage in a situation and expressed your true feelings, or the time you had the strength to ask for something you wanted. *Give yourself a gift whenever you have achieved any objective you have set for yourself.* Keep the significant symbol visible: it is giving you good feedback about yourself.

"Positive Action" Programs

One of the main purposes of the "Positive Action" programs is to start you enjoying other aspects of your life. It is a simple, easy way to begin capitalizing on your strengths and make them work for you, enriching your total being. A "Positive Action" program can be *any activity or experience you have by yourself, or with other people, that you feel will strengthen you, make you feel good, or help you develop some aspect of your potential.*

Such a program allows you to have happy, self-affirmative experiences that nourish the ego and enhance your self-esteem. The idea is to begin and complete a minimum of one positive action a week, for at least five weeks. It is the repetitive, positive impact of the program that contributes to its effectiveness.

To Choose your "Positive Action" program for the first five weeks, consider these criteria:

1 It should be fun, something you will enjoy.
2 It should be something you are certain you can conclude successfully.
3 If possible, it should allow you to act spontaneously and freely in developing it.
4 It should be something that you can complete within a week.

For example, this is not the time to choose to stop smoking or lose weight, for these two actions usually take more than a week to complete and are not fun.

A "Positive Action" program could be planning and going on a long hike; getting involved with a new group of people; going to a dance class; visiting an art gallery; buying a new record; trying new foods and recipes; renting a bike; taking a long walk every day; reading a book; etc.

Begin with the "Positive Action" program that appeals to you most. As you go along, you may find that you have two or three programs in motion—for example, learning to cook Chinese food, exercising, meeting new people, etc.

The "Creativity Encounter" Experience

Using your talents, and discovering some new ones that you have allowed to remain dormant, can be very satisfying and exciting. It is particularly so at this moment in your life, when the possibility for fresh beginnings exists. Everybody has creative potential, and everyone has used creative capacities to some degree throughout a lifetime. However, we often find ourselves trapped in habitual patterns and do not take time to explore other areas we would enjoy developing.

The "Creativity Encounter" is not only helpful in exploring and developing new interests, but has been of great assistance in helping people decide about new careers they wish to pursue. The purpose of the experience is to *help you discover more areas in which you would enjoy being creative.* It also helps you plan the specific steps necessary to develop these areas. This experience is especially effective and enjoyable if done with one or two other people. However, if you do not have a partner, you can write out the answers to all the questions. It takes forty-five minutes to one hour to complete the experience.

Remember, many people are creative and inventive in relation to their work or at home, although they are often not aware of this. Creativity is *not* restricted to the arts—writing, painting, sculpting, hobbies, etc. *You may also be creative in interpersonal relationships and in many other ways, some of which you may not have readily recognized.*

Part 1 Look over your past for times when you have been creative, and begin by sharing with your partner the ways in which you have been creative.

Ask yourself the following question, and share the answers with your partner: "what creative things have I done in childhood? In adolescence?"

It is the task of each partner to ask searching questions and to "tease out" areas and instances where the other has shown creativity. For instance, become aware of an event your partner told you about with great enthusiasm, or ask yourself: "What creative things has my partner done that she particularly enjoyed doing?"

The person writing out the answers should notice where she felt happy and enthusiastic when recalling past experiences. Enthusiasm and joy are often the keys to your creativity. Use your intuition and hunches in this process, and do not be afraid to ask questions.

Part 2 Each partner now chooses and shares what she considers to be the most creative moment in her life (other than childbirth or marriage). To assist yourself in discovering this instance, ask yourself: "What has been my *most* creative moment—the time I remember when I was most proud of a particular achievement? When was I most exultant about having been creative? When was I most pleased with myself for being inventive?"

Think back through your life and review your very happy and productive times. Go back to the time you were eighteen or twenty, to your adolescence, or to your childhood to find your most creative moment.

Share this moment with your partner. Then ask your partner the following questions: "When do you feel most creative now?" "Doing what?"

Part 3 After you have helped your partner recall and survey instances and experiences where she had been creative, ask her the following key question: *"What would you now like to do that would be creative and that you would enjoy doing?"*

An alternative way to ask the key question might be: *"What would be fun for you to do and at the same time would express a creative part of your personality?"*

Each partner may wish to take turns reading these key questions aloud to the other.

Part 4 With your partner, plan some definite steps to take so that you can both have an encounter with creativity. For instance, if your partner is looking for a change in her career, explore together what areas and jobs are available that would use her creative abilities. Go into depth: discuss what steps may be necessary, people to see, where to get further information, etc. For example, as a result of this experience Mary K. has started taking a course one night a week on how to operate a small business.

Part 5   You may want to set up another meeting with your partner to discuss what has been happening since you last saw each other. At this time you may wish to discuss the following question: *"Where and how can I use more of my creativity in my life?"*

Remember, your adventures with creativity are a means of acknowledging your potential.

Enhancing Your Physical Image of Yourself

Now is a good time to make changes in your personal style. The results are often quite dramatic. You can create any image you wish to project of yourself. This is the time to take a long look in the mirror, to check your wardrobe and see *if it expresses the you that you want to be and want the world to see.*

A friend can be helpful in making suggestions, and you can both have fun. This may be a good time to buy or make some new clothes that add zip to your wardrobe and to plan for the changes you want to make in the future. Personal restyling not only can change the image you project to the world, but can make you feel stronger and more self-confident.

SOME ADDITIONAL CONSIDERATIONS

Finances

In most instances, separation, divorce, or widowhood affects the economic aspects of living. There is less money to go around, and this results in a more austere life-style. Feeling under pressure about money can have a marked effect on self-confidence. Many of our class members who have been through this crisis found that budgeting for certain "essential luxuries" (such as movies, an occasional lunch with a friend, etc.) is one way to reduce the impact of the fact that less money will be available.

We have also found that another alternative (when the appropriate resources exist) is to take a temporary loan from parents, relatives, or friends to ease the transition. Since many women must begin to explore the possibilities of gainful employment, it makes a lot of sense to take out such a loan (or dip into one's savings) for additions to one's wardrobe and other expenses of job hunting. Again, class members have reported that one of the best ways of coping with worries about money is to construct a realistic budget—without, however, stinting on the "essential luxuries" previously mentioned.

Separation Without Divorce

When two people separate but do not get a divorce, this often creates special problems. In many instances, women especially seem to have a tendency to be caught up in a serious problem: they do not feel that they are free or independent persons, and in many instances this restricts their capacity to date or establish relationships with men. There are also some women who use the separation as a means of placing themselves in an indefinite state of "suspended animation." As one woman put it, "We are separated for a year now, and I'm just letting things happen. Let him make the first move for the divorce. I want it, but I am just sort of floating along." A separation can often be a devitalizing and sapping experience. One way to get away from the feeling of being "caught" or powerlessness is to seek counseling.

Spiritual Growth and Values

The search for meaning, the reason for continuing to live, usually runs as a basic, perhaps unrecognized current in everyone's life. However, this quest for the meaning of existence seems to come to the surface and demand answers particularly during periods of change. Since our value system is intimately related to our belief system, this is a good time to reexamine what has meaning for you and to explore why you believe you are here.

One way to clarify your values is to find some quiet time, get paper and pencil, and write the following heading: "These are my basic values." (Values are defined as what you really know is of importance to you in the course of your life.)

Taking time to become aware of your inner self, of your relationship with the universe, of your own love and spiritual strengths, can help place everything in focus. It is all part of growth. In this context, asking questions and looking for answers can bring a deep sense of serenity and peace.

Self-communication

We see posters and read advertising slogans everywhere, and they appear to get results by motivating and influencing people. Why not bring this effective technique into your own life? You can give messages to yourself that make you feel happy and creative and give you a sense of well-being and contentment. All the reports from people using such deliberate, spontaneous messages indicate that they are morale builders.

For example, you can leave notes or signs for yourself on your desk, on your bulletin board, on the mirror in your bathroom, near your bed, anywhere. Here are some signs women have used and shared with us:

SMILE
YOU'RE GREAT
EXPECT THE BEST
WALK IN LOVE
YOU ARE IMPORTANT
YOU CAN DO IT
LIFE IS TO ENJOY
I DO NOT WALK ALONE

IT'S TODAY THAT COUNTS, NOT YESTERDAY OR TOMORROW
GOOD WILL
YOU ARE A BEAUTIFUL PERSON
I LOVE YOU

A Cornucopia of Suggestions

During some of our classes and group meetings we have had brainstorming sessions on how to maximize the positive in separation, divorce, and widowhood. The following list contains a collection of ideas drawn from these classes. Read them over—you will probably find several suggestions of interest to you.

Use free time to let creativity flow; take up calligraphy, poetry, painting—something new.

Go to some entertainments—movies, plays, ballets—that he did not like but you do.

Take a break—escape to the mountains or the ocean. Walking and running help take pressure off you.

Take a look at the new freedoms you now have, and make a list of them.

Talk to your minister or priest or rabbi—ask him what positive aspects he sees in your situation.

Throw a party to celebrate your new life-style.

What are some things you would like to do but haven't done in a long time? Make a list of them, and do them.

Go to the library and find some new books to read.

Read a book on the single life, and use at least one positive idea from it.

Ask your closest friend to comment on positive changes he or she sees in you since your separation.

Be good to yourself. Give yourself a present to celebrate your entry into a new life-style.

Make a list of "firsts" since your separation; for example, "I went to a party by myself for the first time." Look at these "firsts" as *positive,* as signs of your independence.

Treat yourself to a massage or facial. Find out where the nearest hot springs or spa is, and plan to go.

Join a singles club or a computerized dating service.

Be courageous and do something you've always been afraid to do before. You can say to yourself: "This is a plus. I would never have dared to do this before."

As one of our recently divorced class members put it, "Let's have the courage and faith to be what we can be." Separation, divorce, and widowhood offer two challenges—to grow with and through the event and to maximize the positive in every aspect of your life.

BIBLIOGRAPHY

Edwards, Morie, and Eleanor Hoover: *The Challenge of Being a Single,* American Library, New York, 1974. This paperback, which addresses itself to the divorced, widowed, and separated as well as the never married woman, has many suggestions on how to cope with loneliness and an excellent annotated list of suggested readings and helpful addresses.

Fromann, Lynn: *Getting It Together,* Berkley, New York, 1974. Subtitled "The Divorced Mother's Guide." This paperback contains many practical tips and a special chapter, "The Newly Working Woman."

Hirsch, Barbara R.: *Divorce: What a Woman Needs to Know,* Regnery, Chicago, Ill., 1973. One of the most recent guides to the legal aspects of a divorce, with a detailed chart of the grounds for divorce recognized in each state.

Krantzler, Mel: *Creative Divorce,* Evans, New York, 1973. Written by a marriage counselor—a valuable book with one of the best chapters on children in divorce and how to help them.

Maas, Henry S., and Joseph A. Kuypers: *From Thirty to Seventy,* Jossey-Bass, San Francisco, Calif., 1975. Many helpful hints for the older woman and widow. Summarizes pertinent recent research.

Shereskey, Norman, and Marya Mannes: *Uncoupling,* Dell, New York, 1972. This paperback has much excellent up-to-date material on legal aspects of divorce.

Chapter 26

The New World
of Retirement

Jaylee M. Duke, Ph.D.

Jaylee M. Duke, Ph.D., was formerly Director of Continuing Education in the Ethel Percy Andrus Gerontology Center, University of Southern California. Her responsibilities included program development and presentation and the administration of the largest summer institute for study in gerontology in the nation. Ms. Duke has taught university graduate classes in the psychology of aging and preparation for the later years.

Retirement is a major event in a person's life. It is both a point in time and a place in one's history as a worker, a homemaker, and an individual. It is an ending and a beginning: the end of years of commitment to a demanding work schedule, and the moment when one can begin to seize opportunities to find new and creative ways to use time. The retired woman finds herself in a bountiful life. She can pursue long-cherished but frequently frustrated desires; she can choose to become all that she knows she is and can be. There is every reason to expect that the retirement years will be personally satisfying.

Each person who considers retirement has problems. Although some of these are individual, many are common to most people. By solving these problems one can reduce much of the anxiety, the fear, and the feelings of uncertainty that often accompany any new venture, change in location, or new purpose. This chapter will respond to the questions commonly raised:

How will adjustments to my life-style be influenced by other members of my family?

What will my health needs be, and what sort of medical services and financial support should I expect?

Should I consider a second career? If so, will I need a résumé, and can I turn a hobby into a profitable enterprise?

What legal matters—such as making a will, selling my home, planning my estate, and other personal rights and responsibilities—should I undertake?

What changes in budgeting, investments, tax considerations, and retirement benefits should I make?

What should I do about my housing? Should I relocate? What services do I require? What climate do I prefer? How close do I really want to be to family and friends?

What will I do with my leisure time? Will hobbies, travel, educational activities, entertainment, and community service be enough?

The material given in this chapter is intended to be practical and comprehensive. It should help to ensure that retirement will be an opportunity and a satisfying and positive stage of life.

THE OLDER WOMAN

Few women reach retirement age without realizing that they have valuable experience with matters that help people get through life: skills in homemaking and dealing with family relationships, insights into other people, and knowledge of the working world. Over a period of forty or more years, these "accidental experts" become successful economists as well as public-relations and efficiency experts. A lifetime of practical experience has given them the ability to negotiate successfully in many marketplaces. They can handle money: they can earn, budget, spend, and invest it. Such women have learned the relationships between time and tasks; any woman who has managed a personal and working life has become an efficiency expert. She has invaluable experience in public relations, too. Working women have learned to meet and relate to the public. They have been members of clubs, service organizations, and church groups; and many have held important positions of leadership. There is really little about management that the retired working woman doesn't know.

These "accidental experts" can apply all their skills during their retirement. For instance, they can be valued members of political groups seeking to improve conditions on a local or national level. They can help to organize and run services for the aged such as a meals-on-wheels program or a volunteer transportation service. Because of their accumulated wisdom, older women are entitled to feel a great sense of personal worth; and they are of unquestioned value to their communities. Having information about being an older woman and about how the world will be experienced during retirement may help such a woman to maintain a sense of self-esteem and to remain a contributing member of her community.

ADJUSTMENTS IN LIFE-STYLE, AND OPPORTUNITIES

Retired women have lived through the pleasures and demands of several social roles. These roles have shifted, overlapped, and required modification. Some women may have elected to remain single. Those who chose to marry may or may not have become mothers; and some may have been divorced, widowed, and perhaps remarried. Relocations, births, and deaths have changed relationships. All these experiences required patience, acceptance, and flexibility. The transition from the working world to retirement, and the roles and opportunities that accompany it, can be smooth and personally satisfying, especially if women will remember that they have lived through many similar changes during the course of their lives.

Anticipating changes in social roles is worthwhile. A personal appraisal of the difference between being employed and being retired is a necessity. If women feel that being over sixty, retired, or simply no longer young makes them inferior or useless, they will accept the picture society all too often has of them. The stereotype of the older woman must be altered from within. Women's feminine levels of consciousness have to be raised. This means searching for and recognizing inner feelings and then giving them a chance to be felt, examined, and assessed. If women will do this, they will be able to develop themselves by renewing their involvement in existing interests or by making themselves open to new experiences. Women who wish to raise their levels of personal awareness try to find out how they really feel about themselves rather than about older women in general. They take an inward look that asks, "Who am I? How do I feel about myself? What do I want?" Often the answers will be positive. They will reflect or lead to feelings of well-being, to saying positive things:

I am a good person.
I like to work.
I have lots of energy.
I am interested in people.
I enjoy having time to myself.
I like politics.
I like to read.

Inspecting one's feelings often inspires an interest in developing them. A woman with a hobby and energy might well develop a marketable product. However, an honest examination need not lead to anything more than a sense of personal satisfaction, which is definitely worth feeling. A careful and honest reading of feelings allows for a sense of satisfaction and for easy transition into and acceptance of being retired.

The process of consciousness raising is not necessarily an easy task. Peer groups—women at the same stage in life—are often better sources of support than one's children, even though they are adults themselves. Many women belong to social groups, and it is quite possible that regular meetings could be expanded to incorporate discussions about personal feelings or that some members might like to meet separately for such discussions. Often topics compatible with those natural to consciousness raising or to self-awareness come up anyway. Membership in the Gray Panthers, the National Retired Teachers Association, or the American Association of Retired Persons can lead to the discovery that many of one's feelings and reactions are shared by others. This support offers encouragement and can mean continued inquiry and personal growth.

So far in this chapter, all questions about the retired husband have been skirted. Though the majority of older women are widows, most older men are married. In 1974, 6.3 million (52 percent) of older women were widows and 6.7 million (79 percent) of older men were married. The critical difference is that there are more older women than men. Again in 1974, there were 143 women for every 100 men sixty-five or older. What this means, of course, is that many retired women are widows.

There are, however, many instances when husband and wife both live on into retirement. When two people are retired together they may spend more time in each other's company than they have spent since the first blush of romance. When this happens, many aspects of their interpersonal relationships have to be sorted out. Two working people have to establish a mutually acceptable routine; this will be strained when both have unlimited time available. Some reassignment of tasks will probably occur. Preferences for household chores will need discussion, routines may change, and sharing and flexibility will be important in the adjustment.

The problem of shifting social roles will have to be faced. Unless the woman maintains associations with some social groups, she will be left with the single role of wife. It is entirely possible that this may be satisfactory, but it does mean giving up other roles that society also recognizes and respects. The married retired woman should consider whether or not she wants to remain involved with people she knew through work, or if she wants to work part time. These two roles, friend and worker, exist in addition to the role of wife. The strength of the need to exist as an individual outside the marital relationship will have to be explored by husband and wife.

MENOPAUSE

Retired women have long since passed a biological milestone known as the menopause or the climacteric. This is a physical reality that all women must experience, but it is rarely welcomed, and rarely understood even by those who have an intimate knowledge of it. Women continue to feel embarrassment about their bodily functions; they seek information from uninformed sources, and old wives' tales persist. Because the complexities of the relationships among hormones and our body clocks are not easily sorted out, information is only recently becoming available. The scientific community still has a lot of research to do. The menopause, a time that belongs to all women but continues to be misunderstood, feared, and often mocked, deserves a brief and simplified exposition.

A woman's body reaches organic maturity early in her life, and this stage covers a period of about thirty years. During this time she can conceive and bear children. Before as well as during this period, she builds the attitudes she needs to be a maternal figure; and when this period is over, she retains all that she has been. The cessation of the menses does not mean a lessening of womanhood or of individual value. A woman remains the sum total of her experiences as she grows, matures, and ages. Being feminine is a total that increases; it never diminishes.

The hormones which determine the stages of the reproductive cycle do diminish, though. Reduced levels of estrogen signal the beginning of the menopause. Estrogen is an important hormone. It is responsible for the development of the inner lining of the uterus (the womb), as well as for the development of the sex organs and the skin adjacent to the vagina. Another hormone, progesterone, is important because it regulates pregnancy and influences the secretory part of the menstrual cycle. When the pituitary gland signals a drop in the level of progesterone and estrogen, the monthly menstrual period begins. Later in life, these hormones, particularly estrogen, are gradually reduced, and ovarian regression slowly begins. Eggs are no longer produced; menstruation becomes erratic and finally ceases. While this is going on, external genitalia and the breasts atrophy: that is, they lose their elasticity.

Sporadic bodily complaints often accompany the menopause. Not all, but many, women experience symptoms such as hot flashes and painful breasts. Some have emotional responses: depression, confusion, crying spells, irritability, and a lack of concentration. Often these symptoms are experienced earlier in association with the normal monthly cycle, but women tend to get used to them over the years; they be problems only if they intensify. They are hard to measure; therefore it is difficult to determine their influence and the number of women experiencing them.

The menopause is more than a lack of estrogen. It is a period in a woman's life when more than hormones must achieve a new balance. Physical distress in the form of disease often accompanies the climacteric, and hysterectomy is a common surgical procedure to correct it. Women have only recently begun to complain about this wholesale removal of their reproductive organs. A perhaps overly cautious medical point of view requires a total hysterectomy for a range of conditions: from fibroid tumors, which are fairly common; to heavy and often erratic vaginal bleeding associated with uneven levels of estrogen without the production of progesterone; to malignancies affecting various organs of the reproductive system. Complaints about hysterectomy are now being heard from women of ethnic backgrounds that identify sexuality and sexual value with menstruation. Having a hysterectomy places extreme pressure on many women to adjust all at once to a condition that is difficult enough to live with when it occurs over a period of years.

MEDICARE

The chances of maintaining good health are greatly increased if a woman will consult her physician at regular and frequent intervals. For instance, a prediabetic condition can be identified and the probable development of diabetes—which is all too often a disease older people must contend with—can be prevented. Monitoring of blood pressure and cholesterol levels is also good—an example of an ounce of prevention being worth a pound of cure. With the increase in medical benefits under Social Security, some form of health care should be within the reach of most women.

Medicare benefits for the aged became available in July 1966. Everyone receives information about Medicare and application forms in the mail as he or she becomes eligible for federal civil-service annuity payments. If the material doesn't arrive, a call to the local Social Security office should ensure that it will be put in the mail. Before reaching retirement age, and certainly before canceling any medical or hospital benefits, a woman should talk with an insurance agent about her needs.

Under Medicare two kinds of health insurance are available. The first, hospital insurance, is automatic for those who are eligible. This insurance helps to defray the high cost of hospital care but does not pay doctors' bills. *At the time of this writing,* if one is hospitalized, a benefit period of up to ninety days of in-patient care in a participating hospital will be covered as follows: For the first sixty days the hospital insurance will pay for all covered services except for the first $92. If a hospital stay continues from the sixty-first through the ninetieth day, the plan pays for all covered services except for $23 per diem. Costs normally covered include bed and board in a two-bed to four-bed room, routine nursing care, and the usual supplies and treatments furnished by the hospital. The plan also partly covers two other kinds of health care: extended care and home health care. Extended care must be authorized by a doctor, be given by skilled nurses, be for the treatment of a condition which previously required hospitalization, and begin within fourteen days of a hospital stay of at least three days. The patient pays $7.50 per day for each day over twenty days. Home health care must be planned by a doctor within fourteen days of discharge from a hospital or extended-care facility. It includes up to 100 visits by registered nurses or therapists to one's home and pays all costs that qualify.

The second major type of health insurance under Medicare, supplementary medical insurance, is a device to provide for paying doctors' bills. Individuals have to sign up for this program; it is not automatic. The plan pays for 80 percent of a doctor's costs and charges not covered by the hospital plan, during a calendar year. The participant pays the first $50. Five services are included: (1) You may choose your own doctor, and his or her "reasonable" charges will be paid. (2) In addition to the 100 home visits allowed under basic hospital insurance, this plan pays for an additional 100 visits. (3) The medical-services section covers such things as laboratory tests, surgical dressings, rental equipment, etc. (4) Hospital outpatient services for diagnosis or treatment will be covered. (5) This insurance can help pay for outpatient physical therapy services. Enrollment in this voluntary plan can take place during the three months *preceding* the month in which one becomes sixty-five or during the three months *afterwards.* It is possible to enroll at other times, to drop out, and to reenroll; but the conditions and costs will vary.

Medicare is financed through payroll deductions made in addition to the regular Social Security tax. Employers also contribute. The costs of voluntary medical insurance are split equally between the individual and the federal government. Under the amendments of 1965 that created Medicare, premiums can be raised and the deductibles varied. The plan also has provisions for the needy: the blind, the totally disabled, and dependent children. Programs change from state to state. To get full and accurate information about the program in a particular state, check with any local Social Security office.

GRIEF, DEATH, AND BURIAL

The role of wife can offer deeply felt satisfactions, especially since it is one long revered as the traditional role for women. Society, though, is still unprepared to deal with widows. Today 52 percent of women sixty-five and older are widows. Because this is true, the fear of loss as well as the actual loss of a husband is of great concern to women, and for a number of interrelated reasons.

Even the retired, sophisticated woman may find herself unprepared to make the major decisions that the death of a husband necessitates. Widows find that they are pressed to make decisions about where to live, what possessions to keep, how to handle the estate, and how to handle their time. Again, the ability to build a life around more than a single person, to establish more than one source of personal support, is clearly essential to a future-oriented life. Friendships and membership in various organizations for the retired woman can be priceless.

Grief is not an easily anticipated emotion, and most of us are not prepared to express it. Anger, guilt, frustration, foreboding, and a sense of inadequacy stemming from the final absence of a best friend are not unusual feelings. They are a normal part of bereavement. These legitimate feelings should be ventilated and shared regardless of one's desire to appear controlled and brave. It is important to recognize that the death of a loved one is a severe loss and one not dealt with quickly or easily. There will be moments of anger because one has been left alone—deserted. There will be feelings of guilt, of not having done enough for the deceased; and it is not unusual to feel frustrated.

All the choices, decisions, and other pressures that confront us as almost routine daily experiences now have to be dealt with alone. If one's feelings are bottled up or suppressed, they will cause far more discomfort than they should. Grief comes to everyone. Admitting that it exists lets one begin a review of one's life that will be colored by the many happy events that typified the relationship. It also allows the hundreds of other experiences, those that were ordinary and those that were unpleasant, to be gradually recalled and put into perspective. As time goes by, the real picture of the marital relationship will come into focus.

And while this is going on, family, friends, religious counselors, and other widows who have lived with and learned to handle their grief can be of great help. There is no reason for not seeking help. It is natural to want help, and help can be found.

Grieving and problems of readjustment are made more serious because widows, like divorcees, find that they are often isolated from old friends. The single woman in a world of couples does find it hard to remain an integrated member of her circle. If one's social group cannot accommodate itself to one's new condition, other associations will have to be found.

Widows must make it a point to stay active. If invitations are not as frequent as they might be, the woman alone can always entertain in her own home. She can also invite friends to go to the movies or shopping, to take trips, or to attend meetings. The best way to avoid loneliness is to make contact with other people. Becoming isolated, brooding about being alone, or refusing to search for new outlets for one's interests will only make mourning harder. As with all new steps, the first are the hardest; but they can be taken. *The widow will find that she is not alone; she will find support, friendship, and a life worth living if she will share her needs with others.*

Though the topic of death is anything but pleasant, it deserves further consideration. It is difficult to discuss the dollars-and-cents aspect of funerals, but a funeral is often a major expenditure that can be calculated in advance. For many reasons some of the world's great people have planned their own funerals— Queen Mary of England, Winston Churchill, and Douglas MacArthur, for example.

In this country, funeral directors usually display a variety of coffins ranging in price from $100 to $2,000. Regardless of the cost, the funeral will be the same. A number of things will be the responsibility of the funeral director. He or she will:

1 Call for the body
2 Obtain a burial permit
3 File the death certificate
4 Help to select or arrange for a place of burial, the pallbearers, and the clergyman
5 Notify those concerned with the service to send the obituary notices
6 Provide the immediate family with automobiles for the procession

There are additional expenses to be considered:

1 Opening and closing the grave will cost between $45 and $250.
2 The plot will cost between $75 and $250.
3 The marker can cost a great deal or relatively little. A satisfactory natural marker will run about $75.

Some people prefer to reduce funeral expenses through membership in a funeral or memorial society. The services of these societies vary, as do the membership fees. Information about nearby societies may be obtained by writing to the Continental Association of Funeral and Memorial Societies, Inc., 59 East Van Buren Street, Chicago, Illinois 60605.

Some other information may also be useful here. For example, if a body must be transported some distance, it is generally cheapest to do so by air freight; and when a body crosses state lines, there is usually a legal requirement that it be embalmed. Enbalming is not generally required under any other circumstance. The costs of burial and cremation are about the same, except that there are no laws requiring the use of a coffin for the cremation. Many crematories, however, have their own rules. For preservation in burial, the least expensive casket will do as well as any other. A person cannot sell his or her body for scientific or educational purposes; therefore, relatives who are likely to survive will have to be convinced of one's wishes in this matter. Finally, if planning for death and burial is done in advance, ask for advice regarding the options available and don't hesitate to ask the opinions of friends.

SOCIAL SECURITY

The Social Security Administration operates for the benefit of everyone. It has set rules that detail the procedures for applying for benefits. Though the system may seem inflexible, it does change from time to time. *Every woman contemplating retirement should contact the office nearest her at least three years before the end of her active working life.* She will probably find it advantageous to acquire from the local Social Security office, or from the Government Printing Office, the brochure entitled "Social Security: What it Means to You" (U.S. Department of Health, Education and Welfare, Social Security Administration, DHEW Publication No. (SSA) 72-10023).

Social Security has become a basic part of American life. Almost everyone contributes to it, and one out of eight Americans gets a monthly check. It is a form of income insurance that provides benefits in case of death, disability, or retirement. Benefits will vary because they are determined by a person's average earnings over a working lifetime. Payments are influenced by the amounts of earnings credited, and this changes from time to time. Congress can raise and has raised benefits so that they will reflect changes in the cost of living. Women, because they assume many roles, can fall into several categories and therefore come under a variety of rules. For instance, a widow has several choices of benefits, which will change upon her remarriage. The working wife doesn't have to depend on her husband's record; and if she has dependent parents, they can receive support if she dies.

Whatever options are available and selected, everyone must apply for Social Security benefits. Local offices will answer questions by telephone if a person is unable to go to the office. *One should apply for retirement benefits two or three months before turning sixty-five.* It is possible for a woman to begin receiving benefits at sixty-two, but they will be less than those received at sixty-five. Some people plan to work after they are sixty-five; they should still apply, so that the paperwork will be complete and payments can begin at their convenience. Medicare coverage is in effect even if one continues to work.

When applying for Social Security there are some documents that will be needed:

1 A Social Security card or number.
2 A birth or a baptismal certificate.
3 The final Form W-2 Wage and Tax Statement, or if one is self-employed a copy of the last federal income tax return.

All these documents are needed to compute earnings and benefits.

It is possible to retire, to receive benefits, and to continue to earn. The present maximum income allowed per year without penalty is $1,680. There is growing pressure to allow people to earn more; it is, therefore, a good practice to stay in touch with a local office to keep track of official changes and new available options.

RETIREMENT AND PART-TIME EMPLOYMENT

In shifting roles, the retired woman can contemplate some good news: more and more women are working. Their numbers increase yearly, and those who join the workforce tend to remain. In 1973, 11.7 million women forty-five and over were working. They represented 13 percent of the workforce. Also in 1973, one-half of 53 percent of women between the ages of forty-five and fifty-four were working; 41 percent of those fifty-five to sixty-four were working; and 9 percent of those sixty-five and over were working. In the same year, twice as many married women forty-five to sixty-four were working as had been working in 1950. By 1973, 44 percent of all married women in the same age category were working. The case for retirement planning for the working woman is, then, easily made.

Though the picture is slowly changing, throughout their working lives women have less prestigious jobs and earn less than men. They also receive smaller pensions and smaller Social Security benefits. For instance, in 1971, the average monthly payment from Social Security was $169 for men and $116 for women. Clearly, the less one earns, the less one's pension will be; but the result is intensified because in effect women are penalized for living too long. Women, on the average, live longer than men. (In 1974, there were 130 women for every 100 men.) The rationale for lower payments is based on the need to equalize the total amounts paid out to retired men and women. The results of this logic can be demonstrated by looking at women's income during 1970. In that year half of all white women and four-fifths of all black women over the age of sixty-five were living below the poverty level. The official poverty level for people over sixty-five is $2,100 per year.

Women make up a large part of the work force, contribute a great deal to the economy, and get shortchanged. Those women who choose to be wives and mothers make significant contributions, too. They deserve some sort of employment compensation, and perhaps some thought should be given to divorce insurance. The point is that a plan might well be devised that would allow homemakers to build credit toward their "retirement" from homemaking in their social security account. Pressure should be brought to bear on the Social Security Administration to broaden its interpretation of the economic worth of women, regardless of the roles they assume during the course of their lives.

HOUSING AND LIVING ARRANGEMENTS

Everyone who is retired or approaching retirement must face and make decisions about where and how to live. Many alternatives are open. Retirement provides an opportunity to select a truly appropriate housing arrangement. The retired woman may choose among several possibilities:

Staying in her present home.
Moving to an apartment, a residential hotel, or a boarding home.
Moving to a retirement home or community.
Buying a mobile home.
Moving to the home of a relative.
Participating in a cooperative or communal living arrangement.
Moving to a nursing home.

Most older Americans, about 95 percent, live in ordinary communities and depend upon normal community resources and services. In 1974, six out of ten older women lived in family settings; fewer than one in twenty lived in institutions; and the rest lived alone or with people who were not their relatives. The general preference seems to be for independent living; habits acquired over a lifetime do not necessarily change with age. But the types of life-styles possible for a woman who opts for independent living do have both advantages and disadvantages.

A common choice seems to be *stay on in the family home.* This allows a person to continue a lifetime pattern and helps to avoid painful changes. It allows privacy and the continuation of a financial investment. However, neighbors do change, and often services which were once easily available are lost. Taxes and utility rates may increase, as well as the need for major home repairs. Making home repairs can strain one's energy as well as one's pocketbook to the limit. Unless land value remains high, the total worth of the homestead may decline; and finally, there may be too much space for one or two people.

Retired women often move into an apartment, a residential hotel, or a boarding home. Some very basic decisions have to be made before consideration of new accommodations even begins. The location, whether in the city or in the suburbs, will have a lot to do with cost and with the location of services. Living out of the city usually costs more and makes it necessary to have an automobile. If existing furniture is kept, an unfurnished apartment will be necessary. In any event, a decision will have to be made about how much room is needed. Some practical consideration should be given to convenience and safety:

Where is the elevator located?

Are there safety features in the kitchen and the bathroom?

Are the outside doors security doors, and is the garage always lighted and locked?

What type of emergency arrangements can be made?

Finally, are there options for cleaning services, getting meals, and maintaining a car?

Once these questions have been answered satisfactorily, the advantages of living in an apartment or residential hotel are clear.

Privacy is easily obtained in individual housing arrangements, whether the residence is a house or an apartment. An apartment, residential hotel, or boarding house requires less physical labor for home maintenance than a house, and uses space efficiently. But the disadvantages of privacy are related to its advantages: privacy can lead to loneliness, to isolation from social interaction; and isloation can make a person vulnerable to illness, accident, and crime. It should also be pointed out that monthly rental does not represent an investment that will develop equity.

Some women choose to move to a retirement community or home. There are many throughout the country, especially in the warmer climates. Retirement communities and homes offer security and an opportunity for homogeneous companionship and many activities. Services offered include taking care of the menial tasks of daily living. This type of living is often expensive, requiring a large commitment of funds. It usually, though not always, means a long-term association, and there will be pressures to conform to a rather unidimensional group. Careful and thorough investigation will ensure a satisfactory selection.

Some people are attracted to mobile homes. These homes can be located, and sometimes relocated, wherever the owner chooses to live. They are cheaper than a standard home and allow for the maintenance of a personal and private life-style. Buying a mobile home does mean taking on financial obligations: used trailers are often hard to sell and depreciate more quickly than houses. It also means finding a suitable site, or "court." Each court is unlike the next and has its own ambience and personality.

Retired people sometimes choose to rent or buy smaller homes. All the advantages of home ownership will be retained, but there will be less maintenance. All the disadvantages remain, too. A move will have to be made and a new mortgage assumed. Privacy will be guaranteed, but some costs of maintenance and upkeep will continue.

It is sometimes possible for a retired woman to live with a relative. Such an arrangement offers family support and comfort and can provide financial relief. It does mean loss of privacy and autonomy, and being subject to the influences and priorities of family members. There is also a potential loss of dignity. This option is most successful for those who know and love their family and when the family has a deep sense of respect for each individual member.

Cooperative communal living is not a new idea in America. It is a concept built on sharing certain facilities while still maintaining a private room. Sharing the cost of food, housing, transportation, and maintenance makes this an attractive choice for many people. It allows for companionship and aid in case of sickness or accident. It offers security, too. Communal living does require cooperation with and an adjustment to others. There can be problems when personal property is used by several people. As group members age, become infirm, have to leave, or die, new participants will have to be found. This is not always easily accomplished. On the whole, though, this type of living arrangement can be most satisfying. There are groups already in existence, and with the numbers of large and older homes available today it wouldn't be hard for a group of friends to set up their own commune.

Because of the many disadvantages connected with all other types of living arrangements, and of course for reasons of health, some women will choose to move to a nursing facility. There all of one's physical and medical needs will be satisfied. All problems regarding quarters and everyday living will be handled. There will be almost no privacy, however; and personal belongings and control over one's life will be minimal. Dependency on others will increase, as will isolation from "normal" living.

In considering one's housing arrangements, it is a good idea to carefully examine all the options available. It is also a good idea to talk with friends who have experience with the acceptable possibilities. Visit them if possible; move in for a short time as a guest or paying guest. If a change in geographic location is desired, a leisurely trip to the area you are considering is a good way to get acquainted with the climate, the available facilities, and the people already living there. Careful planning will reduce the chances of making an unhappy decision. Take lots of time; look around. Investigate carefully and choose something agreeable to your already established life-style.

LEISURE TIME AND RELATED ACTIVITIES

If the retirement years are to be active and pleasant, all available options for using leisure time should be considered. Being future-oriented is important; it will encourage self-esteem. For the woman who has been professionally active throughout her life, retirement will require a "honeymoon period." She will have to test new realities: having time that is no longer given over to a regular work week, for example—time that may be so plentiful that it becomes burdensome.

Many women find it useful to consider activities that will prevent social isolation and the deterioration that accompanies inactivity. Sometimes it is advantageous to find someone to counsel with about leisure time. Many churches have trained lay help. Often communities have counselors available either in local mental-health clinics or through their private or public school systems. Trained people can help suggest alternative uses of time and can offer information about a wide variety of activities. The local Agency on Aging will have an information and referral service, too. The local chapter of the National Organization for Women (NOW) can be most helpful. Using any of these services can save many hours of searching for ways to use time and can avoid frustrations associated with trying to pry information out of inappropriate agencies.

If a retired woman is interested in a second career or is interested in returning to school, counselors in any of the suggested organizations can help her to assess her skills and limitations, the job market, and employers' needs, and arrive at a realistic set of goals. They will help with a résumé, which should be updated before retirement. (See also Chapter 5, page 99.) A good set of professional credentials should contain basic information like height, weight, age, address, education. It should carefully and briefly spell out work experiences. Job responsibilities and additional assignments should be described. Potential employers want to know what prospective employees can do. To that end, one should include volunteer work; clubs; hobbies; interests; and talents, such as typing speed, proficiency in spelling, speed reading, a flair for good grammar, skill in proofreading; etc. Remember, too, that avocational interests have become vocations for many people: not all the florists, potters, artists, weavers, and jewelers in the business today are the very young. A résumé should also include current letters of reference; when a woman retires, she should ask for more than the traditional gold watch.

VOLUNTEER WORK

Some women do not want to work or to go back to school. For many people, volunteer activities are preferable. Working for the Red Cross, the United Fund, the Cancer Foundation, or any of the many societies devoted to medical research and aid to the physically handicapped, can be especially rewarding. A prospective volunteer should not hesitate to investigate the organizations of interest.

Since good programs choose their volunteers carefully, having updated credentials will help you to be placed. A good organization trains its volunteers, seeks feedback regarding its placements, and attempts to provide its participants with public recognition. There are many volunteer groups, and there is no need to choose one that fails in any of these areas. Time spent on a worthy project and in an orderly fashion can be time profitably given. Satisfaction will be deep.

CONCLUSION

In conclusion, it has been the intention of this chapter to provide an overview of the many options available and thus to provide ideas about preretirement planning and to offer suggestions and information that will help to make life truly pleasant, worthwhile, and very much worth living during retirement.

BIBLIOGRAPHY

Bardwick, Judith M.: "The Effects of Body States on the Psyche," in *Psychology of Women,* Harper and Row, New York, 1971, pp. 21–46. This chapter is easily read and is a thorough explanation of the endocrine system and its possible psychological effects during changes such as the menopause. This is an interesting chapter in a book that is a good source of information about the psychology of women.
Carp, Frances M.: *Retirement,* Behavioral Publications, New York, 1972. Retirement is considered from many aspects. This is a complete and professional presentation of

this stage in life. A great deal of statistical information and scholarly insight is provided.

Davis, Richard H. (ed.): *Housing for the Elderly,* Ethel Percy Andrus Gerontology Center, University of Southern California, Los Angeles, 1973. This monograph presents papers covering topics such as design concepts and issues, types and sources of funds, service (needs and delivery), and consumer input to planning design. It is of general rather than specific use but may suggest issues that should be considered when contemplating retirement housing.

DeCrow, Roger: *New Learning for Older Americans: An Overview of National Effort,* Adult Education Association of the U.S.A., Washington, D.C., 1975. This is a readable report covering many aspects of the national scene regarding education and older adults. It summarizes available programs, describes the agencies that provide them, and suggests needed additional programs. The annotated bibliography is thorough and greatly enhances the worth of the report.

Galbraith, Patricia: *What You Can Do for Yourself—Hints for the Handicapped,* Drake, New York, 1974. This book provides a wealth of information for anyone who is physically limited in any way. Clothing and personal care as well as cooking and cleaning are discussed. Many references for matters such as travel and available services are supplied. The book is clearly written and generally very helpful.

Hunter, Woodrow H.: *Preparation for Retirement,* Institute for Gerontology, University of Michigan, Ann Arbor, 1968. Divided into two parts, this book covers topics that are important to the person doing retirement planning and provides some stories about personal reactions to retirement. The book is not a source of facts and figures but an attempt to supply a frame of reference for thinking about retirement situations.

Korim, Andrew: *Older Americans and Community Colleges—A Guide for Program Implementation,* American Association of Community and Junior Colleges, Washington, D.C., 1974. Though this book suggests strategies for community and junior colleges when implementing programs for older adults, these same strategies can be used by interested adults who wish to encourage their schools to serve the unique needs of the mature student.

Kubler-Ross, Elizabeth, and Jeanne Quint Benoliel: *Confrontation with Dying,* Richard H. Davis, (ed.), Ethel Percy Andrus Gerontology Center, University of Southern California, Los Angeles, 1971. This is a brief volume containing papers covering the needs of dying patients, the stages of dying, death and children, and the practitioner's dilemma. Topics are clearly presented and well developed.

Loether, Herman J.: *Problems of Aging: Sociological and Social Psychological Perspectives,* Dickenson, Belmont, Calif., 1967. This is an easily read and useful book. It covers topics important to the older woman. They include health, housing, employment, retirement, and interpersonal relations. It thoroughly surveys the problems of the older American. Any of the chapters will provide interesting reading and practical help.

O'Meara, J. Roger: "Retirement—The Eighth Age of Man," *The Conference Board Record,* October 1974, pp. 59–64. In this article the author presents the results of a survey of companies and their preretirement training programs. Topics considered most important to those in the programs are listed, and the companies' responses to their employees' wants and needs are presented and evaluated.

Pre-retirement Planning Seminar, Action for Independent Maturity/American Association for Retired Persons, Washington, D.C. This program is in common use today as a method of preretirement planning. It is valuable, since it suggests a successful approach.

Epilogue

Making a Political Impact
as a Woman

Patsy Mink

Patsy Takemoto Mink, J.D., has been United States Congresswoman
from Hawaii since 1965. A lawyer and former professor of business law
at the University of Hawaii, she has also had a distinguished career in the
Hawaii House of Representatives and Senate. In the United States House
of Representatives, she is a member of the prestigious Committees on
the Budget and on Interior and Insular affairs, and a member of the
American Council on Education Commission on Women in Higher Education. She was House Delegate to the United Nations Conference on
International Women's Year, held in Mexico City in 1975; and she received the Human Rights Award from the American Federation of Teachers the same year. Congresswoman Mink has published over twenty articles in professional journals and other sources.

At the final convention of the National American Woman Suffrage Association,
held in 1920, the suffragist Carrie Chapman Catt warned that winning the vote
would not automatically give women access to the inner circle of political power
where candidates for office are picked. "You will see the real thing in the center

with the door locked tight," she said. "You will have a long, hard fight before you get inside, . . . but you must move right up to the center."

It has indeed been a long, hard fight. And there are more battles ahead. Men who resent women's recent successes in politics are still trying to put us back "in our place." It is not so very long ago that Mayor Moon Landrieu of New Orleans thoughtlessly remarked that "the women do the licken' and the sticken', while the men plan the strategy." He has lived to regret such a tactless slip: the media pounced on it, and it appeared over and over again in the articles extolling women's victories at the polls in the subsequent elections.

POLITICS: THE LAST BARRIER

Politics may be the last and most difficult "breakthrough" for women. While substantial progress has been made toward removing at least the legal barriers to equal opportunity in many fields, the barriers to women in politics are mostly based on custom, which no court can eradicate. People vote for "the best man" without even thinking that a woman might do the job better. Political parties search for "the best man"; pollsters ask only about our sons' political ambitions. If we can make society rethink its attitudes, rework its mores, only then will women emerge as a new force in American politics. This is our plight and our challenge.

Currently a double standard is employed in politics. A woman has to be right 100 percent of the time to merit your vote. And women in particular exact of a woman candidate extraordinary demands they would never dream of making of a man. There is still too much of this in politics, and this makes it quite difficult for women who will want to run for office. The imposition of subjective masculine criteria for women candidates is a part of our sexist world. Women voters need to free themselves of the need for a father figure in politics.

I find that this discrimination against women is invidious. In a woman, the merest hint of any shortcoming is sufficient cause for rejection. A man might drink, be divorced, miss half of his votes and vote wrong on the other half, be beholden to special interests, and in general abuse his public trust, and still be reelected. But a woman must be flawless.

Women must themselves assume a greater interest in politics and the political process itself. I am often dismayed when women tell me that they have to check with their husbands before they can make political contributions. Equality means freedom to support and work for candidates of our own personal choice, and the fight for equality is nothing more than cosmetic unless these attitudes change. We can have all the legal rights in the world, but they won't make a bit of difference if we choose not to take advantage of them.

As I see it, equal job opportunity is only one aspect of the fight for real equality. Many women put their quest for professional achievement first and argue that because of this struggle they can't get involved in politics. Let's be honest—men don't have any such hesitation. Men have jobs, but they get involved in politics to the point of domination. Women must do the same or be forever satisfied with male domination of our government. If more women are not involved, we have only ourselves to blame.

SOME RECENT HISTORY

It was the national party conventions and elections of 1972 that really signaled the growing role and influence of women in politics. With the impetus provided by the McGovern Reform Commission, the number of women delegates at the Democratic National Convention rose from 13 percent in 1968 to 40 percent in 1972. The Republicans also increased women's representation at their convention, from 17 to 30 percent. A great number of these women returned from the conventions determined to seek office for themselves. Then came Watergate, and suddenly a lack of political experience was no longer a detriment; instead, it was an asset.

Women worked together to create political networks crossing party and state lines. Republicans helped Democrats, and vice versa. Grass-roots efforts across the nation were organized to support qualified women running for office at all levels of government. These efforts paid off. When the votes were counted, women had won in 50 percent of their contests—a rate of victories equal to that of male candidates.

1974: A LANDMARK YEAR

The elections of 1974 were a real breakthrough for women in politics. Figures from the National Women's Political Caucus show that the elections added more than 130 new women to state legislatures, bringing the total to about 600 women members. That does not sound like a significant number when you compare it with the total number of state legislators—about 7,700—but it's double the number of women serving in state legislatures in 1969. In New Hampshire, the number of women members rose from 89 to 107 (more than one-quarter the total membership of 424). In Maryland, the number increased from 11 to 19; in Georgia, from 2 to 9; in my state of Hawaii, from 4 to 10.

Thirty-one of the fifty-one women running as major-party candidates for statewide office were elected, and many of these victories represented important "firsts" for women in politics. Ella Grasso won in Connecticut to become the first woman governor of a state elected on her own merits, without following her husband into that post. New York State elected its first woman lieutenant governor, Mary Ann Krupsak; and California elected a woman secretary of state, March Fong Eu. Only two years previously, no woman even received a major-party nomination for governor or lieutenant governor.

In North Carolina, Susie Sharp garnered 74 percent of the vote to become the first woman in the country popularly elected to the office of chief justice of a state supreme court. Janet Gray Hayes of San Jose, California, became the first woman mayor of an American city of more than 500,000 people. In Minnesota, Ruby Perpich was elected Secretary of State, the first woman elected to statewide office in that state. And for the first time in history a woman, Mary Louise Smith, was named Chairman of the Republican National Committee, replacing the outgoing Chairman, George Bush.

A WOMAN'S PLACE IS . . . ANYWHERE

Women have long provided the backbone of political campaign efforts as volunteers, and today they are finally getting recognition for their efforts and political skills. *They are increasingly attractive to voters because of their independence from vested interests, their integrity, and their leadership on important issues such as the environment, consumer protection, and education.*

The forces pushing women into the political arena are growing stronger. As women become a more potent force in the labor market and assert their economic and social independence, they tend to vote more often and in greater numbers. As they become more educated, taking advantage of the increased opportunities for more and better education for women, they become more politically active.

Beyond their concern for honesty and integrity in government, many of the women who have begun to participate in recent campaigns and elections have something in common: they have been involved with the issues that most concern the voter. They have been active in the woman's movement, in consumer organizations, in aid to the elderly, in environmental causes.

Betty Roberts was a member of the Oregon State Legislature when she received the Democratic nomination to run against United States Senator Robert Packwood. She had led the battle that brought about the nation's first statewide ban on throw-away cans and bottles. Long before Barbara Mikulski ran for the United States Senate in Maryland, she had established a national reputation defending the ethnic neighborhoods of Baltimore, and fighting for lower bus fares, better schools, and improved community services.

The kinds of women who are becoming successful politicians have changed in recent years. In times past, the majority of women elected to Congress, for example, got there through the so-called "widow's mandate"; that is, they took the place of their deceased husbands. Today, however, this is increasingly uncommon. Of the seven new women members of the United States House of Representatives in the 94th Congress, only two are widows who were chosen to replace their husbands on the ticket. And of all the nineteen women serving in the 94th Congress, only four of them got there as widows.

After some years, the Republican administration made good its platform promise to appoint a woman to the Cabinet, and Carla Hills now serves as Secretary of Housing and Urban Development. Talk of a woman on the Supreme Court has increased, and when that day comes, I predict there will be a dramatic shift in the consideration of challenges brought before the Court in the area of equal rights for women *and* men.

SOME HURDLES: PUTTING THE STEREOTYPES TO REST

Instead of women in their fifties entering politics because their children are grown and out of a need to do something worthwhile with themselves, there are now more and more young women in their twenties and thirties who are committing themselves to politics as a full-time, lifetime career. But at whatever age, it cannot be denied that male resistance to female political leadership continues. What is even worse, there are women who still object to other women in politics.

Women are often resented and are forced to run for office outside the regular political organization. They must often raise their own funds, from small contributions, and conduct their campaigns with mostly volunteer support. It is simply a tougher road for women.

What is necessary is a recognition among the voting populace and among potential women candidates themselves that *women have a special contribution to make, because they have special qualities of leadership which are greatly needed today*. These include patience, tolerance, and perseverance—qualities which are no doubt in many cases attributable to the fact that women's aspirations and achievements have been suppressed in the past. We can add to these qualities a reservoir of information about techniques of community action, our concern for human needs, and our crusading spirit for constructive change.

Many women, even many college-educated women, still "just don't want to get involved" in politics. It is a sign of our own self-denigration, our own failure to exorcise the stereotypes that hold women back, to think that a woman is "pushy," or "unfeminine," or "elitist," or "egotistical" if she wants to run for political office. It takes courage to emerge from our private hiding places and risk ourselves, expose ourselves, as we must when we enter the political world in our own right.

If we succeed in uniting women to elect women, we will have the power to confront the bosses and the machines in either party, and to change the power structure. If we use the woman-power that has been used for all the menial work—the mimeographing, envelope-stuffing, canvassing, and doorbell ringing; the coffees, lunches, and teas which have helped elect men; the speeches we have written for men; and the brains that we *haven't* been asked to use—if we use this energy to elect women, women will finally gain their rightful share of political power.

Shall we support any woman against any man? Of course not. But certainly we should support qualified women against less qualified or equally qualified men. There has been too much nonsense about there being "no qualified women" available to run. Thousands of women have had educations equal or superior to those of the men now holding office. Working women, now about 50 percent of the labor force nationwide, have technical and business experience matching that of men. All the women who have run men's campaigns and legislative offices have political expertise, and a whole new group of women have qualified themselves for the new politics by leading the great movements on social issues.

RIGHTING THE WRONGS

The years since 1972, when Congress approved the Equal Rights Amendment (ERA), have seen a tremendous increase in the grass-roots activity among women who have lobbied for ERA at the local level. I point with pride to the fact that

Hawaii was the first state to ratify the amendment, doing so within a matter of hours of its passage by Congress. If ever there was a single issue which has galvanized the women's rights organizations and brought political involvement and political emotions and convictions among women into the open, ERA is such an issue.

But working for the ratification of ERA, I would submit, is only a partial approach to righting the wrongs of these past many years of our nation's discriminatory treatment of women.

A second approach is a judicial attack on those laws which discriminate outright in their application as a denial of equal protection under the Fifth and Fourteenth Amendments to the Constitution. Generally, however, the courts have been unsympathetic, and have never directly addressed the fundamental issue of equal rights for women.

A third approach, which I have diligently pursued as a state and national legislator, is the passage of legislation to prohibit overt discrimination and to eliminate situations which have the effect of discriminating. We seek by this approach to provide adequate access to justice through immediate and timely remedies.

These three approaches to eliminating discrimination must be pursued vigorously if the final legal barriers to equal rights are to be eliminated. In the process, those who involve themselves in this three-pronged effort gain immeasurably. These approaches are not mutually exclusive; indeed, they should be and are being pursued simultaneously.

The Fourteenth Amendment already states, "No State shall make or enforce any law which shall abridge the privileges and immunities of citizens of the United States . . . nor deny to any person within its jurisdiction the equal protection of the laws." It is the failure of the courts to enforce this prohibition of unequal treatment under the law that has resulted in the perpetuation of known discrimination against women, suffered so long by so many.

The language of the Equal Rights Amendment restates this Constitutional principle. It states, "Equality of rights under the law shall not be denied or abridged by the United States or any State on account of sex. Congress shall have power, by appropriate legislation, to enforce this article."

The Equal Rights Amendment still requires case-by-case efforts to implement its provisions, very likely culminating in more Supreme Court cases dealing with the basic issue of equal rights for women. We continue to push for early enactment of specific legislative changes in order to get a head start on the effect of ERA, and have met with some notable, if limited, success. These successes include the celebrated title IX of the Education Amendments of 1972 (Public Law 92–318), and the Women's Educational Equity Act, Section 408, of PL 93–380, which I wrote.

The legal changes cannot help expediting the social, attitudinal changes so necessary if the women's movement is to continue to grow in influence. Along with legally established equality of opportunity comes socially sanctioned equality of aspiration.

GETTING INVOLVED

The transition to a society of true equal rights for all has begun, but it will be up to women to determine, by their own personal involvement or the lack of it, how fast these changes will occur. Those who wish to further the goal of equal opportunity for women will work not only to gain full ratification for ERA, *but also to make known their support of women's rights bills at the state and national level.* They will support, with time and money, those women's organizations working so hard to lobby for those measures. They will attempt to educate those who, whether from ignorance or lack of interest, mistrust or downgrade the importance of the struggle for women's rights.

We can encourage our daughters and friends to make the most of their talents and opportunities, and support women who are willing to run for elective office. I recall a mailing for the National Women's Political Caucus which asked women to remember that the newspapers had said the Caucus was about to fold (but there are now active caucuses in all fifty states); that the idea of an organized women's political movement was once a joke (but over 1,500 women attended the first national convention of the Caucus); that the ERA was thought not to have a chance (but we are awaiting ratification by the final few states); that national political conventions were once an all-male club (but women were 40 percent of the Democratic and 30 percent of the Republican delegates in 1972); and that we were once told to go out and make the coffee (but instead we elected seven new women to Congress and 130 new state legislators). Women as a new force in American politics can continue to surprise the doubters *as long as we never rest in our efforts and continue to believe in ourselves.*

A CHECKLIST

My prescription for political involvement is:

1 Understand what politics is. It is a contest of human ideology. To participate, you must understand the world of ideas, or—more important—have ideas of your own.

2 Be willing to assume leadership roles. Do not stand by and assume that someone else will challenge those now performing poorly in office. Run for public office yourself, or at least support a woman candidate.

3 Don't leave politics to your husband. Women have rights of their own, and these rights include the right to be involved and make political decisions.

4 Dig deeper into your own pocketbook and give financial help as well as lip service to your favorite woman candidate. I can say from personal experience that this is one of the most effective ways to help. Also, offer your services as a volunteer at her headquarters.

5 Join the party of your choice. Don't abdicate by calling yourself an "independent." Join a party, and if it is not entirely to your liking, work to reform it from within. Begin by becoming active on a precinct or ward level. Do volunteer work for your neighborhood political headquarters.

6 Express your views often and with persistence on carefully selected issues. Don't hide your light under a bushel. Make it your business to become involved in the major issues and the decisions which affect us all.

7 Don't operate on a double standard. Don't demand of a woman that she be right 100 percent of the time to merit your support, while supporting a man simply because you "like him"—even if he voted against you half the time.

8 Don't say you can't get involved because you work, or for some other reason. And don't wait for somebody to ask you. Those who dominate our politics have no such reluctance.

9 Write letters expressing your point of view to your elected representatives, to editors of newspapers and magazines. Letters *do* have an effect.

I firmly believe that women's voices in political decision making will help turn politics and government away from war and toward the critical human problems of our society—not because women are purer or better than men, but because our lives have not permitted us to evade human reality as men have. Shana Alexander, one of America's outstanding women journalists, has suggested that our slogan should be "Women's Participation—Human Liberation." It is time now for us to move from the role of observer to that of participant.

BIBLIOGRAPHY

Amundsen, Kirsten: *The Silenced Majority,* Prentice-Hall, Englewood Cliffs, N.J., 1971. The author examines the political position of women at the national and state level and finds that it is very weak. Even women in Congress, the author says, are likely to be excluded from the informal relations that are crucial to the successful maneuvering and power plays within that body.

Jacquette, Jane P. (ed.): *Women in Politics,* Wiley, New York, 1974. Part One of this book examines the individual woman—her position as a voter, her response to socialization, the conflict between motherhood and participation, her response to women in elective office. Part Two views political institutions, from the urban machine to the federal bureaucracy and the Supreme Court, as arenas of female participation and as sources of societal norms for female political behavior.

Kirkpatrick, Jeanne J.: *Political Woman,* Basic Books, New York, 1974.

Tolchin, Susan, and Martin Tolchin: *Clout: Womanpower and Politics,* Coward, McCann and Geoghegan, New York, 1973. The Tolchins and Kirkpatrick conclude that the political process offers a unique opportunity to bring about economic and political change, and that it is possible for women of talent to persevere to positions of influence and power, to their own benefit and to the benefit of men as well.

Index